Life Is Unfair
The Truths And Lies About
John F. Kennedy

Tome I

Eddy J. Neyts

Fortiter Fideliter Feliciter

KENNEDY

GRANDPARENTS

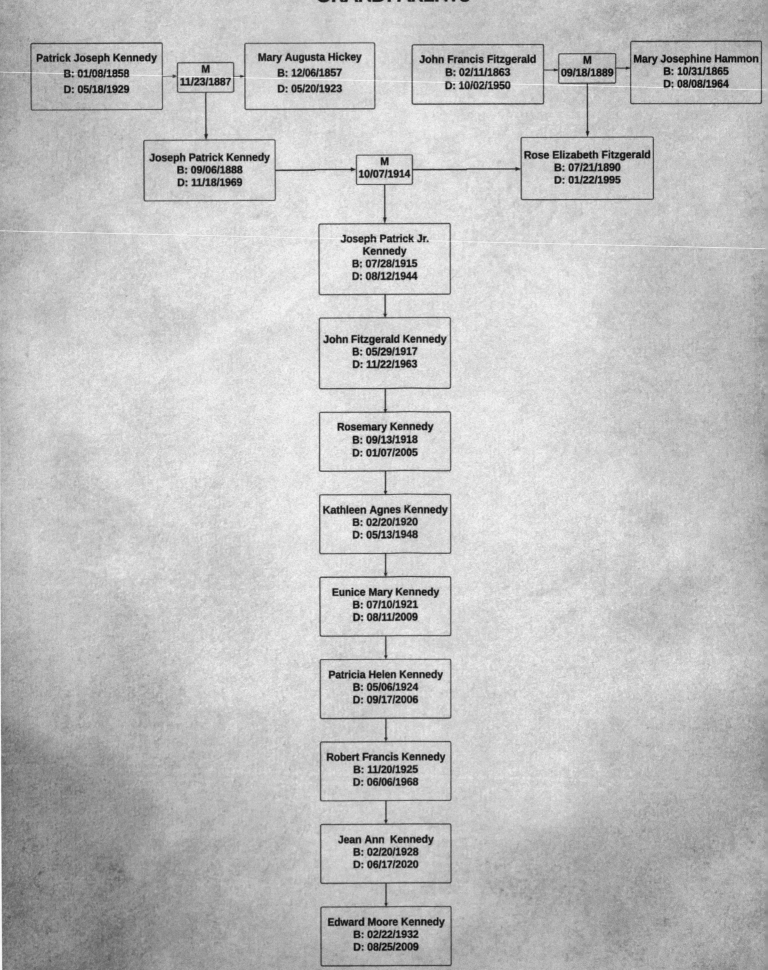

Joseph Patrick Jr.
Kennedy
B: 07/28/1915
D: 08/12/1944

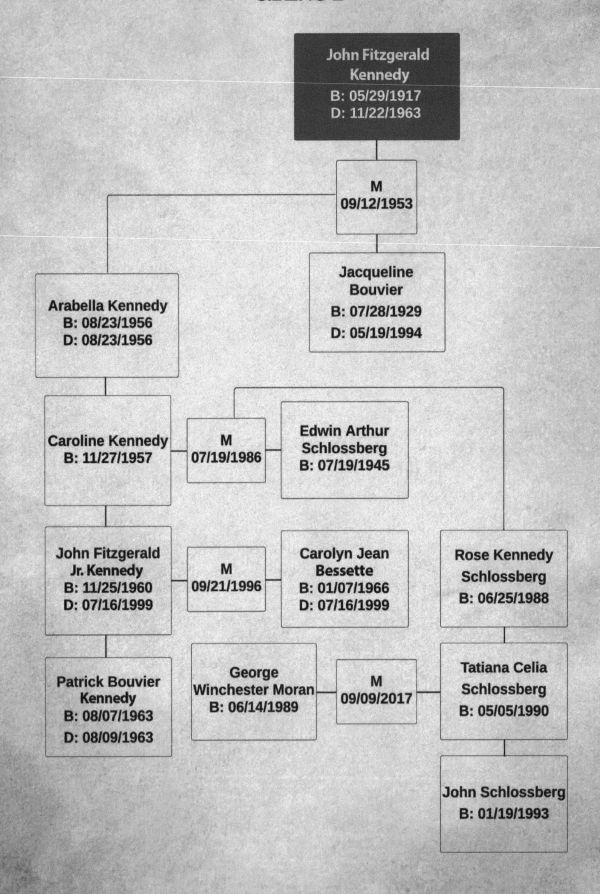

Rosemary
Kennedy
B: 09/13/1918
D: 01/07/2005

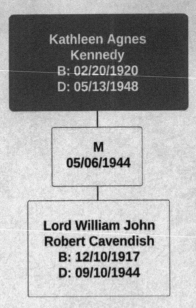

Kathleen Agnes
Kennedy
B: 02/20/1920
D: 05/13/1948

M
05/06/1944

Lord William John
Robert Cavendish
B: 12/10/1917
D: 09/10/1944

SIBLING 5

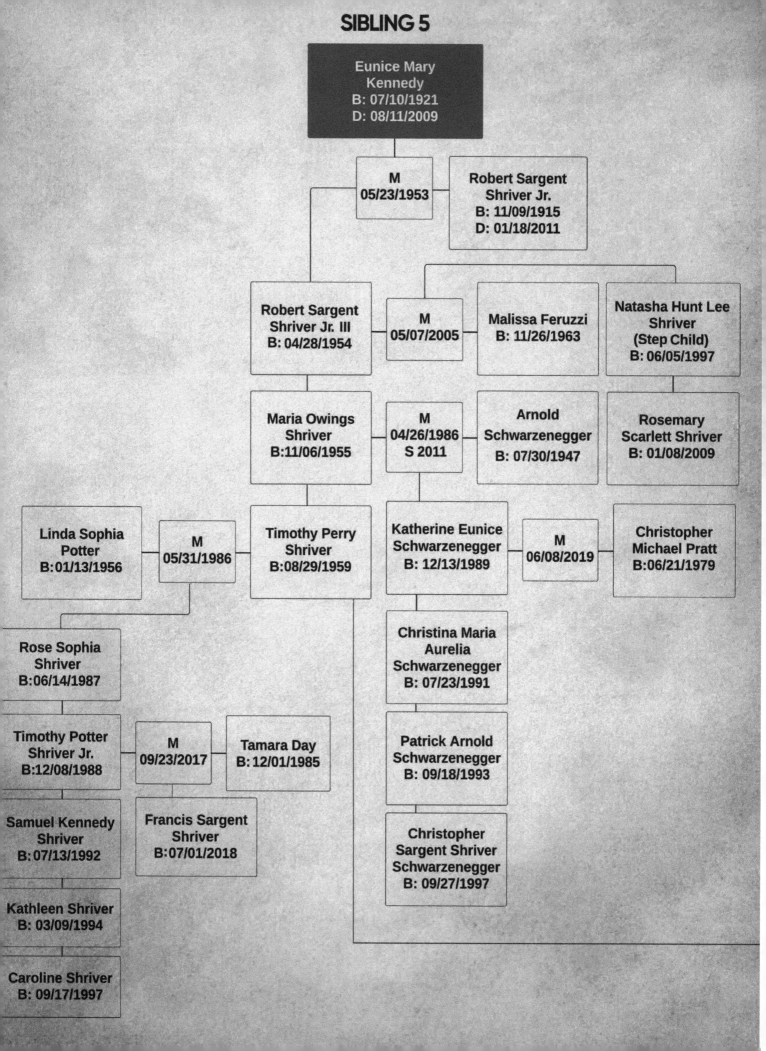

Eunice Mary Kennedy
B: 07/10/1921
D: 08/11/2009

M 05/23/1953

Robert Sargent Shriver Jr.
B: 11/09/1915
D: 01/18/2011

Robert Sargent Shriver Jr. III
B: 04/28/1954

M 05/07/2005

Malissa Feruzzi
B: 11/26/1963

Natasha Hunt Lee Shriver (Step Child)
B: 06/05/1997

Maria Owings Shriver
B: 11/06/1955

M 04/26/1986
S 2011

Arnold Schwarzenegger
B: 07/30/1947

Rosemary Scarlett Shriver
B: 01/08/2009

Linda Sophia Potter
B: 01/13/1956

M 05/31/1986

Timothy Perry Shriver
B: 08/29/1959

Katherine Eunice Schwarzenegger
B: 12/13/1989

M 06/08/2019

Christopher Michael Pratt
B: 06/21/1979

Rose Sophia Shriver
B: 06/14/1987

Christina Maria Aurelia Schwarzenegger
B: 07/23/1991

Timothy Potter Shriver Jr.
B: 12/08/1988

M 09/23/2017

Tamara Day
B: 12/01/1985

Patrick Arnold Schwarzenegger
B: 09/18/1993

Samuel Kennedy Shriver
B: 07/13/1992

Francis Sargent Shriver
B: 07/01/2018

Christopher Sargent Shriver Schwarzenegger
B: 09/27/1997

Kathleen Shriver
B: 03/09/1994

Caroline Shriver
B: 09/17/1997

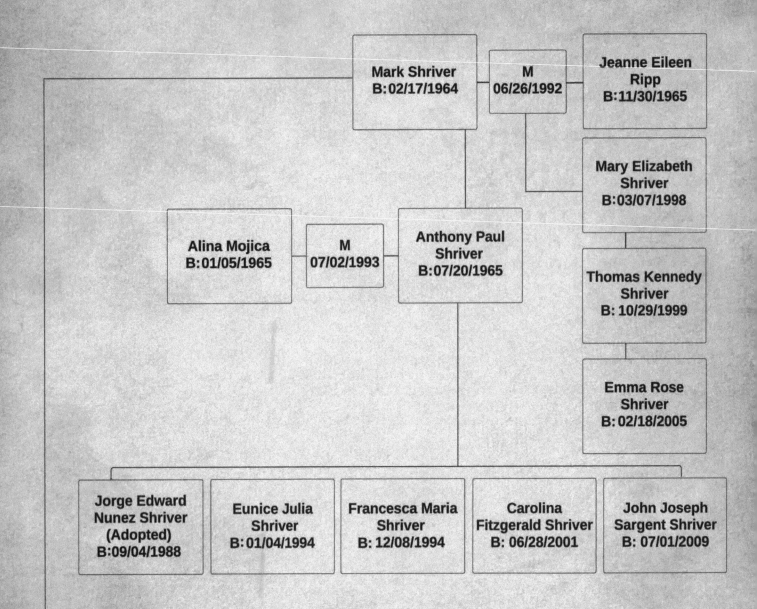

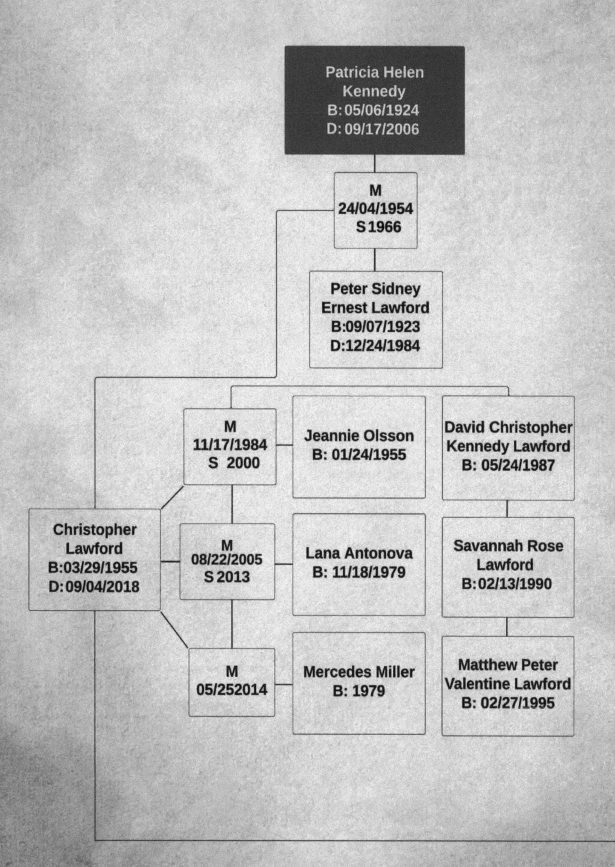

Patricia Helen
Kennedy
B: 05/06/1924
D: 09/17/2006

M
24/04/1954
S 1966

Peter Sidney
Ernest Lawford
B:09/07/1923
D:12/24/1984

M
11/17/1984
S 2000

Jeannie Olsson
B: 01/24/1955

David Christopher
Kennedy Lawford
B: 05/24/1987

Christopher
Lawford
B:03/29/1955
D:09/04/2018

M
08/22/2005
S 2013

Lana Antonova
B: 11/18/1979

Savannah Rose
Lawford
B:02/13/1990

M
05/252014

Mercedes Miller
B: 1979

Matthew Peter
Valentine Lawford
B: 02/27/1995

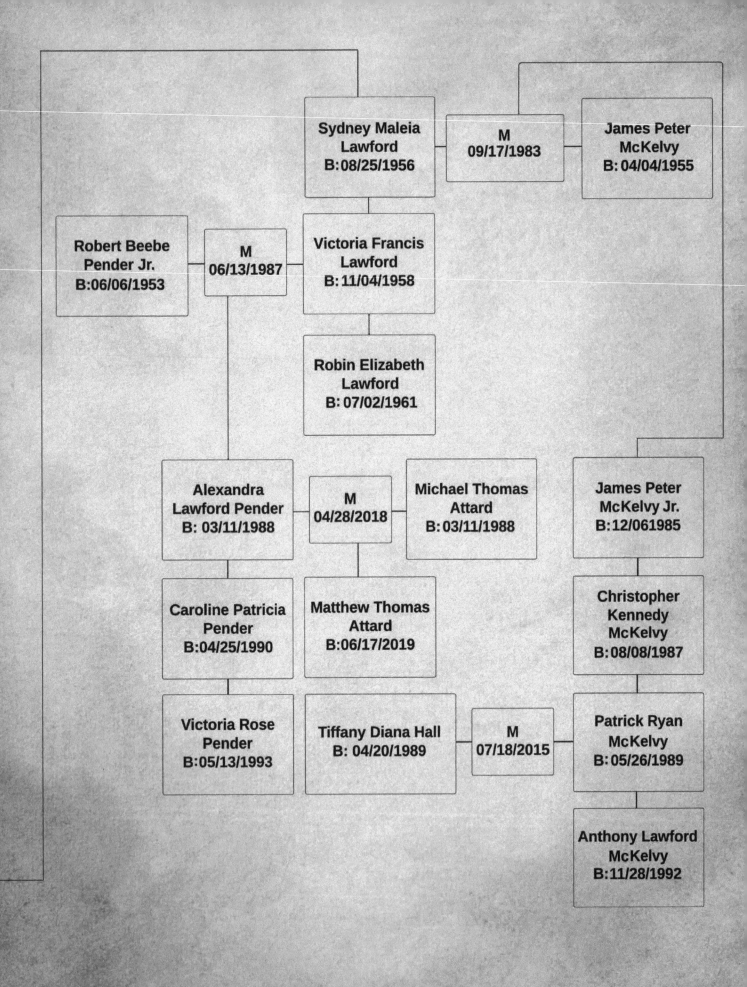

SIBLING 7

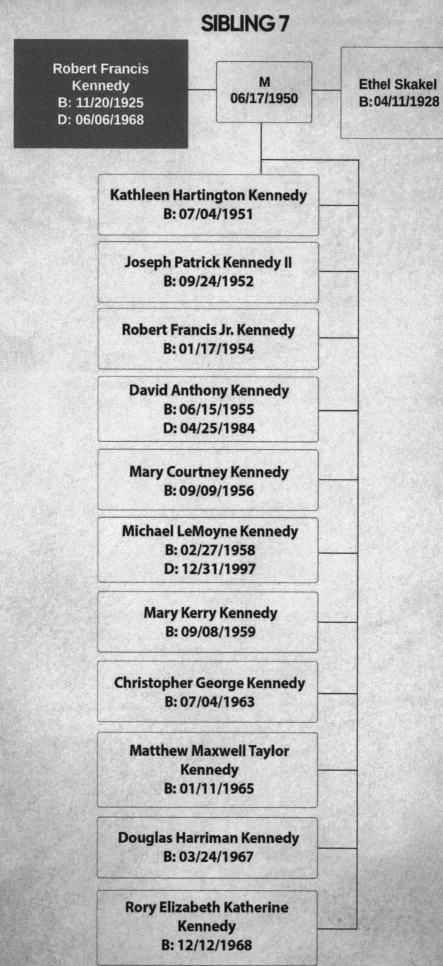

Robert Francis Kennedy
B: 11/20/1925
D: 06/06/1968

M
06/17/1950

Ethel Skakel
B: 04/11/1928

Kathleen Hartington Kennedy
B: 07/04/1951

Joseph Patrick Kennedy II
B: 09/24/1952

Robert Francis Jr. Kennedy
B: 01/17/1954

David Anthony Kennedy
B: 06/15/1955
D: 04/25/1984

Mary Courtney Kennedy
B: 09/09/1956

Michael LeMoyne Kennedy
B: 02/27/1958
D: 12/31/1997

Mary Kerry Kennedy
B: 09/08/1959

Christopher George Kennedy
B: 07/04/1963

Matthew Maxwell Taylor
Kennedy
B: 01/11/1965

Douglas Harriman Kennedy
B: 03/24/1967

Rory Elizabeth Katherine
Kennedy
B: 12/12/1968

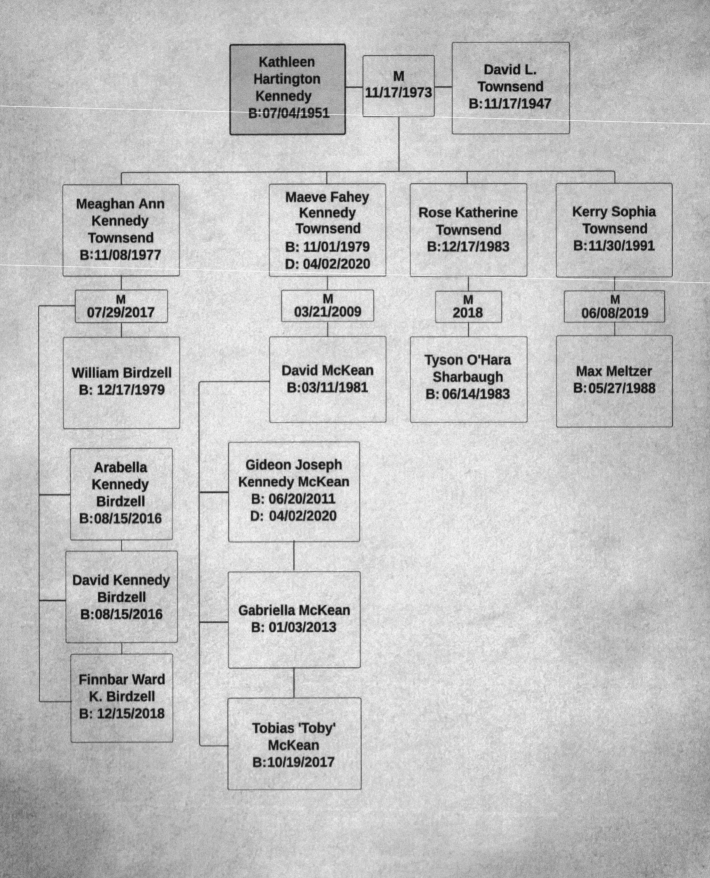

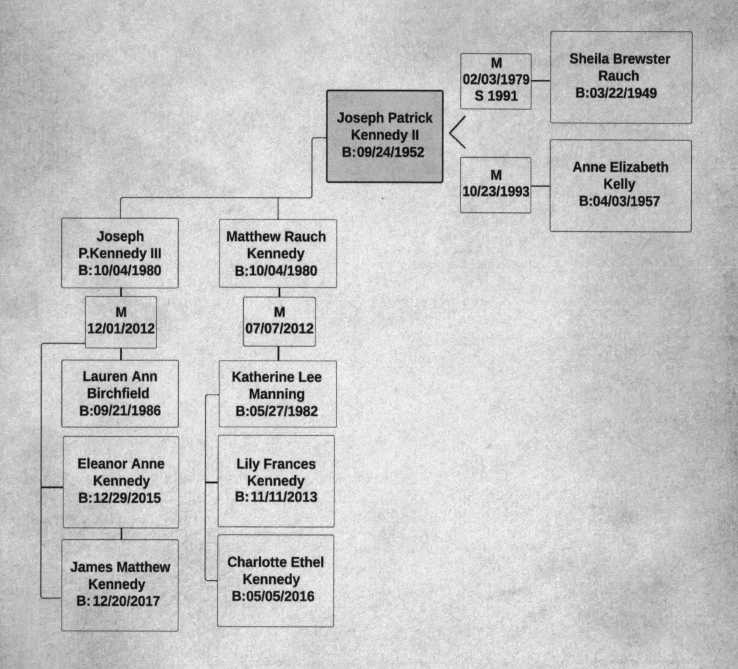

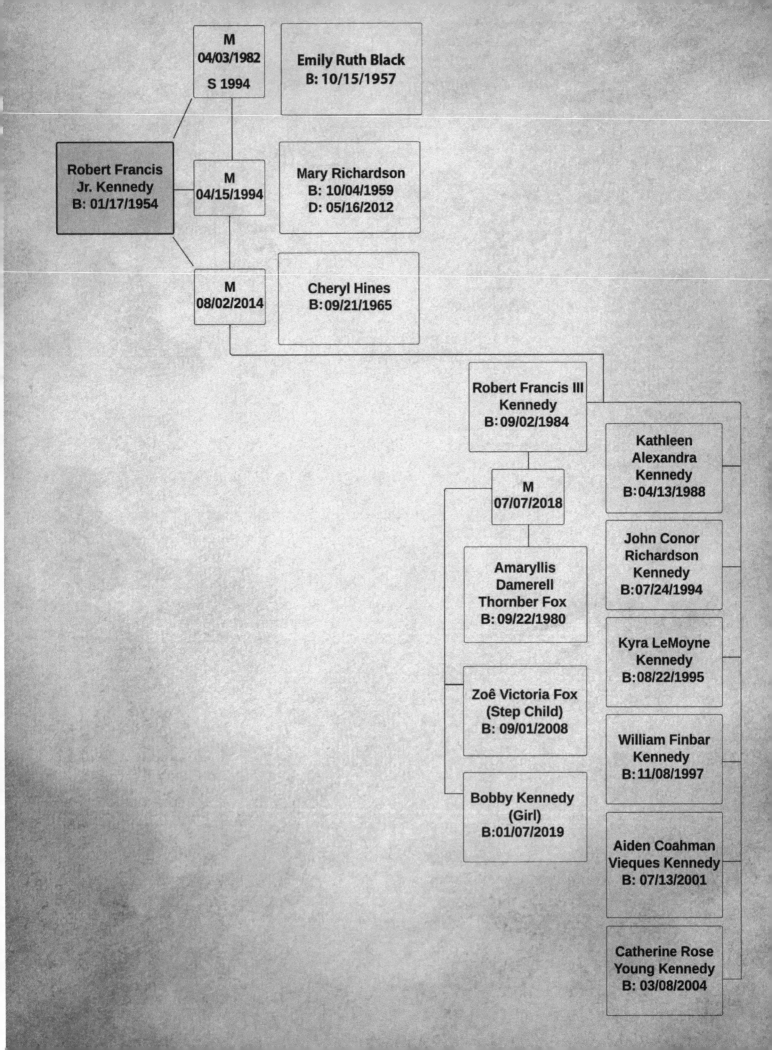

M
04/03/1982

S 1994

Emily Ruth Black
B: 10/15/1957

Robert Francis
Jr. Kennedy
B: 01/17/1954

M
04/15/1994

Mary Richardson
B: 10/04/1959
D: 05/16/2012

M
08/02/2014

Cheryl Hines
B: 09/21/1965

Robert Francis III
Kennedy
B: 09/02/1984

Kathleen
Alexandra
Kennedy
B: 04/13/1988

M
07/07/2018

John Conor
Richardson
Kennedy
B: 07/24/1994

Amaryllis
Damerell
Thornber Fox
B: 09/22/1980

Kyra LeMoyne
Kennedy
B: 08/22/1995

Zoê Victoria Fox
(Step Child)
B: 09/01/2008

William Finbar
Kennedy
B: 11/08/1997

Bobby Kennedy
(Girl)
B: 01/07/2019

Aiden Coahman
Vieques Kennedy
B: 07/13/2001

Catherine Rose
Young Kennedy
B: 03/08/2004

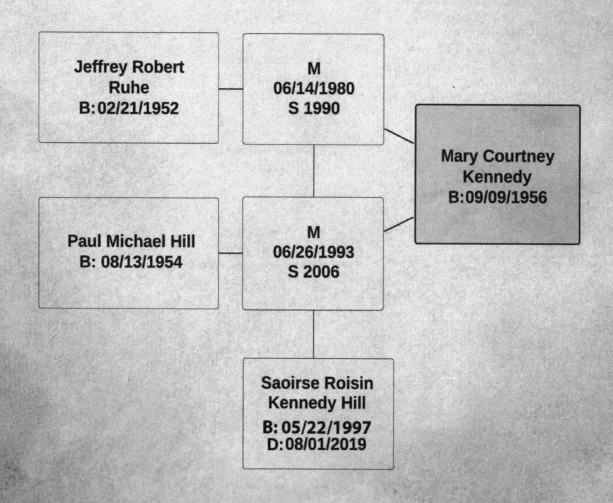

David Anthony
Kennedy
B: 06/15/1955
D: 04/25/1984

Jeffrey Robert
Ruhe
B: 02/21/1952

M
06/14/1980
S 1990

Mary Courtney
Kennedy
B: 09/09/1956

Paul Michael Hill
B: 08/13/1954

M
06/26/1993
S 2006

Saoirse Roisin
Kennedy Hill
B: 05/22/1997
D: 08/01/2019

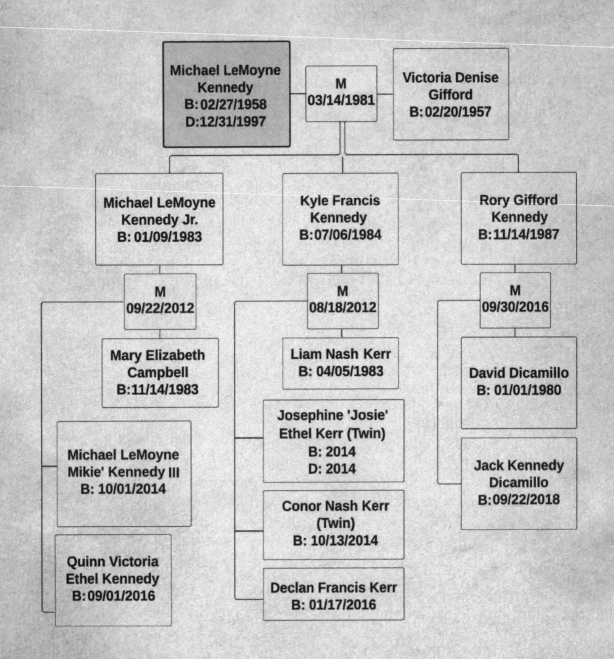

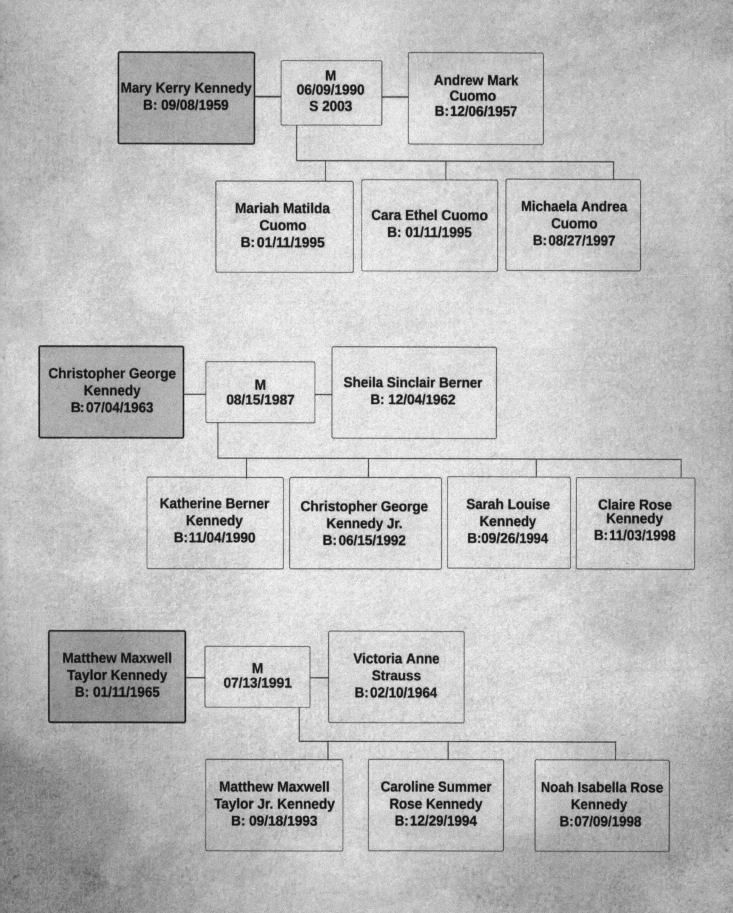

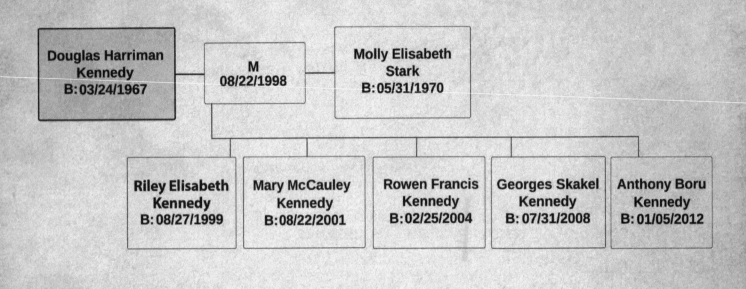

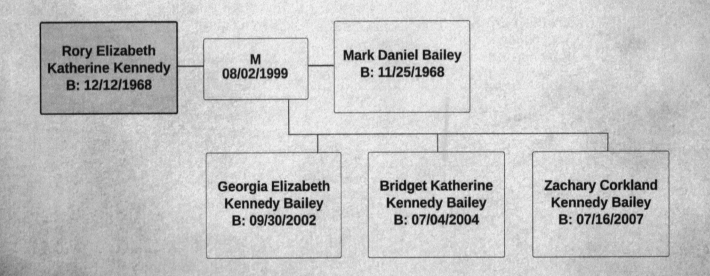

SIBLING 8

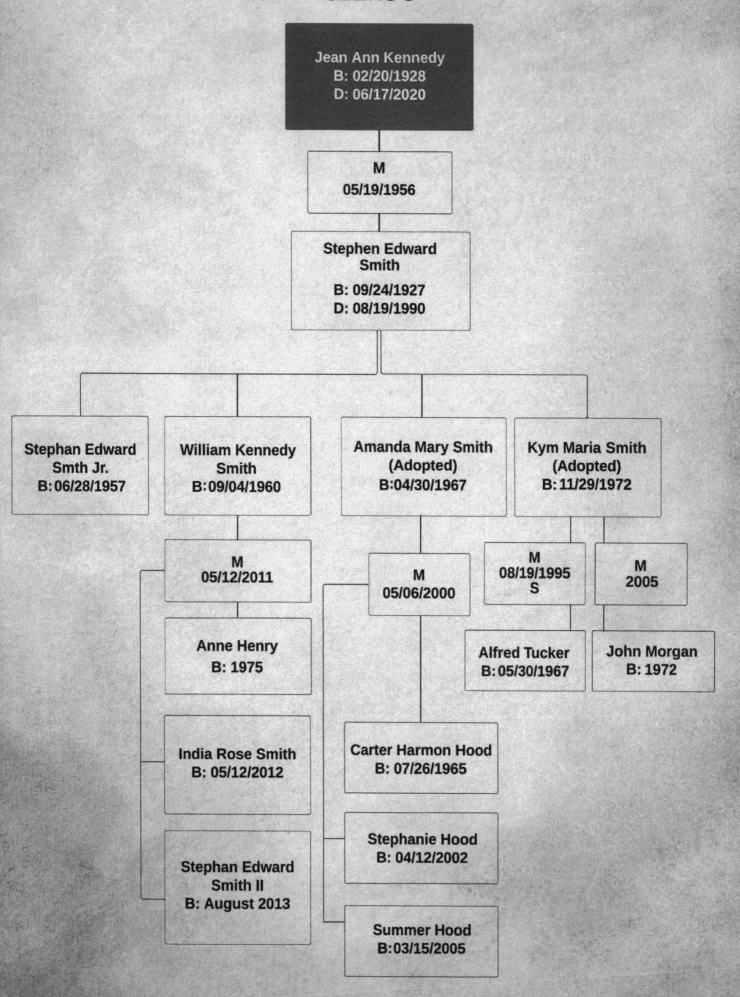

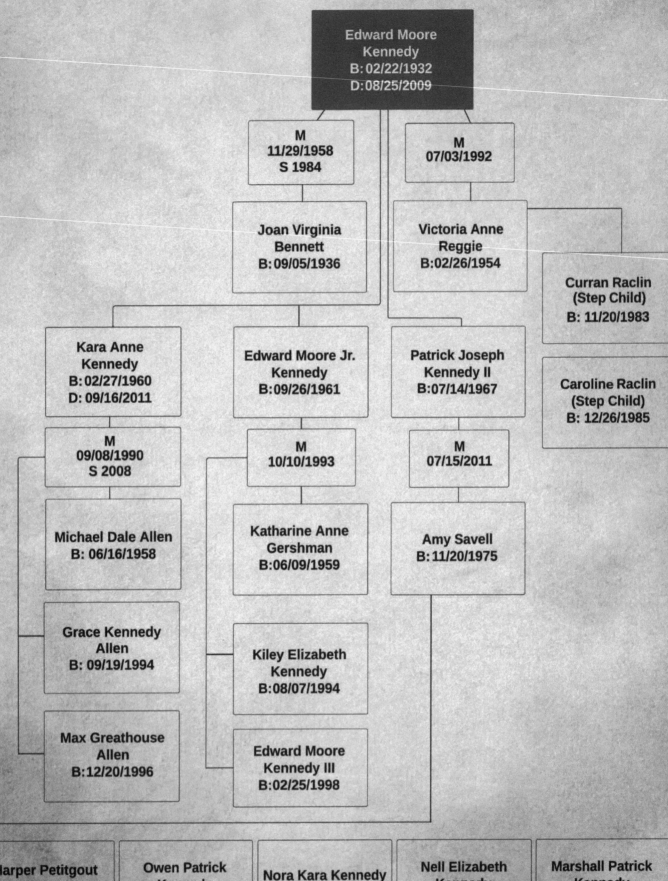

Edward Moore Kennedy
B: 02/22/1932
D: 08/25/2009

M
11/29/1958
S 1984

M
07/03/1992

Joan Virginia Bennett
B: 09/05/1936

Victoria Anne Reggie
B: 02/26/1954

Curran Raclin (Step Child)
B: 11/20/1983

Caroline Raclin (Step Child)
B: 12/26/1985

Kara Anne Kennedy
B: 02/27/1960
D: 09/16/2011

Edward Moore Jr. Kennedy
B: 09/26/1961

Patrick Joseph Kennedy II
B: 07/14/1967

M
09/08/1990
S 2008

M
10/10/1993

M
07/15/2011

Michael Dale Allen
B: 06/16/1958

Katharine Anne Gershman
B: 06/09/1959

Amy Savell
B: 11/20/1975

Grace Kennedy Allen
B: 09/19/1994

Kiley Elizabeth Kennedy
B: 08/07/1994

Max Greathouse Allen
B: 12/20/1996

Edward Moore Kennedy III
B: 02/25/1998

Harper Petitgout (Step Child)
B: 11/14/2008

Owen Patrick Kennedy
B: 04/16/2012

Nora Kara Kennedy
B: 11/19/2013

Nell Elizabeth Kennedy
B: 11/29/2015

Marshall Patrick Kennedy
B: 05/27/2018

Caroline Kennedy and Kerry Kennedy, daughter of Attorney General Robert F. Kennedy, look through hinged panel of President John F. Kennedy's desk in the Oval Office, White House, June 22, 1963, Washington D.C.
(Copyright: JFK Library)

A special thank you to Kerry Kennedy for helping me with the genealogy

Table of Contents

Dedication

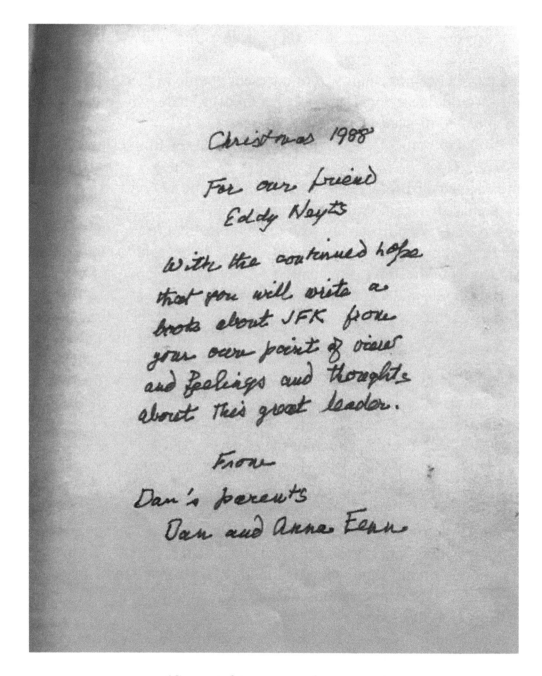

Christmas 1988

For our friend
Eddy Neyts

With the continued hope
that you will write a
book about JFK from
your own point of view
and feelings and thoughts
about this great leader.

From
Dan's parents
Dan and Anna Fenn

(Copyright: personal property)

To My Wife Dorine,
who made the impossible, possible.
To Anna and Dan Fenn Jr.,
who encouraged me to write a book on JFK, my way.

i

Acknowledgments

Writing another book on President John F. Kennedy, in a very different approach and never done by one author, is a difficult and daunting undertaking, as a "hobby" historian.

But I got a lot of encouragements from different people in the shaping of my book. First of all I would like to thank my polisher Geoff Meade, who did an excellent job and was captivated of what I was able to write.

A special thanks to Françoise Pelligrino for allowing me to interview her on Joseph Kennedy Sr.

The John F. Kennedy Library was of great help: The Director Alan Price, Stacey Chandler, archivist, Karen Adler Abraimon, director of archives. A very special thank goes to Maryrose Grossman, who did an excellent job on the selection of the images and the copyright which made my book better. And a great thank you to Jennifer Quan from the JFKL Foundation for her quick response for the picture of President Barack Obama & Caroline Kennedy.

On the family Genealogy edits, I owe a great debt to Robert Francis Kennedy's daughter, Kerry Kennedy, who did a terrific job on making my genealogy almost complete.

Thanks to my friend Lawrence Verhelst, who made my epilogue look better, among many other things. A special word for a special guy, Jurgen Machielse, who made some very positive critics in the shaping of my book.

Thanks to Sarah Alex for the cartoon of the elephant.

Forever in debt to a great man, Bill Marx. I'm humble, honored and so grateful for the picture of his father Harpo Marx.

Thanks to Boudewijn en Marthe Verhelst-Claeys, Klaas Cleppe, Jean-Marie Delattre, Marie Vercruysse, Michael Van Nieuwlant, Jason Jackson, George Greco (and dog Vicky), neighbors Andrée Cohen, Christian Bengsch… for reading and giving your honest opinion and remarks. I thank many other people for their support and a lot of telephone conversations during the Covid isolation: Philippe, Daniel Cruyt, Virginie Bonfils-Bedos…

Not forgetting Fredrik Logevall for his endorsement on the back of my books. Not everybody gets the support of a Pulitzer Prize winner.

Thanks to my publisher, SEO PROHUB UK.

And last but not least, I thank Dan H.Fenn Jr. for believing in my book and all the help he gave me.

Tribute To Dan Huntington Fenn Jr.

President Kennedy with Dan H. Fenn Jr. at Constitution Hall, Washington D.C.,
1962.
(Copyright: JFK Library)

Standing with a man who exemplified grace under pressure, a thoughtful and pragmatic approach to government, and a deep commitment to politics as a noble profession. Dan H. Fenn Jr., January 1995.
(Copyright: a gift to Eddy Neyts from Dan)

Dan H. Fenn Jr. was my mentor and guide for this book on JFK. He supported me throughout this project and read each chapter carefully, providing invaluable feedback and insight as well as constructive criticism. He was my first and foremost critic, and at the end of the day, he acknowledged that he had learned a lot about JFK, too, throughout the process.

I will never forget how we quarreled for over two years about the contents of the chapter, "JFK, the Man, the President, the Character." The exact reasons for that argument will always remain a secret between Dan and myself. One day, to break the deadlock, he sent me a few suggested revisions to the chapter and bluntly told me, "No need to mention my name, just steal it." What he had proposed was a stroke of genius. I could only wonder how he had managed to turn me around and eventually got his way – as he always did. It is fair to say that he greatly helped in making this book what it is today. I thanked him from the bottom of my heart and will be forever in his debt for his counsel on this project and for so many other things as well.

There are two people I admire most in life – my own father, Richard, and my "second" father, Dan. My father had already left us in 2006, and on August 14th, 2020, my friendship of over 38 years with Dan abruptly came to an end. Dan was truly a remarkable man. He helped Eleanor Roosevelt create the World Affairs Council. He was one of the Staff Assistants to President John F. Kennedy from 1961 to 1963. After his service in the White House, Dan was appointed Vice Chairman and a member of the US Tariff Commission (currently known as the US International Trade Commission) from 1963 to 1967. He was the Founding Director of the John F. Kennedy Presidential Library and Museum in Boston, MA, from 1971 until he left the institution in 1986. When Dan became involved with the concept of the JFK Library, the idea of a presidential library being more than a mere repository for papers and a museum of a former president's artifacts was unconventional. That emphasis on the educational aspect "was Dan's huge, huge contribution to the Kennedy library. He literally changed the focus of presidential libraries," said John Stewart, a former acting director of the library who had been its longtime director of education.

Dan was also a true scholar and an academic. His real joy in life was teaching, which he did for over 56 years both in Boston, MA and across the rest of the country. He was a faculty member at the Harvard Graduate Business School, where he still held a class via Zoom during the height of the Covid-19 pandemic and the Harvard Kennedy School of Government. He continued to teach until a few weeks before his death.

Family meant the world to Dan. He was a wonderful father to his four children, Peter, Anne, Thomas, and David Fenn, as well as his three stepchildren, Greg, Marie, and Chris Sheppard. Later in life, he became a fantastic grandfather to his 14 grandchildren and an amazing great-grandfather to his five great-grandchildren. In the eyes of his loving family, he was an example and inspiration – they absolutely adored him. "He knew everything about those kids," Peter used to say of his father's relationship with his grandchildren and great-grandchildren. He was an emotional and passionate man too. I will always remember when, in 2003, on our way to the airport, he asked me to use my cell phone to make a phone call. While letting him use my phone, I was surprised to hear that he was enthusiastically calling Patsy, that very dear friend of his! Dan was 80 years old at the time but still madly in love!

His sense of humor was legendary. It was witty, at times biting, but always to the point. For example, I will never forget his reaction when I introduced him to Dorine, who would become my second wife in 2005. Dan jokingly warned Dorine, "Never marry this guy. You don't know what trouble you're getting yourself into! This guy is crazy..." What Dan really meant was, "Ed, you made a great choice!"

In March 2020, when the rapid spread of the Coronavirus made it impossible for us to travel to Boston to celebrate his 97th birthday, he was pulling my leg and said, "Dorine, leave Ed at home, come alone, you don't need him on this trip." A few months later, he left us after a short illness. The concept of a nursing home was not in his dictionary. However, it provides me some comfort to know that he took the few Cuban cigars that I had sent for his birthday in the spring for his long journey. Dan knew a thing or two about enjoying life.

This book is dedicated to my dear friend and mentor, Dan, an extremely intelligent man who successfully combined the rare virtues of honesty and humbleness. Always prepared to help his fellow citizens, Dan was a true humanitarian with a great sense of empathy.

The secret of Dan's long and rich life? His personal motto says it all, "When you wake up in the morning, recall that you always have something important to do."

I am deeply grateful for everything you have done, and you will be forever in our thoughts.

Author's Note

Like so many of the Baby Boomers, indelibly etched in my memory is where I was on Friday, November 22nd, 1963, at 12.30 p.m., the infamous moment when President John Fitzgerald Kennedy was assassinated.

I was fifteen years old. The silence in my room was shattered when my mother came upstairs to deliver the terrible news that President Kennedy had been shot in Dallas, Texas. Like so many people all over the world, I wept. And I cried again, 45 years later (at Dan's place in Lexington, in Boston, Massachusetts), on November 4th, 2008, when it was confirmed that Barack Obama was being elected the first black President in American history. On that occasion, of course, there were tears of joy. The massive impact of both events for me is difficult to explain.

But Kennedy's death certainly ignited a deep passion within me. I started collecting newspapers, articles, magazines, and books about him, reading everything I could find on the amazing man. As time passed, hundreds of books were written on President Kennedy's life, family, and administration, and I bought every single one I could get my hands on.

Today, my private library is undoubtedly the wealthiest private collection on the subject, and, of course, I have read every one of them!

My goal in this, my own account of his life, is to be as accurate as possible on historical facts and dates concerning John Fitzgerald Kennedy – something which cannot be said of many of the books published on the subject during the past sixty years. While writing this book, I was often asked if I would be the one who tells the whole truth and nothing but the truth. Have I succeeded? Yes and no, because on certain facts in his life, his personal life, it's impossible to find the truth. You, the reader, will decide if I have uncovered some truths in his political accomplishments and failures. I would claim modestly that I have certainly come closer to the truth about JFK – at least as close as an investigator, someone who is fond of history and passionate for the truth, can get.

And if the reader has learned something from the results of my extensive research, it will be a great satisfaction to me. Where I quote other works on JFK, the relevant book is referenced in my notes.

However, in my opinion, many authors have been hasty and very sloppy in their historical approach towards John Fitzgerald Kennedy. Some of them have embellished their research for sensationalism, and their abusive, gossipy approach has marred actual history.

Sheldon Stern, who was the historian at the John F. Kennedy Library in Boston from 1977 to 1999, says, "There is, of course, nothing new about historical participants manipulating the evidence and inventing "truths" to suit their purposes." (1)

Now I have been given the opportunity to write a book with a totally different approach. At least, that is my true hope.

Never before has the subject of JFK been tackled so thoroughly to help a new generation of readers – countless young readers, who I hope will have a better and more accurate understanding of John F. Kennedy, based on the historical facts.

On the assertion that people keep asking me, "Why another Kennedy book?" I respond with the words of the great Dutch historian Pieter Geyl, who, in his view, states that all historians are influenced by the present when writing history, and thus, all historical writing is transitory.

In Geyl's view, there never can be a definitive account for all ages because every age has a different view of the past. Geyl felt that history was the progress of "argument without end."

Finally, about the title "Life is Unfair," I agree with President Kennedy when he said in his press conference on March 21st, 1962, "There is always inequity in life. Some men are killed in the war, and some are wounded. Some men never leave the country, and some men are stationed in San Francisco. It's very hard in military or personal life to assure complete equality. Life is unfair."

- Some people are born poor; some are born rich.
- Some people have a handicapped child.
- Some people commit suicide.

I am convinced that a lot of people won't find this a positive statement, but it is a reality. Moreover, it's an everyday situation for so many people all over the world. *Life is Unfair*, but we should never despair. We need to fight, struggle back, making the best of it because life can be great, worth living, and a great adventure.

There's a heartfelt quote from Jacqueline Kennedy on life, "Every moment one lives is different from the other. The good, the bad, the hardship, the joy, the tragedy, love, and happiness are all interwoven into one single, indescribable whole that is called life. You cannot separate the good from the bad. And perhaps there is no need to do so either."

In my book, I shall illustrate President Kennedy, not as a myth, but as a man. He himself once said at Yale University on June 11th, 1962, "For the greatest enemy of the truth is very often not the lie: deliberate, contrived and dishonest – but the myth – persistent, persuasive and unrealistic."

John Kennedy was an imperfect figure, as a man and as a President. Yet for me, he was still an extraordinary human being; extremely intelligent, charismatic, and graceful. A man who, despite his health problems throughout his life, never, ever complained. He inspired, just as he inspired me, and will continue to inspire future generations of Americans to believe in the power of government and to share the conviction that politics can truly be a noble profession.

I consulted both positive and negative books, which I have placed in three categories:

1. <u>The Court Historians:</u> William Manchester, Arthur M. Schlesinger Jr., Ted Sorensen, Lawrence F. O'Brien, Evelyn Lincoln, Ken O'Donnell, Dave Powers. Also, Pierre Salinger and Paul B. Fay who helped to sustain the Camelot legacy.
2. <u>The Iconoclasts or Revisionists:</u> Victor Lasky, Richard J. Walton, Henry Fairly,

Joan and Clay Blair Jr., Nigel Hamilton, Herbert S. Parmet, Noam Chomsky, Peter Collier, and David Horowitz, Thomas C. Reeves, Seymour M. Hersh, Mark J. White, and many others.

For some (in the second category), he was an incompetent President whose personal weaknesses limited his ability to carry out his duties, a cold war warrior who brought America almost to the brink of nuclear conflict. For some others, he was a compulsive womanizer, a liar, an amphetamine addict, lazy, ruthless, and corrupt.

3. <u>The Political Realists or Post Revisionists</u>: These who take Kennedy on the record, such as Michael R. Beschloss, James N. Giglio, Robert Dallek, Michael O'Brien, James W. Douglas, Larry J; Sabato, Irving Bernstein, Hugh Brogan, Alan Brinkley, Sheldon M. Stern, Fredrik Logevall, and many others.

In this last category, JFK comes out rather well because most authors saw him growing in the office, learning from his mistakes – an above-average-rated President and certainly one of the few transitional Presidents who remain popular after their death. His influence will continue because successive generations in America and around the world have discovered and will continue to learn that he was a man who could inspire – just like he inspired me to write a book about him.

I own no books on his assassination because there are too many murder plots, ranging from the Mob, the Russians, the Mossad, Castro, the CIA, the FBI, his own secret servicemen, all the way up to Lyndon Johnson. Much of it sounds like science fiction to me; many theories are too crazy to be true. However, I have my idea about the assassination, which I will explain in the epilogue.

This book has been in the making for a long time. In 1982, I was preparing an exhibit on President Kennedy and his brother Bobby in Bruges, my hometown in Belgium. With my wife and son, I went to see the director of the Kennedy Library in Boston, Mr. Dan H. Fenn Jr., a former staff assistant to President Kennedy. The first time I met Mr. Dan H. Fenn was at his office in the Kennedy Library at the end of Columbia Point, which just cuts into Dorchester Bay. I told him the following, "If you think Kennedy is God or Elvis Presley to me, you are wrong. Kennedy is my hobby, my reading hobby." I explained to him that I was preparing an exhibition on President Kennedy for the benefit of disabled children, as my late wife was a teacher.

Dan later told me what he thought the first time he saw me, "I said to myself, *what a strange, crazy fellow.*" Then he told me what he thought of me when he met me the second time, "But the second time I saw you, I believed in you." He never imagined Kennedy could be a hobby, a reading hobby, instead of me being another "Kennedy watcher." I spent the entire week at the JFK Library, picking up ideas for my exhibition. I could talk with the director whenever I wanted. I'll never forget what he said to me on a Friday in August 1982, at noon, "You're not coming back this afternoon?"

I replied, "No. You know Mr. Fenn, this afternoon, I am going to Hyannis Port to knock on Rose Kennedy's door." Dan laughed, and a friendship for life was born, based on a determination, perseverance, and wit that Dan and I both share.

The exhibition took place in November 1983, with Kathleen Kennedy Townsend (JFK's niece and the eldest daughter of Robert Kennedy), and her husband David, and Dan Fenn at the opening ceremonies.

Choosing the guest list generated the following fine anecdote (against me). Dan proposed Maria Shriver and her husband Arnold Schwarzenegger because Maria's mother, Eunice Kennedy, was the President's sister. Eunice was married to Sargent Shriver, the Peace Corps Director, during the Kennedy Presidency. I telephoned Dan and said, "No, Mr. Fenn, I don't need a Shriver. And who the hell is Arnold Schwarzenegger?" A year later, he became world-famous through his Terminator movies.

Around Christmas 1988, Dan's parents encouraged me to write a book about JFK. They thought that my perspective, feelings, and thoughts about the 35th President of the United States were fascinating. Anna Fenn died on December 28th, 1998. Thirty years after her encouragement, and twenty years after her death at 99, I finally fulfilled her wishes and my dream. That being said, I had wanted to start years earlier with my project but couldn't find the time. It is very time-consuming to be a certified accountant, defending clients against the IRS.

I am aware that it is a challenging undertaking, writing yet another Kennedy book. It is a daunting task, trying to find an original approach. Not being a scholar, nor a history professor, simply nurturing a deep love of this history, trying to find out historical truth on John F. Kennedy is like a drug to me. My point of view and candor may surprise you. Politics containing excessive lies and too many compromises is completely unacceptable to me.

However, I am fascinated with American political history, along with world history, and always will be. I have the utmost respect for historians, but I want to confront various authors, historians, and scholars, on what they wrote about many events surrounding the Kennedy administration, not least Cuba, Vietnam, the African Americans, the race to the moon, and the personal issues of JFK's life, his health, and his womanizing.

In this book, these subjects have been approached in a non-gossipy nor salacious way while acknowledging that I will not find the entire historical truth. That being said, I am confident that I have been able to expose a lot of falsehoods.

Historian Michael Beschloss asserted during a stimulating television discussion with Thomas C. Reeves, "The burden on all of us who write about those things is to be fair to him (JFK). How much reliability can we place on some of these sources about all these women? Many of them, I'm sure, are true, but again, you have to be fair to someone." That Kennedy's liaisons were extensive is undeniable, but not all of those ascribed to him could have logistically taken place. (2)

On his marriage and his character, not forgetting the influence of his parents on the shaping of JFK, I have looked for the truth in order to discover fabrications, contradictions, inaccuracies, and inconsistencies. I have searched for real truths or blunt lies, determined to set the record straight.

Historically, there are glaring examples of just a day making a tremendous difference, as with the independence of two great countries, July 4th, 1776 or July 5th, 1776, and "l'appel du June 18th, 1940," the famous speech was not delivered on June 19th, 1940, from General Charles de Gaulle.

In 'Conversations with Kennedy' by Benjamin C. Bradlee, Kennedy is quoted as saying, "What makes journalism so fascinating, and biography so interesting, is the struggle to answer that single question: *What's he like?*" (3)

I have tried to find answers to that fascinating question. The Camelot legend created by Jacqueline Kennedy during a Life Magazine interview with Theodore White, and published on December 6th, 1963, is now consigned to its original origins in the Middle Ages. The reference to a fictional, idyllic world in the Kennedy White House seems to have done more harm than good to the legacy of John F. Kennedy. I think President Kennedy himself would not have liked the 'Camelot' idea at all. Indeed, his exemplary display of fortitude while facing adversity would suggest the opposite; that is, he would have been disgusted and outraged by the very idea of it.

As with all politically charged depictions, sometimes the approach to President Kennedy depends on the political affiliation of the author, either democrat or republican. Other authors seem to have more propensity towards writing science fiction stories than actual history. In 1989, C. David Heymann, in his book called '*A Woman Named Jackie*', wrote that according to the actor Peter Lawford, Marilyn Monroe was crazy about Jack. He expounds the theory that the actress had devised all sorts of madcap fantasies with herself in the starring role. Marilyn would have JFK's children, and she would take Jackie's place as First Lady. Marilyn was said to have told Lawford that she had telephoned Jackie at the White House, and Peter Lawford states that according to Marilyn, Jackie wasn't shaken by the call and, in fact, agreed to step aside.

She would divorce Jack, and Marilyn could marry him. She stipulated that Marilyn would have to move into the White House and, if Marilyn wasn't prepared to live openly in the White House, she might as well forget about it. (4)

In his book '*Joe and Marilyn*', which came out in 2014, two years after C. David Heymann's death on May 9th, 2012, Heymann attributed that story to Ralph Roberts, the late actor, and Masseur, a dear friend of Marilyn Monroe. (5)

Subsequently, Christopher Anderson, in his 2013 book '*These few precious days*', tells the 1989 version of the author Heymann's Marilyn Monroe story on 'CBS This Morning'. A so-called new revelation was made when Mr. Anderson told the story of Peter Lawford's claim. (6)

The question is, do you really believe this story? There is another amazing story repeated in a large number of Kennedy books about a quote attributed to the late Senator, Daniel Patrick Moynihan. After President Kennedy was assassinated, Moynihan, the then Assistant Secretary of Labor, was speaking with the Washington Post's star writer, Mary McGrory. Mary sadly commented, "We'll never laugh again." Moynihan replied, "Heavens, Mary! We'll laugh again, but we'll never be young again." This has now become a historical comment. *'We'll never be young again'* is even the title of a book by Chuck Fries and Irv Wilson with Spencer Green from 2003 with recollections on President Kennedy by many famous people. Yet, the simple truth is that the quote *'Heavens, Mary, we'll laugh again but we'll never be young again'* was from Dan H. Fenn Jr. (7)

At that time, Dan was Staff Assistant to President Kennedy. The comment was made in a car on the day of JFK's funeral on November 25th, 1963, on the ride to Arlington Cemetery. The first and the only author who quoted Dan Fenn instead of Moynihan was Larry J. Sabato in 2013. (8)

In future books on JFK, they should give credit to my friend Dan.

With the spiritual help of my friend Dan Fenn Jr., my book on President John F. Kennedy is the fulfillment of a wonderful hobby. I consider Dan to be my second father. He was an exceptional man who combined a great intellect with a great sense of humor and humility. He would have been proud that his encouragement was the catalyst for my years of research, now coming to fruition in these pages. For me, writing a book on JFK is the fulfillment of a never-ending American dream. If you ask me about the link between Kennedy (a man I never met), Dan H. Fenn Jr. (my friend), and me, humbly, I would venture to state that it is our sense of humor. If the pharmaceutical industry could produce a humor drug instead of a drug for less cholesterol, can you imagine taking a humor drug every day? I bet our cholesterol would go down by alleviating stress through humor.

Finally, the photograph on the cover is an illustration as well as an explanation of my title, *'Life is Unfair.'* Depicted is the two-year-old John Fitzgerald Kennedy Jr., climbing around the resolute desk in the Oval Office. The iconic photo has the young John looking through the small door. John Kennedy Jr. has said that it is one of the memories of his father, "I have a few. He had this desk in the Oval Office, and I just remember the inside. You could climb around in it. He used to give us chewing gum because my mother didn't like us to chew gum. So, we used to go over the Oval Office at night, and he'd feed us gum under the desk." (9)

John Fitzgerald Kennedy Jr. died on July 16th, 1999, when the airplane he was piloting crashed into the Atlantic Ocean off the coast of Martha's Vineyard, Massachusetts. His wife Carolyn Bessette and her sister Lauren were also killed. He was on his way to attend the wedding of his cousin Rory Kennedy, the daughter of his father's brother, Robert Kennedy. He was 38 years old and in the prime of his life. How can life be more unfair?

That tragic event taking a toll on the remaining Kennedy Clan was inevitable. The gracious way that John Jr.'s sister, Caroline Kennedy, handled the tragedy was phenomenally dignified. Personally, I was privileged to witness her grace for myself when attending a *'Meet and Greet'* event at the Kennedy Library on November 4th, 2009. Caroline generously signed four books for my library, one of them was titled, *'A family of poems.'* She opened it, then raised the book to her lips and gave it a discrete kiss. Her lovely gesture touched me deeply. I will never forget that moment for the rest of my life.

Each chapter will show some photographs, which will be assisted with explaining what the chapter is about. Those photos illustrate the moments that altered their lives and are shown throughout my book to invoke empathy which, I think, is a wonderful human virtue.

Chapter 1: The Influence Of The Parents On John F. Kennedy's Preparation For The Presidency

"Mothers may still want their favorite son to grow up to be president. Still, according to a famous Gallup poll of some years ago, they do not want them to become politicians in the process."

- Profiles In Courage 1956

1.1. Who Was Joseph P. Kennedy?

To most historians, Joe Kennedy was a crook, a bootlegger, a stock market manipulator, a dictator, a womanizer, ruthless in business, anti-Semitic, and with ties to the mob.

But in *the Patriarch,* David Nasaw comes up with a more credible portrait of father Kennedy. Nasaw was asked to write the biography by Joe Kennedy's two surviving offspring – the former US Ambassador to Ireland, Jean Kennedy Smith, and Senator Edward Kennedy. Nasaw only accepted after the Kennedys promised full cooperation for unfiltered access to Joseph P. Kennedy's papers in the John F. Kennedy Presidential Library, including those closed to researchers and total freedom to cite any document that Nasaw came across. No attempts were made to withhold information or to censor his book in any way. (1)

In the face of all the negative stories about Joe, including the memoirs of Gloria Swanson (with whom Joseph Kennedy had an affair), it was time to have a more balanced and honest picture of Joseph P. Kennedy. Interviewed by Randy Dotinga on December 7, 2012, Nasaw described Joe Kennedy as a man who worked in shipbuilding during World War I and then as a major stock trader during the boom in the 20s, and Joe arrived in Hollywood as a studio operator just when the silent movies were giving way to talkies. He became a Roosevelt confidant, head of the Maritime Commission, chairman of the Securities and Exchange Commission, and Ambassador to Great Britain. Joe Kennedy was an Irish Catholic from East Boston who realized when he left Harvard that he was an outsider, who would have to fight and claw his way inside, trusting no one along the way except family members and maybe a couple of other Irish Catholics.

Unlike other outsiders who make it inside, Joe refused to play by the rules: his self-confidence confirmed he was always the smartest guy in the room, not needing to follow what anyone else said – not even Roosevelt. The result, Nasaw observed, was that Joe ended up on the outside again. (2)

At the age of 25, on January 20, 1914, he boasted that he was the youngest bank president in America – head of the Columbia Trust Bank. Whether it was true or not, no one knows, wrote Ronald Kessler in "the Sins of the Father" in 1996. Joe had learned that the First Ward National Bank was planning a takeover bid for the Columbia Trust Company, in which his father still held a minority interest. Afraid that other stockholders would vote to sell, Joe borrowed $45,000 from family members and friends to obtain control of the bank. (3)

In a radio address on October 29, 1940, in support of Franklin Roosevelt's third-term election bid, Joe said, "I have a great stake in this country. My wife and I have given nine hostages to fortune. Our children and your children are more important than anything else in the world. The kind of America that they and their children will inherit is a great concern to us all. In light of these considerations, I believe that Franklin D. Roosevelt should be reelected President of the United States." (4)

In his 2012 interview, Nasaw said, "Every child got this sense from him (Joe) that

I've struggled. I worked hard, and I struggled for you. I made enough money, so you each have million-dollar trust funds. I expect each of you to do something with your lives, not to make money, but in public service." It's an anomaly because strong fathers don't necessarily yield strong sons, but all of these kids were remarkable, all independent-minded. (5)

Joe Kennedy was a man who lived for his children and who triumphed when they triumphed. Kennedy was always wrapped up in his family. He was convinced they were his greatest accomplishment. In 1943 – not a bright year for Kennedy – Reporter Harold Martin asked him about his family. "It is the finest thing in my life," Kennedy answered with quiet sincerity. "The measure of a man's success in life is not the money he's made. It's the kind of family he has raised. In that, I've been mighty lucky." Kennedy encouraged his sons to expand and grow – indeed, to become bigger men than himself. They did, and he was pleased. In that respect, Joseph Kennedy was generous. (6)

To lose four of them during his lifetime – five if you count Rosemary, who was mentally disabled and underwent a disastrous lobotomy – that's a tragedy.

I think Joseph P. Kennedy made three great mistakes in his life.

First, he believed that American support for the British war effort was going to destroy the US economy: he thought the British would lose the war. His isolationism proved him wrong.

Second, he believed that Hitler was a reasonable statesman who was prepared to negotiate: Joe Kennedy thought he was the man to make that deal. How terribly wrong he was.

The third mistake, and the most personally dramatic one, was the lobotomy operation on Rosemary, performed between November 12 and 28, 1941, at Joe's instigation without consulting his wife. Rosemary had been born mildly retarded, but after her failed lobotomy, she was severely mentally impaired, never recovering her memory or her speech.

Joe Kennedy was the only one in the family who visited Rosemary or consulted with her doctors at Craig House. In this private psychiatric hospital, she was first institutionalized. (7)

When somebody succeeds in life, whether it is in business, sports, the movies, as a singer, model, doctor, accountant, or whatever, people are jealous of that success – and Joseph P. Kennedy used to say, "More men die of jealousy than of cancer." John F. Kennedy said, "My father wasn't around as much as some fathers when I was young, but whether he was there or not, he made his children feel that they were the most important things in the world to him. He was so interested in what we were doing. He held up standards for us, and he was very tough when we failed to meet those standards. The toughness was important. If it hadn't been for that, Teddy might just be a playboy today. But my father cracked down on him at a crucial time in his life, and this brought out in Teddy the discipline and seriousness which will make him an important political figure." (8)

16

In his book "JFK: Reckless Youth," Nigel Hamilton quotes J. Patrick Lannan as saying of Joe, "What impressed me in those days (1945): the telephone would ring, every night at 5 o'clock. Now I know what it is to have a father-son, father-daughter relationship. But I just don't know many fathers who I have ever run into that call their sons like that. At five o'clock – like you'd set your clock – and the phone rings, "How are you? What did you do today? How are things going? Is there anything I can do for you?" (9)

Joe Kennedy was often portrayed as a dictator. Here's an example to the contrary. After dropping out of the London School of Economics because of hepatitis or "jaundice" only one month after arriving in spring 1935, Jack was keen to go to Princeton University to join his Choate roommate, Lem Billings, and several other good friends there. Joe, a Harvard man, was strongly against the idea, but after a serious talk with Jack, he let his son have his way without further argument. (10)

After his stroke on December 19, 1961, Joe Kennedy would spend the last eight years of his life unable to communicate, a crippled monster of a man frightening his grandchildren and uttering only one word, "No." President Kennedy's last visit to his father at Hyannis Port was on Sunday, October 20, 1963. He landed on the lawn in the morning and spent the whole day with his father.

Early the next day, when the helicopter was waiting to take him to Air Force One at Otis Air Base, and Joe (the ambassador) was on the porch in his wheelchair to see him off, the president went over to his father, put his arm around the older man's shoulders, and kissed his forehead. He started to walk away, turned and looked at his father for a moment, then went back and kissed him a second time – something Dave Powers had never seen him do before, "It almost seemed," Dave told Jackie a month later on the way back from Dallas, "as if the president had a feeling that he was seeing his father for the last time."

When the president and Dave were seated in the helicopter, waiting for the takeoff, he looked out the window at the figure in the wheelchair on the porch and, for the first time in all of those years, that Dave had known John Kennedy, he saw his eyes filled with tears. The president said to Dave sadly, "He's the one who made all this possible, and look at him now." (11)

Jack and his brothers and sisters had tremendous respect and the greatest admiration for their incredibly loving and caring father. I have found a French story, a true fairy tale story, about a caddie with a beautiful name, Françoise Pellegrino, who in June 1954 at the age of sixteen, was assigned as a golf caddie to Ambassador Joe Kennedy, father of the future President of the United States.

Her testimony also reveals the softer side of Joe Kennedy as a human being. She started as a caddie in Biot Golf Club (near Antibes, in the South of France) at the age of twelve and has told me she's still astonished to have been the "barefooted caddie" of a president's father.

She knew Joe Kennedy as a man with a generous heart – totally different from the negative Kennedy characterization she read in the newspapers, which upset her very much. The Joe Kennedy she knew was different. He was very respectful to everyone at the golf club. She saw the respect of his sons Jack, Bobby, and Teddy. Before every game, they had to give a handshake to every caddie and say hello.

She saw a very generous man, who, after the 18th hole, checked that every caddie was properly paid by his player; if not, Joe Kennedy paid the difference. In his game, everybody was paid the same.

Françoise was normally paid 3 "anciens francs." Joe Kennedy paid 100 "anciens francs" – about 2.15 euros in 2019. One day he told Françoise, "The sun shines for everybody."

When at the age of twenty, she told him she had a boyfriend, he said, "I want to know him."

Joe took Françoise and her boyfriend Lucien in a big Cadillac to a restaurant in Saint Paul de Vence. "We were embarrassed, not being accustomed to going to a restaurant, but Joe Kennedy did everything he could to make us feel at ease," Françoise told me.

Ambassador Kennedy was a guest at the couple's wedding on September 3, 1961, at a church in Biot, and his gift was a honeymoon reservation in a presidential suite at the Hotel Edison in New York. Joe Kennedy had his stroke.

Although Kennedy was in hospital by that time – he suffered his stroke three months after the ceremony on December 19, 1961 – everything was taken care of, paid for by Joe. The newlyweds were treated like VIPs, and after their child was born, she received presents every year.

Françoise told me Joe talked a lot about his adored granddaughter Caroline, Jack Kennedy's first child, to whom he would often speak by phone when in Antibes. "Caroline's very bright," Joseph Kennedy once commented on his granddaughter to Jack Kennedy. "Smarter than you were Jack at that age."

"Yes, she is," Jack agreed. "But look who she has for a father." That was the French caddie story, or how you see the other side of the ruthless businessman Joseph Kennedy. (12)

Sometime around midnight between Friday, July 18, and Saturday, July 19, 1969, Edward Kennedy drove his car off Dike Bridge at Chappaquiddick. His passenger, Mary Jo Kopechne, drowned. Later, Ted climbed the stairs of the family home in Hyannis Port and walked into his father's bedroom. "Dad, there was an accident," he said. "There was a girl in the car, and she drowned." Joe tilted his head forward as he listened to Ted. Then his head dropped back. Ted sat down and held his face in his hands. "I don't know, Dad. I don't know."

Joseph Kennedy died November 18, 1969, at 11.05, almost six years after Dallas and one year after Los Angeles. (13)

I was 21 years old, and to this day, I feel that Chappaquiddick was too much for him – he would never see another Kennedy becoming President. That had been Ted Kennedy's goal, and it took me until his "True Compass" memoir – honest and very, very touching – for me to forgive his Chappaquiddick mistake. He paid a very high price for it.

He truly said in that memoir, "Atonement is a process that never ends." I believe that. Maybe it's a New England thing, or an Irish thing, or a Catholic thing. Maybe all of those things. But it's as it should be. (14)

1.2. When Did Jack Kennedy Decide to Run for Public Office?

In the introduction to his 1936 book "I'm for Roosevelt," Joseph Kennedy wrote, "I have no political ambitions for myself or my children. I put down these thoughts about our president, conscious only of my concern as a father for the future of his family and my anxiety as a citizen that the facts about the president's philosophy be not lost in a fog of unworthy emotion." (1)

The French philosopher Ernest Renan said, "Woe unto the man who does not change his mind at least three times a day." Joe Kennedy was intelligent enough to change his mind. He was a businessman, after all.

In the August 1957 issue of McCall's, a monthly women's magazine, Joe was quoted as saying, "I got Jack into politics. I was the one who told him Joe (Junior) was dead, and therefore it was his responsibility to run for Congress. He didn't want to. He felt he didn't have the ability, and he still feels that way. But I told him he had to." (2) (3)

After returning from England on the day after the United States dropped the atomic bomb on Hiroshima (August 6, 1945), "Jack spent hours on ends," according to his mother, "discussing his future with his father. He was still pretty unsure at that time whether politics was the right thing for him to do... Looking back on his early days in politics, Jack liked to say that if he initially lacked confidence, his father had confidence for both."

JFK once told a friend, "If I walked out on the stage and fell flat on my face, Father would say I fell better than anyone else." In fact, Joe Kennedy's technique was more subtle than sheer flattery. In politics, there are always plenty of people to tell a candidate he has performed well no matter how badly he had done. Still, with Kennedy, the flattery was always a means of improvement. The praise he gave his son was always based on bits and pieces of facts which he had garnered from someone present. And once the compliment was delivered, the ambassador could go on to shape a critique without ever putting Jack on the defensive. This critique involved his son in a joint enterprise of evaluation. (4)

Rose Kennedy wrote in "Times to Remember," "Many people think that his father made his decision to enter politics, that Joe practically forced him into it. That would have been completely out of character on both sides. Anyone reading Joe's letters to Jack and the others can see that giving orders to his children would have been contrary to the relationship he had with them. And Jack, quite as, obviously would not have submitted to such a parental command, even if it had been given (I can imagine him smiling agreeably and saying, "Yes, Dad," as he used to smile agreeably and say, "Yes, Mother," when I told him to put on a sweater – and then go off without it)."

The combination of time, place, and circumstance made the idea of Jack's running for Congress attractive and reasonable, inexperienced in electoral politics though he certainly was. The plan also appealed enormously to Rose's father, John "Honey Fitz" Fitzgerald. He, at the time, was a healthy eighty-three. The idea that his grandson might be going to Washington to fill the same position that he had held filled "Honey Fitz" with delight. "Thank heavens," concluded Rose, "he lived to see it happen." (5)

In "True Compass," Edward Kennedy wrote, "Jack's initial interest in elective office registered as a mild surprise in our family. He never had, to my knowledge, talked about political ambitions. The last thing I'd heard, he was thinking about a career in journalism. Not even Dad saw this coming. Jack later credited those dinnertime political conversations, steered by our father, as stimulating his interest in the field. Still, as Jack saw it, Dad didn't think he had the stamina for politics. He weighed 120 pounds after the first of three operations on his war-injured back. The igniting spark, as we later learned, seemed to have been a speech – the first public speech – Jack gave. He delivered it to a Boston American Legion Audience in August 1945, on his return to the United States from his reportage in Europe. It covered the wartime fates of Britain, Ireland, and Germany. "Victor, Neutral, and Vanquished," as the title had it. The speech was a big success to Jack's surprise, as were several others he gave not long afterward. The following year, James Michael Curley resigned from his congressional seat to run for a fourth term as mayor of Boston. Jack, at loose ends and not sure of what to do with his life, decided to run for Curley's vacant 11th Congressional District, and he won." (6)

When Joe said in McCall's interview, "I got him into politics and that he had to carry on the mantle after Joe's death," is in contrast to what Lem Billings said, "I think a lot of people say that if Joe hadn't died, that Jack might never have gone into politics. I don't believe this. Nothing could have kept Jack out of politics. I think this was what he had in him, and it just would have come out, no matter what, somewhere along the line, he would have been in politics. Knowing his abilities, interests, and background, I firmly believe he would have entered politics even if he had three other brothers like Joe."

I fully agree with Lem Billings's evaluation of Jack Kennedy's entry into politics. Billings was not romanticizing. Jack had already studied the science of politics, in its domestic and international context, for six long years at college, from 1935 to 1941. (7) Jack Kennedy himself has his account of his entry into politics, "My brother Joe was killed in Europe as a flyer in August 1944, and that ended our hopes for him. But I didn't even start to think about a political profession until more than a year later. When the War came, I didn't know what I was going to do, and in those days and for those few months after the... and I didn't find it oppressive that I didn't know. In '44 and '45, I had been in the hospital for about a year recovering from some injuries I received in the Pacific.

Then I worked as a reporter covering the San Francisco (United Nations) conference, the British Election, and the Potsdam meeting, all in 1945. So there was never a moment of truth for me when I saw my whole political career unfold. I came back in the fall of 1945 after Potsdam, at loose ends, and the head of the Boston Community Fund asked me to help him during the drive. That was Mike Kelleher.

It meant making speeches for the first time in my life, and they seemed to be acceptable. The first speech I ever gave was on England, Ireland, and Germany: Victor, Neutral and Vanquished. It took me three weeks to write, and it was given at an American Legion Post.

Now the speech went rather well. A politician came up to me afterward and said that I should go into politics, that I might be governor of Massachusetts in ten years. Then I began to think about a political career. I hadn't even considered it up until then." (8)

Two authors talk about "a legend" and "a legendary story" concerning Jack Kennedy's entry into politics.

James MacGregor Burns writes, "According to a Boston Legend, Kennedy's decision to enter politics took place on a particular evening a few weeks after Joe Jr's death. Jack, still recovering from his Navy injury, was summoned to his father's presence. In a dramatic scene, the ambassador was supposed to have said that with Joe gone, Jack must now carry on the family tradition of public service, championing the Kennedy clan in politics. The whole family would unite to help him. And Kennedy then and there answered the family call." Burns, in his notes, said that Kennedy's indecision of 1945 is based on Kennedy's and Kennedy's family interviews. (9)

My question is, which Kennedy family members? In "Johnny We Hardly Knew Ye," there's another legendary story, widely told and accepted among the Boston Irish. "The ambassador dramatically summoned Jack to appear at a formal meeting of the grief-stricken Kennedy family a few days after the news of young Joe's death had been received and ordered Jack he picks up the political torch that had fallen from Joe's hand. Jack immediately agreed to carry on for his dead brother, and the whole family pledged him their help and support."

To anybody who knew the Kennedys, that tale does not hold water, mainly because such a theatrical scene, which might happen in many Irish families, hardly could have occurred in the casual atmosphere of the ambassador's home at Hyannis Port, where emotional displays were frowned upon. Jack did not finally decide to go into politics, as a candidate for a vacant seat in Boston's Eleventh Congressional District, until more than a year after Joe's death. (10)

Both legends talk about a dramatic event, according to Burns, a few weeks after Joe's death. Still, for Powers and O'Donnell, "that tale does not hold water" because the claim is that it took Jack more than a year after Joe's death to run for office.

When Joe Jr. died on August 12, 1944, Jack Kennedy was recovering from back surgery, performed on June 23, 1944, during his postoperative eight-week hospital stay.

As for Joe Kennedy summoning and ordering Jack to step in Joe's shoes, Jack once said in a television interview with Walter Cronkite (no exact date found) that he did not feel obliged to go into politics to carry out Joe's unfulfilled ambitions as his father and many other people assumed at the time, but that Joe's death was indeed a decisive factor in choosing a political career, simply because it cleared the path which had been previously reserved for the Kennedys' oldest son.

In "The Search for JFK," the Blairs write, "According to Red Fay's book, "The Pleasure of His Company," Rose invited Red Fay to Palm Beach for Christmas. Since he was far from home, he readily accepted the invitation. Fay recollected, "Behind all the joking and Christmas gaiety, there was a very serious discussion going on between Jack and his father regarding Jack's future course, now that his military service was drawing to close, what would he do in life?" (11)

Red Fay says little about the discussion but delivers two now-famous JFK quotations on the issue, "I can feel Pappy's eyes on the back of my neck," and "I'll be back here with Dad trying to parlay a lost PT boat and a bad back into a political advantage. I tell you, Dad is ready right now and can't understand why Johnny boy isn't all engines ahead full."

Fay recalled, "Early in 1945, when I was stationed at Hollywood Beach, Florida, and came up almost every weekend to visit Jack, he first indicated to me that he had reached his decision. Although at that time, Jack seemed indifferent to the whole idea of a political career, you could sense his movement in that direction." So, Fay wasn't surprised when, early in 1946, JFK decided to run for Congress. (12) However, early 1945 as the point when Jack made his decision is in sharp contrast with what Rose, Edward, and John Kennedy himself said about the timing (namely in the fall of 1945). Do we have a third legend?

In an interview with journalist A. Krock for their book "The Search for JFK," the Blairs asked, "Do you fully subscribe to the theory that when Jack entered politics, he was filling Joe's shoes?" Krock, "Yes, in fact, I knew it. It was almost a physical event. Now it's your turn." When the Blairs asked Krock if he had the impression that Jack wasn't too happy about that, he concurred, saying that it was not Jack's preference. But his father had all the arguments, insisting, "I'll make you the first Roman Catholic president of the United States." (13)

In his memoirs, Arthur Krock wrote of the Kennedy boys, "As the Kennedy boys grew into manhood, although I was early aware of the limitless ambition their father was stimulating in them, I did not foresee that John Fitzgerald Kennedy, the second son, would be the one to attain it; and that the third son would claim the attainment as his rightful heritage." Of Jack specifically, he said, "Although I did perceive potentials of high achievement – though in what field I do not precisely discern – in the young John Fitzgerald Kennedy, in the maturing of his mind and the development of his personality." Krock was also convinced that Jack Kennedy was suited to a career in journalism, or literature, or teaching. (14)

In an Oral History interview on January 8, 1965, with Edward M. Gallagher, a close friend to the Kennedys, I found answers to two very interesting questions on father Joe Kennedy and his pressure on Jack to go into politics.

First Question:

"Who made the decisions in the family? Was that the entire role of the father?"

Gallagher's Answer: "Each child was permitted to express themselves freely. There were so many opportunities available that they were all given these opportunities, and each child elected to go into their own particular field that they wished and were guided and directed by the parents, but never told that they must. The father may have firmly impressed upon Jack that the mantle was his to carry on when young Joe was killed over the English Channel."

Second Question:

"Was there any occasion when there was some conversation about that?"

Gallagher's Answer: "I believe there was, I was not present, but I have heard, and I recall strong discussion to that effect took place in the home, at Hyannis Port, that Jack made up his mind that day, that that's what his father wanted and I think he set out to do it."

The Blairs in their book only quoted a small part of Gallagher's first answer, writing, "Another very close friend of the Kennedy family, Edward M. Gallagher, had a recollection similar to Krock's. In 1965, while giving his oral history for the Kennedy Library, he was asked about the legend. He replied, "The father may have firmly impressed upon Jack that the mantle was his to carry on when young Joe was killed over the English Channel." (15)

By omitting the first paragraph of the answer and failing to mention the positive side of the answer (."..but never told that they must"), the Blairs produced a perfect example of yellow journalism – not good investigative journalism at all.

There's yet another "soft legend" told by Donald C. Lord, "Because Joe Jr. had spoken totally about his desire to become the first catholic president of the United States, the legend grew that the founding father decided that his second son would become the politician of the clan. Supposedly, Joe Kennedy pushed the reluctant, shy Jack into politics against his son's will. Still, concrete evidence to prove this theory is lacking. Joe Kennedy, at first, doubted that the scholarly and quiet-mannered Jack could make it in the rough-and-tumble world of politics. Later in a television interview in 1960, Jack said that he never would have run for office if Joe had lived, but the decision to run for Congress in 1946 seems to have been his. The decision, however, obviously pleased his ambitious father. (16)

Michael O'Brien wrote about Joe Kennedy, bragging, "I got Jack into politics. I was the one, and I told him Joe was dead and that it was, therefore, his responsibility to run for Congress. He didn't want to. He felt he didn't have the ability, and he still feels that way, but I told him he had to."

Jack remembered it differently, "It was the other way around," he said.

"We all like politics, but young Joe seemed a natural to run for office. You can't have a whole mess of Kennedys asking for votes. So when Joe was denied his chance, I wanted to run and was glad I could." (17) Do we have yet another legendary tale?

Herbert S. Parmet thought, "In the ambassador's eyes, it may be said without much exaggeration, Jack became a surrogate for Joe Jr. Still, the much-discussed question of Jack Kennedy having been virtually drafted to fulfill his brother's career objectives has been oversimplified. Jack, in fact, was deeply interested in public affairs long before Joe's death, his flirtation with law school being just one aspect of that. But despite his interest and inherent privileges, Jack's uncertainty about his capacity to become a candidate dissuaded him from rushing into anything prematurely. (18)

James A. Reed, one of the men Jack met en route to the South Pacific in 1943 and who became a close friend as well as a member of his presidential administration, according to Herbert S. Parmet, recalled an evening in the fall of 1945, with Jack, Ambassador Kennedy, Grandfather Fitzgerald, and a few other close friends. In his Oral History interview, Reed wasn't sure if it was in 1944 or 1945 that Grandfather "Honey Fitz" made his toast because he was there on several weekends.

"We were sitting with Grandfather Fitzgerald and a few other close friends who proposed a toast to the future President of the United States – he looked right at Jack – to which everyone joined in. It was not said in any degree of levity or frivolity. It was a serious toast that was proposed to Jack, and I think everyone there thought that one day Jack would be President of the United States." (19)

According to O'Donnell and Powers, "The thing that finally moved Jack Kennedy toward active politics, as he said later, was not trying to carry on for Joe or 'my father's eyes on the back of my neck' but his own experience as a correspondent at the United Nations conference in San Francisco and Potsdam, which sharpened his interest in the National and International issues of the coming postwar period. After getting a close look as a reporter at the postwar leaders in action, he decided that he might be able to find more satisfaction and to perform more useful services as a politician than as a political writer or teacher of government and history, the two careers that he had been considering up to that time." (20)

Barbara A. Perry writes that Joe Kennedy turned his energies to 28-year-old Jack's future political career. "I think it extremely likely that he will run for Congress," Joe wrote to the editor of the Washington Times-Herald, Cissy Patterson, November 26, 1945. "With his background, brains, and courage, he would do a good job if anybody could. I hope for his peace of mind that he does." (21)

"He relished the idea of a campaign," writes Renehan Jr. in "The Kennedys at War," "He had, after all, spoken frequently in the past about the prospect of a political career. And the ambassador himself had told John Bulkeley as early as 1942 that he thought Jack had the stuff to be president. So we know the idea of Jack in politics was not a new one born of Joe's death, although it may well have been honed and sharpened by the fallout of that explosion over the British coast in 1944." (22)

This contrasts with what John Henry Cutler wrote in "Honey Fitz," "I never thought

Jack had it in him," his father said after seeing him working like hell in the 1946 congressional campaign. (23)

At a family meeting in Palm Beach, the ambassador told everyone that this was the race – 1946 congressional election, in the Eleventh Congressional District – they had been looking for. "We're all in this together," he said, looking around the room. Stealing a glance at her frail, sickly brother, Eunice asked, "Daddy, do you think Jack can be a congressman?" The ambassador smiled, "You must remember, it's not what you are that counts, but what people think you are." (24)

Asked by Newsweek correspondent James M. Cannon, "Why do you go in for politics?" JFK answered, "I think the rewards are, first, infinite." Toni Bradlee asked him, "Is being president the ultimate of everybody that goes into politics?" JFK replied, "That is the sense of being head of whatever organization you're in. I suppose. But most important is the fact that the president today is the seat of all power." Jack Kennedy further said he didn't participate in political activities in college. He didn't consider himself the political type, which would mean doing hard work. He thought his grandfather was the national political type who loved to go out to dinners and socialize, to sing with the crowds, to take a train trip, and talk to eighteen people at once. Jack felt himself to be the antithesis of a politician, "As I saw it, my grandfather was the politician. He was ideal. What he loved to do was what politicians are expected to do."

When James M. Cannon asked him, "Don't you?" JFK answered, "No, I don't. I don't enjoy it. I'd rather read a book on a plane than talk to the fellow next to me, and my grandfather (Honey Fitz) wanted to talk to everybody else. I'd rather not go out to dinner." Asked by Ben Bradlee if he had any remote idea that when he ran for Congress in 1946, he would run for president, Kennedy said, "No, I didn't." "Remote?" asked Bradlee, "Not even when you went to bed?" JFK replied, "Never. Never. Never. I thought maybe I'd be governor of Massachusetts someday." (25)

1.3. Joe Jr., 'the Golden Boy' Compared With Jack, 'the Sick One'

Joe Jr., often portrayed as the golden, robust son against Jack the sick and frail one in the Kennedy family, was, in fact, surpassed by his younger brother in publicized achievements.

Alongside Jack's heroic PT-109 escapades and his book "Why England Slept" – the published version of JFK's Harvard thesis on the failure to stop the Second World War – his older brother seemed overshadowed. But the suggestion by some authors that Joe Jr.'s last wartime mission over the English Channel was somehow bravado to counter brother Jack's profile seems foolish to me. However, Jack was kind when he ascribed Joe Jr.'s achievements, not to talent but willpower and exceptional stamina. As Cam Newberry recalled, Joe was heavy, and few people enjoyed his company for long. "He was entirely different from Jack. He didn't have Jack's charm, to begin with. Joe was much more of a heavy-type person. Not only could Joe Jr. be spiteful, but he was a poor loser. Even his youngest brother, Teddy, later recalled how he was thrown into the ocean by Joe Jr. in a fit of pique when they lost a sailing race."

For all his affection for Joe Jr., Dr. Wild felt that the older Kennedy brother was, by comparison with Jack, "kind of slapdash," adding, "He would not put time into reading, and he was not interested in discussing it as thoroughly as Jack."

Here was the difference between Joe Jr. and Jack. Joe Jr.'s famous patience was, as Joe Jr. himself acknowledged, a euphemism for hotheadedness. "He could not mix with those who were not his background." Joe Jr.'s copilot in Puerto Rico, Norman Radd, later remarked that Jack, by contrast, seemed to possess a quiet magnetism that drew people to him from wholly different social backgrounds, religions, educations, and States. Some of Joe's friends, like his Californian friend Tom Killefer, thought he was God, "I thought he was all over himself, totally without humor, totally different from Jack."

Jack, however, never spoke a derogatory word about his elder brother; in fact, he forced one presidential campaign biographer to alter his manuscript rather than allow himself to be quoted as considering Joe Jr. as a "bully."

Jack hadn't got Joe's priceless asset – his good health. Jack's health was awful. But by guts and determination, he'd kept up with Joe. (1)

1.4. Jack Kennedy's Possible Career Instead of Politics

There are many accounts of what path JFK might have taken if family tragedy had not steered him towards politics.

In his 1960 book "The Remarkable Kennedys," Joe McCarthy wrote, "Before young Joe's death, the family expected the reserved and studious Jack to be a writer or a teacher." (1)

John J. Droney told an Oral History interviewer on November 30, 1964, "He (Jack) said that he wanted to be a newspaperman, but his brother was killed during the war, and his father felt that he was best fitted to replace Joe." (2)

Edward M. Gallagher's Oral History interview of August 1, 1965, was also clear, "Jack would never have been President of the United States if young Joe had lived. I think that twist took the bent. I don't know. I mean, he probably would have gone on writing, which he probably wanted." (3)

The same year, Ted Sorensen wrote in his book, "Kennedy" of Jack's ideas, "Early in our acquaintance he told me that he considered careers as a lawyer, a journalist, a professor of history or political science, or an officer in the foreign office." (4)

Schlesinger's Kennedy book, "A Thousand Days" in 1965, stated, "He had expected to become a writer, but the San Francisco experience may have helped him decide that it was better to sit at the conference table than to wait outside with the press. His brother's death also changed things." (5)

Paul B. Fay Jr. took the same line in his 1966 book, "The Pleasure of his Company," writing that, "During those months just after his discharge from the Navy, I'm convinced Jack saw his future as a writer – perhaps a newspaper columnist commenting chiefly in politics. But gradually, his ambitions changed in the months after his brother Joe's death." (6)

Arthur Krock made a strange observation on the matter in his 1968 book, "Memoirs" writing, "It was, I think, after the conclusion that Jack was dying (1954) was dissipated by his partial recovery, that Ambassador Kennedy began definitely to plan for Jack the political career he had designed for Joe Jr. Until then, I think, he shared a belief, which was mine, that Jack was suited to a career in journalism, in literature, or teaching." (7)

In 1970, K. O'Donnell and D. Powers wrote in their book "Johnny, We Hardly Knew Ye," "After getting a close look as a reporter at the post-war political leaders in action, he decided that he might be able to find more satisfaction and to perform more useful service as a politician than as a political writer or teacher of government and history, the two careers that he had been considering up to that time." (8)

Doris Kearns Goodwin's 1987 book, "The Fitzgeralds and The Kennedys" put it this way, "Jack, in those days was rather shy, withdrawn and quiet. His mother and I couldn't picture him as a politician. We were sure he'd be a teacher or a writer." She went on, "From his (Joe Kennedy) letters to Jack, he was thinking more along the lines of public service." (JPK to Joe Kane February 8, 1944). Jack said simply and clearly, "My brother has priority in aspiring for public office."

"I think," Kane concluded, "he prefers a position on a governmental commission." (9)

In 1991, Thomas C. Reeves wrote in his book, "A Life of John F. Kennedy," "Unsure about what to do with the rest of his life after the discharge, Jack thought journalism might be a possible career."

His friend Charles Spalding later observed that Jack never intended to become a serious writer. "He just automatically thought of writing in terms of current events." (10)

In 2009, Edward M. Kennedy wrote in his book "True Compass," "Jack's initial interest in elective office registered as a mild surprise in our family. He never had, to my knowledge, talked about political ambitions. The last I'd heard, he was thinking about a career in journalism. He'd written articles for the Chicago Herald-American and the International News Service after his injuries in the Pacific." (11)

In 2013, Barbara A. Perry wrote in her book, "Rose Kennedy, The Life and Times of a Political Matriarch," "Jack originally intended to be a writer, editor or something in the literary field," Rose explained. (12)

As David Pitts pointed out, Jack had always been interested in journalism and thought that might be the profession that would bring him the most satisfaction. Using his father's connections, he soon found himself with top-notch reporting assignments with Hearst Newspapers, covering the first United Nations Conference in San Francisco, where the United Nations Charter was drafted, and the British elections. He also got a chance to attend the Potsdam summit of the Big Three – the United States, Britain, and the Soviet Union. (13)

Robert Dallek said that in April 1945, shortly before the war ended in Europe, in response to a question from Joe, the Hearst Chicago Herald -American invited Jack to cover the United Nations conference in San Francisco. He jumped at the chance, perhaps seeing his work in journalism as a prelude to a political career – a career whose scope might be hinted at by the fact that writing for Hearst newspapers in Chicago and New York (the Journal-American) was not an especially effective way to win political standing in Massachusetts. Dallek was also convinced that Jack Kennedy did not see journalism as a more interesting profession than life in Congress, where there was a degree of power to determine the nation's direction. "A reporter," said Kennedy, "is reporting what happened. He is not making it happen. It isn't participating. I saw how ideally politics filled the Greek definition of happiness – full use of your powers along the lines of excellence in life-affording scope." (14) Joan and Clay Blair judged Jack's five thousand words of journalism (this time without Krock's skillful fingers) was a dismal performance, on a par with the output of any cub reporter. The Blairs also dismissed as wrong the claims of many authors that Jack Kennedy seriously embarked on a promising career in journalism in 1945, then rejected it for politics. (15)

Michael O'Brien didn't agree with the Blairs comment on Jack's performances as a reporter.

On the contrary, he thought that Jack noticeably improved. By the end of May 1945, he wrote with more confidence and skill. On May 23, 1945, he very effectively explained the veto power given the Big Five nations in the new world organization. (16)

Statistic: Kennedy's possible career before politics:
1. Joe McCarthy (writer, teacher)
2. John J. Droney (newspaperman)
3. Edward M. Gallagher (writer)
4. Ted Sorensen (lawyer, journalist, professor of history or political science, an officer of the foreign office)
5. Arthur Schlesinger (writer)
6. Paul B. Fay Jr. (writer, newspaper columnist)
7. Arthur Krock (journalism, literature, teaching)
8. O'Donnell, Powers (political writer, teacher of government)
9. Rose Kennedy (writer, editor)
10. Doris Kearns Goodwin (public service, a governmental commission)
11. Thomas C. Reeves (journalism)
12. Edward M. Kennedy (journalism)
13. Barbara A. Perry (writer, editor, something in the literary field)
14. David Pitts (journalism)
15. Robert Dallek (journalism as a prelude to a political career)
16. The Blairs (a career in journalism then rejected it for politics is wrong)

1.5. How Did Jack Kennedy Meet With Kenneth O'Donnell and David F. Powers

"Cousin Joe Kane" brought Bill Sutton into Kennedy's orbit one day in January 1946. Sutton, who Kane described as a prize catch, had worked with John Cotter, a fellow native of Charlestown, on two elections in the Eleventh Congressional District, where he knew everybody. "I was quite impressed by Jack Kennedy," Sutton said. "We got along together immediately," Sutton told Jack Kennedy to get Dave Powers in Charlestown because Dave Powers was on first-name terms with every voter there. Sutton and Powers used to sell newspapers together in the Charlestown Navy Yard – so that was 10,000 people Dave knew to start with.

Dave also served as an usher at five masses at Saint Catherine's Church every Sunday, as well as coaching the CYO teams. But Dave told Sutton he had already decided to work for Democratic Party campaigner John Cotter. At Sutton's urging, Kennedy visited Powers – on the evening of January 21, 1946, by Powers' recollection. Jack Kennedy climbed the three flights of stairs to the top floor of the three-decker at 88 Ferrin Street in Charlestown and knocked on the front door. Fifteen years later, when they were swimming together in the White House pool, the president said to Dave, "If I had gotten tired that night when I reached the second floor, I never would have met you."

As Powers opened the door, Kennedy stuck out his hand and said, "My name is Jack Kennedy. I'm a candidate for Congress." When Kennedy said that Bill Sutton had suggested Powers as somebody who might help him in Charlestown, Powers hesitated, "Gosh, if I help anyone, it should be John Cotter," he said. But that didn't discourage Jack Kennedy. Powers found Jack rather ill at ease and shy, but Kennedy knew what he wanted and wouldn't give up. They talked for about twenty minutes about the people in the district and their needs, "He had already then that way of talking to you, asking you questions and listening to you attentively, that made you feel as though you were important, the only person in the world who mattered to him at that moment.

He was really curious about finding out your ideas and your opinions," recalled Powers. When Jack was leaving, he mentioned that he was planning to attend a meeting of a group of Gold Star Mothers two days later at the American Legion Hall in Charlestown and asked Dave if he would go with him. Dave, who minutes earlier had told Jack that he was John Cotter's man – said that he would be glad to. It was early evidence of the soon-to-be-legendary Kennedy vote-winning charisma.

The Gold Star Mothers' meeting was an afternoon party. Jack and Dave went there on the subway. Dave noticed that Jack, unlike every politician that Dave had ever seen, was not wearing a hat. Dave glanced at Jack's hair as the train came out of the subway and climbed the elevated tracks across the bridge to Charlestown, and said to himself, "This guy looks young to be running for Congress." Jack's talk to the Gold Star Mothers was short and earnest.

He spoke for ten minutes on the sacrifices of war and the need to keep the world at peace. After the speech, all the women in the room crowded around Jack, shaking his hand and talking to him excitedly, and wishing him good luck. Dave said he had never before seen such a reaction to political talk in Charlestown, "He's no great orator, and he doesn't say much, but they certainly go crazy over him." (1)

According to Laurence Leamer, "The audience knew that the speech had ended only because the young candidate stopped speaking. By any measure, the speech had been "a disappointment" but the mothers rushed forward to greet Jack as if he had been the most stirring of speakers." (2)

Everybody agrees that Jack Kennedy was no great orator at the beginning of his political career. Still, the content of his speeches was sound. If the content had been disappointing as well as the delivery, the Gold Star Mothers would not have been so enthusiastic.

After the meeting, Jack asked Dave, "How do you think I did?" Dave said, "You were terrific. I've never seen such a reaction from a crowd of people in my whole life."

"Then do you think you'll be with me?" Jack asked.

"I'm already with you," Dave said. "I've already started working for you." They shook hands. Recalling that handshake several years later, Powers, always the sentimental Irishman, added sadly, "And I stayed with him from that day until November 22, 1963, when I was riding in the car behind him in Dallas." (3)

Dave Powers is one of the thousand examples of how Jack Kennedy could mesmerize people. Without being a natural-born politician, he possessed a natural gift, which is rare to find in the political class anywhere in the world. Kennedy convinced people by listening to them.

I was privileged to meet Dave Powers on August 16, 1982, when I was at the John F. Kennedy Library, preparing my exhibition on President Kennedy and his brother Robert for November 1983 in Bruges (Belgium). I asked him to write a small note in his book, "Johnny We Hardly Knew Ye" about what John F. Kennedy meant to him. "Eddy," he said, "John F. Kennedy was the greatest man I ever met, the best friend I ever had. Working with JFK in the White House was like dying and going to heaven."

People can think whatever they want on Powers' silence. He was the man who kept the secrets. If this sounds hagiographic to some, so be it, but Dave Powers has my utmost respect. A true friend doesn't have to "dish the dirt" as many others did on JFK. John Kennedy had in Dave Powers from January 21, 1946, until November 22, 1963, a loyal, devoted, true friend. Hard to find these days. The first day Kenny O'Donnell met with Jack Kennedy was very different from Dave Powers' kitchen encounter with Jack.

In the Spring of 1946, Bobby Kennedy was constantly pestering Kenny to meet his older brother. O'Donnell showed little interest but agreed if only to get it over with. In the end, the meeting was remarkable for what did not happen. Lightning did not strike. Ken did not even shake Jack's hand, unaware, of course, that he was meeting a future president, a man who would change his life. Kenny thought Jack was nice, handsome, and wealthy, but otherwise totally unremarkable, "He seemed too boyish and shy to be running against experienced politicians like Mike Neville and John Cotter in that tough congressional district," Kenny later told his pals.

Nevertheless, he agreed to help Jack's Congressional campaign, telling Bobby, "I'll do it, but as a favor to you – he'll never make it." Later, Kenny would laugh at himself when people asked him about his first meeting with Jack. He wished he had been more perceptive, "Honestly, though, he just seemed like another returned vet – nice guy, rich kid, playboy, good looking, and Joe Kennedy's son. Nothing more." (4)

1.6. The James Michael Curley Pay Off

In May of 1945, Congressman and former Boston Mayor Michael James Curley surprised the city by announcing that he would once again run for mayor. The election would be held that fall. If Curley won against John Kerrigan, he would have to resign his US House seat in the 11th congressional District. It was a tempting launchpad for Jack's political career. The 11th district was packed with Irish voters. It was where Jack's grandfather, Honey Fitz, had launched his political career, and the Fitzgeralds and the Kennedys both had roots and relations in the district. The name John Fitzgerald Kennedy would thus automatically assure many votes. Based on this assessment, the Kennedys made a tentative decision. If Curley won the mayoralty race, Jack would enter Massachusetts politics by declaring for Curley's 11th Congressional District in early 1946 and face an election that year. But first Curley had to become mayor and resign his House seat, and there had to be no hint that a deal had been done with Curley to clear the way for Jack. (1)

Late in December, Joe's cousin Joe Kane had alerted him to an unexpected opportunity. Kane had heard rumors of Congressman Curley's financial problems, following a fraud conviction obliging him to pay back $42,000 from a 1938 illegal backhander.

In an interview, Joe Kane said that Joe Kennedy using Boston's ex-police commissioner Joseph Timilty as his emissary, secretly sent Curley $12,000 in cash to pay off his long-standing debt, with the promise of significant campaign money and help if Curley would vacate his seat in Congress and try for the mayoralty of Boston in the 1945 election. "Curley knew that he was in trouble with the feds over the mail fraud rap," said Kane. "The ambassador paid him to get out of the congressional seat, and Curley figured he might need the money." Nigel Hamilton, the author of "JFK, Reckless Youth" wrote, "How much Jack's father told Jack of these shenanigans when he reached Palm Beach, may never be known." (2) I am pretty sure Joe Kennedy never told his son of his "special, secret business deals."

According to Jack Beatty, Curley announced in November 1944 – on the night of his re-election to Congress – that he would be a candidate for the office of Mayor of

Boston, but he was deeply in debt, "My finances were so depleted when I ran for re-election against Eliot," Curley said in his autobiography. He needed about $100,000 to make the run. He got the money from Joseph P. Kennedy. (3)

Hamilton talks about "a quick $12,000" and $42,000 from a 1938 illegal "backhander" to pay off Curley's long-standing debt and refers to Joe Kennedy's "promise of significant campaign money" for Curley without mentioning the amount. Writer and broadcaster Jack Beatty, who had a private interview with Hamilton, doesn't mention in his book the $42,000 debts but confirms that Curley needed $100,000 to run for mayor – money which Joe Kennedy gave him.

Thomas J. Whalen, using Jack Beatty's "Rascal King" as his source, writes, "In exchange for a pledge not to run, the elder Kennedy gave the aging Democratic leader somewhere in the neighborhood of $100,000 to pay off long-standing personal debts." This contradicts Beatty, who wrote that the $100,000 was needed "to make the run." (4)

Geoffrey Perret, in "Jack: A Life Like No Other," uses Jack Beatty and Ralph G. Martin as his sources to write, "In February 1946, Joe Kennedy and Curley finally cut a deal. Curley had diabetes and some huge medical bills. He was also facing a federal indictment for mail fraud. Joe Kennedy offered to pay off all his medical-legal bills and finance his campaign for re-election as mayor if he'd quit his congressional seat." (5)

Again, Perret mentioned no specific figures on how much Joe Kennedy Sr. spent. However, his sources, Beatty and Martin, gave the $12,000 and $100,000 figures, and Perret is the only author who talks about Joe Kennedy's payments for Curley's medical bills.

Laurence Leamer, using Hamilton as his source, writes, "Joe ran the campaign, but he did it in such a surreptitious way that no one knew just which strings he had pulled and how hard he had pulled them. Even the fact that the congressional seat had suddenly opened up, probably, was the result of Joe's manipulation. "The incumbent congressman, James Michael Curley, was facing an indictment for mail fraud; Joe Kane, who was intimately involved with the campaign, later asserted that Joe had paid Curley $12,000 to retire and had promised more money when Curley decided to run for mayor of Boston." (6)

Robert Dallek, in "Unfinished Life" wrote, "To this end, Joe secretly persuaded James Michael Curley to leave his eleventh Congressional district seat for another run as Boston's Mayor. A fraud conviction and additional legal actions had put Curley in substantial debt, and he welcomed Joe's hush-hush proposal to help him pay off what he owed and to finance his mayoral campaign." (7)

Dallek uses Hamilton as his source but gives no figures.

Michael O'Brien is very vague on the subject, writing, "In the spring of 1945, Curley announced his candidacy for mayor of Boston in the fall election. He was expected to win, and if he did, he would have to vacate his congressional seat. Joe Kennedy eyed the seat for his second son. Rumors spread that Joe Kennedy paid Curley to vacate." (8)

David Nasaw has a different story of Curley's debts, "In declaring his candidacy, Curley made no mention of either his federal indictment for fraud or the six-year-old court order to pay back $37,000, plus interest he had "improperly received" from a city contractor. Six weeks later, on December 26, 1944, he announced that he had paid off all his debts. The funds, it has been whispered from that day to this, had to have come from Joseph P. Kennedy, who had a very good reason to smooth Curley's return to Boston." (Nasaw has no source on the $37,000 plus interest.) (9)

John T. Shaw asserts, "It remains unclear how Kennedy's father worked to encourage Curley to retire. Several historians have argued that Joseph P. Kennedy paid off Curley's debts and took other steps to induce him to retire, leaving an open congressional seat for his son to pursue." (10)

The man who sparked the Curley payoff was Joe Kane, Joseph P. Kennedy's first or second cousin (the first cousin, according to Tip O'Neill; the second cousin, says Doris Kearns Goodwin). It was also Kane who came up with the winning campaign slogan, "The New Generation Offers A Leader."

Was it $12,000, $37,000, $42,000, or even $100,000 to cover Curley for financial problems – medical bills, legal bills, and campaign finance – following his fraud conviction? Goodwin's description of Joe Kane on the Curley payoff story says it all.

She writes, "A unique figure in Boston politics, Kane embodied all the experience of the old ward days complete with a gruff manner long cigar and a fantastic story-telling ability feel for the future."

"Joe Kane had such wonderful stories," Jack later said, "that they could listen to him for hours without thinking about anything else." (11)

As a former certified accountant, I worked for big businessmen. When they do tricky business or make secret deals, they don't tell anybody how much they pay off – certainly not to their wives or mistresses, because, if they did, they would end up spending more of their money on jewels and clothes.

I am convinced that Joe Kennedy paid off Curley, but how much we'll never know. Storyteller and first cousin Kane made up a wonderful "payoff story" and turned it into a legend. Vladimir Lenin said, "A lie told often becomes the truth" – but where's the truth and the lie in the Kane story?

1.7. How Many Family Dollars Were Invested in the Campaign?

As a former certified accountant, figures always do catch my eye. You cannot mess around with wrong figures on a balance sheet – such negligence can get my client into big trouble with his bank or the IRS or even go broke. I always used to joke with my clients that by manipulating figures, I was the perfect guy to get them bankrupt.

In a Kennedy book, you can't do much harm with figures, and they do become legends. But giving a few examples of how renowned authors and historians do believe in those "fairy tale" stories, my humble conclusion is, these aren't accountants.

In 1960, writers Ralph Martin and Ed Plaut started the legend about how much money Joe Kennedy spent in the 1946 congressional campaign.

Joe Kane said, "They spent a staggering sum in the congressional race in 1946, but Jack could have gone to Congress like everyone else for ten cents."

"His father called his friends, his friends worked quickly, and Jack Kennedy could hardly object, even if it were true."

Why shouldn't a father help his son? If he's got money, why shouldn't he spend it on this if he wants to? The point is if it happened – if $250,000 was spent on Kennedy's first campaign, as some circulated rumors claim (and Jack Kennedy – vigorously denies), then it was equivalent of an elephant squashing a peanut.

Why would his father do it? Cousin Kane answered that point, "Because everything his father got, he bought and paid for. And politics is like war. It takes three things to win. The first is money, and the second is money, and the third is money." (1)

This legendary story from 1960 offers no sources. "If it happened" means for me, they weren't sure.

In 1974, David E. Koskoff took over the Martin Plaut story. He says in his notes, Plaut had an interview with Joseph Kane on April 5, 1962, on the matter. (2)

According to Tip O'Neill, "The organization, the newcomers, the slogan, the war record, the reprints, all these played a part in the campaign. But what made the difference was the money." It was said that Joe Kennedy spent $300,000 on that race – six times more than what O'Neill spent in a very tough congressional campaign in the same district six years later.

Although he lived in New York, Joe Kennedy was an ongoing factor in Massachusetts' politics. Every Democrat who ran for governor would go down to see Joe, who would always send him home with a briefcase, full of cash. The word was that if Joe Kennedy liked you, he'd give you $50,000. If he really liked you, he'd give you $100,000. (3)

In an interview with Robert S. Allen for Ralph G. Martin's book of 1995, Allen claimed, "It cost old Joe a million dollars to buy Jack a seat in the House."

"McCormack was the Speaker then and a political force in Massachusetts, but although he spluttered and hemmed and hawed about the Kennedy race, there was nothing he could do. They just bought out all the opposition." (4)

In 1997, Seymour Hersh asserted that Joseph P. Kennedy, in his drive to elect Jack Kennedy in 1946, left nothing to chance. Joe Kane was deemed essential because the elder Kennedy was pouring hundreds of thousands of family dollars into the campaign. (5)

Joe Kennedy went on to hand out somewhere between $250,000 and $500,000, vast sums in those days, for billboards, newspaper ads, and radio broadcasts. "We're going to sell Jack like soap flakes," he cheerfully confided to a friend. No one was ever sure how much money Joe spent or exactly how he spent it. Dave Powers, who became a charter member of Jack Kennedy's so-called Irish Mafia, recalled the secretive way Eddie Moore, Joe Kennedy's henchman, handed out cash – by inviting the recipient into a pay toilet. "You can never be too careful in politics about handing over money," Moore explained. (6)

In 2003, Robert Dallek said that Joe Kennedy might have spent between $250,000 and $300,000 on the campaign. However, the precise amount will never be known since so much of it was handed out in cash by Eddie Moore. His source is Tip O'Neill, but O'Neill speaks of a $300,000, not mentioning Moore. (7)

Mark Dalton's comment, when asked in an Oral History interview whether he considered the 1946 campaign expensive, is telling, "The way congressional campaigns go, I would say it was not an extraordinarily expensive campaign. It was certainly well-financed as it was. We had many, many billboards, and we had the advertising material which was presented all through the community." There certainly was no shortage of funds, but on the other hand, Dalton, in all sincerity, believed that it was not an exorbitant campaign, "There was no vast expenditure of money. That's my estimate of that." (8)

Starting with "no vast expenditure of money," rising to several hundred thousands of family dollars, finishing with $1,000,000, it's a staggering variation in figures. Joe Kennedy spent "family" dollars; so what?

The only people who could tell us about the exact figures are Joe Kennedy's accountants, but they are no longer here to deny or confirm the figures. Joe Kennedy certainly spent a lot of money on the 1946 congressional campaign, but the different figures authors bandy about belong more in the gossip section of the election story rather than in the historical truth part. A businessman doesn't get rich by throwing money through the window. An inflation calculator counts $1,000,000 in 1946 is worth $14,417,846.15 in 2022. Joe Kennedy would have paid $2.46 a vote or a total of $5,474,524 for Jack's congressional election in the Boston eleventh District in 1946. If that were true, that would not have been Joe Kennedy's finest business deal.

1.8. Jack Kennedy's First Campaign for Congress in 1946

When Jack was deciding on politics, his father's friends in Massachusetts tried to interest him in the running for the state's lieutenant-governorship on the Democratic ticket with Maurice Tobin. But a secondary office in the State House held no appeal for Jack. Despite being an outsider in Boston, having grown up in New York and at Hyannis Port on Cape Cod, he saw the Eleventh Congressional District of Greater Boston as an ideal stage for his political debut. The District resonated powerfully with Kennedy. Boston's North End was the birthplace of his mother and his maternal grandfather, John F. ("Honey Fitz") Fitzgerald, who had served as a Congressman for the same district before becoming the mayor of the city. East Boston included the waterfront area where his father was born and raised and where his paternal grandfather, Patrick J. Kennedy, had been the local Democratic ward leader for many years.

The District also included the waterfront community of Charleston, still solidly Irish, with three Catholic churches within its one square mile of the three-docker tenement houses on the slopes of Bunker Hill behind the Charlestown Navy yard, where the frigate Constitution, "Old Ironsides" is docked. Across the Charles River, the constituency covers the whole city of Cambridge, where Jack Kennedy had lived for four years while attending Harvard. However, the world of Harvard was as remote for the working-class districts of Cambridge as Palm Beach was from Boston. (1)

The only person Jack now knew in Boston, he later recalled in a half-joking manner, was his 82-year old grandfather – so he set up his campaign headquarters in a two-room suite at the Bellevue Hotel, just down the hall from the suite where Fitzgerald and his wife had been living for nearly a decade. (2)

Kennedy's many biographers have pointed out after that Jack's popular success in politics, from the start of his first campaign in 1946, was largely due to his disdain for the overblown rhetoric and corny style of the older politicians. Well-suited to the changing times, his air of quiet refinement and an unaffected and sincere platform manner was a welcome contrast to the hard-boiled Curley-era politicians. "Compared to the Boston Irish politicians we grew up with," Bill Sutton says, "Jack Kennedy was like a breath of spring. He never said to anybody, 'How's your mother? Tell her I said hello.' He never went to wake unless he knew the deceased personally." (3)

Jack Kennedy felt his key advantage, apart from having a well-known name, was that he started his political career early. In his opinion, most aspirants in the public office started much too late. "When you think of the money that Coca-Cola and Lucky Strike put into advertising day after day, even though they have well-known brand names, you can realize how difficult it is to become an identifiable political figure."

Jack went on, "The idea that people can get to know you well enough to support you in two or three months is wholly wrong. Most of us do not follow politics and politicians. We become interested only around election time. For the politician to make a dent in the consciousness of the great majority of the people is a long and difficult job, particularly in a primary where you don't have the party label to help you." (4)

Candidates have knocked on doors before, but Kennedy did it with great energy and enthusiasm. If Jack Kennedy would have been campaigning "like being drafted," he would never have been so enthusiastic and would never have been elected. Kennedy's regime quickly became arduous. He woke up around 6.15 – 6.30 a.m. to be on the streets around 7.00. He often went to the dockyards and factories to shake hands with the arriving shift workers. This campaigning method had a positive effect on many voters. Accompanying Kennedy one morning, Dave Powers overheard one of the dockworker's remarks, "If this fellow, you know, gets up at 6.00 in the morning as we do, we're going to vote for him." This was something the laborers were not used to. "None of the other candidates did that," Powers remembered. (5)

After a quick breakfast, Jack would start pounding the pavement, knocking on every door in neighborhoods with triple-decker houses. (6)

After lunch, he and his aides would "hit the barbershops, the neighborhood candy or variety stores and taverns, the fire stations and the police stations. At four o'clock, back at the Navy yard, catching the workers coming out of a different gate from the one where we worked that morning," Dave Powers recalled.

They would ride the trolley cars from Park Street to Harvard Square, with Jack walking like aisles, shaking hands, and introducing himself. In the evening, there would be a rally or a political forum with all the candidates invited to the house parties. "We would arrange with young girls, schoolteachers or telephone operators or nurses, to invite their friends to a party at their house, to meet Jack. The parties would range from small ones, with about fifteen people, to big ones that might take up two or three floors of a three-decker house." (7)

At one big campaign outing, Kennedy, waiting his turn to speak, heard various candidates described as worthy servants of the people who "came up the hard way." Jack, fumbling with his tie, rose to speak, "I'm the one who didn't come up the hard way," he said. The crowd loved it. "Lincoln made fun of his face." Rowland Evans Jr. wrote in the Saturday Evening Post in 1961, "Jack Kennedy's political liabilities were not home-lines, but youth, money, a powerful and controversial father, and religion. Kennedy is cool, detached, and often spontaneous when making fun of his liabilities. He makes fun of himself (sometimes) and others (often) with a flash of natural Irish wit that bubbles near the surface."

"His fondness for teasing, sharpened by the example of his quick-witted father and brightened by his mother's gentler humor, makes political fun, joking as natural for him as breathing." Evans also pointed out, "The touch of blarney was a straight hand-me-down from Honey Fitz." (8)

Any campaign needs money, but it's not a decisive factor. Franklin D. Roosevelt had some personal resources. Lincoln did not. They were both successful political leaders and great presidents.

In that 1946 congressional race, all the other candidates could only be dismayed at the amount Joe Kennedy was spending. But political history in the United States is replete with instances of people spending staggering sums to win elections, only to come up empty-handed. Money in politics works synergistically, adding strength to a strong candidate but often making a weak one look stupid. Jack possessed advantages his father's money could not buy. (9)

His father presided over the campaign's every detail. Still, he stayed behind the scenes so as not to dilute Jack's appeal to veterans and other supporters of the War. He had 100,000 reprints of the Reader's Digest version of John Hersey's PT 109 article printed up and sent one to every registered voter. (10)

Joe Kennedy got his cousin Joe Kane to be Jack's, first man. It was Kane who thought up Jack's campaign slogan "The New Generation Offers a Leader." Joe Kane paid one candidate $7,500 to stay in or get out, depending on how the campaign shaped up. And when Joseph Russo, a potentially strong vote-getter, entered the contest, Kane put another Joseph Russo in the race to cut into his vote. In all, there were ten candidates. (11)

"Your Jack is worth a king's ransom," Kane had told Joe Kennedy even before Kennedy fully recognized Jack's political potential. When Joe first brought Jack together with Kane, he was surprised by Jack's reaction. "I thought Jack wouldn't last five minutes with him," Joe said, "but I was wrong, for he not only stayed for over four hours, but he loved every minute of it." (12)

Kane decided to stress Kennedy's war record. The Kennedy's also put on dozens of cocktail parties and teas. If you agreed to invite a few friends to your house to meet Jack, they brought in a case of mixed booze, hired a caterer, and gave you a hundred dollars, which was supposed to pay for the cleaning woman to come to your house both before and after the party. If they could convince a large family with six or eight voters to host the event, so much the better.

The biggest event of all was a huge Sunday afternoon tea at the Hotel Commander in Harvard Square. Every woman in Cambridge was invited, and fifteen hundred showed up that day in their finest gowns. Jack spoke at the tea, and so did Rose, his mother. His sisters lined up on the stage and shook hands with everybody in the room. Even the older man was there, making his only public appearance in the campaign. (13)

Besides the money and the name, being Joe Kennedy's son had other advantages. There were allies that his father could bring John Kennedy. "I just called people," said Joe. "I got in touch with people. I have a lot of contacts. I've been in politics in Massachusetts since I was ten." Besides his political contacts, Joe Kennedy brought his son's Press allies. Hearst's Boston American had a reporter in Kennedy headquarters every day, but not in those of the other candidates. (14)

In December 1945, Jack Kennedy asked navy veteran Mark Dalton, who had gone to Boston College and the Harvard Law School, to serve as campaign manager. All that winter, Joseph Kennedy and Dalton would confer by telephone. "He was very, very interested, and he would talk at great length and wanted to know every facet of the campaign," Dalton recalled in an Oral History interview for the JFK library. (15) "He never projected himself into the public picture, but if there were an essential campaign manager," Dalton said, "it was Mr. Kennedy, who, according to Dalton, was a very, very able man." (16)

John J. Droney, in another Oral History interview, said, "Of course, his father was well then, and he was wonderful, a great help in the campaign because we were green as grass. Even though he stayed out of it, he wasn't out of it. He was very much in it. Any time I ever had a problem, I'd call him, and he'd help us." (17)

Ex-police commissioner Joseph Timilty told the Blairs for their book "The Search for JFK" that Joe Kennedy was the mastermind of all Jack's campaigns, including his presidential campaign, "When Jack started running for Congress, he truly didn't know ten people in Boston. The ambassador was the mastermind of everything."

Timilty would arrange meetings with political leaders and take Jack to luncheons and political rallies, always acting on the ambassador's orders. "I was his (Joe's) closest friend, but never his confidant. He never confided in anybody, and he was completely in charge of everything, every detail," asserted Timilty. (18)

Rose Kennedy's role in the 1946 campaign was limited to organizing tea parties with her children and playing a Gold Star Mother (a Gold Star Mother is a mother who had lost a son during World War II) to perfection.

Her husband made the decisions. She remained in his shadow and accepted all his moves in getting Jack elected for public office.

The Nomination Papers: A Legendary Story

The Boston Globe ran a big headline in its afternoon edition on April 23, 1946, "Kennedy Papers For Congress Not In As Time Nears." The story began, "The deadline for filing nomination papers for the state primary election expires at 5.00 p.m. today. At an early hour this afternoon, the election commissioners had not received any papers from John F. Kennedy for the Democratic nomination for Congress in the 11th district, the seat to be vacated by Mayor James M. Curley." The commissioners duly closed the office on time with no Kennedy nomination papers submitted.

Fortunately, Kennedy's campaign HQ at the Bellevue hotel was just across the street from the State House, "A series of frantic phone calls were made," Red Fay later recalled, "because the office where the papers had to be filed had been closed since 5 p.m." In the end, money and influence prevailed, "Very quietly, the candidate and some loyal retainers went down, opened up the proper office, and filed the papers. Another couple of hours and all the thousands of hours of work by the candidate and his supporters would have been completely wasted," Fay related. (19)

Chris Matthews called it a loyalist's account of an after-hours escapade that had to have been blatantly illegal. (20)

In "Seeds of Destruction," Ralph G. Martin writes, "Had Jack ever registered and voted before? His answer was no. So, as his mother recorded, "Jack hustled down to City Hall and quietly joined the Democratic Party. They slipped him into City Hall Annex and got his name on the Democratic rolls several days after the deadline."

Author Ed Plaut later photocopied from town Hall files the signed declaration proving that Kennedy had filed too late to qualify for that primary. Plaut later discovered that this bound file had disappeared from the Town Hall – the only volume that was missing – and nobody seemed to know what happened to it. Had all this been revealed at that time, there might not have been any Kennedy candidacy, at least not in 1946. (21)

One puzzle remains to frustrate efforts to verify the truth: where today is the photocopy of that signed declaration, taken by Ed Plaut?

The clear fact is that, on the evening of April 23, 1946, Jack Kennedy became a Democratic Party Congressional Candidate in the eleventh District.

The primary election took place on the morning of June 18, 1946. Jack Kennedy and his two maternal grandparents went to the polls together. They then spent the rest of the day at the cinema watching the Marx Brothers' latest movie, "A Night in Casablanca."

Massachusetts's 11th congressional district, June 18, 1946 (Democratic Primary)

John F. Kennedy – 22,183 (42.41%)
Michael J. Neville – 11,341 (21.68%)
John F. Cotter – 6,677 (12.76%)
Joseph Russo – 5,661 (10.82%)
Catherine E. Falvey – 2,446 (4.68%)
Joseph Lee – 1,848 (3.5%)
Joseph Russo – 799 (1.53%)
Michael DeLuca – 536 (1.03%)
Francis N. Rooney – 521 (1.00%)
Robert B. DiFruscio – 298 (0.57%)

The General election on November 5, 1946, was a pure formality. Jack Kennedy won again by a landslide 69,063 (71.87%) votes against Lester W. Brown (Republican from Somerville) with 26,007 votes (27.05%). Philip Geer (Prohib Boston) got 1,036 votes (1.08%), and there were 9,237 Blank Ballots.

On January 3, 1947, 29-year-old Jack Kennedy was sworn in as congressman, together with another newcomer Richard Milhous Nixon.

1.9. Conclusion

Precisely when Jack Kennedy decided to go into politics and who made him decide, who pushed him to go into politics, will be a source of debate for years to come. JFK's account is that, until his first speech, at an American Legion Post, he hadn't even considered a political life.

The question of how many dollars were spent on the Curley payoff and how much money was consumed by the 1946 congressional campaign will also continue to provide fodder for endless speculation.

The historical value of all this is very doubtful to me.

Joseph P. Kennedy, the Donald Trump of the forties in terms of wealth, if not as a presidential candidate, is proof that being a successful businessman does not make you a great politician.

As John F. Kennedy himself said, "Dad is a financial genius all right, but in politics, he's something else." (1)

Joe's opposition as an American ambassador to the Court of St. James for US entry in World War II, coupled with his inner conviction that Great Britain was going to lose the War, and his position towards Hitler, "a man you could deal with" is in the same line as Neville Chamberlain's coming back from Munich with his historical comment "peace in our time." These were not his finest political hours.

Rose Kennedy said that Joe knew very little about the actual mechanics of organizing and operating a political campaign. Joe was wise in the fields of national and international political affairs, but his interest dwindled as the political unit grew smaller. Events at the level of district, city town, and ward left him progressively bored, particularly in Boston. (2)

Kenneth O'Donnell, in an interview on December 4, 1976, with Herbert S. Parmet, not long before his death, became heated at suggestions that the ambassador had played a prominent role in the 1946 congressional campaign.

He scoffed at stories about Joe Kennedy's expertise and value to the campaign, pointing out that the ambassador had been "out of touch" with Boston politics for a long time, "He no longer knew a goddamn thing what was going on in Massachusetts," O'Donnell argued. (3)

But Mark Dalton had a different view on his involvement in the 1946 congressional campaign, considering Joe Kennedy to be "one of the ablest men I ever met. He was deeply interested in every campaign. He was interested in that congressional campaign." And according to Dalton, "If there were an essential campaign manager, it was Joe Kennedy." (4)

Joe Kennedy's hesitation between Jack "lieutenant governor" or Jack "congressman" proves O'Donnell's point of view justified.

A letter from Joseph P. Kennedy to Joseph Kane, Palm Beach, on March 11, 1946, proves his longtime hesitation between Lt. Governor or Congress. He writes, "Dear Joe, I have read your letter with its very clear outline of Jack's position. Personally, I think I would rather see him, Lt. Governor. Now mind you, I don't say that I would rather see him "run" for Lt. Governor. I would rather see him, Lt. Governor, but I realize his greatest weakness is his lack of experience. Therefore, since he would have an easier chance to win in Congress, I believe I am inclining toward that idea." (5)

Governor Maurice Tobin was up for re-election in 1946. He required a fresh face with lots of money, preferably a veteran, to run on his ticket as lieutenant governor. Joe Kennedy, worried now that his son might be too young and inexperienced to prevail in a wide-open primary, was attracted to the idea of his running with Tobin and gaining the seasoning he needed for a later run for senator or governor. Honey Fitz was bitterly opposed to the idea, as was Jack. I presume that Honey Fitz had more political sense than Joe Kennedy. (6)

Joe Kennedy was eventually won over to their side after commissioning a poll that showed Jack had a much greater chance of being elected congressman in a safe district than the lieutenant governor in a state that was leaning Republican.

Had he been on the Tobin ticket, he would have gone down in defeat in the great Republican sweep of 1946, and that might have been the end of Jack Kennedy's political career before it even got started.

But Joe Kennedy, for all the flaws attributed to him by many historians, was a good father – above all else, his family came first. He was severe, he valued discipline and didn't allow a mistake to be repeated twice, but he wasn't a dictator. His children knew that and respected him for it.

Jack's speeches lacked confidence in his delivery. His sister Eunice recalled her brother's discouragement. "Many a night when he'd come over to see Daddy after a speech, he'd be feeling rather down, admitting that the speech hadn't gone very well or believing his delivery had put people in the front row fast asleep. 'What do you mean?' father would immediately ask. "Why I talked to Mr. X and Mrs. Y on the phone right after they got home, and they told me they were sitting in the front row and that it was a fine speech.

And then I talked to so and so, and he said last year's speaker at the same event had 40 in the audience while you had 90." "And then," Eunice continued, "this was the key – father would go on to elicit from Jack what he thought he could change to make it better the next time." This is a perfect example of Joe Kennedy's role as a father on a mental and psychological approach to a problem, criticizing Jack's performance and stretch his ability at the same time. (7)

Mark Dalton, a member of JFK's staff from 1946-1952, thought Jack, as a young, inexperienced politician from 1946 to the mid-fifties, was an excellent debater but not an excellent orator – certainly not in the league of Daniel Webster. The latter could arouse emotions, JFK never gave an emotional address in that period or later, but as a debater, he was excellent. (8)

As a President, he gave two emotional speeches, the American University speech in Washington, D.C. June 10, 1963, and the "Ich bin ein Berliner" speech in West Berlin on June 26, 1963 – two speeches he will always be remembered for.

Most historians agree that Joe Kennedy wasn't in the limelight of the 1946 Congressional Campaign. Still, he orchestrated it financially and technically almost to perfection, except for the little mishap on his Lt. Governor preference, where he was "saved by the polls."

Jack Kennedy, with no political experience at all, could use his father's business experience along with his determination to get his son elected for Congress, nothing wrong about that, I would think.

In an interview with Herbert S. Parmet, on July 24, 1978, Dave Powers told the author that running for Congress was Jack's decision, "no matter who talked to him about the other." Going into politics was also Jack's decision, of course, encouraged, stimulated, and influenced by his father. Politics was in his blood through the many city tours and conversations with grandpa Fitzgerald. Honey Fitz had spent hours talking to him about the political picture of the Bay State.

Jack was never really interested in local politics in the city of Boston or the state of Massachusetts. His interest lay in international politics. (9) (10)

During his many convalescences, Jack devoured several books a week, mostly books on war and government. To improve his reading rate, he took a speed-reading night course, according to Eric Severeid, a CBS news journalist.

What would Jack Kennedy have done instead of going into politics?

In interviews with various authors, Rose Kennedy said that a possible other career was teacher, writer, editor, or something in the literary field, but no word on a career in journalism.

I am convinced, like Lem Billings, that Jack Kennedy would have gone into politics, even if his brother Joe had lived – even if it involved initially being in his older brother's shadow. After all, younger brothers Bobby and Teddy both became senators and presidential candidates. But because Jack was brighter than his brother Joe, with an internationalist view on politics, he would have outscored his brother.

Kennedy's first congressional campaign, Boston, September 1946
(Copyright: JFK Library)

Despite his inexperience, Kennedy surprised even his supporters by the magnitude of his victory in the June 1946 primaries for the Congressional seat vacated by former Major of Boston James M. Curley, then seeking reelection to the mayoralty. (Copyright: JFK Library)

*The skinny young veteran leads the Bunker Hill day Parade during his 1946
congressional campaign in Boston, Charlestown, Massachusetts. Note that he
carries, rather than wears his hat – Jack never liked to wear headgear.
(Copyright: JFL Library)*

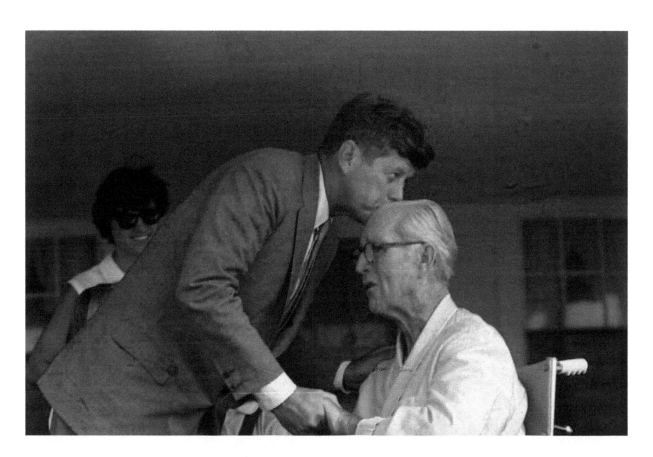

December 20, 1961 West Palm Beach, Flo. JFK visits ailing Joe Sr. Joseph Kennedy Sr. rested comfortably this morning after suffering a stroke yesterday afternoon. On the left is Ann Gargan, a cousin of JFK's, who cared devotedly to Joseph Kennedy after his stroke.
(Copyright: JFK Library)

JFK with Kenneth O'Donnell and David Powers. Trip to Nassau, Bahamas, Meetings with Harold Macmillan, Prime Minister of Great Britain, 18-21 December 1962.
(Copyright: JFK Library)

Chapter 2: Who Wrote 'Profiles In Courage'?

"Our political life is becoming so expensive, so mechanized and so dominated by professional politicians and public relations men that the idealist who dreams of independent statesmanship is rudely awakened by the necessities of election and accomplishment."

- **Profiles in Courage 1955**

"However detailed may have been our study of his life, each man remains something of an enigma."

- **Profiles in Courage 1955**

"The stories of past courage can teach, they can offer hope, they can provide inspiration.
But they cannot supply courage itself. For each man must look into his own soul."

- **Profiles In Courage 1956**

"There are few things wholly evil or wholly good."

- **Abraham Lincoln**

2.1. Where did the Idea for the Book Come From?

Early in 1954, John Kennedy asked Ted Sorensen to read a passage in Herbert Agar's "The Price of Union" (Michael O'Brien talks about Agar's "A Time for Greatness"), which had long intrigued him. It described the political backlash Massachusetts Senator John Quincy Adams suffered when he opposed major economic interest groups in New England by supporting President Jefferson's trade embargo on Great Britain in retaliation for British attacks on American merchant ships.

JFK told Sorensen that, after reading about Adams' experience, he was thinking of writing a piece exploring the willingness of elected officials to defy fierce pressure from powerful lobby groups, or concerned constituents, in the national interest. (1) (2) (3) (4) (5)

Sorensen and fellow Kennedy aides Kenneth O'Donnell and Dave Powers have two different approaches to how his idea of a book on courage started.

Sorensen writes, "It may have been during his 1954 hospitalization for back surgery confronted with the possibility of early death or crippling illness, that he decided to make more of his life, to become more serious about his career as a congressman, even to think seriously about running for higher office." (6)

O'Donnell and Powers write, "There was a noticeable change in Jack Kennedy after his serious illness and a long convalescence. The months that he spent in bed reflecting on his role in politics and studying the courage of great men in political history made him deeper, stronger, and more intellectually and emotionally mature and secure. The Jack Kennedy, who went into the pits and fought William "Onions" Burke and Congressman John McCormack for the leadership of the Democratic organization in Massachusetts in 1956, was much tougher and was more sure of himself than the charming young senatorial candidate of 1952." (7)

Sorensen's approach to Kennedy is one of a collaborator, while O'Donnell's and Powers' approach is one of two friends.

Kennedy always had in mind a bid for high office – strongly influenced by his ambitious father but driven by his ambition.

In December 1954, Sorensen started sending books, memos, and research material to Kennedy in Florida as input for his writing project. In early 1955, while convalescing in Palm Beach from surgery with ample time on his hands, Kennedy decided to expand his planned article on the courage of senators ("Patterns of Political Courage") into a full-length book.

Sorensen flew to Palm Beach in March and again in May, staying for between two weeks and ten days each visit, to lend a hand and taking his Senate secretary with him to help. And while in Washington, Sorensen received almost daily instructions and requests from Kennedy in Florida to check sources, recommend more books to consult for material, and review early drafts of chapters. After JFK returned to the Senate, the collaboration continued at home and work, with Sorensen often putting in 12-hour days. (8) (9)

On May 6, 1955, after seeing a first draft, Harper & Brothers' editor, Evan Thomas, wrote to Jack Kennedy, "I am sending you a signed contract together with a check for $500. I can't tell you how pleased I am to have this in hand." (10) Kennedy donated the $500 prize to the United Negro College Fund (11), and Thomas, as the book's editor, suggested that Kennedy consider titles such as "These brave Men" and "The Patriots." (12) Other titles considered were "Patterns of Political Courage "(the magazine article), "Call the Roll" – Sorensen's favorite at the time – "Eight Were Courageous" (one of the publisher's suggestions) and "Courage in the Senate." (13)

On July 26, 1955, Jack sent a letter asking his sister Eunice that she, Sarge, and their friends mull over the following suggested titles for the book asking, "Let me know as soon as possible which you think is the best:

1. Men of Courage
2. Eight were Courageous;
3. Call the Roll,
4. Profiles in Courage." (14)

No author refers to "Men of Courage" as a possible title, suggested by Jack to his sister Eunice and brother-in-law Sarge.

On August 1, 1955, Jack Kennedy wrote to Evan Thomas, "The more I think about it and discuss it with my friends, the less I like the title, "Men of Courage." "Profiles of Courage" and "Call the Roll" are the two which attract the most interest and support. Perhaps we should spend some more time on this."

Evan Thomas wrote back on August 4, 1955, "I have changed the title to "Profiles in Courage." All of us here are happy with that, but we are most unhappy about the alternative "Call the Roll." (15)

The finished book "Profiles in Courage" is a collection of stories about eight political leaders whose courage at critical moments in their careers had led them to resist their constituents and defy their colleagues to save a broader or national good, much as Kennedy thought he had done on the St. Lawrence Seaway issue.

The first profile in the book was of John Quincy Adams, a Federalist from Massachusetts, son of President John Adams, the second American president. John Quincy Adams – the sixth president – defied the interests of Massachusetts by supporting both the Louisiana Purchase Treaty and Jefferson's 1807 Embargo act.

Hated by the federalists and suspected by the Republicans, John Quincy Adams served in the Congress after his presidency. The second was Daniel Webster, a Massachusetts whig, who ignored most of the North by appealing to the interests of nationalism over sectionalism with his "Seventh of March Speech" defending the compromise of 1850.

Daniel Webster died a disappointed and discouraged man in 1852. His last words in the Senate amounted to his epitaph, "No man can suffer too much, and no man can fall too soon, if he suffers or if he falls in defense of the liberties and constitution of his country."

The third was Thomas Hart Benton, a Democrat who kept Missouri from joining the

Southern confederacy. Benton was defeated for re-election in 1854 and fought in vain to be returned to the senate in 1855. The next year, at the age of 74, he made one last race for governor, dying on April 10, 1858, of throat cancer in Washington, D.C.

The fourth was Sam Houston, a Democrat from Texas who aroused opposition by voting for the Kansas-Nebraska Act of 1854. The Texas Legislature unceremoniously dismissed him on November 10, 1857, and a more militant spokesman for the South was elected as his successor. In the fall of 1859, Houston stood as an independent candidate for governor and won. On February 23, 1861, Texas voted for secession by a large margin, and on March 2 – the anniversary of Houston's birthday and Texan independence – a special convention reassembled at Austin and declared that Texas had seceded. Houston was evicted from his office on March 16, 1861, for refusing to take a call of loyalty to the Confederacy.

The fifth was Edmund G. Ross, a Republican from Kansas. He, along with six other "Courageous Republicans" refused to back an impeachment move against Andrew Johnson. But in "Impeached" by David O. Stewart, there are some strong allegations that Edmund Ross was bribed to vote for Johnson's acquittal, and he was never re-elected to the Senate. When he returned to Kansas, he and his family suffered social ostracism, near-poverty, and physical attack.

The sixth was Lucius Quintus Cincinnatus Lamar, a Democrat from Mississippi who eulogized Charles Summer, the South's most implacable enemy because Lamar was more interested in promoting national unity than in the continuation of sectional strife. It is heartening to note that the people of Mississippi responded to Lamar's sincerity and courage by continuing to give him their support and for the rest of his political life.

The seventh was George Norris, a young insurgent Republican from Nebraska. He was praised for opposing the tyrannical rule of House Speaker Joe Cannon of Illinois. George Norris also supported Democrat Al Smith as a presidential candidate in 1928, despite not only belonging to the opposite party but also being a Catholic and an anti-prohibitionist while Norris was a Protestant. Unable to secure Democratic support in the state in 1942, he was defeated by Republican Kenneth S. Wherry. He parted from the office, saying, "I have done my best to repudiate wrong and evil in government affairs." A 1957 advisory panel of 160 scholars recommended Norris as the top choice for the five best Senators in US history. (16) (17) (18)

The last profile in Kennedy's book was Robert A. Taft, a Republican from Ohio, the elder son of William Howard Taft, the 27th President of the United States. Robert Taft spoke against the Nuremberg trials of Nazi war criminals because the US Constitution prohibited ex post facto laws. It destroyed his chance of ever becoming president, and according to Dan Fenn, he was too conservative and too isolationist and, in the view of the Republican power brokers, unelectable. (19)

Profiles in Courage was published on January 1, 1956. In a New York Times Book

Review the same day, Cabell Phillips wrote, "One of the reasons that the profession of politics suffers from such low public esteem is that it is constantly being run down by politicians themselves. In this unfortunate state of affairs, it is refreshing and enlightening to have a first-rate politician write a thoughtful and persuasive book about political integrity. Kennedy's book is the sort of restoring respect for a venerable and much-abused profession." (20)

But on January 7, 1956, Charles Poore ran a more critical review. According to him, Kennedy's book was "splendidly readable and offered an impressively varied cast of characters,' but it also had weaknesses," he said. One troubling aspect was that the men in the book "showed their most conspicuous courage in defying the very forces that had chosen them for leadership." The book, Poore claimed, did not take sufficient account of "the enduring good sense of the American people as a whole who, as in the past, always will preserve the constitutional government, no matter what the demagogue advocates in any passing time." (21) (22)

Profiles in Courage made the bestseller list and remained there for 66 weeks, selling 124,665 copies by March 1958. Sales would go on to top two million copies. Kennedy's work was translated into 23 languages – Turkish, Italian, Czech, Complex Chinese, Japanese, Portuguese, Spanish, Brazilian, Russian, German, Simplified Chinese, Hindi, Indonesian, Dutch, Amharic, Bahasa, Bulgarian, Danish, French, Finnish, Hebrew, Icelandic and Korean. (23) (24) (25) (26) (27) (28)

2.2. Who Helped Him Write the Book

In the preface of his book, John Kennedy thanked a lot of people who helped him write it. In his preface, Kennedy admits that he got a lot of help in writing his book and that the work "a committee," "a team," or "a group effort" used by some authors is justified and legitimate.

He expressed gratitude to Allan Nevins of Colombia University for contributing to the Foreword.

He went on, "A special debt of gratitude to the Library of Congress, Dr. Georges Galloway, and Dr. William R. Tansill, of the library staff, who made important contributions to the selection of examples for inclusion in the book, as did Arthur Krock of The New York Times and Professor James Mc Gregor Burns of Williams College. Professor John Bystrom of the University of Minnesota, former Nebraska Attorney General C. A. Sorensen, and the Honorable Hugo Sib, clerk of the Nebraska State Legislature. Professor Jules Davids of Georgetown University assisted materially in the preparation of several chapters, as did James M. Landis. Chapters II through X were greatly improved by the criticisms of Professor Arthur N. Holcombe and Arthur M. Schlesinger Jr., both of Harvard and Professor Walter Johnson of the University of Chicago."

He also thanked Evan Thomas of Harper & Brothers for making the book possible. He acknowledged that the greatest debt he owed for research was to Theodore C. Sorensen "for his invaluable assistance in the assembly and preparation of the material upon which this book is based."

He finally thanked his wife Jacqueline, noting that the book would not have been possible without her encouragement, assistance, and criticisms – and her support throughout his convalescence, which he said he could never adequately acknowledge. (1)

Arthur M. Schlesinger Jr. wrote to tell Kennedy that he had read the book "with great interest and admiration," praising it as skillfully written and a genuine contribution to political discussion, and historically sound "in the main." (2) (3)

Professor John Hohenberg, the administrator of the Pulitzer Prize, wrote in "The Pulitzer Diaries," "From the very nature of the book, a lot of research had been required. From my experience with writers and as the author of several books, I have seldom seen so complete a characterization of sources and assistance as Senator Kennedy offered the public for his Profiles in Courage. To have consulted so wide and distinguished a variety of academic and professional figures in itself would have been a creditable feat for any author." (4)

Only John Kennedy knows exactly who helped him in crafting his book, apart from those acknowledged in his preface.

Among them was Joe Kennedy's New York secretary Gertrude Ball, one of whose earliest assignments was to type the research reports that Joe's employees had written and which became chapters in Jack's book.

Both James Fayne and James Landis did some of the research while Jack was in the hospital in New York City, Landis, mainly on the Daniel Webster chapter and Fayne on several of the others. (5)

There are contradictions: Historian Herbert Parmet doesn't associate Landis with the research on the Daniel Webster chapter, but Ted Sorensen says Landis did a research report on Webster for the book.

According to Gertrude Ball, it was Sorensen, the bespectacled, lean, intense, and completely devoted lawyer who became Jack's speechwriter, who wrote final drafts. She said she typed research reports that formed the basis of Profiles in Courage – and later revealed that not only the writing but most of the research for the book was not Jack's. At the time, however, she was not about to go to the newspapers and say that Jack's father had, in effect, written the book for him. Author Ronald Kessler writes that Jack's father had written the book. Still, he also says that Janet Des Rosiers, Joe Kennedy's secretary, recalled seeing Jack working on the book, "I saw Jack write Profiles in Courage in Palm Beach after his back operation," she said. "His bedroom was piled high with reference books. He would sit in bed and write longhand." (5)

Was Joe Kennedy a ghostwriter? I never read a biography on Joe Kennedy in which he was called a ghostwriter. He was called many things; mogul, bootlegger, pro-Hitler, stock-market manipulator, womanizer, and so on, but never a ghostwriter.

On August 15, 1955, Joe Kennedy wrote to Ted Sorensen, suggesting that Harper and Brothers ask an editorial writer to go over the whole book to punctuate and simplifying the structure.

"It's a fine job as it is, but I remember when Lindbergh spoke to me about the real success of his book he said he almost did not recognize it after the editorial writer at Scribner's had finished working on it- he brought so much more clarity and punch to it," Joe wrote. "I think instead of having Harper's take this book just as it is, they should have a man of top-caliber do this same job on it and if he is very good, I am sure you will have a worth-while and profitable piece of literature, and worth-while financially if properly exploited." (6)

In "Johnny We Hardly Knew Ye," by O'Donnell and Powers, there is the following anecdote on the shaping of the book. "Unable to sleep for more than an hour or two at a stretch, Jack worked on the book day and night reading and writing notes and then drafts of the chapters on long yellow legal pads. He clung to the research work doggedly, keeping his mind on it to distract himself from his pain. When he was too tired to write or read, Jackie and Dave read to him."

Dave Powers explains, "I would be reading to him from a book about Texas in Sam Houston's time, and he would be stretched out flat on his back with his eyes closed for a couple of hours listening to every word I said. I would think he had fallen asleep, and I'd stop reading. But he would open his eyes and tell me to keep going." (7)

Arthur Krock, a famous New York Times journalist, said that he had two roles in the book's development – as an observer and as a contributor. When asked by Kennedy to nominate subjects for the profiles, Krock recommended in a letter on April 9, 1954, that an outstanding example might be Robert A. Taft's attack on the ex post facto law of the Nuremberg trials and for defying organized labor's blackmailing tactics to ensure Taft's defeat for re-election as a reprisal for the Taft-Hartley Act.

Kennedy accepted Krock's nomination but with considerable reluctance: during his contest for the 1960 Democratic presidential nomination, he remarked, "One of the things I wish you had never persuaded me to do was to put Taft in the Profiles."

"That," Krock answered firmly, "was probably the best thing I ever got you to do." (8)

According to David Heymann in "A Woman Named Jackie," Jackie helped to shape the overall theme of the book, did much of the initial research, scanning numerous historical volumes sent over by the library of Congress, taking notes, and writing out long passages. (9)

He also acknowledges the help of Sorensen, Davids, James Mac Gregor Burns, Arthur Holcombe, and Alan Nevins. On authorship, he concludes that it is difficult to say who did what concerning the book. Heymann doesn't raise the question of whether it could have been a group effort, with joint authorship, or even the work of a committee.

However, he does emphasize that there is no doubt that Sorensen proved extremely helpful.

Whether this meant that Jack wasn't the book's sole author remains a question that may never be answered.

2.3. Who Saw Him Write the Book?

Arthur Krock was in Palm Beach when Jack was recovering from another spinal operation. He had a suite in the living room, where he lay on a board, his head propped up on pillows. There was a small slanted lectern supporting a pad of ruled yellow foolscap on which Jack was writing incessantly. Once when Krock asked him what he was writing, he replied, "A book."

Later, when Kennedy faced accusations that he hadn't written Profiles in Courage, he simply said the suggestion was "hard to shake off." But surely Krock had seen him writing the book in Palm Beach.

"Of course, I certainly had," Krock insisted when the issue was raised, "I had seen him lying flat on his back on a board with a yellow pad on which he was writing the book. I read enough of those pages at the time to know that the product was his own." (1)

Kennedy's physician Janet Travell saw him sitting at a table in Palm Beach writing his book (2), and Charles Bartlett saw him writing his book in New York while he was recuperating at the Auchincloss house. "It made me a very vehement figure when the charge was later made that he had not written this book because I can remember him lying in that room," said Bartlett. "And I used to go up there, and he was lying on that board of his and writing almost upside down." It seemed to Bartlett that suggesting that Kennedy did not write the book was one of the weirdest charges that have been made. (3)

Rose Kennedy, in "Times to Remember," recalled seeing her son at Palm Beach in an office-studio library, "or whatever the best term is for the working habitat of a writer." She wrote, "So many times I remember looking out from the house across our sturdy green lawn and past the tall royal palm toward the tropical sea, the aquamarine white-capped ocean and blue sky and passing clouds and ships in the distance and there was Jack in his sea-level alcove with his writing board on a thick writing pad clamped on it and a folding table or two piled with books and notebooks and file folders, paperweights or perhaps some rocks on the board to hold things down against the sea breezes and his head would be forward, and he would be writing away on that book from full heart, mind, and spirit." (4)

Gloria Sitrin, Sorensen's secretary, later said, "There's no doubt that Sorensen constructed quite a bit from the research point of view, but I took dictation from Senator Kennedy on the book in Florida." (5)

Lem Billings also confirmed that he saw Jack writing the book, "I saw it all in his handwriting. And I saw him crossing out and rewriting. By God, if at twenty-one years of age, he could write, "Why England Slept," why the hell couldn't he write "Profiles in Courage?" (6)

2.4. The Drew Pearson Episode

After Profiles in Courage was awarded the Pulitzer Prize for biography, Gilbert Seldes, a columnist for the Village Voice, wrote an article claiming that Kennedy had a "collaborator" for his book.

He also dismissed the book as being below Pulitzer quality.

A couple of months later, Kennedy received a letter from Emma Sheehy, a professor at Columbia University, who said she had heard a rumor that Kennedy's book was "entirely ghost-written by somebody else." Kennedy replied that the rumor was "completely and utterly untrue," adding that the "apparent source of this rumor" was Gilbert Seldes' column, which may have been misunderstood. "I suppose the natural growth of a false rumor made the step from "had a collaborator" to "completely ghostwritten" inevitable." Kennedy also noted that "the false rumors" concerning his book did not start until it had been awarded a Pulitzer Prize. (1) (2)

On Monday morning, December 9, 1957, Kennedy called and asked Clark Clifford to come immediately to his home. "Did you see The Mike Wallace Interview Saturday night?" he asked.

Two days earlier, on December 7, 1957, ABC television's "The Mike Wallace interview" featured Drew Pearson, one of the country's most widely read political columnists. In the course of the interview, Pearson referred to Kennedy and his recent book, saying, "Jack Kennedy is the only man in history that I know who won a Pulitzer Prize on a book which was ghostwritten for him, which indicates the kind of public relations build-up he's had."

Wallace: "Do you know for a fact?"

Drew Pearson (speaking over Wallace): "Yes, I do."

Wallace: "...that the book "Profiles in Courage" was written for Senator Kennedy?"

Pearson: "I do."

Wallace: "By somebody else – and he has never acknowledged the fact?"

Pearson: "No, he has not. You know, there's a little wisecrack around the senate about Jack, who is a very handsome man, as you know. Some of his colleagues say, "Jack, I wish you had a little bit less profile and more courage."

Kennedy complained to Clifford: "It is a direct attack on my integrity and my honesty."

Clifford replied that he could sue Wallace, Pearson, and ABC for libel or slander. Still, it would be a lengthy process with court proceedings and substantial public interest, which itself could be damaging to Kennedy. The best solution, Clifford said, would be to obtain a quick retraction from everyone involved before the story grew and developed a life of its own.

During the conversation in Clifford's office, Joe Kennedy telephoned and said, "I want to sue the bastards for fifty million dollars (3) (4) (5) (6) [$60 million according to C. David Heymann (that's what I call inflation) (7)]."

Joe Kennedy was convinced that there was a plot, a deep conspiracy of some kind on the part of his son's detractors. Still, Clark Clifford dismissed the idea. (8)

Two authors talk about FBI involvement at Joe Kennedy's urging.

According to Peter Collier and David Horowitz, Joe Kennedy asked his friend J. Edgar Hoover to go after "the group of New York people" involved in the charges that Ted Sorensen had done almost all the work – and eventually won a retraction by ABC, which had aired the Pearson charges. (9)

But author Herbert Parmet suggested the FBI was pursuing "a group of New York people" to check claims that Arthur Krock had been the real author of Profiles in Courage. (10)

I consulted Parmet's notes, and something seems very strange and implausible to me. That is, it was on Monday morning, December 9, 1957, the "Pearson war" started. So why would Joe Kennedy ask the FBI to intervene on May 14, 1957, seven months before the ABC interview, as Parmet's notes indicate? Even more very doubtful to me is that Arthur Krock was the real author of Profiles in Courage: naming Krock as the ghostwriter seems illogical.

These stories would be great stuff for a novel or a science fiction book on Kennedy. Clifford asked Kennedy to assemble everything that he could find concerning the writing of Profiles in Courage: handwritten notes, notebooks, records, comments by anyone who had seen him writing the book.

Then Clifford set up a meeting with ABC chairman Leonard Goldenson for Thursday, December 12, in New York. In Clifford's presence, the ABC executives and lawyers called Drew Pearson.

Although he had been unable to recall the name of the "ghostwriter" during the television program, Pearson now remembered it clearly, "Theodore Sorensen," he said, "had written 'Profiles in Courage'." Kennedy also admitted that the publisher had paid royalties totaling 6,000 dollars directly to Sorensen. Still, Clifford stressed that this did not constitute an admission that Sorensen had written the book. The ABC executives, after cross-examining Sorensen at length, finally agreed that the senator was the author of Profiles in Courage. Sorensen signed an affidavit, "I wish to state under oath that these charges are wholly untrue. I am not the author of Profiles in Courage.

I did not write the book for Senator Kennedy, and I have not at any time to any person declared myself to be the author. I have never written any book of any kind. I undertook at his (Kennedy's) direction and under his supervision to assist him in the assembly and preparation of research and other materials on which much of the book is based, as acknowledged by the senator in the preface. The author is Senator Kennedy, who originally conceived its themes, selected its characters, determined its contents, and wrote and rewrote each of its chapters.

The research, suggestions, and other materials received by him in the course of writing the book, from me and the others listed in the preface, were all considered by the senator, along with his material, in part rejected by him and in part drawn upon by him in his work. To assert that any one of us who supplied such materials "wrote the book" for the senator is unwarranted and in error."

Pearson was forced to make a public retraction, writing in his diary that Jack had shown him his original notes and that he was fully convinced, "He got a whole of a lot of help in his book," Pearson noted privately. "I'm still dubious as to whether he wrote too much of it in the final draft himself. He showed me the rough chapters, some of them worked out by Harvard professors. But he also showed enough knowledge of the book, made the book many parts of him, that, it is his book." (3) (4)

John Oakes of the New York Times first suggested to Harper editor Simon Michael Bessie the "strong rumor" that Kennedy had not written the book. When Kennedy found out, he contacted Oakes. He arranged for an aide to show to Oakes the actual notebooks he had used in writing the draft of the book during his Florida recuperation. He also showed Oakes the letters from those who had provided help on specific matters. (11)

New York Post editor Martha MacGregor wrote to Kennedy about the rumor that Sorensen had written the book and was receiving half the royalties. As John Hohenberg noted in his diaries, Martha MacGregor admitted she had been "gum-shoeing" around Kennedy probing the claims that he had a ghost-writer for his Pulitzer Prize "Profiles in Courage." She concluded over the phone that he'd had assistance from Ted Sorensen, his secretary, but that he had written the book himself. Nice of her to say so. (12)

2.5. Sorensen's Role in Profiles in Courage

John Kennedy wrote in Profiles in Courage, "However detailed may have been our study of his life, each man remains something of an enigma." (1)

Sorensen was such a man.

From the beginning of my research for this chapter, I was convinced that Sorensen himself had leaked the story privately that he was the author of Profiles in Courage. And in "Counselor," he finally admitted that he was the cause of Kennedy's troubles with Drew Pearson on Mike Wallace's ABC television show of December 7, 1957, "When finally the ABC executives agreed that JFK was the author of Profiles, but then leveled another charge – that I (Sorensen) had privately boasted or indirectly hinted that I had written much of the book, a charge that, I regret to say, may have been – it was all too long ago to remember – partly true."

"Perhaps Sorenson made this statement when drinking," said an ABC executive to JFK, as Sorensen waited in another room. "He doesn't drink," said JFK. "Perhaps he said it when he was mad at you." "He's never been mad at me," replied Kennedy. (2)

But in a 1960 book on Kennedy, "Front Runner, Dark Horse," Sorensen talks very evasively about the Drew Pearson charges, "After all," he said, "Why is it so unbelievable that Jack wrote this book. The first book he wrote, "Why England Slept," was a book-of-the-Month club bestseller, and nobody ever questioned him on that."

He also told the authors Ralph Martin and Ed Plaut that he remembered that Jim Landis did a research report on Webster and maybe somebody else. And Jules Davids, a history professor at Georgetown, did memos on four or five possibilities, and he did four or five. Memos were about five pages each.

Sorensen further told Martin and Plaut, "Now there's no question that I can look in the book and find words and even sentences of mine. I worked damn hard on that book, and I don't want to underestimate what I did. But he (Kennedy) gave me proper credit in the preface, just as he gave all others proper credit. But the basic conception, direction, decisions on what materials to use, digestion of all the research reports and the dictation of the final drafts, the penciling of the final drafts, the rewriting of the final first draft, that was all his."

Martin and Plaut wrote that if Kennedy's book was ghosted, he should admit it. If it was ghosted and he won't admit it, then he was hardly a man of principle, hardly a man to be trusted in the White House. (3)

In his book "Kennedy" in 1965, Sorensen reacted in my view very aggressively to the Pearson charges that he had written "Profiles in Courage" – as if he knew he had leaked the story privately, "The ABC executives, after privately cross-examining me at length, finally agreed that the senator was the author of Profiles in Courage, with sole responsibility for its concept and contents and with such assistance, during his convalescence, as his preface acknowledged." Sorensen insisted. "But they sought to avoid their responsibility for publishing an untrue rumor by making a new and equally untrue charge – namely that I had privately boasted of being the author." (4) This is Ted at his best; as in soccer, the best defense is the attack – but more than 40 years later, he admitted that he leaked being the author of Profiles.

My feelings on Sorensen's attitude are confirmed by what Lem Billings said – that Sorensen was "almost all the way to the left, and that he started the rumor that Jack didn't really write the book." Billings claimed, "I heard Jack Kennedy bawl Sorensen out, frankly because he knew that Sorensen leaked that story." But biographer David Pitts concluded that there was no evidence to support Lem's claim other than his statement, and its accuracy is open to question. Lem was somewhat resentful of Sorensen's growing closeness to Jack at the time, "Sorensen just adored Jack. He was one hell of a speechwriter for Jack," he said grudgingly. (5)

It was Drew Pearson who claimed that Sorensen had written Profiles in Courage. Or was it Professor Jules Davids of Georgetown University, who, in an interview with Herbert S. Parmet, claimed that he drafted a 22-page chapter on Webster, which was forwarded to Schlesinger for an additional opinion?

Davids, with whom Jackie had taken courses, also submitted 26 pages on Sam Houston, 24 on Lucius Q. C. Lamar, a 26-page on George W. Norris, and a 13-page essay on "The Meaning of Political Courage" for the closing section. I read all Davids' drafts, and only fragments appear in the final version of Profiles.

Nevertheless, in a letter to Herbert S. Parmet on November 30, 1978, Davids, who neither a lawyer nor a Kennedy employee, insisted that he and Sorensen carried out the bulk of the research work and the drafting of chapters – an assertion that Sorensen characterized as an "overstatement" of his involvement.

Davids provides additional details of his claim to authorship – including his reaction to what he said was a "pitifully small" payment of $700 for his work.

Parmet subsequently credited Davids with writing parts of the book and characterized the future president as serving "principally as an overseer." (6) (7) (8) (9)

But in "Ghost's Story," Michael J. Birkner wrote, "Before his death, Sorensen admitted more of the truth: He was indeed the main author of Profiles." In an interview conducted by a New York Times writer for use in his obituary, Sorensen confessed that he had drafted "most of the chapters" (as the obituary writer put it) or, as Sorensen said, he had "played an important role and gotten handsomely recompensed for doing so." History professor Birkner said, "It is difficult to say precisely how Profiles was composed, but we have enough documentary evidence to suggest the following, "First, Kennedy hatched the idea and shared it with at least two writers – his young aide Ted Sorensen and Jules Davids, a diplomatic historian at Georgetown whose teaching had impressed Kennedy's new wife, Jacqueline. Both were given the assignment of writing portions of the book, and each was paid for the assignment."

Birkner went on, "Second, Sorensen, by the evidence I have seen, wrote more of the book and was recompensed for more handsomely than Davids. "But none of Kennedy's wit and sagacity should obscure a basic fact that Theodore Sorensen's death has now confirmed: Kennedy did not write Profiles in Courage. He simply took credit for it." (10)

I have two questions on this article: who is the mysterious New York Times reporter, and what evidence has he seen?

I come to the same conclusion as Larry J. Sabato – that Birkner does not support his accusation with incontrovertible evidence.

Professor Davids' 1978 letter also includes the following passage (although it is not quoted in Parmet's book): "Since the book was to be on political courage, I have always felt that my lecture and Jacqueline's presence in my class were connected directly with triggering John Kennedy's interest in the subject of political courage. It is conceivable that this was coincidental, but, I believe, not likely." (11)

But what about Jules Davids' letter to Kennedy dated February 15, 1955 (he must have meant (1956), "It has been a genuine thrill to me to feel that in a small way I was a part of the great book that was written. I felt from the beginning that the theme was excellent. But more than that, you have succeeded in revitalizing our philosophy of American democracy." To which Kennedy replied on February 27, 1956, "Many thanks for your letter of recent date and your very kind remark concerning my book. I certainly appreciate your writing to me, and I wish to thank you for your assistance in the writing of the book. It was very helpful." (12) (13)

Parmet subsequently credited Professor Davids with writing parts of the book and characterized the future president as serving "principally as an overseer."

Davids provides additional details of his claim to authorship – including his reaction to what he said was a "pitifully small" payment of $700 for his work on the book.

The New York Times writer Patricia Cohen provided more evidence in her report about another letter, written by Davids to the Rev. Brien McGrath and dated August 5, 1957.

In the letter, found decades later in Georgetown's library archives, Davids said that he lectured on political courage in the spring of 1956 and that "Mrs. Kennedy" asked him after class if he could suggest for the senator the names of individuals who demonstrated outstanding examples of political courage in American history.

Parmet, in his 1980 biography, "Jack: The Struggles of John F. Kennedy" – considered by historians to be the definitive account of the Profiles project – called it "an important find."

In "A Companion to John F. Kennedy," Michael Brenes writes that Kennedy and Sorensen maintained a rare camaraderie. (14)

I consider it was anything but camaraderie: It was a calculated and compartmentalized relationship between Kennedy and Sorensen. They were never friends, and they didn't socialize: Kennedy needed him, and he needed Kennedy, whom he worshipped.

Brenes's view is that Sorensen was the ghostwriter for Profiles in Courage – and Brenes doesn't mention Davids at all.

According to Geoffrey Perret in "Jack: A Life Like No Other" even the former dean of Harvard Law School, James Landis – Joe Kennedy's old friend – was asked to lend a hand with the book.

But as to the author, Perret writes that much of the manuscript was undoubtedly the work of Ted Sorensen – and Jack Kennedy did very little of the research. Who then really wrote Profiles in Courage?

Sorensen himself referred to the book as "our monumental work," and Jack acknowledged Sorensen's contribution by paying him a $6,000 bonus, equivalent to four months' salary. "In the end," Perret wrote, "The fairest judgment seems to be that it was a work of joint authorship – Kennedy and Sorensen, even though only one author's name appears on the spine." And he mentions Jules Davids just for doing research and not for drafting some chapters for the book. (15)

In "The Kennedy Obsession," John Hellmann cites Herbert Parmet as crediting Jules Davids and Theodore Sorensen for the bulk of the research for the drafting of Profiles in Courage.

He also concludes that the idea for the book seems to have originated with Kennedy as a group project that he sponsored and directed. Kennedy kept up with the research, was a source of ideas and material, and, in the end, decided what would and would not go into the book bearing his name as an author. (16)

Robert Dallek also credits Sorensen and Davids for gathering material for the book and for drafting chapters. Still, he describes the final product as essentially Jack's,

"Jack did more on the book than some later critics believed, but less than the term "author" normally connotes. Profiles in Courage were more the work of a "committee" than of any one person." (17)

Why did Parmet not confront Sorensen closely on this issue when he interviewed him on May 17, 1977? (18)

As an amateur historian who tries to discover the historical truth, I would have asked Sorensen about his 1956-1957 remarks on authorship to James McGregor Burns during lunch at the Student Union at Williams, New England. Burns recalled praising Profiles in Courage and asking Sorenson, who wrote it, "And I, at the time, understood him to say 'I did'. And I have often thought about this. This was a clear impression I had. But it was outside, it was windy, and "he and I" are two words that can easily be confused. It is rather ironic that there should be any question about it now because he said one or the other very definitely, and at the time, I thought he said, 'I did'." Burns went on, "It is something he never would have said, later on, no matter who had done it. If he had said either "I did it" or "he did not" at the time, he would have said it with some emphasis. It was a very brief rejoinder: there was no elaborate discussion on this. So all I can do at this time is to record that my impression at the time was that he said, "I did it," meaning Sorensen did it.

But of course, he might have said that, and that might have still been an exaggeration, and I stick to my view that Kennedy substantially wrote that book. And one reason I stick to this view is later history. At one time, we might have wondered about Kennedy as a man of talent: I don't think now we would raise the question. The evidence I found in manuscript form, the actual manuscript that I looked at, which was in Kennedy's handwriting – not a whole manuscript, but a rather extensive one."

So Burns was sure Kennedy wrote most of the book while observing that "whoever was helping him, presumably Sorensen, gave him more help on the book than you or I could hope to get if we were doing one." (19)

This story shows that Lem Billings' feelings and mine on Sorensen proved accurate and true.

Therefore, although Parmet's book "Jack: The Struggles of John F. Kennedy" (1980) is well-researched and entertaining, his judgment that Profiles in Courage was ghostwritten mostly by Sorensen is for me wrong. He misleads a generation of scholars, historians, students, and myself until I studied his writings extensively and exhaustively.

The flip-flop quotes by Sorensen on the book, such as, "I did it," or "I was not the author," or "The credit ultimately lies with JFK," are examples of Ted Sorensen's mind and psyche. On the one hand, he was a fine speechwriter; on the other, his claims were unreliable.

To finish the Profiles in Courage controversy, I would like to quote Robert Schlesinger, the youngest son of the late Arthur M. Schlesinger Jr., "There is a distinction between authorship of a speech and ownership. Ferreting out the specific author of a memorable line can be an interesting exercise (enough to write whole books about). Of greater importance is not who first sets specific phrases to paper, but the care with which a president adopts them as his own and how well those words express that president's philosophy and policies. The president must ultimately have ownership of his words – for good or ill – not only because he will be held responsible for them, but because to suggest otherwise risks the possibility that he may not." (20)

Towards the end of his life, Ted Sorensen wrote, "Looking back on the issue more than fifty years later; perhaps I can answer the skeptics' the question of authorship by asking my question: Is the author the person who did much of the research and helped choose the words in many of its sentences, or is the author the person who decided the substance, structure, and theme of the book, read and revised each draft, inspired, constructed and improved the work? Like JFK's speeches, Profiles in Courage was a collaboration." (21)

Sorry Mr. Sorensen, but you said in "Counselor" that you had privately boasted or indirectly hinted that you had written much of the book had been partly true; your comments above are once again proof that you often spoke with a forked tongue.

Dan Fenn's view is that Sorensen, of all those involved, did the most work on the book. Dan said, "I suspect that his drafts were based often on the conversations the two had had. I suspect that JFK himself did a great deal on it. I suspect that all the final decisions were his, the shape of it was his, that it was, in the most fundamental sense, his book on which he had lots of help and advice from many people." (22)

Jacqueline Bouvier Kennedy's dislike of Ted Sorensen was triggered in 1956 when he gave people around Washington the impression that he, and not JFK, had written Profiles in Courage. She later reflected, "On that Profiles in Courage thing, Jack behaved like a great gentleman to Ted then, because Ted didn't behave very well that year. I couldn't look at Ted Sorensen for about two years after that. Jack forgave so quickly, but I never forgave Ted Sorensen. I watched him like a hawk for a year or so.

When the Drew Pearson allegations came, where Clark Clifford came and defended him, luckily, Jack had saved all these pages of yellow legal pad that he'd written himself. You know I saw Jack writing that book. I never liked the way Ted behaved. But you know, his life was all around himself, and I think, just in the White House, he got to have one other person beside himself, which was Jack. So in the White House, he was fine." Ted Sorensen received all the royalties from Profiles in Courage until the memorial edition, including Robert Kennedy's preface, was published. Since then, all "Profiles in Courage" royalties have gone to the JFK library. (23)

2.6. Parmet's Prejudicial Approach

I want to give my humble opinion on how Herbert Parmet handled Profiles. Although he did extensive research, I am convinced that it was based on a highly prejudicial approach to prove that Jack Kennedy didn't write Profiles in Courage, but that it was ghostwritten, mostly by Ted Sorensen.

I think I have found some facts to prove my allegation. According to Michael O'Brien, Parmet's research, though extensive, was not exhaustive. Some evidence seems to have disappeared – evidence which might have shown additional Kennedy contributions. Parmet even conceded that newer tape recordings of Kennedy's dictation were taped over old recordings. "So that the existing reels do not represent the full extent of Kennedy's dictation." Missing too are the notebooks, to which Kennedy often referred, and which convinced Drew Pearson and others, that Kennedy did write major parts of Profiles. (1)

And I agree with O'Brien that Sorensen, in correspondence at the time and in subsequent interviews, repeatedly referred to letters and phone calls from the senator concerning the book. Yet, none of these sources appear in Parmet's analysis.

Parmet refers in his notes to an Oral History interview at the Kennedy Library with Jean Mannix in which she said, "Ted Sorensen was up in the office, and he was constantly researching for the book. I'm sure that he did a great deal of research because he was in the position to do this with the library of Congress across the street. But he went down in that time, that winter and spring, to Florida four or five times to confer with the senator. I have seen myself many handwritten drafts of the president's after he came back. I never actually worked on the book because there were two or three girls who did work for Ted Sorensen and worked on this. But I did some when the president came back to Washington. And there's no doubt in my mind that Ted did a great deal of research, but the book was written by the president." (2) (3)

It is a complete mystery to me that Parmet referred in his notes to an oral history without quoting it, even though – or perhaps because – it proved the scale of Kennedy's involvement in Profiles.

Whether Jean Mannix spoke the truth or not is irrelevant, but Parmet should have mentioned it. The same applies to an Oral History interview with Sorensen's secretary, Gloria Sitrin, in which she declared, "There is no doubt that Sorensen contributed quite a bit from the research point of view, but I took dictation from senator Kennedy on the book, giving me his original words while I was in Florida. He sometimes fended talking quicker than I could take it. He didn't object when I asked him to slow down. So, many of the first drafts were his original wording." (4)

Parmet interviewed Sorensen. Why did he not interview his secretary?

Why does he not refer to Sorensen's book "Kennedy" in which he wrote that, except for the introductory and concluding chapters, "the bulk of the manuscript was finished by the time he returned to the Senate on June 1, 1955?" (5)

Parmet said that by the time Kennedy left Florida (at the end of May), the project was well advanced but far from complete. (6) I consulted the same memorandum as Parmet. According to Parmet, four chapters – on Adams, Webster, Benton, and Ross – were finished. Norris needed to be reworked based on a new draft by Sorensen and a Davids' memorandum. A draft on Taft was ready for final approval. Chapter X, which dealt with several miscellaneous minor figures, needed to be rewritten after a comparison with the original draft. (7) But what about the chapter on Sam Houston, which was probably finished, and the final draft on Lamar just to be retyped? – no comment on these last two by Parmet. (8)

In any case, Parmet was incorrect when he wrote that by the time Kennedy left Florida, the Profiles project was well advanced but far from complete. It also differs from Sorensen's account. Parmet further claims, "Neither the chronology of Jack's life in 1954 and 1955 nor the materials accumulated in the preparation of the book even came close to supporting the contention that Jack could have been or was its major author."

Those were the years when, in addition to being in the Senate, Kennedy underwent two major spinal operations and was hospitalized for three additional brief periods. He was also frequently traveling across the country, trying to improve his credentials and visibility as a Democratic leader, and he undertook an extensive European tour from August until. October of 1955. (9)

So, as Michael O'Brien says, it is incorrect to assume that the chronology of Kennedy's life in 1954-1955 made it unlikely that he could substantially contribute to writing the book. In fact, while convalescing from two operations, he had little else to do but work on the book.

Several witnesses saw him writing the book in Washington or Palm Beach, and he stayed in contact with Ted Sorensen during his European tour.

Referring to an Oral History Interview with Charles Bartlett, Parmet writes, "The list of "courageous" profiles grew. That spring, the growing dilemma over McCarthy accompanied by the emergence of the censure question heightened Kennedy's interest in the project." (10)

Bartlett did indeed talk about the McCarthy censure in that interview – but in a completely different context. He said, "I always suspected that he (Kennedy) would have voted to censure Joe McCarthy, but he certainly was pleased, I think, that he didn't have to take that burden. I always thought that the criticism that was leveled against him for being happy that he didn't have to take a vote which would have cost him a lot of skin in Massachusetts was rather ludicrous." (11) Bartlett makes no link between the McCarthy censure and Kennedy's problems with it and the Profiles project, not that it heightened Kennedy's interest in the project.

Herbert Parmet, in his Oral History interview at the Kennedy Library on the Pearson-Clifford negotiations on who wrote Profiles, says this, "And by the way, if you look at Clark Clifford's oral history, it's interesting information that Pearson was right, you don't even have to read between the lines very carefully." (12)

I never read that Clark Clifford said that Pearson was right. But what Clifford said in his oral history interview to his recollection was, "He didn't even talk with Pearson but that Phil Graham of the Washington Post who was close to Pearson at the time talked with him and may have prompted Pearson to come along with that retraction of his, for Pearson valued his place in the Washington Post more than he did any other paper. So Phil Graham became an ally of ours, and I think it was instrumental in getting the final retraction from Pearson." (13)

Parmet quotes James Mac Gregor Burns, "That he expressed this feeling by saying, "I think Sorensen or whoever was helping him, gave him more help on the book than you or I could hope to get if we were doing one." (14)

But what Parmet didn't mention is that in the same Oral History interview, Burns said, "And I think still there is some question as to how completely Kennedy deserves credit for that book. I am just speculating here. Let me say that I satisfied myself in writing my book, that Kennedy had done a significant or a substantial amount on that book. The evidence I found in manuscript form – the actual manuscript I looked at – was in Kennedy's handwriting: not a whole manuscript but a rather extensive one. Then from talking with associates and from seeing a very interesting exchange between Kennedy and a Democratic senator, I believe it was Richard L. Neuberger of Oregon, that Kennedy, upset by rumors that he had not written the book, not only invited but more or less urged Neuberger to stop in at his office sometime and look at the manuscript so that there would be someone who himself was a literary man who could testify that Kennedy had written the book. So I am sure that Kennedy did most of the book, followed by the help of Sorensen and the help Burns was hoping for if he wrote a book himself." (15)

"There is no evidence of a Kennedy draft for the overwhelming bulk of the book, and there is evidence for concluding that much of what he did draft was simply not included in the final version," said Parmet, adding, "If the handwritten evidence is scant, dictation could have justified to authorship. The existing tapes, however, duplicate the pattern of the nearly illegible scrawls on those canary sheets. For all the practical reasons, however – limitation of time, health, and appropriate talent – the senator served principally as an overseer or more charitably as a sponsor and editor, one whose final approval was as important for its publication as for its birth." (16)

Parmet's only concession was to accept, "The existing reels (recordings) do not represent the full extent of (Kennedy's) dictation."

The ghostwriting allegations will always linger, but in two letters from JFK to Profiles in Courage publisher Evan Thomas in 1955, I found some interesting remarks by Kennedy, never quoted by Parmet:

In the first, on June 23, Kennedy wrote, "I am hoping that you or someone on your staff will work over the manuscript to improve style and interest and that you will feel free to suggest the deletion of some of the historical and biographical material which you may feel should be excluded to increase readability."

In the second, on August 1, 1955, Kennedy urged Thomas and his staff to feel free "to do any minor editing of grammar, sentence structure, and style... checking with Sorensen only if some substantive question is involved." He also told Thomas that he was sending a draft of Profiles to Professors Schlesinger, Holcombe, and Johnson and that he would "incorporate their suggestions in the final draft." (17)

In these letters, Kennedy is asking for polishing on style and interest, in no way claiming to be a professional author nor historian, but simply trying to increase readability.

Parmet, however, wrote that it was Sorensen who gave the book both the drama and flow that made for readability: why didn't he refer to Kennedy's letters to Evan Thomas?

This is why I accuse Parmet of prejudice.

Kennedy was the major author of Profiles in Courage. He worked at it while recovering from his spinal operations, putting his heart and soul into something on a subject he valued above all other human virtues – courage.

In theory, the historical approach has to be neutral based on real facts. Still, in practice, it's distorted by personal feelings, beliefs, and political convictions, which makes less plausible "grace under pressure" as Ernest Hemingway defined it. (18)

2.7. Did Arthur Krock Lobby for the Pulitzer Prize?

One reason that Profiles in Courage was a commercial success could be the fact that Joe Kennedy Sr. sent his employees to buy huge quantities at major bookstores to generate enough sales to hit the bestseller lists – just as he had with Jack's previous book. Joe Kane, Joe Kennedy Sr.'s cousin, and political advisor, made a claim to journalist and author Ronald Kessler. Kessler was also the source of the tale of how Joe Kennedy Sr. then persuaded Arthur Krock to lobby the Pulitzer prize Board on behalf of Profiles in Courage. Krock confirmed, "Joe came to me for that." The reason was clear: Krock was a former member of the Pulitzer advisory board and was still able to "log roll" its members, writing letters to most of them. (1)

Geoffrey Perret is, to my knowledge, the only author to take up this crazy story. However, Robert Dallek, in his biography on Kennedy, said that there is some evidence that Arthur Krock may have personally lobbied the Board for Jack. (2) (3) (4) (5)

In "Grace and Power" Sally Bedell Smith wrote that Krock had used his considerable influence to "log roll" the Pulitzer Prize Board into giving Kennedy the award, displacing their first and second choices, acclaimed biographies of Horton Stone and Franklin D. Roosevelt. "I worked as hard as I could to get him that prize," Krock recalled. "Those are the facts. I don't take any pride in them." (6)

On Christmas Eve 1955, Jack ignored seasonal holiday niceties to call his book editor Evan Thomas Sr. to ask that the publication date be advanced from January to December. When Thomas asked why, Kennedy replied, "Well, I've just been talking to Arthur Krock, and I understand it would win the Pulitzer Prize this year." Thomas refused Jack's request – but the book, published in 1956, won the prize anyway, in 1957.

Laurence Leamer in "The Kennedy Women" wrote that one of Joe Kennedy's slogans was, "Things don't happen; they are made to happen." Joe's wife Rose recalled, "For instance, when Jack got the Pulitzer Prize for his book or when he or Bob was chosen as an outstanding man of the year: all of this was a result of their ability plus careful spadework on their father's part as to who was on the committee and how to reach such-and-such a person through such-and-such a friend." (7) Leamer doesn't talk about Arthur Krock's involvement.

Chris Matthews in "Jack Kennedy Elusive Hero" takes over the Leamer version of the Profiles story and the Rose Kennedy quote that "careful spadework" was the key. (8)

By far, the best account of Arthur Krock and Joe Kennedy's involvement in obtaining the Pulitzer Prize can be read in Herbert S. Parmet's "Jack: The Struggles of John F. Kennedy." He writes, "As John Hohenberg has written in his book "The Pulitzer Prizes: A History of the Awards in Books, Drama, Music, and Journalism Based on the Private Files Over Six Decades," Krock did lobby for Kennedy. But Hohenberg later emphasized that Krock's advocacy was not at all instrumental. Krock was such a "drum-beater" that if anything, his efforts could have been counterproductive. Nor was there evidence of visible activities by Ambassador Kennedy. Joseph Pulitzer Jr. also confirmed Joe Kennedy's absence from the scene, saying that there was not a chance in a million that the ambassador could have had any kind of influence, as the Pulitzer board never had "the slightest respect" for outside influence. Neither man, while stressing the board's freedom to overrule the jury, recalled that Joe Kennedy tried to promote his son's cause through personal telephone calls. (9)

Ralph G. Martin, in "Seeds of Destruction" writes, "When family friend Arthur Krock suggested that the book might win a Pulitzer Prize, Kennedy was spurred to the finish. Krock had been on the Pulitzer board and knew most of the board members." Krock himself said, "There was such log-rolling that I thought it had better be taken in hand by somebody, and it might as well be me. So we log-rolled under my direction." What Krock did was simply to talk persuasively with all his friends on the board, some of whom, he later implied, owed him some favors. (10)

Once again, we have a black and white situation with two strong characters – Joe Kennedy and Arthur Krock in the Profiles in Courage Pulitzer Prize saga. What role did they play? Were they involved in trying to influence the board? Had Krock influence or not? Did he regret his intervention? Hohenberg said Krock's involvement was counterproductive, while Joseph Pulitzer Jr. confirmed there was no involvement by Joe Kennedy. What about a fairytale-like story as written in John Hohenberg's diaries, "The board had seemed to me to be ready to accept the book about Justice Stone when there was an unexpected intervention. One of the board members, J.D. Ferguson, the editor of the Milwaukee Journal, raised his hand somewhat hesitantly, and Chairman Pulitzer recognized him. Ferguson wasn't usually very active in Pulitzer affairs. Still, now he wanted to tell his fellow members how he had come across Kennedy's Profiles in Courage, how he had admired the work, and what he had done to test its effect. "I read it aloud to my 12-year-old grandson, and the boy was fascinated. I think we should give the prize to "Profiles in Courage." Then suddenly, the atmosphere changed." (11)

So Dan Ferguson and his 12-year-old grandson carried the day for Kennedy.

I think Krock was involved, having been asked by his friend Joe to intervene – but I don't think Joe Kennedy was directly involved: Joe let other people do his "dirty work" in true businessman fashion. But Arthur Krock's intervention wasn't necessary – because a 12-year-old boy was the reason Jack got the Pulitzer Prize.

Nevertheless, historians and scholars claim that Krock lobbied for the Pulitzer, even though the subject was not raised either in his Oral History in 1964 or Krock's memoirs.

2.8. Conclusion

In Profiles in Courage, published on January 1, 1956, John Fitzgerald Kennedy wrote, "Must men consciously risk their careers only for principles which hindsight declares to be correct for posterity to honor them for their valor? I think not."

He went on, "Our political life is becoming so expensive, so mechanized and so dominated by professional politicians and public relations men that the idealist who dreams of independent statesmanship is rudely awakaned by the necessities of election and accomplishment." (1)

This is John Kennedy's pragmatic approach towards politics – a man who evaluates and resolves events in a business-like way, he is an "idealist without illusions" or a "realist without illusions" – you can choose.

Some authors say that Jack Kennedy had an instinct for avoiding controversial situations. I don't think so, he faced many controversial issues during the Cuban Missile Crisis – choices between the hawks and the doves – and handled them with great skill and success.

Kennedy's interest in political courage dated back at least 15 years before "Profiles" to the time he was writing "Why England Slept" in which he returned again and again to the failure of most English politicians to defy public opinion and re-arm Britain during the Second World War while there was yet time. He has been accused of being obsessed with courage. Still, there was enough suffering in his life to justify him brooding deeply about it, his ill-health as a boy, his wartime plunge into extreme peril, his proximity to death in the months before writing his book, and the long, slow, painful recovery from illness. We need not be surprised that he admired the virtue of courage above all else.

Yes indeed, he was obsessed with courage, political and physical, enjoying life as if every day was his last, the courage, he so admired, was something John Kennedy himself possessed. (2) (3)

Geoffrey Perret wrote that Profiles could be read, too, as a "mea culpa": Jack Kennedy had failed to show courage over Joe McCarthy, and he knew it. (4)

Herbert Parmet and Michael O'Brien conceded that readers could see the book as a "personal catharsis" that Kennedy was driven to expiate his guilt over the McCarthy censure controversy. But O'Brien also pointed out that there was no evidence to support the conjecture – the book's theme of courage pre-dated the McCarthy proceedings. (5) (6) (7)

Parmet doesn't come to that very evident conclusion.

Robert Dallek, on the other hand, was convinced that, when Kennedy was thinking about writing a book on courage, it was partly a retrospective coming to terms with his moral lapse on McCarthy. (8)

Ted Sorensen in "Kennedy" (1965) and in "The Counselor" (2008), clarifies the McCarthy censure controversy, writing, "Others have charged that the book was written to atone for his avoidance of the 1954 McCarthy censure motion while he was in the hospital." But there was no censure vote pending in the Senate when the book's theme was conceived the previous year. (9) (10) (11)

Kennedy and Sorensen's relationship was an enigma, but an extraordinary one-two bright, ambitious guys together, JFK very charismatic and Sorensen devoted to his boss. They would never go on vacation together, but they had mutual respect for each other's skills, and they worked together on one common goal – electing Jack as president.

Robert Schlesinger wrote, "The intellectual communion did not perfectly translate personally."

Arthur Schlesinger Jr. wrote in 1965, "Of Sorensen and Kennedy themselves, two men could hardly be more intimate and at the same time, more separate. They shared so much – the same quick tempo, detached intelligence, deflationary, wit, realistic judgment, candor in speech, coolness in crisis – that, when it came to policy and speeches, they operated nearly as one. But there were other ranges of Kennedy's life, and of these, Sorensen partook very little." (12) (13)

As Charles Bartlett said in an oral history interview in January 1965, "Jack Kennedy was extremely independent and a fairly elusive fellow. I don't think that he ever really spent that much time with any individual over a long period. His relations were compartmentalized." (14)

There is a great contradiction between Herbert Parmet and Micheal O'Brien on the Kennedy-Sorensen correspondence.

O'Brien writes, "In Sorensen's correspondence at the time and in subsequent interviews, he repeatedly referred to letters and phone calls from the Senator concerning the book." Yet, none of these sources appear in Parmet's analysis. (15)

Parmet writes, "Sorensen also wrote long, detailed letters to the Senator in Europe keeping him informed of the book's evolution toward publication and the progress of the subsidiary sales." Parmet, in his notes, refers to two letters that Ted Sorensen did send to JFK. (16) (17)

With O'Brien, Dallek, and others, I agree that Profiles in Courage was a team effort – in economic terms, a joint venture – but the concept of the book was Kennedy's; the responsibility for the book was Kennedy's – even Parmet agrees on that.

And the decisions as to which individuals and which stories should go in the book were all made by Kennedy. Jack Kennedy was known for his humor and for kidding with his friends. Still, as far as his authorship of Profiles was concerned, his attitude

71

was different: questioning his credentials as the writer touched something in him that left no room for humor.

In the basement of the Blackstone Hotel in Chicago during the 1956 convention, Kennedy became involved in a conversation with Joe Alsop and Blair Clark about the rumors of the book have been ghostwritten. Clark, a Kennedy classmate from Harvard days, who was covering the convention for the Columbia Broadcasting System (CBS), cracked a little joke, "Jack," he said, "I'm going to deny forever that I wrote, "Why England Slept..."

It was a joke about Kennedy's Harvard thesis "Appeasement in Munich," which was published as a book in 1940 under the title "Why England Slept?" (18)

That version of the story is as told by Blair Clark to Herbert Parmet on March 18, 1977. But in the version recounted by C. David Heymann, Clark was not making a joke when he said to Kennedy, "Well, of course, Jack, you remember when you and I met in Widener Library (at Harvard) and you asked me to rewrite sections of "Why England Slept?." Clark explained what happened next, "He (Kennedy) became furious at this comment – but in truth, he did ask me to rewrite sections of his first book." (19) That's not at all what Clark said to Parmet.

Arthur Krock, who did some editing and polishing of the thesis in his library in Georgetown, first proposed publication of an expanded, retitled thesis in book form and was rewarded with a generous acknowledgment from Kennedy in the copy he received of "Why England Slept?," "To Mr. Krock, who Baptized, Christened and was Best Man for this book, with sincere thanks."

Garry Wills wrote that Kennedy aided his career in many ways by lying to the nation (it sounds like Watergate to Wills) and conscripted various honorary, in perpetuating his image as a prize-winning author and historian (although Kennedy himself said he was not).

For instance, when JFK wanted Republican Robert McNamara to come to Washington as his secretary of Defense. McNamara – who had read and been impressed by Profiles in Courage – asked him directly if he had written it. Kennedy solemnly assured him that he had. (20)

In an Oral History interview, McNamara said, "I was tremendously impressed by it. I had heard the numerous stories that it had been ghost-written, and I was just interested in how he would answer the question. It was a rather presumptuous thing to ask. Had it been six months later, I would never have asked him because, in that intervening period, I saw him write prose of equal quality on many occasions in my presence." (21)

Sally Bedell Smith records that, when McNamara was asked how Kennedy had replied to his authorship question, he (McNamara) said, "I am not sure precisely how he answered." Smith refers to an undated interview with McNamara. (22)

Wills had not read McNamara's interview, which, as a distinguished author, he should have.

A distinguished figure who took Kennedy to task over Profiles in Courage was

Eleanor Roosevelt, who remarked, "I feel that I would hesitate to place the difficult decisions that the next president will have to make with someone who understands what courage is and admires it, but who has not quite the independence to have it." But the last word on the book should go to the author himself, in response to Arthur Schlesinger Jr.'s suggestion that Kennedy had paid a heavy price for calling his work "Profiles in Courage." Kennedy, his sense of humor restored, replied drily, "Yes, but I didn't have a chapter in it on myself..." (23) (24)

Senator Kennedy autographs his Pulitzer-Prize winning book "Profiles in Courage" (1956).
(Copyright: JFK Library)

Theodore C. "Ted" Sorensen, who joined Kennedy's Staff in 1953, assisted him in researching Profiles in Courage.
(Copyright: JFK Library)

Chapter 3: Who Elected JFK: A Rendezvous With History

"I just received the following wire from my generous Daddy: 'Dear Jack, don't buy a single vote more than is necessary. I'll be damned if I'm going to pay for a landslide.

- **John F. Kennedy**

With a little bit of luck and the help of a few close friends, you're going to carry Illinois.'"

- **Major Daley Richard**

"John Kennedy could sell eggs to chickens."

- **McDonough, West Virginia Campaign Director**

3.1. His Father Bought Him the Election

The Caroline

The Caroline was the first private aircraft used exclusively for campaigning by an American presidential candidate. The Convair CV-240 N 240 K was built in 1948 for American Airlines, bought in 1959 by Welsch Aviation, and sold to Joseph Kennedy. He formed a separate company– the Kenaire Corporation – to manage the plane.

The plane's interior was refurbished to meet the requirements and privacy needs of the presidential candidate and his family. (1)

According to Victor Lasky, it was furnished like an executive suite, with a bedroom in the rear. Kennedy was able not only to work in comfort at a large desk, but he could also even watch his rivals perform on television. (2) It gave Kennedy an enormous advantage against Senator Hubert Humphrey in Wisconsin and the West Virginia primaries. Humphrey had to travel by bus.

After Kennedy's assassination, the aircraft was used by the Kennedy family until it was donated to the Smithsonian Institute in 1967. According to David Pietrusza, Joe Kennedy purchased a $385,000 twin-engine Convair turboprop from his former mistress Janet Des Rosiers. (3)

According to JFK's secretary Evelyn Lincoln, a July 17 1959 news release declared, "Kenaire Corporation, a company jointly owned by the Kennedy brothers and sisters, announced today that it had purchased a Convair airplane from Frederic B. Ayer & Associates of New York." (4)

Ronald Kessler wrote that on September 22, 1959, Stephen Smith, whom Joe had placed in charge of investments at his New York office, announced the "family was about to purchase a Convair for $385,000." (5)

What Did the Caroline Cost?

Herbert E. Alexander, in his 1962 essay "Financing the 1960 Election," was the first to mention a figure of $385,000 and $1.75 a-mile running cost, but he doesn't offer any sources. (6)

Herbert S. Parmet, in 1980, refers to Herbert Alexander for the $385,000, (7) while David Pietrusza relies on Michael O'Brien as his source – and O'Brien cites Parmet. John H. Davis, W.J. Rorabaugh, and Ronald Kessler have no sources for the $385,000 figure: was it $300,000, $339,500, $360,000, $385,000 or $500,000, as other authors have claimed? (8) (9) (10) (11)

None has ever substantiated any of these figures with credible sources: my conclusion is that no author has real proof of what the Caroline cost.

In 1960, Ralph G. Martin and Ed Plaut claimed that the luxury Convair – estimated value $500,000 – was a gift from the Kennedy sisters to their campaigning brother. The plane had two pilots and a lovely stewardess, who doubled as secretary and had previously worked for Jack Kennedy's father. (12)

Martin and Plaut didn't mention that the stewardess, Janet des Rosiers, was also a secret mistress of Joe Kennedy.

In 1963, Victor Lasky quoted James Reston saying, "His father advanced him $270,000 to buy a plane. Six members of his family put up $15,000 each to complete the deal, and they had a contract to return it to the seller for $260,000. It was staffed with two pilots and a secretary- stewardess, Janet des Rosiers." So the plane cost: $270,000 + 6 x $15,000 = $90,000, a total price of $360,000. (13)

In 1964, Richard J. Whalen claimed that a family corporation owned the Convair and then leased it to Jack Kennedy at $1.75 a mile (or $15,000 to $19,000 a month). Because the family kept its $300,000 equity in the plane, it was not considered a campaign contribution. (14)

According to Ted Schwarz in his 2003 book on Joseph Kennedy, Joe arranged for one of his corporations to buy a $300,000 custom-fitted Convair aircraft, which he then leased to his son's campaign for $1.75 a mile. (15)

In 2009, Vincent BZDEK wrote that for Christmas 1959, Jack's brothers and sisters bought him a secret weapon – a two-engine airplane for $339,500, which revolutionized presidential campaigns. (16)

According to Martin and Plaut, the Caroline was staffed by two expert pilots, although no names were mentioned. Parmet said that there was only one pilot retained by the corporation. Evelyn Lincoln wrote that the family hired a pilot – Howard Baird. There were two pilots: Captain Howard Baird and Captain Robert Griscom.

The only figure authors agree upon is the $1.75 a mile leasing cost from the Ken-Air Corporation to Jack Kennedy's presidential campaign – a classic example that history is not necessarily accurate.

The Caroline: Competing Statistics

"They traveled in a luxury Convair (estimated value of $500,000), a gift from the Kennedy sisters to their campaigning brother. The plane had two pilots and a lovely stewardess who doubled as a secretary, for a long time previously she had worked for Jack Kennedy's father."

Martin and Plaut didn't mention that Janet des Rosiers was also a secret mistress of Joseph P. Kennedy. (1)

"Members of the family formed a Ken-Air Corporation to buy a $385,000 airplane, which was leased to the Senator at the rate of $1.75 a mile." (2)

James Reston reported that, "His father advanced him $270,000 to buy a plane. Six members of his family put up $15,000 each to complete the deal, with a clause in the contract to return the plane to the seller for $260,000.

"The plane, a twin-motored Convair, was furnished like an executive suite, with a bedroom in the rear. Not only was Kennedy able to work in comfort at a large desk, but he could even watch his rivals perform on television."

"It cost $15,000 a month to operate, with two expert pilots and a secretary, stewardess, Janet des Rosiers, who had previously worked for the senior Kennedy." (3)

"The Convair was owned by a family corporation and leased to him at $1.75 a mile (or $15,000 to $19,000 a month). The family kept its $300,000 equity in the plane. (4)

According to Evelyn Lincoln, on July 17th 1959, a news release was put out, "Kenaire Corporation, a company jointly owned by the Kennedy brothers and sisters, announced today that it had purchased a Convair airplane from Frederic B. Ayer & Associates of New York." It was to be decorated in light green and beige and was named the Caroline. The family also hired a pilot, Howard Baird." (5)

Parmet, citing Herbert Alexander, repeated the $385,000 and the lease at $1.75 a mile.

He said that the Caroline had one pilot retained by the Ken-Air Corporation. The plane logged 110,000 miles in 1959 and 1960, which would bring the cost for leasing alone to $192,500, not including fuel, maintenance, and insurance. (6)

The Herbert E. Alexander $385,000 and $1.75 a mile. (7)

"Senator Kennedy, for example, had the use throughout the fall of 1959 and the fall of 1960 of a private twin-engined airplane provided by Ken-Air Corporation. This corporation was an effort by his brother and in-laws to provide a $385,000 airplane, the Caroline. It was used by Kennedy and later would be sold by Ken-Air back to the original seller. Kennedy leased it for $1.75 per mile." (8)

On September 22, 1959, Stephen Smith, whom Joe had placed in charge of investments at his New York office, announced that the "family" was about to purchase a Convair for $385,000. It would be the first personal plane ever used by a presidential candidate. Jack was said to have leased it from his father for the ridiculous sum of $1.75 a mile." (9)

According to Ted Schwarz, Joe arranged for one of his corporations to buy a $300,000 custom-fitted Convair aircraft, which he then leased to his son's campaign for $1.75 a mile. This was far below the real operating cost. Still, because the plane was part of a family business, the law did not consider it a campaign contribution. (10)

"In 1959, the Kennedy family formed Ken-Air Corporation, which bought a Convair 240 propeller plane, redesigned to carry eighteen passengers for $385,000. The plane was then leased to the candidate at the rate of $1.75 a mile and logged 110,000 miles in 1959 and 1960." (11)

"In September 1959, Joe Kennedy had purchased a $385,000 twin-engine Convair turboprop from his former mistress, Janet Des Rosiers. The plane would be leased to JFK's campaign at a bargain-basement $1.75 per mile." (12)

"For Christmas 1959, Jack's brothers and sisters bought him a secret weapon, a two-engine airplane for $339,500, and it revolutionized presidential campaigns." (13)

"In 1959, Joe Kennedy arranged for the family to buy the senator a $385,000 jet turboprop Convair." (14)

"The 1948 aircraft, which was purchased in 1959 by Joseph Kennedy – a Convair 240 from American Airlines – was retrofitted to meet the physical and privacy needs of the candidate and his family. After the president's assassination, the aircraft was used by the Kennedy family until it was donated to the Smithsonian institute in 1967. Captain Robert Griscom: During the campaign, the aircraft flew 225,000 miles, with a small crew, frequently carrying the candidate, family members, staff, and reporters. In 1959 it was purchased by Welsch Aviation and sold to Joe Kennedy." (15)

COST

1. $300,000 [Ted Schwarz (2003)]
2. $300,000 equity [Richard J. Whalen (1964)]
3. $339,500 [Vincent BSDEK (2009)]
4. $360,000 [Victor Lasky (1963)]
5. $385,000 [Herbert E. Alexander (1962), Herbert S. Parmet (1980), John H. Davis (1984), Ronald Kessler (1996), Michael O'Brien (2005), David Pietrusza (2008), W. J. Rorabaugh (2009), Dan B. Fleming (1992)]
6. $500,000 (Estimated Value) [Ralph G. Martin & Ed Plaut (1960)]
7. $15,000 to $19,000 a month [Richard J. Whalen]
8. $15,000 [Lasky]

Two Pilots

1. Martin & Plaut
2. Victor Lasky

Hired a pilot

Evelyn Lincoln – Howard Baird

OAC

Captain Baird, Captain Griscom

The two defining primaries in the 1960 election were Wisconsin and West Virginia. Jack originally hesitated to challenge the Wisconsin primary because of Humphrey's popularity. Still, Joe insisted that he could win and goaded him into fighting it by suggesting he would be "yellow" if he didn't. (17)

In the West Virginia primary, Kennedy had run against his father's advice. According to Ben Bradlee, the question of West Virginia came up while he was on holiday with the Kennedys at Ambassador Joseph P. Kennedy's Palm Beach, Florida house. Joe argued strenuously against a JFK visit, "It's a nothing state, and they'll kill him over the Catholic thing." A few minutes later, JFK, "the great listener" spoke out, "Well, we've heard from the ambassador, and we're all very grateful, dad, but I've got the run in West Virginia." (18)

Who was in charge of the Campaign, Jack or his father?

On Election Day, the West Virginia voter was presented with probably the most complex ballot in America: the payoffs involved a system of "slating" – a form of legalized bribery. To sort through dense ballots with long lists of names, voters relied on "slates" given to them by county political bosses, usually the county sheriff. Voters would then vote for those candidates on the slate. It all seemed very simple. The candidate who paid the most to the county Democratic boss (under the guise of subsidizing "printing" costs) would have his list of backers identified as the "approved slate." When one county sheriff told a Humphrey campaign organizer what each name on a slate would cost in his county, and the man passed the word to Humphrey, the response was, "We would pay it, but we don't have the money."

Where Humphrey's total campaign expenditures totaled $25,000, the Kennedys spent $34,000 on TV programming alone. (19)

Larry O'Brien negotiated the payments for campaign expenses. Neither Jack nor Bobby knew what agreements he made; that was his responsibility. But he had to have cash at hand, and he usually left it with his secretary, Phyllis Maddock, for safety. On one occasion, in the lobby of Charleston's Kanawha Hotel, O'Brien completed agreements with the leaders of slates in two extremely important counties, representing the largest single expenditure of the campaign. Then O'Brien called Phyllis on the house phone and whispered, "Bring me five." Phyllis took some cash from her suitcase under her bed and slipped O'Brien $500 – not the $5,000 he'd agreed to. "Not five hundred, Phyllis," he told her, "Five thousand." O'Brien made no apologies about the sums that were spent in West Virginia, "Our total outlay state-wide was about $100,000 including radio and television – less than a candidate for congress in any one congressional district would expect to spend." (20)

There were numerous charges that Kennedy "bought" votes in the West Virginia primary. Still, politics in West Virginia can be violent and complicated and involves money, hot money, under-the-table money. The truth was that everyone who ran for office in West Virginia bought votes – both presidential candidates dealt out the money, but Kennedy was in a better financial position than Humphrey to do so. (21) (22)

Humphrey's frustration was that he was like a "corner grocer running against a chain store" and that he could not afford to run around the state with a little black bag and a checkbook.

He also was honest enough to admit that he was beaten not only by money and organization but, more particularly, by an extraordinary man – Jack Kennedy was at his best in West Virginia, and his best was without equal. He understood the importance of the spectacular, of the unusual, and he knew that the conventional political wisdom – that his background was wrong, his region was wrong – was itself wrong.

Here was Kennedy, the rich son of a richer man, Harvard-educated with a Boston accent, Catholic and Irish, campaigning in one of the most poverty-stricken states, through the hills and valleys and hollows, from little town to smaller village, among coal miners and poor illiterates of Appalachia. It should have been a disaster for him, yet he brought at least a ray of sunshine and glory and glamour into that gloomy, gray atmosphere.

He brought hope to people who had none. The chemistry worked in an almost palpable way, and Humphrey thought that Jack himself learned something vital – possibly his first real understanding and empathy for the "other America" so distant from his own life. (23)

In the mid-1960s French philosopher, playwright, novelist, political activist, biographer, and literary critic Jean-Paul Sartre analyzed the Kennedy-Humphrey Primary, observing that Kennedy's supreme political cleverness was to – temporarily, but totally and sincerely – renounce politics and to transform himself internally for others and himself into a man of exigency, "The West Virginian did not choose the political Kennedy, about whom we knew nothing, but the one whom he had seen with his own eyes," remembered campaign aide Pierre Salinger.

"In short, West Virginians required that the future president put ethical action in the place of politics. (24) It was the first time that he came into direct contact with poverty."

In 1960, Lasky wrote that Arthur F. Hermann of Ganneth News Service reported on July 20, 1960, from Los Angeles that supporters of other candidates were bitter that Kennedy's well-oiled political machine did not even need to launch one fund-raising appeal to raise primary campaign money. Reports had it that multi-millionaire Joseph P. Kennedy spent $7 million on this phase of the campaign alone. (25)

Martin and Plaut claimed in their 1960 book that a rumor spread on the political grapevine that Kennedys were prepared to spend $5,000,000 in the Ohio primary campaign – and many people felt that even if the figure were exaggerated, the real amount would be still a lot more than has ever been spent in an Ohio primary before. Michael W. DiSall, Governor of Ohio, was philosophical, "This business about buying the presidency doesn't bother me. Jack is a good product. All the money in the world couldn't make him president otherwise." (26)

In 1964, Richard J. Whalen says that it was the informed guess of close friends that beginning in 1958, Joe committed at least $1.5 million to his son's pre-convention campaign, a figure far below the estimates of outsiders. (27)

According to Seymour Hersh, the Kennedys spent as never before in American political history. In West Virginia, they spent at least $2 million (nearly $19,456,609.00 at 2022 prices), and possibly twice that amount, much of it in direct payoffs to local officials.

In interviews for Hersh's book, many West Virginia county and slate officials revealed that the Kennedy family spent upward of $2 million in bribes and other pay-offs before the May 10, 1960 primary, with some sheriffs in key counties collecting more than $50,000 a piece in cash in return for placing Kennedy's name at the top of their election slate.

Hersh found two former slate officials who acknowledged during 1995 interviews for his book that they also knew of large-scale Kennedy spending. Benn Brown of Elkins was the personal attorney to W.W. "Wally" Barren, who was elected Democratic Governor of West Virginia in 1960. He estimated that the Kennedy outlay was between $3 to $5 million, with some sheriffs being paid as much as $50,000. Asked how he knew, Brown told Hersh curtly, "I know. If you don't get those guys – the sheriffs – they will fight you." (28)

In 1962, Harry W. Ernst told a softer money version story.

How much did Kennedy spend in West Virginia? After the primary, he officially reported spending of $91,322.62, while Humphrey filed only a pre-election report showing only $13,855.17. At that same time, Kennedy reported spending only $11,211.94, a propaganda coup since Humphrey was running as the poor boy candidate. But Kennedy's West Virginia tab, excluding most staff salaries and personal expenses such as the use of a private plane, probably totaled at least $250,000 – his outlay for advertising alone came to $100,000.

Money gave Kennedy freedom and flexibility, which Humphrey lacked, and Kennedy's hard-won role as the underdog helped counteract Humphrey's charges that he was trying to buy the election. During the primary, Humphrey estimated that Kennedy was spending as much as $500,000 and protested, "I can't afford to run through this state with a little black bag and a check-book. I'm being ganged up on by wealth. "I don't have a daddy to pay the bills."

Kennedy made no apology for his wealth and admitted frankly that his campaign was costing a lot of money. After the votes were counted and the Kennedy triumph had startled the nation, some reporters who had missed the mark returned to West Virginia. Ugly rumors began that the election had been bought. Two Charleston Gazette reporters, Don Marsh, and John G. Morgan, traveled the state trying to find out why Kennedy won. They concluded that Kennedy had not bought the election – and even most Republican leaders agreed that was true. And, after months of investigations in machine-ridden Logan County, no evidence of improper spending could be found by the FBI, West Virginia's Attorney General, or the private investigators dispatched by Vice President Nixon. (29)

In the "bought election," there are a few wonderful money stories...

1. How Cardinal Richard Cushing and Joe Kennedy Elected JFK:

Hubert Humphrey met with Cardinal Cushing during the 1966 Congressional Campaign at his home in Boston. He had come to know and like him, and the feeling, Humphrey thought, was mutual.

By then, Cushing was gaunt from illness and heavy-featured – and very irritated by all the books written by Kennedy's friends and aides.

He had just finished reading Ted Sorensen's book and said, "I keep reading these books by the young men around Jack Kennedy and how they claim credit for electing him. I'll tell you who elected Jack Kennedy. It was his father, Joe, and me, right here in this room."

He continued in his Boston-Irish accent, "You-bert, I believe you should know that the decisions on West Virginia were made here, in this library. Joe Kennedy and I sat and discussed the strategy of that campaign in this room. We decided which of the Protestant ministers would receive a contribution to their church. We decided which church and preacher would get two hundred dollars or one hundred dollars or five hundred dollars." Cushing ended with a whimsical, if not beatific, smile, asking rhetorically, "What better way is there to spend campaign money than to help a preacher and his flock? It's good for the Lord. It's good for the church. It's good for the preacher, and it's good for the candidate." (30)

However, in an interview with Dave Powers for Dan B. Fleming's Jr. 1992 book "Kennedy vs. Humphrey West Virginia, 1960," Powers cast doubt on the Cushing story, claiming that near the end, the Cardinal was slipping mentally and was "losing control." Powers asserted that Cushing often became "really confused" and wanted to seem important when he recalled past events. (31)

Compare that story with that ridiculous story by Hersh in "The Dark Side of Camelot" claiming that the republicans would have used Jack Kennedy's first marriage in the 1964 campaign. Cushing's response to that was, "Well, they won't find anything or any mention of it. The pages are torn out of the register: yeah, Kennedy was married before, but it got taken care of." (32) This proves that Powers' claim on the matter is right. Humphrey met a senile, sick older man.

2. The Cushing – Joe Kennedy "Novel Story"

In providing the cash for Jack's campaign, Joe used the Catholic Church, and in particular, Cardinal Cushing.

In an interview on November 29, 1993, Peter Maas told Ronald Kessler how it worked. If Boston area churches had collected $950,000 on a particular Sunday from collections, for example, Joe would write a check for $1 million to the diocese, deduct it as a charitable contribution, and receive the $950,000 in cash. Thus, in this example, the church got a contribution of $50,000. Joe could deduct the entire amount on his income tax, and he could use the money to pay off politicians without fear that it would be traced.

Maas also cited this money-raising method in his Novel "Father and Son" and this crazy tale about collecting $950,000 in the Boston churches – the equivalent of $8,228,701.01 in 2020 – indeed belongs in a novel or gossip magazine: no historian or scholar should use it as a historical fact. (33) (34)

In 2003 Ted Schwarz wrote, "Was West Virginia bought by Joe Kennedy? Yes. Who was corrupted? No one but the man involved knows for certain. Joe's methods, one of them, was discussed by several writers, including Peter Maas and Ronald Kessler. The arrangement involved the collection of all donated money in all the catholic churches in the archdiocese on a particular Sunday. The sum would be totaled. Then Joe would write a check to the archdiocese for the amount plus many thousands of dollars more. He might give $250,000 when the archdiocese collected $225,000, as an example. Whatever the case, the check would go to the archdiocese and the cash to Joe Kennedy. (35)

In 2009 W. J. Rorabaugh takes over the Kessler story, on the $950,000, but no mention of Peter Maas' "original novel story." (36)

3. Eddie Ford's Suitcase Full of Cash

Eddie Ford, a successful real-estate man with a lot of cash, was a bachelor who lived at the old Statler Hotel, where he'd sit at his regular table in the coffee shop from noon, when he began his day, until eight or nine at night. He loved Jack Kennedy, and a couple of weeks before the West Virginia primary, he filled a suitcase with cash and drove through the state in a big Cadillac with Illinois plates. He'd pick out a powerful sheriff and say, "I'm a businessman from Chicago, and I'm on my way to Miami. I think this young Kennedy would be great for the country, and I'd like to give you $3,000 to see if you can help him. I'll be coming back this way, and I'll be happy to give you a bonus if you're able to carry the town."

"These things happened," said Tip O'Neill, "although Jack didn't always know about them." (37)

Dan B. Fleming Jr., in a telephone interview with Tip O'Neill on the Eddie Ford story, said, "What is not mentioned in the O'Neill book is that Joe Kennedy supplied the money that Ford paid out in West Virginia." O'Neill had personally heard this version from his close personal friend Eddie Ford but didn't know who Ford paid in West Virginia. (38)

So, Tip O'Neill forgot to mention Joe Kennedy as the money man in his political memoirs.

Lawrence Leamer wrote that Eddie Ford was one of Joe Kennedy's rich friends. (39) Ronald Kessler and Richard D. Mahoney tell the same Eddie Ford story as told by O'Neill but they inflated the $3,000 to "Here's $3,000 or here's $5,000. (40) (41)

4. Raymond Chafin Wanted $3,500, Asked for "35," and Got $35,000.

The Raymond Chafin $35,000 story is even more breathtaking than the other three – full of contradictions, guesses, exaggerations, and blunt lies.

By 1960, Chafin, a local political leader, was Democratic chairman in the Logan County primary. He had a well-paying job with the Massey Coal Company. In an interview with Dan B. Fleming Jr., Chafin revealed that he agreed to slate Humphrey if Marshall West, Humphrey's state co-chairman, would give them $2,000, which West did. (42) The problem was that according to Dr. Allen H. Loughry II, "Chafin had originally supported Minnesota Senator and presidential candidate Hubert Humphrey after receiving $2,500 from him to buy votes on his behalf." (43)

Another meeting was set up with Chafin and the heads of the largest coal producer in the area, the Island Creek Coal Company. In attendance was James McCahey Jr., a major coal buyer from Chicago, who wanted to see how he could help Senator Kennedy. After that meeting, McCahey returned with Chafin to the Watts-Humphrey headquarters in the Aracoma Hotel, where McCahey said he could arrange for Kennedy's people to repay the $2,000 Chafin's faction had received from Humphrey, of which about $480 or so had been spent. Believing he was going against his employer, Chafin was in a ticklish position since he had a well-paying job with Massey Coal Company. Chafin decided to switch sides from Humphrey to Kennedy. (44)

Allen H. Loughry II claims that after being handed $35,000 stuffed in sealed briefcases by Kennedy's operatives just days before the primary, Chafin switched his support to Kennedy. (45)

Chafin, in his autobiography, said that McCahey didn't waste any time working on him to back Kennedy, so he told him about the $2,000 Hubert Humphrey had given them. Chafin said, "I can't accept his money and not be for him." McCahey replied,

"Well, then, take two thousand from us and send it back." Chafin's book states it was the first money Chafin accepted from the Kennedy campaign, "We got it from them and sent it right back to Humphrey's people." (46)

This proves that Chafin was working for Jack Kennedy before the $35,000 Pick Up "Literature."

Neither Bob Barry, Humphrey Chairman, nor Humphrey aide Rein Vanderzee recalls the money being returned. (47)

Keith Davis has a different account on returning the $2,000 or $2,500: McCahey met with Chafin secretly at 4 a.m., when no-one would see them together: for Chafin to be talking with a known Kennedy man in broad daylight might be dangerous, especially if certain Logan politicians found out. "What do you want to do, Mr. Chafin?" he asked as he continued talking about what Kennedy could mean for West Virginia and the county. Chafin, "Uh, well, it looks like I'm going to have to be for Kennedy, but I don't know how I can help him. You know I am going to be in a dangerous situation. I could wind up six feet under. Plus, I already have Humphrey's money, and we already spent several hundred dollars of it."

McCahey was horrified, "By golly, send it back to him. And for gosh sakes, be sure you do send it back," he warned. (48)

Two contrasting stories: one told by Chafin, who said that the Kennedy campaign paid the $2,000 back, the other one by Keith Davis, who wrote that McCahey told Chafin on a demanding tone, "Send it back to him, and be sure you do send it back."

In his autobiography "Just Good Politics" Chafin wrote, "One fellow asked me what it would take to take Humphrey's name off the slate and get John Kennedy's name on. He was asking for a dollar figure. I'd already gotten most of the campaign set up. I didn't need much, so I decided to keep the figure real small, just four digits, a little more than what my local candidates donated." "About thirty-five," I said, meaning $3,500. "That's no problem," these fellows replied. "We'll take care of that. No problem."

They agreed to have a whole new batch of slates printed up in New York with Kennedy's name on them.

In his book, "Kennedy vs. Humphrey, West Virginia 1960," Dan B. Fleming Jr., quotes Sargent Shriver as saying he "vividly recalled a private meeting with a top Logan official a few days before the May 10 voting and being able to persuade the leader to switch from Humphrey to Kennedy." When asked how he was able to accomplish such a feat, Shriver laughed and replied, "I'm a lawyer, and I don't know." (49) (50)

A few days before Election Day, someone called from the Kennedy headquarters in Charleston and told Chafin that he should meet a plane coming into Taplan Airport that afternoon. They suggested that he bring a couple of bodyguards with him because they were sending them a little "something to work with." Chafin never needed a bodyguard for himself, but he went to Bus Perry and told him, "You're my man, Bus. I want you to get ready." Chafin gave Bus a little handgun and told him to put it in his pocket. "God," Bus said, "I ain't never carried any gun before!"

"Just put it in your damned pocket," Chafin said. They took his Cadillac through the rain, up to Taplan, just outside Logan. They walked across the swing bridge to get to the edge of the runway, where they waited together in a hangar. A small plane came into sight, circling for some time before landing. The plane came down, and they started there, "Come on." Chafin said as it taxied, "they have some campaign literature for us."

Robert McDonough, an industrialist from Parkersburg, had been running Kennedy's entire show in West Virginia. He was on the plane with two other men. When it landed, McDonough and one of the others climbed out and handed Chafin two briefcases. He asked what was in them. "I don't know," McDonough shrugged. "It's from headquarters." They thanked them and put the cases in the trunk of their car. Bus had noticed the heavy seals on those cases, and he knew right away what was in there. "Boy," he smiled. "This must be some kind of special literature." (51)

According to F. Keith Davis in "West Virginia Tough Boys," Chafin had to sign a paper saying that these fellas had delivered the bags to him. Chafin handed the confirmation to Bus. Chafin turned around and leaned over. Bus placed the document on Chafin's back and signed it as his witness. He handed the document to McDonough. Then the men all boarded the plane and prepared to leave. (52)

They locked the briefcases in Chafin's station wagon. When they arrived at his place, they cut away the seals, opened those cases, and saw all that money, separated into packages of fives, tens, and twenty-dollar bills.

But the more Chafin looked, the more he knew that someone in Kennedy's outfit had misunderstood him. Chafin then realized that those men in Baltimore came from a whole different world than he did. They spoke a different language. Chafin said one thing, but they'd heard something else – a much bigger figure. Chafin said, "Thirty-five," talking in hundreds; they had understood that he meant thousands. The total was $35,000 in those cases, plus more money for some of his contacts in the other counties. Chafin phoned Jim McCahey, "I believe they made a mistake!" Chafin said. "They sent more than I told them to!" "Hell, no!" McCahey said. "There's no mistake! We know you're doing your job."

Chafin thought that he was the only one around there who told them the truth – even if it was kind of an accident. "It would have been the easiest thing in the world for me to keep some of that money," he said, but he maintained that he spent it all, "just the way they wanted me to. I spent it all on that election." (53)

In 2003, F. Keith Davis wrote that because it had been more than 40 years since the Kennedy campaign and the statute of limitations had run out, Chafin was willing to talk candidly about the mysterious bags of money that were dropped off at Taplan Airport before the West Virginia primary. "Nobody will ever know exactly where that money came from. Never! But I'll tell you what we did with it. We bought voters with it! Regardless of what you want to believe, that's the way real politics works. We used up all that money from the bags and won the whole dang election. I'd say there was about two thousand dollars' worth of two-dollar bills, besides the other money. I wish I had kept the two-dollar bills – they'd be worth a fortune now." (54) Chafin had already told that crazy story in his autobiography back in 1994.

Claude Ellis, "Big Daddy," campaign manager "Kennedy for President, Logan County in 1960, claimed that the biggest part of the money that he got during the Kennedy campaign came from his main contact at the Kanawha Motel at Charleston, Kenneth O'Donnell. Some other smaller amounts came from Bob McDonough at Parkersburg. Still, the bulk always came through O'Donnell, even though McDonough and McCahey were usually present. Kenny was in charge of that.

According to Ellis, it was O'Donnell who, with an enormous surplus of financial backing, quietly paid Mountain State political bosses handsomely for their cooperation. It was also rumored that it might have been O'Donnell who supplemented Jim McCahey's enormous resources when he journeyed through southern West Virginia and entertained and bartered with powerful coal operators and union officials.

Ellis continued, "If it was Jack Kennedy's father, Joe, who was funding the bulk of the campaign in West Virginia, he shipped the bundles of currency to Appalachia through Kenny O'Donnell. It's also been suspected that Raymond Chafin's payoff came from the hands of O'Donnell, being delivered to Bob McDonough days before the transfer date. (55)

Ken O'Donnell doesn't appear at all in Chafin's autobiography. At the same time, Dan B. Fleming Jr. only mentions O'Donnell as working for Jack Kennedy in the West Virginia primary and says nothing about O'Donnell being Kennedy's money man in West Virginia.

These four money stories, as attractive as they are, have no historical value for me. They are a treasure for gossip magazines; their readers will love them. But I try to keep, naively perhaps, to the historical facts.

3.2. The Franklin Roosevelt Jr. Factor in West Virginia

FDR had given his son an immortal name, an awesome persona, and natural grace, but little of the strength, will, and ambition that was his essence. FDR Jr. was a self-indulgent, heavy-drinking namesake.

FDR Jr. was a former East-Side Manhattan congressman, an unsuccessful aspirant for New York governor, a failed candidate for New York Attorney General, a lobbyist for Dominican dictator Rafael Trujillo, and, now, an importer of Fiats and Jaguars.

It was not until April 8, 1960, that the Kennedys decided to recruit FDR Jr.

Recruiting Franklin Delano Roosevelt Jr. was once again a Joe Kennedy masterstroke. The ambassador invited young Franklin to Palm Beach and convinced him to stump for Jack in West Virginia because "he and Jack were friends." (1) (2)

Joe Kennedy had already employed FDR Jr. to campaign for Jack in the 1952 Connecticut race against Lodge, and now he thought of using FDR Jr. similarly in the mountain state.

With his precise eye for detail, Joe Kennedy suggested that Roosevelt's endorsement letters be postmarked at Hyde Park to make it seem as though the former president had returned from the grave to urge a vote for Jack. (3) (4)

The West Virginia journalist Charles Peters points out what a masterstroke the use of Roosevelt was, "In a certain sense he was almost God's son coming down and saying it was all right to vote for this catholic, it was permissible, it wasn't something terrible to do. FDR junior made it possible for many people to vote for Kennedy that couldn't have conceived of it as a possibility before." (5)

But Roosevelt Jr. had a poor opinion of Joe Kennedy: he told Ralph G. Martin in an interview, "I think Jack's father was one of the evilest, disgusting men I have ever known. Oh, I know he was a financial genius, but he was a rotten human being." (6) (7) (8)

Roosevelt Jr. was financially strapped, and he needed to revive his defunct political career – but his participation in the 1960 campaign would become his political graveyard. Some say that he and Jack were friends. In 1959, Roosevelt Jr. was invited by Jack Kennedy to dinner at his Georgetown house in Washington to celebrate getting mother Eleanor Roosevelt aboard the Kennedy bandwagon. Roosevelt Jr. left that dinner perplexed, "How can a guy this politically immature seriously expect to be president?" he said to his wife. "The only thing Jack could talk about at dinner was himself and his political problems. I'd never met somebody so completely obsessed in himself as Jack is now." (9) (10)

One of FDR Jr.'s best campaign lines was to raise his hand to the crowds and hold his two fingers close together and say, "My daddy and Jack's daddy were just like that." But for anyone in the Kennedy camp (including John) who knew the stormy wartime relationship between FDR and Joseph Kennedy, that statement was difficult to swallow. (11) Nevertheless, it worked for the West Virginians who seemed to accept it without question. Everybody knew that FDR hated Joe Kennedy, "that SOB," but shrugged it off on the grounds "that's politics."

On April 27, according to Lawrence Leamer and to David Pietrusza (May 6, 1960, for Dan B. Fleming Jr. and Michael O'Brien), FDR Jr. accused Humphrey of seeking deferment from military service several times, during World War II, including to manage a political campaign in Minnesota in 1945. But Humphrey claimed he had been kept from service by a hernia, insisting he had documents to prove that he was fit only for limited service.

"There's another candidate in your primary," Roosevelt said. "He's a good democrat, but I don't know where he was in World War II." (12) (13) (14) (15) (16) (17) (18) (19)

According to Larry F. O'Brien, the Kennedy camp had received from an anonymous Minnesota source supposed copies of correspondence between Humphrey and his draft board. They decided to do nothing with this for the time being. Still, they agreed that if Humphrey hit them with some extremely low blow, they might use the material to retaliate. But, determined that if retaliation were decided upon, it would come from Frank Roosevelt, not directly from the Kennedy camp, and they turned the material over to Frank. (20)

Although FDR Jr. made the allegation, almost everyone outside the Kennedy camp thought that the command to launch the smear came from Bobby Kennedy. Eugene McCarthy later recalled that JFK asked to see him. When he went over to his office, Kennedy told him, "Tell Hubert to lay off in West Virginia, or we will unload on him." Not long afterward, the draft-dodging charge surfaced. (21)

According to Rorabaugh, Robert Kennedy did put heavy pressure on FDR Jr. to attack Humphrey, and Roosevelt agreed to make the false draft-dodging allegation. (22)

Years later, during a discussion with Arthur Schlesinger Jr. on February 12, 1975, Roosevelt Jr. said, "Bobby had been bringing pressure on me to mention it. He kept calling five or six times a day." (23)

And in an interview on November 21, 1985, FDR Jr. told Dan B. Fleming Jr. that the person responsible for the draft-dodging smear was Robert Kennedy.

Fleming Jr. also wrote that there was great doubt that Roosevelt Jr. initiated the attack: Bill Lawrence of the New York Times maintained that "people in Kennedy's organization had given me a file of letters back and forth to Humphrey's draft board and that Kennedy forces were "deciding whether or not this issue would be used." Lawrence recalled, "I was not at liberty to use the documents until they told me Roosevelt had gone ahead with it." (24)

But it was Lawrence's understanding that they had decided not to use it, that the candidate had decided not to use it. (25) Fleming forgot to mention it in his book. On May 6, 1960, Jack Kennedy issued a statement declaring, "Any discussion of the war record of Senator Humphrey was done without my knowledge and consent, and I disapprove of the injection of this issue into the campaign." (26)

According to Theodore H. White, the campaign historian, Kennedy was furious. He'd told Roosevelt he did not want Hubert's war record brought into the campaign, angrily telling White, "I didn't want that." (27) (28)

Dave Powers recalled that Kennedy learned by telephone of FDR Jr.'s attack on Senator Humphrey and demanded, "Why did he do that? He didn't need to do that." Powers thought it possible that Robert Kennedy pressed FDR Jr. to make the attack, observing, "Bobby would do anything for Jack's sake." (29)

White was philosophical, telling Arthur Schlesinger Jr. on July 5, 1976, "Something always happens at the end of a good day."

Meyer Feldman, a legislative assistant to Senator Kennedy, said, "I honestly don't think that John F. Kennedy knew Franklin was going to use it." Feldman thought his campaign aides made the decision. But Feldman also believed Kennedy was committed to a high standard of campaign ethics, "I don't know of any other politician that stuck as rigidly to fair campaigning as John F. Kennedy, and I have seen a good many of them."

Kennedy's initial response to Roosevelt's attack was to say, "Let's get him out of

West Virginia." He felt Roosevelt had served his usefulness. (30)

And according to Lawrence O'Brien, Roosevelt apologized and offered to leave the campaign immediately. (31)

Ultimately Kennedy, who valued Roosevelt's campaign contribution, kept him on the team.

Roosevelt felt he had been used, blaming it on what he saw as Robert Kennedy's determination to win at any cost. He thought that Jack had nothing to do with encouraging him to raise the "draft-dodger" question – a decision Roosevelt said later had been the biggest mistake of his career.

In a recorded interview with Jean Stein on December 9, 1969, Roosevelt revealed that he went to Humphrey the next year to apologize – but Humphrey declared himself still "unforgiving" fifteen years later. (32) (33)

Humphrey recalled that meeting in his memoirs "The Education of a Public Man" but says nothing about refusing to accept Roosevelt's apology: Humphrey was a good man. I think it was not in his character to hold grudges for 15 years.

On the draft-dodging allegation, Humphrey wrote, "They believed me, but they never shut FDR Jr. up, as they easily could have." (34) (35)

David Pietrusza asserts that Roosevelt admitted years later, "Of course, Jack knew – but I always regretted my role in the affair." He went on, "Humphrey, an old ally, never forgave me for it. I did it because of Bobby. RFK was already a full-blown tyrant – you did what he told you to do, and you did it with a smile." (36)

Pietrusza's version of Roosevelt's testimony is not substantiated.

Barry Goldwater, who would have been Kennedy's most likely election rival in 1964, said that he and Kennedy had already agreed that they would ride the same plane or train to several stops and debate face to face on the same platform. (37)

The idea seems incredible today when you look at the modern era's bitter, negative style of campaigning.

3.3. Choosing LBJ as Running Mate: A Labyrinth in Search of a Vice President

Theodore H. White wrote in "The Making of the President 1960," "History is always best-written generations after the event, when cloud, fact, and memory have all fused into what can be accepted as truth, whether it be so or not."

As "a reporter" White said that on Sunday before the Democratic National Convention opened, Kennedy seemingly idly remarked to Washington Post publisher Philip Graham that if he thought Johnson would accept the vice-presidency, he might offer it. Whether Kennedy expected his musing to be transmitted to Johnson is not known, and if White's version is true, Graham, as a very close friend of Johnson, got word of the first "offer" to Johnson as vice-presidential candidate.

However, Graham told White that his facts were wrong and vowed to reveal the truth about how Johnson was nominated – which he did in a memorandum dated July 19, 1960, and published after his death on August 3, 1963. (1) (Graham in no way suggested that he was anything close to being the kingmaker, which I think he was.) Phil Graham, as considered (to Arthur Schlesinger Jr.) to be one of the most brilliant and attractive men of his generation, (2) was also a very sick man, a manic depressive whose moods swung from upbeat brilliance to dark despair. This was in the late fifties when no drug therapy existed for mental illness. (3)

The memorandum states that on Monday, July 11th, Phil Graham and Joe Alsop, a very close Kennedy friend, went together to Kennedy – Phil had urged Joe to go alone – as an intermediary between Johnson and Kennedy.

Graham wrote, "At Joe's request, I did the greatest portion of our talking and urged Kennedy to offer the vice-presidency to Johnson. He immediately agreed – so immediately as to leave me doubting the easy triumph." (4)

This is disputed by Evelyn Lincoln, who, in her diary for July 11, wrote that "those two men did not see Kennedy in his suite." She dismissed the account as a complete fiction, adding that in her "twelve years with John Kennedy," she had never seen him agree immediately to anything as important as this. Joe Alsop did, however, have a five-minute appointment – in company with Lincoln- scheduled with Kennedy on Sunday, July 10, 1960, at 6.00 p.m. (5)

So we have a conflict between the account of a manic depressive – in which mood did he write it? – and of a senator's secretary who mixes updates, hours, and events as she saw them.

Thus the Theodore White and Phil Graham versions of Kennedy asking Graham and Alsop asking Kennedy to put Lyndon Johnson on the ticket is the entry point into my "labyrinth."

In April 1964, Robert Kennedy told his friend Edwin Guthman that there were only three people who knew the whole story, and now one of them – Kennedy himself – was already gone. (6)

This so-called "three-person story" version of the vice-presidential negotiations during the 18-24 hours between Kennedy's nomination on Wednesday, July 13th, 1960, and the announcement of Johnson as his running mate is only mentioned to my knowledge by author, Jeff Shesol. (7)

It is Robert Kennedy's interpretation of the facts – or how he remembered events in his flip-flop narration over several years in oral histories and interviews with his friends A. Schlesinger and John Bartlow Martin.

Although I don't question in any way Bob's loyalty toward his brother Jack – for which he has my greatest admiration – his hatred of Johnson was so great that, in my opinion, he did some foolish things on the afternoon of July 14, 1960.

John Seigenthaler, the administrative assistant to the Attorney General and friend of Robert Kennedy, said of Robert's negotiating with Johnson on the VP ticket, "I think Bobby was trying to talk him out of it and was hoping that he would succeed." (8)

To my knowledge, instead of three people, there were, in fact, four people in the story, three who knew part of it and Jack Kennedy, who knew the whole saga – and who kept the most important details in his head.

John Kennedy compartmentalized his family, friends, and his wife: no one ever knew him completely. He was a very charming man, but he was also an introvert who kept much back and revealed nothing of himself at all. Arthur Schlesinger Jr. goes as far as to say that Kennedy could be a devious and, if necessary, a ruthless man, "I rather think, that he, in a sense, had Ken and me; that he sought our support when he considered it useful before the Convention to have liberal Democratic names behind him, but that, if he thinks our names would cause the slightest trouble when he starts appealing to Republicans, he will drop us without a second thought." (9)

This is how Jack dealt with his brother, making him a messenger boy during the vice-presidential nomination events when he cryptically said, "Bobby's been out of touch and doesn't know what's been happening."

Then there was the father, Joseph Kennedy, who I think was much more involved and almost totally ignored by historians, such as Arthur Schlesinger Jr., Robert Dallek, Michael O'Brien, Geoffrey Perret, and many others.

To me, he was the ghost walking around the events staying quietly at the Davies mansion in Los Angeles, well informed about everything that was happening at the Convention and updated by Jack at breakfast and dinner when he relaxed with his parents at their swimming pool.

When it came to crucial decisions, Jack listened to his father, including about Lyndon Johnson. On the morning of July 14, Jack told Clark Clifford that he had to do something he had never done before in his political career and renege on an offer to Senator Stuart Symington by choosing Johnson as his running mate instead. Kennedy said he had been persuaded overnight during "a family ruckus" that he could not win without Lyndon on the ticket. (10) The strong voice in that family ruckus was, without a doubt, Joe Kennedy. And later on, Clifford and Schlesinger would admit that it was a wise decision – or even a masterstroke.

A Kennedy-Johnson ticket had been Joe Kennedy's dream for a long time. He had talked about it in 1959 – eliciting a short, ugly expletive from Johnson when he was informed of the conversation.

And after his son's nomination, Kennedy was reported by Robert S. Allen (Washington DC correspondent) of the Christian Science Monitor) to have called Johnson to urge him to run as vice-president. But Johnson said that he preferred to stay in the senate. (11)

However, Arthur Schlesinger Jr. wrote in "Robert Kennedy and his Times" that Joe Kennedy had nothing to do with the Johnson decision, despite stories to the contrary: why, Schlesinger said, would he have intervened in favor of Johnson after having been called pro-Nazi by Johnson? (12) Perhaps because businessmen have a different, more calculated approach to politics than historians. "Joe Kennedy," journalist Nancy Dickerson wrote, "was concerned with nothing but victory, and he thought the combination most likely to win was a Kennedy-Johnson ticket. He had broached the vice-presidential nomination with Thomas Corcoran, the famous Washington lawyer. The latter had been a close confidant and advisor of FDR's. Any opinion of Joseph P. Kennedy was highly significant – his influence on his sons was tremendous." (13)

This is also the conviction of Edmund F. Kallina Jr., who says it is very likely that a conversation took place between father and son on the Johnson selection. (14) I am absolutely sure the father-son conversation did happen.

According to Rose Kennedy, the ambassador had been arguing that the Majority leader was a natural choice. As Joe Kennedy saw it, simple arithmetic was decisive: add the votes of New England to the votes of the Solid South, and only a small percentage more was needed to carry the election.

As a former certified accountant, I say, "Sounds like pure logic to me."

Joe even put aside the harsh remarks Johnson had made about him: he had been called much worse things in the past, such as a crook, bootlegger, and stock manipulator.

"Lyndon Johnson and Joseph Kennedy understood each other as kindred souls," Ann Gargan (Joe Kennedy's niece) observed. "They recognized power blocs; they each knew the other was always up to some mischief." (15)

I should add to Ann Gargan's observation that "crooks" understand each other and can make excellent deals together. Lyndon and Joe could be very rough in political or business dealing. Joe ran politics as a business – that's why he made the wrong decision on Hitler – but on the Johnson nomination, he was much more methodical, analyzing the facts and figures and reaching the right answer.

Certainly, Jack Kennedy consulted his father on all important decisions and was hugely influenced by him, something the court historians (Schlesinger, Sorensen, Salinger, O'Donnell, Powers, and others) were well aware of. But I am convinced that they felt they could not – or would not – write about it in the 1960s. To do so would have implied that Jack Kennedy was a pawn on his father's chessboard.

More evidence of Joe Kennedy's involvement comes in Michael Janeway's book "The Fall of the House of Roosevelt."

According to Janeway, Joe Kennedy worked on Johnson through back channels: that way, they could talk away from the heated campaign rhetoric they both attracted. Janeway describes how Kennedy impressed upon Johnson his vision of the future, one in which "these boys" were not ready to run the country, "which means that 'you and I, Lyndon' are going to have to run it for them." (16) This exchange is only quoted in one other book, "Bobby and J. Edgard" by Burton Hersh. Janeway also claimed that Joe Kennedy even offered the Senate majority leader $1 million to settle Johnson's campaign debts, adding, "Offer accepted." (17)

That story came from Janeway's father, Eliot. He claimed he was told it by John Bailey, a key political backer of Jack's run for president. (18) There are many conflicting accounts of how Johnson's selection came about. Edwin Guthman's version in "We band of Brothers" in 1971 is based on Bob Kennedy's response to reading an article by journalist Philip Potter about Johnson's selection. Potter, who had been close to Johnson for many years, had interviewed the president, Bob, and others for the piece and sent a copy to Bob for his approval. Bob asked Potter to make only two changes of importance.

One was to delete a sentence in which Potter recorded Bob as being "actively in favor of putting Johnson on the ticket." The second concerned a denial of claims that Bob had tried to block Johnson's selection. Potter quoted Bob as saying, "He's a lie and unthinkable." Bob crossed it out and replaced it with, "It's untrue and of course made no sense. "The rest of the quote, which Bob did not change, was, "I was not operating independently, I was Jack's agent, and no one knew that better than I. It was unimportant whether or not I concurred with Jack's decision. Jack was happy to have him (LBJ) on the ticket. That was enough for any of us."

It is worth noting that he did not disagree with Potter's findings which were set out at the start of the article as follows, "It was not an unfriendly Robert F. Kennedy, but the telephone – and Lyndon B. Johnson's penchant for keeping it in constant use – that almost upset the arrangements for a Kennedy-Johnson ticket in 1960." This fact has emerged from a series of interviews with the President, Attorney General Robert F. Kennedy, Senator Edward M. Kennedy, and the late President's principal political lieutenants Kenneth O'Donnell and Lawrence F. O'Brien, both of whom served Kennedy and now are serving Johnson as special White House assistants.

"Their recollection of the hectic negotiations between Kennedy and Johnson after the Massachusetts senator's nomination for president late on the night of July 13th repudiates completely conjectures that Kennedy offered his principal rival second place as a "gesture": that Robert Kennedy tried to sabotage his brother's decision to name the Texan; that the Johnson camp took the initiative in getting him on the ticket. "The decision, says the Kennedy brothers and lieutenants, was Kennedy's own, based on his political acumen after weighing the qualifications of various VP candidates including Senators Symington of Missouri and Jackson of Washington and the then Governor Orville Freeman of Minnesota." (19) So, four conclusions from Potter's findings are clear:

1. The VP offer was no "Pro-forma gesture"
2. There was no betrayal on RFK's side
3. No blackmail from the Johnson camp
4. Jack's decision was his own

But this is completely different from what Robert Kennedy told Arthur J. Schlesinger in "A Thousand Days" (1965) and in "Robert Kennedy and His Times" (1978) and also what Kennedy himself said about the Johnson selection in oral histories. (20)

In 1965 Schlesinger implied that Kennedy asked in the hope Johnson would refuse. Still, in the 1978 book, he was more forthright, "On Wednesday evening after the presidential nomination, John Kennedy told his brother that he was going to offer the Vice Presidency to Lyndon Johnson the first thing in the morning. He made me clear that this was entirely pro forma," Schlesinger wrote. "The idea that he'd go down to offer him the nomination in hopes that he'd take the nomination is not true, Robert Kennedy told me in 1965. The reason he went down and offered him the nomination is that he thought that he should offer the nomination because there were enough indications from others that he wanted to be offered the nomination, but he never dreamt that there was a chance in the world that he (Johnson) would accept it." (21)

I think Bob Kennedy had forgotten the Potter story and the few changes he wanted. It is also doubtful, as Bobby argues that JFK offered the vice presidency only to appease Johnson's self-importance and without "any hopes" that LBJ would accept. John Kennedy had clear signals from Graham, Alsop, O'Neill, Corcoran, and Sam Rayburn to expect a positive answer from Johnson. So it could not have been a surprise.

Graham, Alsop, and O'Neill recall JFK enthusiastically singing the praises of a Kennedy-Johnson's ticket, impressing others with his "positiveness."

The oft-quoted sentence from Kennedy after he came back from Johnson's suite – "You just won't believe it. He wants it." (22) – can be seen as a Jack Kennedy maneuver, hiding his true feelings as part of the political game.

Theodore White wrote in 1961, "The labor leaders led by Arthur Goldberg violently and vehemently objected to Johnson. They agreed that it might be expedient, if Johnson seemed to want the vice presidency, to make a pro forma offer of the post while wording the offer to make its rejection almost certain."

But Johnson had made clear that if there was to be an offer of the vice presidency, it must be a genuine offer – a real one, not a fake. (23)

Comparing the story in "We band of Brothers," 1971, to the story in "Robert Kennedy and his Times," in 1978, you'll find a true black-and-white, truth- and- lies situation: why didn't Schlesinger mention what Guthman wrote in his book?

It's also yet more proof that Jack Kennedy didn't tell Bobby the whole story – just what kept Bobby happy and calm for that moment to ensure he was a loyal and dedicated messenger boy for his brother when he went to the Johnson suite two or three times in the afternoon of July 14.

Jack Kennedy's actions could be measured by his answer when asked by New York Post correspondent Robert G. Spivack if Johnson had been offered the nomination. Kennedy shook his head and whispered, "No," – a blunt lie.

On his way down to the press bullpen to file his story, Spivack encountered an old friend, Governor David L. Lawrence of Pennsylvania, and told him of Kennedy's denial. "Bob," Lawrence said in his fatherly way, "Don't write it." "Why not, Governor?" Spivack asked.

Lawrence replied, "Because it's all set for Johnson. It has been for days. We've all known it, and I'm for it."

When many months later, Spivack asked Kennedy about his answer to the columnist's question and why he replied as he did, Kennedy shrugged and said, "That's politics." (24)

Robert A. Caro wrote that a few days after Johnson accepted the nomination, Jack Kennedy remarked to his friend and syndicated communist Charles Bartlett that his offer to Johnson had been merely a Pro-forma "gesture" and hardly an offer at all, "I just held it out like this," Kennedy said, holding his hand two or three inches from his pocket, "and he grabbed at it."

It was an off-the-record remark by Kennedy, and Bartlett kept it out of print until 1964 when he revealed that the Kennedys had been "shocked" when Johnson "seized" the offer and held fast to it. (25)

In a Kennedy Library oral history interview on January 6, 1965, Bartlett said more, "I remember one other time he (Kennedy) said, "I didn't offer the vice presidency to Lyndon – I just held it out to here." The picture I derived from that evening was that they told him this was a gesture, thinking he'd got over with early in the morning. As I understand, Torby MacDonald put in the telephone call and called Johnson (yet another one who called Johnson that morning). Then Jack was going to go down and make the offer and then go on about his business. And then Lyndon said yes, and Jack at that point was completely hooked." (26)

If Kennedy has made these comments, he was playing politics, saying one thing, thinking another. According to Robert, "We changed our minds eight times over the next few hours." (27) According to Hersh, it was seven times. Shesol talks about six times. (28) (29)

When did Kennedy, or someone else, call Johnson, and when did he arrive at the Johnson suite?

According to James W. Hilty, Robert said his brother visited Johnson's suite – solely in a gesture of party unity – at 10.58 a.m. (the timing sounds strange to me because Kennedy had a meeting with labor leaders at 11.00.) (30) In 1968 Evelyn Lincoln talked about a written message delivered to the Johnson suite by her husband, Abe. It said, "Dear Lyndon, if it is agreeable with you, I would like to talk to you in your room tomorrow morning at 10.00 (signed) Jack."

Evelyn was sure that the suggested time was chosen only to give Jack Kennedy a chance to shake Johnson's hand gracefully, but with no plan, at the time the telegram was sent, to offer Johnson the vice-presidential nomination. (31)

But in her 1965 book, "My twelve years with Kennedy," Evelyn Lincoln gave a totally different account, "Bob and Jack were in the bedroom, neither of them said a word. I could tell they were deeply involved in making some decision."

She returned later with a message for the Senator, "Bob was picking up the phone," she recalled. "See if Lyndon is in," the Senator said, "and tell him I will be down to see him." "I gave my message to the Senator and turned to leave. I heard Bobby say, "He'll be available in a few minutes." "Okay," the Senator said, "I'll go down in a little while."

"About eleven o'clock, the Senator went through my office and took the back stairs to Johnson's suite on a lower floor. He was back via the same route in about 20 minutes. When he was back, I also had a message for him to call his father. I trailed him into the living room to hear him say only one word, "Accepted." I turned to one of the men seated in the closest chairs and asked, "What did Johnson say?" "He said yes." (32)

1965-1968: Two different stories, different times: 10.00-11.00 a.m. and one thing all historians will agree upon: neither Bob nor Torby MacDonald makes the first call to Johnson – it was Jack Kennedy, and Lady Bird answered the phone and had to wake her husband.

In an oral history interview for the Kennedy Library on March 9, 1979, Lady Bird Johnson told Sheldon Stern, "I know, I speak for myself, and I think that that was the way Lyndon felt – woken too early by telephone call. I'm a light sleeper, so I woke up quickest to it, and my recollection is that it was John Kennedy's voice."

Stern, "Yes, that's what most of the accounts say."

Johnson, "Let me tell you something, though, because I kept a tape in the White House for five years myself and recollections right then are much, much better than recollections ten or fifteen years later; so I am glad I kept my records then. But my recollections are that it was Senator Kennedy's voice, and he asked if he could speak to Lyndon. Then there was a moment's hesitation on my part because Lyndon was so tired, and it was just too marvelous to just be able to rest. But I knew I couldn't because, after all, he was our party's nominee, so I went over and shook him and said, "Wake up..." (33)

When Johnson met Kennedy around 10.00 July 14, 1960, Lady Bird and Sam Rayburn, in particular, did not want him to go on the ticket, according to Lyndon Johnson himself.

But when Kennedy asked whether Speaker Rayburn had anything against him, Johnson said he did not: Rayburn simply thought that Johnson should stay as a leader and that perhaps Kennedy should talk to him.

The night before, Rayburn had telephoned Johnson and said, "They are going to try to get you on the ticket; you mustn't do that." (34)

Sam Rayburn's involvement in getting Johnson on the ticket is a perfect example of how politics is played – hard, dirty, and full of lies. That's one of the reasons why politics as a noble profession has become degraded: in the USA, losing faith in politicians started with the Vietnam War and Watergate.

On Tuesday evening, July 12, Tommy Corcoran had caught JFK in an elevator and talked about a possible Kennedy-Johnson ticket. Kennedy smiled and said, "Stop kidding Tommy, Johnson will turn me down." (35) Corcoran asked for Kennedy's permission to pursue the matter with LBJ. Kennedy smiled and nodded, "Tommy, you have peculiar abilities." (36)

Then Corcoran sought Johnson's permission "to work out the option with JFK." Johnson told him, "Only if Sam goes along with it – and he hates Kennedys." Rayburn duly refused to "go along with it."

Having been dead set against it on July 12, Johnson had become a convert by July 14 after talking to Senator Kennedy, either by phone late on the 12th as Tip O'Neill said Kennedy promised to, or in-person on that morning of the 14th.

On July 13, after Kennedy was nominated at the Democratic National Convention in Los Angeles, one of the first phone calls to Johnson's suite was from Rayburn. He said there were whispers in the Convention hall that Kennedy was going to offer him the vie-presidency. Rayburn strongly advised against it.

In the early hours of the same morning, Sargent Shriver was awakened by a phone call (no name mentioned of the caller), "Lyndon will." Shriver replied, "All right, I'll get the word to Jack first thing in the morning," Shriver said.

The so-called "opposition" in the Johnson camp to a Kennedy-Johnson ticket was a calculated, reluctant one – a "that's politics" one.

Certainly, Sam Rayburn's decision to back the ticket was influenced by his hatred of Nixon and by the fact that, according to Johnson, he had nothing personally against Kennedy – sentiments expressed in the morning of July 14 when Kennedy asked Johnson whether Rayburn had anything against him.

If the Tip O'Neill account is true, which I think it is, we are talking about July 12, 1960. Rayburn was already converted by then, but Rayburn played his cards very well.

Let's tell the Tip O'Neill – Rayburn story, in brief, one that would never make it into the history books, according to Sam Rayburn.

By July 12, the day before the nomination vote at the Convention floor, the Kennedy brothers were convinced that Jack would win on the first ballot. Sam Rayburn had made it clear that he opposed Johnson taking the second spot on the ticket. But Wright Patman said to McCormack, "John, if Kennedy wants Lyndon for the vice-presidency, Lyndon can't turn it down." To O'Neill's surprise, Rayburn agreed with Patman. "John," he said to McCormack, "if Kennedy wants Lyndon as his running mate, Lyndon had an obligation to this Convention to accept it. You tell Kennedy that if he wants me to talk to Lyndon, I'll be happy to do it. Here's my private telephone number, which you can give to Jack Kennedy." Rayburn handed the phone number to O'Neill and repeated, "If Kennedy is interested in Lyndon being the vice-presidential nominee, you have him call me, and by jolly, I'll insist on it."

Tip O'Neill went to Chasen's restaurant that night, waited 45 minutes, and then told Jack Kennedy what Sam Rayburn had said and handed him the Speaker's phone number. Jack was delighted, "Of course I want Lyndon," he told Tip. "But I'd never want to offer it and have him turn me down. Lyndon is a natural choice, and with him on the ticket, there's no way we could lose. Tell Sam Rayburn I'll call him after the session tonight."

Did Kennedy call Sam Rayburn on the night of July 12, 1960?

Tip O'Neill, "small-part Kingmaker" is convinced he did.

If so, then Rayburn already backed a Kennedy-Johnson ticket on the night of the 12th – but I doubt that Kennedy called Rayburn that night. (37)

That same story is related in short by James W. Hilty. Still, he says the Kennedy call to Rayburn was on the evening of the presidential balloting (July 13th). (38)

Meanwhile, Democratic congressman Hale Boggs says the call was made on July 14th, in the morning, after Kennedy was nominated. Boggs recalled Rayburn asking him for advice. Rayburn said, "What do you think about this?"

I said, "Well, do you want Nixon to be President of the United States?"

He answered, "You know I don't."

"Well," I said, "Unless you approve of Lyndon taking the nomination, that's what's going to happen."

"Well," he said, "That's right. He's got to do it."

That's about how much discussion there was. And in his political mind, and he had a remarkable mind, he immediately started realizing the handicaps, and he knew already the opposition had set in. And he said, "Get Senator Kennedy down here so we can decide immediately." So I wound my way upstairs to Kennedy's suite."

Boggs went on, "A little bit later, Kennedy walked in with O'Donnell, who talked with the Speaker alone than with the Senator."

According to Boggs, "Kennedy walked out of the room positively exuberant. And from that point on, Rayburn was a hundred percent for the Kennedy-Johnson ticket." (39)

Two wonderful stories on how Sam Rayburn went for the Kennedy-Johnson ticket. But what about the version written by Robert A. Caro in 2012 in his book, "The Years of Lyndon Johnson?" In this account, O'Neill credits Congressman Wright Patman as swiftly convincing Rayburn about the Kennedy-Johnson ticket.

Caro says that Johnson himself had begun the persuasion process even before Kennedy made the offer, sending influential emissaries Homer Thornberry and Wright Patman to soften Sam's opposition, "Sam was in the bathroom in his shorts, and he was shaving."

Patman recalled, "He was blistering mad about Lyndon even considering the vice-presidency." (40)

In Caro's account, the same players, Hale Boggs, Patman, Rayburn aides D.B. Hardeman and John Holton, appear, applying the same argument of "Nixon distrust."

But instead of Boggs going to get Kennedy, it was Kennedy who called Rayburn – perhaps the call O'Neill talked about (which I doubt).

In Caro's version, Rayburn told Holton that if Kennedy met certain conditions, he would advise Johnson to accept. In Boggs' version, no condition was imposed. Kennedy came down and agreed with all Rayburn's conditions, according to an account Rayburn gave to his aide D.B. Hardeman.

Rayburn said, "I told him, I'm dead set against this, but I've thought it over, and I'm going to tell you several things: if you tell me that you have to have Lyndon on the ticket to win the election, and if you tell me that you'll go before the world and tell the world that Lyndon is your choice and that you insist on his being the nominee, and if you make every possible use of him in the National Security Council and every other way to keep him busy and keep him happy then the objections that I have had I'm willing to withdraw."

He went on, "Kennedy said to me, 'I tell you all those things'."

Kennedy walked out of Rayburn's suite, "positively exuberant," according to Boggs, who relates that he, Boggs, went to Kennedy's suite and asked him to come down to see Rayburn: in the Caro narrative Kennedy telephoned to come down. There is a big psychological difference between the actions, as described by H. Boggs and written by Caro. (41)

To go to get Kennedy to come down to the Johnson camp means Lyndon wanted to accept the vice-presidential nomination right away. But Kennedy calling the Johnson camp, as Rayburn demanded, "To do the offer meeting certain conditions," makes Kennedy the supplicant.

The moral of the story is that both parties wanted each other desperately.

Another version of events has it that Kennedy met Rayburn downstairs after Johnson recommended that he talk with the Speaker. Rayburn listened carefully to Kennedy and said, "Up until thirty minutes ago, I was against it, and I have withheld a final decision until I found out what was in your heart." No more "conditions" – Rayburn had been charmed by Jack. Johnson's name was never mentioned publicly until after the presidential nomination on July 13.

The most likely candidates being mentioned for the vice presidency in the week before the Convention were Humphrey, Stevenson, Symington, Orville Freeman, and Jackson: the Kennedy people told everyone categorically that Johnson was not in the picture. Ted Sorensen had, by his own account set out in Robert Dallek's book "An Unfinished Life: John F. Kennedy, 1917-1963," submitted to Kennedy several weeks earlier, on June 29, as had many others, a list of potential vice-presidential nominees.

His list of 22 names was reduced to 15 and then to 6. (42) (43) James Hilty wrote that by the time the Democrats convened in Los Angeles, the "Sorensen List" had been pared to four – Governors G. Mennen Williams of Michigan and Orville Freeman of Minnesota, and Senator Stuart Symington of Missouri and Lyndon Johnson. (44) Dallek's book has Robert Kennedy personally favored Washington senator Henry "Scoop" Jackson. At the same time, Sorensen topped his list with Lyndon B. Johnson, as apparently, did many other contributors of suggestions.

This, of course, totally contradicts the suggestion that Johnson's name was "never mentioned" and the notion that the name of Johnson headed many lists.

Sorensen also said that Kennedy respected Johnson and knew he could work with him, making LBJ, in Sorensen's opinion, the next-best qualified man to be president. (45)

Pierre Salinger's memoirs also say that John Kennedy admired LBJ and believed – and often said -that if he, Kennedy, didn't win the nomination, Johnson was the best Democrat alternative. (46)

But Kennedy's friend George Smathers, a senator from Florida, said in an oral history interview, "Kennedy admired Johnson very much: I don't think he liked him personally, but it was very difficult to be around Johnson." (47)

Brother Bobby, in an interview with Arthur M. Schlesinger Jr., said, "I think JFK admired him and he rather amused the president: he admired the obvious ability that he had, but LBJ wasn't helpful at times that he might have been helpful. He was very loyal and never spoke against the president, but he never gave any suggestions. He was opposed to our policy, I mean, the two major matters – The Cuban Missile Crisis and the 1963 Civil Rights bill. He (Johnson) was opposed to sending up any legislation." (48)

This also proves that Jack Kennedy had given the question of a running mate more attention than anyone imagined and that he kept his cards close to his chest.

It's unthinkable and very hard to believe that John Kennedy only thought of selecting a VP nominee until the morning after he was nominated as brother Bobby claims and that only the two of them decided to offer VP to Johnson.

JFK told different versions to different people, but I am convinced he had a pretty good idea whom he would choose. The only potential obstacle was a "No" from Lyndon Johnson.

The Blackmail from the Johnson Camp

The first "Blackmail" story started on July 14, 1960.

Following Johnson's selection as the vice-presidential candidate on Thursday night, Kennedy's press secretary Pierre Salinger returned to the office to face numerous calls from journalists checking a story by John S. Knight, publisher of the Knight Newspapers, alleging that Johnson had forced Kennedy to select him. That night Bob Kennedy insisted to Salinger that the story was untrue: a denial Salinger published under his name before going to bed.

He was woken an hour later by a phone call from Bill Moyers of Senator Johnson's staff, saying the Speaker Sam Rayburn wanted to speak to him. Rayburn was very agitated, insisting that Senator Johnson was extremely disturbed about the story and wanted it nipped in the bud before it got wide circulation. Rayburn demanded publication of a complete denial – in Senator Kennedy's name – and told Salinger to wake Kennedy and have him call John S. Knight personally to say the story was untrue.

Salinger and Bob Kennedy worked out a statement together to issue in the senator's name. Bob said he would call Knight since part of the story related to a conversation between Bob and Senator Johnson before Jack Kennedy even saw Johnson. Salinger and Bob Kennedy tried to find out the source for the Knight story, finally narrowing the list down to Clark Clifford, who had been Senator Symington's campaign manager. Jack Kennedy had told Clifford during the afternoon of July 14 that Johnson was going to be the vice-presidential candidate, even revealing to Clark his surprise that Johnson was willing to make a fight for the second spot nomination.

Bob Kennedy felt that perhaps Clifford had interpreted this remark to mean that Johnson had "forced" his way on the ticket. After talking to John Knight, Bob Kennedy called Salinger back, saying that Knight was going back to his source and checking further on the matter. They later learned that the source was not Clark

Clifford but Governor James T. Blair of Missouri, to whom Clifford had confided his conversation with Senator Kennedy. (1) (2)

There is another "blackmail story" told by Anthony Summers in 1993, and Seymour M. Hersh in 1997, based on a 1993 interview by Evelyn Lincoln, taken over in the Summers book and with an additional interview given by Lincoln to Hersh for his book and Hyman Raskin's account in his unpublished memoir provided to Hersh for his book and buttressed by interviews with him in 1994 and 1995.

A day or two after the Convention, Salinger asked JFK whether he expected LBJ to accept the second position on the ticket or whether the invitation was merely a gesture. Kennedy began giving the facts, then suddenly stopped and said, "The whole story will never be known. And it's just as well that it won't be." Salinger could not explain the cryptic remark, concluding afterward, "I can only report that JFK made it." (3)

Anthony Summers mentions Salinger's cryptical remark but adds this from Kennedy, "The only people who were involved in the discussions were Jack and me. We both promised each other that we'd never tell what happened," said Robert Kennedy. For the Salinger account, he mentioned his source "With Kennedy" by Salinger 1966, p. 46. Still, on Bob Kennedy's statement, he offers no source material. (4)

In her now "historic" 1993 interview, Evelyn Lincoln claimed that she was privy to part of JFK and RFK's conversation in their Biltmore Hotel suite during the Convention, "When I came in there, they were huddled together closely on the bed, discussing this dramatic issue about Lyndon B. Johnson being on the ticket. Bobby would get up and go looking at the window and stare. Kennedy would sit there and think. It was intense. They hardly knew I came into the room. They were so engrossed in their conversation. That went on for 30 minutes, trying to figure out how to maneuver, to get it, so he (Johnson) wouldn't be on the ticket."

Evelyn Lincoln says that what she heard that day convinced her the Kennedy's were being blackmailed, "One of the factors that made John F. Kennedy choose LBJ was the malicious rumors from J. Edgar Hoover about Kennedy's womanizing – so that's one of the reasons that pushed him to go down and offer him the vice-presidency. LBJ and Hoover had boxed him into a hole. They were boxed in." (5)

In interviews with Evelyn Lincoln in 1988-1992, Anthony Summers said Lincoln admitted that her boss was a "ladies man." Then, with a chuckle, she blamed it on the ladies, "Kennedy didn't chase women," she laughed. "The women chased Kennedy. I've never seen anything like it."

But during the 1960 campaign, according to Mrs. Lincoln, Kennedy discovered how vulnerable his womanizing had made him, "Sexual blackmail," she said, "had long been part of Lyndon Johnson's modus operandi, abetted by J. Edgar Hoover."

Lincoln went on, "LBJ had been using all the information Hoover could find on Kennedy, during the campaign, even before the Convention. And Hoover was in on the pressure on Kennedy at the Convention."

Summers concluded that Evelyn Lincoln's account, if accurate, is evidence that Hoover's interference in the American political process was even more insidious than previously feared. It suggests, in effect, that he subverted the democratic system as ruthlessly as any secret police chief in a totalitarian state. (6)

Seymour Hersh followed up Summers' account on Evelyn Lincoln's "blackmail story." Adding evidence from a fresh interview with her for his book "The Dark Side of Camelot," Lincoln told Hersh that she found Bobby and Jack deep in the conversation early on the morning of July 15th (I think it was July 14th). She did not hear any mention then of a specific threat from Johnson on that occasion: Hersh quotes her as saying, "I went in and listened. They were upset and trying to figure out how they could get around it, but they didn't know how they could do it. "Jack knew that Hoover and LBJ would just fill the air with womanizing." (7)

Hersh claims that in an account by Hyman Raskin, a JFK aide overseeing the political operation at the Convention account. Stuart Symington was always at the top of Kennedy's short list of running mates. That list was "precipitously and discarded," Raskin wrote when Kennedy met early on the morning after his nomination with Johnson and Sam Rayburn, the Speaker of the House. At the meeting, Kennedy was "made an offer he could not refuse." In other words, Raskin assumed, Johnson blackmailed his way into the vice presidency. Raskin did not establish which aspect of the Kennedy history was cited by Johnson and Rayburn in making their threats. Still, he did not doubt that that meeting disrupted months of careful planning and caused an uproar in the Kennedy camp.

Raskin told Hersh in an interview, "It was always Symington who was going to be the vice-president because he had the Kennedy family's approval." (8)

In an interview for the Kennedy Library on May 8, 1964, with Sam Vanocur, Hyman B. Raskin said that it had never occurred to him that Lyndon Johnson might be on the ticket, and when it was announced, he found it hard to believe because the Kennedy campaign had discussed many names. Johnson's name was not among them. Vanocur asked for names, noting that Symington was prominent on the list. Raskin answered, "Yes, Symington, Henry M. Jackson, Hubert Humphrey, Orville Freeman, Governor Loveless, Governor Docking..." and he thought there were several others. (9)

There was no hint in the interview of Jack Kennedy being blackmailed.

That leaves us with two "blackmail stories," one of which I call bad communication between two politicians and a journalist, and the second, which is based on Evelyn Lincoln's great sense of imagination: she could make up beautiful stories, thinking they were true. Her 1993, 1988, 1992 interviews are far from the historical truth – I call it historical nonsense.

In 1960, there was no "womanizing trauma." At that time, Jack Kennedy was protected by the press – and Lyndon Johnson was a womanizer too, so in July 1960, he was in no position to subject Kennedy to blackmail.

On one later occasion, Lincoln asked Kennedy, "Who is your choice as a running mate in 1964?" Kennedy answered, "At this time, I am thinking about Terry Sanford of Carolina North. But it will not be Lyndon." Was Kennedy no longer afraid of being blackmailed by Johnson and Hoover, or had he forgotten about the July 1960 blackmail? If true, he would certainly have remembered it. And why did Evelyn Lincoln not talk about the blackmail stories, either in her 1965 book, "My Twelve Years with John F. Kennedy," and particularly, in her 1968 book called, "Kennedy and Johnson?"

But Helen O'Donnell, daughter of Kenneth O'Donnell Sr., wrote on dumping LBJ in 1964 that Kenny explained: "Johnson had not been closely involved in the planning of the upcoming campaign and had begun to suspect that Bobby Kennedy and his allies were planning to dump him as the vice-presidential candidate in 1964 because of his connection with Bobby Baker. According to Bobby, the president "never had any intention of dumping Johnson." It was a position Kennedy concurred with completely: I was sitting with the president and George Smathers on the way to Florida the Saturday before the Texas trip. Senator Smathers asked him if he was planning to get rid of Johnson because of the Baker case. Smathers said rumors were flying all over the Capitol that he planned to dump Johnson, in favor of Bobby. "If I've heard them, then he has," Smathers said.

The president glanced at Smathers and said, "George, you must be the dumbest man in the world. If I drop Lyndon, it will make it look as if we have a really bad and serious scandal on our hands in the Bobby Baker case, which we haven't, and that will reflect on me. It will look as though I made a mistake in picking Johnson in 1960, and can you imagine the mess of trying to select somebody to replace him? Bobby is my brother, and he cares deeply that we succeed in 1964, do you seriously believe he would do anything to jeopardize that success? The dumbest thing we could do is dump Johnson. And, George, I am not dumb." (10)

Conclusion

Navigating the labyrinth of conflicting accounts surrounding the choosing of Lyndon Johnson as Jack's running mate was a difficult undertaking.

Many confusing messages were laying false trails to follow and many issues to ponder. Issues such as "a pro forma offer" or "a genuine offer" numerous presidential kingmakers, with Johnson sometimes on top of the VP candidates' list or never mentioned at all.

And then there was Joe Kennedy's key role – or not: Bobby Kennedy's behavior; blackmail from the Johnson camp – or not; and, finally, Jack Kennedy's exact role in his own final decision.

With all those issues, how could I find the exit gate out of the labyrinth?

Well, I am convinced, after consulting and comparing more than fifty books on the matter, my tentative conclusion is that Joe Kennedy had a more decisive role than most historians thought and credited him for and that he acted in a furtive role still not fully understood and researched on.

Those historic and hectic "18 or 24 hours" in Los Angeles were, first and foremost, a race against the clock: rooms filled with politicians with hidden agendas, having a good time, not afraid to lie, playing kingmakers, through a night with almost no sleep, levels of fatigue which led to bitter encounters and misunderstandings, with all parties involved.... but that's politics.

One man – John Kennedy – was in almost total control, except for his doubts and fears that Johnson would turn him down.

In my view, that fear of rejection prompted JFK to put Stuart Symington high on the list, provoking a lot of confusion. The trouble is that Jack "the listener" kept a lot of his thoughts to himself. Suppose the Johnson offer was Pro-forma and was rejected: having said no to Symington, Kennedy would have been in much bigger trouble than during Johnson's negotiations. I am convinced that Kennedy was sure Johnson would say yes. He chose not to tell his brother Bobby, or Sarge, Pierre, Kenneth, and Dave, and many others who were against Johnson for the vice presidential nominee. But he confided with his father because the wise old fox had also sensed that, logically and mathematically, Johnson was the best choice.

But that leaves us with Kennedy's cryptic remark to Salinger a few days after the Convention, "The whole story will never be known. And it's just as well it won't be."

Could the $1,000,000 offered by Joe Kennedy to settle Johnson's campaign debts help to explain it – or could that remark have fueled the blackmail theory put up by Hersh, Summers, and Evelyn Lincoln in the nineties? But one thing is sure: my exit from this labyrinth has been chosen based on pure analytical analysis, not on sentiment. Bobby's version of the facts has been contradicted even by himself, his own so-called truth, and the Pro-forma and blackmail theories also have been contradicted by a close study of the available facts and opinions. I choose the Joe Kennedy explanation as my exit point from the labyrinth, and if many historians don't agree, so be it.

3.4. A Stolen Election with the Help of the Chicago Mob

John F. Kennedy was elected president on November 8, 1960, with 34,226,731 votes against Richard Nixon's 34,108,157. In the Electoral College, the final returns were Kennedy's 303 electoral votes in 23 states, against 219 votes for Richard M. Nixon in 26 states.

Kennedy had 49.7% and Nixon 49.5% – representing a vote difference of 118,574. The vote difference in Illinois was 8,858, and in Texas, there was a vote difference of 46,257.

However, as you will see in my notes, different authors give different figures. For instance, Victor Lasky in 1963 gave Kennedy 34,227,096 votes, while David Pietrusza in 2008 had 34,220,984 – a discrepancy of 6,112 votes, or 5.15% of the vote difference of 118,574.

In his book "The Making of the President 1960," Theodore H. White dedicated more than three times the number of pages to Kennedy and the Democrats than to Nixon and the GOP.

But, according to Edmund F. Kallina – who wrote "Kennedy vs. Nixon: The Presidential Election of 1960" – White found his hero in Kennedy and his villain in Nixon, long before the election. White even circulated the manuscript for his book to, among others, Robert F. Kennedy, Pierre Salinger, Lou Harris, and Ken O'Donnell and accepted suggestions from them about what material should be included and excluded: the Kennedys and their aides decided what history was and what was not.

Perhaps it is therefore not surprising that White became one of Kennedy's inner circle and sought Kennedy's approval for his work. (1) (2)

A more realistic approach in trying to understand the 1960 election is contained in four revisionist books of the 1960 campaign: "The First Modern Campaign" by Gary Donaldson (2007), "1960 LBJ vs. JFK vs. Nixon" by David Pietrusza (2008), "The real Making of the President" by W.J. Rorabaugh (2009); and "Kennedy vs. Nixon" by Edmund F. Kallina (2010).

These works tell stories far from the fantastical Camelot myth that White, mesmerized by Kennedy's charisma, helped to create and which he later confessed had never existed.

Seymour Hersh's 1997 book, "The Dark Side of Camelot," goes so far as to describe how Joseph P. Kennedy risked the family's reputation and the political future by making a deal with Sam Giancana and his powerful organized crime syndicate in Chicago.

Joe Kennedy's goal was to ensure victory in Illinois and in other states where the syndicate had influence. He achieved it after arranging a dramatic and until now unrevealed summit meeting with Giancana in the chambers of one of Chicago's most respected judges. (3)

Michael O'Brien writes, "Perhaps Hersh's description of their meeting is correct since similar meetings were taken place elsewhere. Joe Kennedy met with scores of the biggest bosses in his attempt to elect his son. What's most important, though, is there isn't evidence of any campaign activity that Giancana used to elect Kennedy. He commanded a few votes. Chicago's Mayor Daley, not Giancana, managed the huge and potent Democratic organization in Chicago. Giancana controlled only two wards, and both were heavily Democratic anyway." (4)

Evan Thomas says that regardless of whether Giancana was somehow working for the Kennedys – a dubious claim at best – there are at least two problems with the mobster's boast. First, Kennedy did not need Giancana, who controlled possibly one or two wards, because they already had Daley, who could deliver the entire city. Second, even if Nixon had won Illinois, Kennedy still had enough electoral votes to win the election. (5)

Did the meeting take place? I doubt it because, in a 1997 interview, Hersh said that Tina Sinatra spoke about a meeting in late 1959 at Hyannis Port with her father Frank and Joe Kennedy:

Over lunch, Joe said (to Frank), "I think that you can help me in West Virginia and Illinois with our friends. You understand Frank, and I can't go. They're my friends too, but I can't approach them. But you can." Frank Sinatra reportedly met Giancana on a golf course because the notion that Joe would meet Sam Giancana was out of the question. (6) So was born one of the more persistent conspiracy theories that organized crime, working with Joe Kennedy, delivered Chicago and hence Illinois, and hence the presidency, to JFK.

Hersh is, to say the least, very contradictory in his statements on a possible face-to-face meeting between Kennedy senior and Sam Giancana, and Tina's interview raises more questions.

Nixon always insisted that he rejected pressure from others, including President Eisenhower, to dispute the Illinois election result. But that was not true: the outgoing president withdrew his support for any challenge within a day of the vote. (7) (8)

In his memoirs, Richard Nixon said that Everett Dirksen urged him not to concede and to request a recount. But Nixon argued that a presidential recount would require up to a half year. During that time, the legitimacy of Kennedy's election would be in question, with a potentially devastating effect on America's foreign relations: "I could not subject the country to such a situation," said Nixon. "And what if I demanded a recount? If it turned out that despite the vote fraud, Kennedy had still won, charges of "sore loser" would follow me through history and remove any possibility of a further political career." (9)

But Nixon doesn't say that Eisenhower encouraged him to dispute the outcome of the election.

According to Gary A. Donaldson, Nixon may also have been worried about strong evidence that downstate Illinois Republicans had initiated their election fraud on his behalf. If so, says Donaldson, it would explain why Nixon refused to support those who were trying to push for a recount. In any case, the matter was eventually dropped. Right or wrong, Nixon appeared statesman-like in defeat. (10)

In 1962 in his book "Six Crises," Nixon was not so statesmanlike as Donaldson asserts. He said that he should have requested the Justice Department to impound the day after the election, all the ballots in Cook County, and other areas where there was evidence of fraud. (11)

But why would Eisenhower support Nixon for a challenge, when during most of the campaign, he didn't work very hard for his vice-president?

Furthermore, according to Nixon's friend Ralph De Toledano, a conservative journalist, Nixon knew Ike's position, yet claimed anyway that he, not the president, was the one advocating restraint. "This was the first time I ever caught Nixon in a lie," Toledano recalled. (12)

In "Conversations with Kennedy" in 1975, Ben Bradlee recalled that one night during the election campaign, while the two were at dinner, Jack Kennedy had called Chicago's Mayor Richard Daley, just as the Illinois result was hanging in the balance, asking how he was doing. "Mr. President," Kennedy quoted Daley as saying, "with a little bit of luck and the help of a few close friends, you're going to carry Illinois." (13)

Twenty years later, in "A Good Life," Bradlee wrote that, as the dinner was explicitly off the record, he, Bradlee, had not published the remarks until he wrote "Conversations with Kennedy" almost fourteen years after the Kennedy-Daley exchange. But when he did, the quote haunted Kennedy's reputation: some Republicans chose to read it as a confirmation that Daley had stolen Illinois from Nixon, and with it the election for Kennedy. They felt the Daley quote revealed the Mayor promising Kennedy that he could and would produce enough votes – one way or the other – to guarantee victory.

"Me, I don't know what the hell Daley meant," Bradlee said. "If it was Irish humor, it seems peculiarly inappropriate, not to say dumb." (14)

If Bradlee didn't find that vote fraud story amusing, John F. Kennedy Jr., on the other hand, did.

In a speech in 1996 in Chicago, he said, "In 1945 my grandfather bought the Chicago Merchandise Mart, and in the 1970s my family bought the Apparel Center – and of course in the 1960 election my family bought 20,000 votes in Cook County..."

I think that quote also haunted Bradlee for many years – I think he wished he had never published it. This historical, legendary, and mythical statement – even Richard Nixon put it in his memoirs – and also taken over by Hersh, contributed to all those voter-fraud-and-mob-conspiracy theories.

According to Edmund Kallina Jr., Bradlee did qualify the quote with an immediate reference to an unnamed Nixon staff member, who allegedly determined that "Republicans could well have stolen in Cook County." (15) (16) (17)

Kenny O'Donnell remembered a conversation with Daley, "Mayor Daley said that they had robbed him blind downstate." "He told O'Donnell about the district that included Peoria. There were areas with only 500 voters, yet Nixon had beaten Kennedy 500 votes to fifty. Impossible numbers. Clearly, there was major fraud downstate."

Mayor Daley said, "Kenny, they do it all the time. They lose their returns, and we have to slow down our returns until we see what they are doing down there and how they are going to come out. But as of right now, we are all right as long as you tell your people to stop calling me. I will tell you, Kenny, and you can tell Jack, we are going to be okay. Jack can count on this." (18)

This is the Kennedy camp version of the vote-stealing in Illinois – putting the focus on the Republicans as vote-stealers too.

In his memoirs, Nixon said they found Washington a lie with the talk of election fraud. Many Republican leaders were still urging him to contest the results and demand recounts. Nixon further claims that Eisenhower himself urged that course, offering to help raise the money needed for recounts in Illinois and Texas. There is no doubt that there was substantial vote fraud in the 1960 election. Texas and Illinois, according to Nixon, produced the most damaging, as well as the most flagrant examples. (19)

According to Victor Lasky, J. Edgar Hoover believed the 1960 election results were more the product of fraud than honest error. Lasky told his close friend Philip Hochstein, editor of the Newark (NJ.) Star-Ledger that Hoover was therefore prepared to launch an inquiry into election fraud – but only involving Joseph Kennedy.

When Hochstein asked Hoover what was preventing him from launching a full-scale probe, Hoover replied, "Ike and Nixon." (20) (21)

Three days after the election, Republican Party Chairman Senator Thurston Morton launched bids for recounts and investigations in 11 states, an action that Democratic Senator Henry Jackson attacked as a "fishing expedition." Eight days later, close Nixon aides sent agents to conduct "field checks" in eight of those states. Peter Flanigan, another aide, encouraged the creation of a Nixon Recount Committee in Chicago. All the while, everyone claimed that Nixon knew nothing of those efforts. This implausible assertion could only have been designed to help Nixon dodge the dreaded "sore loser" label.

The Republicans pressed their case doggedly, succeeding in obtaining recounts, convening grand juries, and involving US attorneys and the FBI. Appeals were heard, claims evaluated, evidence weighed, but the results were meager. New Jersey was typical: the GOP obtained court orders for recounts in five counties, but by December 1, the State Republican Committee halted the process, conceding that the recounts had failed to uncover any significant discrepancies. Kennedy was certified the State's official winner by 22,091 votes.

Texas and Illinois, the two largest states under dispute, witnessed the nastiest fights. In Texas, where Kennedy won the 24 electoral votes by a margin of over 46,000 ballots, the GOP went to court, only to have its claims thrown out by a federal judge who said he had no jurisdiction. In Illinois, the appeal was pursued more vigorously, maybe because, in Cook County (specifically Chicago), Kennedy had won by a suspiciously overwhelming 450,000 votes.

According to David Greenberg, the GOP's failure to prove fraud did not mean, of course, that the election was clean – just that the question remained unsolved and unsolvable. But what is typically left out of the legend is that multiple election boards saw no reason to overturn the results. Neither did state or federal judges. Neither did an Illinois special prosecutor in 1961. (22)

Did the Kennedys steal the 1960 election? We will never know.

What strikes me is that two distinguished historians, Robert Dallek and Michael O'Brien, both concluded that the Daley machine in Cook County did steal the election for Kennedy. But they also concluded that Kennedy would have won in the Electoral College even if Illinois had gone Republican. (23) (24) (25)

And what about Texas, a vote difference of 46,257? Theodore White, in his book "In Search of History," writes, "Even in the most corrupt States of the Union, one cannot steal more than one or two percentage points of the vote." The votes total in Texas was 2,311,084, two percent of which is 46,221 votes... (26)

3.5. Calling Mrs. Martin Luther King

The most celebrated incident in the campaign – after the debates with Nixon and the discussion of church and state at the Houston Ministerial Association – was John Kennedy's phone call to Mrs. Martin King Jr.

According to Arthur Schlesinger Jr., the initial Kennedy interest in Negro affairs was political. The brothers had been entirely devoid of racial prejudice but only intermittently sensitive to racial injustice; the debate over the Civil Rights Act of 1957 had begun John Kennedy's education on the issues.

Harris Wofford, who was appointed in 1961 as a Special Assistant to the President for Civil Rights, was instrumental, "We don't know much about this whole thing," Robert Kennedy told him. "I haven't known many Negroes in my life. It's up to you. Tell us where we are and go to it." (1) (2)

According to Theodore White, Kennedy had tried to enlist Martin Luther King Jr., the Lenin of the Black Revolt, in June of the campaign year. They had met at Kennedy's New York apartment but had not quite hit it off; King was more stubborn and messianic than was generally recognized at the time. The two had met once more after Kennedy's nomination, in a hilarious French-farce mis-scheduling of black leaders in Kennedy's townhouse in Washington in late August. Kennedy was hoping for a meeting of minds: in the tight national race, black votes were vital, and King was the key man to sway them. But King had taken a non-partisan stance and would not be swayed into a commitment unless Kennedy visited the Deep South for a public appearance at King's Southern Christian Leadership Conference.

Kennedy agreed in principle to a meeting but wanted time to work out the place, date, and subject matter. King left disappointed. For the next few weeks, negotiations hung fire. Nashville was discussed as a meeting point, and so was Miami, but King wanted Atlanta. Talks continued, and then Kennedy's hand was forced by events. (3)

According to Evan Thomas, the Kennedys had made no real effort to cultivate Dr. King, who had he not been arrested for sitting in at a segregated lunch counter in Atlanta on October 19, just two weeks before the election, they might never have spoken. (4)

On September 23, 1960, Dr. King had received a $25 fine for traffic violations (expired plates and an expired Alabama license) plus twelve months' probation, predicated on his not violating "any Federal or State penal statutes or municipal ordinances." (5)

On the same day that John Kennedy and Richard Nixon were addressing the American Legion in Miami on the national defense – Wednesday, October 19, 1960 – some seventy-five or fifty-two Negroes, cheered by hundreds of supporters and jeered at by surprised white customers, asked to be served lunch in the Magnolia Tea Room restaurant in Rick's department store in the South. Fifty-two of them, including King, were arrested after staging a sit-in at a segregated lunch counter.

Refusing to put up bail on a charge under anti-trespassing laws, King said, "I'll stay in jail a year, or ten years, if it takes that long to desegregate Rick's." (6) (7)

On October 25, Dc Kalb County judge Oscar Mitchell, a rabid reactionary, revoked King's parole. (8)

And King was taken in handcuffs and leg shackles to the county jail, 230 miles outside Atlanta. He was ordered to serve four or six months' hard labor in a state prison in Reidsville. On the traffic charge – which, unlike segregation, King did not consider unconstitutional – he was ready to post bail and appeal. Still, the judge refused to let him out. (9) (10) (11) (12) (13) (14) (15) (16) (17) (18)

Coretta King, five or six months pregnant, told Harris Wofford that she feared her husband might be lynched. Wofford suggested to Shriver that John Kennedy place a private call to King's wife. (19) (20) (21) (22) (23) (24) (25) (26) (27) (28) (29)

In "The making of the President 1960," Theodore H. White wrote that JFK's reaction to Wofford's suggestion of calling Mrs. King was immediate and impulsive. White wrote in 1978 that Kennedy was impulsive and not calculating, "because no man of goodwill in his position can stand aside when a black leader is imprisoned on a technicality and exposed to a possible knifing in a racist jail." (30) (31)

In "Of Kennedy and Kings," Wofford recalled telling Louis Martin, the wise black newspaperman from Chicago and the DNC's liaison with the black press, "Who cares about public statements? What Kennedy ought to do is something direct and personal, like picking up the telephone and calling Coretta – just giving his sympathy." Louis Martin replied, "That's it; that's it – that would be perfect."

But it was not that simple. Wofford then discussed the matter with Sargent Shriver in Chicago and put it bluntly, "The trouble with your beautiful, passionate Kennedys is that they never show their passion. They don't understand symbolic action."

That prompted Shriver to visit Kennedy at the O'Hare International Inn. Still, when he saw others in the room, he knew someone would shoot down the idea if they heard it. Shriver waited until Ted Sorensen had left to finish writing a speech, Salinger had disappeared to see the press, and O'Donnell went to the bathroom. Then he mentioned King's middle-of-the-night ride to the state prison and said, "Why don't you telephone Mrs. King and give her your sympathy." Kennedy agreed. (32)

Sorensen later wrote in "Kennedy" that a phone call to the pregnant wife of Negro leader imprisoned in Georgia on a traffic technicality could backfire: it was certainly seen by almost all of Kennedy's advisors as a futile "grandstand" gesture which would cost more votes among Southerners than it would gain among Negroes. Many of those who advised against the call to Mrs. King argued decades later that even without it, Kennedy's popularity among Negroes was failing because of the state of the economy. (33)

O'Donnell was just emerging from the bathroom as Kennedy made the call and heard how it went, "You just lost the election," he said to Shriver.

On the plane to Detroit, Jack casually mentioned the call to Salinger, who radioed word to Bobby even before the plane had landed.

Bobby immediately erupted to those around him, in particular, blasting Harris Wofford, Louis Martin, and Sargent Shriver as the "bomb throwers" risking Jack's election.

Wofford recalled, "With his fists tight, his blue eyes cold, Bobby turned on us." He said, "Do you know that three Southern governors told us that if Jack supported Jimmy Hoffa, Nikita Khrushchev, or Martin Luther King, they would throw their states to Nixon? Do you know that this election is razor close, and you have probably lost its focus?"

Bobby was right about the razor closeness of the election but wrong about the outcome and the phone call's effect on it. (34) (35) One thing is certain; Jack acted on his own. He didn't contact his brother nor his advisors to make his decision.

But in an Oral History interview for the Kennedy library, John Seigenthaler, an aide to Robert Kennedy during the 1960 presidential campaign and later his administrative assistant as Attorney General, said that Bobby had talked to the president the night before. He knew that he had been a part of the decision to call Mrs. King. (36)

The Coretta King call puzzles me a lot. Which version of events is the true story?

I think Sorensen's account of "the Coretta King call" is wrong because although there was prior advice about the call, except Shriver's, none of the other "advisors" knew about it in advance.

Kenneth O'Donnell Sr.'s account emerged in 2015 in his daughter Helen's book "The Irish Brotherhood," based on his previously unpublished interviews with NBC White House correspondent Sander Vanocur. O'Donnell said that Jack had resisted making the call, fearing it would be seen as a campaign "gimmick" – a cheap stunt to win the black vote, as Kennedy's aides considered this. O'Donnell himself stood aside, listening to everyone's advice.

But then Jack steered O'Donnell into the bathroom – the same one from which O'Donnell emerged in other accounts to overhear the call to Mrs. King – and asked his opinion.

Kenny recalled his reply as, "While I am sympathetic to what Mrs. King and her family must be going through, from a political point of view, all I can see is that could backfire. We could lose key southern support that we worked hard to achieve." He echoed Kennedy's concerns, saying, "It looks like a cheap stunt. I am afraid that is how it will appear to King and his supporters. You've never thought much about this, then suddenly you make this call. There are a million ways politically; it could be a mess."

When the discussion ended, Jack stayed in his room to rest, and the others left. O'Donnell went to the hotel lounge for a drink and to rethink. That is when Sarge Shriver, fingering the ever-present rosary in his jacket pocket, caught Kenny in the hallway. "I want a few minutes," he said. "I want to reopen the King discussion."

O'Donnell said in his interview, "I was not pleased. The issue had been decided, and I did not want it reopened. We had a heavy schedule the next day, and I wanted to move on, but Sarge would not budge." The two men stood toe to toe in the hallway outside Jack's closed suite door.

According to O'Donnell, Shriver then said, "I never use my family connection or ask for a favor, but you are wrong, Kenny. This is too important. I want time alone with him." O'Donnell admitted in the interview that he was conflicted, "For political reasons, I wanted to tell him to flat out no, but the truth was he had never asked before, and he was a family member. Unlike others, he never asked or abused that relationship, and, at some level, morally, I suspected he might be right, though politically I still was against it." So O'Donnell told Sarge quietly, "I haven't eaten yet." I'm going to get a hamburger and a beer." They shook hands, and O'Donnell left Shriver outside Kennedy's room. "You know I am right," he said to Kenny's departing figure. "Maybe," Kenny said. "If it works, you'll get no credit for it; if it does not, you'll get the blame."

When Kenny returned, Jack had made the decision. He would call Mrs. King. With that single call, he changed the dynamics of the election. "If he'd listened to me instead of Sarge," Kenny said, "who knows?" (37)

Which is the truth? Kenny O'Donnell is seen in this story as taking credit for something to which he was at first heavily opposed. But by letting Sargent Shriver talking to his brother-in-law, he also played his role in risking Negro support only days before the election on November 8th.

Let Sargent Shriver himself have the final word on the Coretta King call.

In an interview with Gerald S. and Deborah M. Strober, Shriver said, "With due respect to everyone else, I am the only one who knows what happened. I was in Chicago, running the "Kennedy for President" operation in Illinois, when I got a call from Harris Wofford. He was in the civil rights headquarters in Washington. He said, "Sarge, I have been thinking about the situations involving Martin Luther King Jr., who is in jail in Georgia. I think it would be a marvelous idea if we could get the candidate to call Mrs. King and express her sympathy. He doesn't have to do anything more than that. He doesn't have to make any kind of political commitment."

Kennedy was in Chicago, and I was in charge of his visit. We had held a breakfast for local leaders, and the Kennedys went back to a motel near the airport where he was staying, and we went into his room. There were people there talking about breakfast, and someone said, "The plane leaves at about ten o'clock. He has to pack."

So everyone else left, and I remained with the candidate, who began to pack his bag. It was miraculous. After all, I had not wanted to bring up the idea of calling Mrs. King with the others there because I knew it would precipitate a debate about the calls, pro, and cons. I said, "Jack, I have an idea that might help you in the campaign. Mrs. Martin Luther King is sitting down here in Atlanta, and she is worried about what is going to happen to her husband. I have her home telephone number. I suggest that you pick up the phone, say hello, and tell her you hope that everything works out well." There was a silence for ten or fifteen seconds, and then he said, "That's a good idea, can you get her on the phone?" So I picked up the phone near the bed and dialed her number, and she answered. I said, "Mrs. King, this is Sargent Shriver" – the King family knew me – "and I am here with Senator Kennedy. He would like to speak with you, is that okay?" She said, "Fine," and I handed the phone to Jack. He spoke for a maximum of three minutes. All he did was to express his sympathy and interest as a citizen and a political leader over the plight of the King family, and then he hung up. I said, "Thanks, Jack. I think that will make a big difference to a lot of people." Jack then went on to Michigan and then to New York, landing at the Marine Terminal at La Guardia Airport.

He was immediately asked about the call to Mrs. King, and shortly after that, I got scorched out by officials of the Kennedy campaign. They asked who the hell I thought I was, getting the candidate to make such a call without consultation with national campaign headquarters. Thirty-six hours later, they changed their tune and started saying how important the call has been." (38)

The call to Mrs. King was placed Wednesday, October 26, 1960.

Morris B. Abram, General Counsel of the Peace Corps, described Shriver as a secular priest – a deeply devout Catholic who was motivated to do good, "I seriously doubt that other than a political motive would have impulsed any of the Kennedys," he opined, "but it certainly would have impulsed Shriver." (39)

Even Robert Kennedy, who had attacked the "bomb-throwers," made an astonishing about-turn, contradicting all he said to Wofford, Shriver, and Martin. While on a flight to New York, Kennedy stewed about the harsh treatment of King. "I thought about it, and I kept thinking it was so outrageous." He told Seigenthaler and Wofford a day later, "When I got off the airplane, I'd made up my mind that somebody had to talk to that judge, Mitchill..." It made me so damned angry to think of that bail and sentencing a citizen to four months of hard labor for a minor traffic offense and screwing up my brother's campaign and making our country look ridiculous before the world."

Bobby finally called the judge, demanding, "Are you an American? Do you know what it means to be an American? You get King out of jail." (40)

According to W. J. Rorabaugh, that call, which could have been construed as an illegal attempt to influence a judge, received only minor coverage. (41)

And Bobby Kennedy's biographer Evan Thomas was sure the call to the judge was not at his initiative, he was carrying out his brother's orders. (42) (43)

Ralph Martin writes that both brothers had acted independently, and neither had acted with any strong feeling for civil rights on the promise that "there are moments when the politically expedient is the morally wise." (44)

According to Arthur Schlesinger Jr., the brothers, in making their phone calls, had acted independently of each other. "The finest strategies," John Kennedy observed to John Kenneth Galbraith, "in this connection, are usually the result of accidents." (45) (46)

Edmund Kallina Jr. asserts that in the Kennedy hagiography, the two telephone calls stand as monuments to Kennedy's passion and brilliance and as a symbolic prelude to their later embrace of the civil rights crusade. (47)

Certainly, the two calls, JFK's call to Mrs. King and RFK's call to the judge, made a big difference to the Negro vote.

On his release, October 28, after paying a $2,000 bail, King said, "I am deeply indebted to Senator Kennedy, who served as a great force in making my release possible. For him to be that courageous shows that he is acting upon principle and not expediency." He added, "There are moments when the politically-expedient can be morally wise." To a reporter, he said, "I hold Senator Kennedy in very high esteem. I am convinced he will seek to exercise the power of his office to fully implement the civil rights plant of his party's platform." (48)

On the other hand, King was scathing about Nixon's silence, "He had been supposedly close to me, and he would call me frequently about things, getting, seeking my advice. And yet, when this moment came, it was like he never heard of me, you see. So this is why I considered him as a moral coward." (49)

Afterward, President Eisenhower blamed "a couple of phone calls" by John and Robert Kennedy for the decisive shift of Negro votes. (50) (51) (52)

According to journalist Scott Stossel, before the Democratic Convention in July 1960, Kennedy had been less popular among blacks than all the Democratic hopefuls, including even the Southerner Lyndon Johnson. On Election Day, three months later, he won more than 70% of the black vote. The call to Mrs. King was the coup de grâce that solidified the Negro vote for Kennedy and secured him the election. (53)

I am convinced that Jack Kennedy didn't talk about the Washington and New York talks of June and August 1960 with Martin Luther King Jr. to his brother or his advisors because Bob, Salinger, O'Donnell and Sorensen, they were all against any involvement of Dr. King on behalf of the Kennedy campaign. Still, once again, Jack Kennedy instinctively made a good decision.

From then on, Dr. King endorsed Kennedy in coded terms, "I never intend to reject a man running for President of the United States, just because he is a Catholic. Religious bigotry is as immoral un-democratic, un-American and un-Christian as racial bigotry." (54)

Even Martin Luther King's father, an influential Baptist preacher, changed his endorsement from Nixon to Kennedy.

Dr. King Sr. made his public announcement on Friday evening, October 28, "I had expected to vote against Senator Kennedy because of his religion. But now he can be my president – Catholic or whatever he is. It took courage to call my daughter-in-law at a time like this. He had the moral courage to stand up for what he knows is right. I've got all my votes, and I've got a suitcase, and I'm going to take them up there and dump them in his lap."

There were just ten days left before the election. (55) (56) (57) (58) (59) (60) (61) (62)

Kennedy later remarked on King's father's statement, "That was a hall of a bigoted statement, wasn't it? I imagine Martin Luther King having a bigot for a father." Then he smiled and added, "Well, we all have fathers, don't we?" (63)

Ultimately one or two million pamphlets describing the incident were distributed at black churches and bars in the north. The pamphlet "The Case of Martin Luther King Jr.," featured on the cover page the headline, "No comment Nixon versus a Candidate with a Heart, Senator Kennedy." This improvised public relations offensive helped tip the balance in the election. (64) (65) (66) (67) (68) (69)

Richard Nixon admitted in "Six Crises" that he should have called the judge in the Martin Luther King case – or done something similar to match JFK's "grandstanding." (70)

W.J. Rorabaugh wrote that when the media later asked Kennedy why he had phoned Coretta King, he said simply that he was a friend of the family. This was an almost comical lie – Kennedy and Coretta had never met and, in fact, never did. (71)

3.6. The TV Debates

According to Gerald S. and Deborah H. Strober in "Let Us Begin Anew," the climactic moment in the debate over Kennedy's religious beliefs came on September 12, 1960, when he addressed the Greater Houston Ministerial Association. There, through his speech and the question-and-answer period that followed, Kennedy was finally able to diffuse the religious issue. The neutralization of the Protestant clergy proved to be the turning point of the campaign. (1)

But according to Ken O'Donnell in "Johnny, We Hardly Knew Ye," the real turning point in the campaign was the first debate with Nixon in Chicago. The contrast on the television screen between Nixon's anxiety and Kennedy's cool composure confounded the Republican contention that Kennedy was too immature and inexperienced for the presidency and established him as a potential winner. (2)

Former President Gerald Ford was also convinced that the debates had an impact, particularly the first one. He suspected that was the turning point for Kennedy. (3)

Nixon began his fifty-state campaign with two trips into the south in mid-August. He bumped his knee, getting into a car in Greensboro. The immediate pain soon passed, and he thought no more about it. But twelve days later, the knee became intensely painful, and tests showed it was badly infected. Nixon required massive doses of penicillin and other antibiotics and two weeks in bed at Walter Reed Hospital. He was finally able to leave on Friday, September 9. (4)

Ironically, Kennedy, whose medical problem greatly exceeded anything Nixon had, appeared to be the picture of robust good health. But somebody in the Nixon campaign thought otherwise: attempts to steal records from two of Kennedy's doctors in New York offices may have been the work of Nixon aides trying to build on Johnson's accusations, which according to New York Times columnist William Safire, had been passed along to them by a 'disgruntled' LBJ supporter unhappy with JFK's nomination.

However, 42 years later, participants in the Nixon campaign and others sympathetic to Nixon emphatically denied the allegation: according to Robert Dallek, the episode certainly can be read as a prelude to Watergate and a break-in at Daniel Ellsberg's psychiatrist's office in Beverly Hills.

Moreover, John Ehrlichman, an advanced man in the 1960 campaign, acknowledged "dirty tricks" on both sides. Dallek concluded that none of this is a clear demonstration that a Nixon campaigner tried to steal Kennedy's medical records. Still, it is plausible: who else but Nixon would have benefited from obtaining them? (5)

Representatives of the two candidates and the spokesmen for the broadcasting networks first met at the Waldorf-Astoria Hotel in New York in September to discuss the conditions and circumstances of the televised debates. There would be a controlled panel of four press interlocutors, no notes, dignity to be safeguarded, with opening statements of eight minutes from each candidate in the first and last debates and two-and-one-half-minute responses to questions. The Nixon negotiators fought to restrict the number of debates: their man, they felt, was the master of the form, and one "sudden death" debate could eliminate Kennedy with a roundhouse swing. The Kennedy negotiators wanted at least five debates rather than let themselves be whittled down to four.

By mid-September, all had been arranged: there would be four debates, on September 26th, October 7th, October 13th, and October 21st. CBS would produce the first out of Chicago, the second by NBC out of Washington, the third by ABC out of New York and Los Angeles, and the fourth, again by ABC out of New York. (6)

President Eisenhower and other Republicans advised his vice president not to participate in the prime-time joint appearances with the young senator. Many believed the telecasts would elevate Kennedy's limited experience in leadership by conveying the image of two equally qualified candidates despite Nixon's fuller résumé. But Nixon had prided himself in being a champion debater at Whittier College. (7)

Nixon, in his first book "Six Crises," said, "I felt it was essential that I not only agree to debate but enthusiastically welcome the opportunity. Had I refused the challenge, I would have opened myself to the charge that I was afraid to defend the Administration's and my record. Even more important, I would be declining to participate in a program which the majority of the American people, regardless of party, wanted to see." (8)

In his second book "RN: The Memoir of Richard Nixon" in 1978, he wrote, "Kennedy would have the tactical advantage of being on the offensive. But there was no way I could refuse to debate without having Kennedy and the media turn my refusal into a central campaign issue." (9)

According to Katz and Feldman, national studies are virtually unanimous in placing the viewing figure for the first debate at 60 to 65% of the total adult population. Some local studies show higher figures because they tend to include respondents with higher education and greater political interest. Altogether, some 70 of the 107 million US adults – and perhaps another 10 to 15 million younger people – watched or listened to the first debate.

The viewing figures are less consistent concerning the subsequent debates. It is difficult to know how to account for the effect of the different days of the week (Monday, Friday, Thursday, Friday) and the different hours of the day (9.30, 7.30, 7.30, 10.00 Eastern Time). The Nielsen ratings show a lower percentage of TV homes tuned in for the follow-up debates (measured by metered readings) but a larger total audience (measured by diary records) for the second and third debates (80 and 82 million individuals) than for the first (77 million) or the last (70 million). This is almost certainly because the second and third debates aired early enough in the evening to have included more children and, possibly, more adults with early bedtimes. In any event, a conservative estimate would be that at least 55% of the total adult population watched or listened to each of the debates and, altogether, that upwards of 80% saw or heard at least one of the debates. (10)

But we will never exactly know how many TV viewers looked at the first televised TV debates in history.

On how many viewers watched the first debate, different authors use different figures, from 70 to 80 million. Most authors use 70 million. (11) (12) (13) (14) (15) (16) (17) (18)

During the first debate in Chicago, only three people were allowed in the control room: Major Daley, his wife, and Roman Puchinski, US Democrat congressman from Illinois. Jack came out first and took his position at the lectern. Nixon followed, and when he walked out onto that stage, Daley said, "My God, they've embalmed him before he even died." (19)

Ben Bradlee thought the vice president looked like "an awkward cadaver." Richard Goodwin believed that Nixon appeared "more like a losing football coach summoned before the Board of Trustees than a leader of the free world." Bradlee added, "What we saw on Nixon's face that night was the panic in his soul." (20) (21) (22) (23)

Behind the scenes, Kennedy had rejected CBS News producer Don Hewitt's offer of make-up, prompting Nixon also to decline – ignoring the fact that his opponent had just spent days campaigning in the California sun. In contrast, he had been hospitalized and was deathly white. (24)

Hewitt, who was directing the broadcast, recalled that, on the day before the debate, both candidates were invited to meet with him to discuss the set design and camera angles to familiarize themselves with the venue.

"Kennedy was very curious," Hewitt said. He wanted to know, "Where do I stand? How long do I have to answer? Will I get a warning when I go too far?" "He wanted to know the nuts and bolts of what we were going to do." But Nixon did not bother, "The opponent declined the same opportunity for a technical briefing." Hewitt confirmed, "I never saw Nixon before they arrived in the studio that night... they (the

Republican campaign) just didn't think it was that important."

Kennedy, however, aware of the significance of the first-ever televised presidential debate in history, prepared thoroughly. (25)

His personal "Brains Trust" of three had settled into the Knickerbocker Hotel in Chicago on Sunday, September 25, 1960. In charge was Ted Sorensen, supported by Richard Goodwin, a 28-year-old lawyer and elongated elfin man with a capacity for fact and reasoning that had made him number one man only two years before at the Harvard Law School, and Mike Feldman, a burly and impressive man, a one-time instructor of law at the University of Pennsylvania and later a highly successful businessman. They had abandoned business to follow Kennedy's star as the head of Senator Kennedy's legislative research. (26)

In "Counselor," Sorensen mentions Feldman but not Goodwin, "Sitting with Mike Feldman and me that morning on the roof of his Chicago Hotel, Kennedy listened closely to every possible issue and the question we would raise, based on Mike's comprehensive card file, setting forth the position of both candidates and both parties in each one. Kennedy responded quickly to those on which he was certain of the facts and asked for more information on others." (27)

According to Donaldson, Nixon studied alone. (28)

According to W. J. Rorabaugh, an exhausted Nixon arrived in Chicago very late on Sunday night, staying in his hotel room through the next morning, banning entry to anyone. Although he reviewed notes for the debate, he made no effective preparation. The staff had compiled a briefing book, but no time had been found to discuss its contents with Nixon. (29)

When the cameras rolled, Kennedy began with a powerful opening, "In the election of 1860, Abraham Lincoln said the question was whether this nation could exist half-slave and half-free. In the election of 1960, and with the world around us, the question is whether the world will exist half-slave or half-free. If we do well here, if we meet our obligations, if we're moving ahead, then I think freedom will be secure around the world. If we fail, then freedom fails. Therefore, I think the question before the American people is: are we doing as much as we can do? I should make it very clear that I do not think we're doing enough. I think it's time America started moving again." (30) (31) (32) (33) (34)

Most historians assert that a majority of television (TV) viewers felt that Kennedy won the encounter. However, some evidence suggested that radio listeners sided with Nixon.

Among them was Lyndon Johnson, who listened but did not see. According to David Pietrusza, reporter Nancy Dickerson was listening with Johnson on a car radio. But Dickerson, in "Among Those Present" said, "We all gathered in the living room to listen on the radio. We all thought Nixon had won, for we could not see how dreadful he looked. Throughout, LBJ kept score, saying, "One for Nixon" or "One for the boy," but the boy always seemed to come out behind. To Johnson, JFK had lost." (35)

Earl Mazo, the political reporter, and Nixon chronicler, later wrote, "Nixon was best on radio, simply because his deep, resonant voice carried more conviction command and determination than Kennedy's higher-pitched voice and his Boston-Harvard accent." (36)

But on television, Kennedy looked sharper, more in control, more firm, he was the image of the man who could stand up to Khrushchev."

Theodore H. White wrote that, according to sample surveys, those who heard the debates on radio believed that the two candidates came off almost equal. Yet every survey of those who watched the debates on television indicated that the vice-president had come off poorly and, in the opinion of many, very poorly. (37)

Ted Sorensen, in "Counselor," disagrees with those Nixon supporters who said their man won that first debate on radio, where the competing visual images could not affect the outcome. In Sorensen's view, if JFK had looked like Nixon, the result of the debate and the election would have been the same. (38)

Richard Nixon himself wrote that "most of the editorial writers who based their opinions on substance rather than the image, even in the pro-Kennedy Washington Post and St. Louis Post-Dispatch, called the debate a draw, but post-debate polls of the television audience gave the edge to Kennedy. Ralph McGill of the Atlantic Constitution, who supported Kennedy, observed that those listening to the debate on the radio reported that I had the better of it." (39)

As for the size of the TV audience for the debates, different authors give different figures.

Theodore White writes in "The Making of the President 1960" that there are many measures of the numbers of Americans who viewed the debates. Dr. George Gallup, America's most experienced pollster, put the figure of those who viewed one or all the debates at 85,000,000. The two most extensive surveys of audience participation were by TV networks NBC and CBS, who conducted produced separate independent polls that produced similar results: NBC estimated that 115,000,000 Americans viewed one or all of the great debates, compared with CBS at 120,000,000. (40)

Michael O'Brien wrote that 75 million viewers watched the first debate, falling to 61 million for the second. (41)

Richard Nixon, in his memoirs, considered that, based on a New York Herald Tribune editorial, he had "clearly won the second round." But 20 million fewer people had watched the second debate than had watched the first one. (42)

The fourth and final debate took place in New York on October 21 – a foreign policy debate that Nixon hoped would attract the largest audience. Instead, the number of viewers stubbornly remained 20 million fewer than the first.

In "Six Crises," Nixon wrote that the audience had been estimated at about 80 million. It had fallen to about 60 million for the second, and it was not to rise above that figure for the third and fourth debates. (43)

White described the fourth debate as to the "dreariest," although the audience remained at least as large as the previous two. Overall, four out of five Americans watched or heard at least one debate during the historic quartet of debate broadcasts. (44) (45)

Ten years earlier, the impact of voters would have been significantly less. In 1950, only 11% of America's 40 million families owned a television. By 1960 and the Kennedy-Nixon debates, the number jumped to 88%. (46)

3.7. Bobby as a Campaign Manager

"It was understood when Jack ran, Bobby would be his campaign manager," wrote Rose Kennedy in "Times to Remember" she said, "Joe wanted Bobby in on all this so he could observe how a national campaign is run, to understand the problems, and benefit from any lessons that could be learned. Jack was very much in favor of this." (1)

Bobby Kennedy already had the experience: in 1956, he had traveled with Adlai Stevenson, the former Illinois governor who ran an ineffective campaign, from which Bobby learned a lot, which he put to good use later – including mistakes to be avoided. He was so horrified with Stevenson's poor organizational skills and indecisiveness that he had quietly voted for Eisenhower. "It was a terrible shock," Bobby said later. "I came out of our first conversation with a very high opinion of him." (2) (3) (4)

Bobby managed the campaign on an 18-hour-a-day basis. A classic puritan, moralistic, and wholly committed to the week ethic, he believed in getting up very early, then working uninterrupted until he virtually dropped from exhaustion at the end of the day. (5)

By October 1960, he was thin, weary, with deep gray bags under his eyes, his shoulders slumped with fatigue. "He's living on his nerves," John Kennedy said. His father, Joe, agreed, "Jack works as hard as any mortal man can: Bobby goes a little further." Once, the two brothers ran into each other at a windswept airport. "Hi Johnny," said Robert Kennedy. "How are you?" The presidential candidate replied, "Man, I'm tired." Bobby retorted, "What the hell are you tired of? I'm doing all the work!" JFK later acknowledged, "I don't have to think about organization. I just show up. He's the hardest worker. He's the greatest organizer. Bobby's easily the best man I've ever seen." (6) (7)

Jack needed Bobby as his presidential campaign manager, not only because they sparked off each other and fitted perfectly together, but because Bobby was one of the very few people who could safely tell him to go to hell when he believed Jack was wrong. (8) (9)

The two brothers had played distinct roles, defined largely by their father. Bobby was tough, Jack the visionary; Bobby, the enforcer; Jack's job was to move forward; Bobby's to cover his back. (10)

For all their professed reluctance to accept the political road, they were political men – for Jack, it was always a game; to Bobby, it was the equivalent of war.

Bobby Kennedy was "a one-man firing squad for Jack." As such, he saw no need for finesse, no need to consider the feelings of those whose help he solicited or whose objections he was sent to placate. (11)

Like his father, Bobby was more aggressive and decisive than Jack. Bobby would neither forget nor forgive. "Anybody who'd ever been against his brother, or who wasn't a hundred percent for his brother, was on Bobby's Absolute Shit-List, the "hell list" observed Newsweek Washington editor Ken Crawford. (12)

Bobby was intense, single-minded in pursuit of a goal, not worried about being liked. He was not afraid to make enemies if it would help his brother win the presidency. He once remarked to New York party officials, "I don't give a damn if the state and county organizations survive after November, and I don't care if you survive. I want to elect John F. Kennedy." (13)

He drove the campaign staff mercilessly and engaged in hardball with the opposition. And while this cemented his reputation as the "ruthless" Kennedy brother, it allowed the candidate to remain above the fray. (14)

Victor Lasky wrote that Bobby never made any effort to compete with his brother on an intellectual level. "He is not at home with abstract concepts," a friend of Lasky's told New York Post's Irwin Ross. "He's fundamentally a deer. Bobby's political ideas are Jack's political ideas." (15)

Paul Johnson, in "A History of the American people" wrote, "Did Kennedy, or for that matter, his, even more, competitive-minded younger brother Bobby – much his superior in intelligence – have any political convictions? No national figure has ever so consistently and unashamedly used others to manufacture a personal reputation as a great thinker and scholar." (16)

Paul Johnson may say that John Kennedy was one of the biggest frauds in American political history – with which I don't agree, of course – but every historian or scholar knows that John Kennedy outscored Robert Kennedy on an intellectual level. The fact was, as Jacqueline Kennedy recalled, that whenever his brother was in trouble, Bobby, the campaign manager, was always there to help and protect him: he would have given his life for Jack. Through Bobby, the bad guy, Jack, could play the good guy.

3.8. The Jacqueline Kennedy Factor

Jack Kennedy had initially expressed reservations about having Jackie play a visible role in his national campaign, worried that many voters may be put off by a cultured, sophisticated, educated wife. He bluntly told Jackie he thought she came across as too aristocratic for the average voter's liking: Americans were not ready for someone like her. His opinion hurt Jackie's feelings, but she remained the dutiful politician's wife, continuing to grant interviews and work behind the scenes. Joe Kennedy, however, saw Jackie's appeal and urged his son to exploit her potential impact. It didn't take Jack long to realize his father was right. (1)

Nevertheless, she was not as involved in politics as Eleanor Roosevelt, Rosalyn Carter, or Hillary Clinton. Neither was she a natural campaigner: it took a lot out of her, and it became increasingly obvious that politics and the political process was not something she enjoyed.

Historian Arthur Schlesinger described Jackie thus, "Underneath a veil of lovely inconsequence, she concealed a tremendous awareness, an all-seeing eye, and a ruthless judgment." (2)

And carefully reading of interviews with her by Arthur M. Schlesinger Jr in "Historic Conversations on Life with John F. Kennedy" in 1964 reveal that this extremely bright young woman was not ignorant about the politics of her late husband's era.

She was also, by nature, extremely shy and uncomfortable with people lacking her sophistication and wide-ranging cultural interests and found the endless small talk – and the vulgarity and political hypocrisy – tiresome. Occasionally she rebelled against it all by sulking and even disappearing from billed events.

Nevertheless, by the time JFK was nominated to be his party's standard-bearer, Jackie had campaigned hard in some sixteen states, from New Hampshire to West Virginia, from Tennessee to California, from New York to Wisconsin.

She captivated audiences in ethnic neighborhoods by addressing them in flawless Spanish, French, or Italian. She reduced her wardrobe to three basic dresses, a string of pearls, and a hat.

Given her problematic obstetric history, Jackie reduced her campaign participation in the second trimester of her pregnancy, staying at the Kennedy summer home in Hyannis Port with Caroline. At the same time, her husband attended the 1960 Democratic Convention in Los Angeles. (3)

But Jackie's importance to John Kennedy's campaign should not be underestimated. Always photogenic, mysterious, reserved, and unpredictable, she made an undeniable impact on the American psyche. She was noticed more than any other of the Kennedy women, primarily because she was different. "She wasn't the girl-next-door," and she knew it, and she didn't try to sell herself as one. She defied political tradition by admitting that she rarely cooked and wasn't particularly interested in housekeeping. She was open about the fact that a governess looked after Caroline and that there were other servants in the house as well. She was refreshingly frank, admitting that she had campaigned with her husband because if she hadn't, she never would have seen him. She said she found it unnerving to go downstairs for breakfast and discover a dozen men in rumpled suits sitting around the table smoking cigars and talking campaign strategy. She admitted spending money on clothes, although not the $30,000 per year that Women's Wear Daily claimed she spent, "I couldn't spend that much unless I wore sable underwear," she said.

The International Ladies "Garment Workers" Union contributed $300,000 to JFK's campaign and lobbied the future president to encourage his wife to "buy American." (4)

It didn't help a lot: Jackie kept buying French and spending large sums of money on her wardrobe.

Today she would have been forced to buy American and cheaper, but the 1960s were extraordinary times, a golden age. Now, for more than a decade, we live in very hard times, where the common man has it hard to support his family and doesn't consider the first lady as a queen, and rightly so.

By early spring 1960, Jackie, who had suffered two failed pregnancies and one successful birth in the late 1950s, was again pregnant, with a due date in December. But despite her medical history, she insisted on campaigning for her husband over three weeks in the critical Mountain State. When she made time to visit an elderly man who was a full-time carer for his invalid wife, he gushed, "Now I believe in Santa Claus – Jackie looks like a real queen." She endeared herself to audiences when introducing Jack by saying, "I have to confess, I was born Republican, but you have to have been a Republican to realize how nice it is to be a Democrat."

When Jacqueline Kennedy became First Lady and ordered new glassware for the White House, she insisted on buying from glassworks in West Virginia to boost the state's economy.

A White House press release on May 20, 1961, duly announced the arrival of a "major order of glassware from the Morgantown Glassware Guild, Inc. of West Virginia, thanks to Jackie's knowledge of the Guild's work from her visits in the primary campaign." (5) (6)

Lester David wrote that Jackie remained at home much of the time during the campaign, giving rise to criticism, repeated even now in books and articles, that she disliked the race for office. (7)

I am sure she didn't "dislike" the race for office because who doesn't want to become "the first lady" and enter the history books?

Clara Shirpser, a California political organizer, thought Jackie had lost interest in the campaign, "She was gracious, not friendly. She was one of the hardest campaign wives to get along with that I have ever known in my life. She just liked the privileges and not the responsibilities." (8)

Dave Powers said Jackie had her ideas about campaigning and often carried them out calmly and coolly without consulting the campaign team, "One day in Kenosha, she walked into a busy supermarket and listened to the manager announcing bargain sale-items over a loudspeaker system," said Powers. "She found the microphone, gave the manager a dazzling smile, and asked if she could say a few words. The next voice heard throughout the crowded store was the soft tone of Jacqueline Kennedy, "Just keep on with your shopping while I tell you about my husband, John F. Kennedy," she said. She talked briefly about his service in the Navy and Congress and then closed with, "He cares deeply about the welfare of his country, please vote for him." (9)

Jackie began writing a syndicated newspaper column from home, called "Campaign Wife," first published on September 16, 1960, in which she explained her views on issues from teachers' salaries ("more teachers must be trained and must be paid for") to the critical importance of health care for the elderly, an issue, she pointed out, which directly affected younger people as well. As well as newspaper syndication, her columns were mailed directly to Kennedy's campaign workers throughout America. Meanwhile, Jackie's routine included meeting with well-known American women to discuss the place of the intelligent woman in US culture (10) (11) (12) (13) – until late October, when her doctor ordered her not to add any more campaign appearances to her schedule, because of her pregnancy.

She fulfilled two previously-arranged October engagements – an appearance with JFK at a rally in Spanish Harlem, where she addressed the crowd in Spanish, and a ticker-tape parade through New York City. Afterward, she recorded in her column how glad she was to be spending more time with Caroline, "who" seeing her father's picture on lapel pins and bumpers, is wondering why so many people are talking about him and why he isn't home so often." Perched on the back seat of a convertible, the couple was cheered by an estimated two million people. Some of them broke security cordons and pressed against the car to shake hands with them. Despite her pregnancy, Jackie looked glamorous in a De Givenchy coat and sporting what would become her trademark a pillbox hat. (14)

3.9. The Help of the Media

Theodore White wrote, "Kennedy, who enjoys words and reading, is a Pulitzer Prize winner himself and a one-time reporter, he has enormous respect for those who work with words and those who can write clean prose. He likes newspapermen and likes their company."

White admitted that by the last weeks of the campaign, the forty or fifty national correspondents who had constantly followed Kennedy had become more than a press-corps – they had become his friends and, in some cases, his most devoted admirers. On the tour buses and planes, they sang songs of their composition about Nixon and the Republicans in chorus with the Kennedy staff. They felt that they, too, were marching like soldiers of the Lord to the New Frontier. (1)

Ben Bradlee described the difference between Kennedy and Nixon as the difference between day and night. (2)

According to Edmund Kallina Jr., long before November 8, White found his hero in John F. Kennedy and his villain in Richard M. Nixon. (3)

Nixon wrote in his Memoirs, "Another new political phenomenon was the way, so many reporters in 1960 became caught up in the excitement of Kennedy's campaign and infected with his sense of mission. This bred an unusual mutuality of interest that replaced the more traditional skepticism of the press toward politicians."

William Edward, the Chicago Tribune's veteran political analyst, wrote to Nixon after the election to state that what he called "the staggering extent of slanted reporting, 'was one of the most' if not, the most shameful chapter of the American press in history." (4)

Kallina further wrote that White's growing friendship with the candidate inevitably limited his ability to criticize the man: the author made no effort to maintain any independence, becoming one of the Kennedy team, and seeking Kennedy's approval for his work. White even circulated the manuscript for "The Making of the President 1960" to Robert F. Kennedy, Pierre Salinger, Lou Harris, and Ken O'Donnell, among others, and accepted suggestions from them as to what material should be included and excluded. The Kennedys and their aides decided what history was and what was not. (5)

According to Gary Donaldson, despite the animosity between Nixon and the press, the vast majority of the nation's newspapers endorsed Nixon by as much as 80%. But an official endorsement did not always translate into support on the page. That was true of the New York Times, which officially supported Nixon and had not supported a Democratic presidential candidate since 1944.

But in fact, the primary editors at the New York Times and most of the reporters supported Kennedy.

Conservative journalist Robert Novak wrote that it was easier to gain an audience with the Pope than to see Nixon privately during the 1960 campaign. (6)

According to W. J. Rorabaugh, although most reporters favored Kennedy, 78% of newspapers endorsed Nixon.

Most magazines that did endorsements, including Life, supported Nixon. One of the few major newspapers to endorse Kennedy was the New York Times, which had backed Dewey in 1948 and Eisenhower in 1952 and 1956. After the election, Kennedy parodied a Times advertising slogan by joking, "I got my job through the New York Times." (7) (8)

Arthur Krock wrote in his memoirs that late in October 1960, The New York Times editorially announced support of the Democratic national ticket. It was definite but not enthusiastic, and in the final couple of paragraphs, certain doubts about Kennedy were expressed. Krock was not consulted about the editorial position or shown the text in advance of publication, it being as well known to the Time's management as to the newspaper's readers that he was deeply disturbed by the

Los Angeles platform and some of JFK's campaign extensions of the pledges. Kennedy was naturally gratified by the general fact of a Times endorsement. (9)

Some journalists were mesmerized by JFK's charisma. So what? Should Nixon not himself take some blame for choosing to believe that the press was intrinsically liberal and against him? He certainly pushed the press farther and farther away from his campaign. In "Six Crises," he admitted that he should have catered more to the working press, but history has shown that Nixon and the press were never going to be a love affair. (10)

3.10. The Economic Factor, Three Recessions

Although Kennedy had developed no cohesive economic program – which normally would have made him vulnerable – he only had to point out the failings of the Eisenhower administration on economic issues. And there were many. During the Eisenhower years, there had been two severe recessions, and economic growth had averaged a paltry 2.4% a year. Between 1939 and 1953, the post-depression years in

127

which the Democrats were in office, the economy had grown at 5.8%. Such weak growth had caused the US to lag behind the growth levels of much of the industrialized world. Western Europe and Japan were growing more rapidly, and according to CIA reports, the Soviet Union was growing at a rate near 7%. The US was also facing rising unemployment, increasing inflation, and an alarming trade deficit. A third recession began in April 1960 and lasted throughout the campaign, giving Kennedy's mantra, "Let's get the country moving again," all the more significance. (1)

These economic figures were compiled by the council of Economic Advisors, headed by Walter Heller (See Heller Memo (Oct. 4, 1960) Box 4, Walter Heller papers, JFKL, Boston). (2)

Sorensen wrote, "The recession which started in April 1960, was the third recession in seven years." (3)

Chris Matthews in "Kennedy & Nixon: The Rivalry That Shaped Postwar America" wrote that there were three recessions in eight years – (4) so did Donald C. Lord in his 1977 book on "John F. Kennedy: The Politics of Confrontations and Conciliation." (5)

3.11. The Missile Gap

On the evening of November 7, 1957, when President Eisenhower addressed the nation on the role of science in national security, Jack Kennedy was in Oklahoma City about to address a Jefferson-Davis twenty-five-dollar dinner. Jack accused the administration of concealing the fact that "we are behind in more than simply space satellites – we may also be as much as several years behind in rocket motors, new fuels, jet engines, radar and several kinds of ballistic missiles. There is every indication that the Soviets will next beat us with nuclear-powered planes which we cannot match for years to come." (1) (2) (3)

In a Senate address on the missile gap on August 14, 1958, Kennedy said, "400 years ago the British Crown and people realized with a sense of shock that they had lost Calais forever. Long considered an impregnable symbol of British supremacy in Europe, this last foothold of English power on the Continent was surrendered to the French in 1558."

He continued, "The time has come for the United States to consider a similar charge, if we, too, are to depend on something more than deep convictions and pious motives to guide the State right. For we, too, are about to lose the power foundation that has long stood behind our basic military and diplomatic strategy. And now we are rapidly approaching that dangerous period which General Gavin and others have called the "gap" or the "missile-hag period" – a period, in the words of General Gavin, in which our offensive and defensive missile capabilities will hag so far behind those of the Soviets as to place us in a position of great peril. The most critical years of the gap would appear to be 1960-1964. There is every indication that by 1960, the United States will have lost its Calais, its superiority in striking nuclear power.

The fact of the matter is that during that period when the emphasis was laid upon our economic strength instead of our military strength, we were losing the decisive years when we could have maintained ahead against the Soviet Union in our missile capacity. Then, why can we not realize that the coming years of the gap present us with a peril more deadly than any wartime danger we have known? And most important of all, and most tragically ironic, our nation could have afforded, and can afford now, the steps necessary to close the missile gap. No Pearl Harbor, no Dunkirk, no Calais is sufficient to end us permanently if we but find the will and the way."

Jack Kennedy ended his Senate speech quoting Sir Winston Churchill in a dark period of England's history, "Come then, let us to the task, to the battle and the toil, each to our part, each to our station. Let us go forward together in all parts of the land. There is not a week, nor a day, nor an hour to be lost." (4)

Victor Lasky, in "JFK: the Man and the Myth," wrote that Kennedy's Calais analogy was far-fetched, arguing that by no stretch of the imagination could the position of the British in 1558 be likened to that of the United States in 1958. (5) (6)

Central to Kennedy's charge that Eisenhower and Nixon had weakened the nation was the missile gap issue, which allowed Kennedy to assert his toughness and show that Democratic doctrine on the value of deficit spending was compatible with the building of American strength. The problem, said historian Michael Beschloss, was that there was no missile gap. Eisenhower had access to closely-guarded U-2 and other intelligence that was enough to convince him that, whatever Khrushchev's boasts, there had been no crash Soviet build-up, and the United States was firmly in the lead.

In August 1960, before CIA Director Allen Dulles went to Hyannis Port for the intelligence briefing offered to all presidential candidates, Eisenhower asked him to stress America's commanding military strength. But when Kennedy asked Dulles how the nation stood in the missile race, the CIA man coyly replied that only the Pentagon could properly answer that question. Dulles later explained his caution by saying that, until America enjoyed full satellite coverage of the Soviet Union, a missile gap could not be ruled out.

Nixon later suspected that Dulles had framed his answer to allow Kennedy to keep exploiting the issue – a favor that a victorious Kennedy might remember after the election when pondering whether or not to replace Dulles.

Nixon believed that Dulles was convinced that he, Nixon, would lose and that Kennedy would win. (7) (8)

Of course, Kennedy used the "Missile Gap" to his advantage because it was an easy issue to explain to voters, and it was hard for Nixon to escape the box Eisenhower and Kennedy had put him in.

"Kennedy Defense Study Finds No Evidence of a Missile Gap" read a two-column headline on the front page of the New York Times written by Jack Raymond on February 6, 1961, and published the next day. The story claimed, "Studies made by the Kennedy administration since Inauguration Day show tentatively that no" missile gap" exists in favor of the Soviet Union."

Defense Secretary Robert McNamara had, rather casually, told reporters that there was no difference in the number of operational Soviet and American nuclear missiles. If there was a gap, the United States was ahead. That, of course, was the opposite of what Kennedy had said during the campaign. (9) (10)

In a televised press conference on February 8, 1961 – his third since becoming president – Kennedy said, "No study had been concluded in the Defense Department which would lead to any conclusion at this time as to whether there is a missile gap or not."

Back in his office, he dictated a memo to his national security advisor, McGeorge Bundy, "Could you let me know what progress has been made on the history of the missile gap controversy?" (11) (12) (13)

Retired General US Army Maxwell D. Taylor wrote in "Swords and Plowshares," "Although in the 1960 campaign he (Kennedy) had used the alleged missile gap as a stick with which to beat the Republicans, he liked to look around the Cabinet Room during a military discussion and ask whimsically, "Whoever believed in the missile gap? Only I would raise my hand." (14)

Journalist Joseph Kraft admitted years later that while he wrote campaign speeches for Kennedy about the "gap," he did not personally believe at any time that it existed. (15)

Roswell L. Gilpatric, Deputy Secretary of Defense from 1961 to 1964, said in an Oral History interview for the Kennedy Library that instead of confronting a missile gap in favor of the Soviets, America had a very definite margin of superiority from a qualitative standpoint rather than a quantitative standpoint. (16)

When John Bartlow Martin, a career journalist, and diplomat, asked Robert Kennedy in 1964, "Do you think in your mind there ever was a missile gap?"

Bobby answered, "No."

When Martin asked, "The president didn't think so either? He thought so at the time he was campaigning and concluded after he got in the White House, there hadn't been. Is that right?" Robert Kennedy answered, "That's right, we were and we are way ahead, considerably ahead of the Russians now in missiles." (17)

3.12. The Religious Issue

According to Ted Sorensen, strange as it seems today, the chief obstacle to John F. Kennedy's nomination and election as President of the United States was based not on doubts about his age or experience, nor about his controversial family, his Senate voting record, or even his health. It was based largely on his Roman Catholic faith. (1)

Having a Catholic in the White House seemed revolutionary because of the Protestant roots of American democracy. Al Smith was the only Catholic ever nominated for president, and his defeat by Herbert Hoover in 1928 set a huge challenge for any future Catholic presidential candidate. During Smith's campaign, anti-Catholic zealots distributed ten million handbills, leaflets, and posters with titles such as "Popery in Public Schools," "Convent Life Unveiled," "Convent Horrors" and "Crimes on the Pope."

In campaigning for President Kennedy, they used a different approach – the New York governor tried to ignore the issue, claiming it wasn't worthy of a response. Occasionally, Kennedy also downplayed the issue, hoping it would disappear, but usually, he faced it squarely. Unlike Smith, Kennedy responded deliberately with logical appeals to pride, fairness, and patriotism. He made his arguments earnestly, but above all, he remained unfailingly courteous, patient, and good-tempered. (2) His opponents fell into four categories – the bigots; the liberal intellectuals; anxious Democrats, tired of losing; and many Catholics themselves, including some Democratic Party Leaders.

But Arthur Schlesinger Jr. claimed that Kennedy's religious denomination had been a help rather than a hindrance during his career, "Jack's Catholicism is the very thing that has brought him into prominence, looking as Jack does and talking as he does, a liberal-minded senator from New England who went to Choate School and Harvard and came from a wealthy family. If he were just another Protestant, nobody would pay much attention to him. But being a Catholic, Jack is a controversial figure. That's why everybody is interested in him." (3) (4)

On September 7, 1960, staunch Republican Rev. Norman Vincent Peale presided over a gathering of 150 Protestant ministers at the Mayflower Hotel in Washington, D.C. It launched the "National Conference of Citizens for Religious Freedom." No Catholics, Jews, or liberal Protestants were invited. Out of it came a 2000-word manifesto which, though aimed at keeping Kennedy out of the White House, did a great deal to put him in there. The document stated that Kennedy's religion made him an unsuitable presidential candidate and expressed concern about whether a Catholic president could resist pressures from the Pope. The Peale group had never heard of Charles de Gaulle, Konrad Adenauer, and other world leaders who happened to be Catholic. During the Conference, Peale was overheard saying, "Our American culture is at stake. I don't say it won't survive (Kennedy's election), but it won't be what it was." On being told about the comment, Kennedy quipped, "I would like to think he was complimenting me, but I'm not sure he was." (5) (6) (7)

In "Six Crises," Richard Nixon wrote, "I know that I would never raise the (religion) question and would not tolerate any use of the religious issue by anyone connected with my campaign, directly or indirectly. I did not believe it to be a legitimate issue. There were several questions as to Kennedy's qualifications for the presidency. Still, I never at any time considered his religion in this category." (8)

A different story emerged in 1979 in "John Kennedy: Catholic and Humanist" by Albert J. Menendez. He wrote that Nixon's campaign was ambivalent about religious issues, with Nixon openly denouncing religious prejudice (except against atheists) and urging voters to ignore both candidates' religious affiliation. However,

Menendez also cited a recent (in 1979) study of the campaign, using long-ignored primary source documents, which revealed that Nixon worked behind the scenes with anti-Catholic underground groups led by an obscure former Republican congressman from the Missouri Ozarks, O.K. Armstrong. Armstrong, the documents revealed, rallied fellow Baptist businessmen to bankroll a campaign designed solely to stir up religious animosity against JFK. (9)

By 1960, Billy Graham, the best-known Protestant evangelist in the country and one of Nixon's closest friends, was growing concerned by the prospect of a Catholic in the White House. He was convinced the Democrats were exploiting the religious issue and urged Nixon to name Congressman Walter Judd, a former Protestant missionary, as his vice-presidential choice.

Nixon, by his own account, cautioned Graham "not to make any public endorsement of him or to associate with the campaign in any way," warning that such actions would discredit Graham's ministry. (10)

On September 11, 1960, Nixon answered lengthy questions on Meet the Press, again calling for an end to religion as a campaign topic and challenging Kennedy to join him in refraining from mentioning it. (11) (12)

But by then, Kennedy had decided to tackle the issue of his religion for once and for all the very next day by going into the lion's den.

Joe Kennedy had strongly advised his son against accepting the invitation from a group of Protestant clergymen – the Greater Houston Ministerial Association – to address them on September 12, "Let's not con ourselves," Joe warned, "The only issue is whether a Catholic can be elected president." Jack Kennedy told a reporter, "You have to understand my father. "He'll throw an idea up in the air, and see how it looks, what the reaction is. I discussed the religious issue with my father, but I didn't get his permission on anything before I made that speech, the relationship doesn't work that way." (13)

The candidate also ignored brother Bobby, Lyndon Johnson, Speaker of the House Sam Rayburn, and other close associates who urged against triggering a confrontation.

Even Tim May, the Kennedy advance man, was under severe pressure from the clergymen for an answer to their invitation, was against it after listening to Democratic leaders in Houston. They regarded the ministers as a hostile group. Rayburn summed up the general feeling in the Kennedy camp, warning Jack, "They're mostly Republicans, and they're out to get you." (14)

But Kennedy, a visionary, perhaps, against strong opposition, was determined to nail the religion issue before it took over the campaign.

Together at the Ambassador Hotel in Los Angeles over the weekend before the Monday, September 12 address, he and Ted Sorensen unilaterally shaped the draft of what he would say. A final caution came from Sorensen even as he helped write the text, "We can win or lose the election right there in Houston on Monday night." (15) (16) (17)

Sam Rayburn, watching the televised speech with Ken O'Donnell, said, "You know Mr. O'Donnell, this is the biggest mistake he made in the campaign." Kennedy began that historic campaign speech by pointing out that there were far more critical things to deal with in the 1960 election than religion, "war and hunger and ignorance and despair know no religious barriers."

He went on, "... but because I am a Catholic, and no Catholic has ever been elected President, the real issues in this campaign have been obscured perhaps deliberately, in some quarters less responsible than this. So it is apparently necessary for me to state once again – not what kind of church I believe in, for that should be important only to me, but what kind of America I believe in.

I believe in an America where the separation of church and state is absolute – where no Catholic prelate would tell the president (should he be Catholic) how to act, and no Protestant minister would tell his parishioners for whom to vote; where no church or church school is granted any public funds or political preference, and where no man is denied public office merely because his religion differs from the President who might appoint him or the people who might elect him.

I believe in an America that is officially neither Catholic, Protestant, nor Jewish – where no public official either requests or accepts instructions on public policy from the pope, the National Council of Churches, or any other ecclesiastical source – where no religious body seeks to impose its will directly or indirectly upon the general populace or the public acts of its officials – and where religious liberty is so indivisible that an act against one church is treated as an act against all.

For a while this year, it may be a Catholic against whom the finger of suspicion is pointed. In other years it has been, and may someday be again, a Jew – or a Quaker – or a Unitarian – or a Baptist.

I want a Chief Executive whose public acts are responsible to all groups and obligated to none – who can attend any ceremony, service, or dinner his office may appropriately require of him – and whose fulfillment of his presidential oath is not limited or conditioned by any religious oath, ritual, or obligation.

This is the kind of America I believe in – and this is the kind I fought for in the South Pacific and the kind my brother died for in Europe. No one suggested then that we might have a "divided loyalty," that we did "not believe in liberty," or that we belonged to a disloyal group that threatened the "freedoms" for which our forefathers died.

Of those who differ, I would cite the record of the Catholic Church in such nations as Ireland and France – and the independence of such statesmen as Adenauer and de Gaulle.

But let me stress again that these are my views – for, contrary to common newspaper usages, I am not the Catholic candidate for President, I am the Democratic Party's candidate for President who also happens to be a Catholic. I do not speak for my church on public matters – and the Church does not speak for me."

In the most controversial paragraph of the speech, Kennedy said, "But if the time should ever come – and I do not concede any conflict to be even remotely possible – when my office would require me to either violate my conscience or violate the national interest, then I would resign the office, and I hope any conscientious public servant would do the same."

That passage which the senator had long deliberated over and which he rightly predicted would be criticized was based on Sorensen's talk months earlier, with Bishop Wright.

"But if the election is decided on the basis that forty million Americans lost their chance of being president on the day they were baptized, then it is the whole nation that will be the loser, in the eyes of Catholics and non-Catholics around the world, in the eyes of history and the eyes of our people." (18)

The Kennedy campaign videotaped the Houston event, and some 300 to 400 copies were made for circulation. Cut and edited into one-minute clips, a five-minute version, and a thirty-minute version, the tapes were shown on local television stations in most parts of the country, often repeatedly in close states. (19)

LBJ was not anti-Catholic, though he was mildly suspicious of the religion: it was a foreign, unknown force to him. But in his barnstorming speeches, he took every opportunity to tell "the Wiley story," a true story much embellished, about a Protestant pilot who was killed in the war. After a dramatic pause, Johnson would roar at the crowd, "Did they ask Wiley's religion when he gave his life for his country?" And the crowd would shout back, "No!" After another pause, LBJ would follow with a story about Joseph P. Kennedy Jr., JFK's older brother, "a young Catholic boy," as he put it, who had lost his life in the war. Poking his finger in the air, Johnson would demand in a stage whisper. "Did anyone ask his religion when he gave his life for his country?"

Of course, the crowd would roar back and even louder, "No!" This made an impact, especially in the Protestant south.

Bobby Kennedy, too, raised the religious question in a well-publicized speech at the opening of Kennedy headquarters in Cincinnati. "Did they ask my brother Joe whether he was a Catholic before he was shot down?" he asked. His eyes seemed to fill with tears. The audience burst into applause. (20) (21)

In a New York Times article on September 14, 1960, the Rev. Dr. David A. Poling said that, although religion would continue to be an issue in political campaigns, Senator John F. Kennedy had "lifted himself above the issue" in his campaign for the Presidency. In a news conference, Poling went further, describing the Houston speech the separation of church and state as "magnificent," and praising as "courageous" Kennedy's declaration that he was not afraid of the Roman Catholic Church's ex-communication powers – occasionally used against heads of other nations. (22) (23)

Theodore White said the Houston speech ranked with Lincoln's "House Divided" speech in 1858 as another moment when politics reach up and touch history. (24)

For O'Donnell, it was by far the best speech of the many Kennedy delivered during the campaign – and probably his best. (25)

Ted Sorensen agreed it was the best speech of the campaign and one of the most important in his life, stating that only Kennedy's Inaugural address as president could be said to surpass it in power and eloquence. (26)

My personal favorite is the "Strategy of Peace" speech at the American University Washington D.C., June 10, 1963, because, although religion is a key issue in the world, it has created many holy wars. Therefore peace is, for me, the most important subject in the world – peace at home, in towns, villages, in the streets, and between countries.

Eugene McCarthy didn't approve of the full text of Kennedy's Houston speech. He thought he had gone too far by even agreeing to address the ministers as if they had a right to pass judgment on him. It may have got him elected. I don't think it did.

According to Jack Valenti, "Kennedy came out of the backroom by himself, no aides around him, and strode confidently, but not arrogantly, with an easy stride, to the rostrum. No one was there to guard him. No one was around him. It's as if he said, "Okay, you bastards, you want me, here I am. Take a look at me, and I'm going to come right back at you." "But that simple act of one lonely man ready to take on the hordes, he threw the first punch, and it was about as brilliant a performance as ever, I've witnessed." (27)

Rayburn, who at the beginning of Kennedy's statement was talking about "his biggest mistake in the campaign," watching Kennedy quietly demolish the ministers in the question and answer period on TV, excitedly clapped his hands. He had considered it stupid for the Democrats to nominate a Catholic, but now he said, "That boy's got it! He's gonna make it, that boy. He's eating them blood-raw. This young feller will be a great president." Then he turned to O'Donnell, looking happier and younger, "Get me a bourbon, sonny!" (28)

A study by the Massachusetts Institute of Technology concluded that religion might have cost Kennedy as many as 1.5 million voters – 2.3% of the electorate – and given Nixon the states of California, Kentucky, Oklahoma, and Tennessee. It estimated that 20% of Protestant Democrats and Independents voted against Kennedy for religious reasons. But the same study concluded that Kennedy won the heavily-weighted Catholic states of New York, Connecticut, Illinois, and Pennsylvania, given him a net gain of 22 electoral votes as a direct result of the religious issue. (29) (30) (31) (32)

3.13. Nixon's Mistakes

From the very beginning, Eisenhower had decided that he would let "Dick" Nixon run his campaign in his way. As early as 1956, he had offered Nixon the choice either of a Cabinet post or reappointment to the Vice-Presidency. Nixon chose the latter, but Eisenhower was convinced that Nixon could have made a better run for the presidency from a Cabinet position, telling his closest aides throughout the campaign Nixon as either Secretary of Defense or Secretary of State could have established a winning record of his own. (1)

There were two reasons for holding back the president. First, Nixon needed and wanted to establish his own identity as a candidate. He feared that too great an Eisenhower presence too early would allow Kennedy to label him as someone who had no program of his own but was simply relying on Ike and his coattails.

Second, limiting the use of Eisenhower was an attempt to maximize his impact when he did appease late in the campaign. During the late summer and fall, the president became politically restless in Washington and Gettysburg. He had never liked JFK, whom he referred to as "Little Boy Blue," and he liked his brother even less. (2)

It was not until Saturday, October 29, that a White House aide heard accidentally from a Nixon aide that Nixon now intended to call heavily on the president for the last week's campaigning.

The aide pointed out that the president was not only eager but anxious to help, but he could not be commandeered – he must be informed and requested to help. (3)

Richard Nixon, in his memoirs, said that from the earliest days of the campaign, he had planned to keep Eisenhower in reserve as a political weapon that would be the more powerful for having been sparingly used. They both felt that Ike's appearances in the last two weeks of the campaign might tip the balance to Nixon in some close areas in key states. According to Nixon, Eisenhower fully agreed with Dick's strategy at the outset.

Nixon had lunch with Eisenhower at the White House on October 31 to discuss a specially expanded campaign schedule, which he had suggested undertaking. The night before the luncheon, Pat, Nixon's wife, received a phone call from Mamie Eisenhower (never a great Nixon fan). She was distraught and said that Eisenhower was not up to the strain campaigning might put on his heart. But he was so determined to get out and answer the attacks on his record that she could not dissuade him. She begged Pat to have me make him change his mind without letting him know that she had intervened. "He must never know I called you," she said.

The next morning, Nixon received an urgent call from the White House physician, Major General Howard Snyder. He told the vice-president he could not approve a heavy campaign schedule for the President. Eisenhower was confused when Nixon opened the discussion with half a dozen rather lame reasons for his not carrying out the expanded itinerary. At first, he was hurt, and then he was angry, but Nixon stood by his ground, insisting that he should stick to the original schedule and to the election-eve telecast with Lodge and him. (4) (5) (6)

In "Six Crises," Nixon said that he should have used Eisenhower more in the campaign. (7)

According to Theodore White, the Eisenhower intervention in these last eight days is remembered by all who followed the campaign as crisp, frail, and dramatic. Eisenhower has and retains magic in American politics that is peculiarly his; he makes people happy. Americans watch Eisenhower, and they are happy. (8)

Another disastrous Nixon mistake was his choice of Henry Cabot Lodge as his running mate. Lodge was a poor campaigner who came across on television as arrogant, aristocratic, and out of touch. "If Nixon ever tries to visit Lodge at Beverly," Kennedy joked, "they will not let him in the door." (9) (10)

Lodge, tall and thin, contrasted physically with Nixon. As a Time reporter noted, when Nixon and Lodge appeared together, "He towers above him, making Nixon look slight, hunched and physically unimpressive." At one point, Nixon appeared to be trying to stand on tiptoe to cut down the height difference between the four candidates, of whom Lodge was the least energetic, made the fewest speeches, drew the smallest crowds, and finally attracted the smaller number of voters. (11)

The 1960 Lodge campaign is known for little more than a statement he made in East Harlem on October 12 that Nixon, if elected, would name an African-American to his cabinet. "There should be a Negro in the Cabinet," Lodge told the primarily African-American audience. To make matters worse, Kennedy appeared just a few days later on Meet the Press and, in answer to a question about Lodge's statement, said all jobs should go to the most qualified person. "If the best person is Negro, if he is White if he is of Mexican descent or Irish descent or whatever he may be." Kennedy added, "But I do believe we should make a greater effort to bring Negros into participation in the higher branches of government." (12)

Nixon wrote in "Six Crises" that Lodge should not have promised that there would be a Negro in the Cabinet and should have been slapped down hard for saying so. (13)

Although Nixon had served as Eisenhower's vice president for eight years, their relationship was never a warm one.

On August 24, at an Eisenhower press conference, a reporter asked the president, "What presidential decisions of your administration have the vice-president participated in?" A smiling Eisenhower replied, "If you give me a week, I might think of one," then signaled the end of the conference before follow-up questions could be asked. There was little he could do except apologize to Nixon, which he immediately did, but the damage had been done, and once again, the public could see the strained relationship between Eisenhower and Nixon and also proof how much he must have disliked him. (14) (15)

Nixon, in his memoirs, asserts that Eisenhower had meant, "Ask me at next week's conference," but he immediately knew that it had come out wrong. He called him that afternoon to express his regret. (16)

Columnist Ralph de Toledano wrote that some Democrats agree with the Republicans that Bobby Kennedy is Nixon's secret weapon, but the Republican candidate did not use it. Nor did Nixon ever refer to Joseph P. Kennedy. (17)

In "Six Crises," Nixon said that "the decision not to drag Kennedy's father and other members of his family into the campaign was one for which I take sole responsibility, and for which I have no regrets. Throughout my political career, I have always held that a candidate's public record should be exposed and attached in as hard-hitting a fashion as possible. But his personal life and that of his family are not fair subjects for discussion unless they somehow bear directly on his qualifications for office.

But on page 419, he wrote, "I should have exposed and exploited Joe Kennedy's background..." (18)

Nixon also felt that he should have refused to debate with Kennedy and should have been more "liberal" – particularly on civil rights, as Rockefeller supporters wanted – and been more "conservative" – again, particularly on civil rights, as Goldwater people argued.

He thought he should have personally repudiated Norman Vincent Peale to win more Catholic votes and that he should have made a speech at the end of the campaign attacking Kennedy for his systematic exploitation of the religious issue to win more Protestants votes.

Nixon found that he should have catered more to the working press. "I should have complained directly to the Republican publishers, as Kennedy did, whenever the reporters appeared to be biased against me." (19)

Nixon forgets that there was never a love story between him and the press. He was always uneasy with reporters. He disliked the press corps, and they disliked him until the very end of his political career with Watergate on August 9, 1974. He estimated that 80% of the working reporters in Washington D.C. disliked him. Remember his famous quote in 1962 when he announced his first retirement from politics, "You won't have Nixon to kick around anymore."

He never had Kennedy's natural charm and wit; he was always "tricky Dicky."

Benjamin Bradlee wrote that Richard Nixon attracted at least as many reporters, including himself, as those who spent most of their time covering Kennedy. The difference was the difference between night and day. In the first place, the men around Nixon, except Bob Finch, the campaign director, Herb Klein, then as later in charge of Nixon's press, and New York political operator Lem Hall, cordially disliked the press and simply spoke a different language, where the men around Kennedy genuinely liked the press and spoke the same language. (20)

Years later, Robert Dallek observed, "It is difficult to believe that voters would want to gamble again on someone with the sort of severe health problems Kennedy suffered. But given the way Nixon performed in the White House, how many people would retrospectively offer him their vote for 1960, even knowing of Kennedy's health problems?" (21)

I think Jack Kennedy would have won by a landslide.

3.14. What Was the Vote Margin in the 1960 Presidential Election?

1. Kennedy 34,221,463 (49.7%) – Nixon 34,108,582 (49.6%) – Others: 502,773 (0.7%) (1)

Vote Margin 112,881

(White used throughout his book the above tabulation of the Associated Press December 17th, 1960)

After the Hawaii Recount

138

Kennedy 34,221,531 – Nixon 34,108,474

Vote Margin 113,057

The Congressional Quarterly sets Kennedy's margin was 111,803 votes.

The official summary of the Republican National Committee sets Kennedy's margin at 112,801 votes.

A "semiofficial-official" tabulation released by the Clerk of the House of Representatives put Kennedy's margin at 119,450.

2. Kennedy 34,227,096 – Nixon 34,107,646 (2)

    Vote Margin 119,450

Electoral College: Kennedy 303 – Nixon 219 – Others 15

3. Kennedy 34,221,000 – Nixon 34,108,000 (3)

Vote Margin 113,000

4. Kennedy 34,226,731 (49.7%) – Nixon 34,108,157 (49.5%) (4)

Vote Margin 118,574

Others: 503,330

Electoral College: Kennedy 303 – Nixon 219

5. Kennedy 34,226,731 – Nixon 34,108,157 (5)

Vote Margin 118,574

Electoral College Vote: Kennedy 303 – Nixon 219

6. Kennedy 34,226,731 – Nixon 34,108,157 (6)

Vote Margin 118,574

Electoral College: Kennedy 303 – Nixon 219

7. Kennedy 34,227,496 – Nixon 34,107,646 (7)

Vote Margin 119,850

Electoral College Vote: Kennedy 303 – Nixon 219

8. Kennedy 34,221,344 (49.72%) – Nixon 34,106,671 (49.55%) (8)

Vote Margin 114,673

Electoral College: Kennedy 303 – Nixon 219 – Byrd 15

9. Kennedy 34,220,984 (49.72%) – Nixon 34,108,157 (49.55%) (9)

Vote Margin 112,827

Others 503,341

Source: Benjamin Guthrie and Ralph Roberts – statistics of the Presidential and Congressional Election of November 8, 1960 (Washington DC (Washington DC) USGPO 1961, p. 50-51

Source: Theodore H. White – The Making of the President 1960 – pages 152

10. Kennedy 34,220,984 – Nixon 34,108,157 (10)

Vote Margin 112,827

Electoral College: Kennedy 303 – Nixon 219

No Source

11. Kennedy 34,221,349 (49.7%) – Nixon 34,108,546 (49.6%) (11)

Vote Margin 112,803

Others: 503,348

Electoral Vote: Kennedy 303 – Nixon 219
Sources: Official returns from "Dave Leip's Atlas of US Presidential elections." And Website: uselectionatlas.org/except Texas returns, which are online at the website of the Texas Secretary of State, www.sos.state.tx.us/elections/historical/index.shtml
12. Kennedy 34.2 million (49.7%) – Nixon 49.5% (12)
<u>Vote Margin</u> 118,600
Electoral college vote: Kennedy 303 – Nixon 220 – unpledged electors 14
13. Kennedy 34,220,984 (49.72%) – Nixon 34,108,157 (49.55%) (13)
"Independent" slates 610,409 (0.42%)
<u>Vote Margin</u> 112,827
Electoral College Kennedy 303 (56.4%); Nixon 219 (40.8%); Harry Byrd 15 (2.8%)

3.15. Conclusion

On December 26, 2006, I was at Dan Fenn's home in Lexington, Boston, Massachusetts. That night I predicted that Barack Obama would be the next president of the United States – the first black president.

I saw it as a rendezvous with a history like the election of John Fitzgerald Kennedy in 1960, the first Catholic president and the youngest ever to be elected to the highest office.

A lot has been written over many decades about what got Kennedy over the top, winning by such a narrow 0.2% margin and by just 118,574 votes (plus or minus...). Was it Bobby as campaign manager, choosing LBJ as his running mate, or the TV debates in which Richard Nixon said in retrospect he should never have taken on Kennedy? Was it the three recessions during the Eisenhower presidency, the religious issue, the Mrs. Coretta King call, the Jacqueline Kennedy appeal, or the help he got from the media and his father's money? And what about Khrushchev, who in the Vienna summit joked with Kennedy that "we had cast the deciding ballot in his election to the presidency over that son-of-a-bitch Richard Nixon?" When Kennedy asked Khrushchev what he meant, he explained that "by waiting to release the U-2 pilot Gary Powers until after the election, we kept Nixon from being able to claim that he could deal with the Russians." Khrushchev boasted that "Our play made a difference of at least half a million votes which gave Kennedy the edge he needed."

Above all, I think that Jack Kennedy made some crucial and important decisions at the end of the campaign – decisions he made against the advice of some of his closest advisors, such as his father, his brother Bobby and Kenny O'Donnell, and his whole campaign staff. He thereby proved that he was totally in charge, that he made the important decisions himself.

Firstly, on September 12, 1960, the appearance he made before a group of Protestant ministers in Houston, Texas, where he confronted them head-on over religion. When he asked O'Donnell what he thought about it, O'Donnell said, "I think it would be a great mistake if you have to meet the religious issue. Houston is not the place to do it." Kennedy went into the bathroom to shave; when he finished shaving, he came back and said to O'Donnell, "Tell them I'm going to do it. This is as good a time as any to get it over with. I've got to face it sooner or later."

Secondly, on Wednesday, October 19, 1960, when Martin Luther King was jailed for picketing an Atlanta department store, and Kennedy made the decision to call Mrs. Coretta King. Nixon, on the other hand, failed to call her. These were defining moments in the 1960 campaign: Kennedy's religion prevented him from winning a decisive victory, but he mastered the art of television as demonstrated by the historic head-to-head debates and in the Houston speech.

Kennedy's journey to the White House involved a mixture of all those factors: all of them contributed in their way along the road of victory and to John F. Kennedy's extraordinary rendezvous with history.

*In the West Virginia primary, coal miners near Mullens, whom Kennedy joined
while they awaited a change of shift, were cool at first, some refusing to shake his
hand. But he won them over discussing their working conditions and job security.
(Copyright: JFK Library)*

Flyers of the Presidential campaign in 1960.
(Copyright: personal collection of Eddy Neyts)

Harpo Marx campaigning for JFK on the 1960 Presidential Election.

"You might say Dad was quite a fan of JFK?" comment from the book "Son of Harpo speaks!" by Bill Marx.

(Copyright: JFK Library + permission of Bill Marx (son of Harpo Marx))

John F. Kennedy and his wife Jacqueline in a ticker tape parade in Manhattan, New York City during the presidential campaign of October 1960. This was Jackie's last campaign appearance with her husband
(Copyright: Getty Images)

John F. Kennedy – President, and Lyndon B. Johnson – Vice President.
(Copyright: JFK Library)

Chapter 4: JFK And Cuba – From The Bay Of Pigs To The Cuban Missile Crisis

"There is an old saying that victory has a hundred fathers, and defeat is an orphan. I'm the responsible officer of the government."

- **April 21, 1961 JFK to Journalist Sander Vanocur**

"I guess this is the week I earn my salary."

- **JFK – Remark Made during the Cuban Missile Crisis**

"The Preservation of work & peace should be our joint concerns."

- **Khrushchev October 26, 1962 – Letter To JFK**

"These brass hats have one great advantage in their favor. If we listen to them and do what they want us to do, none of us will be alive to tell them that they were wrong."

- **JFK (to O'Donnell)**

4.1. The Bay of Pigs: A Brilliant Disaster

The ultimate objective of the American-sponsored invasion of Cuba at the site called the Bay of Pigs (Bahia de Cochinos) was the overthrow of the government of Fidel Castro. (1)

In the spring of 1961, the Kennedy administration had something of the Midas touch – they could do anything they wanted, and it would turn to gold. "Those were the days when we thought we were succeeding because of all the stories about how hard everybody was working," Bobby Kennedy said. (2)

On March 17, 1960, the then President Dwight Eisenhower directed the CIA to bring together Cuban exiles into a unified political opposition to Fidel Castro. This presidential directive resulted in the CIA's establishment of a secret training camp and airbase in Guatemala.

Precisely how much CIA Director Allen Dulles had told Kennedy during a briefing on July 23, 1960, at Hyannis Port on Cape Cod will probably never be known. The men met for two and a quarter hours at Kennedy's summer home. (4) But Nixon, in his book "Six Crises" in 1962, wrote, "I could hardly believe my eyes. As early as September 23, 1960, Kennedy had given an exclusive statement to the Scripps-Howard American newspaper chain in which he said, "The forces fighting for freedom in exile and the mountains of Cuba should be sustained and assisted." On October 20, 1960, he said, "We must attempt to strengthen the non-Batista democratic anti-Castro forces in exile, and in Cuba itself, who offer eventual hope of overthrowing Castro. Thus far, these fighters for freedom have had virtually no support from our government."

Nixon asked Fred Seaton, a senior aide, to call the White House at once on the secure line to find out whether or not Dulles had briefed Kennedy on the fact that for months the CIA had not only been supporting and assisting but training Cuban exiles for the ultimate purpose of supporting an invasion of Cuba itself.

Seaton reported back that Kennedy had been briefed on the operation. "For the first time, and only one time in the campaign, I got mad at Kennedy personally," said Nixon. (3)

But on March 20, 1962, the White House denied that Kennedy had been told about the secret plans before the election. Dulles backed up Kennedy and said there had been an honest misunderstanding by Nixon.

Since there was no "invasion" plans in July 1960 – only plans for guerrilla infiltrations and airdrops – Kennedy probably did not learn of major military plans against Cuba until Dulles and Bissell briefed him in Palm Beach after his election. (4)

On November 17, 1960, two weeks after the election, during a briefing conducted by Dulles, President-elect Kennedy was told of the existence of the Cuban force in Guatemala. And in a second briefing, on November 29, Dulles told the president-elect details of an overall plan for guerrilla action in Cuba. He stated that a force of between 600 and 750 men would arrive in the Trinidad area, on Cuba's Southern coast, and that the force, aided by airstrikes against the Cuban Air Force flown from bases in Nicaragua, would make its way from the beach into the Escambray Mountains. (1)

On November 27, the president-elect received an extensive briefing from CIA Director Dulles on the covert campaign. Eisenhower repeatedly told aides that he hoped Kennedy would go ahead with the invasion plans. In two meetings with Kennedy on December 6 and January 19, he emphasized the importance of ousting Castro. (5)

Allen Dulles told the President, who had his doubts about the operation, "Mr. President, I stood at this very desk and told President Eisenhower, concerning a similar operation in Guatemala, "I believe it will work," and I say to you now Mr. President, that the prospects for this plan are even better than our prospects were in Guatemala." (6)

Eisenhower informed Kennedy on November 29, 1960, of the existence of the army in exile in Guatemala. But at no time was Kennedy ever advised that the troops were being trained in conventional warfare, that morale among the troops was so bad that the CIA had to suppress a mutiny, or that the final plan for assault was full of obvious risks. (7)

At the White House meeting on January 19, 1961, President Eisenhower told Kennedy that "it is the policy of this government to help the Cuban exiles to the utmost. The invasion should be "continued and accelerated."

A year earlier, in January 1960, the Eisenhower administration had made the top-secret decision to overthrow Castro. By the following March, the CIA had developed a plan inspired by and based upon a successful coup in Guatemala in 1954. (8)

On October 30, 1960, Clemente Marroquin Rojas, a journalist well-known in Guatemala and director of the newspaper La Hora, published a story disclosing that the CIA had built a heavily guarded $1 million base near Retalhulen to train Cuban counter-revolutionaries for landing in Cuba. American media ignored the disclosure. Still, at about the same time, Dr. Ronald Hilton, director of the Institute for Hispanic-American studies at Stanford University, visited Guatemala and heard that the existence and purpose of the base were "common knowledge." His discovery found its way into an editorial in the November 19, 1960 issue of the political weekly The Nation, headlined, "Are we training Cuban Guerrillas?" (9)

On January 3, 1961, the United States government announced a complete break of diplomatic relations with Cuba. According to US Secretary of State Dean Rusk, Americans at first wanted to work with Castro. Indeed there is some classic television footage of Castro walking out of the then Vice President Richard Nixon's office with Nixon putting his arm around Castro and declaring, "We're going to work with this man."

Kennedy and Rusk were asked through Rusk's predecessor Christian Herter if they wished to advise Eisenhower to break relations with Cuba, which they chose not to. (10)

A week later, Tuesday, January 10, 1961, a New York Times front-page headline revealed, "The US Helps Train an Anti-Castro Force at Guatemalan Air-Ground Base." Another headline declared, "Clark with Cuba Feared Installations Built With American Aid." Clark Clifford was a Kennedy confidante. (11)

On January 22, two days after Kennedy's inauguration, Allen Dulles and US army General Lyman Lemnitzer, Chairman of the Joint Chiefs of Staff, outlined the project to the leading members of the new administration, among them Dean Rusk, US Defense Secretary Robert McNamara, and Robert Kennedy. Lemnitzer tried to renew the discussion of alternatives ranging from minimum to maximum US involvement. Six days later, President Kennedy convened his first White House meeting on the plan. He was wary and reserved in his reaction. (12)

Schlesinger, just days after returning from Latin America, was summoned to a meeting with the President in the Cabinet Room on March 11, 1961. "An intimidating group sat around the table," recalled Schlesinger. Also, there were Rusk, McNamara, the director of the CIA, three joint chiefs resplendent in uniforms and decorations, the Assistant Secretary of State for Inter-American Affairs, and the chairman of the Latin American Task Force. Schlesinger shrank into a chair at the far end of the table and listened in silence.

CIA Director Dulles warned the meeting that America had a disposal problem, "If we have to take these men out of Guatemala, we will have to transfer them to the United States, and we can't have them wandering around the country telling everyone what they have been doing." Then CIA officer Richard Bissell presented a Bay of Pigs plan, code-named Operation Trinidad. The Trinidad site had several advantages – it was far from Castro's known troop locations, it permitted reversion to guerrilla operations in the Escambray Mountains if the invasion failed, and the local population had shown past sympathy toward anti-Castro guerrillas.

But Kennedy opposed the plan as "too spectacular." He did not want a big amphibious invasion in the manner of the Second World War. He wanted a "quiet" landing at night, and he insisted that the plans be drawn up based on no United States military intervention – a stipulation to which no one at the table objected. (13) (14)

Only nine days before the landing, the Council's president, Dr. José Miro Cardona, told the press in Miami that an uprising against Castro was "imminent." And the very next day, he appealed to Cubans still in their homeland to take up arms against the dictator. The only information Castro didn't have by then was the exact time and place of the invasion. JFK was livid, according to his White House press secretary Pierre Salinger. Kennedy told Salinger a week before the invasion, "I can't believe what I'm reading! Castro doesn't need agents over here. All he has to do is read our papers. It's all laid out for him." (15)

At a press conference, April 12, 1961, Kennedy was asked if a decision had been reached on how far America would be willing to go in helping an anti-Castro uprising against the invasion of Cuba? JFK answered, "I want to say that there will not be under any conditions an intervention in Cuba by US Armed Forces. This government will do everything it possibly can, and I think it can meet its responsibilities to make sure there are no Americans involved in any actions inside Cuba. The basic issue in Cuba is not one between the US and Cuba. It's between the Cubans themselves." (16)

For the next three days, the CIA planners canvassed alternative landing sites, coming up with three new possibilities, of which the most likely was about 100 miles west of Trinidad in the Zapata area around Cochinos Bay, the Bay of Pigs. (13) Michael O'Brien, in his book "John F. Kennedy: A Biography," remarked that at the meeting on March 15, 1961, nobody questioned the extraordinary fact that in only a few days, Bissell had made huge changes in the plan. (17)

The Kennedy team was impressed when they should have been incredulous. The Zapata plan had been prepared so quickly that the Joint Chiefs could give it only a cursory evaluation. Nonetheless, they endorsed the Zapata plan as the best alternative, never indicating at the meeting that they still preferred the Trinidad plan. Most of Kennedy's advisors supported the invasion, and the president himself thought that the operation had already received the scrutiny and blessing of his predecessor. In reality, Eisenhower had only approved the training of Cuban paramilitaries and had not given the green light for a specific attack.

On February 11, 1961, Arthur Schlesinger had sent JFK a warning about the international consequences of a U.S. sponsored attack on Cuba, "The result would be a wave of massive protest, agitation and sabotage throughout Latin America, Europe, Asia, Africa, Canada and of certain quarters in the United States." (18)

On March 31, 1961, Undersecretary of State Chester Bowles – who opposed the plan – told Rusk, "If the operation appears to be a failure in its early stages, the pressure on us to scrap our self-restricted direct involvement will be difficult to resist." He added, "The danger is that a failure would greatly enhance Castro's prestige and strength." And Bowles saw the odds of failure as two to one. He thought it better to scrap the invasion and live with Castro's regime. (19)

Rusk wrote in his memoirs, "I myself did not serve President Kennedy very well. Personally, I was skeptical about the Bay of Pigs from the beginning. But I never expressed my doubts explicitly in our planning sessions. I should have made my opposition clear in the meetings themselves because he was under pressure from those who wanted to proceed." (20)

The former secretary of State Dean Acheson had warned Kennedy in person that it was not necessary to call in Price Waterhouse (the accounting firm) to discover that fifteen hundred Cubans weren't as good as twenty-five thousand Cubans. "It seemed that this was a disastrous idea." Acheson concluded, "It was a completely unthoughtful irresponsible thing to do." (21)

On March 29, 1961, Senator J. William Fulbright, with the assistance of Pat Hilt, a member of the foreign relations Committee staff, wrote a memorandum in which he argued that there were two possible policies toward Cuba: overthrow, or toleration and isolation. (22) (23)

On March 30, 1961, Fulbright hitched a ride with the President aboard Air Force One as Kennedy headed to Palm Beach for a long Easter Weekend. On the plane, he handed over his memorandum.

Cuba, Fulbright said, would become for the United States what Hungary was for the Soviets in 1956 – a propaganda disaster. To conceal U.S. involvement was impossible, and the invasion would violate several US treaties and laws. Better to liberate and isolate Castro, who was a "thorn in the flesh," but not a "dagger in the heart." (24)

Historian Arthur Schlesinger, who had been appointed special assistant to Kennedy, described it as "a brilliant memorandum." Yet the President returned from Palm Beach more militant than when he had left. But he did ask Fulbright to attend a climactic meeting on April 4, 1961. (25)

Present at this last major meeting on the invasion plan were: Dean Rusk; Defense Secretary Robert S. McNamara, General Lyman L. Lemnitzer, Treasury Secretary Douglas Dillon; Allen Dulles, Richard Bissell; National Security Advisor McGeorge Bundy; Thomas Mann, US State Department Latin America specialist; Adolf A. Berle, head of an interdepartmental task force on Latin American affairs; Richard Goodwin, speechwriter, and aide to Kennedy; Arthur M. Schlesinger and William Fulbright. Much has been written about the objections raised by Senator Fulbright. Some people feel he deliberately said little during the conference, waiting instead until he had the President's ear. At that April 4 gathering, the president went from man to man and put the question to each one: except for Fulbright, not a dissenting voice was raised. According to Malcolm E. Smith, author of "John F. Kennedy's 13 Greatest Mistakes in the White House," the vote for the invasion was unanimous.

But still, Kennedy hesitated. He was young, he was wholly inexperienced in these matters, and some say he had had strong doubts about the operation from the beginning. Now he was torn between two opposite points of view – to invade or not to invade. In his quandary, he made a fatal mistake: he tried to straddle both horses and fell between them. He gave grudging consent for the operation, but he imposed ruinous conditions – and once again, still vacillating and indecisive, he reserved the right to cancel the invasion at the last minute. (26)

C. Douglas Dillon said later that Kennedy's only weakness – a big one – was inexperience. But the president was a quick learner, and he never made the same mistake twice. "The Bay of Pigs," says Dillon, "I laid to inexperience rather than being too interventionist. This was a plan that had been set up earlier during the Eisenhower administration without any commitment to carry it out. Still, it was on the table so it could be carried out." Dillon thought that was one of the main mistakes President Kennedy made. (27)

On April 10, Schlesinger wrote to Kennedy, arguing that the operational planning for the invasion was much further advanced than the political, diplomatic, and economic planning, which should ideally accompany it. He warned that the Cuban operation could sully Kennedy's excellent start in conducting foreign relations. (28)

On Thursday, April 7, 1961, in the usual Cuba meeting, Schlesinger and Goodwin tried once more to reverse the decision, but Bundy and Rostow discouraged their efforts. At the end of the afternoon, Schlesinger went to see the President. It was apparent that he had made his decision and was not likely to reverse it. Kennedy felt he had pared down the operation from an invasion to a mass infiltration. "If we have to get rid of those 800 men, it is much better to dump them in Cuba than in the United States." (29)

April 5 was the new date for the invasion. Later it was postponed to April 10 and finally to April 17. (30)

In a communiqué issued in Havana on Saturday, April 15, 1961, Cuban Prime Minister Fidel Castro announced that at six o'clock that morning, United States B-26 bombers had simultaneously bombed several Cuban cities. The air assault – actually carried out from a secret CIA airbase in Nicaragua – had begun.

In New York, the cover story issued by Miro Cardona, president of the Cuban Revolutionary Council, contended that the bombing of Cuban airfields that morning had been conducted by "certain members of the Cuban Air Force," a claim the Revolutionary Council had encouraged.

On the afternoon of April 15, 1961, the UN General Assembly began considering the conflict developing in Cuba. Raul Roa, Castro's UN delegate, accused the US of aggression against Cuba. At the same time, the Soviet representative, Valerian A. Zorin, warned that "Cuba has many friends in the world who are ready to come to its aid, including the Soviet Union."

America's ambassador to the UN, Adlai Stevenson, poorly briefed, believed the cover story. He defended the American position, replying that the air raids had been carried out by defectors from the Cuban Air force who had subsequently landed in Florida and had asked for political asylum. When this was quickly proven false, Stevenson was embarrassed and furious. (31)

By Sunday afternoon, April 16, 1961, six B26 planes painted with Cuban insignia had already destroyed almost half of Castro's air force. (32)

On Monday at Glen Ora, the phone next to the President's bed rang at 5.15 a.m. It was Rusk. The invasion of Cuba had begun thirty minutes before, he said. More than 1400 commandos motored in small boats to the beaches at Bahia de Cochinos. The invaders immediately tangled with Castro's militia. Fighting ferociously, the brigade nonetheless failed to establish a beachhead. Kennedy turned down CIA appeals to dispatch planes from the nearby USS Essex. Still, he did permit some jets to provide air cover for a new B26 attack from Nicaragua. Manned this time by American CIA pilots, the B26s arrived an hour after the jets had come and gone.

Cuban aircraft downed the B26s, killing four Americans. With Castro's boasting that the mercenaries had been foiled, the final toll was grim: an estimated 114 of the exile brigade 2506 drowned or were killed in action, and 1,189 were captured, tried and imprisoned. (33) (34) (35)

The failure became evident by Tuesday afternoon, April 18, 1961, and Mac Bundy told Kennedy that "the situation in Cuba is not a bit good. The Cuban armed forces are stronger, the popular response is weaker, and our tactical position is feebler than we had hoped." But Kennedy had no intention of sending in a US rescue mission, however bad the situation might be. He later told his special assistant Dave Powers "They couldn't believe that a new President like me wouldn't panic and try to save his face. Well, they had figured all wrong." (36)

At the cabinet meeting Thursday, April 20, and an NSC meeting on Saturday, April 22, Bowles took notes and remembers these meetings as "grim as any meeting I can remember in all my experience in government." President Kennedy looked shattered, Bowles observed. (37)

A Presidential breakfast on Friday morning, April 21, 1961, to prepare for the president's press conference on Cuba was attended by Dean Rusk, Pierre Salinger, Mac Bundy, Dick Goodwin, and Ted Sorensen, a key Kennedy speechwriter and aide. Kennedy said rather pointedly, "There is only one person in the clear in Cuba, and that's Bill Fullbright – and he probably would have been converted if he had attended more of the meetings." When Mac Bundy reminded him that Schlesinger too had been opposed to the invasion, Kennedy concurred, "Oh sure," the president said, in a typical flash of sardonic humor, "Arthur wrote me a memorandum that will look pretty good, when he gets around to writing his book on my administration – only he better not publish that memorandum while I'm still alive!" He added, "and I know what the book will be called: Kennedy: The Only Years." (38)

That same day Kennedy set up a task force to study "military and paramilitary guerrilla and anti-guerrilla activities which felt short of outright war. The task force chairman was General Maxwell Taylor, a World War II hero whose 1960 book "The Uncertain trumpet," said Kennedy, "reoriented our whole strategic thinking." (39)

Ex-president Eisenhower visited JFK at the presidential mountain retreat, Camp David, on April 22. Kennedy, who had also called in Nixon, did not want the Republicans to start launching uninformed attacks on his failure. Ike found him "very frank but also very subdued and more than a little bewildered."

Kennedy told Ike, "No one knows how tough this job is until after he has been in it a few months" Eisenhower replied, "Mr. President, if you will forgive me, I think I mentioned that to you three months ago." Kennedy admitted, "I certainly have learned a lot since." (40)

Privately Eisenhower told friends, "Any second lieutenant with combat experience could have done better." (41)

When Eisenhower was asked to evaluate Kennedy's first hundred days, he generously sidestepped criticism by saying that "this Administration is preoccupied with the most important question there is in the world "at the moment." He also declined to say whether he thought American troops should be sent to Laos. Privately, however, Eisenhower showed his contempt. As he did so often, he confined his impressions to paper. Speculating that there would be a public outcry, "if the whole story ever becomes known to the American people," he concluded that "it could be called a "Profile in Timidity and Indecision." (42)

Meanwhile, Kennedy was asking himself how he could have been "so off base." He said, "All my life, I have known better than to depend on the experts. How could I have been so stupid as to let them go ahead? "He vowed that professional military advisors would never again over-awe him. (43)

Georges Clemenceau, a French Statesman, said in 1886 that War is much too serious a matter to be entrusted to the military.

General Maxwell Taylor, appointed by President Kennedy to lead an inquiry into the failure of the invasion, observed that an amphibious landing against a hostile enemy shore was one of the most difficult of all military manoeuvres, requiring surprise, air superiority and exceptionally good logistics. "Our government had expected that an amphibious landing on a hostile shore by amateur soldiers directed by US amateurs could succeed under the circumstances of the landing at the Bay of Pigs," he declared, adding, "In all the staff schools of the Armed Services we are taught that such an operation is the most complicated and difficult operation in War." (44)

Walt Rostow, Kennedy's deputy national security advisor, told journalist Peter Wyden that the Bay of Pigs invasion was the most screwed-up operation there has ever been.

Richard Bissell first spoke up in his defense in an interview with The Washington Evening Star in 1965. He insisted that the venture failed "because of lack of control of the air," and said, "if we had been able to dump five times the tonnage of bombs on Castro's airfields, we would have had a damned good chance." He told Wyden that the smallness of the expedition's air force was the plan's "worst mistake." He said that the impossibility of the guerrilla option had simply not been "thought through," and the lack of contingency planning was "sloppy."

Mac Bundy agreed in 1977 that the air strength was not only too small, it was much too small, but he pointed out that the planners said nothing about it. (45)

Bob McNamara admitted that although President Kennedy assumed full responsibility for the decision, the fault lay not with the President, in McNamara's opinion, but rather with his senior advisors- McNamara himself included. Not a single advisor to the President, other than Senator Fulbright, recommended against the operation. McNamara claims that several factors influenced it. First and perhaps most important, most of the senior advisors had been in office less than ninety days. (46)

I'm very sorry to contradict McNamara's excuse as bullshit because they were called "the best and the brightest."

Dean Rusk said that President Kennedy later took the view that had there been more newspaper discussion, it might have saved him the decision. The New York Times had a pretty full account of the story but did not run it at the request of President Kennedy. Rusk later said, "I think that, had the New York Times run this story, it might have led to the decision not to go ahead with the operation." An interesting insight into the relationship between secret operations on the one side and press disclosures on the other. (47)

Can you imagine the Press reacting like this in 2022? They were pussies in those days.

A six-month secret review by Lyman Kirkpatrick, the CIA inspector general, and executive director, blamed the Bay of Pigs failure largely on the CIA and confirmed Kennedy's conviction that both Dulles and Bissell would have to resign. "Under a parliamentary system of government, it is I who would be leaving office," Kennedy told Dulles. "But under our system, it is you who must go." Although Dulles and Bissell blamed the cancelled airstrikes for the defeat, Kirkpatrick concluded that this was not the chief cause of failure, as a better-conceived plan would never have confronted Kennedy with such a decision in the first place. Kirkpatrick saw "the root cause in the CIA's poor planning, organization, staffing, and management." (48)

Grayston Lynch, one of the two CIA officers who accompanied Brigade 2506 despite presidential orders that no US citizen participate, blamed Rusk for rejecting the original Trinidad invasion plan, which would have allowed a guerrilla war and for insisting on an impossible night-time landing. Most galling to Lynch and others, especially Cuban exiles, was Kennedy's decision to call off the second round of airstrikes against Cuba, a choice also motivated by political- and erroneous-calculations.

Lynch completely exonerates the CIA and the Joint Chiefs of Staff and never takes Kennedy's political caution seriously, concluding simply that "a successful invasion could have won the approval and acclaim of the entire free world." (49)

An important oral interview, one overlooked by historians, writes Hersh, was recorded in the early 1970s at the US Naval Institute. Admiral Robert L. Dennison, commander in chief of the US Navy forces in the Atlantic, told of being ordered by the Pentagon to have his destroyers set up a haven fifteen miles off the coast of the Bay of Pigs and wait there for possible survivors of the debacle. The orders, as relayed by General Lyman L. Lemnitzer, not only instructed Dennison what to do but how to do it. "It was a tactical order," Dennison recounted. "I wouldn't have sent the thing to a captain. So I called up Lemnitzer on the scrambler phone and said, "I've gotten a good many orders in my life, but this is a strange one. This is the first order I ever got from somebody who found it necessary to interpret his orders." Lemnitzer said, "Where did you get this directive?" I said, "You did." He said, "No, I didn't send it. That order was written at 1600 Pennsylvania Avenue." (50) (51)

That's what I call a perfect example of science fiction history.

The President's determination to get the prisoners released, at any cost to his pride, led him into one of the most ill-advised moves in his career.

In May 1961, he quickly accepted an offer from Castro to release the survivors of the Cuban relief brigade in return for five hundred tractors or bulldozers or $28,000,000.

156

President Kennedy talked with Milton Eisenhower, younger brother of Eisenhower, Eleanor Roosevelt, Walter Reuther, and Cardinal Cushing, among others, into organizing a "Tractors for Freedom Committee." Still, the vulnerable project was soon scuppered by political controversy. The Republicans denounced the idea of bartering with Castro for human lives. James B. Donovan, a New York lawyer, negotiated with Castro, but talks dragged on into the fall of 1962 – the tense period of the Cuban Missile Crisis when Bobby Kennedy and Donovan persisted in seeking to get the prisoners freed before Christmas. Finally, in December 1962, Castro agreed to exchange the survivors for $53m-worth of food and medicines. Then, only a few days before the Christmas Eve deadline that Bobby was eager to meet, Castro demanded another $2.9m in cash, which he said was owed to him by the Cuban refugee organizations in the US as payment for sick and wounded Bay of Pigs veterans already released.

In desperation, Bobby hastily raised $1.9m in a hurry with the help of General Lucius D. Clay and, at the suggestion of the President, asked the Archbishop of Boston, Cardinal Cushing, a prolific fundraiser, to muster the other million. (52)

Bobby Kennedy, reminiscence on the Bay of Pigs episode in 1964, said that it drastically altered the President's approach to government – and posited that it might have been the best thing that happened to the administration. (53)

In later months, Joe Kennedy Sr. would tell his son that, in its perverse way, the Bay of Pigs was not a misfortune but a benefit – although Schlesinger doubted whether Jack Kennedy fully believed this. (54)

Mark J. White said that Cuba was emblematic of the Kennedy presidency in that it so clearly demonstrated JFK's skills as a crisis manager and his shortcomings as a crisis preventer. (55)

Would he have been a crisis preventer if he had not ordered the Bay of Pigs invasion? There were tensions before Kennedy became President. The Russians were aware of that, and who can state that without the Bay of Pigs invasion, in which Kennedy wanted no American military intervention, the Russians wouldn't have put missiles in Cuba? Cancelling the Bay of Pigs invasion would have made Kennedy seem like a weak president, and the Republicans would have destroyed him.

Barton J. Bernstein, Professor Emeritus of History at Stanford University, has said, "a different president than Kennedy might well have chosen not to launch the Bay of Pigs venture." Bernstein believes that the Bay of Pigs invasion and others provoked Khrushchev into his Cuban missile adventure. (56)

I agree that Bernstein's argument has merit, but Kennedy never wanted to invade Cuba with American troops. Khrushchev must have known that. Dan Fenn, Founding Director of the John F. Kennedy Library in Boston, agreed that it was probably part of the reason. However, Khrushchev may not have thought the whole thing through, and putting missiles close may have appealed to him as a countermeasure to our missiles in Turkey. (57)

Or Kennedy could have chosen the Reagan US Invasion of Grenada on October 25-29, 1983 (4 days), code-named Operation Urgent fury, which the United Nations General Assembly Resolution 38/7 on November 2, 1983, by a vote of 108 to 9, with 27 abstentions, condemned as "a flagrant violation of international law." There is an interesting oral history interview at the Kennedy library of Walt W. Rostow, being questioned by Richard Neustadt on the Bay of Pigs, and never, to my knowledge, quoted in a Kennedy book. "Rostow saw him (Kennedy) in a morning briefing, at a time he was going around the Mansion on crutches in the post-Bay of Pigs Period. It was a soul-searching time for him. He knew he had been set back in his performance as a President. Rostow also said in the interview that Kennedy never met Nasser, but their correspondence was interesting. Nasser, Rostow asserts, wrote a remarkable letter to the President after the Bay of Pigs, expressing respect for the way JFK handled it and almost saying what Gunnar Myrdal, a Swedish economist and sociologist, said. Rostow thought that Nasser's letter showed an understanding of the dilemma the President faced. Shortly after the Bay of Pigs, Myrdal announced firmly: you have a great President because if Kennedy had called the Bay of Pigs off, he would have been dead politically in the United States. The Republicans could have argued that Kennedy didn't have the guts to go through with something that would have eliminated Castro once and for all. Everything unpleasant that happened subsequently in Cuba would have been directly blamed on Kennedy.

On the other hand, Myrdal argued, if Kennedy had sent US troops in to make a covert operation stick, which would otherwise have failed, he would be internationally dead. This is an act that is intolerable for a great power." "So that in releasing the operation, but holding the line on the use of US forces," Myrdal argued, "that Kennedy preserved the possibility of going on and becoming a great American President. And that was the best he could do with the situation he inherited." (58)

Maxwell Taylor said that the cancelations of the Bay of Pigs operation would have been the cautious course of action, but it would have wasted the asset represented by the Brigade, comforted Castro, and vastly discouraged the thousands of Cuban Exiles dedicated to restoring the freedom of their country. The President's political opponents at home would have accused him of timidity in abandoning a course of action which his Republican predecessor would presumably have carried out. (59)

Economist J. K. Galbraith stated in a JFK library interview that "Eisenhower is said to have warned him that that was the one thing from which he must not back off." (60)

Richard Reeves wrote that Kennedy was determined to turn that kind of talk around, but he still thought he could do it on the cheap, with some hard thinking, a little bluff, and a few good men – or even all by himself. He thought that he could straighten out a few things himself if he had just had a reasonable opportunity to get together face-to-face and alone with Khrushchev. But the nation didn't let its humiliated President down.

The national Gallup Poll that came out after the Bay of Pigs, on the same day as Time Magazine, reported that Kennedy's approval rating had jumped ten points: 83% of taking part in a survey approved of the job Kennedy was doing as President, and only 5 percent disapproved.

"Jesus, it's just like Ike," Kennedy said, reading the poll. "The worse you do, the better they like you." (61)

US-Cuba historian Thomas G. Paterson wrote that Kennedy's foreign policy had sometimes been explained as an inheritance from Eisenhower – including the Cuban problem. But Kennedy did not simply continue his predecessor's anti-Castro policies.

Kennedy greatly exaggerated the Cuban threat, attributing to Castro a capability to export revolution that the Cuban leader never had and lavishing on him the attention he did not deserve.

Political commentator Walter Lippmann wisely wrote that Castro was "an affront to our pride" and a "mischief-maker," but he was not a "mortal threat" to the United States. And Paterson concludes that because he was obsessed with Cuba, Kennedy significantly increased the pressures against the upstart island. He then helped generate a major crisis, including the October 1962 Missile Crisis. In short, Kennedy inherited the Cuban problem and made it worse. (62)

Answering a press conference question on April 21, 1961, from journalist Sander Vanocur, JFK made a memorable remark about the Bay of Pigs disaster, "There's an old saying that victory has 100 fathers and defeat is an orphan." (63)

Historian Arthur Schlesinger asked him where he had come upon this felicitous observation. JFK looked surprised and said vaguely, "Oh, I don't know, it's just an old saying." He then told the newspapermen, "I'm the responsible officer of the government."

Emily Morison Beck, who edited the reference book "Bartlett's Familiar Quotations," told Schlesinger that she knew of no previous use of this "old saying." (64)

Jacqueline Kennedy, in her historic interviews with Arthur Schlesinger in 1964, was asked if she knew where her husband found the quotation. She answered, "I don't know. We could see if it's in Mao Tse-Tung because I told you he had an awful lot of Chinese proverbs (chuckles). But he was always collecting things like that." (65)

But writer Richard Reeves and broadcaster Robert Siegel set the record straight. They assert that while John F. Kennedy gets credit for saying victory has a thousand fathers, people forget that he called it an old saying. It is actually during World War II that Count Galeazzo Ciano, the Italian dictator Benito Mussolini's son-in-law and foreign minister, wrote in his diary: victory finds a hundred fathers, but defeat is an orphan. (66) (67)

Shortly after 10.00 a.m. on Wednesday, April 19, 1961, Kennedy met for three hours with the members of the Revolutionary Council. Schlesinger, who was present, had never seen him so drawn and tired, but as usual self-possessed. (68)

Kennedy apologized for the way the Cubans had been treated. He assured the Council members that he shared their grief and reminded them that he, too, had seen combat. "I lost a brother and a brother-in-law in the war," he said. "I know something of how you feel." (69)

As the Cubans prepared to leave, Kennedy said, "I want you all to understand that as soon as you leave the White House, you are all free men, free to go wherever you want, free to talk to anyone you want."

Schlesinger thought he had never seen President Kennedy so impressive. Despite themselves, his visitors were deeply moved. (70)

Thursday, April 20, 1961, John Kennedy invited Richard Nixon to the White House and told him about the meeting with the members of the Revolutionary Council. He told Nixon that several of Council members had lost their sons, brothers, or other close relatives or friends in the Bay of Pigs action."

Then he confided, "Talking to them and seeing the tragic expressions on their faces was the worst experience of my life." (71)

Rose Kennedy wrote about Jack's first crisis of his presidency, "Phoned Joe, who said Jack had been on the phone with him, much of the day, also Bobby. I asked him how he was feeling, and he said "dying" as a result of trying to bring up Jack's morale after the Cuban debacle."

Jackie told Rose that Jack had been upset all day. "He had practically been in tears, felt he had been misinformed by the CIA and others. I felt so sorry for him. Jackie, so sympathetic, said she had stayed with him until he had lain down that afternoon for a short nap. She said she had never seen him so depressed except at the time of his operation." (72)

Jacqueline Kennedy remembers the Bay of Pigs episode as an awful time and Jack looking awful.

Schlesinger remarked that it must have been unbearable to go to a Greek dinner amidst it all. Jacqueline replied, "Then we had to go to the Greek dinner that night. But I remember so well when it happened, whatever day it was, it was in the morning. Jack came back over to the White House to his bedroom and started to cry, just with me, you know, just for one, just put his head in his hands and sort of wept." She said she could only remember seeing him cry three times, "Once was the winter he was sick in the hospital, out of sheer despair. He wouldn't weep, but some tears would fill his eyes and roll down his cheek. And then when Patrick died, this summer 1963, when Jack came back from Boston to me in the hospital, and he walked in the morning at about eight in my room and just sobbed and put his arms around me. And it was so sad, because first his hundred days and all his dreams, and then this awful thing to happen. And he cared so much. He didn't care about his hundred days, but all those poor men who you'd sent off with all their hopes high and promises that we'd back them and there they were, shot down like dogs or going to die in jail. He cared so much about them." (73)

One morning when Kennedy was at his desk, he remarked to O'Donnell that he had had no sleep the night before. "I was willing to make any kind of deal with Castro to get them out of there."

Bobby came over to see Jackie and said to her, "Please stay very close to Jack, just be around all afternoon, just to sort of comfort him, just because he was so sad." (74)

Pierre Salinger will never forget the night that the Bay of Pigs came to its dismal conclusion on the beach in Cuba. At two o'clock in the morning, Schlesinger, McGeorge Bundy, Dick Goodwin, and Pierre gathered in the Oval Office. "After we talked to the President for about a half an hour, he left us and walked out the French doors and onto the South Lawn of the White House. He walked completely alone for an hour. From time to time, we could see him through the windows as he walked by. Salinger added, "I doubt if any of us had ever seen, or would ever see, a more dramatic example of the loneliness of the presidency and the lonesome burden of ultimate responsibility." (75)

O'Donnell also remembered watching Kennedy walking in the Rose garden and saying to Pierre Salinger, "He must be the loneliest man in the world tonight." (76) The only difference is that Salinger does not mention O'Donnell's presence that night.

In an interview with Richard Reeves, Pierre Salinger said that Kennedy was crying in his bedroom when he woke up after sunrise that Wednesday morning, April 19, 1961.

Senator Albert Gore Sr. had the first appointment with Kennedy on the morning after the Bay of Pigs, "His hair was disheveled, he was disheveled, his tie was askew, he talked too fast, and he was extremely bitter, especially towards Lemnitzer. He didn't use that word, but he felt he was framed, especially after he was asked to release jets from an aircraft carrier." (77)

Wire service journalist Henry Raymont, who had been in Cuba during the invasion, had a similar recollection of Kennedy's distress. Arriving at the Oval Office, Raymont found the president so full of self-recrimination and so sad at his short-sightedness that Raymont only gently reinforced what Kennedy already understood about the reasons for the failure.

The president's poor health problems continued to emerge. Immediately before and during the invasion on April 17 and 18, Jack Kennedy struggled with constant acute diarrhea and a urinary tract infection. He was treated with increased amounts of antispasmodics, a puree diet, and penicillin, and his doctor scheduled him for a sigmoidoscopy. (78) (79)

When Clark Clifford entered the Oval Office for the first time after the Bay of Pigs, he could see a change in the President. His mood was somber, his normal grace buried in a shell of regret, anger, and distress. Clifford had never seen him so depressed. "Let me tell you something," Kennedy said, "I have had two full days of hell. I haven't slept; this has been the most excruciating period of my life. I doubt my presidency could survive another catastrophe like this." (80)

Cardinal Richard Cushing thought that Kennedy's decision to refuse American armed support was a good one. Without that support, those who took part in the invasion of that Bay of Pigs were doomed. Cushing further said that President Kennedy felt very, very sad about it all. "It was the first time in my life that I ever saw tears coming to his eyes. The second time was when we buried little Patrick Bouvier Kennedy from the chapel of the Archbishop's house in Boston." (81)

Paul B. Fay, his personal friend and Under Secretary of the Navy, remembered driving with Kennedy to Middleburg on a grey, foggy, raining Saturday afternoon when the President was still pre-occupied with the Bay of Pigs disaster. There were very few people there. Generally, there's always a pretty good crowd, but the weather kept them away. Fay recalled JFK saying to him, "If they think they're going to get me to run for this job again, they're out of their mind." (82)

According to Ted Sorensen, the Bay of Pigs had been, and it would be the worst defeat of Kennedy's career, the kind of outright failure to which he was not accustomed. Kennedy had handed his critics a stick with which they would forever beat him. Sorensen walked with JFK on the South lawn Thursday morning, April 20, 1961, and he seemed to him a depressed and lonely man. (83)

One of Kennedy's closest long-standing friends, LeMoyne 'Lem' Billings, gave his insight into Kennedy's state of mind in the wake of the Bay of Pigs fiasco. As he often did, Lem joined Jack at Glen Ora, the president's private retreat in Middleburg, Virginia, for the last weekend of April 1961. Recording an oral history interview years later, Lem vividly recalled the president's mood on Sunday, April 30, 1961. Kennedy was feeling guilty and distressed, said Lem – even admitting that he hated reading the newspaper editorials, as he found the coverage of the Bay of Pigs too depressing. The only thing that lightened the mood was when Kennedy laughed as he confessed that he had thrown the latest copy of Time Magazine into the fire to avoid reading it.

All during that weekend, he told Lem that he certainly wasn't interested in a second term in what had turned into the most unpleasant job existent. When Lem told him that he had heard that the Vice President was reckoning he might have a chance at the presidency in 1968, Kennedy said he was welcome to it in 1964. When they talked about his legacy library, Kennedy said he didn't think anyone would be interested in building one, as this looked like it would be a rather tragic, legacy-light administration. (84)

The Friday, May 5 edition of Time declared, "One prediction in President Kennedy's State of the Union Message last January has proved to be dismally accurate. "The News," he said, "will be worse before it is better." Last week, as John F. Kennedy closed out the first 100 days of his administration, the U.S. had suffered a month-long series of setbacks rare in the history of the Republic. First came Russia's man-in-space triumph. Then the shockingly bungled invasion of Cuba. Finally, and belatedly, came the sickening realization that US-backed Laos was about to go down the Communist drain."

Kennedy's reaction to the article was blunt, "Sons of bitches... If they want this job, they can have it tomorrow."

From then on, whenever he was asked how he liked being president, Kennedy replied that he liked it better before the Bay of Pigs. He also described himself as "always on the edge of irritability."

Yet, however, frustrated he was by events and his stumbles, Kennedy was determined to use the problems of his first months as object lessons in how to become effective. (85)

4.2. The Cuban Missile Crisis: President Kennedy in Total Control

Khrushchev said that it was during his visit to Bulgaria that he had the idea of installing missiles with nuclear warheads in Cuba without letting the United States find out they were there until it was too late to do anything about them. But first, he had to talk to Castro and explain the Russian strategy to him to get the agreement of the Cuban government.

"The main reason was that the installation of our missiles in Cuba," Khrushchev said, "would restrain the United States from precipitous military action against Castro's government. In addition to protecting Cuba, added Khrushchev, our missiles would have equalized what the West likes to call "the balance of power." The Americans would learn just what it felt like to have enemy missiles "pointing at their country and people." (1)

So the idea of installing the missiles came from the Russians, but Castro, with characteristic loquacity, produced a confusion of explanations. He told a Cuban audience in January 1963 that sending the missiles was a Soviet idea, repeating this to Claude Julien of Le Monde in March 1963. In May, however, he described it to journalist and broadcaster Lisa Howard as a simultaneous action on the part of both governments. In October, he told Herbert Matthews of the New York Times that it was a Cuban idea, only to tell Jean Daniel of L'Express in November that it was a Soviet idea.

In January 1964, when Matthews called him about the Daniel story, Castro claimed again that it was a Cuban idea, and when Cyrus Sulzberger of the New York Times asked him in October 1964, Castro, pleading that the question raised security problems, declared, "Both Russia and Cuba participated."

According to Arthur Schlesinger, Khrushchev had told the Supreme Soviet back in December 1962, "We carried weapons there at the request of the Cuban government." (2)

I think that Khrushchev gave the correct version in his memoirs. But why did Khrushchev gamble with the Missiles? What was his reason for acting?

Sheldon Stern, John F. Kennedy library historian from 1977 till 1999, says that Kennedy and his administration, without question, bore a substantial share of the responsibility for the onset of the Cuban missile crisis. The secret war against Cuba may have been successfully kept from the American people. Still, it was no secret to the leaders of the Soviet Union and Cuba. (3)

Most historians and scholars agree with Stern, but George Carver said that the seeds of the crisis lay in Kennedy's meeting with Khrushchev in Vienna, which gave Khrushchev the impression that Kennedy was an idiot who could be and had been, out bluffed. The result was the Berlin Crisis and the Cuban Missile Crisis. Khrushchev judged that Kennedy was a lightweight, pretty boy who could be had. (4)

Bobby Kennedy acknowledged that the Berlin crisis resulted from the fact that Khrushchev got the idea at the Vienna summit that he was dealing with a young, rather weak figure because Kennedy didn't do what he, Khrushchev, would have done in Cuba, in not going in and taking Cuba. Khrushchev thought that if Kennedy was so weak and so vacillating at the time of the Cuban Bay of Pigs, that he was a pushover, and all he had to do was show strength, and Kennedy would back down. And that's what he tried to do at the Berlin Wall. (5)

On the contrary, Raymond Garthoff, who was part of the US government's Cuban Crisis discussions, said that it was very unlikely that Khrushchev thought Kennedy was weak in the spring of 1962 when the decision was made to put the missiles in Cuba, principally because we had been through the Berlin crisis, where Kennedy and the alliance had been very staunch. (6)

In his book "Counselor," Ted Sorensen writes, "Contrary to speculation that Khrushchev had gambled with Soviet missiles because he had judged Kennedy at their Vienna summit meeting to be weak, Khrushchev's son later recalled that his father returned from Vienna "with a very high opinion of Kennedy as a worthy partner and a strong statesman, a sensible politician."

Sorensen's view was that Khrushchev, who was determined to see his country regarded as a superpower equal to the United States, deemed Soviet missiles in Cuba the equivalent of NATO missiles in Turkey. Once the weapons were there, Khrushchev did not want to back down and thereby look soft to his Chinese and domestic critics. (7)

Sorensen's book on Kennedy, entitled simply "Kennedy," recounts that Kennedy, after receiving a detailed briefing from top CIA officials on the morning of October 16, 1962, was prompted not just to ponder on what action he should take in response, but also on why the Soviets had made so drastic and dangerous a departure from their usual practice. Sorensen put forward different motives on why Khrushchev acted that way.

Theory 1: Cold War Politics. Khrushchev believed that the American people were too timid to risk nuclear war. It was a probe, a test of America's will to resist.

Theory 2: Diverting Trap. Some speculated that Khrushchev also calculated that any strong U.S. reaction would help him prove to the Stalinists and Chinese that the West was no paper Tiger.

Theory 3: Cuban Defense. A Soviet satellite in the Western Hemisphere was so valuable to Khrushchev, in both his drive for expansion and his contest with Red China that he could not allow it to fall.

Theory 4: Bargaining Barter. Khrushchev intended to use these bases as effective bargaining power to trade them off for his kind of Berlin settlement or a withdrawal of American overseas bases.

Theory 5: Military Power. The Soviets could no longer benefit from the fiction that the missile gap was in their favor. By establishing medium-and intermediate-range ballistic missiles in Cuba, the Russians wanted to overcome by comparatively inexpensive means the American lead in international missiles.

Kennedy's analysis regarding the third and fifth theories as an offering but insufficient motives, and he leaned most strongly towards the first. (8)

On Monday morning, October 22, at ten o'clock, Kennedy told Arthur Schlesinger that the Soviet Union had done it for three reasons: first, because it would help bring Russia and China closer together, second, because it would radically redefine the setting in which the Berlin issue would be reopened after the election and, third because it would deal the United States a tremendous political blow.

When Schlesinger said that the Russians must have thought there would be no US response, Kennedy said America was caught either way – doing nothing would mean "we would be dead." On the other hand, any reaction was likely to leave the White House in an embarrassing and exposed position, whether concerning Berlin or Turkey or the UN.

Schlesinger thought that the most plausible reason Khrushchev had for putting missiles in Cuba was to repair his missile gap. Castro told Schlesinger that he didn't want nuclear missiles – he was only persuaded to accept them on the grounds of socialist solidarity, and he was furious about not being consulted on their withdrawal.

Diplomat and banker George Ball thought Khrushchev was "not an elegant thinker" and took his "crude" decision to put missiles in Cuba based on Kennedy's apparent youth. The weakness he displayed in Berlin and the Bay of Pigs. So sitting in the Kremlin, suspicious and vindictive, Khrushchev figured that he could teach this young man a lesson. "The fact that we (the US) didn't do what he thought we would do in the Bay of Pigs," Ball said, "and despite his awareness of massive American nuclear superiority, he believed that he could bring the US down a peg, strengthen his position concerning China, and improve his standing in the Politburo with one bold stroke."

Neither political scientist Richard Ned Lebow nor Ted Sorensen agreed with George Ball.

Ned Lebow said that the claims about Khrushchev's negative views on Kennedy are either not supported by the evidence or the evidence cuts both ways.

Khrushchev remarked that "Kennedy is young and young people do brash things" – but brashness isn't a weakness, and it makes Kennedy look unpredictable. Making it difficult for Khrushchev to form any firm expectation of his reaction to Cuban missiles. Ted Sorensen said that the Sovietologists in 1962 were convinced that the Soviets would never deploy missiles outside the Soviet Union. (9)

If you read Khrushchev's memoirs, you'll see that Khrushchev had a very high opinion of JFK and did not see him as a weak person.

At a Press Conference on August 29, 1962, senator Capehart of Indiana suggested to Kennedy that the US intended to invade Cuba. JFK gave a firm and clear answer, "I'm not for invading Cuba at this time. No, the words do not have a secondary meaning. I think it would be a mistake to invade Cuba because I think it would lead... an action like that, which could be very casually suggested, can lead to very serious consequences for many people." (10)

On August 29, U-2 surveillance of Cuba detected Soviet surface-to-air missiles (SAMs) but no ground to- ground missiles or other offensive weapons. On September 4, Kennedy issued a policy statement outlining the nature of the Soviet build-up to reassure Americans and warning Khrushchev about provoking policy changes in the Western hemisphere, if he did, "the gravest issues would arise." (11) (12)

In his September 13, 1962, Press Conference Kennedy said, "Ever since Communism moved into Cuba in 1958, Soviet technical and military personnel have moved steadily onto the island in increasing numbers at the invitation of the Cuban Government. Now the Movement has been increased. It is under our most careful surveillance.

But I will respect the conclusion that I reported last week that the new shipments do not constitute a serious threat to any other part of this hemisphere." But Kennedy cautioned that if at any time the Communist build-up in Cuba were to endanger or interfere with US security in any way, or the lives of American citizens, "then this country will do whatever it must be done to protect its security and that of its allies." (13)

The same month, Kennedy also requested congressional authority to call up 150,000 reservists, probably to defuse Republican criticism.

James N. Giglio, author of "The Presidency of John F. Kennedy," says that Kennedy's September statements were ambiguous and most likely reinforced Khrushchev's belief that the United States would not respond to Soviet offensive missiles in Cuba. (14)

On August 31, New York Republican Senator Kenneth Keating complained in a floor speech that the administration had no effective response to the installation of Soviet rockets in Cuba under the control of 1,200 Soviet troops. Nor, Keating added, did the administration seem prepared to deal with the troubling construction of missile bases. (15)

Keating also referred to the lessons of Munich. "Remember, too, what happened before the outbreak of the Second World War. Had Hitler been stopped decisively when he marched into the Rhineland, into Austria, or even when he went to

Czechoslovakia, the Second World War would probably never have occurred. If we do not act decisively in Cuba, we will face more or less trouble in Berlin and elsewhere in the World." (16)

This Hitler comparison makes no sense at all. It is absurd, out of proportion. Khrushchev was no Hitler, Mr. Keating.

On Sunday, October 14, 1962, a U-2 reconnaissance aircraft flown by Air Force Major Rudolf Anderson Jr. over Western Cuba brought back photographic evidence of medium-range ballistic missile sites.

By 8.30 p.m. the next day, October 15, the analysts were fairly certain of their findings. McGeorge Bundy, notified by the top CIA officials, immediately recognized that this was no unconfirmed refugee report or minor incident. He decided, however, not to call the President but to brief him in person and detail the next morning. Over four months later, almost as an afterthought, the President asked why he didn't telephone him that night, and Bundy responded with a memorandum "for your memoirs." (17)

On October 15, Eisenhower delivered a speech in which he charged that the Kennedy administration's foreign policy had not been "firm." In the eight years of his administration, Eisenhower claimed, "we witnessed no abdication of responsibility, we accepted no compromise of pledged word or withdrawal from principle. No Berlin Wall was built. No foreign bases were established. On the other hand, domestic pressure on Kennedy to do something about Cuba should not be overemphasized."

Three separate polls, including a Gallup poll, taken a week before the crisis, indicated no increase in public support for an invasion of Cuba since April 1961. It showed 63 percent opposing invasion, 24 percent in favor, with 13 percent registering no opinion. (18)

"Well, what are we going to do?" the President responded to Bundy's news the next morning, Tuesday, October 16. Kennedy's initial reaction was to "take them out" with an airstrike. (19)

America's ambassador to the UN, Adlai Stevenson, first heard about the missiles from the President himself on October 16, 1962, immediately after the 1 p.m. luncheon for the Libyan crown prince. Kennedy showed his UN ambassador photographic evidence when the two were alone together. "We'll have to do something quickly," the President said. "I suppose the alternatives are to go in by air and wipe them out or to take other steps to render the weapons inoperable." Stevenson replied, "Let's not go to an airstrike until we have explored the possibilities of a peaceful solution." Four months before his death in July 1965, Stevenson recalled, "I was a little alarmed that Kennedy's first consideration should have been an airstrike. He told Kennedy that sooner or later we would have to go to the UN and it was vitally important we go there with a reasonable case." (20)

The worst-case scenario for Kennedy was the do-nothing option.

Michael O'Brien, author of "John F. Kennedy: A Biography," said that no US President could politically survive if he allowed the Soviet Union to brazenly enter the Western Hemisphere and establish missile bases ninety miles off the US coast. It would have undermined NATO's confidence in the will and determination of the United States and disturbed all the nations in North and South America.

On October 16, at 11.45 a.m., thirteen men joined the president in the White House cabinet room for an hour-and-ten-minute discussion. The members of the ad hoc group, called the Executive Committee of National Security Council (ExComm), were Dean Rusk, McGeorge Bundy, Robert McNamara, Maxwell Taylor, Douglas Dillon, Robert Kennedy, Paul Nitze, George Ball, Llewellyn Thompson, Ted Sorensen, John McCone, Dean Acheson, and Lyndon Johnson. (21) (22)

Dean Rusk, Us Secretary of state, said that if each of them wrote their account of the Cuban Missile Crisis and ExComm deliberations, there would be sixteen different stories, each true from the author's perspective. (23)

On Wednesday, October 17, at 8.30 a.m., the ExComm met at the state department without the president who was campaigning for the November congressional elections. There was still a great deal of uncertainty and vacillation, but support seemed to be coalescing around some combinations of airstrikes, a blockade, and diplomatic approaches to the USSR. The former secretary of State, Dean Acheson, invited by the president, insisted on immediate airstrikes to eliminate the nuclear threat and demonstrate American resolve to the Soviets. (24)

That same Wednesday, Kennedy special assistant Kenneth O'Donnell said, "We heard later, Bobby Kennedy had it out loudly with Dean Acheson, arguing in favor of the blockade. "Bobby insisted that a surprise attack on Cuba would be a Pearl Harbor-type deception that would blacken the reputation of the United States." Bobby warned, "We're not going to make my brother the Tojo of the 1960s."

Acheson denounced Bobby's comparison with Hideki Tojo, the Japanese Prime Minister responsible for ordering the attack on Pearl Harbor, as a poppycock. (25) But Robert Weisbrot, author of "Maximum Danger: Kennedy, the Missiles, and Crisis of American Confidence Paperback," wrote that RFK seriously considered an invasion. At the afternoon meeting, he drew inspiration from the sinking of an American ship in Havana Harbor in 1898 that helped trigger a war with Spain and asked, "Whether there is some other way we can get involved in this through the US naval base in Guantanamo Bay or something." Weisbrot remarked that "we too scribbled his now-famous wry and rueful remark." "I now know how Tojo felt when he was planning Pearl Harbor," his meaning was both ironic and literal. (26)

In "Thirteen Days: A Memoir of the Cuban Missile Crisis," RFK wrote, "The general feeling, in the beginning, was that some form of action was required. There were those, although a small minority, who felt the missiles did not alter the balance of power and therefore necessitated no action. Most felt, at that stage, that an airstrike against the missile sites could be the only course. RFK continued, "Listening to the proposals, I passed a note to the President, "I know how Tojo felt when he was planning Pearl Harbor." (27)

At the same meeting within the ExComm, Under Secretary of State George Ball became the first advocate of a blockade. Anticipating Robert Kennedy's now celebrated stand, Ball opposed a surprise air strike on Cuba as no worthier than the Japanese sneak attack on Pearl Harbor. He hinted his concerns during the first evening of the ExComm's deliberations, urging hardheaded considerations of likely Soviet reprisals launched a Pearl Harbor attack. Ball voiced his fear about what would follow: Ball was sure such action would not be the end, but the beginning. (28)

On Wednesday, October 18, 1962, Dean Rusk met his Russian counterpart Andrei Gromyko at the State Department, and during their long after-dinner talk, Gromyko let on nothing about the missiles.

In his memoirs, Gromyko said that Rusk expressed his particular dissatisfaction with the appearance of Soviet weapons in Cuba. However, like Kennedy, he did not ask specifically about Soviet rockets.

Gromyko also said to Rusk, "You obviously will not deny the presence of American military bases and numerous military advisors in Turkey, and Japan let alone Britain, Italy and other West European countries, as well as Asia and Africa. Thus the USA may have bases in those countries and conclude military treaties with them. Yet, you do not believe the USSR has the right to help Cuba to develop its economy and strengthen its defensive capability, precisely that, its defensive capability." (29) (30)

Robert Kennedy later wrote on that Wednesday, October 17, 1962, "I supported McNamara's position in favor of a blockade" (31), but Sheldon Stern says that the evidence on the tapes is far more convoluted and contradictory. On October 18, McNamara abandoned the caution he had recommended on the evening of October 16 and boldly endorsed the Joint Chiefs of Staff (JCS) demand for an all-out air-land attack on Cuba, "In other words," he announced, "we consider nothing short of a full invasion as practicable military action." President Kennedy, taken aback by this reversal, reacted uncharacteristically harshly, demanding, "Why have you changed? Why has this information changed the recommendation?"

Referring to one of those ExComm meetings, Stern writes in "The Cuban Missile Crisis in American Memory," "Early in the discussion, the defense secretary had passionately endorsed invading Cuba, but by the end of the meeting, undoubtedly responding to JFK's determined resistance, he did not even list invasion as an option."

Stern points out that "The final resolution of the crisis, which of course included McNamara and virtually the entire ExComm opposed the secret Cuba-Turkey missile trade. But he concludes, "However, Robert McNamara's myth that "I was trying to help President Kennedy keep us out of war," can no longer be taken seriously after listening to the ExComm tape recordings." (32)

On October 18, 1962, at 5 p.m., on the instructions of the Soviet leadership, Gromyko met with President Kennedy in the White House. Understandably most of his talk with Kennedy was devoted to the Cuban problem. At the same time, other international issues, in particular, Germany and West Berlin, took a back seat. (33)

American journalist Hugh Sidey wrote about the two hours and fifteen minutes Kennedy-Gromyko Oval Office meeting as follows, "Kennedy would let Cuba come up naturally in the discussions, but the main subject would be Berlin, which seemed to be more on the minds of the international politicians than any other subject. The two men and their aides met in the Oval Office Room, and indeed Berlin was the next topic." (34)

James Giglio writes, "Kennedy's apprehension that Gromyko might raise the missile issue likely elevated the anxiety level. With relief, he heard the Soviet say that he had come primarily about Berlin." (35)

This could be true, but why would Gromyko raise the missile issue to say to Kennedy, "We put missiles in Cuba, but they are defensive?"

During their conversation, Gromyko stated that Cuba belonged to the Cuban people, and neither the US nor any other state had the right to interfere in Cuba's internal affairs. He told President Kennedy in the name of the Soviet leadership, "Should the USA undertake hostile actions against Cuba, the Soviet Union cannot play the part of a bystander." Kennedy asserted that his administration had no plans to attack Cuba, and the Soviet Union could take it that no threat to Cuba existed.

Kennedy then made an important admission, "The action in the area of the Bay of Pigs was a mistake. I don't deny that the Cuban problem is a serious one. Still, I am restraining those who are in favor of actions which could lead to war, as long as the other side does not provoke such actions." Gromyko said later that "contrary to later assertions made in the West, at no time in our conversation did Kennedy raise the question of the presence of Soviets rockets in Cuba. Consequently, there was no need for me to say whether there were any or not." (36)

Kennedy recalled, "I was dying to confront him with our evidence, but to do so at that time would have spoiled our chance to make the first surprise move which could catch Khrushchev at a disadvantage and reveal him to the world doing something that he was pretending not to be doing."

Kenneth O'Donnell said that if Kennedy had tipped his hand to Gromyko that Thursday, before he was ready with a plan to make a public demand for the removal of the missiles, the Russians could have come out first with an announcement of threats and demands, putting the White House on the defensive. (37)

Gromyko thought that his conversation with Kennedy had been full of sharp turns and inconsistencies. He found Kennedy nervous, though he tried not to show it and kept contradicting himself. One minute he would make threats against Cuba; the next, he would insist that Washington had no aggressive intentions against that country. Gromyko thought that Kennedy was under pressure from the hawks who were insisting on a test of strength. But the fact that common sense eventually gained the upper hand shows that Kennedy, who had been visibly thrown out of balance, was, in fact, a statesman of outstanding intelligence and integrity. Gromyko concludes, "My conversation with him was perhaps the most difficult I have had with any of the nine presidents with whom I had dealings in my forty-nine years of service." (38)

Dean Rusk said that "if President Kennedy had shown Gromyko the pictures that might have allowed the Soviets to issue an ultimatum, which would have made things more difficult to resolve." (39)

In what I call the Gromyko episode at the White House, there are two crazy anecdotes.

First, Geoffrey Perret – an English author specializing in American History – writes that one of Khrushchev's speechwriters, Fedor Burlatsky, was told a short time before the missiles went into Cuba. Khrushchev was certain he would prevail because although Kennedy was intelligent, he was also weak. "He will crumble when tested," said Khrushchev. The cable that Khrushchev received from Gromyko reporting on his Oval Office meeting with Kennedy had caught Kennedy so completely by surprise he would be unable to respond. (40) Perret refers to Gromyko's Memoirs and Dobrynin's book "In confidence," but I have checked these books, and there is nothing about it.

Jury Barsukov said it is quite possible that Gromyko didn't know about the missiles because, at that time, he wasn't a member of the Politburo. He was just a foreign minister. Khrushchev formulated a foreign policy. Barsukov said that he could imagine that John Kennedy felt that Gromyko lied to him. Still, the tragedy is that Gromyko didn't know about the missiles. (41)

Garthoff makes the same reflection as Barsukov that Gromyko probably didn't know about the missiles because he wasn't a member of the politburo. He supposed that we would never know for sure whether he did or not. (42)

Viktor Sukhodrev, a Russian-English interpreter for the highest Soviet politicians, thought that Gromyko in the Oval Office with Kennedy was tenser than usual. "I think he was sort of steeling himself to the possibility that Kennedy might just come out with it. I don't know whether or not Gromyko knew or could know that Kennedy had aerial photographs. I think he was steeling himself to being confronted with a direct statement. But Kennedy decided against it. Kennedy had those photographs in a drawer by his side and didn't take them out, although the temptation to show them to Gromyko was high." (43)

John A. Barnes makes a very good point about the Kennedy-Gromyko meeting at the Oval Office. He said that if the president had revealed his knowledge of the missiles secretly to Gromyko, the initiative would have passed to Khrushchev. The Soviet leader could then have delayed responding until the missiles were operational. He could publicly announce the presence of the missiles and declare that two sovereign states, the Soviet Union and Cuba, could engage in any agreements they liked. Barnes says Khrushchev could also have pointed to the presence of similar

U.S. Missiles on the periphery of the Soviet Union, especially in Turkey, and placed Kennedy on the defensive internationally.

Kennedy had ordered the removal of the obsolete, inaccurate, and unreliable Jupiter Missiles from Turkey several times, but both the U.S. Air Force and the State Department had dragged their collective feet: They didn't want to upset the Turks. The latter had lobbied Eisenhower hard for the missiles. John Barnes concludes that by making the crisis public, Kennedy kept the initiative, obliging the Soviet Leader to react to him, rather than Kennedy having to react to Khrushchev. When your opponent is in such a position, he had less time and mental energy to plan his countermoves. (44)

Khrushchev speechwriter Fedor Burlatsky was convinced that if John Kennedy said when he met Gromyko, "We know everything about rockets in Cuba," maybe there would have been no crisis because Khrushchev would surely have understood that he was exposed and that he would need now to negotiate in a new situation. (45)

On Friday, October 19, when Kennedy left Washington to make his scheduled campaign trip to Cleveland and Springfield, Illinois, and Chicago, he had made up his mind to start his action against Khrushchev with a naval blockade of Cuba. He considered a blockade to be a strong opening move, posing the least immediate risk of starting a war.

O'Donnell questioned whether Kennedy would get a consensus:

"I'll make my own decision anyway," JFK said. "I'm the one who has the responsibility, so we'll do what I want to do." He then told O'Donnell the story about Abraham Lincoln, who once told a Cabinet meeting, "All in favor vote "Aye." The whole Cabinet voted aye, but Lincoln voted no and then announced that the no's had it. (46)

Michael P. Riccards called it "the apocryphal story about Lincoln." (47)

Before he left at 9.45, Kennedy briefed the Joint Chiefs of Staff on his decision to impose a blockade. Curtis LeMay, US Air Force Chief of Staff, objected, commenting, "I'd emphasize a little strongly perhaps, that we don't have any choice except military action." Kennedy asked more questions and tried to empathize with the Chief's perspectives. LeMay finally said, "I think a blockade, and political talk, would be considered by a lot of our friends and neutrals as being a pretty weak response to this; you're in a pretty bad fix, Mr. President."

Kennedy replied, "What did you say?" LeMay replied, "You're in a pretty bad fix," Kennedy retorted, "Well, you're in there with me. Personally." (48)

There was strained laughter to this comment, but the fact remained that the president, once again at odds with his principal advisors, concluded Goduti. (49)

After the meeting, JFK expressed amazement at LeMay's blithe assurance that Khrushchev would fail to react to the bombing of the missile sites and the deaths of hundreds of Russians.

He told Kenneth O'Donnell, "These brass hats have one great advantage in their favor. If we listen to them and do what they want us to do, none of us will be alive later to tell them that they were wrong." (50) (51)

American historian Jeremy Suri compared the Cuban Missile Crisis with Pearl Harbor, and he says that unlike Roosevelt after the Pearl Harbor attack, Kennedy could not devote maximum time and energy to this world-changing challenge. His agendas recount a breakneck marathon of other crises, commitments, and obligations. They reveal that Kennedy had to work more hours, greet more people, and manage larger meetings than Roosevelt, just to keep up with all his presidential responsibilities.

Kennedy struggled to find time to deliberate with his closest advisors about a crisis that could trigger a nuclear war.

Suri claims that scholars of the Cuban Missile Crisis, particularly those who correctly praise Kennedy's judgment, miss this point. (52)

But can you imagine what would have happened if Kennedy had cancelled all his appointments and campaign trips? Total secrecy was a major part of the whole operation. What would he have told the press? It would have been chaos at the White House. Pearl Harbor happened Sunday, December 7, 1941, in totally different times and circumstances.

Ted Sorensen said The ExComm meetings had a sense of complete equality – protocol mattered little when the nation's life was at stake. Experience mattered little in a crisis that had no precedent. Even rank mattered little when secrecy prevented staff support. Sorensen said that he felt freer than he had ever had in an NSC meeting, and the absence of the president encouraged everyone to speak his mind. (53)

On Saturday, October 20, at 2.30 p.m., President Kennedy asked Rusk to begin the meeting with a recommendation. He had written on a small piece of paper "a naval quarantine" of Cuba, with his reasons why. Bob McNamara spoke next and supported a quarantine. Kennedy then asked Lyndon Johnson for his comments. Johnson told the President, "You have the recommendation of your secretary of state and your secretary of defense. I would take it." (54)

McNamara, who endorsed the blockade, admonished the president that "there were differences between his advisors. JCS Chairman General Maxwell Taylor insisted that attacking the missiles was less dangerous than allowing the sites to become operational, while RFK argued that this might be the last chance "to destroy Castro." (55)

Robert Kennedy in "Thirteen Days" said he did not attend all ExComm meetings to avoid inhibiting free discussion and because President Kennedy did not want to arouse attention. This was wise, said Robert Kennedy, because personalities change when the President is present. Frequently even strong men make recommendations based on what they believe the President wishes to hear. (56)

Donald WilsonPhil, an ExComm, said that President Kennedy wasn't in the room that much – deliberately. "Whenever the President is there, it makes a hell of a difference. Everybody is in awe of the President. It is very hard to differ with him. If he is not there, there is a much greater opportunity for free discussion. Without him, it is a level playing field, with a lot of powerful and articulate people playing. Without the president, you were freer to express your thoughts even though you knew whatever you said would get back to him." (57)

Sunday, October 21, early morning at 2.30 A.M

The discussions turned to the implementation and enforcement of the blockade defined as a "strict quarantine of offensive missile equipment under shipment to Cuba." Kennedy expressed the hope that Soviets would "turn back their ships rather than submit to inspection."

Kennedy also ordered the evacuation of US dependents from the Guantanamo naval base within twenty-four hours. 2,500 military family members were given fifteen minutes to pack one bag each before boarding navy transport ships for Norfolk, Virginia. (58)

Monday, October 22, 1962

At 6.55 p.m., Kennedy walked past Salinger and other aides, reporters, lights cameras, and cables, to his naval desk, covered with canvas and marking tape. His face was thinner than usual, with dark rings around the eyes and deep creases in the forehead. At seven, Evelyn Lincoln moved toward him with a hairbrush. As the television announcer began to speak, he waved her aside. Staring into the camera lens and then down at his script, Kennedy began reading perhaps the most important address of the Cold War. It lasted for seventeen minutes and forty-five seconds. (59)

"Good evening, my fellow citizens: This government, as promised, had maintained the closest surveillance of the Soviet military build-up on the island of Cuba. Within the past week, unmistakable evidence has established the fact that a series of offensive missile sites is now in preparation on that imprisoned island. The purpose of these bases can be none other than to provide a nuclear strike capability against the Western hemisphere. There is evidence that those medium-range ballistic missiles, capable of carrying a nuclear warhead for a distance of more than 1,000 nautical miles.

Each of these missiles is capable of striking Washington D.C., the Panama Canal, Cape Canaveral, Mexico City, and any other city in the Southeastern part of the United States or in the Caribbean area. Additional sites not yet completed appear to be designed for intermediate-range ballistic missiles, capable of traveling more than twice as far and thus capable of striking most of the major cities in the Western hemisphere, ranging as far north as Hudson Bay, Canada and as far south as Lima, Peru. The size of this undertaking makes it clear that it has been planned for some months. Only last Thursday, as evidence of this rapid offensive build-up, was already in my hand.

Soviet Foreign Minister Gromyko told me in my office that he was instructed to make it clear once again, as he said his government had already done that Soviet assistance to Cuba. I quote, "pursued solely the purpose of contributing to the defensive capabilities of Cuba." I quote him, "training by Soviet specialists of Cuban nationals in handling defensive armaments was by no means offensive, and if it were otherwise." Mr. Gromyko went on, "the Soviet government would never become involved in rendering such assistance." That statement also was false.

The 1930s taught us a clear lesson; aggressive conduct, if allowed to go unchecked and unchallenged, ultimately leads to war. This nation is opposed to war."

President Kennedy then announced that the following initial steps be taken immediately, "I have directed the armed forces to prepare for any eventualities, and I trust that in the interest of both the Cuban people and the Soviet technicians at the sites, the hazards to all concerned of continuing this threat will be recognized."

And then followed what I call "a very dangerous warning by President Kennedy.

"It shall be in the policy of this nation to regard any nuclear missile launched from Cuba against any nation in the Western Hemisphere as an attack by the Soviet Union on the United States, requiring a full retaliatory response upon the Soviet Union. I call upon Chairman Khrushchev to halt and eliminate this clandestine, reckless and provocative threat to world peace and stable relations between our two countries. I call upon him further to abandon this course of world domination and to join in a historic effort to end the perilous armor race and to transform the history of man."

His critics say that there seems to be two Kennedys, the confrontationist and the conciliator, the hawk and the dove.

I should say that JFK, at first, was the Cold warrior and a few lines further requesting a peaceful solution, and there's nothing wrong with that.

President Kennedy said that he "didn't wish a war with the Soviet Union, for we are a peaceful people who desire to live in peace with other peoples."

President Kennedy finished his speech by stating "that the greatest danger of all would be to do nothing. The cost of freedom is always high, but Americans have always paid for it. And one path we shall never choose, and that is the path of surrender or submission. Our goal is not the victory of might, but the vindication of right, not peace at the expense of freedom, here in this hemisphere, and, we hope around the world. God willing, that goal will be achieved. Thank you and good night." (60)

Before setting down the previous Friday night to draft the speech, Ted Sorensen had quietly reviewed Franklin Roosevelt's 1941 speech on Pearl Harbor and Woodrow Wilson's 1917 speech declaring war on Germany. Kennedy's final line – "Our goal is not the victory of might, but the vindication of right" – came from Wilson's speech. But Sorensen made clear that the Kennedy 1962 speech was not a declaration of war. (61)

"By confronting Mr. Gromyko privately," the columnist Walter Lippmann wrote in the New York Herald Tribune, "the President would have given Mr. Khrushchev what all wise statesmen give their adversaries – the chance to save face. Lippmann added, "Kennedy's subsequent speech on the missiles would then have been more effective, Lippmann added, "For it would not have been subject to the criticism that a great power had issued on an ultimatum to another great power without first attempting to save face."

Hersh claims that Kennedy was confounded by Lippmann, who seemed unmoved by his charms. "You have lunch with Lippmann or Reston, and they go back and knock the shit out of you to prove their integrity." Kennedy told Charles Bartlett. "The hell with them." According to Hersh, Bartlett told the anecdote to Richard Reeves. (62) (63)

On October 23, 1962, at 5 p.m., Khrushchev sent a telegram to President Kennedy in which he stated, "I should say frankly that measures outlined in your statement represent a serious threat to peace and security of peoples." Khrushchev once again claimed that "armaments now on Cuba, regardless of classification to which they belong, are destined exclusively for defensive purposes," This was a lie to prevent any acts of aggression. Khrushchev concluded that he 'hoped that the Government of the United States would show prudence and renounce actions pursued by you, which could lead to catastrophic consequences for peace throughout the world." (64)

Michael Beschloss called the Kennedy address, which triggered this Soviet response the most alarming address ever delivered by an American President – a judgement Ted Sorensen regrets because he said it was neither JFK's intention nor his. (65) (66)

The pacifist British philosopher Bertrand Russell wired Kennedy, "Your action desperate, no conceivable justification." He wired Khrushchev, "Your continued forbearance is our only hope."

Kennedy rightfully replied that Russell's attention might well be directed to the burglar rather than to those who caught the burglar. (67)

Richard Neustadt wrote Sorensen a memorandum a few days after the President's address. He described the significance of the speech and of the fear it generated. "The reaction among students here to the president's speech of Monday last was qualitatively different from anything I ever witnessed before in moments of foreign crises since I started to teach nine years ago. This time these kids were scared for their lives. They were astonished somehow that this American initiative could risk their lives." (68)

I fully agree with author John Barnes' rejection of Kennedy critics who believe that the President should have quietly informed Khrushchev of his knowledge of the missiles and worked for a behind-the-scenes diplomatic settlement, rather than making public a crisis that nearly led to nuclear war. Barnes, in his book "John F. Kennedy on Leadership: The Lessons and Legacy of a President," pointed out that such criticism ignores the fact that Kennedy had been engaged in "backchannel" negotiations with the Soviets as well as public discussions before the discovery of the missiles, and he had been lied to repeatedly. (69)

Gromyko's meeting with Kennedy on October 18 is a perfect example. McGeorge Bundy thought that the speech was excellent. However, in retrospect, he felt it was a little overstated and overemotional. Overall, it was a good speech which "did the job," said Bundy, who believed it had been necessary to state a clear public position.

Speechwriter Sorensen responded that Kennedy was indeed worried that the world would say, "What's the difference between Soviet missiles ninety miles away from Florida and American missiles right next door to the Soviet Union in Turkey?

It was precisely for that reason that there was so much emphasis on the sudden and deceptive deployment. Sorensen concluded, "Look at the speech very carefully. We rely very heavily on words such as those to make sure the world didn't focus on the question of symmetry. We felt that helped justify the American response." (70)

In the late hours of October 23, 1962, Robert Kennedy called Russian Ambassador Anatoly Dobrynin. RFK was in a state of agitation, and what he said was markedly repetitious, observed Dobrynin. He summarized it as follows. Robert had called on his initiative to explain just what had led to the current grave state of events. What preoccupied RFK most was the serious damage that had been done to the personal relationship between the President and the Soviet Premier, a relationship that meant so much.

And now Soviet medium-range missiles had appeared in Cuba, where their range covered almost the entire territory of the United States. Surely those were not the "defensive" weapons that the ambassador, Gromyko, the Soviet government, and Khrushchev had been talking about.

Dobrynin himself was unaware that medium-range missiles capable of hitting the United States had already been delivered to Cuba and that they were not intended to defend Cuba against attack on the approaches to that country.

Dobrynin said that because he had no real information from his government, the conversation was tense and rather embarrassing to him. (71)

A Gallup Poll taken Tuesday, October 23, 1962, showed that 84 percent of Americans favored the blockade, with just 4 percent opposed. One in every five thought that World War III would result. (74)

The reactions from the American Press and the American people reflected overwhelming support for the President.

Time Magazine predicted that Kennedy's resolve could prove one of the decisive moments of the twentieth century.

Barry Goldwater called Kennedy's action "welcome but belated." (72)

However, the British quality press was, at first, not very supportive. The Guardian was markedly critical in tone, "In the United Nations, the Americans, have taken the initiative themselves. In this, at least, and in their consultation with other governments beforehand, they had acted wisely. But even a limited military action will be hard to justify. In the end, the United States may find that it has done its cause, its friends, and its own true interests little good."

The Times wrote, "In judging whether President Kennedy is right in military blockading Cuba, almost everything depends on the accuracy of the evidence that the Russians are in fact building missile bases on the island. Once the evidence is accepted as true, it has to be recognized that the President had urgently to face and disturbing change in Russian policy in Cuba." (73)

177

If you want the true story of the Cuban Missile Crisis, you should listen to the tapes JFK recorded secretly.

Author Seymour Hersh claims that because the President and his brother were the only people involved in the deliberations who knew that there could be a record for posterity, their historical value is diminished because JFK could turn his tape recorder on and off when he wanted. (74) Stern, however, pointed out that the on/off switch was under the table in front of the President's chair in the Cabinet Room, making it difficult to prevent other participants from seeing what he was doing. To stop recording, since there was no visible counter, he would have stuck his head under the table. (75)

James Giglio wrote that Kennedy, one of six presidents who secretly taped White House meetings, used a concealed switch in the Oval Office and Cabinet Room to activate the recorder. Only a few White House personnel knew about this, including Evelyn Lincoln, Robert Kennedy, and close aides Kenneth O'Donnell and David Powers.

If Dave Powers knew about the women, he must certainly have been told by Jack about the taping system.

But Giglio was puzzled about what motivated Kennedy to record specific meetings beginning in July 1962. He thought that a likely explanation was that JFK intended to employ those recordings as an invaluable source for his memoirs. (76)

Kennedy had a sense of history and loved it: he wanted to ensure his place in history; he would have liked to be part of history, so these tapes are the answer.

Sheldon Stern wrote that only JFK and RFK knew of the taping system (I think Lincoln, O'Donnell, and Powers knew about their existence). Still, RFK took a persistently hawkish stance, pushing for a tough strategy that would remove Castro and demonstrate American resolve to the Soviets. Yet when he decided to write a book on the missile crisis meetings and to run for president in 1968, he downplayed his aggressive posture, never imagining that the tapes would one day be made public, painting himself as a persistent dove and conciliator. Stern claims that half a century after the event, it is surely time to document, once and for all, that RFK's book "Thirteen Days" cannot be taken seriously as a historical account of the ExComm meetings. (77)

The once-secret tapes of the Executive Committee of the National Security Council (ExComm) since they have been available, some writers, Sheldon argues, likely put off by the demanding and labor-intensive effort required to listen to those technically primitive recordings. Still, for once and for all, says Stern, there is no substitute for listening to those tapes.

William Safire, the former Nixon speechwriter and New York Times columnist, wrote in an Essay headlined "White House Tapes" on October 12, 1997, for the New York Times, "the JFK tapes inherently lie. There pose the Kennedy brothers, knowing they are being recorded, taking care to speak for history, while their unsuspecting colleagues think aloud and contradict themselves the way honest people do in a crisis."

The ExComm tapes do not present pure raw history. On the contrary, when the central character is the only one to know the tape is rolling, he can turn the meetings into a charade of entrapment, half history-in-the-making, half image-in-the-manipulating.

And Safire concluded, "And you can be sure of some outright deception. Not only had the editing of tapes by Kennedy acolytes with uncool, uncareful comments snipped out but the turning-off of the machine at key moments." (78)

I agree with Sheldon Stern that Safire's arguments, however, are nonsense. I remember one poignant argument from Stern that JFK would never, even in his most vivid imagination, have conceived of the possibility that we, the public, would ever hear these tapes. He thought of them, quite correctly, as private property, which they were legally at the time. Stern concludes, "Why would he need to "control" the content of the tapes when he was certain that historians and the public would never hear them unless he or his state-granted special access to this unique portion of his personal history.

This is what Stern calls the way Safire interprets history. They are historical participants manipulating the evidence and inventing "truths" to suit their purposes. (79)

According to conventional wisdom, Robert Kennedy suggested accepting the proposal in Khrushchev's first letter and ignoring the second message. This allegedly brilliant diplomatic strategy came to be called the "Trollope play," a reference to a plot device by nineteenth-century British novelist Antony Trollope, in which a woman interprets a casual romantic gesture as a marriage proposal. RFK's idea has been hailed for decades as the ingenious and cunning diplomatic breakthrough that led to resolving the crisis.

"Written a dozen of times in books of the Cuban Missile Crisis, RFK urged the president to ignore the second letter conveying a much stiffer tone" and to accept the proposal in the first, more hopeful letter."

Sheldon Stern claims that RFK's inspired strategy makes a great story, but the ExComm tapes prove that it never actually happened. Today, however, Stern continues his RFK attack, while historians can finally get it right by turning to the ultimate primary historical source: the audiotapes of the ExComm meetings. (80)

In his book, "Councelor" Ted Sorensen honestly admits "the hazards of memory, inevitably influenced by selectivity and hindsight." He never kept a diary to write his book to rekindle his memory and to reinvigorate his conscience.

A quarter of a century later, Dean Rusk wrote Sorensen a letter stating that Thompson "was the one who originally came up with the idea of ignoring the second message from Khrushchev, and responding to the first message, a point which had been discussed with Bobby Kennedy before the meeting in which Bobby Kennedy made that suggestion. (81)

Hersh claims that Khrushchev wrote in his memoirs published in 1970, "I'm not saying we had any documentary proof that the Americans were preparing a second invasion (after the Bay of Pigs). We didn't need documentary proof. We knew the class affiliation, the class blindness of the United States, and that was enough to make us expect the worst." (82) But that's not what Khrushchev wrote. He said, "We welcomed Castro's victory, of course, but at the same time, we were quite certain that the (Bay of Pigs) invasion was only the beginning and that the Americans would not let Cuba alone.

The United States had put its faith in the Cuban emigres once, and it would do so again. The emigré conspirators had learned some lessons from their defeat, and they wouldn't refuse a chance to repeat their aggression." (83)

I think Khrushchev deals with the matter in a different way. The way Hersh deals with it is not the way history should be written.

McNamara's recollection of the Cuban Missile Crisis is a self-serving travesty, observes journalist Fred Kaplan.

In the documentary film of his life "Fog of War," he tells director Errol Morris that "Kennedy was trying to keep us out of the war. I was trying to help him keep us out of war." (84)

McNamara, RFK, Rusk, Bundy, John McCone, George Ball, Paul Nitze, Douglas Dillon, Llewellyn Thompson, Maxwell Taylor, and Ted Sorensen tenaciously and unanimously exhorted the president to reject any deal involving U.S. Missiles in Turkey. (85)

A full hearing of the tapes indicates that Kennedy didn't need anybody to steer him toward negotiation. From the third day of the crisis, Kennedy was looking for a peaceful solution, pondering a way to let Khrushchev save face and was virtually alone in doing so. A week before Khrushchev brought it up, he mused about the possibility of trading away the Turkish Missiles. In short, Kaplan concludes that McNamara tries to paint himself as no less doveish than Kennedy in dealing with the Russians, yet, as he must know on some level, the opposite was true. (84)

In "The Fog of War," McNamara concluded that the fact, the Cuban Missile Crisis didn't become the start of World War III was only due to the fact, "we lucked out, it was luck that prevented Nuclear War," although "Kennedy was rational, Khrushchev was rational, Castro was rational." (86)

Sheldon Stern says that the assertion about Castro is certainly debatable in light of Soviet Ambassador to Cuba Alekseyev's recollections about Castro's demeanor when he cabled Moscow, demanding a nuclear strike against the U.S, in the event of an attack on Cuba.

Sergei Khrushchev says that when his father heard that Castro wanted a nuclear strike at America, his father responded calmly, "Is he proposing that we start a Nuclear War, that we launch missiles from Cuba? That is insane. We deployed missiles there to prevent an attack on the island, to save Cuba, and defend socialism.

But now not only is he ready to die himself, but he also wants to drag us with him." (87)

On October 24, Khrushchev, even as he was dispatching a harshly-worded and uncompromising letter to the White House refusing a blockade, also invited William C. Knox, the head of Westing House International who was in Moscow on business, to meet with him at the Kremlin.

During a three-and-a-quarter-hour conversation in which Khrushchev was "calm, friendly and frank," he acknowledged that he had ballistic missiles with both conventional and thermonuclear warheads in Cuba and that if the US government wanted to learn what kind of weapons were available for the defense of Cuba, all it had to do was to attack Cuba and Americans would find out very quickly. Khrushchev then said that he was not interested in the destruction of the world, but if we all wanted to go to hell, it was up to us. Khrushchev declared himself "anxious" to have a meeting with President Kennedy, saying he would be glad to receive him in Moscow or to visit him in Washington. (88)

On October 24, 1962, Soviet ships reached the quarantine line and stopped dead in the water. President Kennedy received a letter from Khrushchev in which the Chairman states, "Just imagine, Mr. President, that we had presented you with the conditions of an ultimatum which you have presented to us. How would you have reacted to this? I think that you would have been indignant at such a step on our part. And this would have been understandable to us." Khrushchev also accused Kennedy of acting not only out of hatred for the Cuban people and its government but also for selfish considerations of the US election campaign.

"What morality, what law can justify such an approach by the American Government to international affairs? No such morality or law can be found because actions of the United States concerning Cuba constitute outright banditry or, if you like, the folly of degenerate imperialism."

Khrushchev went on, "When you confront us with such conditions, try to put yourself in our place and consider how the United States would react to these conditions. I do not doubt that if someone attempted to dictate similar conditions to you, the United States, you would reject such an attempt. And we also say no. The Soviet Government considers that the violation of the freedom to use international waters and international air space is an act of aggression which pushes mankind toward the abyss of a world nuclear-missile war."

He finished his letter with a warning that "we will not simply be bystanders about piratical cuts by American ships on the high seas. We will then be forced on our part to take the measures we consider necessary and adequate to protect our rights. We have everything necessary to do so." (89)

Except for words and expressions like "intimidate," "banditry," "the abyss of a world nuclear-missile war," and "piratical acts," this Khrushchev letter invokes to me a beautiful human virtue which JFK also possessed, written on the brink of nuclear war, "Empathy."

The more I read and research the Kennedy-Khrushchev letters, of course, the situation was tense; the smallest mistake could lead up to the nuclear war. Nevertheless, those letters are at no time written by two people who wanted to go to war. They are proof of a desire on both sides for peace.

Among many other factors involved in the search for peace – including individual efforts, the ExComm meetings, and back-channel negotiations, the Kennedy-Khrushchev correspondence played a decisive role in avoiding nuclear disaster.

Dean Rusk stated later that" the moment of truth would not come until we stopped Soviet ships that carried missiles. Fortunately, we never got that far since on Thursday, October 25, 1962, several ships we suspected of carrying missiles stopped dead in the water, then turned around and headed back to the Black Sea. When we heard this news, Rusk said to his colleagues, "We are eyeball to eyeball, and the other fellow just blinked." (90)

After the crisis was over, Khrushchev bestowed the highest praise on President Kennedy. To a top Western diplomat, he said in effect, "Kennedy did just what I would have done if I had been in the White House instead of the Kremlin." (91)

On the afternoon of October 25, 1962, the US ambassador to the UN, Adlai Stevenson, presented photographic evidence of the Missiles at a UN gathering, while Kennedy watched the televised confrontation between Stevenson and Soviet ambassador Valerian Zorin. With the help of photo interpreters, Stevenson was going to show large-scale prints of photographs that revealed storage bays and missile launchers. But before Stevenson had a chance to show even one picture, Zorin (who had been kept in the dark by his government as well as Ambassador Dobrynin, as for some who claim foreign Minister Gromyko) ridiculed the presentation. It was all fake, and he snorted – all fabrication straight from the laboratories of the CIA. "All right, sir," said Stevenson, "do you deny that the Soviet Union has placed and is placing medium- and intermediate-range missiles and sites in Cuba, yes or no?" Zorin protested, "I am not in an American courtroom!" Stevenson fired back, "You are in the court of world opinion right now!" Zorin blustered for a while, concluding weakly, "In due course, sir, you will have your reply." Stevenson responded vigorously, "I am prepared to wait for my answer until hell freezes over." Stevenson then embarrassed the Russians by putting U2 photos of the missiles before the Security Council. "I never knew Adlai had it in him," Kennedy said of his performance. "Too bad he didn't show some of his steam in the 1956 campaign." (92)

Stevenson told Powers and O'Donnell that "when we met Khrushchev at the signing of the nuclear test ban treaty in Moscow the following summer, the Soviet Premier growled at him and said, "Stevenson, we don't like to be interrogated like a prisoner in the dock."

At an ExComm meeting the next day, October 26, 1962, Adlai Stevenson felt courageous enough to question the President's refusal to compromise. If the removal of the Soviet missiles from Cuba was worth any price, Stevenson asked, why not offer to exchange their removal for withdrawal of US Jupiter missiles from Turkey and the closure of the US Naval base at Guantanamo Bay? Any such diplomatic bargain was worth considering, Stevenson said, if it would save the world from nuclear war.

Dulles, Loveth and McCone sharply criticized him, and when the meeting broke up, the President walked out onto the Truman Balcony with Bobby and O'Donnell to discuss what had been said. Bobby was so furious with Stevenson he wanted him sacked and replaced at the UN job by John McCloy. But typical, JFK – unlike his brother- could see both sides of the argument, "Now wait a minute," the President said. "I think Adlai showed plenty of strength and courage, presenting that viewpoint as an appeaser (it was called "A Munich"). It was an argument that needed to be stated, but nobody had the guts to do it. JFK acknowledged to the others that he thought Stevenson might have gone too far but added, "Remember we're in a situation where that may cost us millions of lives, and we should consider every side of it and every way to get out of it. I admire him for saying what he said."

According to Kenneth O'Donnell, the President was deeply upset when Stewart Alsop and Charles Bartlett wrote an article in the Saturday Evening Post on December 18, 1962, called "in Time of Crisis," which summed up Stevenson's compromise plan, in the words of a critic, as "Adlai wanted a Munich,"

Because Bartlett was a personal friend of the Kennedys, it was assumed that the article had the President's approval, but O'Donnell asserts that he strongly disapproved. (93)

On Saturday, December 1, President Kennedy informed Arthur Schlesinger about the upcoming Bartlett and Alsop article. "You had better warn Adlai that it is coming. Everyone will suppose that it came out of the White House because of Charlie. Will you tell Adlai that I never talked to Charlie or any other reporter about the Cuban Crisis and that this piece does not represent my views." (94) Kennedy made a missile swap and so proved Stevenson – partly: Guantanamo stayed – right. Richard Reeves wrote, "The President did not disagree all that much with the ambassador's words, saying at one point that perhaps the only way to get the missiles out of Cuba was invading or trading, that the quarantine alone probably could not do that job. "But he thought that it was foolish to begin negotiating by revealing your final terms. Kennedy himself had twice moved toward the removal of the Jupiters from Turkey during the past year, but nothing had happened because after they were in place, the missiles had become the symbol of Turkey's international maturity." ExComm member Clarence Dillon, who had been Eisenhower's Undersecretary of State when the decision was made to install the weapons, told a meeting, "Well, everyone knows that those Jupiter missiles aren't much good anyway. We only put them in there because we didn't know what else to do with them, and we made the Turks and the Italians take them."

"Did you hear that from Dillon?" Kennedy asked in a telephone call to Sorensen after the meeting broke up. "Put that down for the book! The Memoirs." (95)

Dean Rusk said that Adlai Stevenson was unfairly criticized for his advocating a "Munich" and "selling out to the Russians." But John Kennedy took a more generous view, pointing out that representing the UN and making such proposals were Stevenson's job. America was fortunate to have him at the UN. (96)

In Khrushchev's emotional letter of October 26, 1962, he appealed to Kennedy to weigh carefully what the consequences would be of "the aggressive, piratical" actions proposed by the US in international waters. "You know that any sensible man simply cannot agree with this, cannot recognize your right to such actions," Khrushchev insisted. "Mr. President, you and we ought not now to pull on the ends of the rope in which you have tied the knot of war because the more the two of us pull, the tighter that knot will be tied. And a moment may come when that knot will be tied so tight that even he who tied it will not have the strength to untie it. Then it will be necessary to cut that knot, and what that would mean is not for me to explain to you because you understand perfectly of what terrible forces our countries dispose of." (97)

O'Donnell said that "the irony and irritating side of this question was that the Jupiter missiles were more or less useless to the US militarily. He went on, "President Kennedy had asked repeatedly over the past year to have those Jupiters removed from Turkey, but the Turkish government, anxious to keep the American missile base payrolls in their country, had pleaded against the closing of the bases, and our State Department had given in to the Turks' request." (98)

David Horowitz said that the fact that the removal of the Turkish Missile bases had been considered before the Cuban crisis raises the question as to why there was a crisis at all.

Why, for example, was not the Soviet Ambassador given an ultimatum in private before the presence of the missiles was disclosed to the world, and the prestige of the United States had been put on the line? Such a move would have been a normal diplomatic procedure and was proposed by Stevenson. I think that the Cuban Missile Crisis problem was far more complicated than the "no crisis at all" scenario of Horowitz. (99)

The former American Ambassador to the Soviet Union Llewellyn Thompson is mentioned only twice in RFK's "Thirteen Days," once a member of the ExComm and the second time in the following paragraph, "President Kennedy wanted to hear from Secretary Rusk, but he also wished to hear from Tommy Thompson, former (and now again) Ambassador to the Soviet Union, whose advice on the Russians and predictions as to what they would do were uncannily accurate and whose advice and recommendations were surpassed by none." (100)

Even Thompson's superior Secretary of State Dean Rusk acknowledged the ambassador's status as the ExComm's prime expert on the Soviet Union.

Tommy Thompson and his wife Jane had occasionally lived with Khrushchev and his wife. McNamara in "The Fog of War" singles out Thompson for urging JFK to reject the "hard" Saturday, October 27, 1962 message from Moscow's hawks and to respond instead to the "soft" Friday, October 26, 1962, from Khrushchev himself. The President said to Tommy, "We can't do that; that'll get us nowhere." Tommy replied boldly, "Mr. President, you're wrong." Now that takes a lot of guts. Kennedy insisted that "We're probably not going these missiles out of Cuba anyway by negotiation." The Ambassador replied, "I don't agree with Mr. President; I think there's still a chance." Kennedy asked, "That he'll back down?" Thompson explained that "the important thing for Khrushchev, it seems to me, is to be able to say, "I saved Cuba. I saved the invasion." (101)

Indeed Khrushchev wrote in his memoirs, "The Caribbean crisis was a triumph of Soviet foreign policy and a personal triumph in my career as a statesman and as a member of the collective leadership. We achieved, I would say, a spectacular success without having to fire a single shot." (102)

Khrushchev's memoirs prove Thompson was right. Thompson knowing Khrushchev as he did, thought Khrushchev would accept that. That's what I call empathy. McNamara's view was that it was Thompson (rather than RFK) who preserved the peace by persuading President Kennedy to adopt a shrewd and subtle strategy (essentially the Trollope play) based on the ambassador's empathy and personal knowledge of Khrushchev – and it worked.

Ted Sorensen, on the "two letters Oct 26, 27, wrote that "on Friday night October 26, we received a long letter that appeared to be the work of Chairman Khrushchev himself, but the next morning we received a second letter distinctly cooler in tone, and more likely to be the handwork of the Politburo. "During the ExComm meeting Saturday afternoon," Sorenson continued, "I joined RFK, Ambassador Thompson is urging the President to respond to the positive elements buried in the Friday Evening letter." (103)

Sorensen doesn't explicitly credit Thompson as the man who convinced Kennedy – which is Sorensen at his best, don't you think?

Just before nine o'clock Sunday morning, October 28, Moscow radio announced that it would broadcast an important statement to broadcast at nine sharp: It was a letter from Chairman Khrushchev.

"To eliminate as rapidly as possible the conflict which endangers the cause of peace, the Soviet Government has given a new order to dismantle the arms which you described as offensive, and to crate and return them to the Soviet Union." (104)

As the crisis wound down, President Kennedy said that he didn't want the US to gloat about a diplomatic victory, and if Khrushchev wanted to play the role of peacemaker, let him do so. Kennedy didn't want to make life any more difficult for Khrushchev than it already was. (105)

Pierre Salinger recalled that it was not a case of "We won, we lost," which became Kennedy's mantra strong point from the minute the crisis came to an end. He said to Pierre, "This is not our victory, this is a joint victory of the two nations, we did it together. Don't let anybody go out and say this was America's victory."

That's what I call JFK's empathy, putting himself in Nikita Khrushchev's place.

In his letter of October 30, 1962, Khrushchev asked Kennedy, "I do not know what you will think about it, but if you were prepared already now to proclaim the liquidation of your base in

Guantanamo, this would be an act which would give world public opinion real satisfaction and would contribute to the easing of tension."

On November 3, 1962, Kennedy answered Khrushchev's letter of October 30, 1962, but didn't respond to Khrushchev's request on closing Guantanamo Base. (106)

"Whatever doubt his father might have had about his decision to remove the missiles had vanished completely," said his son, Sergei, "Remove them and as soon as possible. Before it's too late. Before something terrible happens." (107)

Dean Acheson, who had opposed the quarantine strategy and wanted an immediate air strike on Cuba, said after the quarantine had proven successful, "It was just plain dumb luck. We were lucky, the Russians were lucky, the whole world was lucky." But Acheson overlooked Dean Rusk's assertion that you can make your luck. Or you can force your luck. (108)

On October 29, 1962, Dean Acheson wrote to Kennedy, "Only a few people know better than I how hard these decisions are to make, and how broad the gap is between the advisors and the decider." (109) (110)

McNamara stressed, "I don't believe it's primarily a military problem. It's primarily a domestic problem." He urged his colleagues, "What do you expect Castro will be doing after you attack these missiles? Does he survive as a political leader? Is he overthrown? Is he stronger, weaker? How will he react? How will the Soviets react?" (111)

After a brush with death in 2006-2007, Fidel Castro decided to devote the bulk of his remaining energy to a single cause – the abolition of nuclear weapons from the face of the earth. As Castro remembered it, almost everyone around him was skeptical about his idea, everybody except Fidelito, his son, the nuclear scientist. The latter thought it would be a very good idea.

In August 2010, Fidel met for three days with Jeffrey Goldberg, a reporter for US Magazine, The Atlantic.

Goldberg, a provocateur, asked him how he squared his pursuit of nuclear abolition with his infamous, ("infamous" was Goldberg's word, Castro recalled) letter to Khrushchev asking the Soviet leader to blow the US to smithereens. Fidel simply told Goldberg that, back in October 1962, he had been wrong. (112)

Or how an old man, but wise man, almost fifty years later got a second chance from God to repair his mistakes.

On Saturday morning, October 27, 1962, Major Rudolf Anderson Jr., the pilot of the U-2 reconnaissance plane, was shot down by a Soviet SAM. No one knew who had fired the missile, even though American intelligence identified the Los Angeles, Cuba missile site as the culprit. In 1985, a Washington Post report concluded that during a Soviet-Cuban military conflict, the Cubans had seized temporary control of the SAM site and fired the missile. Two years later, the Soviets denied the assertion. Sergei Mikoyan, formerly personal secretary to his father, First Deputy Premier Anastas Mikoyan confessed that a Soviet general in Cuba had violated instructions in ordering the SAM fired. Khrushchev, in his memoirs, says that the incident caused an uproar. At first, he was concerned that President Kennedy wouldn't be able to stomach the humiliation. Fortunately, however, nothing happened except that the Americans became more brazen in their propaganda.

When Kennedy asked McNamara on the U-2 being shot down, "How do we interpret this?" McNamara admitted that he didn't know. The defense chief nonetheless declared emphatically, "If we're gonna carry out surveillance each day, we must be prepared to fire each day." Kennedy warned, "We can't very well send a U-2 over there and have a guy killed again tomorrow." (113) (114) (115)

Kennedy once again exercised considerable restraint in arguing that the shooting might have been accidental. But there's also a human story to that tragic death.

JFK was at that particular moment more disturbed by the death of Major Anderson in Cuba than he was worried about Khrushchev. He had asked the Defense Department to find out if the U-2 pilot had a wife and family. McNamara telephoned to tell him that Anderson was married and had two sons, five and three years old. The President hung up the telephone and turned to Dave Powers with a stricken look on his face. "He had a boy about the same age as John," he said. (116) (117)

Finally, I agree with Mark J. White that from October 22 to October 28, the day the missile crisis was essentially resolved, caution was the admirable hallmark of Kennedy's approach. Ultimately, he was willing to make concessions to Khrushchev to end the confrontation. Had the Soviet premier not backed down on October 28, Kennedy, moreover, would probably have compromised further before ordering military action against Cuba. (118)

4.3. The Scali-Fomin (Feklisov) Meetings

According to Kennedy aide and advisor Roger Hilsman, there are five basic elements of communication between the Soviet and American governments.

The first is by formal letter between the heads of government, using embassy facilities. Second, the Soviets characteristically maintain alternative sets of channels that bypass their embassy in Washington and probably are handled in special ways at the Moscow end as well.

Third, views can be exchanged formally and officially by note or by letters between officials lesser than the heads of government.

Fourth, there can be an informal but still official exchange, orally, for example, between the ambassador and an official in the State Department or the White House. Finally, fifth, the Soviets not infrequently use entirely unofficial channels. Roger Hilsman asserts that the decisive channels were probably used first – the letters between Kennedy and Khrushchev – as well as one very unusual channel of the last type, the very informal and unofficial. It was from this, the most unofficial channel that the first hint of a blink came in.

At one-thirty Friday afternoon, October 26, 1962, ABC television's State Department correspondent John Scali – a man, according to his friend Hilsman, trusted as a reliable and accurate reporter by the highest levels of the US Government – received an urgent phone call from a senior Soviet official, Aleksander Fomin, asking for an immediate appointment. They met at the Occidental Restaurant on Pennsylvania Avenue, and Fomin went straight to the point. He asked Scali to find out immediately from his "high-level friends in the State Department" whether the United States would be interested in a solution to the crisis along the following lines:

(1) The Soviet Union would agree to dismantle and remove the offensive missiles in Cuba.

(2) It would allow United Nations inspection to supervise and verify the removal.

(3) The Soviet government would pledge not to reintroduce missiles, ever, to Cuba.

(4) And in return, the United States would pledge publicly not to invade Cuba.

In 1967, Hilsman called Fomin "a man with his direct channels of communication to the Kremlin." In 1996, Hilsman wrote that Fomin repeatedly assured Scali that the message came from Khrushchev himself. (1) (2)

Anatoly Dobrynin, the Russian ambassador to the US, has a different version of the Scali-Fomin meeting. According to him, Scali maintained contact with Alexander Fomin, the resident of the Soviet intelligence service in Washington – allegedly with the knowledge of the White House. Fomin (his real name was Feklisov) contacted Scali, codenamed MIN, because he regarded him, rightly or wrongly, as an important CIA agent. In the Washington restaurant, where the two met during the crisis, an enterprising owner has even hung a sign commemorating "The Place." Dobrynin later recalled, "I was briefed on these contacts by Fomin, who also held the rank of the counselor in our embassy, but I found their importance was relatively insignificant given my direct and ongoing dialogue with Robert Kennedy." After the crisis subsided, Robert Kennedy complained to Dobrynin that the Soviet side should not have searched for other communication channels. Kennedy said that Scali had been acting on his initiative without any approval from the White House. For their part, Scali and Fomin, each claimed the other had sought him out first as a contact. (3)

In a December 14, 1962 letter to Khrushchev, President Kennedy wrote that "by accident or misunderstanding, one of your diplomats appears to have used a representative of a private television network as a channel to us. This is always unwise in our country, where the members of the press often insist on printing at some later time what they may learn privately." (4)

Dobrynin thought that the real reason behind the use of this very informal channel was that both intelligence services were looking for contacts with each other during the crisis in a desperate search for information. In any case, that was the end of the Scali-Fomin affair, and nothing like it ever occurred again.

When they met by chance many years later, they were not even on speaking terms, and both gave contradictory versions of their meeting during the crisis itself. (3)

Perhaps, the Scali-Fomin meeting was not approved by the White House, but according to Hilsman, Rusk saw the possibilities in an entirely unofficial exchange of views with the Soviets. After a short discussion with other members of the ExComm, he asked Hilsman to bring Scali up to see him – using the private elevator. After their meeting, Scali came directly to Hilsman and typed out the gist of his conversation with Fomin.

Rusk asked Scali to go back to the Soviet official and tell him that the United States was interested, and Rusk authorized Scali to tell the Soviet official that the statement came from the "highest" levels in the US government. Rusk told Scali, "You have served your country well."

Informed of Scali's talk with Fomin, Rusk took the newsman to the White House. Via Rusk, he got an appointment with Kennedy, who wanted to hear Scali's story from the horse's mouth and to allow him to tell Fomin that he had consulted the highest level of his government. (5)

According to Beschloss, Kennedy and Rusk operated under the very possibly false assumption that Fomin was acting as Khrushchev's agent, just as Bolshakov had done for seventeen months.

Historian Michael Beschloss confirms the Scali-Fomin meeting at the Occidental restaurant. By Scali's account, he and Fomin had lunched seven times after their first meal at Duke Zeibert's restaurant in the fall of 1961. Scali found him a quiet, reasonable, intelligent man who did not hesitate to depart when he felt it necessary from the standard Communist line. Scali and other Americans thought that Khrushchev had authorized Fomin's approach. In 1989, Fomin said he acted on his own. However, the conversation was reported to Dobrynin, who may have cabled it to Moscow. By then, Fomin was ailing, and time may have distorted his memory concluded Beschloss. (6) But if you believe the Dobrynin version of the meeting, I doubt that he will have cabled it to Moscow.

Raymond L. Garthoff, a participant in the crisis deliberations of the U.S. Government, said that Fomin himself informed a Soviet scholar in 1987 that he had been acting on his authority. He repeated this statement at the Moscow conference in early 1989.

Georgi M. Korniyenko told Garthoff in Moscow in May 1988 not only that Fomin had been operating on his initiative, under general guidance from Ambassador Dobrynin to sound out possible American positions, but also that Fomin had reported his discussion with Scali in a way that left unclear how much had been Scali's initiative and how much Fomin's, leaving Dobrynin and Korniyenko very dubious of the report: Fomin even claimed that Scali had initiated the contact. At the Moscow conference, Fomin himself gave an account that was even more bizarre, including an alleged contact with Scali on October 22, in which Scali had informed him of the missiles in Cuba even before the president's speech. Scali hotly denies such a meeting ever took place and also denies Fomin's account of their meeting on October 26.

Garthoff concludes that Fomin's, Korniyenko's, and Dobrynin's denials of authorization for Fomin's exploratory sounding with Scali are not, of course, proof certain that Fomin was not making a probe authorized through KGB channels. However, Garthoff says that, in retrospect, it seems very unlikely that it was. (7)

In 1987 during a conference on the Cuban Missile Crisis, including American scholars and three Soviet officials, the Soviet representatives said that the approach by Fomin, the head of the KGB in Washington, was his idea – an assertion Hilsman dismissed as not credible. Fomin, Hilsman said, stressed from the beginning that the message came directly from Khrushchev and that he, Fomin, was acting on Khrushchev's instructions. And Fomin repeated these statements several times. Indeed without those emphatic assurances, Hilsman said that he Hilsman would not have taken the message to the secretary of state and the President. (8)

After Scali publicized his Rendezvous with Fomin in Family weekly in 1964, Charles Bartlett was told by his friend Alexander Zinchuk of the Soviet Embassy that Scali's story was "a phoney" and that Fomin had been "acting on his own." As Bartlett recalled, I think the implication was that Scali might have been making more out of it than was there, that he was trying to get a little publicity. Georgi Korniyenko, a Soviet diplomat attaché at the Soviet Embassy in Washington DC during the 1962 Cuban Missile Crisis and later Dobrynin's deputy, insisted in 1991 that Fomin was indeed freelancing, that the KGB and others in the Washington Embassy were working, whatever American contacts they had, to find a way out of the crisis. (9)

Kennedy's press secretary, Pierre Salinger, in his book "With Kennedy," deals for almost seven pages on the "Scali-Fomin" meetings. He calls the role of ABC newsman John Scali in settling the Missile Crisis, a fascinating footnote to history. It highlights both the dangerously obsolete nature of our communications with the Soviet Union before the "hotline" and the Byzantine-like character of Soviet diplomacy.

Salinger said that he participated in the decision to ask Scali to hold his silence on the secret negotiations in which he was a principal. Still, the story has since been leaking out in dribbles from other sources. Now, and with Scali's permission, Salinger, for the first time, talks about the significant sections of his reports to President Kennedy and Secretary Rusk.

He further tells how Rusk brought Scali to the White House to secure the President's reply. He describes extensively the October 26, 1962 meeting at 7.35 p.m. in the Statler Hotel lobby, which lasted for twenty minutes, and from other meetings as well.

Salinger is persuaded that Fomin was acting on orders from Ambassador Dobrynin and was speaking directly for Khrushchev. Salinger concludes that the Nation and the world owe John Scali a great debt of gratitude. He chose to put aside his tools as

190

a newsman in favor of the greater National interest at a crucial time in history. This meant neutralizing himself as a reporter and permitting others to end up with what was the greatest story of his life.

Salinger calls John Scali not only a great reporter, but he considers him a great American. (10)

In an oral history interview, Dean Rusk had this comment to make on the Scali-Fomin meetings, "It was unexpected, but it was, in effect reassuring, because what we were getting from that channel helped us to figure out which communications from Khrushchev were real. We thought we had clear contact with the KGB through John Scali's channel, and as it turned out, it was very useful information. Now, it was not as central to the solution of the problem as Scali sometimes thinks. Nevertheless, it was a very helpful and useful interchange." (11)

In his memoirs of JFK in "Johnny, We Hardly Knew Ye," Kenneth O'Donnell said that he led Scali and Rusk into the President's office, where the President listened to Fomin's proposal and told Scali to take back a reply that it was completely acceptable as a basis for a settlement. "But don't use my name," Kennedy added. "That's against the rules. Give them the impression that you talked to me, but don't say so. Tell them you've gotten a favorable response from the highest authority in the government." (12)

Walter Lippmann, in his 25 October column, advocated trading the Cuban missiles for those in Turkey. This proposal was explored at the United Nations and finally espoused by the Soviets. Lippmann's column, apparently read and considered by the Soviets to be somewhat official, was discussed in a secret meeting between ABC's John Scali, who was acting as an administration negotiator with the Russian embassy in Washington, and State Security Committee (KGB) operative Alexander Fomin.

In explaining the unacceptability of this Lippmann idea, Scali informed Fomin that "everything Mr. Lippmann writes does not come straight from the White House, and if the Soviets were going to seek to judge administration intentions by following the words of reporters, they should listen to different reporters than the ones they have been following." Again, Lippmann's international readership had proved him influential. (13)

Sergei Khrushchev had his version of the Scali-Fomin meeting at the occidental restaurant. He claims that a plaque later appeared on the wall, where the two men had lunch, with this inscription, "At a tense moment of the Cuban Crisis (October 1962) a mysterious Russian Mr. X advanced a proposal here to John Scali, a newsman at ABC news. That meeting averted the threat of nuclear war." So is history made?

When Fomin returned to the embassy after his lunch with Scali, he wrote out a telegram to Moscow describing the proposal he had received and gave it to Ambassador Dobrynin to sign. It was growing late on Friday, but Dobrynin said nothing to him for more than three hours and then returned the telegram unsigned, explaining that no one had authorized him to carry on such negotiations. President

Kennedy, afraid to make a mistake and with no great faith in the Scali-Fomin connection, decided to ask his brother Robert to talk to the ambassador. (14)

Michael Dobbs wrote that the encounter between the KGB agent and the reporter was a classic example of miscommunication between Moscow and Washington at a time when a single misstep could lead to nuclear war. Dobbs concluded, "There is no evidence that the cable played any role in Kremlin decision making on the crisis or was even read by Khrushchev." But the Scali-Feklisov meeting would become part of the mythology of the Cuban Missile Crisis. (15)

There was another channel – the fourth – involving less formal exchanges between Robert Kennedy and Dobrynin, of which Hilsman only vaguely refers to in his two books.

Private conversations between Robert Kennedy and Anatoly Dobrynin were held at the Russian Embassy or in Robert Kennedy's office at the Department of Justice from about 1 a.m. to 3 a.m.

Late Saturday night October 27, 1962, Dobrynin was invited by Robert Kennedy for an urgent tête-a-tête at the Justice Department. It turned out to be a decisive conversation that sent the signal to Khrushchev that he could save face by eventually arranging for a missile trade in Cuba and Turkey.

 This account was written immediately afterwards and is to be regarded as authoritative, claims Dobrynin. During their conversation, the ambassador asked Kennedy, "What about the missile basis in Turkey?" It turned out that Robert Kennedy was ready with an answer, which the President had authorized me but had not yet been given to Khrushchev. He replied that if the missiles in Turkey represented the only obstacle to a settlement on the terms that had just been outlined, the president saw no insurmountable difficulties.

His main problem was a public announcement: the siting of missile bases in Turkey had been a result of a formal decision adopted by the NATO Counsel. For the president now to announce a unilateral decision to withdraw the missiles from Turkey would damage the structure of NATO and the position of the United States as its leader. Nevertheless, President Kennedy was ready to come to terms with Khrushchev on this subject as well.

"I believe," Robert Kennedy said, "that it will take probably four or five months for the U.S. to withdraw its missiles from Turkey. This is the minimum time the administration will require because of rules of procedure with NATO." Robert Kennedy warned that what he was telling Dobrynin about Turkey was strictly confidential and that only a couple of people in Washington, besides his brother and himself, were aware of it.

Before they parted, Robert Kennedy gave the ambassador a telephone number so he could ring him directly at the White House. Dobrynin found that "throughout the whole meeting, Robert Kennedy was very nervous, and it was the first time he had seen him in such a state. Kennedy did not even try to argue with the various points as he normally did. He just kept repeating that time was pressing, and the two of them should not waste it.

In earlier meetings, the tense atmosphere in Washington had been accentuated by the fact that Robert Kennedy was far from being a friendly person and lacked a proper sense of humor, always a great help whenever discussions become complicated, as these certainly were. Moreover, he was impulsive and excitable. "Nevertheless, we managed to keep our conversations, which as a rule were lengthly, strictly businesslike," Dobrynin observed. According to Dobrynin, in his memoirs, Khrushchev leaves no doubt that his report of his conversation with Bob Kennedy, October 27, 1962, turned the tide in Moscow. He called it the "Culminating point of the crisis." (16)

I checked Khrushchev's memoirs but couldn't find that comment on the RFK-Dobrynin meeting.

But Anatoly Dobrynin reported, according to Khrushchev, that five or six days into the crisis, Robert Kennedy came to see him on an unofficial visit, looking exhausted. RFK even admitted that he had not been home for six days and nights. "The President is in a grave situation," Robert Kennedy said, "and he does not know how to get out of it. We are under severe stress. We are under pressure from our military to use force against Cuba. If the situation continues much longer, the president is not sure that the military will not overthrow him and seize power. The American army could get out of control." (17)

Not for one moment was Kennedy acting out of fear of a military takeover – this was North America, not South America. That's what I call Khrushchev's sense of exaggeration. Remember his shoe incident at the United Nations on October 12, 1960 (he removed his shoe and furiously pound a table with it in protest against a speech critical of Soviet policy in Eastern Europe). He had a great feeling for dramatizing events, and he could have been a great actor.

It is hard to find out, as always in politics, who is telling the truth. I am convinced that Scali and Fomin are both unreliable. I think Bartlett is right when he claims that Scali made up the whole story. In the Cuban Missile Crisis, different channels were consulted, but which one was the opening of a settlement of the Crisis?

How could President Kennedy and Dean Rusk know Scali invented the story? Perhaps he did not because, at first sight, his story was reliable, being backed by Roger Hilsman.

Could it be that Roger Hilsman was fooled by Fomin when he was "acting on Khrushchev's instructions?"

Why would Khrushchev send Fomin to negotiate with Kennedy if he could deal with JFK directly through their correspondence?

I think Scali invented the story, as Bartlett said, to gain publicity. But what about Salinger's comment on Scali being "a great reporter and a great American?" Was Pierre so naive at that time when he made that observation?

Unknown at that time, the RFK-Dobrynin meetings were more important and decisive to get a way out in the Missile Crisis. But even a "lying" option must be consulted, and that was what Rusk and Kennedy did.

If you look at the different stories of the backchannel Scali-Fomin meetings, I think it's frightening, two guys searching for recognition and fame on a very, very serious matter, avoiding nuclear war. They distrusted each other, lied to each other, fooled Hilsman, Salinger, and Rusk. JFK had to take into consideration their advice, which turned up to be of no significant value.

4.4. McNamara's Ambiguous Point of View on the "Castro Assassination"

Before the Church Committee, McNamara stated that he had never heard either the President or the Attorney General propose Castro's assassination. But he conceded later, "We were hysterical about Castro at the time of the Bay of Pigs and after that, and there was pressure from President Kennedy and the Attorney General to do something about Castro."

The Minutes of August 10, 1962, SGA meeting contains no reference to an assassination.

Dick Goodwin testified before the Committee that he had a recollection of "limited certainty" that the subject of a Castro assassination was raised at the August 10 meeting. Still, he was unable to say "with any certainty" who raised the subject.

Harvey and McCone recalled that the question of assassinating Castro was raised at the August 10 meeting. Harvey recollects that the question of the assassination was raised by Secretary McNamara but only in the context of inviting the meeting to "consider the elimination of the assassination" of Castro.

Lansdale also recalled that the subject of Castro's assassination had surfaced at the August 10 meeting. But Rusk, Bundy, Gilpatric did not recall the August 10 discussion at all.

In a staff interview before his testimony, Goodwin recalled the date of the meeting at which a Castro assassination was raised as falling in early 1961 after the Bay of Pigs.

After reviewing the minutes of the August 10, 1962 meeting and the Lansdale and Harvey memoranda of August 13 and 14, he testified he had misplaced the dates of the meeting in his memory.

McNamara testified that although he did not recall assassination being discussed at the SGA meeting, he did remember having expressed opposition to any assassination attempt or plan when he spoke with McCone several days later. Harvey said that shortly after the meeting, McCone informed him that he had told McNamara that assassination, or involvement in any such plan, should not be discussed. Walter Elder, McCone's Executive Assistant, was present when McCone telephoned McNamara after the August 10 meeting and testified that McCone told McNamara,

"The subject you just brought up, I think it's highly improper. I do not think it should be discussed. Such action should never be condoned. It is not proper for us to discuss, and I intend to have it expunged from the record."

Although Bobby Kennedy was not present at that August 10, 1962 meeting when McNamara discussed the assassination of Castro as the only solution, my logical reflection is that Bob McNamara must have discussed it with Bobby Kennedy in private because they were very close friends.

In a magazine article in June 1975, Goodwin was quoted as stating that at one of the meetings of a White House task force on Cuba, it was McNamara who said that Castro's assassination was the only productive way of dealing with Cuba. In his testimony at the Church Committee on July 18, 1975, Goodwin said, "That's not an exact quote," and explained. "I didn't say that it was McNamara, but that very possibly it was McNamara. When the interviewer asked Goodwin about McNamara's role, he said it very well could have been McNamara."

Goodwin told the Committee, "It's not a light matter to perhaps destroy a man's career based on a 15-year-old memory on a single sentence that he might have spoken at a meeting without substantial certainty in your mind, and I do not have that." (75-15=60: not possible, in 1960 Kennedy was not yet President). (1)

It is difficult to reconcile this testimony with Goodwin's testimony that he told the author of the article that McNamara might very have made the statement about assassination at the August meeting.

In 1988 Goodwin regained his memory. He recalled that in the middle of May 1961 at another meeting of the Cuban task force, this time at the State Department, about twenty people were gathered at a conference table when Secretary of Defense, McNamara, having sat through an hour of discussion, rose to leave for another appointment and firmly grasping Goodwin's shoulder with his right hand, announced, "The only thing to do is to eliminate Castro." Goodwin was puzzled; wasn't that just what they had been talking about for a month? When the CIA representative looked toward McNamara and said, "You mean Executive Action," McNamara nodded, then said to Goodwin, "I mean it, Dick, it's the only way." Goodwin had never heard the phrase "executive action" before. But its meaning was instantly apparent.

Two divergent thoughts raced through Goodwin's mind. Could McNamara mean it? Did we do such things? And: It's absurd even if you killed Castro, you would accomplish nothing. His brother Raoul and Che would take his place, both if anything, more fanatic, more devoutly pledged to international Communism than Fidel. (2)

Robert McNamara suggested a possible Castro assassination three times in the presence of Dick Goodwin. In the Harpers article, Goodwin quoted McNamara as saying that a Castro assassination was" the only productive way of dealing with Cuba." But before the Church Committee, Goodwin testified that he told the author, "it very well could have been McNamara, but he wasn't sure." As for the August 10,

1962 meeting, he said he misplaced the date with early 1961. But thirteen years after the Church Committee investigation, he told another McNamara-Castro assassination story, which happened in May 1961, with a CIA representative present. If true, it was not very smart on McNamara's part because for the CIA, and this could have been an unofficial encouragement from a senior Kennedy Cabinet member considered by Stewart Alsop as the highest IQ of the country top public officials. But the most disturbing testimony comes from Walter Elder. He testified before the Church Committee, "The subject you just brought up, I think it's highly improper. I do not think it should be discussed." No doubt about it that "the subject" was a Castro assassination. Did McNamara bring up a possible Castro assassination with Goodwin present? Yes, McNamara never disputed Goodwin's claim. But Goodwin's allegation loses credibility because he changed his story too much and too often.

And I agree with my friend Dan when he said that Dick, for all his great talents and good ideas, was prone to exaggeration. I feel that fame was important to him. (3)

Was McNamara perhaps one of the "pressures" Kennedy felt he was under to assassinate Castro?

4.5. Three Cuban Cigar Stories

The first opportunity for talks with a high-ranking leader of the Cuban revolution came at the founding meeting of the Alliance for Progress in Punta Del Este, Uruguay. Spontaneous and informal, the encounter, in the early hours of August 18, 1961, came at the initiative of Ernesto "Che" Guevara. During the conference, Guevara saw a young White House aide named Richard Goodwin smoking a cigar across the room.

"I see Goodwin likes cigars," he remarked to a young member of the Argentine delegation. "I bet he wouldn't dare smoke Cuban cigars." When the Argentinian repeated this to Goodwin, he told him he would love to smoke Cuban cigars but that Americans couldn't get them. The next day, a large polished-mahogany box, hard inlaid with the Cuban flag from a brass key and crammed with the finest Havanas, arrived at Goodwin's room. With it was a typewritten signed note from Guevara, reading in Spanish "Since I have no greeting card, I have to write. Since writing to an enemy is difficult, I limit myself to extending my hand." (1)

On his return, Goodwin was invited by Kennedy to the White House. After a brief statement of congratulation, Goodwin walked into the mansion with him and told of the meeting with Guevara. There was no sign of annoyance from the president, no limit of reproof, only curiosity about Guevara and interest in what he had said. "Write a complete account," Kennedy instructed, "and circulate it to Rusk, Bundy, and the others." Then, pointing to a small package Goodwin was holding, he said, "What's that?" It was the still untouched box of Cuban cigars that Guevara had sent to Goodwin. He handed the box to Kennedy, who put it on his desk and promptly opened it. "Are they good?" he asked. "They're the best," Goodwin replied, as

196

Kennedy lifted one from the box, lit it, and took a few puffs. Suddenly the president turned to Goodwin, exclaiming, "You should have smoked the first one." "It's too late now, Mr. President," Goodwin responded. He grimaced slightly and then resumed smoking. (2)

In their notes to their book "Back Channel to Cuba: The History of Negotiations between Washington and Havana," William M. LeoGrande & Kornbluh write that "The President was alluding to the possibility the cigars could have been poisoned." It is not clear if Kennedy was aware of that, among several CIA assassination schemes aimed at Castro, one was to lace Castro's favorite cigars with a toxic substance. They were referring to the Church Committee, which says, "CIA's Office of Medical Services, indicates that on August 16, 1960, an official was given a box of Castro's favorite cigars with instructions to treat them with lethal poison." (3) (4) Kennedy was at the height of his presidential campaign. I doubt that the CIA did inform him, and the Church Committee's conclusions are from 1975-1976. I think he enjoyed his cigar, and that's all we have to think about.

But there are two other wonderful cigar stories involving Pierre Salinger, Kennedy's press secretary. Before signing the executive order on February 3, 1962, that put an embargo on all trade with Cuba, the President called Pierre into his office in the early evening.

"Pierre, I need some help," he said solemnly.

"I'll be glad to do anything I can, Mr. President."

"I need a lot of cigars."

"How many, Mr. President?"

"About 1,000 Petit Upmann's."

Salinger shuddered a bit and asked when Kennedy needed them. "Tomorrow morning."

As a staunch Cuban Cigar smoker himself, Salinger knew many stores, and he worked on the problem into the evening. The next morning Pierre walked into his White House office at about 8 a.m., and the direct line from the President's office was already ringing. He asked Pierre to come in immediately. "How did you do, Pierre?" he asked. Indeed Salinger had done well – acquiring 1,200 cigars. Kennedy smiled and opened up his desk. He took out and signed a substantial document – the decree banning all Cuban products from the United States, including, naturally, Cuban cigars. (5)

Dick Goodwin complained that lacking the means for such a gesture, and he had to be satisfied with a single box, which he rationed over weeks. (6)

On May 5, 1962, Pierre Salinger flew to the Soviet Union to meet with his counterparts in communications. He spent fourteen hours with Nikita Khrushchev, and when he bounded out of the line, a smile stretching from ear to ear (Salinger had been warned about his mercurial temper) and his first words to Salinger were, "I thank your president for having my daughter to lunch at the White House. No other American President has dared to do that."

Shortly before Salinger was due to leave, the Soviet Premier said, "I hear you are a great lover of cigars. I do not smoke cigars myself, but I just received a wonderful present which I have decided to give to you. It's from my friend Fidel. With that, he handed a stunned Salinger a huge box containing 150 Cuban cigars. Salinger, well aware of the illegality of the gift, nevertheless decided that, as an emissary of the US president, it would be churlish to reject Khrushchev's generosity, particularly as his boss loved cigars. Besides, his status meant no customs checks on returning home. So Salinger packed the cigars, beautiful box and all, breezed through US customs, and went straight to the White House to deliver a very detailed report of his trip. Afterwards, he produced what he thought would be a welcome surprise, but instead of smiling, JFK frowned at the cigars and asked: at the end of which he told him that he had a special surprise, "What's it? I've got one hundred and fifty Cuban Cigars." Instead of smiling, as I'd anticipated he would, JFK frowned and said, "You didn't smuggle those into the country, did you?" "No," Salinger said, "I brought them right through customs." "Pierre," the President said in a lecturing tone, "do you realize what a scandal it would be if the media found out?" Salinger was unfazed, "How are they going to find out, Mr. President? There are only three people in the world who know about it, you, me and Khrushchev." But Kennedy was unmoved and ordered Salinger to take the cigars to the head of the US Customs and hand them over to him personally.

"And because I think you might take some of those cigars out of the box, I want him to count them and then sign a paper saying all one hundred and fifty survived the trip." Kennedy insisted. So sadly, Salinger went to the head of the customs, turned over the cigars, which he counted and signed a paper certifying that, yes, all 150 were there. Salinger asked what would happen to them. "Why destroy them," he said in a formal tone. "I know," I said, "one by one." Relenting, but only a bit, this hard-hearted civil servant said, "Here, take the box." Salinger's hopes leaped, but he took the box, turned it over, and dumped out all 150 cigars. It was, however, a lovely box and Salinger kept it for the rest of his life. (7)

A cigar story before and after the trade Embargo with an overzealous reaction by Jack Kennedy on Salinger's cigar story – JFK was obviously more afraid of Cuban cigars than women.

4.6. The William Attwood – Lisa Howard – Jean Daniel – Castro Rapprochement

Mark J. White says that while Castro and Soviet leader Nikita S. Khrushchev could be dangerously erratic, particularly in respect to the Soviet premier's risk-taking propensities, both were keen to have better relations with Kennedy than had existed with President Dwight D. Eisenhower. Khrushchev and Castro, moreover, did not keep their interest in better relations with the United States under wraps. In private correspondence with Kennedy advisors such as seasoned diplomat W. Averell

Harriman, Khrushchev made his hopes clear. Castro and his advisors, in statements and interviews, did the same. Even after the Bay of Pigs invasion, Cuban officials continued to explore possibilities for a rapprochement with Kennedy.

Mark J. White refers to an August 17, 1961 conference in Uruguay, where Ernesto Che Guevara told Kennedy to aid Richard N. Goodwin of his government's interest in a modus vivendi with Washington.

White concluded that, with a bold, innovative US president, the overtures of Castro and Khrushchev might have been explored. Under Kennedy's leadership, however, they were not. Instead, Kennedy implemented policies that helped trigger the most severe crisis in the Cold War. (1) (2)

Mark J. White tells only one side of the story about the Cubans wanting a rapprochement. Dick Goodwin told Arthur Schlesinger on June 11, 1977, that the timing and psychology of the Che Guevara meeting on August 17, 1961 – only four months after the Bay of Pigs humiliation – were both wrong. It was too soon. What White also forgot to mention is that Goodwin qualified his account of his talks (meeting) with Ernesto Che Guevara by adding, "If he means it." This is a striking example of historical participants manipulating the evidence and inventing "truths" to suit their purposes, so well defined by Sheldon M. Stern. (3) (4) (5)

On October 18, 1963, William Attwood talked with noted Greek architect and town planner Constantinos Apostolou Doxiadis – often known as C.A. Doxiadis – who had just returned from an architects' congress in Havana, where he talked alone to both Castro and Guevara. He told Attwood that he was convinced Castro would welcome a normalization of relations with the US if he could do so without losing too much face. He said that Guevara and the other Communists were opposed to any deal and regarded Castro as dangerous and unreliable. Doxiadis also made clear that they would get rid of Castro if they thought they could carry on without him and retain his popular support. (6)

In a memorandum for President Kennedy on January 4, 1963, McGeorge Bundy reported that "there is well- a high universal agreement that Mongoose (the secret program against Cuba aimed at removing the Communists from power, which was a prime focus of the Kennedy administration) is at a dead end. We should identify our investigation of ways and means of communicating with possibly dissident members of the Castro regime, perhaps even Castro himself (Donovan, for example, had an invitation to be Castro's guest at Cuba's resort beach of Varadero). There is work to be done in our relations with men like Manolo Ray. The role of intelligence officers needs to be redefined. The very large commitment of the CIA to Mongoose activities should be reexamined and probably substantially reduced. The role of CIA as an apparent spokesman and agent of the United States government in Cuban affairs should probably be reduced still further." (7)

In an interview on March 22, 1996, six months before his death, McGeorge Bundy said, "We wanted to make a reality check on what could or could not be done with

Fidel Castro. The President thought this was an exploration worth making because it might lead to something." (8)

William Attwood, U.S. Ambassador to Guinea, who also served as an advisor to Adlai Stevenson, was the leading advocate inside the Kennedy administration for talking to Castro about the potential for improving relations.

In September 1963, the Guinean Ambassador to Havana assured Attwood that Castro, in contrast to his Communist "entourage," was unhappy about his own "satellite" status and was looking for a way out. Attwood also received information from other sources indicating that Castro wanted an accommodation with the US and would make substantial concessions to this end. There was also a rift developing on this issue between Castro and his chief pro-Communist associate, Che Guevara, who considered Castro dangerously unreliable. (9)

The CIA was determined to derail the administration's secret peace bid. At a White House meeting on Cuba on November 5, 1963, Helms urged that the administration slow down the Attwood initiative and proposed that the government "war game" the peace scenario "and look at it from all possible angles before making any contacts" with Castro. (10)

In an interview on September 11, 1980, with Herbert Parmet, Attwood said, "I saw Castro last October and saw him two years before, and he keeps referring to that little period and how he was on the other end of the plans." Parmet asked how, in the face of all the clandestine activities going on against him, how did Castro think he would go through to Kennedy? Castro thought he could go through to Kennedy. "He read a lot about them," Attwood replied. "He understood that these things were being done by a police or a Secret Service bureaucracy. I think he probably felt that Kennedy was not fully in control of the CIA." (11)

Attwood said he believed that the only people who knew about his contacts with the Cubans were the President, Ambassador Averell Harriman, Ambassador Stevenson, and Attorney General Robert Kennedy, McGeorge Bundy, Bundy's assistant, and journalist Lisa Howard. (12)

On November 12, 1963, Bundy advised Attwood that the president saw the visit of any U.S. Official to Cuba now as impractical. Instead, he, as Bobby had before him, suggested that Castro send his envoy to see Attwood in New York. Kennedy wanted Castro to say first whether there was any prospect of Cuban independence from Moscow and an end to hemisphere subversion. "Without an indication of readiness to move in those directions, it is hard for us to see what could be accomplished by a visit to Cuba." Bundy advised Attwood to make clear to the Cubans "that we were not supplicants in this matter, and the initiative for exploratory conversations was coming from the Cubans."

On November 18, Castro put a word to Attwood that the invitation to come to Cuba remained open and that the security of the visit was guaranteed.

On the same day, Kennedy delivered a speech before the International Press Association in Miami. He declared, "The hard reality of life in much of Latin

America will not be solved simply by complaining about Castro, by blaming all problems on Communism, or generals, or nationalism. It is important to rotate what now divides Cuba from my country and the other countries of this hemisphere.

It is the fact that a small bond of conspirators has stripped the Cuban people of that freedom and handed over the independence and sovereignty of the Cuban nation to forces beyond the hemisphere. They have made Cuba a victim of foreign imperialism, an instrument of the policy of others, a weapon in an effort dictated by external powers to subvert the other American Republics." Kennedy went on: "This, and this alone divides us. As long as this is true, nothing is possible. Without it, everything is possible. Once this barrier is removed, we will be ready and anxious to work with the Cuban people in pursuit of those progressive goals which a few short years ago stirred their hopes and the sympathy of many people throughout the hemisphere."

Robert Dallek remarked that the Cuban community in Florida did not miss the president's implied receptivity to a fresh start in relations with Cuba. In general, the exiles saw the speech as "expressions of willingness to accept Fidelismo sin Fidel." This did not please the substantial number of conservatives in the community. If they had known about the Attwood initiative and the Daniel conversation, and I should add the Howard secret meetings, they would have been up in arms. (13) (14)

Schlesinger, who helped write the speech, later told Attwood that it was meant to help his diplomatic effort by signaling that the president was truly interested in opening a peace channel with Castro.

But Kennedy's November 18 speech carried harsh rhetoric as well, maligning the Castro government as a "small band of conspirators," which "once removed" would ensure U.S. support for a democratic, progressive Cuba. Desmond Fitzgerald took credit for injecting this militant language into the speech, and the CIA spun the president's remarks to its friendly media contacts as a get-Castro tirade. The fact that both Schlesinger and Fitzgerald could claim credit for the same speech demonstrates how the administration's Cuba policy was a battlefield between competing factions. Arthur Schlesinger explained to Anthony Summers in 1978 why the CIA did not want John F. Kennedy to negotiate with Fidel Castro during the summer of 1963, "The CIA was reviving the assassination plots at the very time President Kennedy was considering the possibility of normalization of relations with Cuba – an extraordinary action. If it was not total incompetence, which in the case of the CIA cannot be excluded, it was a deliberate attempt to subvert national policy." (15) (16)

Ted Sorensen believed that a neutral Cuba was exactly what Kennedy wanted. While he continued to deplore its politics and repression, JFK hoped that he might someday be able to turn Castro into another Marshal Tito, the Yugoslav Communist leader who broke with the Soviet System and Moscow without adopting anti-Communist policies. (17)

After months of her cajoling, the Cuban mission in New York, Lisa Howard was finally granted a visa to travel to Havana in early April 1963. Castro ignored her for several weeks as he finished negotiations with New York lawyer James Donovan for the release of U.S. prisoners in Cuban jails and prepared to take a long trip to Russia for his first summit with Khrushchev.

To get his attention, Howard wrote Castro a letter after she arrived, "I beg you to say yes," it pleaded in Spanish. "Give me this interview, please," and passed it on to various interlocutors, among them Donovan, whom she beseeched to put in a good word for her.

Finally, at midnight on April 21, 1963, Castro arrived at the nightclub in the Havana Riviera hotel, and the two talked until 6 a.m. discussing Kennedy and Khrushchev. Howard was impressed by Castro's breadth of knowledge. "Never, never before have I found a Communist interested in the sentiments of Albert Camus."

Castro enjoyed the conversation so much that he agreed to a formal interview, the first granted to a U.S. television journalist since 1959.

In the early hours of April 24, Howard put a series of forceful questions to the Cuban commandant, "When had he become a Communist? Did he ask Khrushchev for the nuclear missiles? Why were hundreds of thousands of Cubans fleeing to Florida?"

And then came the question, "Under what conditions might he support a rapprochement with Washington?" Castro cited his successful talks with Donovan on the prisoner release as a positive step forward. A rapprochement "was possible," Castro noted in halting English, "if the United States wishes it."

When "Fidel Castro: Self Portrait" aired on ABC on May 10, 1963, it dominated the news cycle. "Castro applauds U.S. "Peace Steps," declared the New York Times. "Castro would like to talk with Kennedy," announced the Cleveland Plain Dealer. Howard's interview was a great success, the front page of nearly every paper in the country. Howard wrote in a private note for Castro, "The entire interview is now being discussed on the highest levels."

Unbeknownst to Howard, however, the CIA vigorously opposed her message of potential reconciliation and lobbied Kennedy to ignore it. In a secret memo to the White House, dated May 2, 1963, CIA Director John McCone recommended "the Lisa Howard report be handled in the most limited and sensitive manner" and "that no active steps be taken on the rapprochement matter at this time."

Howard's initial efforts went nowhere. (18)

After she returned to the US, she went to see Kennedy at the White House, sharing details of her Castro encounter with the gossip-hungry Kennedy – including the revelation that she had slept with the Cuban leader. "She talked with Jack about it," Howard's friend, the equally dishy Gore Vidal, later reported, "and mentioned that Castro hadn't taken his boots off. Jack liked details like that." Do you believe that story? I don't.

In her diary, Howard wrote that Castro "made love to me efficiently." Her daughter Fritzi Lareau said that her mother fell for him because she liked powerful men, and Fidel was very macho. And, of course, the peace mission appealed to her sense of drama because it was being played out in a global spotlight. But at the same time, it was secretive and exciting. (19)

Getting no traction at the White House, Howard redrafted her letter to the president into the article "Castro Overture," which appeared as a cover story in the September 1963 issue of the liberal journal War/Peace Report. William Attwood read the article and called Howard on September 12, 1963. Together they agreed on a plan of action. First, Attwood approached UN Ambassador Adlai Stevenson to get a green light from Kennedy to make "discreet contact" with Cuba's UN ambassador Carlos Lechuga. Then, Howard approached Lechuga in the UN lounge and told him that Attwood urgently wanted to talk to him. A cocktail party at her East 74th Street townhouse would serve as a cover for the two diplomats to meet. (20)

On September 23, 1963, off in the corner of the living room, Attwood and Lechuga discussed how negotiations between their two hostile countries might be initiated. Lechuga hinted that Castro was indeed in the mood to talk. "If the peace meeting succeeded," Attwood observed, "it could remove the Cuban issue from the 1964 campaign." Stevenson was intrigued but cautioned that "unfortunately, the CIA is still in charge in Cuba."

Nonetheless, Stevenson took the proposal to Kennedy, who gave him clearance to pursue the dialogue. Harriman, too said he was "adventuresome enough" to like the idea but advised Attwood also to get the approval of Bobby Kennedy. Stevenson was not keen for Attwood to meet with the Attorney General, whom he still considered bull-headed on Cuba. But Attwood dutifully phoned the Justice Department, arranging to see RFK on September 24, 1963, in his office.

Instead of pouring cold water on the rapprochement idea, as Stevenson had feared, Bobby responded favorably. He thought it would be too risky for Attwood to visit Cuba since it would probably leak out and create a political furor in Washington. But he nevertheless felt the peace dialogue was "worth pursuing," and he suggested that secret talks with Castro could be held in another country such as Mexico or at the United Nations.

JFK was even more enthusiastic. At a White House meeting on November 5, Bundy told Attwood that the president was "more in favor of pushing towards an opening toward Cuba than was the State Department, the idea being to get them out of the Soviet fold and, perhaps, to wipe out the Bay of Pigs and maybe get back to normal." Once again, Kennedy himself was the most forward-looking person on his foreign policy team.

Milt Ebbins – talent manager and impresario, who helped produce JFK's 1961 Inaugural Ball – told Daniel Talbot that Kennedy would have recognized Cuba. Kennedy had told Ebbins that if the US recognized Cuba, Cuba would buy American refrigerators and toasters, "and they'll end up kicking Castro out."

Red Fay was also convinced that Kennedy was determined to make peace with Cuba. (21) Howard set up a meeting for Attwood to talk directly with Castro's top aide Vallejo.

Around 2 a.m. November 18, 1963, Howard managed to reach Vallejo and put Attwood on the line to discuss arrangements for the two to meet clandestinely. This was the moment Howard had long-awaited. Attwood would recall many years later that at the other end of the line, Fidel Castro was listening in, in the presence of Lisa Howard – as Castro himself would tell Attwood many years later. (22)

Jean Daniel working at that moment for the French weekly news magazine L'Express got an appointment with President Kennedy. At William Attwood's request, Ben Bradlee arranged for Daniel to go to the oval office before he went to Havana.

On October 24, 1963, at 17.30, Jean Daniel interviewed President Kennedy for twenty-five minutes.

The visitor before him was Marshal Tito, of whom Kennedy remarked that he had a better relationship than he had with de Gaulle.

On November 19, 1963, after been waiting for days to get an interview with Castro, Daniel and his friends decided to leave to take a plane to Mexico. At 10 p.m., picking up their luggage, the telephone rang. Castro was waiting in the hotel lobby downstairs. Castro asked Daniel to go back to his hotel room to talk. Fidel, Vallejo, his top aide, Juan Orocha, the interpreter, Marc Riboud, Michèle, and Daniel were to stay in this hotel room from 10 p.m. until 4 o'clock the next morning.

A good part of the talk revolved around the impressions Daniel recounted to Castro of the interview, which President Kennedy had granted him on October 24, and about Fidel Castro's reactions to these impressions. He told Daniel that he wasn't in the least fearful for his life since danger was his natural milieu. If he were to become a victim of the US, this would simply enhance his radius of influence in Latin America as well as throughout the socialist world. He was speaking, Castro said, in the interests of peace in both of the American continents. To achieve this goal, a leader would have to arise in the United States capable of understanding the explosive realities of Latin America and of meeting them halfway. Then, suddenly, he took a less hostile tack, "Kennedy could still be this man. He still has the possibility of becoming, in the eyes of history, the greatest President of the United States, the leader who may, at last, understand that there can be coexistence between capitalists and socialists, even in the Americas. He would then be an even greater President than Lincoln."

Castro explained that Khrushchev considered Kennedy was a man you can talk to and added:

"I consider him (Kennedy) responsible for everything, but I will say this: he has come to understand many things over the past few months... in the last analysis, I'm convinced that anyone else would be worse." Then Fidel said with a broad and boyish grin, "If you see him again, you even tell him that I'm willing to declare Goldwater my friend if that will guarantee Kennedy's re-election."

At the end of that extraordinary night, Fidel told Daniel, "Because you will see Kennedy again, be a messenger of peace." When they finally got out of the hotel, Daniel said that he could have listened to Castro for a couple of hours more.

The next morning Vallejo came to the hotel telling Daniel and his friends that they were invited for the weekend to the humble summer residence which Fidel Castro owned on magnificent Varadero Beach, 120 kilometers from Havana. During lunch in the living room at around 1.30 in the afternoon on November 22, the telephone rang. A secretary announced that Osvaldo Dorticos, Cuba's President, had an urgent communication with the Prime Minister. Fidel picked up the phone, and Daniel heard him say, "Como? Un atentado." He then turned to Daniel and his friends to say that Kennedy had just been struck down in Dallas. He came back, sat down, and repeated three times the words "Es una mala notica" (This is bad news). Castro remained silent for a moment awaiting another call with further news. Another call came through: it was hoped they would be able to announce that the United States President was still alive, that there was the hope of saving him.

Fidel Castro's immediate reaction was, "If they can, he is already re-elected." He pronounced these words with satisfaction.

But finally came the announcement that President Kennedy was dead. Castro stood up and told Daniel, "That's the end of your mission of peace. Everything is changed; everything is going to change. And I'll tell you one thing: at least Kennedy was an enemy to whom we had been accustomed. This is a serious matter, an extremely serious matter." (23) (24)

William Breuer has his version when Castro announced to Daniel that Kennedy was dead. He wrote, "Daniel was surprised that the maximum leader displayed no emotion over the sudden demise of his bitter Yankee foe, not even asking the caller who had performed the deed; Daniel later reflected that "It was almost as though Castro was expecting it." (25) This is once more a perfect example of marginal science fiction history. Jean Daniel never made that reflection. Jean Daniel, who died February 19, 2020, at the age of 99, was convinced that Kennedy would have made peace with Castro.

But on the very day that Daniel was conveying JFK's conciliatory message to Castro, CIA officials were taking covert steps to strangle the peace initiative. On November 22, in a stunningly duplicitous act of insubordination without informing the president, the Attorney General or CIA director Richard Helms and Desmond Fitzgerald arranged for a poison pen to be delivered in Paris to a disaffected Castro military officer named Rolando Cubela for the assassination of Castro. Like the agency's plan to kill Castro with a toxic wet suit, hatched during the Donovan peace mission, the Cubela plot was designed to snuff out the Attwood-Howard initiative. (26)

Dallek wrote that Kennedy's dual-track Cuban policy in 1963 did not, however, include assassinating Castro.

A CIA scheme (or more precisely a Desmond Fitzgerald scheme) set in motion on November 22, to have Rolando Cubela Secades, an anti-Castro member of the Cuban government, kill Castro with an injection from a hypodermic needle hidden in a ballpoint pen, was directly at odds with Kennedy's policies. (27)

Stephen G. Rabe writes that some scholars have suggested that Kennedy showed interest, during his last months in office, in improving relations with Castro. He responded to Castro's peace overtures, opening indirect lines of communication. Intermediaries were authorized to speak with Cuban officials. The United States wanted Castro to renounce his faith in Communism. In short, President Kennedy was prepared only to accept Castro's surrender. His administration never renounced its policy of either overthrowing Castro or plotting his death. (28)

Robert Dallek formulates an excellent conclusion on what the future of Cuban-American relations would have been after November 22 or during a second Kennedy term, when he would not have had to answer American voters again. Whatever the uncertainties in November 1963 about future Castro-Kennedy dealings, it is clear that they signaled a mutual interest in finding a way through their antagonisms, which were doing neither of them any good. (29)

President Lyndon B. Johnson was told about those negotiations in December 1963. He refused to continue those talks and claimed that the reason for this was that he feared that Richard Nixon, the expected Republican candidate for the Presidency, would accuse him of being soft on Communism.

In December 1963, President Johnson came to New York and lunched with William Attwood and his delegation after reassuring the General Assembly that he'd be carrying on Kennedy's policies. At lunch, he told Attwood that he'd read his chronological account of the US-Cuban initiative "with interest." And that was it. Attwood was named ambassador to Kenya in January 1964, and during his Washington briefings, he saw Chase. The latter told him there was no desire among the Johnson people to do anything about Cuba in an election year. (30)

This is a strange observation because Nixon was considered politically dead in 1963 (Barry Goldwater was considered as Kennedy's opponent.) after his gubernatorial elections in California. In the so-called "last press conference" November 7, 1962, he made his famous remark, "you won't have Dick Nixon to kick around anymore." Six years later, Nixon was elected President of the United States. (31) According to Michael Beschloss, Johnson was not interested in a Cuban rapprochement. Helms found that Johnson lacked Kennedy's emotional commitment to covert action against Castro, and thought Vietnam absorbed Johnson, civil rights, the 1964 election, and by "whether or not the Kennedy assassination was a conspiracy." Helms concluded, "Maybe Johnson saw Cuba as an obsession of Robert Kennedy's." (32)

In 1964, Howard continued her talks with Fidel Castro, but Castro thought that there was evidence that some change was taking place in the mind of the US government.

But after July 1964, the Johnson administration appears to have cut Howard out of the loop. There are no more memos about contacts between Howard and Castro and no more diary entries about communications with the White House. (33)

4.7. Operation Mongoose

Operation Mongoose, the secret US program aimed at removing the Communists from power – a prime focus of the Kennedy administration – was named after the animal that fights and kills venomous snakes – particularly cobras.

On November 4, 1961 (According to Evan Thomas, it was November 3), Cuba was the subject of a White House meeting.

Present, according to Robert Kennedy's handwritten notes were, McNamara, Dick Bissell, Alexis Johnson (Deputy Undersecretary of State and an Excomm member), Paul Nitze, and Ed Lansdale (the Ugly American). "McNamara said he would make the latter available for me," wrote Kennedy. "I assigned him to survey the situation in Cuba, the problems, and our assets. My idea is to stir things up on an island with espionage, sabotage, and general disorder, run an operated by the Cubans themselves with every group but Batistaites & Communists. Do not know if we will be successful in overthrowing Castro, but we have nothing to lose in my estimate." (1) (2)

On November 30, 1961, President Kennedy signed a memorandum with a summary of the major decisions which had been made concerning the Cuba operation. "We will use our available assets to go ahead with the discussed project to help Cuba overthrow the Communist regime." (3)

Richard Goodwin had written a memo to the president on November 1, 1961, arguing that RFK would be "the most effective commander." But Bobby Kennedy wanted none of that, "Eliminate my name, as a Commander," he insisted.

Although RFK was the real commander of Mongoose, they chose Edward Lansdale as chief of operations, reporting to a new review committee known as the Special Group (Augmented). Operation Mongoose was born. (4)

The regular Special Group – Taylor, McGeorge Bundy, Alexis Johnson, Gilpatric, Lemnitzer, and McCone – would meet at two o'clock every Thursday afternoon. When its business was finished, Robert Kennedy would arrive, and it would expand into the Special Group (e.i). Cuba would become the subject, and the group, with mainly the same people, would metamorphose into a special Group (Augmented). (5)

According to Evan Thomas, Lansdale was a cross between a Boy Scout and a street hustler. He was brave and risk-taking, and uninhibited by bureaucratic protocols. At once corny and cunning, the gung-ho Lansdale was the model for both Graham Greene's The Quiet American (1956) and William Lederer and Eugene Burdick's The Ugly American (1958). Within the CIA, Lansdale was seen as a loner, a free spirit who did not take orders well, and a bit of a con man who promised more than he could deliver. (4)

Journalist and author David Talbot described Lansdale as a dashing-looking mustachioed Erol Flynn type – a romantic aspect of the Lansdale legend that strongly appealed to the Kennedys. (6)

And it was Lansdale who urged President Kennedy on the bureaucrats that the Cuban people were not likely to rise against Castro.

A National Intelligence Estimate by the CIA on November 28, 1961, flatly declared, "The Castro regime has sufficient popular support and repressive capabilities to cope with any internal threat likely to develop within the foreseeable future."

But in a memo on November 30, Lansdale urged Kennedy to ignore the intelligence experts. They were just playing bureaucratic warfare, Lansdale insinuated. By trying to discourage Kennedy from setting up a separate command that would be outside the agency control. Robert Kennedy, author Even Thomas wrote, was easily swayed by Lansdale, in part because he was still so angry at the CIA for the Bay of Pigs. (7)

Dick Goodwin wrote in "Remembering America" that the Defense Department assigned Lansdale to work with him to devise measures for the overthrow of Castro. Together they called upon the National Security Agency, the CIA and even the Joint Chiefs of Staff to conjure up plans that might lead to Castro's undoing. After the first week, while Goodwin and Lansdale sat in Dick's office, preparing another in a series of endless memoranda, Lansdale looked toward Goodwin, "You know, Dick, it's impossible." "What's impossible?" Goodwin asked. "There is no way you can overthrow Castro without a strong, indigenous, political opposition," Lansdale answered. "And there is not much opposition, either in Cuba or outside it." Goodwin concluded later, "He was right, of course, and although we kept trying, it was hopeless from the beginning."

Within two weeks, Goodwin had drafted a memorandum for the President, which came much to the same conclusion that had unjustifiably discredited Bowles: that our most "effective" immediate steps would be an effort to organize collective action, help democratic parties in other countries, and most important of all, accelerate the Alliance for Progress. "This program," Goodwin wrote to Kennedy, "with its emphasis on the social and economic advance, is the real hope of preventing a Communist takeover." (8)

Lansdale's plan to eliminate Castro had called for an escalating effort to create an opposition to Castro inside Cuba, followed by insurgency and a general uprising. When Lansdale spoke of a March in Havana in October 1962 – conveniently just before the November congressional US elections – he meant a triumphal entry like Castro's own just three years earlier. But as an American author and intelligence expert, Thomas Powers rightly asserts that "Lansdale's plan was a fantasy." Castro's effective opposition was very close to being a class without members. (9)

Evan Thomas agreed, "Lansdale's plan was grandiose, a fantasy, and it was ridiculed by CIA subordinates who began mockingly calling Lansdale "the FM, for field marshal." Lansdale was a general, but he still needed an army, so he depended on

CIA handlers and their Cuban exile foot soldiers whose barracks were safe houses scattered about Miami. (10)

Roger Hilsman of the State Department's Bureau of Intelligence and Research described the "Lansdale approach" as "fragmentary to say to the least and wondered whether"an even worse fiasco than the Bay of Pigs was on the way. (11)

Mary Hemingway, Ernest's widow, may have "irked" Kennedy during an April 1962 White House dinner when she told him that his Cuban policy was "stupid, unrealistic, and worse, ineffective," but her point was not entirely lost in him. (12) (13)

I think General Lansdale, with his big ideas, dreams, tremendous imagination, and a lot of fantasy, would have been able to write a great show on Broadway on Mongoose.

There is not much agreement among notorious historians on what Operation Mongoose cost the American taxpayer. RFK had decreed that "no time, effort, money or manpower was to be spared in the assault on Castro."

Michael R. Beschloss writes, "The contamination of Cuban sugar exports, the counterfeiting of Cuban money, ration books, other sabotage, paramilitary raids, propaganda, espionage, and guerrilla warfare enjoyed a budget of fifty to one hundred million dollars and a massive nerve eater on the campus of the University of Miami called JM/Wave, said to be the largest CIA installation in the world outside Langley. (14)

Thomas C. Reeves says that by November 1961, the President had effectively approved an "Operation Mongoose" effort that would cost $50 million a year. (15)

Sheldon Stern, the John F. Kennedy Library historian, also put a $50 million-a-year price tag on the various covert economic and psychological operations involved in Mongoose. (16)

However, Richard Reeves wrote that Mongoose, including the Task Force W., involving more than four hundred Americans and two thousand Cubans, a fleet of small boats, and some planes operating from U.S. Air Force bases in Florida, cost more than $100 million a year. (17)

So did John H. Davis, "The CIA's special Mongoose unit, Task Force W. under the direction of William K. Harvey, established a huge nerve center, on the campus of the University of Miami code-named JM/Wave, which had some four hundred men working for it in Washington and Miami, maintained over fifty business fronts in Florida, a small navy of high-speed vessels, and air force, and employed over 2000 Cuban Agents, the whole at the cost of $100 million a year." (18)

Seymour Hersh also put the price of Mongoose, including Task Force W., at a minimum of $100 million a year. (19)

Evan Thomas writes that since RFK had decreed that "no time, effort, money or manpower was to be spared in the assault on Castro, the CIA quickly spent about $100 million to create a base for clandestine operations out of Miami, Code-named

JM/WAVE, the Miami station had hundreds of agents, exotic weaponry, and its own fleet of airplanes and speedboats. But it didn't accomplish much (20)

Whatever the true cost, operation Mongoose did nothing to jeopardize the security of Fidel Castro or his standing with the Cuban population. On the cost of the Operation Mongoose, I have two comments to make: First, was it "$50 million a year," or "more than $100 million a year," or "at about $100 million," or "the CIA quickly spent about $100 million to create a base?"

Secondly: between $50 million and more than $100 million, it is a hell of a difference: $100 million in 1962 is the equivalent of $930,953,642.39 in 2022. These are dazzling figures wasted on an operation based on revenge and frustration. It was a manhunt that never succeeded. The painful moral of that story is that governments spent too much money on lost causes or unnecessary ones, like the war in Iraq.

I am persuaded that John Kennedy didn't believe in Operation Mongoose and that he rightfully resisted his Brother Bobby's pressures. It was his brother's preposterous adventure and obsession that overthrowing Castro was "the top priority of the United States government" and that all else was secondary, requiring no time, money, effort, or manpower to be spared.

RFK also said that the president said to him that "the final chapter on Cuba has not been written" and "that this has to get done."

I can't agree with the Kennedy debunkers when they claim that the spirit behind the creation of Operation Mongoose was an act of revenge for the humiliation not only to the United States but to the Kennedy family. The Bay of Pigs was a big Kennedy mistake; he admitted it, he felt sick about it, but it had nothing to do with the Kennedy family.

Attwood, Howard, and Daniel's actions prove that those who advance the case that JFK's main motive was a Castro assassination at all costs are wrong. JFK was for pragmatic and practical solutions, but of course, the iconoclasts can perhaps rightly claim that Kennedy was playing it both ways, a sort of dual-track policy in 1963 – operation Mongoose in combination with negotiations.

No Kennedy apologist can argue that Operation Mongoose under the direction of Robert Kennedy wasn't "his finest hour," and that's what I call dealing with the matter politely. Kennedy debunkers write that John F. Kennedy and his brother Robert ordered a Castro assassination, although a written and signed order from the Kennedys was never found, nor a witness who could confirm explicitly having received such an order personally.

I consider operation Mongoose far worse than the Bay of Pigs. It was stupid, poorly conceived, reckless, and badly executed, a Robert Kennedy folly and obsession.

Arthur Schlesinger Jr. called it Robert Kennedy's most conspicuous folly. James W. Hilty claimed that Robert Kennedy's excitable and amateurish handling of Mongoose bore the marks of a neophyte adventure.

The iconoclasts blame Robert Kennedy's character, ruthlessness, arrogance, recklessness, temper, and habit of insulting people all the time. There is some merit in their accusations. I even can agree with them with their assumption that, due to his character, he gave orders to kill Castro.

But I have two reflections to make: First, he couldn't order it: JFK was the President, and he would never have agreed. JFK would see further ahead and had a broader view than Bobby. Second, a bad character does not make you a cold-blooded murderer. In the Church Committee papers, they discuss four aspects of the Kennedy Administration's Cuba policy in 1963.

1. The standing group's discussion of possible developments in the event of Castro's death.
2. The standing group's discussion of policy options
3. The covert action program approved by the Special Group and
4. The diplomatic effort to explore the possibility of re-establishing relations with Castro.

The first three took place in the spring or early summer of 1963. The fourth, the effort to communicate with Castro, occurred at the same time the CIA offered AM/LASH – the codename for a trusted Castro aide who told the CIA he would organize a coup – a poison pen device for Castro's assassination. (21)

4.8. Did President Kennedy Order the Assassination of Fidel Castro?

In 1975 the Senate established the Select Committee to Study Government Operations concerning Intelligence Activities, commonly known as the Church Committee.

Relying on sworn testimony and written records, the Committee investigated illegal and improper activities by the CIA and FBI, uncovering spectacular evidence about Kennedy's presidency, including reports of assassination plots and covert operations to overthrow Fidel Castro. (1)

The Church Committee stated that they had found concrete evidence of at least eight plots involving the CIA to assassinate Fidel Castro between 1960 to 1965. In August 1975, Fidel Castro himself gave Senator George McGovern a list of twenty-four alleged CIA-backed attempts to assassinate him.

The Committee forwarded the list to the CIA, which responded with a 14-page report insisting that, according to the CIA's files, the agency had no involvement in fifteen of the cases.

The Church Committee further stated that although some of the assassination plots never got beyond the planning and preparation stage, one plot – involving the use of underworld figures – twice progressed to the point of sending poison pills to Cuba and dispatching teams to commit the deed. The proposed assassination devices ran the gamut from high powered rifles to poison pills, poison pens, deadly bacterial powders, and other devices that defy the imagination. (2)

They defy my imagination, too, because the assassination attempts (plots) were either extremely badly organized, or Fidel Castro was a genius in escaping them. There is some truth in both.

On November 8, 1961, Tad Szulc, the Polish-born and Spanish-speaking New York Times reporter, was asked by Richard Goodwin to meet with Robert Kennedy to discuss the situation in Cuba. The meeting was "off-the-record," and Szulc, who attended as a friend of Goodwin's, not as a reporter, later claimed that the subject of the assassination was not mentioned.

The day after the meeting, at Robert Kennedy's request, Szulc, accompanied by Goodwin, met with President Kennedy for over an hour in the Oval Office. (3)

According to Schlesinger, Talbot, and Hersh, Goodwin asserted in an interview with Hersh that "Tad was auditioning for a job, and Kennedy was recruiting him." But, says Hersh, Szulc's typed notes of the meeting, provided by him to the Church Committee and published in scores of books, say nothing about a job offer from Jack Kennedy. (4) Why would Kennedy offer a job to a journalist? I cannot find a plausible answer.

According to notes Szulc made immediately after the talk, the President asked what the United States might do about Cuba, "either in a hostile way or in establishing some kind of dialogue." Then Kennedy said, "What would you think if I ordered Castro to be assassinated?" Szulc replied that murdering Castro would not necessarily change things and was not something the United States should be doing. According to Szulc, the President responded, "I agree with you completely." JFK told Szulc he was raising the question because he was under intense pressure from advisors to okay a Castro murder, but he was resisting. (5) (6)

Szulc remembered President Kennedy going on for a few minutes to emphasize how strongly he and his brother felt that the US, on moral grounds, should have recourse to the assassination. Szulc thought Kennedy might have mentioned the pressure coming from "someone in the intelligence business" but could not be sure: interviewed in 1998, Szulc said, "Now as I look back, I don't think he meant intelligence officials. I think he was talking about Bobby." (7)

Schlesinger and Goodwin both agree that if Kennedy was involved in a plot to kill Castro, he would hardly have told a reporter from the New York Times. (8)

On the so-called "intelligence people," Evan Thomas wrote, "It is hard to know which "intelligence people" might have been badgering the president in 1961. The CIA was on the defensive, Dulles was gone, and the once-mighty Bissell was a lame duck on his way out."

John Nolan, later RFK's administrative assistant, thought the pressure to kill Castro came from wealthy friends of the Kennedys in Palm Beach. (7) That's what I call a wonderful, invented story.

A day or two later, Goodwin, out of curiosity, raised the question with Kennedy, observing that it sounded like a crazy idea to him. "If we get into that kind of thing," Kennedy said, "we'll all be targets." (9)

Goodwin recalled that, after asking Szulc for his reaction to the idea of assassinating Castro, Kennedy said, "Well, that's the kind of thing, I'm never going to do." (10)

A few days after the meeting with Szulc and Goodwin and some six weeks after the issuance of NSAM 100, President Kennedy, speaking at the University of Washington in Seattle on November 16, 1961, stated, "We cannot, as a free nation, compete with our adversaries in tactics of terror, assassination, false promises, counterfeit mobs, and crises." (11)

But Harris Wofford's claim about who was actually behind the pressure on the president is astonishing, "If Robert Kennedy understood and supported this secret plan within the larger covert operation, he might have been the source of "terrific pressure" for the assassination. Nothing in the testimony before the Senate Committee suggests that the circumlocutious and evasive leaders of the CIA would have put such direct pressure on the President. Then who did? "Terrific pressure" is what anyone, including his brother the president, would have felt if he tried to resist a course strongly advocated by the Attorney General." (12)

Do I have to persuade the readers that Harris and Bobby weren't the best of friends? On two occasions, separated by more than 20 years, Tad Szulc had the chance to discuss the Bay of Pigs and President Kennedy with Fidel Castro. The first time was in June 1961, less than two months after the invasion, when he joined Castro on a tour of the battlefield. The next time was at Castro's office at the Palace of the Revolution in Havana late in January 1984, almost twenty-three years later.

Szulc told Castro about the November 9th meeting in 1961, explained the pressure Kennedy was under and put the historical question, "What would you think if Kennedy ordered your assassination?" Castro, of course, knew by 1984 that numerous attempts had been made by the CIA in the 1960s to murder him. Still, he could never bring himself to believe that President Kennedy would have authorized them. "What you tell me is very interesting, and I had never heard it before," Castro told Szulc.

In a letter June 23, 1961, from Tad Szulc to Arthur Schlesinger, who send a memorandum to President Kennedy on June 26, 1961, Szulc wrote, "Castro indicated that he would be interested in the resumption of some form of relationship with the US, provided that the US agree to quit trying to destroy his revolution. Castro said that a successful negotiation on the rebels-for-tractors affair could lead to further US-Cuban negotiations. In all the talks with us, Szulc said that Castro made a point of speaking with utmost respect about the President." (13) (14) (15)

"Smathers," Herbert S. Parmet writes, "would not be the most credible witness about a Kennedy involvement, especially with Castro." I would add: look at the health chapter, and you'll find George Smathers a funny guy, a great storyteller, but unreliable.

George Smathers recalled in a 1964 oral history interview that while walking in the White House grounds in March 1961 with Kennedy, the talk turned to what to do about Cuba. Smathers could not recall whether he brought it up or I brought it up, "We had a further conversation of assassinating Fidel Castro, what would be the reaction, how the people would react, would people be gratified. I'm sure he

213

(Kennedy) had his ideas about it, but he was picking my brain on this particular question as I had heard many times he picked the brains of others." As Smathers recollected, Kennedy was just throwing out a barrage of questions, seemingly certain it could be accomplished and that it would be no problem. (16)

In 1975, fourteen years after that stroll in the White House grounds, Smathers testified to the Church Committee that President Kennedy raised the subject of assassination (with Smathers) because someone else "had discussed this and other possibilities concerning Cuba" with the president.

According to Smathers, President Kennedy asked him what reaction he thought there would be throughout South America where Castro was to be assassinated. Smathers said he thought it would not be a good idea to consider assassinating him. Kennedy completely agreed with Smathers, pointing out that no matter how it was done and by whom, the US, and its president, would be condemned for it. In other words, Smathers and the president were united in their disapproval of any such plan.

Smathers said that on a later occasion, he had tried to discuss Cuba once more with President Kennedy – but the President had made it clear that Smathers should not raise the subject with him again. One night at a dinner with Smathers, the president emphasized his point by cracking his plate at the mention of Cuba. (17)

In a 1988 interview with Michael Beschloss, Smathers claimed that the President had told him that he had been "given to believe" by the CIA that when the invaders hit the beaches of the Bay of Pigs, Castro would no longer be alive. (18)

Seymour Hersh writes in "The Dark Side of Camelot," "Smathers provided one hint of Kennedy's real attitude in his March 1964 oral history for the Kennedy library. JFK's concern, Smathers noted, was not about the morality of political murder but about the political difficulty of getting it done without leaving any evidence." (19)

Hersh made this grave accusation, but according to George Smathers' oral interview on March 31, 1964, JFK never mentioned those incriminating words. Hersh has a right to criticize JFK, but he should have done it honestly. However, his whole book is dishonest, full of fabrications, and untrustworthy sources. As one critic wrote in the Los Angeles Times, Hersh's book "turns out to be, alas more about the deficiencies of investigative journalism than about the deficiencies of John F. Kennedy." (20)

Thomas Powers is certain that the conversations with Smathers and Szulc indicate Kennedy was troubled by the matter. Still, if he was clear in his mind that it was wrong, it does not seem likely that he would have invited the reaction of two knowledgeable but disinterested outsiders. The fact that Kennedy said he was against it, too, in both instances, should not be taken at face value. Maybe he was against it, but even if he had been for it, he probably would not have tried to argue Smathers and Szulc around. (21)

Thomas Powers considered that Helms was "like an amnesia victim" – and I consider Powers as "a Kennedy mind reader." Did Kennedy wanted Castro dead or overthrown? The Kennedys no doubt felt a personal animus toward Castro, admits

Arthur Schlesinger. Still, if a vendetta consumed them, they would have had the perfect pretext when the Soviet Union sent nuclear missiles to Cuba in October 1962. No one who knew John and Robert Kennedy well believed they would conceivably countenance a program of assassination. Like McCone, they were Catholics. Robert certainly was as devout as McCone asserts Schlesinger. (22)

Thomas Powers wrote, "Could anyone believe the Kennedy people would all have been chewing on pencils and murmuring disbelief if the CIA had truly been off on its own where Castro was concerned?

They would have raised the roof. Could anyone believe that the CIA, as an institution, much cared who ruled Cuba? Could anyone doubt the response of the Kennedy people, and very likely the Senate Intelligence Committee itself, if some CIA officials had risked the complete absence of a single piece of paper to back him up and had said, "Well, who do you think ordered Castro's assassination, the office boy?" It was John F. Kennedy and his brother Bobby."

If Helms had said that, which in Powers opinion he could have, he not only would have been the target of some extremely Caustic comment but from that day forward, he would have lunched alone. (23)

Thomas Powers' book "The Man who Kept the Secrets, Richard Helms and the CIA" is considered as possibly the best book ever written about the CIA: it is indeed a well-written book, but I have one reflection to make, there is not a single word on his executive assistant George M. Manus who ran the Cuba operation and who contradicted his boss about RFK's go-ahead for a Castro assassination.

According to John H. Davis, "in April-June 1962, a three-person assassination team was sent by Roselli to ambush the Cuban premier, and it also failed. To what extent were the Kennedy brothers involved in these murder attempts? John Kennedy is on public record as denouncing the assassination of foreign leaders as an instrument of national policy. Still, we have seen that Kennedy's public pronouncements were often at odds with his intended actions." (24)

Thomas G. Paterson read the Helm's and Bissell's Church Committee testimonies and concluded that President Kennedy may or may not have known about the assassination plots, but he did set the general guidelines. (25)

The fact that no authorization appears on paper or in the memories of Kennedy's lieutenants does not prove that the president never signaled the CIA that he would not object to Castro's murder. Richard Helms told Michael Beschloss in 1988 that "a lot of people probably lied about what had happened in the effort to get rid of Castro."

Beschloss further wrote that whether Kennedy gave a clear go-ahead for the CIA's assassination plots against Castro will probably never be conclusively resolved.

Bissell told the Church Committee that during the Palm Beach Meeting at which he and Dulles briefed the president-elect on Cuban invasion planning, the CIA director told Kennedy "obliquely" of this auxiliary operation, the assassination attempt. It is only remotely possible, concludes Beschloss, that the President was told of the murder plots, so obliquely that he did not know what he was hearing. Helms further told Beschloss, "There are two things you have to understand: Kennedy wanted to get rid of Castro, and the Agency was not about to undertake anything like that on its own."

Michael Beschloss examined possible motives: Decades later, investigation of the Kennedy, Mafia, Castro connection has become a cottage industry. Kennedy's severest critics argue that in 1960 he made some kind of secret unholy alliance with Giancana and other organized crime leaders. The result: once Kennedy was President, he had to navigate between his brother's insistence on prosecuting the mob and whatever pledge he or his representatives might have made to Giancana and his men. Such a pledge might have included a promise to move slowly on prosecuting the Mob and fast on removing Castro. (26)

I would like to ask Michael Beschloss if he agrees with Kennedy's severest critics on what they claim.

James Giglio writes, "Whether the President knew of the efforts to kill Castro is uncertain." (27)

Richard Reeves, however, was convinced that the Kennedys knew of and encouraged attempts on Castro's life. "So liquidation was off the record – but it was never off the table," Reeves wrote. Helms said, "It was made abundantly clear to everybody involved in the operation that the desire was to get rid of the Castro regime and to get rid of Castro. No limitations were put on this injunction." (28)

According to Seymour Hersh, "The Bay of Pigs was the first political defeat of Jack Kennedy's life, and he sought revenge, but not on the advisors and the government agencies that, so he told everyone, had misled him. His target was Fidel Castro, and he spent his remaining days in office determined to make Castro pay with his life, preferably for staining the Kennedy honor."

Hersh asserted that the President's files would reveal that Jack and Bobby Kennedy were more than merely informed about the CIA's assassination plotting against Prime Minister Fidel Castro of Cuba: they were its strongest advocates. The necessity of Castro's death became a presidential obsession after the disastrous failure of the Bay of Pigs invasion in April 1961 and remained an obsession until the end.

Hersh further claimed bluntly that White House files also dealt with three foreign leaders. They were murdered during Kennedy's thousand days in the presidency. Patrice Lumumba of the Congo, Rafael Trujillo of the Dominican Republic, and Ngo Dinh Diem of South Vietnam. Hersh insists that Jack Kennedy knew of and endorsed the CIA's assassination plotting against Lumumba and Trujillo before his inauguration on January 20, 1961. (29)

Probably Kennedy knew of the CIA assassination plotting against Lumumba. However, I doubt it, but he wasn't President when Lumumba was assassinated. The execution of Lumumba is thought to have taken place on January 17, 1961, between

21.40 and 21.43, according to a Belgian report. His death was formally announced over Katangan radio on February 13, 1961. (30)

If a respected journalist goes that far in blaming a "President-elect," I call this badly conducted investigating journalism.

James Hilty, another Kennedy author, points out that, although the Church Committee never discovered a written order to kill Castro, the lack of a paper trail does not necessarily prove that the Kennedys had no knowledge of or involvement in plots to kill Castro. Presidents have reportedly instituted covert activities with a nod of the head or with vague verbal instructions that later could be refuted under the doctrine of plausible deniability.

Precisely how much Robert Kennedy knew of these plots is unclear. CIA General Counsel Lawrence Houston testified under oath that he had informed Kennedy in May 1962 of the CIA's hiring of Roselli, Maheu, and Giancana to act as the go-betweens with Cubans presumably to overthrow Castro's regime. Richard Bissell also briefed Kennedy on some aspect of the same operation.

Asked by the Church Committee if that briefing indicated that the purpose of the operation was to kill Castro, Bissell replied, "I thought it signalled just exactly that to the Attorney General I'm sure, Robert Kennedy, however, believed that he had terminated the CIA – Mafia plots." When rumors surfaced attaching Kennedy's name to attempts on Castro's life, he complained to Richard Goodwin, "I'm tired of all these Latins attacking me for going after Castro. The fact is that I'm the guy who saved his life." (31)

Mark J. White asserts that CIA attempts to assassinate Castro, which were ongoing during the Kennedy years, were almost certainly made with JFK's knowledge and approval. (32) Evan Thomas writes, "The CIA – Mafia plots never came close to killing Castro, but, by a perverse ripple effect, they had a greater impact on others, most especially on Robert Kennedy."

A careful examination of the evidence suggests that Kennedy may or may not have been a perpetrator of the assassination plots – "enabler" is probably a more accurate term – but he was the victim, not physically, but rather psychologically. It appears most likely that RFK's involvement in the plots was at worst peripheral – but that, after his brother died in 1963, he became very fearful about what they might have wrought.

Thomas concludes his assassination plots theory by stating that if Bobby Kennedy was aggressively trying to kill Castro, he surely would let Lansdale in on the secret. And if Lansdale were complicit in the CIA's Mafia operation, he hardly would have written a memo about "liquidation of leaders." What the August 10 flap demonstrates is that the second phase of the Castro assassination plots, the Harvey-Rosselli connection, was small, feckless, and closely guarded.

The Kennedys may have discussed the idea of assassination as a weapon of last resort. But they did not know the particulars of the Harvey-Rosselli operation or want to, asserts Thomas. Roberto San Roman was a quiet, dignified man from a middle-class Cuban family, one of the survivors of the Bay of Pigs. They had escaped off the beachhead and floated for three weeks in an open boat before rescue. He met with Bob Kennedy at his office and at Kennedy's Virginia home, Hickory Hill, where the two men talked about the Cuban situation.

"He never created false hopes," said San Roman. "He said he wanted a second shot at Castro, but that it would not be easy." In an interview 35 years later with Evan Thomas, San Roman said that Kennedy did not push the assassination option. But San Roman did push it, as the two men sat alone, in the living room at Hickory Hill. San Roman asked RFK directly if he would help the Cuban exiles kill Castro. Bob Kennedy responded, "Couldn't you get five or ten Cubans to do it." "His reaction," San Roman asserted, was that "it's not my job, it's not something the United States would do, but if the Cubans can, fine." (33)

On May 7, 1962, at 4.00 at the Attorney General's request, RFK met with Houston Lawrence and Sheffield Edwards to be briefed on the CIA operation involving Maheu, Rosselli, and Giancana.

Describing the Attorney General's anger, Lawrence Houston later testified, "If you have seen Mr Kennedy's eyes got steely and his jaw set and his voice got low and precise, you got a definite feeling of unhappiness." (34)

Lawrence Freedman writes, "There is no evidence that Kennedy ordered the assassination of Castro. All one can say is that the obsession with Castro, and Robert's constant goading of the CIA, created a climate in which CIA officials might have been forgiven for believing that the higher authorities would not be unhappy with the Cuban leader's demise."

In the fall of 1961, with the Castro issue still unresolved, the possibility of the assassination was on Kennedy's mind. On October 5, in NSAM 100, Bundy wrote to Rusk, asking for a plan for a particular Cuban contingency. The contingency conveyed orally was that "Castro would in some way or another be removed from the Cuban scene." Freedman concluded, "It seems reasonably clear that Kennedy had asked for the plan." (35)

The CIA's Samuel Halpern, who served as the executive assistant to three deputy directors for clandestine operations, told Hersh, "They were just absolutely obsessed with getting rid of Castro. I don't know of any senior official that I talked to who felt, aside from the pressure from the Kennedys, that Castro had to go.

You don't know what pressure is until you get those two sons of bitches laying it on you." Halpern told Hersh, "We felt we were doing things in Cuba because of a family vendetta and not because of the good of the United States. The Kennedys were taking on Castro for personal reasons because the Bay of Pigs besmirched the family name." (36)

According to Ray Cline, deputy director of intelligence at the CIA, overthrowing Castro was also a very personal matter for the Kennedys. They were a couple of Irish men who felt they had miffed it, and they vented their wrath on Castro for the next two years.

Michael O'Brien concludes that, in the first analysis, circumstantial evidence leans toward the fact that the Kennedys did, authorize the CIA to kill Castro. He cites the conversations the president had with Smathers and Szulc are telltale.

Michael O'Brien says that Robert Kennedy hadn't expressed surprise or anger at the plot to kill Castro, only that the killers being used were gangsters. Plotting with the Mafia would jeopardize his goalG of putting Giancana and Rosselli in prison. In 1967 Drew Pearson and Jack Anderson revealed that the CIA might have contracted with the Mafia to murder Castro, but they mistakenly reported that Robert Kennedy took part in the planning. "I didn't start it," Robert told aides after the column appeared. "I stopped it. I found out that some people were going to try and attempt on Castro's life, and I turned it off."

In his oral history interview for the Kennedy library, Robert Kennedy disavowed any involvement with plots to kill Castro. Still, for Michael O'Brien, his perfunctory denial is unconvincing.

Did he know of any attempt to assassinate Castro?

"No," responded the Attorney General.

None tried?

"No"

Contemplated?

"No"

O'Brien further claims that if Helms lied to the Church Committee, the entire controversy becomes clear. Robert Kennedy met secretly with Helms and verbally ordered him to try to assassinate Castro, and both maintained the secret. Helms had a record of lying, says O'Brien.

The sense of urgency emanating from the White House was intense. More than once, Helms told Larry Houston, "My God, these Kennedys keep the pressure on about Castro."

O'Brien concludes, "If we assume that Robert Kennedy directed the assassination plans, it is certain he discussed them with the president. The brothers were so close, and the matter was too important. President Kennedy must have authorized the plots." (37) We know that JFK listened to his brother but not always followed his advice. There's plenty of proof of that in my book.

David Talbot writes, "Robert Kennedy's meeting with the two CIA officials still looms large in historical debates about the Kennedy administration. Bob Kennedy found out that the CIA was using the Mob to kill Castro. He was outraged. He told them, "I trust that if you ever do business with an organized crime again -with gangsters," he said in a voice seething with sarcasm. "You will let the Attorney General know." CIA Officials and other political opponents of the Kennedys would insist many years later that Bobby's outrage that day had been an act.

Was he truly shocked and enraged by the agency's dark dealings? Or was the younger Kennedy the driving force behind the government's murderous plots against Castro? Two warring camps have angrily engaged each other over these questions in the past four decades, with Kennedy partisans on one side and CIA apologists on the other. At stake is nothing less than the Kennedy brothers' moral standing in history and the reputation of the intelligence agency.

RFK's right-hand man at the Justice Department, John Seigenthaler, told David Talbot that he believes that Kennedy's anger that afternoon was genuine. "I remember when Bob found out about the plots against Castro, he was furious."

When the two fellows from the CIA came over, Seigenthaler took them into Bob's office. "It was a testy, cold discussion. I could tell that Bob was genuinely furious at that meeting. He was not putting on a show for me," said Seigenthaler. Whatever anybody might think about him, you just don't know the man if you think that's something he might go for. It violated his most basic principles.

Advance knowledge of a conspiracy to assassinate Castro would have been antithetical to his most basic beliefs." Seigenthaler concluded, "I don't think there's any evidence of it, and I don't believe you'd ever find it." (38)

Michael Dobbs has his theory linking the Kennedy brothers to a Castro assassination, "While there is no smoking gun tying the Kennedy brothers to the Castro assassination plot, there is some circumstantial evidence Jack Kennedy discussed the possibility of Castro's assassination with a journalist, Tad Szulc, only to agree that it would be "immoral" and "impractical." (39)

Bissell testified before the Church Committee that Allen Dulles never told him that he, Dulles, had informed President Kennedy about the underworld plot. But Bissell told the Church Committee that he believed Dulles had so informed President Kennedy and that the highest authority had accordingly approved the plot. Bissell never asked Dulles whether Dulles had informed President Kennedy's National Security advisor McGeorge Bundy about the plot, and Bissell characterized his belief that the president had been informed as "a purely personal opinion."

On another occasion, however, Bissell was more forthright in his answer to a question from Senator Morgan, "I gather that you think it (assassination plot information) came out because of the seriousness of the accusation you are just extremely cautious, is that a fair assumption to make?" Morgan asked. Bissell responded that Morgan's assumption was "very close to a fair" and that he, Bissell, had no direct knowledge, firsthand knowledge, of President Kennedy being advised about a plot. However, Bissell believed that Kennedy knew of the assassination plans.

The Committee had taken testimony from all living officials in the Kennedy administration. None of them – Dean Rusk, Bob McNamara, Roswell Gilpatric, Maxwell Taylor, McGeorge Bundy, and Walt W. Rostow, Richard Goodwin and Ted Sorensen – had heard of an assassination effort against Castro.

Sorensen testified (further) that such an act (an assassination) was foreign to his character and conscience, foreign to his fundamental reverence for human life and his respect for his adversaries, foreign to his approach to US foreign policy; foreign to his concern for this country's reputation abroad and foreign to his pragmatic recognition that so horrendous but inevitably counterproductive a president committed by a country whose own chief of state was inevitably vulnerable, could only provoke reprisals and inflame hostility.

Notes taken by Helms' executive assistant, George McManus, of a meeting in the Attorney General's office on January 19, 1962, included the following passages, "Conclusion – the overthrow of Castro is possible. A solution to the Cuban problem today carried top priority in U.S. Government. No time, no effort, or manpower is to be spared. Yesterday the President had indicated to him that the final chapter had not been written, it's got to be done, and will be done." McManus attributed the words "the top priority in the U.S. Government and no time, money, effort or manpower is to be spared" to Robert Kennedy."

Richard Helms stated that those words reflected "the kind of atmosphere" in which he had perceived that assassination was implicitly authorized. McManus agreed that Robert Kennedy "was very vehement in his speech" and "really wanted action," but McManus disagreed with Helms' perception, stating that "it never occurred to me that Kennedy's exhortation included permission to assassinate Castro." Nor did the spirit of the meeting as a whole leave McManus with the impression that assassination was either contemplated or authorized.

There was a great deal of evidence showing that Castro had a high priority in the Kennedy administration. On the other hand, Sorensen testified that "there were lots of top priorities and it was the job of some of us to tell various agencies their particular subject was top priority continually, and although Cuba was important, it was fairly well down on the list of the President's agenda.

Richard Helms noted in a memorandum of a meeting on October 16, 1962, that Robert Kennedy, while expressing the general dissatisfaction of the President with Mongoose, pointed out that Mongoose had been underway for a year, that there had been no acts of sabotage and that even the one which had been attempted had failed twice.

In a memorandum to Helms by McManus, who worked full time on Cuba matters, reviewed the Mongoose program in the aftermath of the Cuban Missile Crisis and stated, "During the past year, while one of the options of the project was to create internal dimension and resistance leading to eventual U.S. Intervention, a review shows that policymakers not only shied away from the military intervention aspect but were generally apprehensive of sabotage proposals." On October 30, 1962, the SGA ordered a halt to all sabotage operations.

Helms testified that the "intense" pressure exerted by the Kennedy administration to overthrow Castro had led him to perceive that the CIA was acting within the scope of its authority in attempting Castro's assassination, even though assassination was never directly ordered. Helms said, "I believe it was the policy at the time to get rid of Castro, and if killing him was one of the things that was to be done in this connection, that was within what was expected. I remember vividly the pressure to overthrow Castro was very intense."

Senator Mathias put the following to Helms "Let me draw an example from History; when Thomas Beckett was proving to be an annoyance, like Castro, the King said, "Who will rid me of this man." He didn't say to somebody, "go out and murder him." He said who will rid me of this man and let it go at that."

Helms answered that it was a warming reference to the problem. Senator Mathias' next question was, "You feel that spans the generations and the centuries?" "I think it does," answered Helms. Mathias, "And that is typical of the kind of thing which might be said, which might be taken by the Director or by anybody else as Presidential authorization to go forward, don't you think so, Mr. Helms?"

Helms agreed, adding, "but in answer to that, I realize that one sort of grows up is traditional of time, and I think that any of us would have found it very difficult to discuss assassination with a President of the U.S." "I just think," Helms concluded, "We all had the feeling that we're hired out to keep those things out of the Oval Office."

Helms said that "he never was told by his superiors to kill Castro, but that no member of the Kennedy administration ever told him that assassination was proscribed or ever referred to in that matter, but nobody ever said that assassination was ruled out."

Helms was asked during one appearance before the Committee by the chairman, "Since he (RFK) was on the phone to you repeatedly, did he ever tell you to kill Castro?"

Helms: "No."

The Chairman: "He did not?"

Helms: "Not on those words, no."

Helms testified that he had never told Attorney General Robert Kennedy by any assassination activity. Still, Helms also said that the Attorney General had never told him that assassination was ruled out. Helms added that he did not know if Castro's assassination would have been morally unacceptable to Bob Kennedy. Still, he believed that the Attorney General would not have been unhappy if Castro had disappeared off the scene, whatever that means. Helms also said that he never liked assassination and banned its use five years after he became CIA Director.

The lead paragraph of Martin's report for the Church Committee stated, "Retired Maj. Gen. Edward G. Lansdale said Friday that acting on orders from President John F. Kennedy, delivered through an intermediary, and he developed plans for removing Cuban Premier Fidel Castro by any means including assassination."

Martin testified that this paragraph was an accurate reflection of his conclusion based on the totality of his interview with Lansdale on May 30, 1975. (40)

John H. Davis, Jackie's cousin, Thomas C. Reeves and William B. Breuer, who cannot be described as "Kennedy admirers," quote carefully the Church Committee "through an intermediary "and" including assassination," but they forgot to mention the reaction of Lansdale, who after reading Martin's story, told the reporter, "Your first sentence is not only completely untrue but there is not a single thing in your story that says it is true." (41)(42)(43)

222

Given Martin's testimony that the report's lead paragraph was a conclusion based on his entire interview with Lansdale, it should be noted that the remainder of Martin's story does not state that Lansdale was ordered by President Kennedy or the Attorney General to develop plans for Castro's assassination.

The report quotes Lansdale as stating, "I was working for the highest authority in the land, the President, and then states that Lansdale said he did not deal directly with the President, but "worked through" an intermediary who was more intimate with the President than Bundy. Lansdale refused to provide Martin with the intermediary's name.

Subsequent paragraphs in the Martin report indicate that Lansdale told the reporter that the decision to undertake assassination planning was his own – as Lansdale testified to the Committee. According to the Martin article, Lansdale said that assassination was "one of the means he considered, that he believed assassination would not have been "incompatible" with his assignment and that he just wanted to see if the U.S. had any such capabilities."

Martin asked Lansdale, "Who were you working for?" In a subsequent conversation on June 4, 1975, Martin said he asked Lansdale specifically, "Were you ever ordered by President Kennedy or any other Kennedy to draw up plans to assassinate Castro?" Martin testified that Lansdale replied, "No." Martin further testified that in the June 4 conversation, he asked Lansdale whether "any assassination planning you did was alone on your initiative" and that Lansdale replied "Yes."

On reading Lansdale and Martin's testimony, you get a different view on "assassination ordered through an intermediary." Still, doubt remains because the Martin report says that the intermediary was more intimate with the President than Bundy, and according to Martin, Lansdale refused to give the intermediary's name. But on the other hand, Lansdale told Martin that he disagreed with what he wrote on the subject.

When the Committee chairman asked Lansdale if he had ever discussed with the Attorney General a plan or a proposal to assassinate Fidel Castro, he said "No." And I am very certain that such a discussion never came up either with the Attorney General or the President because he "had doubts" that assassination was a useful action and one which he had never employed in the past during work in coping with revolutions. He had considerable doubts about its utility, and he was trying to be very pragmatic.

The O'Leary report states, "Retired Maj. Gen. Edward G. Lansdale has named Robert F. Kennedy as the administration official who ordered him in 1962 to launch a CIA project to work out all feasible plans for "getting rid of" Cuban Prime Minister Fidel Castro."

Lansdale, in an interview with the Washington Star, never used the word assassination and said Robert Kennedy did not use it. But Lansdale further said that "there could be no doubt that project for disposing of Castro envisioned the whole spectrum of plans from overthrowing the Cuban leader to assassinating him."

Lansdale testified that he had submitted a statement to the Washington Star-News stating that O'Leary's report was a "distortion of my remarks." (44)

In February 1996, RFK's son Robert Kennedy Jr. and his brother, Michael, traveled to Havana to meet with Fidel Castro. As a gesture of goodwill, they brought a file of formerly top-secret US documents on the Kennedy administration's covert exploration of accommodation with Cuba – a record that stated of what might have been, if Lee Harvey Oswald, seemingly believing the president to be an implacable foe of Castro's Cuba, had not fired his fateful shots in Dallas. Castro thanked them for the file and shared his impression that "it was President Kennedy's intention after the Missile Crisis to change the framework of relations between the United States and Cuba. It's unfortunate," said Castro, "that things happened as they did, and he could not do what he wanted to do." (45)

Robert Kennedy's widow, Ethel, raised the subject of the assassination plots with Castro during a visit with the Cuban leader in Havana. I asked Kathleen Kennedy when her mother visited Castro, but I didn't get any answer.

She waited until his translator had left the room before broaching the matter. Castro pretended not to be fluent in English, but he spoke it very well. When they were alone, Ethel addressed Fidel directly. "I want you to know something," she said, looking up at the tall, greying figure whose story was so entwined with that of her family. "Jack and Bobby had nothing to do with the plots to kill you." Castro met her eyes, "I know," he said. (46)

At the end of NBC's weekly television news program Rock Center (which ran from late 2011 until June 2013), host Brian Williams touted an "unexpected" moment with the widow of Robert F. Kennedy when he asked her what she remembered about Fidel Castro, whom she met several times. Ethel Kennedy replied, "He was very warm, very emotional. He clearly would have liked to have been friends with President Kennedy and Bobby." (47)

John Kennedy Jr arrived in Havana on October 23, 1997, during the 35th anniversary of the Cuban Missile Crisis, hoping for an interview with Fidel Castro for his monthly glossy magazine "George," which had launched in 1995. Kennedy took with him "George" writer Inigo Thomas.

But after four lunchless days and no word of an interview, John's standing joke was that a meal before 6 p.m. was as elusive as Castro himself. It, therefore, seemed fitting that when John finally received a call at five on Sunday afternoon telling him to be ready for dinner with Castro at nine o'clock, he thought of it as yet another late lunch. Castro reputedly had seven homes in Havana, never slept in the same place two nights in a row, and never decided on a rendezvous until the last minute.

The dinner took place at the Council of Ministers, a large 1950's building just behind the Plaza de la Revolucion. A tape recorder would not be welcome, John was told: it was to be a private meeting, not an occasion for an interview. Castro delivered one of his legendary five-hour performances. Some of his remarks, though, were particularly striking. He spoke of his admiration for President Kennedy, how brave he had been to accept the blame for the Bay of Pigs, and how US – Cuba relations might have been repaired had the President lived.

When John Kennedy Jr. was leaving the dining room with the gift of cigars he had received, Castro abruptly stopped walking. "You know, Lee Harvey Oswald was trying to come here," he said, half a question, half declaration. (In October 1963, Oswald had applied for a visa at the Cuban embassy in Mexico City, but his request had been denied) "Yes, I did know that," John replied. Castro paused, then said, "It was a difficult time, and you know we didn't let many Americans into Cuba." John simply replied, "Yes," then Castro lifted his head and walked on. The exchange is a riddle of sorts, and exactly what Castro meant is impossible to say, but immediately he heard John's last answer, a sense of relief washed over his face. Maybe he was offering a veiled apology: Castro knew that if Oswald had been allowed into Cuba in October 1963, then he might not have been in Dallas a month later.

Sitting on the Mexicana flight back to New York, Inigo Thomas mentioned the possibility to John. He thought about it for a few moments, nodded, and said nothing. (48)

On July 26, 1963, tens of thousands of perspiring Fidelistas and some 950 guests from foreign countries packed Havana's José Marti Plaza to hear Castro speak. Castro said that he was "willing to discuss differences with the United States," but President Kennedy had refused all offers to negotiate. He also expressed "screw" for the American people who had to pay for Kennedy's "stupid, incorrect policy." "This gentleman (Kennedy), like a horseman, is riding from blunder to blunder, stupidity to stupidity," Castro declared. (49)

On September 8, 1963, Fidel Castro launched a bitter attack on the president during a reception at the Brazilian Embassy, "Kennedy is the Batista of his time, more demagogic than former President Eisenhower, and the most opportunistic American President of all times."

Castro went on, "Kennedy is a Cretin, a member of an oligarchic family that controls several important posts in the government. For instance, one brother is a Senator and another Attorney General. And there are no more Kennedy officials because there are no more brothers." Puffing on a cigar, Castro leaned back in an easy chair and said, "Kennedy is thinking more about re-election than about the American people. He thinks only of Kennedy and nothing else." (50) (51)

Castro forgot to mention Sargent Shriver, Kennedy's brother-in-law, who was head of the Peace Corps and Eunice Shriver, the president's sister, who was a member of a mental retardation board.

On June 10, 1963, President Kennedy gave his historic "Peace Speech" at the American University in Washington, hailed by Khrushchev as the best speech delivered by an American President since FDR.

In some excerpts of the speech, he reached out to the Soviet Union, "Let us re-examine our attitude toward the Soviet Union. It is discouraging to think that their leaders may believe what their propagandists write."

"No government or system is so evil that its people must be considered as lacking in virtue. As Americans, we find Communism profoundly repugnant as a negation of personal freedom and dignity. But we can still hail the Russian people for their many achievements in science and space, in economic and industrial growth, in culture and acts of courage. Among the many traits the people of our two countries have in common, none is stronger than our mutual abhorrence of war." (52)

But a couple of weeks later, on June 26, 1963, in the Rudolph Wilde Platz in Berlin, he spoke a different tone, like Kennedy, the cold warrior:

"There are many people in the world who really don't understand, or say they don't, what is the great issue between the free world and the Communist world. Let them come to Berlin. Some say that Communism is the wave of the future. Let them come to Berlin. And there are even a few who say that Communism is an evil system, but it permits us to make economic progress. Lass sie nach Berlin kommen, let them come to Berlin. Freedom has many difficulties, and democracy is not perfect. Still, we have never had to put a wall up to keep our people in, to prevent them from leaving us." (53)

I view Kennedy's and Castro's sordid comments, Kennedy on Communism and Castro on JFK, as "that's politics," keeping your constituents happy, taking a tough stand on your adversary, like Ali and Frazier before a fight, not giving the impression of being weak in the face of the enemy.

How else can you explain Kennedy's Peace Speech against his hostile Berlin address and Castro insulting Kennedy in Havana against his private comments to Attwood, Howard, and Daniel?

John Kennedy, in his 1961 campaign book wrote, "The Strategy of Peace," recognized Fidel Castro as part of the legacy of Bolivar, who led his men over the Andes Mountains, vowing "war to the death" against Spanish rule, saying, "Where a goat can pass, so can an army." Kennedy mused, "Whether Castro would have taken a more rational course after his victory had the United States Government not backed the dictator Batista for so long and so uncritically, and had it given the fiery young rebel a warmer welcome in his hour of triumph, especially on his trip to this country, we cannot be sure." (54)

White House correspondent and Senior Editor at Look Magazine Laura Bergquist told Sheldon Stern that Kennedy talked to her at great length about Castro. She felt he admired Castro in many ways, something he couldn't admit to publicly. But there was something about Castro that fascinated him. (55)

However, Sorensen believed that one of Kennedy's mistakes in the Bay of Pigs invasion was that JFK should never have permitted his deep feelings against Castro (Unusual for him), nor considerations such as public opinion, especially his fear of condemnation for calling off a plan to get rid of Castro – to overcome his innate suspicions. (56)

Parmet thought Kennedy did admire and respected Castro. A mutual hate/hate was feeling between the two, and each was determined to bring down the other. (57)

4.9. Conclusion

From the Bay of Pigs, a complete failure, some authors call it a brilliant disaster, overconfidence the so-called Midas touch or due to inexperience, call it whatever you want, to the Cuban Missile Crisis, his finest hour, or his need to prove himself by confronting Khrushchev, or JFK's ego as a driver of the crisis.

Hagiographs or revisionists, if they reflect in a rational way, which many historians tend to forget, answers to very difficult questions can be very simple. John F. Kennedy, during his short stay in the White House, had a horror of war. He had experienced one himself, and he was well aware of the cost of modern war to people and nations, not least the threat of a nuclear war conflict that could destroy the world. There would be no winners, only losers.

And above all, Nikita Khrushchev felt the same way. "Any fool can start a war, and once he's done, even the wisest of men are helpless to stop it, especially if it's a nuclear war," Khrushchev stated in his memoirs. (1)

Sergei, his son, who with his wife Valentina became naturalized citizens of the United States on July 12, 1999, (2) said that his father, at the end of May 1962, decided to send strategic nuclear missiles to Cuba. In making this decision, he relied on Russian and European experience and history. For centuries enemies had constantly replaced one another on Russia's borders: the Mongols, Swedes, Poles, Lithuanians, Turks, Napoleon, the British, Germans, and again the Germans. After the Second World War, the Germans had been replaced by US airbases. (3)

Nikita Khrushchev wrote in his Memoirs, "Everyone agreed that America would not leave Cuba alone unless we did something. We had an obligation to do everything in our power to protect Cuba's existence as a Socialist country and as a working example to the other countries in Latin America. We had to establish a tangible and effective deterrent to American interference in the Caribbean, and the logical answer what to do exactly, Missiles. The United States had surrounded the Soviet Union with its bomber bases and missiles. We knew that American missiles were aimed against us in Turkey and Italy, to say nothing of West Germany."

Khrushchev further stated that "the main thing was that the installation of our missiles in Cuba would, I thought, restrain the United States from precipitous military action against Cuba's government. In addition to protecting Cuba, our missiles would have equalized what the West likes to call "the balance of power."

Khrushchev concluded that "the Americans had surrounded our country with military bases and threatened us with nuclear weapons, and knew they would learn just what it feels like to have enemy missiles pointing at you, we'd be doing nothing more than giving them a little of their own medicine. And it was high time America learned what it feels like to have her land and her people threatened."

Who can argue or disagree with Khrushchev's honest observation?

But Khrushchev wanted to make one thing absolutely clear, "When we put our ballistic missiles in Cuba, we had no desire to start a war. On the contrary, our principal aim was only to deter America from starting a war. We were well aware that a war that started over Cuba would quickly expand into a world war. Any idiot could have started a war between America and Cuba. Cuba was eleven thousand kilometers away from us. Only a fool would think that we wanted to invade the American continent from Cuba." (4)

And Khrushchev was no fool. June 3, 1961, when Kennedy and Khrushchev met in Vienna, an extensive report on Khrushchev compiled by psychologists and psychiatrists under the direction of the CIA proved that Khrushchev was not the Machiavellian villain pictured in the American Press, but a predictable pragmatic man. The premier, the report said, was quick to grasp and utilize existing situations. Because he was flexible and impulsive, he could also exploit his opponents' weak spots as adroitly as a chess master. Khrushchev, the report continued, was an earthy, direct man who quickly came to the crux of the matter, particularly in personal relationships.

Finally, the report emphasized that despite Khrushchev's bluster, he basically was a man of peace. (5) (6) Sergei Khrushchev wrote on the 50th anniversary of the Cuban Missile Crisis, "So the Cuban Missile Crisis was resolved. We survived, and I could write this article, and you can read it. But everything might have turned out differently. You, I and all mankind might have disappeared from the face of the earth. The fact that this did not happen is the greatest achievement of those cold warriors President John F. Kennedy and my father, the premier of the Soviet Union, Nikita. Father said more than once that we differed from Kennedy in every respect. He defended his capitalist belief, his world, and we defended ours, our concept of justice. We had one thing in common: Both he and I did everything to preserve peace on earth." (7)

Many historians have written that Khrushchev didn't have great esteem for Kennedy, but if you read Khrushchev's memoirs carefully, you will think differently.

If Khrushchev had to compare – Eisenhower and Kennedy – the two presidents with whom he dealt – the comparison would not be in favor for Eisenhower. Khrushchev considered Eisenhower to be a mediocre military leader and a weak President, a good man, but not very tough. And as Khrushchev discovered in Geneva, he was much too dependent on his advisors. It was always obvious that being the US President was a great burden for him.

Kennedy, on the other hand, impressed Khrushchev, at their Vienna summit meeting in 1961, as a better statesman than Eisenhower, with a precisely formulated opinion on every subject.

He had already been impressed by Kennedy two years before, during his visit to America, when Lyndon Johnson introduced him to the young Senator at a Senate Foreign Relations Committee reception in his honor. Khrushchev later recalled liking Kennedy's face – sometimes stern but often breaking into a good-natured smile. (8)

Sergei Khrushchev said on the Cuban Missile Crisis that the world was lucky. Neither President Kennedy nor his father stumbled. (9) Nikita said that both sides showed that if the desire to avoid war was strong enough, even the most pressing dispute could be solved by compromise. And a compromise over Cuba was indeed found. The episode ended in a triumph of common sense. Khrushchev later said he would always remember the late president with deep respect because, in the final analysis, Kennedy showed himself to be sober-minded and determined to avoid war, showing neither fear nor recklessness. He didn't overestimate America's might, and he left himself a way out of the crisis.

Khrushchev found it a great victory for the Russians. However, we had been able to extract from Kennedy a promise that neither America nor any of her allies would invade Cuba.

He also found the Caribbean crisis as a triumph of Soviet foreign policy and a personal triumph in his career as a statesman and as a member of the collective leadership. And, Khrushchev concluded, Kennedy's death was a great loss of a man gifted with the ability to resolve international conflicts by negotiation, as the whole world learned during the so-called Cuban Crisis. Despite Kennedy's youth, Khrushchev saw the American as a real statesman. Had Kennedy lived, Khrushchev believed, relations between the Soviet Union and the US would have been much better than they became after his death. (10)

The Kennedy-Khrushchev relationship could be likened to that of sporting rivals: great opponents in soccer, tennis, boxing, and football respect each other – and so did these two leaders.

Kennedy, as British Prime Minister Harold McMillan would later say, earned his place in history by this achievement alone.

Ted Sorensen in "Counselor" wrote that the discovery that the Soviet Union had secretly rushed nuclear missiles into Cuba tested JFK's wisdom, courage, and leadership as no president since Lincoln and FDR had been tested. No other test so starkly put at risk, depending on the president's choices, the survival of America. It was for that moment that he had been elected, and it was for that moment, concluded Sorensen, that he would most be remembered. (11)

Aleg Daroussenkov, a Soviet specialist on Cuba at the time of the invasion, recalled that the Soviet Union had little interest in the island in April 1961 and had no ready response to a US invasion. It was the attempt itself that led the Soviets to begin the rapid military build-up that led to the CMC. (12)

The Kennedy revisionists and there are a lot, such as Mark White, states that the consequences of the Bay of Pigs invasion for the Cold War were profound. One of Khrushchev's main motives for sending nuclear weapons to Cuba was to deter a US invasion of the island he thought likely as Kennedy had already sanctioned a similar sort of attack in April 1961. In short, without the American backed invasion, the Cuban Missile Crisis would most likely not have taken place. (13) (14)

White's argument has merit, and he also has the historical honesty to say that Castro, by agreeing to go along with Khrushchev's missile play, also shares some of the responsibility for averting the Crisis.

The Bay of Pigs was a big mistake, but Kennedy was trapped. If he had cancelled it, he was politically dead, harassed by the republicans as being soft on Communism and Castro. As I already before asserted, Kennedy didn't do it the Reagan way in Grenada by sending in American troops.

A Cold War hawk in public, he distrusted the military, was skeptical about military solutions to political problems and horrified by the prospect of global nuclear war. President Kennedy often stood virtually alone against warlike council from the ExComm, the Joint Chiefs, and the leaders of Congress during those historic thirteen days.

JFK's handling of the Bay of Pigs and the Cuban Missile Crisis proves two things for me. Once again, he took his brother's advice when it suited him, and he would never have "Americanized" the Vietnam War.

There is a very interesting story told by Fidel Castro to Pierre Salinger when they met on August 21, 1975, in Cuba. They discussed the Bay of Pigs and the Cuban Missile Crisis for a long time. Castro said he understood why the US had had to impose sanctions on Cuba after the Bay of Pigs, adding that JFK had been seen as failing in his effort to overthrow him and had, therefore, had to do something tough. Yet, at the same time, and much to Salinger's surprise, Castro kept saying he had great admiration for Kennedy. Castro further declared, "If Nixon had won the election in 1960, I am sure that the US marines would have come into Cuba during the Bay of Pigs, and it would have been a dirty war."

He was sad that Kennedy had been assassinated and was persuaded that "Relations between Cuba and The United States would probably have been renewed under the Kennedy administration. (15)

You will never find that story in a Kennedy revisionist book. Still, I think that story told by a member of "the Camelot school" has a right to be told in a Kennedy revisionist assessment. I have done my best to combine positive and negative stories side by side.

At the initial meeting of the crisis, President Kennedy had little of his famed coolness. He was "much clipped, very tense," Gilpatric noted. I don't recall a time when I saw him more preoccupied and less given to any light touch at all. The atmosphere was unrelieved by any of the usual asides and changes of pace that he was capable of. He seemed to believe that the Soviets meant business in the most real sense, and this was the biggest national crisis he'd faced." (16) (17)

Dean Rusk said that Kennedy was very calm and composed, and determined and handled himself beautifully throughout the crisis. There was never any undue nervousness, never any sense of panic, and never any feeling of despair or anything of that sort. Rusk said that he acted like a real President. He had ice water in his veins. That was one of his greatest moments. (18) (19)

Charles Bartlett told Hersh, as the tension grew, that he and his wife had dinner at the White House with the President and his wife on the night that Russian ships were approaching the US blockade. "That's when I admired him the most. He was very cool and yet very sensitive to the implications of what was going on. It was scary. He did not know what the Russian reaction was going to be when they reached the blockade. We went home early, and he hadn't heard..." And Kennedy called Bartlett at about ten-thirty that night and said, "Well, we've got the word they turned around."

For Bartlett, the president had been "perfectly normal" the whole time. (20)

Philip A. Goduti Jr. saw a different JFK than the one at Vienna and the Bay of Pigs. This JFK was cool and calculating. His style in the ExComm meetings was to listen, not talk over the group. It was an exemplary performance of leadership under stressful situations. Also, his strong position with the Joint Chiefs demonstrates that he was not afraid to stand up to the military advisors. (21)

Stephen G. Rabe said that Kennedy deserved credit for standing up to the Joint Chiefs of Staff. Their constant advice could be crudely but accurately put as, "bomb now, ask questions later." He responded calmly to the news of the loss of the U-2 over Cuba. By October 27, discussions in ExComm were becoming unfocused and disorganized. The advisors, exhausted and under extreme stress, rambled and expressed incomplete thoughts. Kennedy remained poised, lucid, and capable of analytic thinking, as was later revealed in the tapes and the transcripts of the meetings. (22)

And what about Martin Luther King, who wrote a draft of a previously unknown private letter to the president in which King stated, "At a time when so many are saying that the most impressive achievement is the result, I find myself as much impressed by the method. In resisting any impulses to overestimate or overstate the result, you allowed your adversary to count some again, thereby preventing psychology of desperation. This laid a firm basis for future negotiations. Equally, your fair and generous characterization of Mr. Khrushchev's responses as "statesmanlike" created an example for him.

In the combination of these approaches, I feel you have utilized some of the elements of non-violent creativity in international conflict, despite the presence of latent force." Martin Luther King concluded that he hoped that Kennedy would continue, despite conflicting pressures, to pursue the difficult quest for settlements. In this direction may be the greatest achievement of the twentieth century, the emergence of statesmen who are equal to the colossal risks a racing technology has imposed upon the world. (23)

Dallek wrote that despite Kennedy's part in provoking the crisis, historians generally have high praise for his performance. One need only compare it with that of Europe's heads of government before World War I – a disaster that cost millions of lives – to understand how important effective leadership can be in times of international strife. October 1962 was not only Kennedy's finest hour in the White House, but it was also an imperishable example of how one man prevented a catastrophe that may yet afflict the world. (24)

But apart from the praise, you have dissenters and others who deal with it in sometimes an ambiguous way. James Giglio said that neither Robert Kennedy nor anyone else could keep the meetings on track.

However, Dean Acheson, unaccustomed to such freewheeling during his Truman days, labelled the gatherings "repetitive, leaderless and a waste of time." Psychological stress became yet another hurdle – something experienced by every participant over the grueling, tension-filled thirteen days.

Sorensen later wrote of waking in the middle of the night that "no other decision in his lifetime would equal this." A raw-nerved president found himself losing his famous "cool" at least a dozen occasions, and McNamara claimed that this crisis induced "the most intense strain" I have ever been under. (25)

Barton Bernstein, a notorious dissenter, used declassified documents at the Kennedy library to argue that the missiles were not an imminent military threat but a political one and that Kennedy could have negotiated privately rather than chosen a public confrontation.

Michael Beschloss says that Kennedy needed to prove himself by confronting Khrushchev. (26)

Khrushchev, in a letter to President Kennedy, October 24, 1962, wrote, "This action you are taking, a quarantine," you're not doing it, not only out of hatred for the Cuban people and its government but also because of considerations of the election campaign in the United States." (27)

Anatoly Dobrynin wrote in his memoirs that President Kennedy, like a gambler, actually was staking his reputation as a statesman, and his chances for re-election in 1964, on the outcome of this crisis. (28)

Mark J. White wrote that while Kennedy's handling of Castro and Khrushchev before October 1962 was flawed, his management of the missile crisis itself proved effective. A quick but not a deep thinker, he was better at grasping immediate dangers than anticipating those down the road. There were weaknesses in Kennedy's performances in the missile crisis, especially during the first few days. But in general, he handled the confrontation adroitly. The salient decision made by Kennedy in the first week of the missile crisis -to opt for the quarantine instead of an airstrike- was prudent.

Mark J. White concludes that although it is worrying that JFK's initial reaction was so belligerent and fortunate that he did not feel compelled to respond instantaneously to the missiles in Cuba. On the other hand, he deserves credit for being open-minded as the debate over options progressed, willing to listen to advice and alter his views. (29)

My observation on White's ambiguous remark about Kennedy's "weaknesses" and JFK's "initial reaction was belligerent," is that the fact that Kennedy was at first for an airstrike, he not only quickly changed his mind to a blockade, but he had to face his hawkish ExComm members, even his brother. Does one has not the right to change his mind and in this Nuclear War threat for the better?

Michael P. Riccards considers the Cuban Missile Crisis not a good example of how foreign policy should be made and implemented. Instead, the crisis itself was partially a consequence of an administration that wildly vacillated between weak expressions of accommodation and dangerous overreaction. The Kennedy presidency, especially in the first of its three years, was not a brief interlude of brilliant statecraft. Rather, it was an immature collection of belligerent, rhetorical, over-idealistic interventions and misdirected overtures. (30)

I agree with what the revisionists call "the Camelot school" writers, that this was JFK's finest hour and will still be praised decades from now.

Michael K. Bohn has researched 17 international crises from 1950 through 2014. He picked at least one illustrative incident from each of twelve consecutive administrations – Harry Truman's through Barack Obama's: six Republicans and six Democrats.

The upshot: There is a big gap between what a president can realistically accomplish in a crisis and what the public expects and political opponents demand. Everyone wants bold and decisive action to right wrongs, punish evil perpetrators, and rescue the innocent. But Bohn concludes, "This is a fairy-tale model of presidential crisis management. In real life, it's been almost unachievable."

There are some of the factors that have limited presidents from acting boldly:
1. Fears of nuclear war,
2. A lack of situational awareness – often called "the fog of war,"
3. Turf battles among senior advisors,
4. Minimal U.S. leverage in the situation,
5. Underestimating adverse consequences of military action.

Conversely, some factors cause presidents to take ill-advised bold action, including:
1. Presidential scandal,
2. Election campaigns,
3. Groupthink within a small, insular presidential advisory team,
4. Planning military operations without meaningful participation by military experts.

During his research, Michael Bohn had gathered observations from foreign policy experts on the 17 crisis and rated them on a maximum of five stars.

The only president who got five stars was President John F. Kennedy for his dealing with the Cuban Missile Crisis, which Bohn gave as a reason for the five-star ratings: Kennedy took incremental steps, made a deal with the Soviets, and avoided war. (31)

After the Cuban Missile Crisis was over, JFK presented a gift of remembrance to his wife Jacqueline and those around him, who had been most involved in deliberations on the Cuban Missile Crisis. Each was given a little silver Tiffany calendar for October 1962, with the fateful thirteen days highlighted in bold and engraved with "JFK" and the recipient's initials. (32)

Kennedy and Khrushchev meet in Vienna on June 3, 1961. They held inconclusive talks on nuclear testing, Laos, and the braining crisis in Berlin and Germany, which are still divided by the major powers.
(Copyright: JFK Library)

Excomm meeting during the Cuban Missile Crisis, October 16 and October 28, 1962
(Copyright: JFK Library)

The 20-month negotiations for the 1118 prisoners captured at the Bay of Pigs were finally successful shortly after resolution of the Cuban Missile Crisis. Freed members of Brigade 2506 were flown to Miami two days before Christmas of 1962, after payment of a ransom of $55 million in food, drugs and cash. President and Mrs. Kennedy addressed the group on December 29 at the Orange Bowl. (Copyright: JFK Library)

After the Cuban Missile Crisis, President Kennedy gave calendars to members of his inner circle. He presented his wife with this calendar, which was on her desk in the White House family quarters. Kennedy had thirty made of them by Tiffany's.
(Copyright: JFK Library)

*President Kennedy was honored by presentation of the brigade flag for his efforts on behalf of the Cuban exiles. His brother had been instrumental in raising the ransom demanded by Fidel Castro. December 29, 1962
(Copyright: JFK Library)*

Cartoon of President Charles de Gaulle with President John F. Kennedy and Khrushchev on his legs.
(Copyright: private collection of Eddy Neyts)

Fidel Castro, his brother Raoul Castro and "Che" Geuvara
(Copyright: free photo internet)

Chapter 5: Kennedy And The Civil Rights Issue. Did He Act Too Slowly?

"One hundred years of delay have passed since President Lincoln freed the slaves. Yet their heirs, their grandsons are not fully free."

- **June 11, 1963, the White House**

"I have a dream that my four little children will one day live in a nation where they will not be judged by the color of their skin, but by the content of their character. I have a dream today!"

- **Martin Luther King Jr., Lincoln Memorial, August 28, 1963**

"Greater than the tread of mighty armies is the idea whose time has arrived."

- **Victor Hugo**

5.1. The RFK-Baldwin Meeting May 24, 1963

The suggestion that Bobby Kennedy should meet James Baldwin, the gay, 38-year old novelist son of a Harlem minister, was made by the militant black comedian Dick Gregory. (1)

Baldwin's 20,000-word essay "Letter from a Region in My Mind" - part of his new book entitled "The Fire Next Time" – had impressed Kennedy when it was published in the New Yorker on November 17, 1962. (2)

On May 24, Robert Kennedy, Burke Marshall and Edwin Guthman met with James Baldwin and a group of Negroes in Joe Kennedy's apartment at 24 Central Park South, Manhattan, wherein 1960 Martin Luther King first met with Senator John Kennedy, the presidential candidate.

Bob Kennedy and Baldwin had met the year before April 29, 1962, at the White House dinner for Nobel Prize Laureates and had agreed then that they wanted to talk some more.

Thus on May 23, 1963, Kennedy invited Baldwin to breakfast at Hickory Hill. "We had a very nice meeting," Kennedy later said. But the meeting lasted just half an hour, as Baldwin's plane was late and Kennedy had to leave for another engagement in New York. So the two agreed to meet in Manhattan the next day – this time with Baldwin and a group of thirteen people.

Among those present were Kenneth B. Clark, the social psychologist; Edwin C. Berry of the Chicago Urban League; Clarence B. Jones, an attorney representing Martin Luther King; and Lorraine Hansberry, the first black woman to have a play produced on Broadway and author of the Raisin in the Sun. Kennedy also invited the singers Lena Horne and Harry Belafonte. Jerome Smith, a young civil rights worker who began as a Gandhian pacifist, became a Freedom Rider and a field worker for the Congress of Racial Equality (CORE). According to CORE historians, Smith had probably spent more time in jail and been beaten more often than any other CORE member. Also present were Edward False, James Baldwin's secretary; Baldwin's brother David; Thais Aubrey, a friend of David Baldwin's; and three white men – actor Rip Torn; magazine editor and literary agent Robert P. Mills; and Henry Morgenthau III, a television producer. (3)

Jerome Smith opened the meeting and, according to Burke Marshall, began with a bitter attack on the Attorney General. Smith boasted that, on his command, all Negroes would come onto the streets with guns and kill the Whites. "Then they all started sort of competing with each other in attacking us, the President, the federal government, and the white system of government in addition to the United States. They said that Negroes wouldn't fight for the United States anymore that we ought to recognize that. They thought the President should have sent the Army into Birmingham. And then, according to Robert Kennedy, Lorraine Hansberry said that they were going to go down and get guns. They were going to start to kill people," Marshall said. (4)

Marshall recalled, "Bobby got redder and redder, and in a sense accused Jerome

Smith of treason, you know, or something of that sort. Kennedy said as he had before, that his grandparents had faced discrimination and now two generations later, his brother was President; a Negro would be President within forty years – and Bob Kennedy was right with his prediction."

Baldwin replied furiously, "Your family has been here for three generations: my family has been here for longer than that. Why is your brother at the top while we are still so far away? That's the heart of the problem."

Kennedy said he had come in search of ideas, and Baldwin suggested that John Kennedy personally escort two black students whom Governor Wallace was loudly threatening to bar from the University of Alabama.

Kenneth Clark described the encounter as "one of the most violent, emotional, verbal assaults that I had ever witnessed before or since." (5) (6)

Clark left the meeting convinced that Robert Kennedy was an extraordinarily insensitive person, unusually loyal to his brother. "I did not leave there feeling that he was a racist by any means, but he did not have empathy." (7)

I disagree with Clark's point of view. I respond to him later.

The meeting went on for three hours. At one point, Clarence Jones, King's lawyer, took Kennedy aside and said, "I just want you to say that Dr. King deeply appreciates the way you handled the Birmingham affair." Kennedy's response was blunt. "You watched these people attack me over Birmingham for forty minutes, and you didn't say a word. There is no point in your saying this to me now." (8)

When Kennedy asked Harry Belafonte privately why he had not spoken up in the meeting to correct some false statements, the singer replied: "I'd lose my position with these people if I spoke up and defended you."

According to Schlesinger, Baldwin was not even aware that the president had delivered a civil rights Message in February. "They (Baldwin's supporters) don't know what the laws are, they don't know what the facts are, they don't know what we've been doing or what we're trying to do, you couldn't talk to them as you can to Roy Wilkins or Martin Luther King. They didn't want to talk that way. It was all emotion, hysteria. They stood up and orated. They cursed. Some of them wept and left the room." (9) (10) (11)

According to Larry Tye, it was Kennedy's frustration with King and Wilkins that made him ask Baldwin to gather other black voices. And there was more. "None of them lived in Harlem. Bobby complained to another interviewer that "they were wealthy Negroes" – although his wealth dwarfed theirs, and their fame didn't exempt them from the humiliations faced by every dark-skinned American. Worse still, to Bobby, three of the black guests that night "were married to white people," which he said exacerbated their insecurities and encouraged them to talk tough. He concluded that he should never have gotten involved with that group, it was a terrible mistake on Bobby's part, and he regretted it deeply. (12)

Bobby had called Arthur Schlesinger when he got back from the meeting. "He was particularly shocked when this fellow said he wouldn't fight for his country, but his later reaction was that it was a good step in education – he got a sense of the rage and the despair from that meeting that enabled him to widen his understanding of the problem." (13)

New York Times journalist Tom Wicker thought that Robert didn't realize the depth of black feeling. "These guys (The Kennedys) were from Massachusetts, they didn't know anything about that. They didn't campaign very much in the South." He saw James Baldwin later that night. "That meeting was significant, because they opened Robert Kennedy's eyes, not only to the seriousness of the matter but to the depth of feeling in the black community. Baldwin at that time was a very intense, charged up-gay, and when I saw him, he was angry: If you had a white skin that night, he was going for you," concluded Tom Wicker. (14)

Fellow journalist John Seigenthaler said that when he talked to Bobby after the meeting, he was down about it. "A few days later, he was mad at himself, not at them: he was angry, furious at himself." Seigenthaler added, "I don't believe after that, I ever visited his home for anything larger than a party of a couple or three couples, when there was not a black (person) present. It wasn't spoken that there had been a charge, but there was a heightened sensitivity that hadn't been there before." (15)

But James Baldwin informed the New York Times on the secret meeting, commenting in print on Kennedy's failure to influence Negroes at the "secret talks." Robert Kennedy never saw or spoke to Baldwin again. (16) (17)

According to Layhmond Robinson, one of the first black reporters at the New York Times, the meeting "was seen as evidence of growing concern over criticism voiced by Negroes across the country on its handling of the Civil Rights issue." Robinson observed that Baldwin had been "sharply critical of President Kennedy for not moving more forcefully in civil rights in the South," and had claimed that the president "has not used the great prestige of his office as the moral forum it can be," adding that Baldwin had also urged the Attorney General to "use his influence to get the president to make a series of talks to the nation on the civil rights issue."

History shows that Bob Kennedy used all his influence on Jack to make a moral stand, which he did a couple of weeks later on June 11, 1963. (18) (19)

Baldwin and his friends so angered Robert Kennedy that at his request, the FBI forwarded dossiers on all those present, a few of whom belonged to organizations suspected of being "subversive." (20) (21)

Robert Kennedy's capacity for showing empathy for the poor and the socially excluded was a great help for his brother in dealing with the Civil Rights issue – although Kenneth Clark will not agree with my point of view.

A few days later after the Baldwin confrontation, Bobby told Ed Guthman after he had been troubled when Jerome Smith, the 24-year-old Congress of Racial Equality (CORE) chairman in New Orleans, said that he would not fight for the United States. "I guess if I were in his (Smith's) shoes if I had gone through what he's gone through, I might feel differently about this country."

Later Baldwin and Clark would credit the meeting has caused a significant shift in Bob's thinking.

Only a couple of weeks before the civil rights riots in Tuscaloosa, Alabama, May 4, 1963, Robert Kennedy shifted his thinking on the Negro issue and begun urging his brother to deal with it primarily as a moral problem.

The Kennedy-Baldwin meeting on May 24, 1963, undoubtedly shaped the direction of the weeks leading up to JFK's address to the nation on June 11, 1963.

Edwin Guthman wrote, "What I didn't fully appreciate, and what most critics did not understand, was the relationship between the President and Bob, that it was remarkably close even for brothers, that John Kennedy felt a need to have his brother's counsel." (22)

I agree with Guthman's assessment that John Kennedy needed Bob's advice, he didn't always listen but in the case seeing the civil rights issue as a moral question – he listened and followed his advice when he thought it was the right time to act and the right thing to do.

Harry Belafonte said that Bobby was undergoing "one of the most profound transformations" he had seen in any human being. He found in Bobby Kennedy, a man wrestling with profound moral questions and always coming down on the right side of the answer." (23) (24)

According to the author and journalist Simeon Booker, Robert Kennedy became perhaps the first American white man really to impress Negroes with his civil rights actions, leaders and followers alike. For the New Frontier, the Attorney General was the messenger, the wonder boy, the Negroes' crusader. No individual, including the late FDR, gained such billing and such respect. Not even his brother rivalled him in popularity among Negroes during the first years of that administration. (25)

5.2. The June 11, 1963 Address – August 28, 1963, The March on Washington

On June 11, 1963, two Negro students, Vivian Malone and James Hood, both twenty, turned up to register at the University of Alabama in Tuscaloosa, with the Kennedy administration determined to avoid a repeat of the tragic violence nine months earlier when James Meredith became the first African-American student to be enrolled at the segregated University of Mississippi.

At 10, 10.15 or 10.48 a.m., Governor Wallace arrived at the university campus and stood in the Schoolhouse door at Foster Auditorium in a symbolic attempt to keep his promise at his inaugural on January 14, 1963, to maintain "segregation now, segregation tomorrow, segregation forever" and to try to block the entry of the two African -American students.

There were two separate confrontations with Wallace during the day.

At the first meeting late in the morning, Kennedy decided to "let Wallace have his show."

Otherwise, Kennedy told his representative at the schoolhouse door, Deputy Attorney General Nicholas Katzenbach, "God knows what could happen by way of violence." He instructed Katzenbach to approach Wallace alone, without the students.

Wallace read a prepared statement, "I George C. Wallace, as Governor, do as a result of this denounce and forbid this illegal and unwanted actions by the central government, unwelcomed, unwarranted and force-induced intrusion upon the campus of the University of Alabama, today by the might of the central government offers a frightful example of the suppression of the rights, privileges and sovereignty of this state."

When, as expected, Wallace blocked Katzenbach from entering the building, Katzenbach telephoned Robert Kennedy, who called the President.

The President issued Executive Order 11111 at 11.34, 11.35 a.m. or 1.34 p.m., according to Bernstein, Richard Reeves or Nick Bryant and Michael O'Brien. It federalized the Alabama National Guard.

The second confrontation came in the mid-afternoon when Brig. General Henry Graham, assistant commander of the 31st Infantry, Alabama National Guard, asked Wallace to stand aside "so that the order of the court may be accomplished."

Wallace moved two steps to the left, saluted Graham, and left in the flashing light of a motorcade. Moments later, Vivian Malone and James Hood walked through the doorway to be registered as students of the University of Alabama. It was a happy ending to a stressful situation – no riot, no violence and no need for troops: what the Kennedys had hoped. (1) (2) (3) (4) (5) (6) (7)

When Wallace stepped aside, Robert Kennedy heaved a sigh of relief and lit a cigar. The instant it became clear that Wallace would go peacefully was a "pleasant moment," he recalled.

George Corley Wallace later told Kennedy's Deputy Assistant Secretary of State, Carl T. Rowan, that his biggest mistake came during his 1963 inauguration as Governor when he stood in the state Capitol Building and shouted, "Segregation now! Segregation tomorrow! Segregation forever!"

Wallace admitted, "I should never have said it because it wasn't true." I didn't write those words about segregation now, tomorrow and forever. I saw them in the speech written for me and planned to skip over them. But the wind-chill factor was five below zero when I gave that speech. I started reading just to get it over and read those words without thinking. I have regretted it all my life."

At the end of the interview, Wallace told Rowan that he didn't support white supremacy. "I'm the one who made them take "white supremacy" off the roster that was the symbol of the Democratic Party in this State."

He concluded by saying, "I did nothing worse than Lyndon Johnson: he was for segregation when he thought he had to be; I was for segregation, and I was wrong. The media rehabilitated Johnson, why won't it rehabilitate me?" (8)

His daughter Peggy Wallace Kennedy, just 13 at the time, says that her father never once discussed the events of June 11, 1963, and that his motivations then remain a mystery even now. "He never talked with me about it. I never heard them (her parents) have a conversation about the schoolhouse door stand at all." (9)

In June 2012, George Wallace Jr. commented on his father's legacy, mentioning Bob Dylan's reference to the Alabama confrontation in his 1964 song "The Times They Are Changin". Come, Senators, Congressmen, please heed the call. Don't stand in the doorway; don't block up the hall." Wallace Jr. said that when he was 14, he sang the song for his father and thought he saw the look of regret in his father's eyes. (10)

Two Speeches that Changed the Course of Civil Rights

John F. Kennedy's legendary speech at 8 pm on June 11, 1963, lasted for thirteen minutes and six seconds and was, according to Arthur Schlesinger Jr., the boldest presidential step in U.S. civil rights since Reconstruction. Robert Kennedy was key in urging him to deliver an address of moral commitment, which gave birth to what indeed can be called the Second Reconstruction. (1)

In the speech's most memorable lines, he eloquently said, "Today we are committed to a worldwide struggle to promote and protect the rights of all who wish to be free. And when Americans are sent to Vietnam or West Berlin, we do not ask for whites only. It ought to be possible, therefore, for American students of any color to attend any public institution they select without having to be backed up by troops."

Kennedy emphasized that civil rights were neither a sectional issue nor a partisan issue. "In a time of domestic crisis, men of goodwill and generosity should be able to unite regardless of party or politics. This is not even a legal or legislative issue alone. It is better to settle these matters in the courts than on the streets, and new laws are needed at every level, but law alone can make men see right."

Kennedy repeated that legislation could not solve the civil rights problem alone. "It must be solved in the homes of every American in every community across our country."

In one of his most stirring appeals, he said, "We are confronted primarily with a moral issue. It is as old as the scriptures and is as clear as the American constitution."

"If an American, because his skin is dark, cannot eat lunch in a restaurant open to the public, if he cannot send his children to the best public schools available if he cannot vote for the public officials who represent him if in short, he cannot enjoy the full and free life which all of us want, then who among us would be content to have the color of his skin changed and stand in his place?"

In a direct allusion to Lincoln, Kennedy said, "One hundred years of delay have passed since President Lincoln freed the slaves, yet their heirs, their grandsons, are not fully free. They are not yet freed from the bonds of injustice. They are not yet freed from social and economic oppression. And this nation, for all its hopes and all its boasts, will not be fully free until all its citizens are free."

"Now the time has come for this Nation to fulfill its promise. We face, therefore, a moral crisis as a country and as a people."

He went on, "Next week, I shall ask the Congress of the United States to act, to make a commitment it has not fully made in this century to the proposition that race has no place in American life or law."

In the end, President Kennedy extemporized the speech, of which Robert said that the speech was good. He thought that probably if he had given it extemporaneously, it would have been as good or better.

In his closing words, he asked the American people for help. "Making it easier for us to move ahead and to provide the kind of equality of treatment which we would want ourselves; to give a chance for every child to be educated to the limit of his talents. As I have said before, not every child has an equal talent or an equal ability or an equal motivation. Still, they should have the equal right to develop their talent and their ability and their motivation to make something of themselves. We have a right to expect that the Negro community will be responsible, will uphold the law. Still, they have the right to expect that the law will be fair, that the Constitution will be color blind, as Justice Harlan said at the turn of the Century." (2)

Before that historical television and radio address, Kennedy gave two other speeches, which showed his growing public commitment to the civil rights cause, and acted as "warm-ups" to the June 11 address – one of the finest moments of his presidency.

The first came on May 18, when Kennedy used a speech at the Vanderbilt University in Nashville to reinforce his civil rights credentials. "The Nation is now engaged in a continuing debate about the rights of a portion of its citizens. That will go on, and those rights will expand until the standard first forged by the Nation's founders has been reached. All Americans enjoy equal opportunity and liberty under law."

Towards the end of his address, he said. "No one can deny the complexity of the problems involved in assuring to all our citizens their full rights as Americans. But no one can gainsay the fact that the determination to secure these rights is in the highest traditions of American freedom."

In the second speech, on June 9, at the U.S. Conference of Mayors in Honolulu, Kennedy asked for peaceful solutions to black demands. "The problem is growing, the challenge is there, the cause is just," he said. I think this demonstrates how convinced he was by the moral force of the black movement.

Historians and scholars have seized on Kennedy's declaration in the June 11 civil rights speech that "We face therefore a moral crisis as a country and as a people," as the high point of his rhetorical passion. But he had already shown his moral commitment in the speech of two days before. I quote, "We face a moment of a moral and constitutional crisis, and men of generosity and vision must make themselves heard in every section of this country." (3) (4)

What's the difference between those two speeches? The June 11, 1963 address, unlike the June 9, was another John F. Kennedy Rendez-Vous with History.

The Preparation of the June 11, 1963 Address

Presidential speechwriter Ted Sorensen in his first book on Kennedy in 1965, claimed that, in many ways, the June 11 speech had been in preparation by the President himself for some time. It drew on at least three years of evolution in his thinking about the development of the equal rights movement, plus at least three weeks of meetings in the White House, many drafts of a new message to Congress, and on his remarks just two days earlier to the June 9 Conference of Mayors. Kennedy also drew on his civil rights message four months earlier when he said, "Just as 1863 did not mark the beginning of the struggle to abolish slavery on this continent, so we cannot congratulate ourselves that in 1963 full equality has been attained for all our citizens. Too many of the bonds of restriction still exist. The distance still to be traveled 100 years after the signing of the Emancipation Proclamation is at once a reproach and a challenge. It must be our purpose to continue steady progress until the promise of equal rights for all has been fulfilled."

In the speech itself, Sorensen said, "No other President had ever before so forcefully recognized the moral injustice of all racial discrimination, and no President could ever, after that, ignore his moral obligation to remove it." (5)

Arthur M. Schlesinger Jr. said that some had criticized Kennedy for not having delivered such a speech earlier, but the timing was a vindication of his approach to mass education. He had been preparing the ground for it from his first day in office. On February 28, in his speech Message to the Congress on Civil Rights, he had already spoken about the Negro baby born in America today that had far less chance of succeeding in life than a white baby – a message repeated in his June 11 address. Arthur M. Schlesinger Jr. noted just after June 11 how differently the two speeches were received. "The President's civil rights message in February, though less impressive in substance, was as urgent in tone as his civil rights message this week, but no one paid any attention to it."

James Baldwin, for example, had not been even aware of the February speech, remarking, "If the President had given his June 11 speech six months ago, it would have died before an indifferent nation."

On a question from New York Times columnist Anthony Lewis on reaction to the speech, Robert Kennedy answered, "We used to laugh a little about the fact that I'd gotten him into so much trouble. I used to say that it was Burke Marshall (head of the US Justice Department's Civil Rights Division during the civil rights movement) who had gotten both of us in trouble." (6) (7) (8) (9)

Sorensen didn't mention who was against the address in his 1965 book "Kennedy" but in Counselor: "A Life at the Edge of History," he said that O'Donnell and O'Brien were both opposed to JFK making a speech because of the potential damage on his political future and legislative program and that he (Sorensen) had his reservations for the same reasons, despite his long-held wish for Kennedy to exert leadership on the issue.

Burke Marshall also said that Kenny O'Donnell and Ted Sorensen urged Kennedy not to deliver a speech in case it cost him his political support in 1964 – O'Donnell quite firmly, while Sorensen expressed reservations: Ted as always had his ambiguous view on the situation.

But what about the Attorney General? Burke Marshall said Bob Kennedy was very much in favor of sending a moral, civil rights message from the White House.

Marshall recalled, "The President didn't think for a minute about not giving a speech. He listened to the arguments against it, and of course, Ted and Kenny – I'm pretty sure I'm right – they spoke against it, giving the arguments against it.

Sorensen thought that such a major civil rights speech should await the completion of relevant legislation and cover its contents.

But the Attorney General urged his brother on the morning of the Tuscaloosa schoolhouse confrontation to deliver the speech then.

However, Vice President Johnson warned that a civil rights bill might fail if submitted now. He suggested that instead of a nationally televised address, Kennedy should give "a major speech in each of the main Southern states on the moral principle of ending discrimination." (10) (11) (12) (13)

By 4.30 p.m., on June 11, Ted Sorensen had prepared a speech – an unsatisfactory draft, according to Robert Kennedy. However, Sorensen said later that he had no draft.

RFK had arrived with Burke Marshall, saying, "Don't worry, we have a lot of good material at the justice department that we can send to you."

But when Sorensen came back in, and Robert Kennedy with Burke Marshall met in the Cabinet Room, they gave their views, and Ted Sorensen simply took notes and then went back into his office. For a time, John Kennedy thought that he was going to have to deliver the speech extemporaneously. Bob and Jack talked about what he'd say in the speech. He made notes on the back of an envelope or something, outlining and organizing.

Indeed, the President was still preparing his longhand notes on a scratch pad at three minutes before 8.00 p.m., urging Marshall, "Come on, come on now, Burke, you must have some ideas." (14) (15)

But according to historian Andrew Cohen, there was a draft of a presidential speech. However, Sorensen may never have seen it. If he did see it, he did not use it. It was prepared by Bobby Kennedy's gifted new speechwriter, Richard Yates. He had only been working for the Attorney General for two weeks when Bobby asked him to draft a civil rights text. So Yates shut himself in a room on the evening of Sunday, June 9, armed with coffee and cigarettes, and hammered out a draft, which he polished and delivered on Tuesday morning. (Blake Bailey mentions the speech in a biography of Richard Yates.)

Apart from Cohen's account, there are no other references to this in any of the leading Histories of the period or this presidency, not even as a footnote. (A stapled copy of these undelivered words lies, nearly anonymously and almost forgotten, among Robert Kennedy's papers in the John F. Kennedy Library). (16)

If true, which I am sure it is, there are two questions to be asked. Did Sorensen see Yates's draft? We'll never know, but the second question is: Why did Robert Kennedy never talk about it in his oral history interviews? The answer is another Kennedy enigma because if you examine Richard Yates's draft of his Civil Rights speech, he deserves his place in the history of the June 11 address.

Two comparisons between Yates and JFK's speech will prove it.

Yates: "It is a moral problem. Something is wrong, in the full sense of the word – something is wrong North, South, East and West in our Country."

JFK: "We face, therefore, a moral crisis as a country and as a people."

Yates: "But legislation is not enough."

JFK: "But legislation, I repeat, cannot solve this problem alone."

Perhaps, Robert Kennedy never acknowledged Richard Yates' role because Yates was an alcoholic and a manic-depressive while Bobby was a puritan – although according to Cohen, Robert Kennedy was personally kind to him. (17)

US Secretary of Commerce Luther H. Hodges vividly recalls having a conversation with President Kennedy quite some time before the civil rights legislation went to Congress, in which he urged him to address the Nation on television. He told the president, "You're being blamed for really encouraging the Negro to disobey the law. I know that isn't completely fair, but that's what is being said. I wish you would do the other thing." But Kennedy did not, despite Hodges pointing out some of the pitfalls from the standpoint of legislation and the next election. However, the president did make a statement – in a "Profiles in Courage" style – which deeply impressed Hodges.

"Governor," said Kennedy, "I may lose the legislation, or I may even lose the election in 1964, but there comes a time when a man has to take a stand, and history will record that he has to meet these tough situations and ultimately make a decision." (18) (19) (20)

Robert Kennedy said that his brother worried that the June 11 speech could be his "political swan song." Indeed, a Gallup poll conducted on June 16 found that 36% of Americans thought he was pushing integration "too fast," 32% "about right," and 18% "not fast enough." (21) (22)

The remaining 14% had no opinion. The comparable percentages for southern whites were 62%, 4%, 21% and 13%, and for whites outside the South, 30%, 17%, 33% and 16%. Moreover, Kennedy's popularity plummeted in the south, obviously because of adverse white opinion. In June, he attained only a 33% approval rating compared to 60% in March and 52% in late May. (23)

But what were the reactions to the Speech?

Among Black Leaders, Martin Luther King, who watched it in Atlanta, immediately wrote to compliment the President, telling reporters the speech was a "masterpiece." A year later, King said, "Ike never spoke to the moral issue, and I think this is something that President Kennedy brought to the nation that is desperately needed, the insistence on the morality of integration and the fact that the issue was more than a political or an economic issue – that it was at bottom a moral issue." King said that the speech was the "most eloquent, passionate, and unequivocal plea for civil rights ever made by any president. Kennedy's message will become a hallmark in the annals of American history." (24) (25) (26) (27)

Decades later, Reverend Walter Fauntroy, one of Dr. King's closest associates, said that he and Dr. King sat together watching the speech on television. At its conclusion, Dr. King leapt to his feet and said, "Walter, can you believe that white man not only stepped up to the plate, but he also hit it over the fence." (28) (29)

An equally excited Stanley Levison called King that night to say that President Kennedy had done "what you have been asking him to do." To Levison, the historic speech underscored the importance of their decision to make Congress, not President Kennedy, the focus of the Washington demonstration. (30) (31)

Roy Wilkins, executive secretary of the National Association for the Advancement of Colored People (NAACP), said that President Kennedy had rightly posed the moral issue in racial matters but had failed to emphasize "the most pressing problem confronting Negro Americans today" – discrimination in employment. (32)

In Newsweek, Walter Lippmann lauded Kennedy's "momentous and irrevocable steps." The president had "committed himself to lead the movement toward equality of status and opportunity for the American Negro. No President has ever done this before. None had ever staked his personal prestige and has brought to bear all the powers of the Presidency and the Negro cause. I count very high the speech, the intelligence, the imagination, and the courage of the Kennedy reaction."

An editorial in The New Republic wrote. "If the President proves as good a politician in the next few months as he has shown himself a statesman, who can tell what higher roads the Republic may be traveling before the year has ended." (33) (34)

Jackie Robinson, a Republican stalwart who had campaigned vigorously against Kennedy in 1960, was almost stupefied, declaring in a statement on June 13, 1963. "If I were to vote for a president tomorrow, I would cast my ballot for John F. Kennedy. No previous president has ever been as forthright about human rights and race relations as Mr. Kennedy was." Robinson said the president had emerged as the most forthright chief Executive in American History and one who had inspired leadership "in the sensitive civil rights field." (35) (36) (37)

Reaction from Congress was mixed. Southern legislators despised the speech, with Senator John Stennis of Mississippi, a staunch segregationist, vowing to resist Kennedy's proposals, declaring that they were "clearly unconstitutional and would open the door for police control of employment and personal associations in almost every field." Stennis warned, "These bills will be fought to the limit and their invalidity exposed." Kennedy's old friend, George Smathers, doubted that a bill was necessary. "I could agree with almost everything the president said, but I don't believe we need additional legislation."

Louisiana Senator Allen Ellender predicted that Kennedy's proposals would lead to violence, claiming later that the bill would not have passed if the president had lived because of Kennedy's consistently ineffective approach toward Congress.

The Wall Street Journal, one of Kennedy's reliable critics, said that Kennedy had left the impression that "90% of the American people are engaged in a bitter and unremitting oppression to the other 10%." (38)

But how did historians react to Kennedy's speech?

Thomas C. Reeves, always critical of Kennedy's performance, pondered it highly likely that the "moralistic rhetoric" of the June 11 speech was designed in large part for a pragmatic purpose: the president was wrapping the proposed legislation in the loftiest possible language in the hope of securing its passage – a tactic familiar to students of American history. (39)

Carl M. Brauer praised it as one of the most eloquent, moving and essential addresses of Kennedy's presidency, despite the lack of detail required for legislation. It was a speech, he said, directed more at the public than Congress. (40)

The speech did indeed represent a commitment on the part of the federal government to fight against discrimination, and he sought a "consensus" to support it.

According to Henry Fairlie, he had himself moved on the issue only when the Negro had already moved out of the courts into the streets. At the beginning of the administration, Robert Kennedy had said of the pressure for civil rights. "There has got to be – and there is going to be– leadership from the White House. That is going to make the difference." For two and a half years, this leadership had been absent, and the form in which it was now offered was predictable. (41)

Bruce Miroff noted that the June 11 address contained Kennedy's first words ever on the racial crisis during his presidency and described the content as "excellent, appropriate, timely, and eloquent." Yet, there was still something lacking in it. Once again, Kennedy had failed to give the civil rights movement its due credit for illuminating America's moral crisis and had been unable to pay public tribute to its dedication and courage. Miroff observed that once again, Kennedy had missed an opportunity to create a positive appreciation of the movement among white Americans. Miroff had probably forgotten the June 9 speech in Honolulu.

Miroff also claimed that when Kennedy said, "We have a right to expect that the Negro community will be responsible, will uphold the law. Still, they have a right to expect that the law will be fair, that the constitution will be color blind," it was a veiled warning to militant civil rights activists.

But another Kennedy remark seems addressed equally to white, black, Hispanic and all races. "I want to pay tribute to those citizens north and south who have been working in their communities to make life better for all. They are acting not out of a sense of legal duty but out of a sense of human decency." (42)

In his special message to Congress on June 19, 1963, Kennedy said, "I urge all community leaders, negro and white, to do their utmost to lessen tensions and to exercise self-restraint." This was a warning to both communities to uphold the law. (43)

I think A President has the right, and it is his duty and obligation to ask his citizens

253

to uphold the law.

Peniel E. Joseph, writing in the New York Times of June 10, 2013, said that June 11, 1963, may not be a widely recognized date these days. Still, it might have been the most critical day in civil rights history.

He thought that Kennedy's speech was almost immediately overshadowed by the murder of civil rights activist Medgar Evers – and overshadowed again two months later by the massive March on Washington for Jobs and Freedom, which became symbolic of the civil rights movement's heroic period.

Kennedy's death made him a martyr for many causes, and, in a cruel twist, it provided a considerable boost to the civil rights bill, which his successor, Lyndon B. Johnson, signed on July 2, 1964. But without the moral forcefulness of the June 11 speech, the Bill might never have been passed.

Kennedy's words anticipated some of the key themes found in King's soaring March on Washington address two months later. And that shared moral force, that commonality of thinking between the two speeches, is the most important reason to remember the president's address 50 years later.

Peniel E. Joseph concluded that it reminds us of a forgotten moment of the civil rights era when presidential leadership and grassroots activism worked in creative tension to turn the narrative of civil rights from a regional issue into a national story promoting racial equality and democratic renewal. (44)

On June 12, 1963, at 12.20 a.m., 37-year-old civil rights leader Medgar Evers returned home from a mass meeting at the New Jerusalem Baptist Church. Byron De La Beckwith, age 42, a white supremacist and Ku Klux Klan member, was waiting for him across the street from his house with an Enfield 30-06 caliber rifle. Evers, a member of the NAACP (National Association for the Advancement of Colored People) and veteran of the D-Day invasion, was shot in the back and died an hour later. His wife Myrlie Evers, and their three children, James, Reena and Darrell, were home at the time of the assassination.

Beckwith faced two trials for murder in 1964, but they resulted in hung (all-white) juries. Finally, in 1994, a jury consisting of eight blacks and four whites convicted him of first-degree murder.

Why did it take 30 years to convict Beckwith?

The answer came from Kennedy himself in his civil rights address. "Legislation cannot solve this problem alone, it must be solved in the homes of every American." (45) (46) (47) (48) (49)

On June 13, President Kennedy wrote a condolence letter to Myrlie Evers, "I attend to you and your children my sincerest condolences on the tragic death of your husband. Although comforting thoughts are difficult at a time like this, surely there can be some solace in the realization of justice for the cause for which your husband gave his life. Achievement of the goals he did so much to promote will enable his children and the generations to follow to share fully and equally in the benefits and advantages our nation has to offer."

In the margin of the letter, he scribbled a handwritten message, "Mrs. Kennedy joins me in extending her deepest sympathy." (50) (51) (52)

Robert Kennedy attended Evers' funeral in Arlington Cemetery and gave Charles Evers, Medgar's older brother, his telephone numbers at the office and home, inviting Evers to call any time, day or night, if negroes were being harassed or intimidated. Charles Evers said later, "Whenever I needed to call him, and I've never found it too late or too early." (53)

On June 19, 1963, Kennedy asked for the enactment of the most far-reaching Civil Rights bill in the country's history.

His statement began, "I have emphasized that 'the events in Birmingham and elsewhere have so increased the cries for equality that no city or state or legislative body can prudently choose to ignore them'. It is time to act."

In his conclusion, he emphasized that "many problems remain that cannot be ignored. The enactment will not solve all our problems of race relations."

The problems of race relations all over the world are still with us at the beginning of the 21st century. In the end, he affirmed, "The enactment of the "Civil Rights act of 1963" at this session of the Congress – however long it may take and however troublesome it may be – is imperative. It will go far toward providing reasonable men with reasonable means of meeting these problems, and it will thus help end the kind of racial strive which this Nation can hardly afford. Rancour, violence, disunity and national shame can only hamper our national standing and security. To paraphrase the words of Lincoln: In giving freedom to the Negro, we assure freedom to the free, honorable alike in what we offer and what we preserve." (54)

The New York Times editorial described it as "a bold and admirable attempt to erase the barriers that now stand in the way of the full enjoyment by every American of the constitutional guarantees that are his birthright." (55)

On June 19, Majority Leader Mike Mansfield introduced the bill to the floor and then joined Minority Leader Everett Dirksen in sponsoring bi-partisan legislation. The proposed law would ensure any citizen with a sixth-grade education the right to vote. It would eliminate discrimination in all places of public accommodation, hotels, restaurants, amusement facilities, and retail establishments.

Jonathan Lewis remembered Burke Marshall telling him that Senator Mansfield was gloomy during the proposing of the June legislation, believing that it had no chance at all – and Robert Kennedy agreed.

Mansfield had several discussions with the President about the difficulties he thought he would face in getting such a bill passed. Kennedy said, "You've got to get it done. It's the heart of the matter. These people are entitled to this consideration, and I depend upon you to see that what I recommended is passed." "Well," Mansfield said, "I'll do my best Mr. President, but I'm just explaining the situation to you." (56) (57) (58) (59)

Burke Marshall recalls, "When President Kennedy sent up that Civil Rights bill, every person spoke about it in the White House, every one of them was against

President Kennedy sending up that bill; against his speech in June, against making it a moral issue, against the March on Washington. The unmistakable voice within the government at that time, there's no question about it at all, that Robert Kennedy was the one. He urged, he felt it, he understood it. And he prevailed. I don't think there was anybody in the Cabinet, except the president himself, who felt that way on these issues, and the president got it from his brother." (60) (61) (62)

In Montgomery, Alabama, Governor Wallace reacted to the proposed Civil Rights legislation by saying to the president by television, "You're going to have to bring the troops back from Berlin if you pass the law." (63)

President Kennedy had called Dwight Eisenhower to Washington on June 12 to try to enlist him to the cause, but the former president reportedly told Kennedy, as well as a group of Republican Congressmen, that passing a "whole bunch of laws" would not solve the civil rights problem, although he did favor voting rights. (64)

Even Vice President Lyndon Johnson privately expressed pessimism about the success of any civil rights legislation at this time, at least until the appropriations were passed.

Joseph L. Rauh Jr., one of America's foremost civil right lawyers, thought that the bill contained the administration's best estimates of what could be enacted rather than what was needed. Still, as Rauh told the Civil Rights leaders, "It is the most comprehensive Civil Rights bill ever to receive serious consideration from the Congress of the United States." (65) (66) (67)

The March on Washington August 28, 1963

The John Lewis speech Controversy

John Lewis, a 23- year old student, chairman of the Student Nonviolent Coordinating Committee, was to give an inflammatory and incendiary speech.

Julian Bond, at the time spokesperson for the SNCC, the press guy, remembers Patrick A. O'Boyle, Roman Catholic archbishop of Washington, DC, raising a fuss over John Lewis' speech and threatening to boycott the event by not delivering the opening invocation unless Lewis softened his words.

Bond didn't remember things the way they are recounted in a great many books. He remembers last-minute changes being made on the podium that day after other changes had already been made beforehand. He remembers distributing copies of both versions of the speech and telling the press people, "Look at the difference."

Bond explained, "There was an understanding among us that you couldn't say there was a difference or what had happened, and he (Lewis) was irritated that not as many people as he would have liked said, "Oh, my God! He's changed his speech."

In an interview, Lewis diplomatically said that some people saw copies of the text and said it would have to be changed because, "they didn't like the words "revolution" and "masses." (1)

According to Victor Navasky, Lewis changed his speech only after an appeal from the civil rights movement's grand old man, A. Philip Randolph. He was urged by Walter Reuther, who had been pressured in turn by Robert Kennedy. But Navasky questioned what was gained by the changes and what would have been lost had Lewis spoken his mind? He felt that the future of SNCC might be different without such government intervention.

Murray Kempton reported Malcolm X's observation that "Kennedy should win the Academy Award for direction." (2)

Although who first read the first draft of the Lewis speech is up for speculation.

Trouble over the speech began on Tuesday afternoon, August 27. Author and civil rights historian Taylor Branch says that a Catholic prelate took the Lewis draft to Washington's Archbishop Patrick O'Boyle, whose complaints about the "incendiary" language soon spread to Burke Marshall, Walter Reuther, and to other white clergymen who had agreed to participate. (3)

David J. Garrow claims that Robert Kennedy's assistants, overseeing everything concerning the March, had collected the advance text and passed it to the Attorney General and Burke Marshall for scrutiny. In his notes, he says, "As Ahmann recalled the Cardinal's unhappiness with Lewis's text, "It was the administration that drew it to O'Boyle's attention."

Robert Kennedy and Burke Marshall spoke with O'Boyle, and on Wednesday night in a small room just behind Lincoln's statue, Lewis, James Foreman, and Courtland Cox from SNCC were huddled with Randolph, Wilkins, King, Eugene Carson Blake, and other March leaders, plus the harried march Deputy Director Bayard Rustin and his assistant Tom Kahn. They made Lewis agree to let them edit the speech. Marshall said that he didn't know how he got hold of the edited speech, but somehow he acquired it and delivered it – in the sidecar of a police motorcycle, right past the marchers – to the Lincoln Memorial. He got it there and then gave the edited speech. (4) (5)

The polishing of the speech was a joint venture of Robert Kennedy, Burke Marshall, Walter Reuther and the Negro leaders.

King said to Lewis, "John, I know you as well as anybody. That doesn't sound like you." King changed a few words while insisting that it was merely an adjustment of style and context, not substance. (6)

According to Richard Reeves, President Kennedy himself did the editing, and Lewis finally agreed to drop the Sherman line. (7)

I doubt that President Kennedy intervened in the editing. Robert Kennedy thought it was a bad speech. I think it was a speech from a bright young student frustrated and with reason after more than a score of civil rights confrontations, arrests and beatings.

Philip A. Goduti Jr. wrote, "Reverend Eugene Carson Blake of the National Council of Churches, a white pastor who was arrested during the movement, had a particular objection to the language. He objected to the use of the terms "revolution" and "the masses," which had a communist connotation. However, A. Philip Randolph defended the language saying that Lewis had used it for years. Randolph noted that Lewis changed the word "citizens" instead of "masses," and although he was angry about the edits, he felt that "the speech still had fire." (8)

David J. Garrow thought the speech was like a leftist ideological tract, with passages such as, "We are involved in a serious revolution. This nation is still a place of cheap political leaders who build their careers on immoral compromises and ally themselves with open forms, of political, economic and social exploitation."

What Lewis said was, "By and large, American politics is dominated by politicians, who build... and he added a crucial sentence, "There are exceptions, of course, we salute those."

Do you think this is a leftist ideological tract? I don't. By leaving out this last sentence by Garrow, Lewis' words became more inflammatory.

Many authors refer to the words "revolution" and "the masses" as offensive or an alien dogma. But the fact is that the word revolution was punctuated seven times and six times in the revised draft and that the word "black masses," not "citizens," was kept in the edited selection by Robert Kennedy, Burke Marshall and the Black leaders.

John Lewis said in the final edited speech, "I appeal to you to get into this great revolution that is sweeping this nation. Get in and stay in the streets of every city, every village and hamlet of this nation, until true freedom comes, until the revolution of 1776 is complete. We must get into this revolution and complete the revolution. For in the Delta in Mississippi, in Southwest Georgia, in the Black Belt of Alabama, in Harlem, in Chicago, Detroit, Philadelphia, and all over this nation, the black masses are on the march for jobs and freedom."

What angered O'Boyle, Marshall, Bobby, and some black leaders was what Lewis wrote in the original draft, "In good conscience, we cannot support the administration's civil rights bill wholeheartedly, for it is too little and too late. There's not one thing in the bill that will protect our people from police brutality. I want to know: which side is the federal government on?" Nick Bryant called the question the "most trenchant" in the original speech.

The – unedited – speech declared:

"The Revolution is a serious one. Mr. Kennedy is trying to take the revolution out of the streets and put it into the courts. Listen, Mr. Kennedy, listen Mr. Congressman, listen fellow citizens. The black masses are on the march for jobs and freedom, and we must say that there won't be a "cooling-off period."

And finally, "We won't stop now. All the forces of Eastland, Barnett, Wallace and Thurmond won't stop this revolution. The time will come when we will not confine our marching to Washington. We will march through the South, through the heart of Dixie, the way Sherman did. We shall pursue our own scored earth policy and burn Jim Crow to the ground – non-violently." (9) (10)

Bruce Miroff called this a statement of hope and anger that the Kennedy administration could never grasp (11): marching through the south the way Sherman did cannot be placed in the category of non-violence.

But the first amendment of the Constitution of the United States of America says, "Congress shall make no law respecting an establishment of religion, or prohibiting the free exercise thereof; or abridging the freedom of speech....

I think the federal government violated the provision on freedom of speech in censoring the Lewis text, and particularly by objections to Lewis' words "the administration's Civil Rights bill, for it is too little and too late." On "too little," he was right, I believe.

In December 1962, Bayard Rustin had called on A. Philip Randolph, the revered president of the Brotherhood of Sleeping Car Porters. Recalling Randolph's 1941 victory in threatening a march on Washington and getting the wartime Fair Employment Practice Committee (FEPC) in exchange to implement Executive Order 8802, Rustin proposed a new march.

But Rustin had a few personal problems – he was a draft dodger who was jailed for two years, and in 1953 he had been jailed for 60 days on a morals charge for publicly engaging in homosexual activity. And he was also a socialist, and many people thought that socialism and communism were the same things. He had belonged to the Young Communist League.

Thus, on July 2, 1963, as the black leadership was gathering for the March on Washington, Roy Wilkins (NAACP) tried to block the nomination of Rustin as director for the march.

Whitney Young of the Urban League proposed that Randolph be named march director, free to choose his deputy. Wilkins, being in no position to object to Randolph, consented, and Randolph appointed Rustin as his deputy.

Wilkins' effort had failed. Rustin would run the March, in fact, if not in name. (12) (13) (14) (15)

Rustin was a talented organizer who oversaw the tiniest details. The provision of many toilets was one of his top practical priorities. "We can't have any disorganized pissing in Washington," he said in his somewhat affected British Accent. (16)

According to Burke Marshall, Bayard Rustin, and A. Philip Randolph must be taken a good deal of credit for organizing the March. But the key person behind the arrangements was the Attorney General, who assigned Assistant Attorney General John Douglas to the project almost full time for at least four weeks, making sure that there were enough toilets and food and that there was an effective liaison with the police on vetting the marchers. And so Marshall thought that that made a lot of difference all that work, to which Robert Kennedy added, "We had several people who just spent all their time. It was very, very badly organized." (17)

The White House had set a date for the march, choosing a Wednesday, hoping that people would come and go in one day because they would need to be at work the day before and the day after. Rustin had negotiated round the clock on every detail with Douglas and Jerry Bruno and sometimes Robert Kennedy until they signed off on a plan for a three-hour rally rather than a protest march. The ceremonies would end by four o'clock in the afternoon, leaving enough time for the crowds to leave town before a late summer sunset. Robert Kennedy and Burke Marshall got tough with the Washington Police Department when the District's chief said he wanted to use dogs for crowd control. No Dogs decided Kennedy and Marshall. (18)

Robert Kennedy favored the Lincoln Memorial rather than the Capitol to keep the crowd controlled – it certainly would help his case in Congress if he kept the demonstrators at bay. The reflecting pool, he believed, reduced the possibility of violence. Also, Kennedy ordered Washington's bars and liquor stores to stay shut. (19)

Two thousand five hundred National Guardsmen were mobilized to assist city police, and 4,000 regular army troops, code-named "Task Force Inside," were moved by helicopters to a U.S. navy station inside the district and Fort Myers, across the Potomac River in Virginia. Fourteen thousand men (15,000 according to Irving Bernstein) of the 82nd Airborne Division were on standby alert at Fort Bragg in North Carolina. All were ready to move or execute orders which had been prepared in advance, stating, "An extraordinary assemblage of persons constituting a threat to life and property in the District of Columbia are ordered to disperse and retire peaceably."

The papers waited only for the president's signature. (20)

Also on emergency medical care were 50 doctors and 100 nurses at 15 first-aid stations, plus a volunteer group of New York doctors at the Willard Hotel. (21)

Robert Kennedy knew from reports that many groups of communists were trying unsuccessfully to take part. Civil rights leaders worked hard to keep them out, including monitoring the plans of the Communist Party organization, which complained that it was denied a more prominent role. (22)

Kennedy's team also monitored the American Nazi Party and the Ku Klux Klan, who were both planning counterdemonstrations. (23) (24)

The Kennedy's were as enthusiastic about the March as Roosevelt had been 22 years earlier. On June 22, 1963, President Kennedy met in the cabinet room with the Black Leaders; the Big Six, ML King (SCLC), J. Farmer (Core), J. Lewis (SNCCC), R. Wilkins (NAACP), Whitney Young (Urban League) and A.P. Randolph (BSCP). The president told them, "We want success in Congress, not just a big show at the Capitol. Some of these people are looking for an excuse to be against us, and I don't want to give any of them a chance to say, "Yes, I'm for the bill, but I am damned if I will vote for it at the point of a gun." It seemed Kennedy thought it would be a great mistake to announce a march on Washington before the bill was even in committee, in case it provided some members of Congress with an "out."

The polls had shown that the public was not receptive to further demonstrations: violence, which Kennedy was worried about, could be counterproductive. (25)

Randolph then spoke about the president's effort to shift the matter from the streets to the courts.

"The problem of the streets is challenging," Randolph said. "The Negroes are already on the streets. It is very likely impossible to get them off," he warned. "If they are bound to be on the streets in any case, is it not better that they are led by organizations dedicated to civil rights and disciplined by struggle rather than leave them to other leaders who care neither about civil rights nor about non-violence."

Kennedy agreed that the street demonstration had forced Congress to entertain legislation which had had no chance a few weeks ago and that it has made the executive branch act faster, adding, "This is true, but now we are in a new phase, the legislative phase, and results are essential." (26)

On the March itself, Martin Luther King said, "I think it will serve as a purpose. It may seem ill-timed. Frankly, I have never engaged in any direct action movement which did not seem ill-timed. Some people thought Birmingham ill-timed."

The President interjected, including the Attorney General. Kennedy went on to say, "This is a severe fight. The Vice President and I know what it will mean if we fail. I have just seen the new Gallup poll. National approval of the administration has fallen from 60% to 47%.

According to Stern (1992) and Dallek (2013), the Gallup poll that JFK was referring to, mentioned by Schlesinger in his June 22 journal, was never located. I couldn't find it myself. His Gallup approval rating at the time was, in fact, 61%. Joseph L. Rauh Jr., who was at the June 22 meeting, told an Oral Hearing Interview for the Kennedy library in 1965 that Kennedy "read the famous poll that nobody's ever been able to find, where he said that his popularity had gone down to 42%." (Was it 47% or 42%) (27) (28) (29)

"We're in this up to the neck. What would be the worst trouble of all would be to lose the fight in Congress. We'll have enough trouble if we win – but if we win, we can deal with those," said Kennedy.

President Kennedy told the black Leaders that "we preserve confidence in good faith of each other. I have my problems with the Congress: you have yours with your groups. We will undoubtedly disagree from time to time on tactics. But the important thing is to keep in touch."

Then he concluded with remarks often overlooked by historians, "What seems to me important is to get and keep, as many Negro children as possible in schools this fall. It is too late to get equality for their parents. However, we can still get it for the children if they can go to school and take advantage of what educational opportunity is open to them. I urge you to get every Negro family to do this at whatever sacrifice." (30)

Arthur Schlesinger considered the June 22 meeting as about the best he had attended in government. The President – who was in much better form, it seemed to him, than in the larger march meetings – gave a crisp, precise, articulate account of the civil rights situation.

And Kennedy repeated his words on black children's education, now cited by historians such as Taylor Branch, at the White House reception after the march, "This doesn't have anything to do with what we've been talking about," he said. "But it seems to me with all the influence that you gentlemen have in the Negro community, that we could emphasize, which I think the Jewish community has done, on educating their children, on making them study, making them stay in school and all the rest" (secretly taped by the president).

Kennedy's remarks of June 22, repeated August 28, can be seen as historical, going to the heart of the black community problem, "An uneducated child makes an uneducated parent who, in many cases, produces another uneducated child." (31) (32) (33)

Burke Marshall said that after the June 22 meeting, the president knew they were going to have their march, and he accepted that fact. (34)

On June 23, 1963, Lawrence Spivak, host of NBC's Meet the Press, asked Bobby Kennedy if he thought that a march on Washington would "hurt" the cause of Civil Rights or "help get Civil Rights legislation through?" Bobby said that he didn't think that the president's bill "should be discussed under an aura of pressure" and called the announcement of a march "premature." But he also expressed support for the people's "right to petition" and said that black citizens "as well as others" had the right to make their views known. (35)

On June 25, at a rally in Harlem, the black Leaders announced August 28 as the day for the "March on Washington for Jobs and Freedom." (36) (37)

In preparation for the march, John R. Reilly said that the President said, "Well, how the hell do you expect to get a Civil Rights bill passed if these people come down here without any control or guidance," and used a rather earthy expression about what they might do to the Washington Monument in regard with relieving themselves thereabouts.

Alan Raywid said on the same incident that "The president is reported to have said, "They're liable to come down here and shit all over the monument. I've got a Civil Rights bill to get through. We'll run it." (38) (39)

Evan Thomas writes, "Reverting to his prep school, navy man profanity, the president wondered, "What if they pee on the Washington Monument?"

Thomas refers to an interview with John Reilly and Alan Raywid OH. In the John Reilly OH, there's no mention about "pee or shit," just about "a rather earthy expression." (40) (41)

"A rather earthy expression," "shit all over," and "What if they pee," sorry historians, stay to the facts and the historical truth.

In a press conference on July 17, 1963, Kennedy said, "I think that the way the Washington march is now developed, which is a peaceful assembly calling for a redress of grievances, the cooperation with the police, every evidence that it is to be peaceful, they are going to the Washington Monument, they are going to express their strong views. I think that's in the great tradition. I look forward to being here. I am sure Members of Congress will be here. We want citizens to come to Washington if they feel that they are not having their rights expressed. But, of course, arrangements have been made to make this responsible and peaceful. This is not a march on the capitol."

Kennedy said he had warned against demonstrations which could lead to riots and bloodshed, adding:

"But you just can't tell people "don't protest," but on the other hand, "we are not going to let you come into a store or a restaurant." It seems to me it is a two-way street." (42)

But not only the Kennedys had reservations about the March, John Lewis, King and Randolph also lobbied Roy Wilkins of the NAACP and Whitney Young of the National Urban League to participate. Those more conservative leaders resisted so long as the march envisioned sit-ins at the Capitol with "Senator Eastland stepping over supine bodies to get to his office."

George Meany, the powerful head of the AFL-CIO (American Federation of Labor, Congress of Industrial Organizations), also kept his distance, much to the irritation of Randolph and the UAW's Walter Reuther. (43)

"How can our country endure when we legislate based on threats and intimidations from mobs?" was Richard Russell's rhetorical question to former Senator William Knowland.

And Senator A. Willis Robertson of Virginia warned, "If Kennedy permits two or three hundred thousand Negroes in violation of the law, swarming over the Capitol grounds and into all committee rooms, offices, etc. if Kennedy permits that to happen, I guess that the people in the north and other sections who don't endorse priority in jobs and everything else for the non-whites will not endorse Kennedy for reelection in 1964." (44)

The march would be a tactical error. Emanuel Celler and House Majority Leader Carl Albert feared it would create opposition to the bill, which was also Kennedy's fear in the beginning when the march was announced. (45)

But Cardinal Francis Spellman of New York endorsed the march, and the National Catholic Conference for Interracial Justice helped sponsor it, as did the American Jewish Congress and the National Council of Churches of Christ in America. (46)

At a news conference on August 1, 1963, a reporter asked Kennedy to comment on indications that "your policies on civil rights are costing you heavily in political prestige and popularity and would you tell us whether civil rights are worth an election?"

Kennedy's reply was, "Well, I assume what you say is probably right. On the other hand, this is a national crisis of great proportions. I am confident that whoever was president would meet his responsibilities. Crises come in different forms. I don't think anyone would have anticipated the exact form of this particular crisis. Maybe last winter we were dealing with other matters. But I think it has come, and we are going to deal with it." (47) (48)

President Kennedy expressed a little concern to Arthur Schlesinger on August 15th about the march – because it might not be large enough. The leaders had committed themselves to produce 100,000 people, and the president feared that any significant shortfall would persuade some members of Congress that the public demand for action on civil rights was greatly exaggerated. He need not have worried: on August 28, nearly a quarter of a million people, black and white, came to Washington. (49) There is an ambiguity about whether Kennedy wanted to meet the civil rights leaders before or after the march.

Louis Martin said that the last issue to be resolved was whether the White House meeting would be before or after the march, with Kenny O'Donnell pushing for the meeting with the president before the program.

Louis Martin's representative inside the march committee said there was no way to convince King and Roy Wilkins to meet before it took place. They wanted the meeting afterwards because the chances were high that everyone would behave well: they wouldn't want to spoil a positive day. (50)

According to Ted Sorensen, Kennedy declined to appear before the march because he feared they might present him with a list of demands he could not meet, risking turning the march into an anti-Kennedy protest. He did agree to comply with them at the end of the day, and that turned out to be very successful. (51) (52) (53)

While planning for the great march went apace, King laid low that August to work on a quick book about Birmingham and the summer revolution, to be called "Why We can't Wait (in answer to whites who said the Negro should). Alfred Duckett, a Negro journalist, gave unstinting editorial and rewrote help as King labored on his manuscript. Still, he ran out of time and had to leave it, despairing of ever meeting his book deadlines.

King flew to Washington with Coretta and an entourage of aides and advisors on August 27, the day before the great march. He prepared his speech in a suite at the Willard Hotel, spending an hour or so thinking through what he would say. Then he put the outline together and worked on the text until 4.00 a.m. on the morning of August 28. (54) (55)

In "Why We Can't Wait," King wrote, "They came from almost every state in the union. They came in every form of transportation. They gave up from one to three days' pay plus the cost of transportation, which for many was a heavy financial sacrifice. It was an army without guns, but not without strength. It was an army into which no one had to be drafted. (56) It was white and Negro, and of all ages. It had adherents of every faith, members of every class, every profession, every political party united by a single ideal. It was a fighting army, but no one could mistake that its most powerful weapon was love."

The March totaled as many as 250,000 people, more than one-quarter of them white. FBI agents, on order from Hoover, were calling Charlton Heston and other celebrities in their Washington Hotel rooms, warning them to stay indoors because the government expected violence. But they didn't stay indoors: among the Negro, and White entertainers were present Mahalia Jackson, Bob Dylan, Joan Baez, Peter, Paul and Mary, Harry Belafonte, Marlon Brando, Paul Newman, Sidney Poitier, Lena Horne, Josephine Baker, Ossie Davis, Marian Anderson,

Sammy Davis Jr., Diahann Carrell and Dick Gregory.

Before lunch, on August 28, the President chaired a full-scale meeting on Vietnam. Then he left the mansion at 1.40 and did not return to his office until 4.25 – a gap of almost three hours in the appointment calendar which coincided almost perfectly with the speech-making schedule around the reflecting pool. (57) (58)

Ralph Martin claims that Edward was the only Kennedy scheduled to speak at the march, and he had a speech prepared, but the President vetoed it. (59)

Do you believe that Ted Kennedy, freshman Senator, would have asked his brother to deliver a speech at the march?

Edward Kennedy had asked his brother to attend the march, but Jack thought that his presence might be counterproductive. He believed that Ted should be in his office to greet any of the people who might come there, and in the end, that's what he did. But Ted still managed to slip out of the Capitol at one point, unnoticed and alone, and he made his way to the Reflecting Pool surrounded by thousands of people. (60)

I think Martin Luther King Jr.'s speech was historical, an address that changed the United States of America. Forty-five years later, the American people elected Barack Obama.

Standing before the Lincoln Memorial, with the bright sun glistering on the reflecting pool with thousands of people around him, he poetically and with the phrasing and cadences of the Bible and the pulpit, expressed his immortal ideal, "Five score years ago, a great American, in whose symbolic shadow we stand today, signed the Emancipation Act."

Then gospel singer Mahalia Jackson shouted, "Tell them about the dream Martin." He pushed his text aside and went on extemporaneously:

"I say to you today, my friends: so even though we face the difficulties of today and tomorrow. I still have a dream. It is a dream deeply rooted in the American dream. I have a dream that one day this nation will rise and live out the true meaning of its creed, we hold these truths to be self-evident that all men are created equal." He ended his "helluva speech," according to Robert Kennedy with the following, "And when this happens when we allow freedom ring when we let it ring from every village and every hamlet, from every state and every city, we will be able to speed up that day when all of God's children black men and white men, Jewish and Gentiles, Protestants and Catholics, will be able to join hands and sing in the words of the old Negro spiritual – "Free at last, free at last. Thank God Almighty we are free at last." (61)

It was, according to James N. Giglio, perhaps his greatest speech.

But Taylor Branch writes, "The speech was politically sound but far from historic, nimble in some streaks, while club-footed through others." (62) (63) W. J. Rorabaugh called Martin Luther Jr's "I Have a Dream" speech the most moving piece of rhetoric in the twentieth century. (64)

Kennedy, watching at the White House, remarked to his aides, "He's damn good."

As the principal leaders filed into the Cabinet Room from the march, he greeted King with a smile and the words "I have a dream." King asked President Kennedy if he had heard the excellent speech of Walter Reuther. The latter had indeed delivered a fiery oration containing the day's most pointed barbs at the president. ("We cannot defend Freedom in Berlin so long as we deny freedom in Birmingham!") And the president replied, "Oh, I've heard him plenty of times." (65) (66) (67)

Steven Levingston wrote, "President Kennedy was a man who had hit rhetorical highs himself, and he appreciated eloquence: he knew he had just seen performance for the ages." (68)

Laurence Leamer observes that in King's glorious words, there had been not one sentence about what blacks do for themselves. The overwhelming burden of black oppressions lay elsewhere, but the civil rights leaders risked fostering a disquieting sense of entitlement. (69)

Henry Fairlie, the number one British Kennedy Iconoclast, was scathing about the president welcoming the leaders of the march at the White House with the greeting "I have a dream" – in much the same way as Lyndon Johnson addressed a joint meeting of the two houses of Congress nineteen months later with the slogan – "We shall overcome." Fairlie claimed and dismissed this manner of political leadership as false, having little to do with the real political struggle and even making that struggle harder to win. He believed it distracted from the task of developing the kind of political strategy which, 30 years earlier, had carried the New Deal genuinely and irresistibly into the heart of the political process of the country and the political attitudes of the people. (70) "I have a dream" and "We shall overcome" were political slogans that had nothing to do with political leadership. But that struggle was won on July 2, 1964, and August 6, 1965. The FBI's Domestic Intelligence Division described this "Demagogic speech" as yet more evidence that Dr. King was "the most dangerous and effective Negro leader in the Country. (71)

James Reston of the New York Times placed King in the historical tradition of America's great reformers. "Roger Williams calling for religious liberty; Sam Adams calling for political liberty; old man Thoreau denouncing coercion; William Lloyd Garrison was demanding emancipation and Eugene V. Debs crying for American rights and liberty."

King's cry, "I have a dream," was a similar cry for American rights and liberty. But as Reston wondered, "The question of the day, of course, was raised by Dr. King's theme – was this all a dream or will it help a dream come true?" (72)

Hubert Humphrey said of the March, "If I had to pick one day in my public life when I was most encouraged that democracy could work when my spirit soared on the wings of the American dream of social justice for everyone, it was that day." (73)

John Lewis, who had heard King many times, felt something was lacking. "As he moved toward his final words, it seemed that he, too, could sense that he was falling short." Lewis recalled. "He hadn't locked into that power he so often found." (74)

Among the few critics was King's rival Malcolm X of the Black Muslims, the voice of Negro rage and retaliation, condemning the march as "The Farce on Washington."

From a jail cell in Louisiana, James Farmer, co-founder of the Congress of Racial Equality, wept at seeing the huge crowd on television. (75)

"I do not object," said the black novelist James Baldwin publicly, "to the fact that Senator Eastland (a symbol of southern resistance to racial integration) is alive, but I do object to his power. I certainly reject with vehemence any notion that I, as a Negro, should ever become "equal to such a man. Furthermore, if racism was purged from America's heart, as King recommended, how would Americans of all races work with and relate to each other? King's speech suggested compassion, charity, and Christian love. It did not present a method for implementation."

On August 29, after finding the upbeat newspaper coverage of the march on Washington much to his liking, Kennedy contacted Rustin and Randolph at their hotel. He did so partly to apologize for having called initially for the cancelation of the protest. Now that the demonstration had passed off so successfully, the White House mood was more relaxed. The polls were looking reasonably healthy as well. Kennedy's approval ratings in the South has taken a predictable hit, dropping from 60% in March to 44% in September. But his nationwide rating remained steady at 62%.

More gratifying still, a series of polls taken in August, pitting him against the three most frequently mentioned Republican hopefuls – Governor George Romney of Michigan, Arizona Senator Barry Goldwater and Rockefeller – suggested he was heading for a comfortable victory. Since the introduction of the Civil Rights bill and his televised address to the nation, Kennedy's approval rating among blacks had skyrocketed. And polls showed that he was likely to receive support from 95% of blacks, a huge improvement from 1960. (76)

5.3. Who Ordered King Wiretaps?

Was it Robert Kennedy or J. Edgar Hoover, who first called for telephone wiretaps surveillance on Martin Luther King? The answer is surrounded by confusion, misinformation, misunderstanding and plenty of controversy.

Hoover's involvement emerged on June 4, 1969, when it was revealed in a court hearing in Houston – during an appeal by former heavyweight boxing champion Cassius Clay against his conviction for refusing to be drafted – that the FBI had tapped Dr. King's telephone calls.

In his televised news conference on June 19, 1969, President Nixon said that he checked to see whether J. Edgar Hoover "had acted on his own or with proper authority" in ordering wiretaps on Dr. King and Elijah Muhammad, the black Muslim Leader said, "I found that it (the wiretapping) had always been approved by the Attorney General, as Mr. Hoover testified in 1964 and 1965," Nixon said. He did not mention the two Attorneys General – Robert F. Kennedy and Nicholas De B. Katzenbach – who held the office during the period in which the wiretapping is known to have taken place. Still, Nixon seemed in his news conference to support Hoover when he said he had established that the Attorney General had approved the wiretap.

Hoover said in a rare newspaper interview with the Washington Star's Jeremiah O'Leary that he had a memorandum from Courtney Evans, then assistant bureau director, the FBI's liaison to the Attorney General, showing that Kennedy was the initiator, having first proposed tapping Dr. King's phone in June 1963: the Evans memorandum proves it, Hoover insisted.

However, Ramsey Clark and his immediate predecessor as Attorney General, Nicholas de B. Katzenbach, labelled Mr. Hoover's statements "misleading." (1) (2) (3) (4)

Evans himself, in an interview for the Kennedy Library, said the following, "The June 1963 memorandum in which I reported a conversation I had with the Attorney General concerning his concern about reports that Doctor King was a student of Marxism and was allegedly associating with a New York attorney with known Communist connections, and if it was technically feasible to use electronic devices to prove or disprove these allegations." The text of this memorandum, to the best of my knowledge, has never been released publicly, which raises in my mind some questions as to what else there is in the memorandum.

When Evans was asked during testimony for the Church Committee whether the idea of installing a wiretap originated with the Attorney General, he answered, "No, this is not clear in my mind at all. The record that has been exhibited to me doesn't establish this definitely. However, that inference can be drawn from some of the memoranda. But it is my recollection, without the benefit of any specifics, that there was much more to it than this. And I have the feeling that pressures were existing at the time to develop more specific information that may have had a bearing here." (5) (6)

Cartha DeLoach, the Number three man in the FBI, claimed that, contrary to public opinion, Bobby Kennedy first asked the FBI to put a wiretap on Dr. King. Mr. Hoover told Courtney Evans to go back and try to talk him out of it because he realized the ramifications if it ever became public. (7) (8)

On Saturday, June 22, 1963, Martin Luther King had two meetings at the White House, the first between 10.10-10.30 a.m. with Robert Kennedy and Burke Marshall, and the second, from 10.30-12.17 a.m., when King was among a group of 31 civil rights leaders who met with the president. (9)

According to Richard Reeves, Kennedy wanted to talk to King alone, inviting him to stroll in the White House Rose Garden after the other civil rights leaders left. (10) The president told King, "I assume you know you're under close surveillance." He placed one hand on King's shoulder and half-whispered that he had to get rid of both Jack O'Dell, director of the Southern Christian Leadership Conference (SCLC) and Stanley Levison, a white attorney and King's closest white friend, "They're communists," the president said. Levison was O'Dell's "handler," and O'Dell was the number five Communist in the US. King tried to laugh it off, but Kennedy was dead serious and determined. He also brought up the Profumo sex scandal in Britain, in which John Profumo, British secretary of state for war, was compromised by a gorgeous call girl, Christina Keeler, who was involved with a Soviet diplomat. The affair threatened the government of Prime Minister Harold Macmillan. Kennedy cautioned King, "That's an example of friendship and loyalty carried too far. Macmillan is likely to lose his government because he has been loyal to a friend. You must take care not to lose your cause for the same reason."

He told King that getting the civil rights bill through Congress was going to be difficult. "If they (the opponents of the bill) shoot you down, they'll shoot us down too, so we're asking you to be careful." King finally said, "I know Stanley, and I can't believe this, you will have to prove it." Kennedy noted that Burke Marshall would show the proof to Andrew Young – but when Young asked Marshall for evidence, he said he had none and could not get anything out of the Bureau, "We ask the Bureau for things, and we get these big memos, but they don't ever really say anything," Marshall insisted.

King told Andrew Young afterwards, "The president is afraid of Hoover himself. I guess Hoover must be bugging him too." (11) (12)

The private meeting was scheduled between two other private sessions with Roy Wilkins, head of the NAACP, and Walter Reuther of the United Auto Workers (UAW), the white leader of the labor union with the largest Negro membership. We have here a small distortion of history because I checked the White House appointment book, and Kennedy didn't talk only with King in his now historic stroll in the Rose Garden, in the afternoon.

In his July 17 press conference, one reporter said to the president, "Mr. President, in the last week the Governor of Alabama, the Governor of Mississippi, and the Attorney General have all testified before the Senate Commerce Committee insisting that the integration move was communist-inspired. And this has led to some fears on the part of some senators that we may be entering into a period of McCarthyism that will submerge this issue."

The president's answered:

"We have no evidence that any of the leaders of the civil rights movements in the US are communists. We have no evidence that the demonstrations are communist-inspired. There may be occasions when a communist takes part in a demonstration. We can't prevent that. But I think it is a convenient scapegoat to suggest that all the difficulties are communist and if the communist movement would only disappear that we would end this." (13)

According to James W. Hilty, Robert Kennedy believed by 1963 in an international communist conspiracy, and he had first-hand proof from the FBI of the Soviet Union's internal spy apparatus. This contradicts what Burke Marshall said to Andrew Young, "We get big memos, but they don't ever really say anything." (14)

Arthur Schlesinger Jr. wrote that the Attorney General saw communism as a danger but hardly in the Republic. "It is such nonsense to have to waste time prosecuting the Communist Party," he told Henry Branson of the London Sunday Times in

December 1961. "It wouldn't be less of a threat, and besides, its membership consists largely of FBI agents." An outraged patriot sent the clipping to Hoover, who quickly replied, "It was good of you to make this item available to me." Hoover enclosed five statements expressing his views of the communist threat and described the Communist Party as "a Trojan Horse of rigidly-disciplined fanatics unalterably committed to bringing this free nation under the joke of international communism." (15)

Immediately before the Washington march, the bureau's domestic intelligence division prepared a comprehensive 68-page report laying out all Communist party efforts to influence or join in civil rights movement efforts and noting the party's total failure in such attempts, given only 4,453 active members. Hoover refused to accept domestic intelligence's implicit conclusion that the Communist Party was of no relevance to the American racial problem. (16)

Sullivan wrote, "So I had to play this dusty conclusion that King was a Marxist, no matter how mistaken he was. Hoover berated me – I kept saying that Castro was a communist, and you people wouldn't believe me. Now you're saying that King is not a communist, and you're just as wrong this time as you were with Castro."

On Levison and O'Dell being communists, Robert Kennedy believed Hoover. When New York Times columnist Anthony Lewis asked Robert Kennedy in December 1964, in the presence of Burke Marshall, whether he knew while he was Attorney General that there were some communists close to Dr. King, his answer was "Yes." Concerning Stanley Levison, Burke Marshall said the Bureau's information was that he was a secret Communist Party member. Robert Kennedy described him as "A High Official," so he was quite a big figure.

Copies of a Hoover memorandum, attacking Dr. King, classified as top secret and referring to Levison, were sent to the President, the Attorney General, to Navy Intelligence, Army Intelligence, Air Force Intelligence and the Secretary of Defense. Bobby thought the document was one-sided and painted a very unfair picture of King, despite the link to Levison: Marshall and Kennedy did not indicate that King went to communist meetings or was otherwise involved with communists – although they were convinced that Levison influenced King. (17) (18)

It was Levison who recommended Jack O'Dell (Hunter Pitts O'Dell) Levison as SCLC director, and King knew that O'Dell had been a Communist party member in the 1940s and 1950s. So when Kennedy warned that he had to go, O'Dell temporarily resigned from his SCLC position.

Then on July 3, 1963, King wrote to him, "We conducted what we felt to be a thorough inquiry into these charges and were unable to discover any present connections with the Communist Party on your part. The situation in our country is such, however, that an allusion to the left brings forth an emotional response which would seem to indicate that SCLC and the Southern Freedom Movement are communist-inspired. In these critical times, we cannot afford to risk such impressions.

We, therefore, have decided in our Administrative Committee that we should request you to make your temporary resignation permanent." (19)

But Martin Luther King found it hard to fire O'Dell because he was excellent at doing mailings to raise funds. After the FBI found out that O'Dell continued to work for King almost a year after his "resignation," Hoover concluded that King was a "vicious liar." (20)

Meanwhile, Levison, a white attorney and businessman from New York City initially introduced to King by Deputy Washington March director Bayard Rustin in 1956, had become King's closest white advisor as well as a friend. The FBI forwarded memoranda to Robert Kennedy warning that Levison represented a danger to King, alleging he was a "known," or "secret" high official of the Communist party," possibly "engaged in espionage," an "associate of foreign nationals" or a "conduit of foreign monies." (21)

All available evidence indicates that Levison had been closely involved in CP financial activities between 1952 and 1955 but that he ended that association sometime in 1955 and that he had no active CP ties once he became associated with King in 1956.

The FBI sources were a pair of double agents, the brothers, Jack and Morris Childs (code-named Solo), and their reports of Levison's earlier activities were in all likelihood quite accurate. (22) (23)

However, from late 1955 on, the FBI had no direct or convincing evidence that Levison had continued to work with the party – the Bureau had even tried unsuccessfully to recruit him as an informant in February 1960. (24)

Levison's relatives recall that he ended a number of his previous associations once he became close to Martin Luther King in 1956-57. In short, the FBI's information tied Levison to the CP only for the years before 1956 and no later.

According to King biographer David Garrow, "the FBI possessed no evidence that connected Levison to any CP activity in the years after he and Martin Luther King Jr. first became acquainted. The FBI's lack of interest in Levison between early 1960 and late 1961 ended suddenly when it learned in very early 1962 that Levison and King were close friends rather than just acquaintances." (25)

William C. Sullivan told A. Schlesinger Jr. that he had never seen any evidence that Levison was a party member. (26)

On January 8, 1962, Hoover reported to the Attorney General that the FBI had identified Stanley D. Levison, King's friend, financial advisor and ghostwriter, as a "high official," "a member of the Executive Board of the Communist Party." (27)

In fact, Levison negotiated a book contract for King's account of the Montgomery bus boycott, "Stride Toward Freedom," and then offered King line-by-line criticism and assistance in editing and polishing the book's text. Levison also took charge of other tasks, ranging from writing King's fundraising letters to preparing his tax returns – and always firmly refused King's offers of payment. (28)

On March 6, the formal FBI memo requesting approval for the wiretap was sent by the Director's office to the Attorney General. A microphone was installed in Levison's office on March 16, 1962, and a wiretap installed on his office telephone on March 20, 1962. The Attorney General authorized the wiretap – the microphone was approved only at the FBI division level. It was planted by Bureau agents who broke into Levison's office on the night of March 15-16. (29) (30) (31) (32)

Installation of the tap and mike dramatically increased the Bureau's flow of information on Levison – but none of the overheard conversations lent any support, even indirectly, to the claims about Levison. Most of the intercepted dialogue was of no real value, and also, the Levison-King phone conversations proved only that Levison was an influential advisor to King.

According to Harris Wofford, King finally agreed with Levison's consent to break their ties, and they did not meet again for about a year. By the fall of 1963, however, King had started telephoning Levison to check matters they had been working on. (33) This seems to be a strange observation on Wofford's part when we know that "the stroll in the Rose Garden," where Kennedy asked King to get rid of Levison and O'Dell, took place June 22, 1963.

Journalist and author Victor S. Navasky wrote, "And so, despite King's promise to break with Levison, he would call from time to time, to find out a date or a location or to get some files." And Levison explained to Navasky, "You don't sever a long relationship just like that."

In a tribute after King's assassination, Levison displayed true friendship credentials, writing, "Few people know how humble this giant was. He had an inexhaustible faith in people, and multitudes felt it with their hearts and their minds, and went beyond respect almost to worship."

And Coretta King called Stanley Levison "our trusted friend."

Martin Luther King himself couldn't believe that his close friend, who had been at his side long before King became the country's leading civil rights figure, would abuse his trust. (34)

Michael O'Brien calls this poor judgement on King's behalf, claiming that Levison lied to King about his communist past, telling him merely that he had "known" some Communists and had worked with some in Henry Wallace's 1948 presidential bid, but that those activities were history.

I think that "true friendship, not political" friendship is hard to find, and if so it was, it's hard to separate as friends from one day to another.

O'Brien further wrote that Levison claimed he had never been a card-carrying member of the Communist party.

Did Levison break with Communism after 1955? Where did his ideology lie after he met King? Did he have an insidious hidden agenda in befriending King? O'Brien says that biographer Garrow, despite his brilliant research and exceptional insights, has not adequately answered those questions, partly because of his naive faith in Levison. (35)

Having interviewed Levison and talked with countless members of the civil rights movement and the Justice Department, Navasky believed Stanley Levison when he said, "I can tell you I'm not a member of the Communist Party, and I never was."

The most suspicious "fact" about him is that he took the Fifth Amendment in 1962 when testifying in executive session before the Senate Internal Security Committee. His lawyers had urged him to invoke the Fifth Amendment because he was reluctant to rehash sensational and misleading charges, which could only end up smearing Dr King's reputation. (36)

Garrow argued, says O'Brien, that after 1955, "The FBI had no direct or convincing evidence that Levison had continued to work with the party. In "legal terms," Garrow added, the FBI's case against Levison after 1955 was "so weak as to be virtually worthless." To which O'Brien replies:

"History, though, need not be judged strictly in "legal terms" and the grounds for harshly judging Levison should be his essential, secret work for the Communist Party before he met King."

In the final judgment, O'Brien concluded that it was regrettable that King associated with the two Communists. (37)

Fellow Kennedy biographer Burton Hersh wrote, "Both Kennedys were quite peeved that, whatever King told them, Stanly Levison was still around, involved in the ghosting of King's new book about the Birmingham protests, and patiently advising the SCLC." (38)

According to Thomas C. Reeves, Arthur Schlesinger described Levison as "a good-hearted and undiscriminating liberal of the type for whom there was no enemy to the left." (39)

Schlesinger, who interviewed Levison, told him that he was "neither an international agent nor even a domestic party member, but at that time Hoover's credibility was unchallenged: it would have diverted the movement at a critical stage to take on so difficult a civil liberties battle." As for Robert Kennedy, "I understand his position. You have to recall the time. We weren't too far away from the McCarthy period. They were so committed to our movement, and they couldn't possibly risk what could have been a terrible political scandal when I realized how hard Hoover was pressing them and how simultaneously they were giving Martin such essential support. I didn't feel any hostility about their attitude toward me."

Stanley Levison died in September 1979, at the age of 67, without ever honestly acknowledging how far his political journey had gone: he was never forthcoming about what he had been before 1957, just as the FBI was never forthcoming about what he no longer was after 1957. (40)

William C. Sullivan, former head of FBI intelligence operations, said that Hoover told him that he felt King was, or could become, a "serious threat" to the security of the country. He pointed out that King was an instrument of the Communist party. He, Hoover, wanted it proved that King had a relationship with the Soviet bloc, "Hoover didn't like King on general principles, but though we had been tapping King's telephone in Atlanta since the late 1950s, no damning information on him had been unearthed," Sullivan said.

Sullivan invited King for an interview, approved by Hoover. Still, King, in a brief note, replied that he was too busy to join in a discussion at the FBI – something Sullivan felt was a severe mistake by King.

So Sullivan had to stick to his conclusion that King was a Marxist, no matter how mistaken he was. What was Hoover's proof?

Hoover believed that King was a communist because King once publicly said that he was a Marxist. Hundreds of memos were written to Hoover during those years from all the top men at the bureau, including Sullivan, all of them telling Hoover that King was a dangerous menace and that Hoover was doing the right thing. "We gave him what he wanted, under the threat of being out on the street if we didn't agree" said Sullivan.

Sullivan thought Hoover's motives in pursuing King were:

1. Hoover was opposed to change, to the civil rights movement and blacks.
2. Hoover believed that King was a communist, or at the very least pro-communist, all evidence to the contrary, notwithstanding.
3. Hoover resented King's criticism of the FBI.
4. Hoover was jealous of King's national prominence and the international awards that were offered to him. Martin Luther King, at the age of 35, was the youngest to receive the Nobel Peace Prize, December 10, 1964, in Oslo. (41) (42)

I have a few remarks on William Sullivan's statements.

First, as Garrow writes, "William Sullivan was the key decision-maker in the King case in the Summer, and the Fall of 1963, and Sullivan was an almost ideal example of what one scholar has termed the bureaucratic "climber," someone whose principal or the only goal in a job is to maximize the power of his position, the number of resources under his control, and the prestige that accompanies such an expanding role. Climbers are particularly noted for telling their superiors only what they believe those superiors want to hear."

I fully agree with Garrow's observation.

And what about Sullivan's view of King as a human being? In a letter of recommendation to Hoover, Sullivan wrote, "It should be clear to all of us that Martin Luther King must, at some propitious point in the future, be revealed to the people of this country and his Negro followers as being what he is – a fraud, demagogue and scoundrel."

Compared to what he wrote in his book, "I was one hundred per cent for King at that time because I saw him rising as an effective and badly-needed leader for the black people in their desire for civil rights." (43) This flip-flop attitude can be regarded as the approach of a chameleon. No wonder that the Church Committee, when faced with Sullivan's flawed credibility, viewed his very reasonable account of the fall 1963 conflict with mistrust.

Out of fear of losing his job at the Bureau, Sullivan constantly lied about Martin Luther King. People who are afraid can be dangerous, or, as Franklin Delano

Roosevelt put it, "The only thing we have to fear is fear itself."

If Sullivan had gone to Robert Kennedy and told him about all those falls memos, the history of the civil rights movement would have been different.

On July 16, 1963, the day after Governor Wallace's charges that Dr. King was dominated by Communists and the day before the President denied communist influence in the civil rights movement, the Attorney General raised with Courtney Evans the possibility of wiretap coverage of Dr. King and Clarence Jones, King's attorney. Asked where the idea came from, Sullivan said, "Not from Bobby. It came from Hoover, and the whole impetus came from us."

Reports from the FBI offices indicated that wiretaps were feasible, and Director Hoover requested on July 23, 1963, the Attorney General to approve wiretaps on phones in Dr. King's home, SCLC offices, and at the New York attorney's home and law office.

The next day, on July 24, 1963, warned by Evans about the dangers of wiretapping King, Bobby Kennedy informed Evans that he had decided against technical surveillance of King but had approved supervision of Jones.

There were no allegations that Jones was a communist. His mistake was to have raised Bobby's ire by saying nothing at the infamous Baldwin meeting and then approaching the Attorney General to compliment him on all the good he was doing. At the time Robert Kennedy asked for such surveillance, he was told there was considerable doubt that what it might produce would be worth the risk because King traveled most of the time and because there might be serious repercussions if it ever became known that the government had approved surveillance. (44) (45) (46)

On September 6, 1963, William Sullivan first recommended to Director Hoover that the FBI install wiretaps on Dr. King's home and the offices of the SCLC. Sullivan's recommendation was part of an attempt to improve the Domestic Intelligence Division's standing with the director by convincing him that Sullivan's division was concerned about alleged communist influence on the civil rights movement.

Sullivan's recommendation was viewed with scepticism by the FBI leadership since Bobby Kennedy had rejected a similar proposal in July.

Associate Director Clyde Tolson noted in the memorandum containing Sullivan's proposal, "I see no point in making this recommendation to the Attorney General since he turned down a similar recommendation on July 22 (in fact it was July 24) 1963."

Hoover scrawled below Tolson's note, "I will approve though I am dizzy over vacillation as to the influence of CPUSA." (47)

On October 4, 1963, William Sullivan, avidly seeking redemption, formally recommended that Hoover once again seek Bobby Kennedy's approval for a wiretap on King's home in Atlanta. The proposal was a watershed to Hoover, especially since Kennedy had turned him down in July. "I hope you don't change your mind on this," he scribbled to Sullivan in a reminder of his brief apostasy. (48) (49)

In late September 1963, the FBI conducted a survey and concluded that wiretap coverage of Dr. King's residence and of the New York SCLC office could be implemented without detection.

On October 7, 1963, citing "possible communist influence in the racial situation," Hoover requested the Attorney General's permission for a wiretap "on King at his current address or at any future address to which he may move" and "on the SCLC office at the current New York address or to any other address it may be moved." Attorney General Kennedy signed the request on October 10 and on October 21 also approved the FBI request for coverage of the SCLC's Atlanta office.

Two memoranda by Courtney Evans indicate that the Attorney General was uncertain about the advisability of the wiretaps: Evans and Bobby Kennedy met to discuss the FBI's request for the wiretaps on October 10, after which Bobby Kennedy signed the authorization, even though he was still vacillating about technical coverage. Evans reminded him of their previous conversation when he had been assured that all possible would be done to ensure the security of this operation. Robert Kennedy thus approved the wiretaps but asked that this coverage and that on King's residence be evaluated at the end of thirty days – a kind of "probation period," after which time the results would be evaluated to decide whether to continue or not. Wiretaps were installed on the SCLC's New York office on October 24, 1963, and at Dr. King's home and the SCLC's Atlanta office on November 8, 1963.

The FBI made an internal evaluation of the wiretaps in December 1963 and decided on its own to extend them for three months.

Reading the Attorney's authorization broadly, the FBI construed permission to wiretap Dr. King "at his current address or at any future address" to include hotel room phones and the phone at the home of friends with whom he temporarily stayed. That's what you can read in the Church Committee transcripts. Still, the Committee was not able to ascertain why Attorney General Robert Kennedy approved the FBI's request for wiretaps in October 1963 after refusing an identical request in July 1963. (50) (51)

On "who ordered the King Wiretaps, and what was the reason Bobby Kennedy finally after three months gave Hoover what he wanted," there is a pro and a contra Kennedy version.

According to Arthur M. Schlesinger Jr., the Kennedys authorized the taps on King for defensive purposes, to protect King, to protect the Civil Rights Bill, to protect themselves.

"What was less excusable," Schlesinger said, "if understandable for a period after November 22, 1963, was the failure of the Attorney General to terminate the taps." Sullivan explained, "Bobby Kennedy resisted, resisted and resisted tapping King. Finally, we twisted the arm of the Attorney General to the point where he had to go. I guess he feared we would let that stuff go in the press if he said no. I know he resisted the electronic coverage. He didn't want to put it on." (52) (53)

Burton Hersh writes, "Already under pressure from Hoover over the Ellen Rometsch incident, Kennedy passed the word to the FBI that he had decided to augment the

Levison surveillance with wiretaps on Clarence Jones and Martin Luther King. "This was a switch – normally, wiretap requests went up from the Bureau to the Attorney General, who signed off without too many questions being asked."

In an interview with Hersh, Cartha DeLoach insisted years later, "We were against putting a wiretap on King. We told him that it would be wrong to do that, an embarrassment if it were found out." (54)

Anthony Summers says that Edgar Hoover had again pressed the Attorney General to authorize a wiretap on King. Three months earlier, Kennedy had refused a Bureau request to wiretap Martin Luther King. On October 26, the morning he and Hoover discussed Ellen Rometsch, the Attorney General had found himself in an impossible situation. When Kennedy tried to remonstrate, Hoover just stonewalled. The Kennedys had lost control of J. Edgar Hoover.

There would have been "no living with the Bureau," Kennedy told an aide, "if he had not approved the King wiretaps."

I thought that Bobby Kennedy had already signed Hoover's request on October 10 and October 21. (55)

Taylor Branch wrote, "It was a trap. How could Kennedy hope to control Hoover once he had agreed to wiretap King? There was a Faustian undertow to Kennedy's dilemma, and he did not feel strong enough to resist." (56)

But according to William Sullivan, Kennedy was aware that Hoover was an enemy, of course, and he kept his distance, never asking Hoover for any gossip or any favors. Kennedy couldn't stop Hoover from talking behind his back. Still, he could do something about Hoover's public statements, and he did. Kennedy would also call Hoover over to the White House two or three times to remind him who was the boss. Kennedy didn't say it bluntly, but Hoover got the message. (57) This is what I call a Black and White situation.

David Garrow, in an article for the Atlantic, writes, "On October 10, 1963, the U.S. Attorney General committed what is widely viewed as one of the most ignominious acts in modern American History."

But Michael O'Brien says Garrow's accusation is wrong, and I would add that it is exaggerated and out of proportion. Although considering what we now know about the hundreds of false memos written by top men at the Bureau to please and to satisfy Hoover's paranoia to destroy Martin Luther King, it was indeed ignominious. (58) (59)

Ramsey Clark, who succeeded Nicholas Katzenbach as Attorney General in 1967, says in an oral history interview that three bugs were placed on King in three different hotels in the summer and fall of '65 after Bobby Kennedy had left. "There's a vast difference between wiretaps and telephones and bugs in hotel rooms," Clark pointed out. "The talk that you hear about scandalous conduct, so to speak, could not, and does not come from any wiretaps authorized by Bob Kennedy. That's just a rap he should not take in history."

Clark also believed that it was deceitful of Hoover to pose as a reluctant eavesdropper on King because he repeatedly requested Clark to authorize FBI wiretaps on King while Clark was Attorney General. The last of those requests – none of which was granted – came two days before King's murder. (60) (61) (62) (63)

Edwin O. Guthman, the Justice Department public relations chief during Robert Kennedy's tenure as Attorney General, told the Church Committee that Robert Kennedy finally agreed in the fall of 1963 to give the FBI permission to wiretap the phones because Guthman thought that if he did not do it, Hoover would move to impede or block the passage of the Civil Rights Bill. (64)

Katzenbach, who was Attorney General from 1964 to 1966, said that while Hoover didn't organize the telephone taps on his own, he did all the hotel room bugs on his own. He is sure Bobby didn't know about them. (65)

But Bobby was the one who signed the wiretap on October 10, 1963, which was finally discontinued on April 30, 1965.

Senator Walter Mondale and later Vice President in 1977, said, "The way Martin Luther King was hounded and harassed is a disgrace to every American."

Hoover's jealousy and King paranoia were ignominious. Joseph P. Kennedy, Jack's father, once observed, "More people die from jealousy than cancer."

Maybe the time has come to rename the J. Edgar Hoover building headquarters of the FBI in Washington.

5.4. Was Harris Wofford Sent to Africa, or Was It His Own Decision?

In two oral history interviews in 1965 and 1968, Harris Wofford, American attorney, civil rights activist and advisor to Martin Luther King, recalls his appointment as a Special Assistant to the President for Civil Rights.

After the election, he was working with Sargent Shriver on the so-called "talent hunt" but was not then on Kennedy's staff. The day the Civil Rights Commission had its first meeting with the president, he told Chairman John A. Hannah and Father Theodore M. Hesburgh before they saw the president that he was going to work on the Peace Corps because he knew "they were discussing why I shouldn't work in civil rights." "They" must have been John and Robert Kennedy.

Wofford felt he had worked hard during the election campaign and wanted and deserved the role of assistant Attorney General. Still, there were several obstacles to his selection: he was very close to Martin Luther King. He had clashed with Robert Kennedy and Byron White during the campaign. (1) (2) (3) (4)

On top of that, John Kennedy's priority was not the civil rights issue but foreign affairs.

By choosing Burke Marshall as his assistant, Robert Kennedy admitted that he was influenced a good deal by Byron White – not Wofford's best friend. He had considered Wofford to head of the Civil Rights division. Still, he was reluctant to appoint him because he was so committed to civil rights emotionally – and Bobby thought that Wofford was in some areas a slight madman. Bobby had called Wofford

278

one of the "bomb throwers" – the other was Sargent Shriver – when Wofford proposed calling Coretta King. Harris Wofford came up with the idea during the election to give Coretta King a phone call while her husband was in jail in Georgia. Robert Kennedy wanted a tough lawyer who could look at things objectively and give advice and handle things properly. That's why he finally settled on Burke Marshall.

Fortunately, Harris and Burke were close friends, notwithstanding very different personalities. According to Sargent Shriver, Wofford was the most qualified man to lead the Civil Rights Division. Still, there was no love lost between Wofford and Byron White. According to C. David Heymann, Wofford had lobbied RFK in vain against the appointment of White, whom he considered stubborn and humorless. At the same time, the latter persuaded Bobby that Wofford's well-established ties to Martin Luther King and his sympathies for the doctrine of civil disobedience would not sit well with Dixie legislators. In the mid-fifties, Harris Wofford and Martin Luther King Jr. were drawn together by their interest in nonviolence: Wofford arranged for King to visit India and became King's advisor.

So White selected for the post Burke Marshall, a high-powered corporate lawyer and another graduate of Yale Law School. As the new appointee's law partner and friend, Wofford was in no position to protest the choice, even though Marshall's prime qualification in White's mind was his utter lack of civil rights experience. (5)

Marshall thought Wofford was a terrific fellow – a man who had been shunted aside and had difficulty getting attention when he was in the White House but remained loyal. Marshall was convinced that Bob Kennedy liked him but thought that he didn't like that job in the White House. (6)

So John Hannah, Father Theodore M. Hesburgh and one other member of the Civil Rights Commission went to the president and told him how important it was that he has somebody on civil rights in the White House that Eisenhower hadn't. Kennedy pointed out that he already had someone, "One of my special assistants, Harris Wofford, is working on it full-time." They told Kennedy that the last time they saw Wofford, he had an office in the Peace Corps. Kennedy answered, "Oh, that was just temporarily, with Sarge."

A few minutes later, Ralph A. Dungan called Wofford and said, "The president wants you to come over." And Harris said, "Well, I can guess what it's about Ralph. I sort of committed myself to Shriver in the Peace Corps," and Ralph said, "Well, come over here and see what the president has to say." While Wofford waited in an outer office to see the president, White House Executive Clerk William J. Hopkins appeared, carrying the Bible and asked, "Are you Mr. Wofford? Take the oath of office after me, please." Wofford asked why and Hopkins replied, "Well, I just got word from the president to come up and swear you in this minute as Special Assistant to the President."

Wofford said he hadn't seen the president. Still, Hopkins insisted he had been ordered by the president to swear Wofford in immediately, "So here's the Bible, please raise your right hand and repeat the oath of office." That is how he got to be a Special Assistant to the President on Civil Rights.

Kennedy told Wofford that he could continue to work with Sargent Shriver if he wanted to half the time but that he needed Harris to get the issue of civil rights on track at the White House. (7) (8) (9)

Wofford never knew for sure in whether his White House assignment resulted from his meeting with the Civil Rights Commissioners on February 7, 1961, or was already set in his mind and just not conveyed to him during his first two weeks in office: Wofford was sure that, between the election and the inauguration, Kennedy paid only fleeting attention to civil rights. (10)

Wofford was convinced that Kennedy genuinely wanted to resolve the civil rights controversy and end discrimination. Still, he felt that the president, wrongly, did not make it a top priority.

It turned out that it was a greater issue and problem and more urgent than he thought. Kennedy preferred, in the style of Lincoln, "to let a thing ripen before you move on it" – similar to a lawyer's concept of dealing with concrete cases rather than things in the abstract.

In other words, do not initiate action on difficult matters unless necessary: Wofford thought that was, more or less, the president's attitude towards civil rights. (11)

Wofford was in post for nearly five hundred of Kennedy's thousand days in office, with some high points but some lows – the lowest being the occasions when the president delayed signing the Order against discrimination in housing. As pens marked "one stroke of the pen" poured into the White House mailroom in a campaign to remind him of his campaign promise, Kennedy said, "Send them to Wofford!" (12)

President Kennedy was busy preparing his forthcoming encounter with Khrushchev and did not appreciate the crisis the Congress of Racial Equality (CORE) had deliberately precipitated in Alabama, with The "Freedom Riders" riding interstate buses in the South in mixed racial groups to challenge segregation laws.

Wofford received an angry phone call from the president, "Tell them to call it off.....Stop them!" But it was too late – Kennedy wasn't satisfied, and not even his brother nor the ever-persuasive Burke Marshall could halt the Freedom Riders. (13)

In a June Gallup Poll, 63% of those questioned disapproved of the rides, while 70% approved Kennedy's action in sending marshals to protect the Riders, including 50% of those polled in the South.

Wofford's highest point came just before he left for a new assignment in Africa in August 1962. Kennedy, with great sincerity and warmth, said, "It will take some more time, but I want you to know that we are going to do all these things." He was referring to a list Wofford had prepared of difficult civil rights actions awaiting a presidential decision, including the still postponed housing order.

Wofford had, at John Kennedy's request, worked out a civil rights strategy for 1961 and submitted it in a lengthy memorandum on December 30, 1960.

When Wofford left, Kennedy smiled reassuringly and repeated, "You will see, with time, I'm going to do them all." He didn't get the time to fulfill his promise. (14) (15)

The "stroke-of-a-pen" comment has an exciting history of its own.

According to Richard Goodwin, a Kennedy advisor and speechwriter between the election and inauguration, the campaign team had, by December 1960, compiled a formidable list of campaign promises, eighty-one in all. Promise number 52 was an executive order ending discrimination in federally-supported housing, thus abolishing racial barriers "with a stroke of a pen." Later Kennedy asked Ted Sorensen, "Who the hell wrote that?" When Sorensen answered, "I didn't," Kennedy retorted, "Well then, I guess nobody wrote it." The promise was contained in Goodwin's draft for a campaign trip to Los Angeles and delivered by Kennedy without the slightest hint of doubt or equivocation. (16) (17) (18)

Wofford remembers that he had used the phrase in his speeches and that Kennedy adopted it in one of the debates with Richard Nixon. Whatever the origin of the phrase, it became an albatross for Kennedy by 1962.

Wofford was aware of the fact, as he predicted that federal civil rights policy would be centered on Robert Kennedy and the Justice Department. Still, unknown to him was that Byron White had been urging that the White House be the coordinator of overall federal civil rights action so that the Department of Justice could remain an objective enforcer of the laws. However, Robert Kennedy, according to Burke Marshall's oral history interview, did not favor such direct White House involvement and thought that Justice's Civil Rights Division was the appropriate agency. (19)

I agree with Byron White's vision of the facts: the White House is the center for action on civil rights.

Harris Wofford saw his function as a buffer between Kennedy and the civil rights forces pressing for presidential action. However, according to Taylor Branch, Wofford was far too earnest about racial segregation to enjoy the role. By the spring of 1962, the more congenial atmosphere of Sargent Shriver's Peace Corps was worth more to him than the opportunities at the White House, "The spirit of your administration and your spirit makes me want to go and work on a frontier of my own," he wrote to President Kennedy on resigning to take a job in Ethiopia.

If his heart was working for the Peace Corps, he should never have accepted the "Special Assistant" appointment for civil rights. He knew that he wasn't the first choice for the job and that Bobby didn't want him for the job, and we know what happens if Bobby doesn't like you. Wofford was naive, but as a passionate, engaged wonderful man, an idealist – some of his White House colleagues found him arrogant – he was overjoyed to get that post in the White House. I am convinced that he went to Africa half-heartedly: as an ambitious man, he left out of frustration, because his wings had been clipped: President Kennedy gave him the job he relished, but he was too much involved in the civil rights cause, wanting to go too fast with a reluctant President in the first two years in office. Ultimately, Wofford went out through the back door instead of being fired – although John Kennedy would not "fire" Wofford because he was grateful for what he did in the campaign: Lem Billings said that a Kennedy weakness was that he hated firing anybody, private secretary or a Cabinet member. "Kennedy," said Billings, "held tremendous feeling of loyalty towards all those who worked for him." (20) (21)

I asked my friend Dan if my feeling about Wofford, civil rights and the Peace Corps was right. He said, "I took over Wofford's office in the Executive Office Building, and I recall seeing him as he was leaving. He did not look like a happy camper to me. The next time I saw him was in Ethiopia, where he was head of the Peace Corps group. I recall at the time how downcast he looked. He had the look of an ambitious person who felt he had been shunted on a sidetrack." (22) This confirms my views on Wofford and civil rights at the White House.

5.5. Would Kennedy Have Replaced J. Edgar Hoover in 1965?

Historians have searched for hidden meaning in the reappointment of Dulles, CIA chief, and FBI boss Hoover, questioning the wisdom and rationale for both decisions. On November 10, 1960, Kennedy asked his political advisor Clark Clifford for his views on the retention of both men. Clifford's view was that, in light of Kennedy's narrow margin of victory, these decisions were neither controversial nor challenging to make: any other choice would have provoked a partisan debate that the president-elect did not need at that time. It would, therefore, be appropriate to retain both men "for the time being." However, he had despised and distrusted Hoover since the Truman years. (1)

Richard Neustadt, a prominent political scientist who counseled Kennedy on staffing the presidency in the fall of 1960, also recommended Hoover's retention, "His reappointment seems a matter of course." Neustadt advised. "You might as well make the most of it by an early announcement, particularly since you may well find some things you would like him to do for you, quite confidentially, before inauguration." (2) (3)

On Wednesday night, November 9, 1960, Ben Bradlee and his wife Tony, with the ex-journalist and Kennedy ally, Bill Walton, were invited to supper at the Kennedy house in Hyannis Port. After dinner, in a relaxed and mischievous mood, Kennedy turned to Bradlee and Walton and said, "Okay, I'll give each one of you guys one appointment, one job to fill: what will it be?"

Walton spoke up first and told Kennedy he should replace J. Edgar Hoover, FBI director since 1924.

Bradlee wanted to replace Allen Dulles, head of the CIA, who had run the agency since 1953 and was the "godfather" of the American intelligence community.

The next morning, Bradlee was back at the Kennedy compound in Hyannis Port when suddenly, John Kennedy's friend, Lem Billings, came out into the hall. Bradlee heard him pick up the phone and say, "Operator, the president-elect would like to place two calls urgently, one to Mr. J. Edgar Hoover at the FBI and one to Mr. Allen

Dulles at the CIA." Kennedy was telling Hoover how much he was counting on him and wanted him to stay on: a few minutes later, the whole scene was repeated with Allen Dulles. Thus Bradlee said, "There ended my career as a presidential consultant." Kennedy had listened to Clifford and Dick Neustadt, played it safe in "a strategy of reassurance" because Hoover and Dulles were still national icons in 1960. (4) (5)

The fact that the "amateurs" Walton and Bradlee were right and President Kennedy was wrong would not be apparent until at least fifteen years later. (6)

In "Counselor: A Life At the Edge of History," Kennedy speechwriter Ted Sorensen wrote that his biggest personal error, which he never corrected or -publicly- regretted, was to endorse the continuance in office of the "tyrannical" FBI director J. Edgar Hoover: Arbitrary and undemocratic, Hoover became too powerful and complicated for either President Kennedy or Attorney General Robert Kennedy to manage adequately.

Reportedly JFK later justified his retention of Hoover with the statement, "You don't fire God." (7)

According to author Ralph G. Martin, Kennedy told Timothy Selder, a Double Day editor, years later that he couldn't fire FBI director Hoover because he had all the tapes of him and Inga (Inga Arvad, the suspected Nazi spy who captivated both JFK and Hitler). (8) (9)

But in 1983, Martin wrote that Kennedy had kept his growing complaints file against Hoover. The American consulate refused a visa to a British Communist who wanted to visit his dying sister in the United States. Kennedy ordered the visa issued and asked Alba Schwartz of the State Department to request a 24-hour FBI surveillance while the communist was in the country. "I want to show how ridiculous the whole business is," the president said. Hoover refused, claiming he didn't have the money or the staff to do it. Then he told Schwartz, "You know, I have practically financed the Communist Party to keep tabs on them."

When Schwartz reported this to the president, Kennedy answered, "Tell it to Kenny – he's keeping a record of all this." According to Martin, Schwartz took this to mean that "Kennedy planned to get rid of Hoover after the re-election."

Martin concludes that if Kennedy had been re-elected, he would not have had to worry about the folder in the Hoover file that connected Kennedy during the war with lovely Inga Arvad, accused of being a Nazi spy. (10)

In Martin's 1983 book, he wrote that Kennedy didn't have to worry about the Inga Arvad file, kept by Hoover. But In his 1995 version, the Inga Arvad tapes were dynamite: two versions, one black, one white, but both of them are science-fiction to me.

On November 10, at his first formal news conference, the president-elect announced the reappointment of J. Edgar Hoover as FBI Director and Allen W. Dulles as head of the CIA.

For some authors, such as Robert Dallek and Michael O' Brien, Kennedy kept

Hoover in place because the director had files of embarrassing material about Kennedy's womanizing. (11) (12) Thomas C. Reeves, Richard Reeves, Michael O'Brien, among others, highlight in particular the fact that Hoover had the tapes of Jack's wartime escapade with Inga Arvad, better known as "Inga Binga," suspected of being a Nazi Spy, which she wasn't. (13)

According to another Kennedy profiler, David Nasaw, Joe Kennedy kept a close watch on his children, wherever they happened to be, and knew that Jack had many lovers. As a rule, Joe left them alone, but not in the case of Arvad. Inga Arvad, born October 6, 1913, was Danish, Protestant and older than Jack.

She was divorced from her first husband but still married to her second, a mysterious Hungarian film director who was employed by a Swedish millionaire suspected of being a Nazi sympathizer or operative.

It was his sister, Kathleen, Inga's roommate, who introduced Jack to Inga. When Joe Kennedy found out– from Kick or Krock- that Jack might be serious about the relationship, he intervened: what he said to his son is not known, but whatever it was, Jack listened, took it to heart, and that was the end of the wartime romance.

Joe Kennedy's informant was his friend J. Edgar Hoover, of whom Joe remained a fawning, outspoken admirer for many years. (14)

I think the turning point in the Joe Kennedy-Hoover relationship was in December 1961, when he suffered a debilitating stroke. His right side and face were paralyzed, and he was never to speak intelligibly again.

Anthony Summers writes, "The FBI surveillance had been a legitimate way of handling a potential risk, and the lovers had done nothing disloyal. It was, however, the start of a lasting bitterness between John F. Kennedy and Edgar.

His observation is based on an interview by the Blairs with Inga Arvad's son Ronald McCoy.

When they asked Ronald if Inga had told him anything about the trouble with the FBI, he said, "Jack was furious. Through his father or Arthur Krock, he and his mother went to see J. Edgar Hoover. Hoover told them his investigation showed that she was not a Nazi spy or had ever been employed by the Nazi's or did anything for them. So Jack asked Hoover if he would give them a letter saying she wasn't a Nazi spy. Hoover said he couldn't because if he gave her a letter and then she went out and started working for them tomorrow, his ass was on the line." (15) (16) (17)

According to Anthony Summers, columnist Jack Anderson said to him that John Kennedy was afraid not to reappoint Hoover, fearing it would have been politically destructive. Ben Bradlee confirmed to Summers that the bottom line was fear, saying, "All the Kennedys were afraid of Hoover." (18)

According to the Blairs, Langdon Parker Marvin Jr. was a close social friend as well as a legislative aide to Jack Kennedy in his early House days. Marvin claimed that when Kennedy came down to Congress, one of the things on his mind was getting hold of the "Inga-Binga" tape in the FBI files – the tape he was on. Marvin's advice would have been not to ask: he'd never get it. But later, when Kennedy was elected to the Senate, he was determined to get the tape, and Marvin told him not to be stupid. (19) (20)

According to my friend Dan, Langdon Marvin was a jerk – a Harvard student council president, a lightweight, very ambitious, and above all, he was unreliable. (21)

"A close social friend," as the Blairs suggested? I doubt it because I never saw him mentioned in other Kennedy biographies. It looks to be a fabricated story. I think in his Congress and early Senate days, JFK had other things on his mind than the Inga-Binga tape.

Anthony Summers adds some spice to Blair's Marvin story, claiming Kennedy told Marvin, "That bastard – I'm going to force Hoover to give me those files." And Marvin supposedly replied, "Jack, you're not going to do a thing. You can be sure there'll be a dozen copies made before he returns them to you, so you will not have gained a yard. And if he knows, you're desperate for them, and he'll realize he has you in a stranglehold." (22) (23). That's what I call a "totally inflated fabricated story" – a demonstration that some authors have no problem to write their historical truth.

Did President Kennedy reappoint Hoover out of fear that his womanizing and the "explosive" Inga Arvad tapes would be revealed? All those theories are easy to posit with hindsight – but this happened in November 1960, long before Kennedy's personal life was thoroughly scrutinized and concerned a wartime romance, like a million others. I don't think the claims pass the "so what?" test – and I see no merit in the contention that this issue was the start of a lasting bitterness between Kennedy and Hoover.

In 1960 only a few knew about his personal life, including his very closest personal friend Dave Powers, so why would he worry about those tapes? I think they didn't even cross his mind, not least because his father and Hoover were longstanding friends, and Hoover continued to visit Joe Kennedy after his stroke.

Finally, I think that too many authors are obsessed with the impact on the presidency of Kennedy's personal life, which was unknown at that time in history. Many historians have speculated with hindsight that Kennedy's womanizing would have been exposed and would have destroyed him in his second term.

But what about Lyndon Johnson, who finished his presidency in 1969? Johnson had no wish to hide his sexual conquests, "Why I had more women by accident than he ever had by design," Johnson liked to say when people spoke of Kennedy's philandering. (24)

So why would Kennedy, with better press relations than Johnson, not complete a second term? I think he would have.

There's an interesting comment from Courtney Evans, Assistant Director of the FBI's Special Investigative Division, who said, "It is well known that in his bachelor days President Kennedy had a reputation for playing particular attention to the fairer sex. Hoover knew this, but it was also widely known among those concerned with the political picture in Washington.

I've never seen evidence that there was anything of substance that would cause any undue influence that if Hoover released it, was going to be devastating to the presidency." (25)

Whether JFK would have replaced Hoover at the beginning of his second term is another "Kennedy enigma" where gossip, rumors, falsehoods and half-truths, collide with the historical truth.

J. Edgar Hoover had been director of the FBI since May 10, 1924, serving under eight presidents, from Calvin Coolidge to Richard Nixon. He died on May 2, 1972, at his home in Washington from a heart attack at the age of 77.

All presidents had their problems with their dictatorial director, but no one fired him. According to Anthony Summers, Mrs Roosevelt and her husband were very upset with Hoover because of the Lash affaire: did the president's wife sleep with Joseph P. Lash at the Blackstone Hotel in Chicago or anywhere else? Lash, who obtained the FBI and army files in 1978, denied it.

His widow, Trude Lash, recalled, "I had the impression the president had asked her not to discuss the details, but it was clear he was turning away from Hoover. Hoover knew it and tried to make himself seem indispensable by finding out things Mr. Roosevelt needed to know. As I understood it, however, the president said privately that he would dismiss Hoover as soon as possible."

According to Kenneth D. Ackerman, Hoover had particularly good relationships with at least two presidents he served under Franklin D. Roosevelt and Lyndon Johnson. (26) (27)

President Truman considered dismissing Hoover as FBI director but ultimately concluded that the political cost of doing would be too great. As a Senator, he had objected publicly when the FBI was absolved of all blame for Pearl Harbor. Now in his first weeks as president, Truman was alarmed by what he learned about the FBI – bloated in size and power – that Roosevelt had left behind. A month after taking office, Truman expressed these feelings in one of his celebrated memos to himself on May 12, 1945, "We want no Gestapo or secret police – FBI is tending in that direction. They are dabbling in sex-life scandals and plain blackmail when they should be catching criminals. They also have a habit of sneering at local law enforcement officers. This must stop. Cooperation is what we must have." (28) (29)

William J. Sullivan told John Dean that "there were only two presidents that he knew of who never made any political requests of the FBI, and they were Truman and Kennedy. Truman detested Hoover, while Hoover was frightened out of his life by Truman: during his entire career in the White House, Truman had nothing to do with Hoover and wouldn't let Hoover get anywhere close to him, and when Hoover tried very hard. Truman had General Vaughan as a buffer."

"As for Kennedy," Sullivan said, "He distrusted Hoover and wouldn't have dared to make a political request of him." (30)

J. Edgar Hoover stepped out of his limousine at the northeast gate of the White House on March 22, 1962, at one o'clock. He was ushered into the Oval Office, and then he and the president took the elevator to the dining room in the Executive Mansion. The only other person present was Kennedy special advisor Kenneth O'Donnell.

The meeting was a long one. Four hours later, J. Edgar Hoover left when Theodore Sorensen and Arthur Schlesinger were on the way in. According to Antony Summers, "It may never be known whether or not Kennedy tried to fire Edgar that day." The Kennedy library says it has no record of what was said at lunch. Nor does the FBI, even though Hoover usually wrote a memo following a visit to the White House. (31)

O'Donnell has maintained that his boss and the FBI Director had no private conversation that day or that the name of Judith Campbell – alleged mistress of Kennedy and two mafia bosses – ever came up.

Interviewed by Herbert S. Parmet, Kenneth O'Donnell later recalled Kennedy telling him, "Get rid of that bastard. He's the biggest bore" because Hoover was "seeing commies under every bed." (32)

But when O'Donnell was asked by Ovid Demaris if he was aware that Bobby was telling his people that Hoover would not be around after 1964, O'Donnell replied laconically, "Well, wouldn't he retire automatically at seventy? He'd have to submit his resignation, right? That's the law."

Asked if Bobby discussed his problems with the president, O'Donnell said that he wasn't sure that Bobby had many conversations with his brother because "he (Bobby) thought they had a hell of a lot more problems than J. Edgar Hoover." (33)

O'Donnell changed from a friendly quote, "resignation automatically at 70, that's the law," and Kennedy's quote, "Get rid of that bastard. He's the biggest bore"—two wholly different approaches between 1975 and 1983. I believe in what O'Donnell said in his interview with Parmet.

Demaris asked Dave Powers if Hoover had heard that he was going to get "dumped" after the 1964 election. Powers, typically diplomatic, replied, "The answer in that is that the word would not be "dumped." The President would never, never use the word. He (Hoover) would have been seventy years old, and it would have been time for him to retire." But Demaris pointed out that Hoover didn't want to retire, which would have caused a conflict. Dave Powers, still diplomatic, answered wonderfully, "Not really because the president would have thought that "conflict" was too strong a word. It would be a difference of opinion, he would have felt, which maybe requires a little more work, and maybe that could have been what he was talking to him about that three weeks before the assassination when he saw him. But the president never mentioned any of that to me." (34)

That's what I call a lesson of profile in loyalty from a friend.

Robert Kennedy, interviewed by New York Times columnist Anthony Lewis on December 4, 1964, said, "I don't think Hoover liked me. I knew he didn't like me much. Courtney Evans used to say he was disturbed at me because for the first time since he had been director of the FBI, he had to take instructions or orders from the

Attorney General of the United States and couldn't go over his head."

Burke Marshall confirmed that Hoover didn't like having Robert Kennedy as Attorney General because that put someone between the FBI director and the president. At the same time, Hoover wanted to deal with the president directly. Marshall explained, "The FBI didn't have any agents who knew how to talk to black people in the South. There were bureaucratic reasons – they were trained to chase communists and find stolen cars. Mr. Hoover viewed the civil rights activists as lawbreakers. The FBI was worse than useless, given his mindset. I would send them one-hundred-page memoranda telling them what to do, but they didn't know how to do my cases." Marshall conceded that Hoover had "enormous" support from the public and in Congress, but did not doubt that Hoover would have been retired in a second Kennedy term." (35) (36)

Pierre Salinger thought Hoover was a very anti-Kennedy person, "He didn't like Bobby because Bobby had started the whole team looking into the Mafia – something the FBI had never done – and it angered Hoover a lot." (37)

According to William Hundley, who worked for Internal Security in the Department of Justice, the thing that finally destroyed the relationship between Bobby and Hoover was Bobby's well-known promises of "just wait" to the many people who complained to him about Hoover: they all got the message that the Kennedy's would retire him after Jack got reelected and Hoover hit seventy.

Hundley also thought that it was too dangerous to fire him before the election because Hoover had too many friends on the Hill and he had done a lot for the country. (38)

Emanuel Celler, chairman of the House Judiciary Committee, said that the Kennedys wanted to get rid of Hoover but held back because it would be political dynamite. They hated him and had no use for him at all but were afraid to let him go – even though Hoover never ran counter to what the president wanted. (39)

Curt Gentry writes, "In early May 1964, the Newsweek editor Ben Bradlee learned from Lyndon Johnson's press secretary, Bill Moyers, that the president intended to replace J. Edgar Hoover.

"We finally got the bastard," Moyers told Bradlee. "Lyndon told me to find his replacement." The leak was so momentous that Bradlee prepared a cover story about LBJ's search for Hoover's successor.

On May 8, 1964, the President summoned reporters to the Rose Garden for a special announcement – the reading of an executive order exempting Hoover from the Federal retirement law for an indefinite period.

Moments before appearing before the TV cameras, Johnson had turned to Moyers. He whispered, "You call up Ben Bradlee and tell him, "Fuck you." For years afterwards, Bradlee would recall, people said, "You did it! Bradlee. You did it – you got him appointed for life." (40) (41)

When an aide questioned Johnson's decision to extend Hoover's term as director, he replied, "I'd rather have him inside the tent pissing out than outside the tent pissing in." (42)

But Burton Hersh has a different story on Hoover's possible replacement. In November 1964, Newsweek printed a story alleging that the president was about to replace Hoover, prompting FBI Associate Director Clyde Tolson to write to the magazine complaining about "a new low in reporting." (43)

And what about Ben Bradlee's version of a possible Hoover replacement as FBI director?

Bradlee wrote, "In my role as a facilitator for reporters in the Newsweek Bureau, one of the most intriguing stories of the day involved J. Edgar Hoover, the more or less permanent director of the FBI – how long could he go on, and what president would have the guts to fire him?" Requests for interviews with Hoover, who disliked all but the most fawning journalists, were denied, and Bradlee's efforts via Cartha J. "Deke" Deloach, the FBI's number three, failed.

He was so frustrated he walked out on Deloach and sat back to wait for a sign that LBJ was going to move.

The sign came some months later during a lunch with LBJ's special assistant, Bill Moyers, who told Bradlee that the administration was looking for a new FBI director. He even mentioned a few names, giving Bradlee all he needed, and we went with the Hoover cover on the following issue on December 7, 1964. The White House denied the story, as Moyers had thought they probably would. Still, later in the week, LBJ scheduled a special Rose Garden briefing with Hoover in attendance, at which the president announced that he had persuaded Hoover to stay on as FBI director, apparently forever. On his way out to make his announcement in the Rose Garden, President Johnson muttered to Moyers under his breath, "tell your friend Ben Bradlee, fuck you." (44) (45)

This discrepancy in dates is not resolved by Johnson's daily presidential diary, according to which Hoover was at the White House on Friday, May 8, 1964, from 5.35-5.45 p.m. "The President went to the Rose Garden and participated in a ceremony honoring J. Edgar Hoover – 40th Anniversary as Director of the FBI," as reported by the New York Times May 9, 1964.

Hoover was there again November 17, 1964, from 1.31-2.00 p.m., after the Newsweek story on November 9, about a possible Hoover replacement. Finally, he was there again on December 4, 1965, from 1.16-1.20 p.m., for a concise visit.

Ben Bradlee, as well as Curt Gentry, talk about a Rose Garden briefing, but in Bradlee's case, the meeting lasted only four minutes. The diary mentioned the Rose Garden meeting on May 8, but not on December 4, 1964.

Curt Gentry takes the LBJ quote "fuck you," which was delivered on May 8, although Gentry mixed up historical facts. Still, Bradlee says it happened on December 4. One thing is certain that LBJ tried to get rid of Hoover but didn't succeed.

One important aide to Johnson remembers the day Johnson did try to fire Hoover. "Hoover walks in with an armful of files, smiling," the aide recalls (Gus Russo private citation quoting Martin Underwood). "Twenty minutes later, he walks out, still smiling, and LBJ is white as a sheet. He's got everything, the son of a bitch. The president told me."

My conclusion to this episode is that some authors go once again for sensationalism instead of telling the historical truth. (46)

Just before Christmas 1968, weeks after their meeting at the Pierre Hotel in New York, Nixon announced Edgar's reappointment as Director. He also gave him a raise to $42,500 a year, a fortune at the time. Yet Nixon, in his term, had collided with Hoover: early on, the elderly director had become impossible to live with.

In October 1971, the President of the United States, his Attorney General and key advisors were wrestling with an intractable problem – J. Edgar Hoover. Richard Nixon said, "For a lot of reasons, he ought a resign. He should get the hell out of there. Now it may be, which I doubt, that I could just call him and talk him into resigning. There are some problems: if he does go, he's got to go of his own volition, that's why we're in a hell of a problem – I think he'll stay until he's a hundred years old."

Hoover's erratic public performance made him an embarrassment to the administration. Still, Nixon did not dare fire him, despite trying to do so, on several occasions.

In the fall of 1971, aware that Nixon had summoned Hoover for a showdown meeting, officials sat watching the clock, waiting for news that the director had finally been forced out of office. The news never came. Though Nixon never admitted it, the old man fought off disaster with his most trusty weapon: knowledge. (47) (48)

Richard Helms, CIA director under President Nixon, said that Nixon was the only one he knew who wanted to retire Hoover.

So, would Kennedy have replaced Hoover if he had been re-elected in the '64 elections?

Nicholas Katzenbach was very clear-cut on the subject. He said, "Firing J. Edgar Hoover – Jesus Christ- let's go back to those times to realize what that meant: I seriously question whether President Kennedy could have made a firing stick: he'd have been in a brouhaha for months."

Roger Hilsman said that "Every president from Roosevelt on wanted to fire J. Edgar Hoover, but none of them dared. A president could have, but the political costs would have outweighed the gain: It was better to go on and live with him." He went on, "Kennedy was pissed at him and wanted him out, so he said, what we are going to do is this: we'll have the army band walk down one side of the Mall playing "The Star-Spangled Banner" and the navy band at the other side. The air force band will parachute, playing the national anthem as they descend. From a platform in the middle of the Mall, I will present Hoover with the Medal of Freedom and every other medal we can think of. Then I will whisper in his ears, you are fired." However, Hilsman concluded, "But he couldn't touch him..." (49)

Jacqueline Kennedy also believed that he was going to get rid of J. Edgar Hoover. (50)

John Connally, then Governor of Texas, told Bobby Kennedy, "You're not going to be able to get rid of J. Edgar Hoover." But Bobby assured Connally that the time would come when he would be fired. Justice department aide William Hundley said that the president had said to Bobby, "I can't do it now, but when I'm re-elected, I'm going to get rid of him, make him Boxing Commissioner or something." "It was common knowledge." recalled Norman Ollestad, "that in 1964 the Director would be out." (51)

Courtney Evans said that he, if the circumstances worked out and the directorship of the FBI became vacant, he could count on support from Robert Kennedy to be appointed to that position, "Even if we were good official friends, the fact is, he never said anything to me about a change in the leadership of the FBI. The rumors about his mandatory retirement January 1, 1965, were known to Hoover, and I got the very distinct impression that he was very resentful that any consideration at all would be given to replacing him." (52)

William C. Sullivan, who worked in the FBI for thirty years, writes that Evans remained loyal to the Kennedys in deed if not in word. It was rumored that when JFK was re-elected, Hoover would be out and Courtney Evans would become replace him, "How I wish that that had happened," said Sullivan.

Hoover heard that rumor too, and the day after Kennedy's assassination, Evans was as good as dead himself as far as Hoover was concerned. And Evans, being constantly harassed by Hoover, decided to give up and retire. If he hadn't retired, Sullivan concluded, Hoover would have fired him. (53)

There are a few authors who have a name for the FBI director succeeding Hoover. Ted Schwarz claimed Hoover was certainly blackmailing Jack, knowing that the Kennedys wanted him fired. Schwarz was sure they had chosen William Parker, the innovative chief of police of Los Angeles and the man for whom its headquarters would eventually be named, to take over the FBI.

By this account, the Kennedys thought they could get Hoover to quietly resign when he knew they had access to the photographs taken of the director with his lover, Clyde Tolson. But unfortunately, according to Schwarz, Hoover had access to images and sound recordings of Kennedy with a myriad of women other than his wife. (54) The author doesn't mention any sources, so I can put it in the "gossip and sensationalism" part of my book, but with this humoristic reflection. If Kennedy had fired Hoover, they could have exchanged photographs of their respective lovers – a solution to a difficult situation which I am sure Kennedy would have enjoyed.

On January 6, 1962, columnist Drew Pearson predicted that the Attorney General would get rid of the FBI director, naming the State Department security director William Boswell as the brothers' chosen replacement. (55)

But what did Robert Kennedy say on the Hoover replacement in 1965?

Responding to interviewer Anthony Lewis, when asked, "Do you think he would have remained in his position after January 1965?" Robert Kennedy answered clearly, "No, the relationship that we had was not difficult. I mean, it wasn't an impossible relationship. But President Kennedy would have gotten a replacement before he left office."

This was a political and very ambiguous answer, with RFK first saying that Hoover would have been out January 1965 but then suggesting that he would undoubtedly have been gone before January 1969, outlasting a second Kennedy term. (56)

Hoover had heard the rumors of his possible replacement during Kennedy's second term, and according to Courtney Evans, "it caused great bitterness on Hoover's part."

Evan Thomas, writing about the "Rometsch spy case" in which Hoover told the Kennedys about FBI information linking them both to suspected Soviet intelligence agent Ellen Rometsch, points out that the FBI director ultimately concluded that there was no evidence that Rometsch was a spy or that she had had sex with anyone at the White House. Observing that "Hoover's services" were never free, Thomas concludes that Hoover extracted from RFK a promise of lunch with the president and -more to the point- a testimonial from the Attorney General that Hoover's job was secure. With obvious satisfaction, Hoover recorded Kennedy's avowal that any gossip about replacing the FBI director was "vicious" and baseless. (57) (58) (59)

According to FBI agent James Hosty, President Kennedy had decided early in his administration to force Hoover to retire at seventy, carefully setting the stage by not granting retirement exceptions to any directors of the Secret Service, the Bureau of Prisons, the Immigration and Naturalization Service, and the Narcotics Bureau. Hoover was next. (60) (61)

Would John Kennedy have fired J. Edgar Hoover in 1965 during his second term? That is a one million dollar question.

Or do we believe Pierre Salinger, Jacqueline Kennedy and Bobby Kennedy? They were sure that, had Kennedy been re-elected in 1964, Hoover would have been gone? Or would Nicholas Katzenbach, Roger Hilsman have been proved right that Hoover was untouchable?

And what about Lyndon Johnson's private comment to friendly reporters over drinks, "J. Edgar Hoover has Jack Kennedy by the balls?" (62)

Courtney Evans said that he stopped the Kennedys from firing Hoover on the occasions when they were incensed by him. Evans thought they would wait until after the 1964 election, when Hoover would reach his seventieth birthday, the mandatory retirement age, and they expected the law to take its course. (63)

With hindsight, the conclusion seems obvious: John Kennedy would have retained J. Edgar Hoover until the mandatory retirement age early in a second Kennedy term, and that would have been the end of Hoover as FBI director. But we will never know. "The answer, my friend is blowing in the wind," as Bob Dylan so poetically sang.

5.6. Conclusion

Did John Kennedy mention the civil rights issue in his Inaugural? The speech's only domestic change added on the final day after being suggested to Sorensen by the chief civil rights campaign advisors, Harris Wofford and Louis Martin, was an expansion of a reference to "those human rights to which this nation has been committed and to which we are committed today." Six words were added to that sentence: ..."at home and around the world."

Sorensen suggested to Kennedy a possible question to the audience at this point, "Are you willing to demonstrate in your own life, in your attitude toward those of other races and those from other shores, that you held these births to be self-evident?" But, said Sorenson later, "That line did not make the final cut." (1)

Philip A. Goduti Jr. wrote that Kennedy's reference of passing the torch to "a new generation of Americans" had a great deal of symbolism that many in the country defined as their own. Many in the civil rights movement took that line as a reference to their cause. (2)

But Henrie Fairlie claims that Kennedy did not mention civil rights in terms during the address, so civil rights were the only significant area of domestic policy in which he did not have a task force. (3)

Civil rights, says Evan Thomas, was not of grave concern to JFK, as he did not even mention the subject in his famously expansive inaugural address (4), which of course, focused mainly on foreign policy – Cuba, Berlin, dealing with Khrushchev and de Gaulle, not to mention the ongoing Cold War.

Whether Kennedy acted too slowly on civil rights is up for debate. Arthur Schlesinger Jr. said that "legislation was not possible until the days of the peaceful marches in Birmingham in 1963. Kennedy had sent out a civil rights message the month before, and it had gotten nowhere. Resistance in Congress to any civil rights legislation was intense. "He could have done more by executive order on housing," observed Schlesinger, who thought that they all underestimated the moral dynamism that the civil rights movement was acquiring by the early 1960s. It wasn't until the spring of 1963 that they began to understand the importance of what was happening. (5)

Ted Sorensen admitted that there was no Kennedy administration civil rights program in 1961, and JFK had decided to do what he could through executive orders. Sorensen said that it was easy for his critics in the civil rights movement to urge him to be bold and send up a bill, but there was no hope of getting one passed at that stage.

Even Sorensen felt frustrated by Kennedy's caution in mobilizing the full powers of his presidency behind the civil rights movement. Still, he was also sufficiently pragmatic to understand the importance of blacks of both his legislative program and to future reelection – a typical Sorensen reflection. (6)

And if an "early bill" had been submitted and did not pass, the critics would have said Kennedy was moving too fast, engaging in bad politics and should have waited.

Prominent civil right lawyer Joseph L. Rauh thought that not enough was done, criticizing Kennedy for waiting for two years to complete an executive order on housing which the president had promised would require just a "stroke of the pen." (7)

Fred Logevall also thinks that JFK acted too slowly, not because he was a bigot (he wasn't) but because of political calculations. But Kennedy began to act, partly because of Bobby's influence – and the speech in June 1963 was significant. (8)

My answer to Logevall is there is a Yes and a No.

Yes: I fully agree with "Rauh's point of view that he waited two years (November 20, 1962) before signing Executive Order 11063 banning segregation in federally funded housing.

No: Martin Luther King had a cause to defend: JFK had a country to run and defend. JFK was always cautious in making his decisions. That was part of his character. He listened to his brother, following his advice when he thought it was the right time to act and the right thing to do. Did JFK listen to RFK in choosing LBJ as his running mate? No. On the Cuban Missile Crisis? No. On making the civil rights issue a moral one? Yes.

On those three matters, JFK made the right call each time rather than blindly follow his brother's advice. On the first No, he would not have been elected if he had backed Bobby's advice. And on the second No, we know what he prevented in not listening to his hawkish brother.

New York Times journalist Tom Wicker felt that if Kennedy had introduced an early civil rights bill in the Senate, it would surely have provoked a major filibuster, delaying other legislation. Wicker said that at the time, there seemed a good deal more to be gained by leaving the issue alone than by pursuing it. Still, in retrospect, that analysis was questionable: fighting for a strong civil rights bill, whether it could pass or not, would have done a great deal to store up the notion of Kennedy as a vigorous liberal, holding his supporters together in loyalty and enthusiasm.

The measure might even have passed because it would have been hard for the Republicans to refrain from supporting it. (9)

Michael A. Genovese writes that Kennedy was a reluctant reformer, avoiding civil rights until it became politically unacceptable to do so. Was this wisdom on cowardice? As FDR knew, it was dangerous to get too far out in front of public opinion, so Kennedy waited until the civil rights issue gained prominence, then became its champion. (10)

According to John A. Barnes, "The great insight, of course, was King's white America had to be convinced of the need for action. Birmingham and the great March on Washington in August 1963 helped achieve that. But that would have been in vain had John F. Kennedy not been prepared to admit he had misread the situation initially and been willing to change his mind. (11)

But what did the "Father and Soul" of civil rights, Martin Luther King, think of JFK on civil rights?

Before and during the first two years of his presidency Kennedy did not have the grasp and deep understanding of the problem as he later did. He knew that segregation was morally wrong, and he indeed intellectually committed himself to integration. Still, King could see that he didn't have the emotional involvement then, having never been involved enough in the issue. After the election when King was at Harris Wofford's home for dinner, he said, "In the election, when I gave my testimony for Kennedy, my impression then was that he had the intelligence and the skill and the moral fervor to give the leadership we've been waiting for and do what no president has ever done. Now, I'm convinced that he has the understanding and the political skill, but so far, I'm afraid that the moral passion is missing." (12) (13) King believed that Kennedy didn't know many Negroes personally – but I don't think that was the problem. Looking back on his own and his brother's approach to the status of the Negro, Robert Kennedy in 1964 conceded that, before 1960, "We didn't lie awake nights worrying about it." Indeed, the problem, which would keep the Kennedy brothers awake, only hit home in 1963.

Jack Kennedy did know a few blacks personally. In the late fifties, he employed a black secretary in his Boston office as well as two well-connected black attorneys from Washington D.C. as advisors. (14)

George E. Thomas, his valet, began serving Jack Kennedy in 1947 on the recommendation of Arthur Krock. The latter was at that time close to Joe Kennedy. Thomas accompanied the president to Dallas, and Kennedy joked with him after Air Force One landed at the airport. The president, knowing that Thomas came from the tiny town of Berryville, Virginia, paused before stepping out onto the airport ramp, turned to his valet, winked and said, "You know George, I think this is a bigger town than you came from." (15) (16)

Then there was Andrew T. Hatcher, associate White House press secretary, the first black man to hold the number two communications spot in The White House.

Then there was White House doorman Preston Bruce, lean and courtly in his dark suit and trim white moustache, who developed a bond with the president and First Lady. Kennedy made him feel that he was part of the family, sometimes inviting him to join the couple to watch a movie in the White House theatre. When Bruce's son was appointed principal of a school in Vermont at age twenty-four, the president asked the proud father for a chat. Bruce brought his son in at 12 O'clock, and Kennedy stopped in the middle of some of his busy schedule and talked with his son for more than 25 minutes.

The doorman often heard the president say to visitors, "This is Bruce. He runs the place." (16) (17)

Martin Luther King said that President Kennedy was a man who was big enough to admit when he was wrong, as he did after the Bay of Pigs incident. But Lyndon Johnson seemed to be unable to make this kind of statesmanlike gesture in connection with Vietnam. (18)

King studied John Fitzgerald Kennedy with the cold insight of an enemy and the warm concern of a friend. "The basic thing about him, he could respond to creative pressure," said King. "I never wanted – and I told him this – to be in the position that I couldn't criticize him if I thought he was wrong. And he (Kennedy) said, "It often helps me to be pushed." He had the vision and wisdom to see the problem in all of its dimensions and the courage to do something about it. He grew until the day of his assassination." King added, "Historians will record that he vacillated like Lincoln, but he lifted the cause far above the political level." (19)

Lewis J. Paper wrote, "Time and time again, civil rights leaders would travel to speak to various communities and to criticize the administration only to find that blacks erupted in spontaneous applause at the mention of the president's name." (20)

Simeon Booker, a black journalist at the Washington Post, said that Kennedy arrived at a time when everything was beginning to go downhill and gave everyone a "shot in the arm." And not necessarily through programs – often through "a sense of freshness, a sense of new life, a hope, and he did it not only at our middle class, but he did it at the area of people in the ghettos, slums." (21)

Roy Wilkins said that Kennedy create the setting in which the Civil Rights bill could be enacted and could become law. "I don't think anybody begrudges the fact that in its critical stages through the House and the Senate it had the support of President Johnson, but it's essentially a creature of Kennedy." (22)

Kennedy's handling of the civil rights issue shows that, from a cautious, reluctant reformer in 1961-1962, through his passionate brother and the 1963 events, he became involved intellectually and morally in the black cause for equality.

*After the March on Washington for Jobs and Freedom, August 28, 1963, 5.00 p.m.,
King and participants were invited to the White House to meet with President
Kennedy and Vice President Johnson in the Oval Office.
(Copyright: JFK Library)*

After Alabama governor George C. Wallace refused to register two black students at the state university, JFK federalized the Alabama National Guard (June 11, 1963) and made an impassioned address to the nation, June 11, 1963 on Civil Rights Crisis.
(Copyright: JFK Library)

On May 14, 1961, the Ku Klux Klan attacked and set afire the Greyhound bus carrying the Freedom Riders near Anniston, Alabama. Several were severely beaten.
(Copyright: Getty images – UPI/Bettmann Newsphotos)

A 17-year-old right activist is attacked by police dogs in Birmingham, Alabama, May 3, 1963.
(Copyright: Getty images – Bill Hudson/Associated Press)

Chapter 6: The Health Issue: A Perfect Cover Up And A True Profile In Courage

"How is your aching back?"
"Well, it depends on the weather, political and otherwise. It is very good, though today."

- **Presidential Press Conference, August 1, 1962**

"When we were growing up together, we used to laugh about the great risk a mosquito took on biting Jack Kennedy – with some of his blood, the mosquito was almost sure to die."

- **Robert F. Kennedy, December 18, 1963 Profiles in Courage Memorial Edition**

6.1. Kennedy's Family Members on His Health

Rose Fitzgerald Kennedy

When Rose Kennedy became a mother for the first time, she began a ritual that she was to endure for many years. With the birth of each of her children, she dipped into her plentiful supply of file cards and index tabs and started charting the course of their development – including medical problems. As each new baby came along, he or she was indexed, and the card contained all the primary vital statistics such as date and place of birth, the church of baptism, names of godparents, and any other pertinent data.

Each card evokes a biography. Joe Jr. was a healthy infant and child, big and strong for his age, and there are few remarks about him in Rose's notes in the early years. Jack was a healthy infant too, although Rose recorded, "Has whooping cough, measles, chicken pox"- childhood diseases that were common enough in those days but which raised concerns about him.

More concerning was this entry on Jack's card, "Had scarlet fever – February 20, 1920." Scarlet fever was a dreaded disease, fairly often fatal and very often with crippling after-effects on the heart, eyes, and ears. It was also highly contagious, and in the small Kennedy house on Beals Street, there were fears that it could spread from Jack not just to newly-born Kathleen and 15-months old Rosemary, but also to Joe Jr. – and even to Rose herself. But there was no place in Brookline where Jack could be taken – the hospital wouldn't admit patients with contagious diseases.

The little boy was very sick by the time he was finally admitted to a specialist unit in Boston City Hospital, thanks to the influence of Rose's father, John "Honey Fitz" Fitzgerald, a Democratic US congressman who had also served twice as Boston's mayor. Jack recovered without serious complications. But Rose always felt she had neglected her second-oldest, rather sickly child, reflecting in later life that Jack had needed "perhaps more attention than I gave him, in my worry and distraction about Rosemary." Jackie reassured her that Jack never mentioned any feelings of neglect – but Rose's concerns never completely left her. He was certainly troubled with health problems for much of his life.

At age 18, in September 1935, Jack, accompanied by his parents and sibling Kathleen, sailed for Britain and Europe. He had graduated with reasonable success from Choate, the Wallingford, Connecticut, and boarding school, favored by the upper-class New England Elite. Now it was time for a year with Professor Harold Laski at the London School of Economics. But illness intervened almost at once, forcing Jack to drop out after just a month with hepatitis or "jaundice." His most enduring ailment -his acute back problem – was exacerbated by Kennedy's heroic efforts to save his surviving boat crew after the sinking of PT-109 in a war-time collision in the Pacific in 1943.

He was seldom, if ever really, free of pain after his months of subsequent hospital treatment, although he bore it so well that nobody but his doctors, family, and a few close associates realized the seriousness of his condition. But within a decade (during 1954), the problem had become so bad that he needed crutches, finally agreeing to a spinal operation rather than face spending the rest of his life as a cripple. Not only was the operation a failure, but an infection set in, leaving him so close to death that he received the last rites. When the danger was past, he was flown – still on a stretcher- to his parents' Palm Beach home for recuperation in the warm climate.

A few months later, he was well enough for the doctors to try the operation again, this time with a little more success. But the result still left Jack in discomfort, which he learned to live with. (1) (2) (3) (4)

Edward Moore Kennedy

Edward considered Jack almost a second father. In fact, Jack was his godfather, a role he had requested in a letter to Rose, written from Choate in 1932.

"Jack," Ted said, "was bedeviled by health challenges for all of his life, but he refused to let illness slow him down for long. He was resilient enough to play junior varsity football at Harvard, work as a ranch hand in Arizona, and sail competitively in Hyannis port and elsewhere. He was fearless enough to tear around Europe in his own convertible in 1937, and, amid the tensions of 1939, to explore the Soviet Union, the Balkan countries, parts of the Middle East, Czechoslovakia, and Germany, returning to London on September 1 – the day Germany invaded Poland."

"Far from these hijinks in Massachusetts, the war that Joe Kennedy Sr. had tried to keep at bay from his country and his children exploded onto American territory on December 7, 1941. World War II proceeded to draw several of Joseph Kennedy's "hostage to fortune" into its maw. Joe was the first. He earned his naval aviator wings in May 1942 at the Jacksonville Naval Air Station. My father was on hand to pin them on him. Jack followed his brother a few weeks later, despite his fears that his numerous health problems would prevent military service. Indeed, he failed the army physical, mostly because of his torturously bad back. But he would not give up, throwing himself into a rigorous exercise program." Edward Kennedy later admitted candidly something not mentioned at all by Rose – the fact that Jack ultimately persuaded his father to use his influence to get him accepted. "After some behind-the-scenes prodding by Dad's friend and former naval attaché in London, Admiral Alan Goodrich Kirk, Jack passed a second physical and joined the navy as an ensign two months before Pearl Harbor. He served in the Office of Naval Intelligence in Washington, where he socialized with his sister Kathleen and her friends.

Joseph P. Kennedy didn't think his son had the stamina for politics in the wake of his health problems. Jack weighed just 120 pounds after the first of three operations on his war-injured back. He still felt and showed the effects of malaria he'd contracted in the Pacific, and there were still the after-effects of the synthetic drug known as Atabrine that was used to treat the disease, which tended to discolor the skin.

In "True Compass," Edward Kennedy wrote, "There were conversational boundaries in our family, and we respected them. For example, I had no idea how serious Jack's health problems were while he was alive. It would never have occurred to us to discuss such private things with each other." (5)

In a letter from the French Riviera, July 18, 1956, Joseph P. Kennedy wrote to his son Edward, "Talked to Jack twice. After a conversation with Bill Blair, Governor Adlai Stevenson's former administrative assistant, 1950-58, on Cape on Sunday, he is giving serious consideration to the job (for the vice-presidential nomination on the Stevenson ticket). Last night, however, he was worried because the New York Evening Post was coming out with an article that said he had Addison's disease; I told him he should cooperate with the reporter and admit that he had it, but that the disease was not a killer as it was eight years ago, and I feel it should be brought out now and not after he gets the nomination if he gets it. He thought he might come over for a week to talk things over, but I doubt it." (6)

Jack didn't listen to his father, but I agree with Joseph Kennedy. He should have been more candid about it. But on the other hand, as Dan Fenn Jr. said, "He was very private on his health and other than to his doctor's, he never complained."

Neither Rose Kennedy, Jacqueline Kennedy, Bobby Kennedy nor Edward Kennedy mention that Jack had Addison's disease. I regret their reluctance on this sensitive subject, certainly on Edward's part, 46 years after his brother's death. They were wrong. They should have been more candid about it. It would have served his memory. Having a disease is not a sin. Coping with it as Jack Kennedy did, is a virtue, a true profile in courage.

Jacqueline Bouvier Kennedy

In her interviews with Arthur Schlesinger Jr. in 1964 for the "Historic Conversations on Life with John F. Kennedy," Jackie talked a lot about Jack's back problems, at the beginning of their marriage, during the Presidential 1960 campaign and during his Presidency.

Historian Arthur Schlesinger, except for the rumors on Addison disease during the campaign, didn't question Jacqueline on it. And he could not question her about "miracle" physician Max "Dr. Feelgood" Jacobson – on whom Jack Kennedy came to rely for pain-relieving drugs – because Schlesinger had not heard of him when he interviewed Jackie.

When Schlesinger asked, "The back had been an overhanging thing for some time before?" Jacqueline answered, "With the back, it had just gotten worse and worse. I mean, the year before we were married, when he'd take me out, half the time, it was on crutches. You know, when I went to watch him campaign before we were married, he was on crutches. I can remember him on crutches more than not. And then, in our marriage, he'd be off it a lot, and then something would go wrong. It was really, I mean, the problem everyone found later. He didn't even need the operation. It was that he'd had a bad back since college, and then the war, and he'd had a disk operation that he never needed, so all those muscles had gotten weak, had gone into spasm, and that was what was giving him pain, the muscles."

She explained that Dr. Shorr, a New York Hospital endocrinologist told Jack Kennedy about a Dr. Travell who had been doing terrific things with muscles, "Jack went to see her. She put in this Novocain for spasms. Well, she could fix him, I mean, life just changed then." At that time, Jacqueline also said, "No one can underestimate her contribution then." But later on, she clarified, "It was apparent that what Jack should be doing was building up his back with exercises. She (Dr. Travell) was very reluctant to let him leave her Novocain treatments, which by then, were not doing any good. This is once we're in the White House. But she changed his life then."

When Schlesinger asked Jacqueline if his back troubled him during the 1960 campaign, she answered, "He had the best health in the world. I think one reason was he was doing so much, too much. When he got in the White House, he took this nap every day. It was just forty-five minutes. Then all his back and his stomach and everything wasn't always plaguing him. He just always overtaxed himself."

And, she said, when he arrived in the White House, his physical condition was the best it had ever been, "He had muscles and everything. He played golf, sort of eighteen holes – all these things he hadn't been able to do for a long time. And then he sat at his desk, without moving for six weeks. He didn't walk around the driveway, he didn't swim, and suddenly his back went bad. He'd lost all the muscle tone. So, then it was awful because he was really in pain. Dr. Travell would come and pump him full with Novocain. But all that Novocain, it didn't do any good anymore."

She continued, "It wasn't until the next October 1961, I got so mad at her because then other doctors were trying to bring in Dr. Hans Kraus, who could build you up through exercises. Well, all these doctors are so jealous of each other, and she wouldn't let Kraus come in. But then once Kraus started, then that was, you know, encouraging because he'd get so discouraged. That's when you'd seen him in the black periods. Well, he'd tried, and he had every doctor, and Dr. Travell had given him the tenth treatment, and before, she always helped. And now, there didn't seem to be any answer. So then Kraus helped him, and that cheered him up."

Schlesinger asked, "Would he ever get depressed or was his temperament just terribly equable?" She responded, "His temperament was terribly even, except when he'd be in pain for a long period of time – for instance, his back – and when he'd done the three or four usual things, which is stay on crutches four days – if that doesn't work, go to bed for two days, or have a hot pack or something. And if it just seemed to stay on and on, he couldn't shake it. Then he'd get very low, but just because of that. But if he had something to do, he'd get up and do it. And then eventually it would get better. But in the beginning years of our marriage, ill-health was – just seeing Jack in pain. It used to make me so sad all the time, but really after – when? I guess, after the Senate thing, it didn't seem to be as much of a problem anymore." (7)

Robert Francis Kennedy

"At least one-half of the days that he spent on this earth were days of intense physical pain. He had scarlet fever when he was very young and serious back trouble when he was older. In between, he had about every other conceivable ailment. When we were growing up together, we used to laugh about the great risk a mosquito took in biting Jack Kennedy – with some of his blood. The mosquito was almost sure to die. He was in Chelsea Naval Hospital for an extended period of time after the war, had a major and painful operation on his back in 1955, campaigned on crutches in 1958. In 1951, on a trip we took around the world, he became ill. We flew to the military hospital in Okinawa, and he had a temperature of over 106 degrees. They didn't think he would live. But during all this time, I never heard him complain. I never heard him say anything that would indicate that he felt God had dealt with him unjustly. Those who knew him well would know he was suffering only because his face was a little whiter, the lines around his eyes were a little deeper, his words a little sharper. Those who did not know him well detected nothing." (8)

In the 1960 election, two days before polling day, a statement from Travell was issued by Robert Kennedy, "John F. Kennedy has not, nor has he ever, had an ailment described classically as Addison's disease, which is tuberculous destruction of the adrenal gland. Any statement to the contrary is false. In the post-war period, he had some mild adrenal insufficiency, and this is not in any way a dangerous condition." And it is possible that even this might be corrected over the years since ACTH (Adrenocorticotropic hormone) stimulation tests for adrenal function were considered normal in 1958. Doctors have stated that this condition might have arisen out of his wartime experiences of shock and malaria. (9)

6.2. Kennedy's Addison's Disease

Kennedy's ailment is named after Thomas Addison, a graduate of the University of Edinburg Medical School, who first described the condition in 1855 – a failure of the body's adrenal glands, located above the kidneys, and vital to life. They produce hormones that regulate certain body metabolisms, fight infection and, in times of stress, provide extra strength. If the adrenals fail, a person can die of a simple infection. Addison found the disease to be caused primarily by tuberculosis, which attacks the adrenal glands and finally destroys them.

Years later, medical research revealed that the adrenal glands could also fail through atrophy, a premature wasting away or degeneration not associated with tuberculosis. In 1949 George W. Thorn of the Harvard Medical School, who was then one of the leading world experts on Addison's disease, reported that about half of all Addisonians he had treated were tubercular in origin, the other half atrophy. Addison's disease is difficult to diagnose, especially in its early stages.

The early symptoms are fatigue, general weakness, poor appetite and weight loss. The late stages are nausea, vomiting, diarrhea, and circulatory collapse.

According to "The Search for JFK" by Joan Blair and Clay Blair Jr., Addison's disease is relatively rare. In the early days following its discovery, it was considered as a fatal affection. Thorn points out that prior to 1930, the mortality rate five years following the onset of the disease was 90%. Then, in the early 1930s, endocrinologists experimented with a high-salt, low-potassium diet – lowering the mortality rate five years after onset to 78%. Within a few years, endocrinologists probing the frontiers of hormone research began to extract, in a very complicated and expensive process, adrenal hormones (adrenal cortical extracts) from cows and hogs. In 1939, they developed a synthetic substance – desoxycorticosterone acetate (DOCA), which as Thorn states, "was found to possess cortical hormone-like activity." (1) (2)

From 1938 to 1946, when extracts of the whole adrenal cortex and imperfect hormone replacement were available, one of every two patients died within the five-year period of observation. From 1950 to 1955, with the advent of oral preparations of new corticosteroid adrenal hormones, optimal replacement of the deficiency and a normal life span became possible for the first time.

Jack Kennedy was wholly dependent on the cortisone therapy that Addisonians rely upon for survival. Initially, he took 25 milligrams of cortisone by mouth. He then took it through injection. Also, he had implanted in his thighs DOCA tablets of 150 milligrams, which were replaced several times a year. There are even reports that the Kennedy family kept a reservoir of DOCA and cortisone in safety deposit boxes around the country so that Jack would have ready access to those medications wherever he traveled. (3)

Robert Dallek said that it is now well established that Kennedy was treated with DOCA after Addison's disease was diagnosed in 1947. But it is possible that Jack was taking DOCA as early as 1937. Early that year, in a handwritten note to his father, Jack worried about getting a prescription in Cambridge, Massachusetts, where he was a freshman at Harvard College. "Ordering stuff here very (illegible word)," he wrote to his father. "I would be sure you get the prescription. Some of that stuff as it is, very potent, and he (Jack's doctor) seems to be keeping it pretty quiet." Given that corticosteroids had just become clinically viable and were being touted as a therapeutic cure-all, it is reasonable to hypothesize that the prescription Jack asked for was DOCA.

Dallek argues that Jack Kennedy paid a high price for taking DOCA early and for so many years. Physicians in the 1930s and 1940s did not realize what is common medical knowledge today – namely, that corticosteroids are effective in treating acute colitis but have deleterious long-term effects, including osteoporosis of lower back bones and increased incidence of serious infection (owing to suppression of the body's immune system). (4)

Michael O'Brien, in June 2003, met at the Kennedy library with three medical experts, and the four studied the Travell records. His committee of medical experts comprised Edwin Cassem, professor of psychiatry at Harvard Medical School;

endocrinologist Gilbert Daniels; and Robert Boyd, formerly assistant clinical professor of orthopedic surgery at Harvard Medical School. They all disagree with several of Dallek's major contentions. (5)

Dr. Forest Tennant doesn't agree with criticism ascribed to JFK's cortisone use in that he should never have taken it because it may have caused osteoporosis and degeneration of his adrenal glands. This criticism, Tennant believes, is grossly wrong. In his view, the invention of DOCA in the 1930s was a marvelous advance that undoubtedly saved many people's lives, including JFK's.

However, Dr. Tennant concluded that, although JFK's intestinal problems and pain responded to DOCA, the treatment may have contributed to his osteoporosis and adrenal degeneration. How often JFK used the pellets is unknown, but he undoubtedly used them for flares of his colitis and pain. (6)

So, different doctors, different conclusions; who is right and who is wrong is a matter for speculation – yet another Kennedy enigma without a definite answer.

Dr. Elmer C. Bartels, an endocrinologist at the Lahey Clinic in Burlington, Massachusetts (now the Lahey Hospital and Medical Centre), who subsequently treated him for his Addison's, recalled that Jack was negligent about taking his medicine with him on trips. In an interview with Robert Dallek, Dr. Bartels told how Jack became very ill in London while on a trip to Ireland with his sister Kathleen in 1947. He was admitted to the London Clinic, where physician Dr. Sir Daniel Davis diagnosed Addison's disease.

According to Dallek, Jack's sister Eunice also suffered from Addison's, raising the possibility that the disease had an inherited component. Yet whatever the etiology of the problem, it was yet another potentially life-threatening disorder for Jack. (7)

When in 1959, rumors circulated that Jack had Addison's disease, his aides, doctors, and Jack himself, denied it. Jack described his condition as a "partial adrenal insufficiency." (8)

Denying Addison's disease was a perfect cover-up.

In 1960, during the heat of the political convention in Los Angeles, aides of Lyndon B. Johnson, who was competing for the nomination, told the press Jack had Addison's disease and had been kept alive for many years by drugs. Again Kennedy's aides, including his doctors of that period, and Bobby, Sargent Shriver and Pierre Salinger denied the claim. After the election, on November 11, Jack was asked by a reporter if it were true. Again a flat denial.

Salinger also asserted that it was not Addison's that it was not fatal, that it had always been under control and was going to stay that way. And all through the democratic primaries and the 1960 presidential race, the Kennedy campaigners consistently flatly denied that their candidate had Addison's disease. The reason why is clear, says Former British foreign secretary David Owen. Senator Kennedy was himself in denial, as illustrated in a conversation with his doctor Janet Travell, which she recorded in her book. Travell told him, "Senator, I think a series of reviews in the medical journals and popular magazines should be written right away. People don't realize how the outlook has changed in Addison's disease." Kennedy replied, "But I don't have it, doctor."

Travell's response was, "That's right, senator, you don't have classical Addison's disease. But the language is changing too, and doctors disagree maybe because they aren't talking about the same thing."

Kennedy then declared, "You'll never educate all those Republicans." (9) (10)

When Arthur Schlesinger asked him about the rumors about Addison's, Kennedy insisted that, after the war, fevers associated with malaria had produced a malfunctioning of the adrenal glands, but that this had been brought under control. He also pointed out that he had none of the symptoms of Addison's disease – yellowed skin, black spots in the mouth, unusual vulnerability to infection, "No one who has the real Addison's disease should run for the presidency, but I do not have it," he said. (11)

Ben Bradlee wrote the following in his book "Conversations with Kennedy," "Kennedy's Addison's disease was always a mystery to him. It was a not-so-hidden issue in the 1960 campaign, especially in the primary. India Edwards, the onetime Democratic National Committeewoman who was campaigning on behalf of Lyndon Johnson, once told a bunch of reporters that Kennedy was so sick from Addison's disease that he "looked like a spavined hunchback" – one of the least lofty moments of that tense episode. Kennedy's entourage would say only that he had "an adrenal insufficiency." (12)

On January 5, 1960, John F. Kennedy and his wife Jacqueline held a small dinner party in Washington DC. Their guests included Ben Bradlee, then Newsweek's Washington bureau chief, and his then-wife Tony and Newsweek correspondent James M. Cannon. Cannon taped the conversation for research on a book he was writing.

When Bradlee asked JFK if he had run for Congress with this greenness, JFK said, "Oh yeah, greener. It was atabrine, malaria, and probably some adrenal deficiency." Bradlee asked, "Addison's disease, what is that damn disease?" JFK answered, "Addison's disease, they say I have. Jack Anderson, Drew Pearson's man asked me today if I have it." Jack's response to that was, "No, God, a guy with Addison's disease looks sort of brown and everything. Christ! See, that's the sun," and everyone in the room had a good laugh. (13) (14)

After his election, Kennedy did speak out during a press conference at Hyannis Port on November 10, 1960. The following day the New York Times reported, "When someone asked about reports circulated in the campaign that he had once suffered from Addison's disease, Senator Kennedy answered without hesitation, "I have never had Addison's disease," he said, "In regard to my health, it was fully explained in a press statement in the middle of July, and my health is excellent. I have been through a long campaign, and my health is very good today." (15)

Journalist Joan Braden said that, more than any man she'd ever known, Kennedy cared about what people said. She recalled an occasion when she told him that she had heard that he had Addison's. Kennedy's reaction was as if an alarm had gone off within him, "Where did you hear that? Who told you that?" he asked. She said she heard it from a doctor in New York. "What's his name? What's his hospital? Where were you when he told you this?" Kennedy went on. She refused to say, but his tone startled her, making her regret raising the matter. She never mentioned Addison's disease in John Kennedy's presence again – or to anyone else. But she always believed that he had uncovered the doctor's name by checking up on where she had dined in New York and who else had dined there. (16)

It appears that Richard Nixon may have tried at one point to gain access to Kennedy's medical history. In the fall of 1960, as he and JFK battled in what turned out to be one of the closest presidential election ever, thieves ransacked the office of Eugene J. Cohen, a New York endocrinologist, who had been treating Kennedy for Addison's disease. When they failed to find Kennedy's records, which were filed under a code name, they tried unsuccessfully to break into Janet Travell's office. Although the thieves remain unidentified, it is reasonable to speculate, said Robert Dallek, that they were Nixon operatives. The failed robberies have the aura of Watergate and of the break-in at the Beverly Hills office of Daniel Ellsberg's psychiatrist. (17)

Herbert S. Parmet writes, "In an interview, January 14, 1980, Sargent Shriver, married to Jack's sister Eunice, another Addisonian, confirmed that his brother-in-law was on cortisone for the rest of his life. In another interview with Dr. Kraus, December 8, 1980, he found that he was taking cortisone "all the time." The medication had relieved the life-threatening condition, and the disease had little to do with the ability to do his job. (18)

6.3. How Did Kennedy Injure His Back?

There are different accounts of how and when Kennedy's back problem began.

Rose Kennedy, in "Times to Remember," identified the start of his serious back problems during World War II and the injuries he suffered when his PT-109 was demolished by a Japanese destroyer. Jack was seldom, if ever, free of pain from then on. But she also says that football was a root cause, following Jack's decision to try out for the varsity team, although he weighed only 149 pounds – a display more of Kennedy's courage than his common sense. According to his mother, he dropped back to the "junior varsity" side and was doing well until one day, during practice, he was hit by a hard block or tackle and landed at the wrong angle, rupturing a spinal disk. This injury ended his football days. (1)

Kennedy author David Pitts notes that Rose Kennedy described that as "the beginning of troubles with his back that were to haunt him for the rest of his life" – although Pitts adds, that in fact, he had suffered back problems even at Choate. (2)

James Mac Gregor Burns confirms that Kennedy was plagued by illness during his freshman year at Choate but insists his back problems began with his football injury, which Kennedy speechwriter Ted Sorensen says happened at Harvard in 1939. (3) (4)

And everyone points to the PT-109 wartime incident as turning a sporting injury into a chronic condition. The Blairs said, "The world knows that Jack Kennedy had a "bad back – all the Kennedy books talk about it."

Dr. Elmer C. Bartels of the Lahey Clinic explained to the Blairs that "unstable back is something you are born with and it doesn't maintain itself properly. An unstable back lasts a lifetime." When they asked Bartels, "You say Jack Kennedy was born with an unstable back?" he answered "Yes." (5)

British biographer Nigel Hamilton, however, tells a very different story. According to him, Jack and his friend Holton Wood were Junior Varsity substitutes but were not called upon to play, as far as Wood could later recall. But at the conclusion of the match, the Kennedy family chauffeur came racing across the field to say hello to Jack, and in the spirit of the morning's game, launched a "half-baked tackle," and the unsuspecting boy was knocked to the ground. Though Jack struggled to his feet, it was obvious he was in great pain, and although he played for a few minutes in the subsequent Dartmouth game, it was clear that his back injury was serious. By this account, his football career had ended thanks to the family chauffeur.

Hamilton further writes that Jack's already unstable back was aggravated by a car accident in France, which forced him to wear a special corset for the rest of his life. Hamilton doesn't mention in what year the car accident happened, but he does record an occasion in August 1940 when Kennedy pulled something in his back while serving at tennis. Apparently, he continued the match, but the back problem recurred when he played again. Gradually his back got stiffer, and he had to stop athletics. (6)

Another Kennedy author, Geoffrey Perret, has yet another take on Jack's back in a fascinating Italian beach story.

It was August 1937, and Jack wanted a swim in the Mediterranean sea of history, poetry and legend. He drove off the road and across the beach, almost to the water's edge, changed into a pair of shorts and plunged in. At this point, Perret claims, Jack had suffered numerous ailments before but never any problems with his back. Following the swim, he climbs back into his Ford and tries to drive off the beach, but the tires keep spinning in the sand. Kennedy, Billings and two Germans deflate the tires and start to push the car across the beach. It takes two hours of unremitting effort before the Ford is on the asphalt again. Over the next few days, Jack Kennedy's back will become increasingly stiff and painful.

The story is based mainly on the journals that Jack Kennedy and his close friend Lem Billings kept during their trip, as well as Billing's recollections in the New Yorker, May 1, 1961, and David Michaelis in his book, The Best of Friends.

In his notes, Perret says that Jack Kennedy does not hint at his back problem, but Billings describes it. Some important details are missing, such as where and on which day Kennedy bought back support, but it seems possible to work out roughly the week when that occurred. At all events, Perret concludes, that pushing the car off the beach caused the original back problem, although the convertible top might have been to blame – it was difficult even for two young men to get it up and down. What is certain is that Jack's back troubles began during this trip. (7)

I have a couple of remarks to make. Perret writes that "He, Billings and two Germans deflate the tires and start to push the car across the beach," while in his notes, he writes, "even for two young men," it was hard work to get the car out of trouble.

And there's another problem concerning Billing's apparent recollections in the New Yorker magazine of May 1, 1961 – this New Yorker May 1, 1961, doesn't exist. It's on April 29, 1961, or May 6, 1961. There is no such recollection, nor in the previous or subsequent edition. There simply is no "Italian beach story" to find, and David Michaelis doesn't talk about the "Italian Beach Story." One thing is certain, Jack Kennedy's back troubles didn't start in Italy, August 1937.

There are other suggestions. David Owen says that Kennedy's back problems began, after a car accident at Harvard in 1938, while some have suggested they were mainly due more to the steroids he was receiving, which produced the well-known side-effect of osteoporosis.

Probably both contributed, with the osteoporosis coming later. (8)

James N. Giglio takes over the Hamilton story and supports the idea that his back problem was aggravated while playing tennis in the summer of 1940 (9), while Dr. Forest Tennant says the idea that JFK's back pain problem began when the PT 109 incident is a 'common misperception. The problem already existed but was worsened by accident, which required an operation in 1944.

Already at the age of 15, JFK had aches in various parts of his body and severe pain in his knees. Although not diagnosed at the time, today, doctors may have diagnosed JFK with juvenile rheumatoid arthritis or Still's disease. (10)

Robert Dallek writes that in 1938, he began to have "an occasional pain in his right sacroiliac joint. It apparently grew worse, but at times he was completely free from symptoms. According to a medical report in December 1944, "In the later part of 1940, while playing tennis, he had experienced a sudden pain in his lower right back. It seemed to him that something had slipped. He was hospitalized at the Lahey Clinic for ten days. Low back support was applied, and he was comfortable. Since that time, he has had periodic attacks of a similar nature." Although he had suffered football injuries and other mishaps that could help account for his emerging back pain, the onset of his back problem could have been related to his reliance on adrenal extracts and/or parathyroid hormone to control his colitis. They may have caused osteoporosis and deterioration in his lumbar spine. (11)

After studying the Kennedy Medical Records, O'Brien's team of physicians drew the same conclusion that Dr. Park and Giglio had months previously – that steroids did not cause Kennedy's gastrointestinal problems and back problems, as Dallek suggested. (12)

How medical teams can differ – a prime example of a black and white situation. I am not surprised at all because of my own experience in the case of my late wife when doctors did not agree for years on the diagnosis of her state of depression or manic depression.

American historian Thomas C. Reeves claims that in mid-November 1943, Jack's back suddenly began to trouble him, and a physician ordered him the relief of his command. Jack would tell writer John Hersey that the PT- 109 crash was responsible for his back problem, but he was more candid with the examining physician. (13)

John A. Barnes said that whenever Kennedy's back problems became too severe to hide, they were simply ascribed to "an old war injury." (14)

Michael O' Brien tells a similar tennis story to those told by Hamilton and Dallek. In 1938, Jack began experiencing back pain, but when it subsided, he continued to swim, golf and play touch football. Then in August 1940, he felt "something pull" in his back while he was serving at tennis, and the pain recurred the next time he played. He often felt something "slip out in his back, and if he sat in a certain position for a while, it would "go in again." Gradually his back became stiffer and more painful. (15)

What Janet Travell thought really happened to his back was the fact that he was born with the left side of his body smaller than the right. The left side of his face was smaller as well, and his left shoulder was lower.

Travell had reviewed pictures of Kennedy when he was at Harvard and in his childhood, and while standing straight, it can be seen his left shoulder is always lower, and one leg is appreciably shorter.

One of the first things Travell did, was to use a heel lift, a correction for the difference in leg length, which on the outside of the shoe was approximately five-sixteenths to three-eighths of an inch, slightly over a quarter of an inch. A disparity in the length of the lower extremity, one leg being longer than the other, produces a tilting of the sacrum and the pelvis. The major mechanical distortion is in the sacroiliac joint. Travell believes that when Jack Kennedy began to have his earliest attacks of back pain that these were due to left-sided sacroiliac joint strain. (16)

According to Collier and Horowitz, suffering from his back problem in the South Pacific, he would later blame his problem alternately on Harvard football and Navy Service. (17)

According to Garry Wills, his bad back had been with him since childhood, but he told John Hersey that it originated in the strain of rescuing his comrades after his boat was sunk. (18) Those comrades do not remember his mentioning any back injury at the time, asserts Wills. But what about Lennie Thom's letters to his wife, in which he wrote, "Jack feigned being well."

Michael Beschloss wrote, "Superimposed upon Kennedy's history of Addison's disease was his ancient back problem. He once told Billings that he would trade all his political successes and all his money "just to be out of pain." One of his doctors thought that he was "born with an unstable back', perhaps aggravated by football. He badly injured his back when the PT 109 was split in half by a Japanese destroyer. He submitted to a life-threatening spinal fusion operation because "he couldn't take any more pain." (19)

For Pierre Salinger, Kennedy's press secretary, it had been clear from the day they met that the President was a man who lived with pain and his back, injured in World War II, was the source of his problem. Even a serious operation in 1954 (from which he almost did not recover) failed to adequately cure his condition. (20)

A Statistic

1. 1960 James McGregor Burns
Playing football at Harvard and the PT boat explosion had aggravated his old back injury.

2. 1965 Ted Sorensen
He injured his back in 1939 playing football at Harvard and re-injured when his PT boat was rammed.

3. 1966 Pierre Salinger
His back was injured in World War II.

4. 1968 Janet Travell
She gives a very technical, very convincing explanation of how Kennedy's back problems started.

5. 1974 Rose Fitzgerald Kennedy
War and his injuries during the PT 109 ordeal and a football injury at the "junior varsity," and a hard block or tackle ended his football days and the beginning of troubles with his back.

6. 1976 The Blairs
Cite Burns and others, a football injury while Jack was at Harvard, and it exacerbated during the PT 109 incident. They refer to Dr. Bartels, who claimed that JFK was born with an unstable back.

7. 1981-1982 Garry Wills
Since childhood, but he told Hersey it was due to the PT 109 episode.

8. 1984 Collier – Horowitz
Harvard football and Navy Service.

9. 1991 Michael Beschloss
He says that one of his doctors said that he was born with an unstable back, perhaps aggravated by football and the PT 109 incident.

10. 1991 Thomas C. Reeves
Jack would tell John Hersey that the PT 109 crash was responsible for his back problem.

11. 1991 James N. Giglio
He takes over the Hamilton story. August 1940, he aggravated his back while playing tennis.

12. 1992 Nigel Hamilton
A car accident in France had aggravated his already unstable back. October 30, 1937, his football career had ended thanks to the family chauffeur.

August 1940, he pulled something in his back while serving at tennis.

13. 2001 Geoffrey Perret

The Italian Beach Story, August 1937. Two or four men pushed the car across the beach to the asphalt.

One thing Perret is absolutely certain of is Jack's back troubles began during this trip.

14. 2003 Robert Dallek

In 1938, "an occasional" pain in his right sacroiliac joint. He, like Hamilton, also cited the tennis mishap in 1940.

15. 2005 John B. Barnes

An old war injury.

16. 2005 Michael O'Brien

A similar story like Hamilton and Dallek. The August 1940 tennis incident.

17. 2006 James N. Giglio

Three different teams of physicians, two different conclusions.

18. 2007 David Pitts

He had suffered back problems even at Choate.

19. 2008 David Owen

A car accident at Harvard in 1938.

20. 2012 Dr. Forest Tennant

Back problem started at the age of 15.

Doctors today would diagnose JFK with rheumatoid arthritis or Still's disease.

And so, we find that Jack Kennedy injured his back, which could be from a football injury at Harvard, the PT 109 ordeal, a car accident in France or a car accident at Harvard 1938. Or the Italian beach story August 1937 or August 1940 while serving tennis. Dr. Elmer Bartels, who treated John Kennedy at the Lahey Clinic, says that JFK had been born with an unstable back. Janet Travell convinced me with her technical explanation that Kennedy was born with a malformation of his body. He was subject to back and spinal discomfort that was so intense. So his disparity in leg length was a potential source of low back pain.

6.4. Kennedy's Doctors During His Presidency

1. Admiral George C. Burkley, physician to the President of the United States, his personal doctor.
2. Janet Travell, pharmacologist, treatment of muscular disorders, internist and JFK's personal physician.
3. Preston A. Wade, the surgeon who had operated on Kennedy's back.
4. Eugene J. Cohen, internist, endocrinologist.
5. Hans Kraus, a physiotherapist.
6. Paul F. de Gara, an allergist.

7. Max Jacobson, the amphetamines steroids injections.
8. William P. Herbst Jr., urologist.
9. Roger Boles, a gastroenterologist.
10. James M. Young, White House physician.

6.5. Three Back Doctors in the White House

6.5.1. Janet Travell "The Procaine Injections"

On May 24, 1955, Dr. Ephraim Shorr telephoned Dr. Janet Travell and made an appointment for Senator Jack Kennedy to see her in her 9 West 16th Street office at 1.30 p.m. on Thursday, May 26, 1955. She cleared her calendar of other work for the length of time that she thought the Senator's medical problem might need. On this visit and on subsequent ones, she made sure that he encountered no other patient in her office. At their first meeting, the thin young Senator on crutches could barely navigate the few steps down from the sidewalk into her ground-floor office. Left-sided pain in his back and leg made it almost impossible for him to bear weight on that foot, and a stiff right knee since a football injury in his youth made it difficult for him to step up or down with his weight on the right leg, became that required bending the right knee.

As Travell and Shorr talked, Kennedy seemed tired and discouraged. He listened intently, but he answered Travell's questions briefly, almost reluctantly, as if he were retelling a boring story. He looked thin. His weight of about 155 pounds did not adequately cover his generous frame and statue of six feet.

It was decided that Kennedy would be admitted to New York Hospital as soon as possible. He remained there, according to Travell, for a week under her care. He left the hospital on Tuesday noon, May 31, 1955. (1)

Richard Reeves wrote that three weeks after the 1956 Democratic National Convention, Dr. Travell, who had been treating Kennedy's back problems with massive injections of novocaine for the past five years, asked him, "You weren't really disappointed when you lost the nomination, were you?" JFK answered, "Yes, I was, but I learned that it should be as easy to get the nomination for President as it was for Vice President." (2)

I thought Janet Travell met Jack Kennedy for the first time at her office on May 26, 1955.

On a question from Ted Sorensen, "Did he tell you how early he had the back pain?" Travell answered, "Jack said he had it in college. He had a football injury at Harvard." In her autobiography, she wrote, "Senator Kennedy incurred an injury to his back in 1939 and reinjured it in 1943 during the war.

"The Harvard student health record, I believe, does show that he had complained of back injury at the time. Of course, when the PT boat exploded, he incurred a second

316

severe back strain."

"I think," Travell went on, "he incurred both muscle strain and low back joint strain. The very extraordinary physical exertion that he put into the swimming and out reaching for help produced tremendous muscular strain-overuse of the muscles under conditions of poor nutrition, lack of vitamin C, lack of all kinds of things, and this was a severe strain to his back." (3) (4) (5)

Forest Tennant, Md, Dr. PH., considered Dr. Travell as probably the best pain specialist in the world at the time. Her medical records kept over the course of her 8-years treatment reveal that JFK was prescribed the following medications; codeine, meperidine, methadone, methylphenidate, meprobamate, barbiturates, liothyronine, gamma globulin, cortisone, testosterone, and procaine injections.

Dr. Travell was clearly an expert in the use of injectable procaine, injecting the president up to 2 to 3 times per day if he had a severe pain flare.

Within about three months after starting Dr. Travell's treatment regimen, JFK's pain was immensely better, and he was back to work as Senator. (6)

Paul Fay saw him implant a pellet. He described it this way, "He used a little knife, and he would just cut the surface, or just barely cut the surface of the skin, try not to get blood, and then get underneath and put his tablet underneath the skin, and then put a bandage over it. And then hopefully, this tablet would dissolve by the heat of the body and be absorbed by the bloodstream."

There's a great story between Fay and Jack when Fay had some trouble with his shoulder as a result of an old football injury. Jack sent him to Travell, telling him that "After a little of Doc Travell, you'll know what I've been going through for the past few years." Fay went to Dr. Travell's office and was immediately placed in a chair and stripped to the waist. One of the longest needles he ever saw was waved in front of his face, the first injection going in around the top of his shoulder. He was in a cold sweat. The improvement was almost immediate, and as he relaxed, Travell answered a ringing phone in another room.

Fay could not quite hear the conversation, but Travell was laughing with whoever had called. When the conversation concluded, Dr.Travell came back in and told Fay, "That was Senator Kennedy," "He wanted to know if you had cried or screamed." (7) (8)

Dr. Tennant praises Dr. Travell very highly, mentions Dr. Jacobson, once – when he accompanied Kennedy to Paris to meet with Charles de Gaulle, where he continued giving the president injections, but not a word about Dr. Kraus. (9)

Janet Travell had her merits in the second half of the fifties with her procaine injections, but Kennedy's body soon became more tolerant of the drug, and she was forced to inject him as often as six or seven times a day – more than double the dose at the beginning, which did not help, but even Jacqueline Kennedy said that "no one can underestimate her contribution then." (10)

But Dr. Travell was definitely a doctor of the past – an injection doctor, not an exercise doctor.

In May 1961, Dr. Burkley and his colleagues at Bethesda Naval Hospital were becoming increasingly worried by Dr. Travell's promiscuous use of novocaine. It was not a drug to be injected two or three times daily, day after day. Eventually, its effect would be deadened, and the president might move on to using narcotics to ease his pain. Dr. Dorothea E. Hellman, a highly regarded doctor at Georgetown University and at the renowned medical research centre National Institutes of Health, was growing dismayed and highly critical of Dr. Travell. Dr. Cohen reluctantly concluded, as he wrote his colleague Dr. Burkley later, that Dr. Travell was "a deceiving, incompetent, publicity–mad physician, who only had one consideration in mind, and that was herself." Dr. Cohen was concerned only with the care of his patient.

Dr. Travell was certainly a woman of immense political ambition who sought to advance herself through her relationship with Jack. (11)

Lem Billings, in his oral history interview, revealed that his own brother – a doctor who also had a bad back – was worried when he heard that Dr. Travell had never prescribed exercise for Jack's back. Lem voiced these concerns to Kennedy, who would not listen. It was only after the Canadian accident happened and she couldn't help him, he began to look around for help, and then, at last, he found Dr. Kraus, with whom Jack exercised until his death. (12)

In November 1961, Kennedy asked Ken O' Donnell to fire Travell. O' Donnell delegated the task to Cohen, who wrote to Kennedy on November 12 that he regretted he had been "burdened with initiating a housecleaning in your medical staff." Speaking of Travell, he said, "In spite of repeated advice against her personal publicity, her own interests were placed above yours." Cohen flew to Washington and was flabbergasted when Travell demanded several years' worth of severance pay. On Christmas Day, a Washington newspaper reported that she was leaving, and Salinger informed Cohen that he was about to issue a statement announcing her resignation.

He called back an hour later to say that Travell had just met with the president and would not be resigning. Furthermore, the White House would deny the newspaper story. "I hate to use the word blackmail," Cohen wrote in his 1964 letter to Burkley, "but essentially this is how she has kept her tentacles stuck to the White House."

Thurston Clarke concludes on the "resigning episode" that just as Kennedy's womanizing made it risky for him to fire J. Edgar Hoover, the perilous state of his health made it too dangerous to dismiss Travell.

Dr. Travell kept her office in the White House, though many members of the staff no longer visited her. She had the title that she wanted above all things, but she was relegated to treating Jackie and the children. (13) (14)

I don't agree with Thurston Clarke's observation that President Kennedy couldn't have fired Dr. Travell because of the perilous state of his health. She could have gone to press with her story of Kennedy's illnesses. Clarke compared it to his difficulty firing Hoover because of his womanizing, but at the time of the "Travell problem,

December 1961, there was no Hoover problem. That only could have started March 22, 1962, the day Kennedy met with Hoover and was confronted with the issue of Judith Exner, who claimed to be Kennedy's mistress.

Moreover, Janet Travell would never have exposed JFK's health problems to the press because she had tremendous respect and admiration for her president.

Jack Kennedy was a man who was very respectful to people who worked with him and were loyal to him, and it is well known that President Kennedy had problems firing anybody. Dr. Janet Travell had helped him a lot in the late fifties with her "afterwards" controversial Novocain injections. He was thankful to her for her help at a time he was in a lot of pain.

Janet Travell also has her version of "the resigning story."

On December 25, 1961, she saw President Kennedy in his bedroom and handed him the front page of the Washington Post. "I read this morning that I'm resigning," she said. "Mr. President, I will do anything I can do for you as long as you wish. But I am ready to leave at a moment's notice if that is your pleasure." Kennedy replied, "I don't want you to leave ... if I do, I will let you know." He stepped to the door and called down the hall, "Pierre, Pierre – come in here." When Pierre Salinger joined them, the president spoke to him as they were continuing a conversation. "That story about Dr. Travell... deny it completely. And you can announce that she has arranged for Dr. Wade to fly down and give me a year-end checkup."

On December 26, 1961, the newspapers carried more headlines about Travell. The Miami Herald announced, "Dr. Travell to resign?" In Palm Beach, Press Secretary Pierre Salinger said, "There is nothing to the report." Asked whether that meant Dr. Travell was staying on indefinitely, Salinger said that was the case. (15) (16)

6.5.2. Max Jacobson "The Quack"

Max Jacobson, born in Germany, July 3, 1900, was a New York physician, nicknamed "Miracle Max" and "Dr. Feelgood," who administered amphetamines and other medications to several high-profile clients. Jacobson fled Berlin in 1936 and set up an office on the Upper East Side of Manhattan at East 72nd Street and Third Avenue, where he treated many famous individuals, including Lauren Bacall, Humphrey Bogart, Maria Callas, Truman Capote, Judy Garland, Marlene Dietrich, Andy Warhol, Marilyn Monroe, Elvis Presley among others. (1)

His nickname, Dr. Feelgood, is now commonly used to refer to numerous modern doctors whose misuse of drugs caused their patients harm or death, such as the late Michael Jackson's physician Dr. Conrad Murray. Even the widespread use of methamphetamines has been blamed on Jacobson.

In their exposé of Jacobson published on December 4, 1972, Rensenberger, Brody and Altman of the New York Times wrote that despite Max Jacobson's rich clientele of patients, he lived very modestly in what could be called a middle-class apartment. His best friend Michael Samek noted that Max Jacobson never got rich. "He never set up a proper billing system. He was never paid by many patients, and that includes President Kennedy. Max was a very compassionate person. He wanted to help his patients. Max always said, "It's better to feel good than to feel sick." Treating his patients was his life, not money. He saw his practice as a sort of a mission."

Jacobson's license to practice as a medical doctor was revoked in New York in April 1975, and an application to restore it was rejected in 1979, on evidence taken from him starting around February 1966. During an interview with Jacobson in 1969, agents from the Bureau of Narcotics and Dangerous Drugs noticed he had needle tracks on his hands. He admitted that he injected himself with 25 grams of methamphetamine (speed) every two or three days. Presumably, the bureau meant milligrams, not grams, injected intravenously. Jacobson died on December 1, 1979. (2)

There's a funny story, told by Frank Saunders. Joseph P. Kennedy's chauffeur, who recalled that "Miracle Max" came to Hyannis Port on one occasion, "I guess to give the president injections for his back." Years later, he read of Dr. Jacobson as "Dr. Feelgood and learned that the vitamin shots he gave rich and famous patients were laced with speed. But Frank admitted, "The story made it sound as though it was a big secret the way he had given President Kennedy amphetamines, but it wasn't that way at all. Anybody at the Kennedy place could have a shot from Dr. Jacobson. The nurses even asked me, "Dr. Jacobson's here, Frank. Do you want a vitamin shot?" (3)

Jacobson claimed that amphetamine – stimulant drugs – are not an addiction drug, unlike heroin and morphine, but most experts would strongly disagree. And although amphetamines were not illegal in the 1960s, their dangers and addictive properties were not widely known at the time, and they were widely used to treat depression and to prevent fatigue. Amphetamines were the favorite drug of professional cyclists in Western Europe throughout the 1960s. During the 1967 Tour de France, world champion Tom Simpson died July 13 on the famous mountain "Mont Ventoux" from a combination of amphetamines, alcohol and heat. Two empty tubes were found and a half-full tube of amphetamines in the rear pocket of his racing jersey. Erik De Vlaminck, a Belgium seven times World Cycle Cross Champion, was treated for amphetamine addiction after his racing career. Proof of the addictive power of a very dangerous drug.

Jack Kennedy's old college roommate, Chuck Spalding, introduced Jacobson just before the first televised debate in the 1960 presidential campaign, and Max Jacobson became JFK's unofficial doctor. (4)

However, John A. Barnes claims that Frank Sinatra introduced Jacobson to Kennedy – because, in the celebrity circles in which Kennedy moved, the use and abuse of chemical stimulants were far more widespread and tolerated than in American society at large. (5)

But it was Spalding who later voiced concern about Max's irrational behavior, "I am not ashamed that I went to him as a patient, but Max's medical miracles shouldn't be overrated. It had reached a point where, though initially intrigued by the guy. I felt I'd had enough. At first, he gave me a big lift, but later he seemed to become increasingly erratic," he said. (6)

In Jacobson's professional relationship with the president, Kennedy was given the code name "Mrs Dunn" from the start – but exactly how many times the doctor visited "Mrs Dunn" (7) in the White House, in New York, at Palm Beach or Hyannis Port – and until when in his presidency is something on which authors disagree. The issue is yet another John F. Kennedy labyrinth, full of contradictions.

C. David Heymann writes, "John Kennedy's first contact with Max came in the fall of 1960, one week after addressing a group of Protestant clergymen in Houston and a week before his first televised debate with Nixon." According to Heymann, Jacobson continued to medicate the Kennedys for the duration of Camelot, never once requesting (or receiving) a single penny above or beyond immediate expenses. On November 15, 1963, he flew to Palm Beach, where he ministered to the President for the last time. (8)

According to Herbert S. Parmet, Jacobson was one of the unofficial White House visitors and also traveled with the Kennedys, treating Jacqueline along with the Radziwills and Mark Shaw, the Kennedy photographer. A published collection of Shaw's pictures shows the doctor with Kennedy, Charles Spalding and Prince Radziwill near Palm Beach in February of 1963. But the Kennedy reliance on the hyperactivity-inducing drug had actually begun early in his administration. (9)

Richard Reeves writes that on May 23, 1961, Jacobson was called to Washington to treat the President's back pain after a tree-planting ceremony in Canada and was asked to go to Europe with Kennedy the following week. Kennedy asked, "Will you rearrange your schedule? You can send a bill." (10) This is totally in contrast with Heymann's version of sending bills.

Thomas C. Reeves wrote that Kennedy was introduced to Jacobson by his friend Chuck Spalding in the fall of 1960, a week after the speech in Houston on church and State. "After his first shot, much of Kennedy's weariness and pain seemed to vanish. Soon he and Jackie were using the physician's services on a regular basis. The Kennedys took injections not only throughout the European trip but for the balance of the "Thousand Days," using Jacobson's services at least once a week and sometimes three or four times weekly. By the summer of 1961, they had both developed a strong dependence on amphetamines." Reeves source was Heymann. (11)

As recalled by Heymann, after the Kennedys returned from their European trip in June 1961, they began using the services of Jacobson on a regular basis, at least once a week, and occasionally as often as three or four times weekly. By the summer of 1961, they had both developed a strong dependence on amphetamines, asserts Heymann. (12)

Richard Reeves relates that Dr. Jacobson had treated Kennedy during the 1960 campaign, but on specific occasions like before the first debate. Later he was injecting his amphetamine mixes at the White House or Palm Beach or wherever the President was, two or three times some weeks.

Gate logs indeed confirm that Jacobson visited the White House more than thirty times in 1961, 1962.

Richard Reeves puts the date of Jacobson first treating Kennedy at the White House as of May 24, 1961, noting that a concerned Jackie showed him a vial of Demerol that she had found in her husband's bedroom. Later that day, she told Jacobson that a Secret Service agent had given Kennedy the drug and that he had been dismissed – and Jacobson stated that he was "in principle absolutely opposed to the use of opiates" as they were addictive and would interfere with his medications. (13) (14)

Seymour Hersh said the doctor attended to the president and the first lady, who was also his patient, in Palm Beach and Hyannis Port, and said Jacobson made more than thirty visits to the White House, according to gate logs, but gives no dates. (15)

In "Counselor," Ted Sorenson remarked, "I was uncomfortable about a doctor of questionable reputation visiting the White House – Max Jacobson, known as "Dr. Feelgood" for his reportedly dubious prescriptions – but upon inquiry, I was informed that he was treating Jackie, not the president." (16)

Schlesinger, Salinger, O'Donnell, Powers and Ted Sorensen ("Kennedy" 1965) ignored the Max Jacobson episode in Jack Kennedy's life, but this is not the way to treat history and doesn't do any good to President Kennedy's legacy and image.

Mark J. White says that Jacobson treated Kennedy during the 1960 campaign and accompanied Kennedy to Paris and Vienna prior to his meetings with French Leader Charles de Gaulle and Soviet Premier Khrushchev. Thereafter, the president used Jacobson's services on a regular basis, at least once, and sometimes as many as three or four times each week.

Moreover, Kennedy had Jacobson treat him at critical moments in his presidency, such as the time of the civil rights dispute at the University of Mississippi in September 1962 and during the Cuban Missile Crisis a month later, while also treating Jackie Kennedy. (17) Mark J. White's source is C. David Heymann of which we have seen in other chapters, is not always very reliable, which I consider a gossip author first class.

Laurence Leamer writes that in the six months period from mid-May to mid-October 1961, Dr. Jacobson spent thirty-six days with the president, based on his billing for incidental expenses and travel, attending the president in Palm Beach, Washington, New York City and Hyannis Port, seeing him on average more than once a week. The bill did not even include the days Dr. Jacobson had been with the president on his European trip. (18)

In his notes, Leamer claims that he has in his possession the bills that Dr. Jacobson submitted for May 13 to October 17, 1961, confirming that in that six-month period, he charged $25 daily for incidental expenses for thirty-six days, plus travel expenses. This does not include the days he was with President Kennedy on his European trip. Gretchen Rubin supports the Leamer version, also claiming that on November 15,

1963, Kennedy flew to Palm Beach with the ever-present Dave Powers and Torbert Macdonald, as well as two regular White House pool-party girls. He'd also asked "Dr. Feelgood" to fly to Florida separately to treat him for back pain. (19) She doesn't refer to any author in her notes, but November 15, 1963, was already mentioned by Heymann in his 1989 book.

Geoffrey Perret says that at the time when Dr. Travell had to give Kennedy a shot of procaine before he could get out of bed, Jacobson was also coming to the White House every two weeks to give the president a shot of amphetamines. (20) Perret doesn't mention the period Jacobson was treating Kennedy. Robert Dallek, with Richard Reeves as his source, said that through much of 1962, Jacobson made occasional professional visits to the White House. (21)

John A. Barnes says that "Miracle Max" began treating Kennedy during the 1960 campaign and continued to do so during Kennedy's presidency. There were people around Kennedy who tried to pry him away from Jacobson, notably his brother Bobby. But Jack would have none of it. Kennedy kept seeing Jacobson sometimes, as often as twice a week, until his death. (22)

Michael O'Brien writes, "Dark haired, with horn-rimmed glasses, Jacobson was sixty years old when he first treated Kennedy in the fall of 1960 during the presidential campaign, and he continued to treat Kennedy for the next three years. (23)

James N. Giglio had an interview with Jacobson's son Dr. Thomas Jacobson on May 5, 1990, in which he says that his father injected the president with ten to fifteen milligrams of amphetamines as often as twice a week. Once again, no mention of what period.

Jacobson exaggeratedly contended that he came to Kennedy's assistance during the steel crisis, the University of Mississippi civil rights incident and the missile crisis of 1962, enabling him to function efficiently with little sleep. He afterwards claimed that Kennedy "never could have done it without me." (24)

Giglio's essay "Writing Kennedy" says that the allegation made about the White House gate logs by Richard Reeves does not suggest that Max Jacobson treated Kennedy with amphetamines after May 1962, as first conveyed in Jacobson's unpublished autobiography. Unlike other Kennedy presidential studies published during the decade, Reeves' book contained no manuscripts from either the Kennedy library or from other research libraries save for oral histories.

Giglio concluded that, in all likelihood, by the end of May 1962, Kennedy ended his association with Dr. Feelgood and White House physician Dr. James M. Young confirmed that Jacobson was long gone by the time he came on board in June 1963. (25)

David Pitts says that in addition to sexual promiscuity, there was another issue that was potentially damaging to Jack, although this, too, was unknown to the public during the years in the White House. Jack had used the services of a doctor named Max Jacobson, nicknamed Dr. Feelgood, who sometimes gave injections to Jackie as well. It is not known whether Lem ever availed himself of Dr. Feelgood's services, but it is likely that he did. According to Pitts, Max Jacobson was barred from treating Jack. (26)

By May 1962, all that needed to be done to fully control Kennedy's medication was to get rid of Max Jacobson, according to David Owen. In November 1961, it had been Cohen who had written to the President, warning him in particular about the injections he was receiving from Jacobson, but Kennedy ignored that warning. Secret Service files and the White House gate logs substantiate that Jacobson visited Kennedy as President no fewer than thirty-four times through to June 1962, when he ceased to visit the White House.

Jacobson's treatment of the President, however, continued outside the White House for some months. Jacobson claimed to have seen Kennedy frequently during the Cuban Missile Crisis, implying that he did so when the President flew out of Washington to New York and Chicago. Owen refers to Dallek, who wrote that Kraus told Kennedy in December 1962 that, "if I ever heard he took another shot, I'd make sure it be known. No President with his fingers on the red button has any business taking that stuff." Owen concludes everything points to Jacobson seeing the president during the Cuban Missile Crisis, but less frequently than he claimed. The unresolved question is how many injections of amphetamine and steroids Jacobson was still giving Kennedy and in what quantities.

Owen believes that Kennedy went on seeing Jacobson into 1963 even if there were fewer injections of amphetamine.

Jacobson claims he saw Kennedy in Hyannis Port in July 1963 and flew to Florida to see Kennedy on November 3 at West Palm Beach but does not mention whether any treatments took place. (27) (28)

Nassir Ghaemi writes that the role of Jacobson is documented well by Dallek and Owen and that Robert Kennedy's June 1962 intervention against Jacobson was likely the beginning of the end. Thus, though Jacobson injected the president as late as September 1962, his injections were less frequent and thus influenced the president for the worse, or to a lesser degree than had been the case in 1961.

Ghaemi refers further once again to Dallek and Owen's assertion that Jacobson saw Kennedy less frequently in 1962, and it is highly probable that his last visit was during the Oxford, Mississippi crisis of September 1962. (29)

If you read carefully what Dallek and Owen wrote on the September 1962 episode, you won't find any answers. Moreover, Owen writes that Jacobson claimed to be at the White House during the Cuban Missile Crisis in October 1962 and that Kennedy went on seeing Jacobson into 1963.

Thurston Clarke says that on multiple occasions between 1960 and 1962, Jacobson gave him a cocktail of vitamins and speed. Dr. Burkley became so alarmed that he wrote a stern letter cautioning JFK, "You cannot be permitted to receive therapy from irresponsible doctors like M.J. who by the form of stimulating injections, offer some temporary help." He added that Jacobson's injections should not be taken by "responsible individuals who at any split second may have to decide the fate of the universe." (30)

How Many Vials Were Examined?
Max Jacobson, "Dr. Feelgood," "Miracle Max," or the "Quack," was distrusted by the other White House doctors, Kraus, Travell, Burkley and Cohen, and hated by Robert Kennedy, who passed on to the president the concerns of his other doctors about the disastrous side-effects of Jacobson's amphetamines and steroids could have in the long term, including dependence and serious addiction.

And David Heymann wrote that Dr. Janet Travell tried to discuss the matter of amphetamine addiction with the President, but he ignored her just as he ignored his brother Bobby's frequent warnings. FBI records indicate that in 1961, Bobby sent five vials of medications Jacobson had left at the White House to FBI laboratories for chemical analysis. The subsequent FBI report showed the presence of amphetamines and steroids at high concentration levels in each of the five vials.

Robert Kennedy was determined to get rid of Jacobson and kept up a steady campaign to discredit him, including suggesting to Jack that all medications he took be submitted first for analysis by the Food and Drug Administration (FDA). After much pressure, the President finally asked Max if he would mind complying with this suggestion. Max agreed and forwarded to the Attorney General's office fifteen vials of medication. A week later, the FDA confirmed the findings of the FBI laboratories. The medications contained amphetamines and steroids. "I don't care if it's horse piss," Kennedy replied, "It works." (1)

Thomas C. Reeves in 1991 takes the Heymann account over. (2)

According to Richard Reeves, Robert Kennedy was trying to get rid of Dr. Jacobson. Jacobson wrote that in the spring of 1962, JFK told him that Robert Kennedy had demanded samples of his medication for FDA testing. Jacobson claimed that he forwarded fifteen vials to the Attorney General's office and that the President told him a week later that "the material had been examined, tested, and approved."

Jacobson's FBI file states that on June 4, 1962, Robert Kennedy's "executive assistant" asked that certain medicine be analyzed by the laboratory for the Attorney General. Jacobson's name and address were printed on the label of the bottle received by the FBI, but the contents could not be analyzed because of the "limited quantity furnished." (3)

If Jacobson had provided fifteen vials containing amphetamines and steroids, the FDA would have recorded it. The alternative is that Jacobson gave vials without speed in it – or that his story is totally invented.

According to Seymour Hersh, FBI records, made available under the Freedom of Information Act, show that in June 1962, one of Bobby Kennedy's aides in the Justice Department sought to have a vial of Jacobson's drugs analyzed by the FBI's laboratory, but the laboratory could not do so because the sample supplied was insufficient. In his memoir, Jacobson claimed that the president hesitantly told him "that his brother Bobby had demanded a sample of all my medications for testing by the FDA." The doctor said he had sent fifteen vials of medicine to the Attorney General's office but heard nothing further. (4)

According to Evan Thomas, RFK demanded that his brother get Dr. Jacobson to turn over samples of his elixir to be tested. Jacobson was informed by the Food and Drug Administration. Actually, Bobby sent several vials to the FBI labs. Noting the Attorney General's "intense personal interest," the Justice Department aide passing along the request speculated that the drugs were for RFK's father. But on June 7, 1962, the FBI had reported back that the sample was too small to thoroughly analyze. The sample did not test positive for narcotics – but then Jacobson never used opiates. The FBI apparently did not test for amphetamines, concluded Evans. Thus, JFK told Jacobson that his injections were now government approved. (5)

Geoffrey Perret wrote, "Kennedy's agony from his back while in Paris, he needed a shot of whatever it was that Dr. Feelgood, Max Jacobson, was giving him. Bobby had been trying to get his brother to allow a government lab to figure out just what was in Jacobson's hypodermic, but JFK had brushed that aside." "I don't care if it's horse piss. It works." (6)

Leamer tells a similar story that quite resembles Richard Reeves' and S. Hersh's account but has much more detail on the number of vails that were given to the FBI laboratory.

In June 1962, the Attorney General's assistant, Andrew Oehmann, left a vial of orange-colored liquid at the FBI for analysis. The bottle had Dr. Jacobson's name and address and appeared to be the sort that he gave to patients so that they could inject themselves at home. Bobby had shown such "obvious personal interest" that Oehmann speculated that the medicine might have been for the Attorney General's father. The FBI laboratory received not one small vial but five vials containing probably between thirty-five and forty milligrams of liquids, far more than would have been in the original container. Moreover, the FBI technicians described the liquid as yellow, not the orange-colored liquid that Bobby's assistant had delivered. Amphetamines were usually dispensed in brown-colored vials, and either orange, yellow colored liquid would have been quite peculiar if these samples were indeed Dr. Jacobson's injection. These may be meaningless anomalies, or they may suggest that the FBI did not analyze the sample originally given to its laboratory. In any case, the FBI showed that the specimen contained a solution of vegetable oil and water and did not contain "any barbiturates or narcotics, such as Methadon, Demerol or opium alkaloids." It is unclear, concludes Leamer, whether the FBI tested the liquid for amphetamines, or if it did, whether the test was positive. The vial was undated, and in his memoir, Dr. Jacobson wrote that when tested after two weeks, "there was no trace of amphetamine in the solution." (7)

Mark J. White wrote that Kennedy was alerted to the dangers of his association with Jacobson. Pierre Salinger, Robert Kennedy and Janet Travell all tried to point out Jacobson's exentriuties to JFK but to no avail. Robert Kennedy, in particular, waged a fruitless campaign to discredit Jacobson. In 1961, he sent vials of Jacobson's medications to the FBI scientists, who reported the presence of high levels of amphetamines and steroids. When sent to the FDA, the FBI results were confirmed. White's source is Heymann, he takes over in 1961, but I think it was (June) 1962. (8)

Robert Dallek is very short on the control of the vails. It is well known, he said, that in June 1962, Bobby instructed an FBI laboratory to analyze the substance Jacobson was injecting into his brother's back. Bobby was concerned that the president might become addicted to amphetamines Jacobson was using. Inconclusive lab tests, however, allowed Jacobson to continue treating Kennedy through at least the fall of 1962. (9)

Michael O'Brien supports Evan Thomas' account. (10)

David Owen supports Richard Reeves and Robert Dallek's version on the investigation of the vials. (11)

Richard Lertzman and William J. Birnes, who wrote a biography on Max Jacobson called "Dr. Feelgood," wrote that in early 1962, Bobby had asked Jacobson for a sample of the medicine he was administering to the president. He secured fifteen vails of the drugs from his brother's own stash and another five directly from Jacobson to make sure the medicines were identical. Bobby turned all of these samples over to the FBI laboratory for analysis. When the results came back that Jacobson had formulated a substance with significant amounts of amphetamines, at least thirty milligrams, Bobby confronted his brother about it. According to Mike Samek, Jacobson's best friend told the authors in an interview that JFK was blunt, telling Bobby that the ingredients were inconsequential to him, "I don't care if it's horse piss, it makes me feel good."

Jacobson, according to Samek, continued to visit the White House, often flown to Washington by his patient Mark Shaw, the Kennedy family photographer, or Mike Samek. In April 1962, Bobby confronted Jacobson and his friend Samek in the White House. According to Samek, Bobby said, "What are you fuckin' kikes doing in the White House? Your Jews aren't welcome here. Go back to New York with the other Jews." (12)

I have tried to compile a statistic on "how many vials" were examined and on the laboratory results. I found out once again another Kennedy labyrinth, enigma, obfuscating the historical truth, mixing years and dates in the search for JFK's-Jacobson's medical concoctions, how long they were injected, if they were drug-related or if really there was no trace of amphetamines or steroids found and his drugs were government-approved, as Jacobson claimed in his unpublished memoirs. We have a story of one vial, four vials, five vials, fifteen vials, or maybe a certain medicine, unable to thoroughly analyzed because the sample was too small. It was not even clear whether the FBI lab tested the liquid for amphetamines.

But then we have accounts of the FBI, and the FDA found significant amounts of amphetamines, at least 30 milligrams.

Some claimed that in 1961 (spring-summer – fall or winter?), Bobby sent five or fifteen (?) vials to the FBI lab. Most authors talked about June 1962, when Bobby started working against Jacobson. I am persuaded that June 1962 is the most probable time that Robert Kennedy took action and that Kennedy ended his professional association with Max Jacobson – or was it the end of May 1962, as stated by James N. Giglio? Other authors said that it was on November 15, 1963 that Jacobson last ministered to the president – but I think we could put that in the science fiction and gossip part of my book – but unfortunately, I have no chapter on it. There are too many vials' accounts to find out the true "vial story." Heymann was the first one to write on it extensively. The period that Bobby acted in 1961 (referring to FBI records) is very doubtful to me, knowing that Heymann proved with his "Marilyn Monroe story" that he is a great story inventor.

A Statistic on "How Many Vials, and the Laboratory Results"

<u>1989</u>

1. David C. Heymann, 1961 Bobby sent five vials to the FBI, Amphetamines and steroids. Max forwarded fifteen vials to the Attorney General. One week later, the FDA confirmed the FBI findings

<u>1991</u>

2. Richard Reeves, spring 1962 samples of medication to the FDA. Fifteen vials forwarded by Jacobson. 1 week later, material examined, tested and approved. June 4, 1962, certain medicine to the FBI. Notable to analyze, limited quantity furnished.

<u>1997</u>

3. Seymour M. Hersh, June 1962 "a vial" to the FBI, sample insufficient. Jacobson sent 15 vials to RFK. Heard nothing further.

<u>1998</u>

4. Mark J. White supports David C. Heymann.

<u>2000</u>

5. Evan Thomas, Bobby, send several vials to FBI labs. June 7, 1962. The sample too small to thoroughly analyze. FBI did not test for amphetamines. JFK told Max's injections were now government approved.

2001

6. Geoffrey Perret, Bobby, tried his brother to allow FBI labs to figure out, no vails mentioned. JFK brushed that aside.

2001

7. Laurence Leamer, June 1962, Oehmann left a vial of orange colored liquid at the FBI for analysis. The FBI received not one vial but four vials, between thirty-five and forty milligrams of liquids. Unclear if the FBI lab tested the liquid for amphetamines or if it did, if the test was positive. Jacobson, in his memoir, after two weeks, no trace of amphetamines in the solution.

2003

8. Robert Dallek, in June 1962, Bobby instructed an FBI lab to analyze Jacobson's substance giving injections to JFK in his back. Inconclusive lab tests, Jacobson continued treating JFK in, fall of 1962.

2005

9. Michael O'Brien supports Evan's account.

2008

10. David Owen supports Dallek and Richard Reeves.

2013

11. Lertzman & Birnes fifteen vials of his brothers own stash and five directly from Jacobson, a substance with significant amounts of amphetamines, at least thirty milligrams.

6.5.3. Hans Kraus "The Exercise Doctor"

Hans Kraus was born on November 28, 1905, in current-day Trieste, Italy, which at that time was part of the 1867-1918 Austro-Hungarian Empire. He was taught English as a youth by James Joyce, and throughout his life, Kraus could always recite by heart long passages from Dante's Inferno that he had learned from Joyce. In 1938, the Kraus family fled to the US, just ahead of World War II, settling in New York City. (1)

In June of 1961, Kraus got a phone call from the White House. On the line was one of Kennedy's White House doctors, Dr. Gene Cohen, asking him to treat the president in the White House. It was the chance of a lifetime, which most doctors would seize upon. Not Kraus, he listened to Cohen, neither flattered nor excited, and then politely refused. Cohen was surprised and dismayed as Kraus explained his problem, "You know I can't see Kennedy unless his current back doctor personally asks me. It wouldn't be ethical." Kraus later explained his thinking, "I couldn't treat anyone I didn't like. Too many people judge other people on their rank or money. But to me, it wasn't that. What mattered was whether I felt they were a good person." Kraus also knew from Cohen that Kennedy had been through several (three) failed back operations. "Once someone has had a back operation, even once, you never know," Kraus explained. "Backs don't like to be operated on."

By the spring of 1961, Kennedy's inner circle was split into two camps over Janet Travell and her back treatments. Aligned on one side were Burkley, Cohen and Evelyn Lincoln, with the powerful bloc of Travell and her supporters, on the other. They included the Kennedy clan and powerful aides Ted Sorensen and Pierre Salinger, who recognized her immense political value.

In 1967, Burkley recalled, "At that time, I had attempted to secure the aid of a physical medicine specialist, Doctor Hans Kraus of New York, and had requested contact with him from Dr. Travell. She had resisted doing this, and I said if she did not call him personally, I would call him."

Finally, in October of 1961, Burkley and Cohen issued an ultimatum to Travell, either she personally called Kraus to invite him to see Kennedy, or they would go to Kennedy themselves and explain that Travell was inept, should be fired, and Kraus brought on as a replacement. Given those options, Travell had no choice. "At that point, he was called," Burkley said about Kraus. On October 14, 1961, Travell phoned Kraus to invite him to the White House to examine Kennedy, and he flew to Washington the next day. (2)

According to David Owen, citing Suzan E.B. Schwartz, Kraus examined Kennedy on October 17. (3)

Robert Dallek was sure that Kennedy's ailments were not life-threatening, unlike those of several earlier presidents, principally Cleveland, Wilson and Franklin Delano Roosevelt. But because ignoring Kraus's advice might have eventually confined him to a wheelchair, Kennedy accepted that something had to be done. (4)

When Kraus examined Kennedy, he was able to learn a lot about Kennedy from Kraus's old-fashioned physical exam and K-W tests. At that time, Kennedy was so weak that he couldn't do a single sit-up and his leg muscles were so tight that they felt "as taut as piano wires." When Kraus asked his patient to touch his toes, Kennedy's fingertips dangled a good twenty inches off the floor, not even reaching his knees.

Kraus had no doubt about one thing, Kennedy needed exercise. Otherwise, his muscles would grow weaker and tighter, causing more pain and immobility. Kraus's diagnosis was blunt, "You will be a cripple soon if you don't start exercising. Five days a week. And you need to start now," he told Kennedy. Kraus made clear to the other White House doctors that he, Kraus, must have "absolute control," without compromise. He would need no interference from any of them and would entertain no second opinion unless he sought it. If the other doctors, Kennedy, or any member of the Kennedy family didn't like his conditions, that was fine with Kraus. In that case, he wouldn't take Kennedy on as a patient. Kennedy himself and Travell were reluctant, although for different reasons. Travell didn't want to be fired or give up power. Kennedy didn't want to draw attention to his health problems by having reporters notice Kraus's regular presence in the White House.

Kennedy hesitated, asking Kraus, "What if reporters start writing again about my health problems?" Kraus was clear, "It's your decision – but when you get worse, what will they write then?" But Kennedy had a condition for Kraus, too – absolute discretion and secrecy.

In 1961, Kraus and the other Kennedy White House doctors Gene Cohen and George Burkley swore a vow of secrecy to Kennedy and to each other. They faithfully kept their word throughout their lives.

Neither Kraus nor Kennedy mentioned money. Kraus didn't even raise the issue for over a year and then, in a letter to Evelyn Lincoln, requested reimbursement for his plane fares. He never charged for his time or the treatments, reasoning that, as he had not been able to fight for America in World War II, he could heal its president as a way of giving back to his country.

Kraus was dubious about a rocking chair's medical utility, which Travell had made into a personal trademark by recommending it to all her patients with back pain.

Kraus's treatments of Kennedy consisted almost entirely of exercise. In his two years of treating him, Kraus found on a couple of occasions that Kennedy had developed a muscle-knot or "trigger point" from stress, ultra-sensitive to touch and pressure. This required trigger point injections – and, apart from the name, Kraus's trigger point injections had little in common with Travell's injections or those of other practitioners.

Also, unlike Travell, Kraus never used procaine in his trigger point injections. Instead, he filled his needle with a plain saline solution or else the mild, non-narcotic lidocaine (which, unlike procaine, does not provide temporary pain relief).

Kraus had voted for Nixon in the 1960 election but was soon caught up in the

Kennedy spell. As he would say, "Kennedy was very easy to like. He treated a person like a person. He was a really likeable fellow." For Kraus, the turning point in his relationship with Kennedy was Monday, October 22, 1962, a day on which Kraus was scheduled to treat Kennedy.

It also was the day the Cuban Missile Crisis came to a head. Afterwards, Kraus's devotion to Kennedy was absolute, although the reasons were personal rather than political.

After his historical speech, Kennedy walked stiffly downstairs to the Dispensary, still wearing his thick television makeup, and took his doctor's hand gently. "I know, Doctor, you've come a long way to take care of me," Kraus recalled Kennedy said, "But please forgive me. Tonight, I simply have no time." Then aides whisked Kennedy away to deal with averting a nuclear holocaust. Kraus recalled, "I was struck that after such a momentous occasion, Kennedy took the time to personally come down to excuse himself. It only took a minute, but almost anyone else"- Kraus rattled off Eisenhower, Nixon, Robert Kennedy and Lyndon Johnson – "would have sent an assistant or secretary down to say, "Get rid of this guy, this doctor, I'm busy." "You know I really liked Kennedy before that incident. But after that, I liked him even more." (5)

A proof once more that Jack Kennedy possessed an outstanding and honest tremendous amount of empathy.

But Kraus remained uncompromising, once telling Evelyn Lincoln that if Travell was going to continue making injections and innuendos concerning the President's health, he would "get out of the picture." It had to be "yes" or "no," and that he was not interested in "half-way tactics."

By late 1962, Kraus was down to seeing Kennedy twice a week, with markedly fewer weekend emergencies. Then it was once a week. By the spring of 1963, Kraus sometimes saw Kennedy only once every few weeks. This didn't mean that Kennedy did his exercises less often. Kraus had trained head White House therapist "Chief" Hendrix in the K-W method.

By May of 1963, the previously unthinkable happened. Kennedy was so well that Kraus gave him permission to resume playing golf – grudgingly though because Kraus was no golf fan and did not think it provided real exercise. Worse, it caused stress for most players and tightened their muscles.

He warned Kennedy, "A couple of holes would be okay, but avoid driving practice." By the end of that summer, Kraus's work with Kennedy was done. Kraus said, "I continued to see Kennedy at Burkley's insistence, but my work with Kennedy was really over. If he had been a regular patient, I wouldn't have continued to see him at all."

By September of 1963, it was clear even to Burkley that Kennedy was cured. Kennedy's muscles were so strong and flexible, Burkley declared, that Kennedy could execute a series of exercises that would do credit to a gymnast. (6)

The positive observation on Jack Kennedy's back, made by Kraus and Burkley in the summer and September of 1963, is in sharp contrast with how Geoffrey Perret described the medical situation, "During his presidency, Kennedy's back was deteriorating so inexorably that long before he finished a second term, he, like FDR, would have been in a wheelchair." (7) One of his sources was Richard Reeves, who deals with Jack's back problems and other ailments but without mentioning a wheelchair. He refers to the work of Dr. Hans Kraus and the fact that Kennedy used a small gymnasium built for him next to the White House swimming pool for forty-minute sessions of stretching routines prescribed by Dr. Kraus. (8)

Perret doesn't mention the existence of Dr. Kraus in the White House at all.

John A. Barnes said that John Kennedy's serious physical problems might have confined him to a wheelchair or perhaps even killed him before very long, but also makes no mention of Dr. Kraus either. (9)

Evelyn Lincoln asserts that it was due to Dr. Kraus's persistence that the trouble of the President's back almost vanished. One day when Dr. Kraus was in the office, she overheard the President say to him, "I wish I had known you years ago," prompting Kraus to reply, "I appreciate your saying that very much." (10)

Nearly 30 years later, in a letter she wrote to Kraus, from her home in Chevy Chase on July 29, 1993, Lincoln said it was due to Kraus that Kennedy, for the first time in his life, could fully play with his children, "A thing he was able to do, was to pick up little John and toss him around – something that had been lacking in his life. And all of this was made possible because of your treatment."

Michael Beschloss noted an unusual observation about Kennedy. Without knowing anything about Kraus or his treatments, Beschloss wrote that JFK was a rare American president who looked better at the end of his term than at the beginning.

By the fall of 1963, Kraus knew that Kennedy's back corset represented the one last piece of unfinished medical business, but Kraus understood the president's reluctant stubbornness to give it up – because it could take years for a patient's mental image to catch up to the physical reality. Both Cohen and Burkley agreed with Kraus, "Kennedy had worn his corset too long." Kraus kept pushing, explaining to Kennedy, "Your corset isn't needed anymore since there are enough muscles in your hips and low back to support it without outside help." Finally, in October 1963, Kennedy agreed. Kraus confidently jotted down in his medical notes that Kennedy had assured him that after the New Year of 1964, he would throw out his corset and begin Kraus's regular exercise program. That was the last time that Kraus saw Kennedy.

For Dr. Eugene Cohen, Dr. Hans Kraus was one of the great unsung medical pioneers of the 20th century. George Burkley, John F. Kennedy's chief White House doctor, sent a note to Hans Kraus on November 30, 1963, in which he wrote, "You will always remain on the top of the list by those who dearly loved and worked with the president." (11)

Dr. Kraus was an outstanding human being with great physical strength. Legendary rock climber, humble, workaholic, he retired at age eighty-nine. His practice boomed, even though Kraus treated many for free. Three (for me) unnecessary back operations which did more harm than good; too much of Travell and Jacobson's injections. If Hans Kraus had been able to treat Jack Kennedy at the beginning of the fifties with his K-W tests and K-W exercises, Jack Kennedy, I believe, would have been a more healthy man with a much more stable back. But we must be fair to the doctors in the 1940s who prescribed him exercises which he didn't always do.

Pierre Salinger says that the closest Kennedy ever came to permanent relief resulted from the work of Dr. Kraus, who put him on a simple exercise regime and gradually strengthened his back to the point where he could play golf and do other physical activity with a bare minimum of pain. (12)

Even as early as 1966, Pierre Salinger talked about the presence of Dr. Kraus at the White House. Twenty-five years later, Thomas C. Reeves talked about Max Jacobson, Janet Travell, but not a word was said about Dr. Kraus.

Thanks to this doctor, John Kennedy was in better physical shape in the last weeks of his life than he had been in 1961. His weight was more healthy, 171 pounds, down from 186 pounds two years earlier, and his medication for Addison's disease was much better regulated in the post-Jacobson period. And on the morning of his fateful departure for Texas, Kennedy told Ken O'Donnell, "I feel great. My back feels better than it's felt in years."

Giglio said that had Kennedy lived, his health problems would have persisted, but there is no evidence that he would have been physically disabled in a second presidential term. (13)

Powers and O'Donnell admit that for the remaining eight years of his life, he was never completely free from pain but never again as crippled as he was in 1954, before the two spinal fusion operations. In his later years as a Senator and after he became president, Dr. Janet Travell and White House physician Admiral George Burkley gave him periodic injections of Novocain, which deadened his back pains. The Novocain injections relieved his discomfort but brought no real improvement to the muscular condition that was causing it.

O'Donnell and Powers said that in 1963, Kennedy began callisthenics to strengthen his back muscles, but it was in fact since October 1961, when Kraus started treating Kennedy. (14) This is another example of how Kennedy compartmentalized even his best friends. They didn't know about the presence of Dr. Kraus.

6.6. Thursday, June 22, 1961: The day President Kennedy Almost Died in the White House

Worn out from the stress of meeting Khrushchev at Vienna June 3-4, 1961, perhaps Kennedy suffered from strep throat. By June 22, 1961, his fever had risen to 105 degrees, which resulted in massive dosages of penicillin for the next two days, and the arrival of endocrinologist Cohen from New York.

According to Giglio, Kennedy was probably the only president to have had intravenous therapy in the White House.

He also claimed that the Kennedy medical records alluded to a potential Addisonian crisis that Kennedy experienced in June 1961 – an episode serious enough, asserts Giglio, to have posed a threat to his presidency, politically and otherwise, but which was not mentioned in Dallek's biography. (1)

I believe that Janet Travell was the most qualified person to witness this "near-death" episode because she was there the whole night. She recalls that this was about the only day he missed being in his office because of illness. "He had a beta-hemolytic streptococcus, acute sore throat, coughing, chills, and onset of fever. She took blood cultures in the middle of the night. He was given large doses of penicillin on the basis of the history that we had that he was extremely tolerant of penicillin. This was not a simple viral infection. Kennedy was quite sick." Jackie had called Travell at about midnight when his temperature had reached 101 degrees. By the time she got there, it was about 103, and it went straight up to 105. Travell began with an intravenous infusion and cold alcohol sponge baths, and by morning it was back down to 101 – the figure was given to the media. Kennedy was kept in bed that day, while Dr. Wade came down from New York to make sure that there was no problem such as a recurrence of infection of his back – which there was not. His temperature remained normal all day, and by evening we found that he was up and "greeting guests." According to Janet Travell, this was Kennedy's most acute illness in the White House. (2)

Travell talks about the "June 22" episode in an oral history interview for the Kennedy library in 1966, but in her autobiography in 1968, she doesn't mention it at all.

According to Nassir Ghaemi, Dr. Travell's handwritten note on June 21, 1961, was ominous, describing a fever of 104.5 and "shivering," blood cultures being drawn at 3.15 a.m., and symptoms of being "very chilly," and "perspiring profusely."

Ghaemi, an academic psychiatrist and author, says that on the night of June 22, 1961, barely five months after he first took office, President Kennedy almost died in the White House. (This episode is documented in his medical records, which have been available to scholars since 2002. No biographer, Glaemi claims, and he believes, has ever written about JFK's near-death in 1961. He believes he is the first psychiatrist to review his medical records).

But at some point, all the steroids and penicillin kicked in, and Kennedy came back to life. Ghaemi concludes that despite the medical cover-up, Kennedy deserves respect for all the suffering he endured for his mere survival in the face of long odds and for his remarkable resilience. Most normal people with half his medical problems and a fraction of his wealth would have retired to a quiet easy life. (3)

Journalist Hugh Sidey wrote that a virus caught the president, and for a day and a half, Dr. Janet Travell and Dr. Preston Wade, summoned from New York, made sure the presidential temperature was unconnected with the back ailment. In his version, concern had been crowing in the country about the president after people saw television footage of him hobbling on crutches to his place in Palm Beach, to be lifted in a cherry-picker crane up to his cabin door, then returned to the ground in another hydraulic lift when he arrived at Washington's Andrews Air Force Base. Dr. Travell had seen him in the evening, and he had been feeling well, with no hint of a virus. Then around 1.30 a.m., he awoke and felt ill, with a sore throat, aching head, his upset stomach. Kennedy took his own temperature and found he had a fever. He called Dr. Travell, who sped over shortly after 2 a.m., after alerting her assistant, Dr. George Burkley. Worried, Jackie had gotten out of bed to help her husband. Dr. Travell gave him an intramuscular shot of penicillin (1,2 ml units) and then some tetracycline by mouth. She also increased the number of corticosteroids that he normally took for adrenal insufficiency to help combat the infection. Travell and her patient stayed awake all night, and at about 7 a.m., the temperature reached 101.6, then broke. By 11 a.m., it was normal, and John Kennedy was asleep. The details flashed over the wires. "Now we've got an invalid President," snorted one Republican on the Hill.

Hugh Sidey concludes that Kennedy grumbled from his bed, "How much longer do I have to hang around here?" Hour after hour, while the virus receded, the President summoned his Berlin advisors.

He met with them in the mornings in his office, sometimes he invited them to lunch, and sometimes they gathered around his bed in the early afternoon as he rested and had hot packs on his back. (4)

Richard Reeves tells the saga differently. After a couple of days with a sore throat, the President was hit with a debilitating fever, probably a viral infection. His temperature reached 105 degrees as doctors and aides gave him massive doses of penicillin and cold sponge baths through the night to bring it down to 101 degrees. That was what the thermometer showed in the morning as he stepped painfully out of the elevator from the second floor living quarters of the White House, handing his crutches to a secret service man and walking slowly into a meeting with the prime minister of Japan, Hayato Ikeda.

Day after day, the President's aides clustered around his bed as he puffed on a cigar or sorted through stacks of newspapers and "Top Secret" reports. One of his meetings after his temperature returned to near normal was with Judith Campbell, who was able to minister to his sexual needs without disturbing his atrophying back muscles. (5)

Laurence Leamer wrote that at the end of June, Kennedy became seriously ill with a cough, chills, a sore throat and high fever. By the time Dr. Travell was called in the middle of the night, the president was running a temperature of 103 degrees, rising to 105 soon after she arrived. (6) Leamer doesn't say it was life-threatening.

Barbara Leaming's account has it that on Wednesday, June 21, 1961, following a two-hour Potomac cruise with the Japanese Prime Minister Ikeda, the president fell ill. What began as a sore throat escalated to a 101-degree fever, and by the time Dr. Travell arrived after Jackie had summoned her at midnight, the fever had risen to 103. The extreme stress of any sort poses a grave danger to a sufferer of Addison's disease, and it seemed as if the acute pain of recent weeks, coupled with tension over

Berlin, where a misstep could set off a nuclear war, might have triggered an Addisonian crisis. In the course of the night, Kennedy's fever rose to 105, while Travell took blood cultures and started the president on large doses of penicillin for what seemed to be a recurrence of infection at the site of the 1954-55 bad surgery. Travell administered an intravenous infusion and alcohol sponge baths, and by daybreak Kennedy's temperature had returned to 101.

Leaming claims that the White House tried to minimize the incident, with Travell's press release omitting the fact that Kennedy's temperature had spiked at 105 and simply saying it had reached 101 both when she was summoned to his bedside and the next morning. Leaming says there was, of course, no mention of its having been an Addisonian crisis, as Kennedy through the years had persistently denied that he had Addison's disease. But Leaming further asserts that though the crisis was over, the president remained so unwell that he had to cancel all of his Thursday appointments.

He remained in bed, where Dr. Preston A. Wade, summoned from New York, determined that, despite Dr. Travell's fears, there was no infection in his back after all.

By evening Kennedy's temperature was normal, and he insisted on getting up to greet visitors, despite Travell's admonitions. (7)

But Barbara Leaming never mentions that it was life-threatening or that "he almost died."

Conclusion

If it would have been that life-threatening, as Ghaemi claims, why then no biographers such as Giglio, Parmet, Perret, Dallek (who in his extensive research on the medical ordeals of JFK didn't mention it), nor did O'Brien mention the "near-death" episode? They forgot to mention the illness, there Ghaemi has a point, but the only ones who can testify how sick Jack Kennedy was on June 22, 1961, are Jacqueline Kennedy, Janet Travell and Dr. Wade.

6.7. How Did Health Affect His Presidency?

A legitimate question to be asked is how Jack Kennedy's various ailments affected his presidency. Once again, some historians differ on his ability to govern with all his disabilities, but others claim that Kennedy's physical ailments directly contributed to his character and political personality development. Once again, the iconoclasts and the political realists, of course, don't agree with each other. I'll put them opposite each other so that the reader can form his own opinion.

I'll start with Robert Dallek, who has done the most "thorough" research on Jack Kennedy's health problems. He concluded that there is no evidence that JFK's physical torments played any significant part in shaping the successes or shortcomings of his public actions, either before or during his presidency. Prescribed medicines and the program of exercises begun in the fall of 1961, combined with his intelligence, knowledge of history and determination to manage presidential challenges, allowed him to address potentially disastrous problems sensibly. His presidency was not without failings. "Which Presidency was?" (The invasion of Cuba at the Bay of Pigs and his slowness to act on civil rights were glaring lapses of judgment), but they were not the result of any physical or emotional impairment.

Judging from the tape recordings made of conversations during the Cuban Missile Crisis in October 1962, his medication was no impediment to lucid thought during those long days; on the contrary, Kennedy would have been significantly less effective without them and might even have been unable to function. But these medications were only one element in helping Kennedy to focus on the crisis. His extraordinary strength of will cannot be underestimated, concluded Robert Dallek. (1)

But David Owen does not share Dallek's view. In his judgment, when Kennedy met Khrushchev in Vienna in June 1961, his presidential performance was seriously impaired. A combination of back pain and steroids interacted with his replacement drug therapy of testosterone and steroids for his Addison's disease to cause a state of exhaustion, restlessness, and fluctuations of mood that considerably reduced his ability to do the job of president. Owen believes that the balance of probability is that Kennedy's decisions over the Bay of Pigs were significantly undermined by his medical condition, treatment and drug abuse.

Owen further comments on the Bay of Pigs episode that this was not the behavior of a fit, resilient Commander in Chief, nor that of a man suffering from depression. It was instead the behavior of a man physically unwell buoyed up by a variety of drugs but then brought to a low ebb by failure. (2)

I don't agree with Owen because I think Kennedy's greatest mistake in the Bay of Pigs episode was inexperience, combined with overconfidence, his sort of Midas touch.

Nassir Ghaemi claims that the military presence in Vietnam, later disastrous, was a mistake made in 1961 when Kennedy was medically ill and psychiatrically erratic. By 1963, Kennedy expressed reservations about further involvement in that conflict. Had he lived, he probably would not have responded the way Lyndon Johnson did. (3)

Admiral George G. Burkley, in an oral history interview on October 17, 1967, insisted Kennedy's medical problems in no way affected his normal routine and his conduct in the office of President.

He tended his office and went back and forth, occasionally on crutches, but that did not deter him from his full duty as president. (4)

Robert E. Gilbert, a professor of political science at Northeastern University, said that Kennedy's long bouts with illness seem to have given him the strength of character, a sense of stoicism and a cool detachment that served him well as President. (5)

John A. Barnes says that there is certainly something admirable about Kennedy's ability to face up the challenges of the presidency with an utter absence of whining about his hard-luck at having such a weak body. At the same time, a president who needs to be high on various narcotics administered by a quack in order to function hardly inspires confidence. Some have pointed out that Franklin D. Roosevelt disguised his disabilities, but that hardly clinches the argument. More than a few historians think the dying FDR was a disadvantage near the end of his life in negotiations with Joseph Stalin. Kennedy, Barnes asserts, should have been more forthcoming about his health problems and let the American people decide. (6)

Dr. PH Forest Tennant met JFK in Hutchinson, Kansas, to campaign in 1959. He was a student at the local junior college, though like most other persons who met him, he was warm, personable, and after shaking his hand, you felt he was a lifelong friend. He thinks that practitioners of pain management, as well as pain patients, should study the case of JFK. There are many lessons to be learned. Above all, his pain story is one of a strong will, desire and discipline on the part of both patient and physician. (7)

Gretchen Rubin, however, is sure that Kennedy's ailments and medication affected his personality and performance. Addisonian taking cortisone has noticed side effects, including an increase of well-being and confidence, unusually high social functioning energy, concentrating power, muscular endurance, and heightened libido, all of which seem applicable to Kennedy. Cortisone made Kennedy restless and gave him insomnia. At the same time, Kennedy also secretly consulted Dr. Max Jacobson "Dr. Feelgood," who injected his patients with "vitamin shots" that contained amphetamines. Amphetamines are potentially addictive and can cause nervousness, impaired judgment, overconfidence, and depression side effects that could have serious repercussions. (8)

James N. Giglio said Kennedy missed only two days of work (Travell said he missed just one day) because of illness. Instead, he conveyed an image of robust health via his continually youthful trim appearance, his limited but publicized physical activity and the rigorous escapades of associates, particularly brother Robert. Even his physicians, who knew better, privately marveled that he "looked like a million bucks." The public admired Kennedy for his supposed vigor, but his friends, who knew the extent to which he overcame daily pain, found him an inspiration. (9)

Janet Travell claims that "he was in good health from 1958, 1959, 1960. Then in the White House, the easier control of all small details and better furniture and more rest, we had better control over his environment. We were able to go through with a course of vaccine, to do many things with the diet that we'd never been able to do. His health improved steadily through the presidency, and I believe that at the time of the assassination, he was in his best health since the time I first knew him in 1955." (10)

Dr. Jeffrey Kelman, who helped Robert Dallek with his biography on JFK, describes the types of drugs the President had to take daily, "By the time he was president, he was on ten, 12 medications a day." Dr. Kelman was convinced that JFK was heroic in the way he managed his public and private life. "The lesson that I got out of it was that this guy had a real disability, I mean, he was living with a disability which probably would get him federal disability or retirement if he was around today, and it was known. He was on enough pain medications to disable him. And he survived through it. He came out of it and performed at the highest level." (11)

Paul Gileno, president of the US Pain Foundation, which he founded in 2006, is a history buff well-read on JFK's chronic back pain and how he kept it hidden. "It had to be hush-hush back then. But in some ways, he was a role model for people living with pain today. I wish he'd been able to talk about it– to begin tearing down some of the barriers we face," Gileno said. (12)

Paul Johnson wrote that the lies centered on certain areas. One was Jack's health. Old Joe had learned many tricks in concealing the true state of health of his daughter, Rosemary, banished to a care home, and Joe used them to gloss over the seriousness of Jack's back problems too – his back pain, his functional disorder, and the eventually diagnose of Addison's disease. Strictly speaking, Jack was never fit to hold any important public office, and the list of lies told about his body by the Kennedy camp over many years is formidable. Johnson highlights how Jack's suffering from back pain seemed only to increase after he became president, requiring daily injections of Novocain administered by White House physician Dr. Janet Travell. (13)

What Paul Johnson forgot to mention is that by the summer of 1963, Dr. Kraus considered Jack Kennedy cured. Johnson either discounts or doesn't know of Kraus' existence and work in the White House.

In an interview with Ed Plaut, Abraham Ribicoff, Kennedy's secretary of health, education and welfare confided, "Kennedy could never be president because he is so frail. He lives on pills. He had blue pills for this and pink pills for that." (14)

The interview took place in the 1990s, when Ribicoff was in his eighties. He had been able to read a lot of books on JFK's illnesses, but the fact is that when he worked in the Kennedy government (January 21, 1961 – July 19, 1962), he didn't know about Kennedy's ailments – he learned about them later.

According to Thomas C. Reeves, it was reckless, if understandable, of Kennedy to become dependent on Jacobson's shots. The amphetamines, while alleviating pain, might have affected his decision-making faculties, endangering the nation and the world. Even first-time users, an expert said later, are often restless, confused and aggressive. Many individuals experience an exaggerated sense of personal power. Although we may never know the effects of Jacobson's chemicals on Kennedy's decision making, it is clear that the president placed his constituents at risk by taking them. (15)

According to Mark J. White, Kennedy's use of drugs could be regarded as a weakness of character and as harmful to the lucid thinking required for effective policy-making. It is no exaggeration to say that Kennedy probably developed an addiction to Jacobson's concoctions. As these drugs can impair judgment, promote aggression, and cause other troubling side effects, the question that must be asked is, did the drugs influence Kennedy's thinking on critical issues?

Additionally, what does it say about Kennedy's character that he took these medications even when warned about their contents? While the decision to use Jacobson is understandable in light of Kennedy's daily physical discomfort and the desire for relief – however unconventional the treatment – he should have dispensed with the eccentric doctor's services once he learned from the FDA that the medications were dangerous. His failure to do so showed poor judgment, according to Mark J. White. Although it is difficult – I say impossible – to establish that Jacobson's speed-steroid cocktails influenced Kennedy's policy-making. The fact that there is even a possibility that his thinking was impaired at crucial moments of his presidency is disturbing. (16)

6.8. Was Grace De Monaco the "New Night Nurse" at Jack Kennedy's Bedside Late 1954?

In late 1954, after his back operation October 1954, he was at the New York Hospital. Meanwhile, according to Christopher Andersen, while attending an intimate Park Avenue soirée, Jackie asked one of the guests to return with her and pay a surprise call to Jack. (1)

According to Donald Spoto, the film actress, hearing of the handsome senator's illness, asked if she could visit. Jackie thought this a wonderful idea. (2)

For Sarah Bradford, the story that she took Grace Kelly to cheer him up is a myth. (3)

According to Edward Klein, it was Jack's old flame, Flo Pritebelt Smith, who arranged for Grace Kelly to dress up as a night nurse and pay Jack a surprise visit. (4)

Heymann wrote that when Grace Kelly visited Jack, he smiled but was so groggy from medication that by the next morning, he could hardly remember having a visitor. (5)

I consulted nine authors on the nurse episode. Only one, Michael O'Brien, mentions the OH interview at the Kennedy Library with Grace Kelly. (6)

On June 19, 1965, Grace De Monaco said, "The first time I met Jack Kennedy was before he became President. During that year, he was in the hospital in New York with his back. I had been to a dinner party where I had met Mrs. Kennedy and her sister (Lee Bouvier) for the first time. They asked me to go to the hospital with them to pay a visit and help to cheer him up. They wanted me to go into his room and say I was the night nurse.

At first, I hesitated. I was terribly embarrassed. Eventually, I was sort of pushed into his room by two girls. I introduced myself, but he had recognized me at once and couldn't have been sweeter or quicker to put me at ease." (7)

The true story can be very simple.

6.9. An Extensive Chronology

Lem Billings knew Kennedy's different maladies, and they were many. "We used to joke about the fact that if I ever wrote his biography, I would call it "John F. Kennedy, A medical History." Jack never wanted us to talk about this. I seldom ever heard him complain." (1)

February 20, 1920

On the day his sister Kathleen was born, Jack fell ill with scarlet fever. It was highly contagious, requiring separation from his family, and was potentially life-threatening for so small a child.

Brookline, however, had no hospital for contagious diseases. Once again, it was Rose's father who came to rescue, prevailing upon Dr. Place of Boston City Hospital to take Jack there.

Jack was "a very, very sick little boy," often perilously close to death. For three months, he was sent away at the Mansion House in Poland Springs, Maine. By the early summer of 1920, when finally he returned to Beals Street, Jack had so captured his nurse's heart that she begged to be allowed to stay on with him, a fun-loving and precociously humorous little boy who never complained. (2) (3) I think Jack Kennedy's ability to never complain was in his genes.

During the 1920s

Undated City Hospital, Dr. Hill, Dr. Reardon took care of the ear.

During the 1920s, he suffered from a variety of other childhood maladies, including bronchitis, chicken pox, ear infections, German measles, measles, mumps, and whooping cough. His illnesses filled the family with anxiety about his survival. (4) (5)

1926

Joe Jr., bigger and stronger than Jack, bullied him, and fights between the two – often fierce wrestling matches – terrified younger brother Bobby and their sisters. Jack particularly remembered a bicycle race Joe suggested. They sped around the block in opposite directions, meeting head-on in front of their house. Never willing to concede superiority to the other, neither backed off from a collision that left Joe unhurt and Jack nursing twenty-eight stitches. (6)

1928

German measles. Schick test – Bronchitis occasionally. (7)

1930

Jack, at age 13, wrote a letter to his mother. "I got the suit the other day, but I did not like the color, and it was a pretty itchy looking material. So if it is alright with you, when I go to the occultist, I can pick out a suit. Is that OK? Doctor Hume said he was going to write to you about my right eye. I see things blurry even at a distance of ten feet. I can't see many colors through that eye either. So if you make the appointment with the oculist, I can get my suit fitted and kill two birds with one stone." (8)

In another letter to his mother, from Canterbury School (he signed in on Sept. 24, 1930), New Milford, Connecticut, he said, "I have only lost a pound up here. I have hives that is a sickness in which everything begins to itch. I have a cold. My knees are very red with white lumps of skin. But I guess I will pull through." (9) (10) (11) (12)

1930

According to Robert Dallek, in 1930, at age thirteen, Jack was affected with an undiagnosed illness that restricted his activities. From October to December, he lost four to six pounds, felt "pretty tired," and did not grow. One doctor attributed it to a lack of milk in his diet, but that failed to explain why at a chapel service at Canterbury School, he felt "sick, dizzy, and weak." (13)

June 15, 1930

Examined at Lahey Clinic, tonsils and adenoids OK. (14)

October to December 1930

While at Canterbury, his weight fell from 99 ¾ to 95 ½. (14)

December 31, 1930

According to the Blairs, he was examined by Dr. Schloss, December 31, 1930. Good condition, loss of weight attributed to lack of milk diet. (14)

March 21, 1931

Jack indicated that he had blurred vision and could not see much color from his right eye, which led to his wearing glasses temporarily prescribed by Dr. John Wheeler. If the glasses were really for reading, this would be an indication Kennedy had presbyopia (far-sightedness) at age 13, a very rare occurrence. (14)

May 2, 1931

Jack assured his father on April 15 there was no chance of improving his academic performance. In Late April of 1931, Jack collapsed with abdominal pains, and surgeon Dr. Verdi concluded that an appendectomy was necessary. An emergency operation was carried out at a hospital in Danbury Connecticut. Normally routine, the surgery proved traumatic, and Jack was slow to recover. On May 2 it was agreed that he would not go back to Canterbury School that term, but would convalesce at home and be tutored. The Blairs say that the appendicitis operation was performed on May 2, 1931 by Dr. Verdi of New Haven at Danbury Hospital.

In One Six-Day Stretch in Early 1932

Clare St. John, the headmaster's wife, sent five separate updates to Rose Kennedy.
January 20: "Keeping Jack in the infirmary...because he does not yet seem to be entirely himself."
January 21: "Jack is up and dressed...regaining his pep...He will be himself again after another 24 hours of taking things easy at the infirmary."
January 22: "The weather is so unpleasant we don't dare run the risk of releasing Jack."

January 23: "Don't be discouraged with me for writing that Jack is still in the infirmary! We are in no way troubled about him but he still has quite a cough...We are starting Kepler's Malt and Cod Liver Oil (as per Rose's request). I will see that his House Master will follow him up on it."

January 25: "You will rejoice with us (that) Jack is being allowed to go out into this glorious sunshine today. We are so glad." (15) (16) (17) (18)

Fall 1932

The appendicitis operation did not solve the problem.

In the fall of 1932, while boarding at the Choate School in Wallingford, Connecticut, Jack complained of abdominal discomfort and fatigue. He weighed only 117 pounds, less than robust for a 15-year old boy. (19)

At the age of 15 – 1932

According to Forest Tennant, by the age of 15, JFK had aches in various parts of his body and had severe pain in his knees. Over the next two years, he lost weight, had fevers, and developed hives. Although not diagnosed at the time, today, these presenting symptoms may have caused doctors to diagnose JFK with juvenile rheumatoid arthritis of Still's disease. (20)

January-February 1933

Throughout most of January and February 1933, Jack was confined to Choate's infirmary with strange "flu-like symptoms." He also suffered pain in his knee, which his mother in Bronxville had no hesitation in ascribing to the fact that "he had persisted in wearing cheap, rubber-soled shoes, during the last two or three years." The headmaster's son, Seymour, later recalled that "Jack's winter term sounded like a hospital report, with correspondence flying back and forth between Rose Kennedy and Clara St-John. Again, eyes, ears, teeth, knees, arches, from the top of his head to the tip of his toes, Jack needed attention." (21)

Summer 1933

Over the summer of 1933, after he turned sixteen, he gained no weight. And matters got worse the following year. (22)

August 31, 1933

Dr. Kahill of St. Margeret's Hospital Boston removed tonsils and adenoids out. (23)

January 1934

Giglio writes in January 1934 (but according to Dallek in the winter of 1934), Jack was stricken with a mysterious infection that necessitated a stay at New Haven Hospital and then at the prestigious Mayo Clinic in Rochester, Minnesota. He had a high fever, hives that covered his entire body, an abnormal blood count and jaundice, causing physicians to suspect leukemia.

Joe Kennedy secured the services of Dr. William P. Murphy of Peter Bent Brigham Hospital in Boston. Murphy diagnosed the illness as agranulocytosis, a rare syndrome characterized by a low blood count, fever and jaundice caused by drugs or bacteria. Murphy suggested that Kennedy's condition bordered on leukemia and that he faced odds of about 5 in 100 of survival. (24) (25)

Lem Billings recalled that he came very close to dying. It was diagnosed at one time as leukemia, but Lem asserted that it couldn't have been leukemia. "It must have been some form of leukemia. (26) It was a very serious blood condition. In fact, we prayed for him in the chapel. Jack missed several months of school and recuperated in Palm Beach. He returned to Choate after Easter." (27)

Mrs. St. John reported to Rose that even when he felt most miserable, Jack's sense of humor hadn't left him for a minute. (28)

May 4, 1934

Writing to Joe Jr., Joe Kennedy Sr. said, "Last winter Jack came to Palm Beach in terrible shape weighing about 125 pounds, but he gained 15 pounds in the five weeks he was there and went back in reasonably good condition. His case is the subject of an article now being prepared by Doctor William P. Murphy of the Peter Bent Brigham Hospital in Boston for discussion before the American Medical Association. Because it is only one of the few recoveries of a condition bordering on leukemia, and it was the general impression of the doctors that his chances were about five out of one hundred that he ever could have lived. He is still taking the treatments, and I am going to have him go to the Mayo Clinic at the close of the School." (29)

June 1934

Jack spent most of June 1934 at the Mayo Clinic in Rochester, Minnesota, undergoing a battery of tests. When he entered the hospital, he complained of cramping, abdominal pain, and alternating bouts of diarrhea and constipation. Jack wryly reported to Billings that all the staff thought he was an "interesting case" but continued, "Nobody is able to figure out what's wrong with me...God, what a beating I'm taking. I've lost 8 lbs, and still going down."

In another letter, he wrote nonchalantly, "I've got something wrong with my intestines. In other words, I shit blood." He feared he might be dying. After two weeks, he was transferred to nearby St Mary's Hospital. Tests on his colon were normal. Paul O'Leary, his primary physician at the Mayo Clinic, didn't mention agranulocytosis in his report. O'Leary concluded that Jack had a blood infection and a decrease in the number of white blood cells. (30) (31)

Summer 1934

Joe Kennedy Sr. sent Jack to the Mayo Clinic under the care of Dr. Paul O'Leary, who had treated Joe Kennedy in the past. After a thorough, one-month examination, O'Leary wrote to Joe Kennedy that as a result of bone marrow medication taken orally, Kennedy's white cell count had risen from 3,400 to 5,800 – within the normal range – and his mild anemia had abated. (32)

From September 1934 to June of 1935

From September of 1934 to June of 1935, Jack's senior year of prep school, the school infirmary had kept a close watch on his blood count. Joe Kennedy passed these records on to the Mayo doctors. At that time, there was still concern that Jack might be suffering from leukemia.

Shortly after leaving Choate, he had to spend two months at the Peter Bent Brigham Hospital in Boston.

According to a letter Jack wrote to Lem Billings, his white-blood-cell count was 6,000 when he entered the hospital and down to 3,500 three weeks later. "At 1,500, you die," Jack joked. "They call me 2,000 to go Kennedy." (33)

September 1935

Jack attended the London School of Economics under Professor Harold Laski, but Jack developed hepatitis, or jaundice and had to drop out after only a month. On October 17, he returned to the US. (34)

September or October 1935

The Blairs wondered how long Jack had had Addison's disease. Dr. Bartels could not recall Jack's prior medical history nor precisely date the onset. Every case of Addison's disease is different. If the cause of Jack's adrenal disorder was atrophy, then the dissolution had occurred gradually over a number of years. The Blairs thought that might explain various illnesses beginning with that severe illness in his fifth-form year at Choate and the "jaundice" in September or October 1935. Did he have a mild form of Addison's disease? Had doctors confused his "jaundice" for the pigmentation associated with mild Addison's? (35)

October 21, 1935

He enrolled at Princeton with his friend Lem Billings.

According to Lem, he stayed at Princeton for about two months, but he was sick the entire time he was there. It had the appearance of jaundice, but it was probably hepatitis. He spent the rest of the year recuperating in Arizona. (36)

December 12, 1935

Jack was taken sick and dispatched to the Peter Bent Brigham Hospital in Boston for observation by Dr. Murphy. The doctors in Boston recommended getting a second opinion from a Richmond specialist, Dr. Warren T. Vaughan. Thus on December 12, 1935, Dr. Vaughan cabled Jack from Virginia to say he would see him the next morning for a medical examination, warning him that "the study may require three or four days." The University physician, Dr. Raycroft, was not disposed to wait. (37)

December 13, 1935

Dr. Raycroft wrote to Dr. Gauss, dean of the college, "You are probably familiar with the interesting case of John Fitzgerald Kennedy (class of '39). We have been in touch with his doctors ever since he came here, and it now appears advisable for him to withdraw from the university for the purpose of having such examinations and treatment as his condition may require in the hope that he will improve sufficiently to return as a freshman next fall." This arrangement for withdrawal should be dated December 12th. (37)

Fall 1936

Jack enrolled at Harvard in the fall of 1936, eventually majoring in economics, political science, and history. Unfortunately, while there, Jack further injured his back playing football. According to Rose Kennedy, this was "the beginning of troubles with his back that were to haunt him for the rest of his life." But, in fact, he had suffered back problems even at Choate. (38)

August 1937

Jack bought a beautiful dachshund for $8.00 as a gift for Olive Cawley and named him Office. But leaving Nuremberg, Lem and Jack set off for England via Frankfurt and the Rhine, though having to stop in Würtenberg due to Jack's wheezing. "Jack discovered, for the first time in his life, that he was allergic to dogs," Billings explained, "The dachshund gave him asthma." It was a new malady to add to his already long medical history. From then on, until the day he died, he could never have a dog in the room with him. (39) (40)

August 28, 1937

Saturday, August 28, 1937, "Still sick," Jack scrawled in his diary, "had a very tough night. Billings got a "neat" doctor who wondered if I had mixed my chocolate and tomato juice in a big glass. Finally convinced him I hadn't. Got another Dr." (41)

Sunday, August 29, 1937

In London, as Lem Billings recalled, Jack's illness was serious. "Jack broke out in the most terrible rash, and his face blew up, and we didn't know anybody and had an awful time to get a doctor."

Jack's diary noted a few laconic lines. "Still with the hives." It was the first time he missed church since the journey began. A third doctor, a specialist, was summoned. "A new doctor for my hives + blood count is 4,000." The next day a fourth doctor looked in. The crisis was passing, however, and there were fewer swellings. (41)

By the age of 21–1938

By the age of 21, an ominous symptom began to appear. JFK began having occasional pain in his right sacroiliac joint. Although the pain would disappear, it kept returning and was a little worse each time. (42)

February 1938

Jack went back to the Mayo Clinic for more studies, but with no good results. (43)

March 1938

By the second week of March 1938, Jack was in the New England Baptist Hospital, trying to get rid of an intestinal infection he had had for two weeks. (44)

October 1938

Still "in rotten shape" but refused to re-enter the hospital.

In 1938 he had begun having an occasional pain in his right "sacroiliac joint," according to a Navy medical history recorded in December of 1944.

January 1939 – James N. Giglio

February 1939 – Robert Dallek

According to Giglio, by January 1939 (Dallek says February 1939), John Kennedy's recurring gastrointestinal problems combined with his listlessness just before a scheduled trip to London brought him to the Mayo Clinic for a second opinion, undoubtedly at the urging of his father. For weeks, specialists conducted the most thorough examination on him. They performed every test imaginable, including one for syphilis, and found nothing originally wrong with him aside from his various allergies.

According to Dallek, in October 1938, he was still "in rotten shape," but he refused to re-enter the hospital for more of what now seemed like pointless tests.

In February 1939, however, he gave in and went back to the Mayo Clinic. It was the same old routine; a diet of bland foods three times a day and another inspection of his colon and digestive system. (45) (46)

February 1940

In February 1940, tired and thin, Kennedy returned to the Mayo Clinic after recurring gastrointestinal problems, exacerbated by irritable bowel problem. Mayo found that he had diffuse duodenitis – an inflammation of the duodenum – treatable by medication. Dr. Paul O'Leary reminded Joe Kennedy that Jack "has a nervous system that pushes him along at a fast pace, in fact at least for his physical endurance." (47)

Harvard College 1940

It was not just Jack's physical breakdowns and pain he had suffered throughout his life, but the infection that blighted the end of his Harvard career, venereal disease. Nigel Hamilton refers to a letter on March 20, 1953, from Dr. Vernon Dick to Dr. William Herbst.

This latest infection occurred "when he was in college in 1940," the Lahey Clinic's chief urologist later confided, adding that the urethritis cleared after "local urethral treatment and sulfonamides." (48)

In the Latter Part of 1940 or August 1940

According to Dallek, "in the latter part of 1940," Hamilton says, "August 1940."

While playing tennis, he experienced a sudden pain in his lower right back. It seemed to him that "something had slipped." He was hospitalized for ten days at the Lahey Clinic. Gradually his back got stiffer, and he had to stop all athletics, asserts Hamilton. (49) (50)

Just before Christmas 1940

Giglio writes that just before Christmas 1940, the Lahey Clinic, by its own admission, had taken less than adequate X-rays of his back, which mistakenly pinpointed the cause of Kennedy's pain as a "very unstable type of lumbosacral joint" (instead of the left sacroiliac (joint), located in the midline at below waist level. The consultant orthopedist recommended manipulation of the back, followed by intensive exercises and the wearing of a supporting belt. (51)

1941

John Kennedy began that year with back manipulation treatments at Boston Baptist Hospital, and after a vacation in the Bahamas, he joined his mother and sister Eunice on a tour of South America. (52)

1941

Jack failed the physical exams for admission to first the army's and then the navy's officer candidate schools and turned to his father to pull strings on his behalf. Only a denial of his medical history would allow him to pass muster, and he was able to ensure this through Captain Alan Kirk. (53)

January 1942

In January 1942, in Charleston, South Carolina, his back and stomach bothered him so much that he took ten days' leave to visit the Lahey Clinic, where he was advised that he had an ulcer and needed back surgery, a procedure Kennedy wanted "speeded up." His anxious parents persuaded him to obtain a second opinion from the Mayo Clinic, which advised against surgery that probably would not correct the problem. Dr. M.N. Smith – Petersen, a consultant for Chelsea Naval Hospital, reached the same conclusion, given the absence of an identifiable herniated disc. (54)

April 9, 1942

To Lem Billings, Jack wrote on April 9, 1942, to record his latest plans, "I expect to be leaving here (Charleston) in about ten days for my operation." The same day he formally requested six months' leave in order to have the operation and subsequent period of convalescence. "The operation," he said, was "to be performed by the family surgeon at a private hospital for a condition which existed prior to entrance in the Navy. The physician of the Sixth Naval District (Charleston) concurs that the operation is necessary. There followed a veritable marry-go round of hospitalizations and diagnoses." (55)

April 11, 1942

Two days later, on April 11, 1942, Jack was transferred from his duties in the Sixth Naval District to the Charleston Naval Hospital "for the determination of your physical condition." About a month later, on May 9, Jack was transferred to the Naval Hospital Chelsea (in Boston) for further treatment. **(56)**

April 13, 1942

On admission to the Charleston Naval Hospital on April 13, 1942, it was noted that "during the past six months his attacks have been more severe. Recently he has been examined at the Lahey Clinic and the Mayo Clinic. They have advised fusion of the right sacroiliac joint. The Naval doctors disagreed, however, about the advisability of surgery as the best way resolve such chronic dislocation." Only after a month of tests, examinations, and physical and pharmacological treatments in Charleston's Naval Hospital was Jack finally authorized to go to Boston, and then it was to the Naval Hospital in Chelsea, rather than the Lahey, though he traveled at his own expense.

May 9, 1942

About a month later, on May 9, 1942, Jack was transferred to the Naval Hospital Chelsea (in Boston) for further treatment. He was then also able to consult his doctors at the Lahey Clinic about possible back surgery. Since such an operation might end his naval career, Jack and the doctors were reluctant to do it. Besides, the navy physicians at Chelsea concluded that it was unnecessary.

So instead of having the back operation, Jack underwent a battery of new tests, X rays and anatomical examinations over the next month. (57) (58) (59)

June 24, 1942

In Boston, after a month of examinations and medical debates, the naval doctors charged with Jack's case concluded that Jack was indeed suffering muscular strain rather than a ruptured disc, and on June 24, 1942, he returned to duty in Charleston, South Carolina. Jack, however, agreed with the less drastic diagnosis of the Chelsea Hospital doctors. (60)

December 1943

Kennedy received a transfer to the United States in December 1943. After a short visit to California, he went directly to the Mayo Clinic, where doctors found him anemic (hemoglobin 11.6), albeit with the same degree of duodenitis that existed in March 1942. Nor were they able to detect an ulcer. They also found his back worse than it had been when the aching was confined to the left sacroiliac area. Now the pain extended to the left thigh as far as the knee and included weakened gluteal muscles. Not able to detect a disk problem, the doctors concluded that any changes in the sacroiliac area were not sufficient to warrant surgery at this time. They recommended more conservative measures, including physical therapy. (61)

February 21, 1944

"I'm in the hospital for another couple of weeks on my back, then down to report at Melville. Then in a month or so later, I'm afraid I'm going to have an operation on it," Jack confided to Red Fay on February 21, 1944. (62)

The Lahey Clinic, where Kennedy was examined in February 1944, claimed, however, that oxygen programs had disclosed a protruding disc on the left side above the fourth lumbar vertebra requiring surgery to correct. (63)

June 23, 1944

Dr. Poppen performed the surgery on June 23, 1944, at New England Baptist Hospital, and on removing some "degenerative" cartilage, the surgeon found "very little protrusion of ruptured cartilage" – in other words, no real disk herniation. Making matters worse, Kennedy thereafter suffered "severe muscle spasms" in his lower back that required "fairly large dosages of narcotics." Dr. James White of Chelsea Naval Hospital, who described Kennedy as a "high-strung individual" suffering from combat strain, concluded that Poppen "may well have failed to get to the bottom of the situation and the pathology seen at the operation was not a clear-cut disk." (64)

August 17, 1944

On August 17, 1944, Jack underwent rectal surgery by Dr. Hensen at the Chelsea Naval Hospital. Once more, the operation failed. While the back pain and leg pain was less, and the patient could walk without less discomfort, Hensen reported, the abdominal symptoms remained. Shortly after the doctor's report, Jack's back pain returned as well. (65)

October 16, 1944

US Naval Hospital Chelsea, Massachusetts. Report of Medical Survey.

Diagnosis Hernia, intervertebral disc. Disability is not the result of his own misconduct and was incurred in the line of duty.

Existed prior to enlistment: No

Present condition: Unfit for duty. Probable future duration: Indefinite. (66)

November 1944

During his post-operative eight-week hospital stay, John Kennedy's weight plummeted to 126 pounds, and only codeine provided relief from the constant pain now coming from his gastrointestinal tract and back. Dr. Jordan attributed the gut problem to spastic colitis and duodenitis, along with a possible duodenal ulcer.

In November 1944, John Kennedy's incomplete recovery set the stage for a disability discharge after thirty-seven months of active duty.

Surprisingly, he listed the primary disability as chronic colitis instead of his back, which was supposedly linked to his ordeal in the South Pacific. (67)

He wrote a letter to his friend Paul "Red" Fay Jr. from the Pacific. He did not tell Red of the despair that he surely must have felt but covered his emotions with joking bravado, "sometime in the next month, I am going to be paying full price at the local," he wrote. "I will no longer be getting the 40% off for servicemen for the simple reason that I'm going to be in mufti." (68)

January 1945

In January 1945, he left Palm Beach and his father to go to Castle Hot Springs, Arizona, where he planned to spend the year restoring his health. There, he rested, worked on the book ("As We Remember Joe"), and rode horses. Dr. Lahey, vacationing in Arizona, reported that Kennedy was not well because his stomach and back continued to bother him. Yet, as his worried father acknowledged, he remained his "gay self." (69)

February 20, 1945

Jack wrote Lem Billings on February 20, 1945, "I've been cut here for about a month, but the back has been so bad that I am going to go to Mayo's about the first of April unless it gets a little better." (70)

July 1945

Thanks to arrangements made by Joe Kennedy, Jack flew to Paris at the end of July to meet the secretary of the Navy, James Forrestal and his party on the way to the Potsdam Conference, the Allied Summit with Stalin. On July 30, 1945, Jack accompanied the Forrestal party on a tour of German ports and cities and Nazi landmarks.

After returning to London from Germany, Jack mysteriously fell ill at the Grosvenor House and was hospitalized at the U.S. Naval dispensary in London with fever, nausea and stomach discomfort. As mysteriously as it began, the fever, nausea and stomach pain ended. The report concluded that he had suffered from "Gastro – Enteritis, Acute." (71) (72)

June 17, 1946

The most frightening moment came on June 17, the last day of the primary campaign, when Kennedy walked five miles in a Veterans of Foreign War parade in Harlem on a hot day. "Jack was exhausted," Powers said. They stopped in the home of the State Senator and Kennedy supporter, Bobby Lee. Lee recalled in his oral history, "Jack went ill. He turned yellow and blue and collapsed. He looked like he had a heart attack." Lee called Joe Kennedy, and he was instructed to wait until a doctor came. His father asked Lee if Jack had his pills. He did, and he took some. (73) (74)

September 21, 1947

A ghastly chapter in the life of Jack Kennedy began.

Pamela Churchill told the Blairs that "on the day we arrived in London, Jack called me up from Claridge's and asked if I had a doctor. He wasn't feeling well." So she called up her doctor, Sir Daniel Davis. "I asked him to go around and see Jack at Claridge. He did, and put him straight in a hospital, the London Clinic." A couple of weeks later, when Pamela Churchill got back from the South of France, she saw Dr. Davis, and he said to her, "That young American friend of yours, he hasn't got a year to live." That was when they first knew that Jack had Addison's disease, which is rare – it affects about four people in 100,000.

The family arranged for Annie McGillicuddy, the American nurse who had taken care of Jack at the Chelsea Naval hospital in 1944, to fly to London to help look after him. On his way home to the US on the Queen Mary, Kennedy became so sick that upon arrival, a priest was brought aboard to give him last rites before he was carried off the ship on a stretcher. (75) (76) (77)

October 11, 1947

Jack was in the London Clinic, and he sailed from Southhampton on the Queen Mary on October 11, 1947. In one (news)paper, it was written that Jack had been "a patient in the ship's hospital." (78)

October 16, 1947

The Queen Mary docked October 16, 1947, in New York, or October 17, according to Giglio.

Jack's passport was stamped with an entry mark on that day, and he was wheeled into the ambulance, then taken to a chartered plane at La Guardia Airport. The plane flew him to Boston, where he would be cared for by the doctors at Lahey Clinic. When Jack arrived at the New England Baptist Hospital on a wheeled stretcher, a reporter who saw Jack described him as being "thin and wan." (79) (80)

1951

Seven straight weeks on crutches. Only freely walking in September.

October – November 1951

Jack took a 25,000-miles seven-week trip to the Middle East and Azia with sister Patricia and brother Bob. In Tokyo, he fell seriously ill from a severe Addisonian crisis when he apparently neglected to take his steroids medications. He was transferred to Okinawa to a US Navy Hospital. His temperature rose to 106 or 107 degrees, and he lapsed into a coma. He wasn't given the last rites, although some authors such as Evan Thomas, Geoffrey Perret and Chuck Wills claim the contrary. His brother Bobby would surely have known but did not mention it in his oral history. In the Memorial Edition of Profiles in Courage, all he says is, "They didn't think he would live."

Sometimes afterwards, his father arranged to have DOCA placed in safety deposit boxes around the country where he would most likely travel.

There were three last rites: September 21, 1947 – October 24, 1954, November 22, 1963. (81) (82) (83) (84) (85) (86) (87)

July 1953

Two months before his marriage, he was admitted to George Washington Hospital for a sore throat, nausea, vomiting, fever and weakness. Two days later, he was discharged for an undisclosed illness that proved not to be suspected malaria. (88)

May 26, 1954

During Travell's first examination on May 26, Kennedy complained of pain in the left lower back and right knee, making it difficult for him to navigate the two steps into her office. She treated the knee with a vapocoolant spray, which lessened the muscle spasm in the joint. Soon thereafter, Dr. Travell began treating his back pain with procaine or Novocain trigger point injections. (89)

Summer 1954

To Jack, life on crutches was no life at all, and he set out to find a remedy so that he could live as he felt he must live. In the summer of 1954, he traveled to Boston to consult with Dr. Elmer Bartels and other specialists at the Lahey Clinic about an operation. Dr. Bartels had been treating Jack for seven years. The doctor had a realistic if disheartening approval of his patient's prospects. Bartels believed that Jack had been born with an unstable back and that his Addison's disease made an operation even less feasible. Bartels was eminently aware of the limitations of his profession and believed that Jack would simply have to exercise carefully and live a sedentary life. (90)

October 10, 1954

Jack entered New York's Hospital for Special Surgery on October 10, 1954. The team of endocrinologists and surgeons postponed the operation three times until October 21 to ensure an "extended metabolic work-up prior to during and after surgery."

The operation performed by Dr. Philip D. Wilson with Ephraim Shorr, there in an advisory capacity, was a deemed success. Three days later, however, Jack was stricken with a urinary tract infection and slipped into a coma. The priests arrived and administered the last rites, and the death watch began. Jack's father was devastated. Arthur Krock saw Joe cry as he had not cried since the death of Joe Jr.

According to David Owen, the three-hour operation took place on October 22, 1954. According to the Blairs, Jack entered a New York Hospital on October 21, 1954. They said he remained there until February 26, 1955.

In fact, Jack left the hospital on December 21, 1954, two months after the operation.

Jack was wrapped up in a plaid blanket, placed on a stretcher, and taken by ambulance to La Guardia Airport to fly to Florida. He was going to recuperate in the warmth of Palm Beach, Florida, where the family had gathered for Christmas. Jack arrived, weighing 115 pounds. There was an eight-inch suppurating wound in his back. From time to time, it opened up, revealing to horrified friends and family the dull grey, glinting off a sinister-looking steel plate inserted to brace his damaged spine.

Perret refers to an oral history interview with Charles Bartlett to visiting Jack during his recuperation, but in New York, and not in Florida, "And then I saw a lot of him when he came down and was recuperating at the Auchincloss' house here, and when he was writing his book." (91) (92) (93) (94) (95) (96) (97)

February 15, 1955

On February 15, 1955, he underwent a third back operation – according to Doris K. Goodwin, his second – at the same New York hospital to remove the plate. Extracting it meant removing three screws that had been drilled into the bone and replacing shattered cartilage with a bone graft. After another three months recuperating in Florida, Jack returned in May to Washington, where he received a warm welcome from Senate colleagues who admired his determination to maintain his career in the face of such debilitating medical problems. (98) (99) (100)

May 26, 1955

According to Robert Dallek, terrible back pain triggered a weeklong hospitalization on May 26, 1955. This time his continuing back miseries were compounded by a chronic abscess at the site of his 1954-55 surgeries, repeated bouts of colitis with abdominal pain, diarrhea and dehydration and prostatitis marked by pain when urinating and ejaculating, as well as urinary tract infections. (101)

But according to Janet Travell, Kennedy came the first time to her office on May 26, 1955, at 9 West 16th Street in New York City. He was brought there by Dr. Ephraim Shorr. So it's almost impossible that he was admitted to the hospital the same day. Because in her book, Travell writes that in May 1955, John Kennedy remained in Room 1502, on the fifteenth floor of the Baker Pavillon at the New York Hospital, for a week under her care, and Sorensen recorded Jack's return to the US Senate on June 1. According to Janet Travell, three days earlier on May 23, 1955, Washington newspapers had headlined his Senate return after seven months of convalescence from back surgery. The Senator's 38th birthday fell on Sunday, May 29, and he left the hospital for the day on a pass. The Senate had recessed over the Memorial Day weekend, from 10.30 a.m. On Friday, May 27, until noon on Tuesday, May 31. No notice was taken by the press of Senator John F. Kennedy's whereabouts during that holiday period. (102) (103)

July 3, 1955

On July 3, he spent one day at New England Baptist being treated for severe diarrhea caused by colitis. Eleven days later, he entered New York Hospital for a week to relieve his back pain and treat another attack of diarrhea.

January 11, 1956

On January 11, 1956, he returned for three days to New York Hospital, where he received large doses of antibiotics to counter respiratory and urinary tract infections. To learn more about his prostate troubles, his doctors performed a cystoscopy under anesthesia. When nausea, vomiting, dehydration, and continuing urinary discomfort occurred at the end of the month, he spent two more days in the hospital. (104)

July 18, 1956

Jack spent forty-eight hours at New York Hospital for abdominal cramps. Fevers of unknown origin, severe abdominal discomfort, weight loss, throat and urinary infections, a recurrence of his back abscess, and his all too familiar acute back pain and spasms resulted in three hospitalizations for a total of twenty-two miserable days in September and October. (105)

January 1957

When nausea, vomiting, dehydration and continuing urinary discomfort occurred was it at the end of January 1957, he spent two more days in the hospital.

July 1957

In July 1957, abdominal cramps put him in the hospital again for forty-eight hours, and his all too familiar acute back pain and spasms resulted in three hospital visits for a total of twenty-two miserable days in September and October. (106)

Was it at the end of January 1957 that he spent two more days in the hospital, plus three more for a total of twenty-two miserable days in September and October, as Dallek writes in his Atlantic article on the Medical Ordeals of JFK in 2002, or was it July 18, 1956, as he wrote in his 2003 biography on JFK and three hospital visits for a total of 22 miserable days in September and October?

Giglio: From 1953 Through 1957

Kennedy's compromised health required hospital treatment on nine separate occasions, eight occurring in New York City under Travell's direction. Several stays involved back pain that required procaine injections. Any one of these may have contributed to the lumbar abscess in 1957, necessitating further antibiotics and draining. Moreover, Kennedy continued to suffer from prostatitis and urinary tract infections that were also treated with penicillin. (107)

Dallek: From May 26, 1955, until October 28, 1957

As he tried to get the 1956 vice-presidential nomination and then began organizing his presidential campaigns, Kennedy was in hospital nine times for a total of forty-five days, including one nineteen-day stretch and two-week-long stays. The record of these two and a half years reads like the ordeal of an old man, not one in his late thirties, in the prime of life.

All Kennedy's confinements at this time were at New York hospital, except for one in July of 1955, at New England Baptist. Terrible back pain triggered an eight-day hospitalization beginning on May 26, 1955. Records from this period noted continuing back miseries, with a chronic abscess at the site of his 1954-1955 surgeries.

Dallek in his notes says that JFK's hospital visits were May 26- June 2, 1955; July 3, 1955; July 14-20, 1955; January 11-13, 1956; January 31 – Feb 1, 1957; July 18-19, 1957; September 3-4, 1957; September 13 – Oct 1, 1957; October 28, 1957.

The records of these admissions, with diagnoses and treatments, are in the Dr. Janet Travell medical records, JFKL. Also, see Travell OH. (108) (109)

Janet Travell, in her Oral History interview for the Kennedy Library, says that he was seven or eight times in New York Hospital for two or three nights, the last time being in October 1957. When he was first hospitalized was in May 1955.

Nassir Ghaemi: From 1953 to 1957

John Kennedy had seven hospital visits, mostly at GWU in Washington or at New York hospital, generally for stays of a few days, usually caused by various infections, either in the urinary tract, ear, or throat, followed by Addisonian crisis symptoms of fever, malaise, and altered mental status, and later improvement with antibiotics and intravenous steroids. (110)

I think Dallek has the right account.

October 1960

According to David Heymann, JFK's first contact with Jacobson came in the fall of 1960, one week after addressing a group of Protestant clergymen in Houston and a week before his first televised debate with Nixon. **(111)**

November 5, 1960

John F. Kennedy and his wife Jacqueline held a small dinner party in Washington DC. Their guests included Ben Bradlee, then Newsweek's Washington bureau chief, and his then-wife Tony and Newsweek correspondent James M. Cannon. Cannon taped the conversation for research on a book he was writing.

When Bradlee asked JFK if he did run for Congress with this greenness, JFK said, "Oh yeah, Greener. It was atabrine, malaria, and probably some adrenal deficiency." Bradlee asked, "Addison's disease, what is that damn disease?" JFK answered, "Addison's disease, they say I have. Jack Anderson, Drew Pearson's man, asked me today if I have it." Jack said, "No, God, a guy with Addison's disease looks sort of brown and everything. Christ! See, that's the sun," and everyone in the room had a good laugh.

Thurston Clarke said that Kennedy confirmed that he had Addison's and was willing to keep it secret to him. If he had said that to two journalists, Cannon, who then worked for Drew Pearson, it would mean JFK's political suicide. In the same interview, Jack Kennedy himself was mistaken on the year of his first back operation. He said it was 1945, but in fact, it was June 23, 1944. (112)

November 10, 1960

After his election, Kennedy did speak out during a press conference on November 10, 1960, at Hyannis Port. The New York Times reported it the following day: When someone asked about reports circulated in the campaign that he had once suffered from Addison's disease, Senator Kennedy answered without hesitation, "I have never had Addison's disease," he said. "In regard to my health, it was fully explained in a press statement in the middle of July, and my health is excellent. I have been through a long campaign, and my health is very good today." (113)

April 17-18, 1961

Ill-timed health problems further rattled Kennedy. Immediately prior to and during the invasion on April 17 and 18, he struggled with "constant" acute diarrhea and a urinary tract infection. His doctors treated him with increased amounts of antispasmodic, a puree diet and penicillin, and scheduled him for a sigmoidoscopy. (114)

May 17, 1961

During his first foreign trip to Canada – Ottawa, while for the ceremonial planting of a small oak tree, he had thrown his back out and was in terrible pain. He was on crutches at Andrews Air Force Base when he landed. Travell's injections failed to alleviate his pain. Cohen recommended that he consult Dr. Hans Kraus, a renowned New York orthopaedic surgeon. It took five months to get Dr. Kraus examining and helping Kennedy through exercise. (115) (116)

Paris, June 1961

Travell and Burkley accompanied him on Air Force One. Unknown to Travell and Burkley, Jacobson flew on a chartered jet to Paris, where he continued giving the President back injections.

June 22, 1961

The day President Kennedy almost died in the White House. See subchapter 6.6

Spring-Summer 1961

Although he got procaine injections from Travell two or three times a day, his suffering had become unbearable. (117)

Summer 1961

According to Ghaemi, Dean Rusk, Kennedy's secretary of state, would have told a White House meeting in the summer of 1961 when the President was out of the room, "this country is without leadership." Needing extra testosterone injections even to handle state dinners, Kennedy struggled through his annus horribilis. (118) I don't think Ghaemi has any idea of Rusk's character, a very private man, loyal to his president, and he would never have made such a statement.

August 27, 1961

Travell noted in her records that Kennedy's cry of pain in response to the injections brought Jackie in from another room to see what was wrong.

Travell's shots were in addition to the concoction of painkillers and amphetamines that Max Jacobson was administering. White House physician Admiral George Burkley believed that the injections, as well as the back braces and positioning devices that immobilized Kennedy, were doing more harm than good. (119)

October 14, 1961

Burkley and Cohen issued an ultimatum to Travell – either she personally asks Kraus to examine Kennedy, or they would go to Kennedy themselves and explain that Travell was inept and should be fired and replaced by Kraus. So, on October 14,

1961, Travell phoned Kraus to invite him to the White House to examine Kennedy. The next day, Kraus flew to Washington.

October 17, 1961

On October 17, 1961, Hans Kraus, a small, athletic and blunt man who had once been the trainer of Austria's Olympic ski team, and was a legendary rock climber, examined President Kennedy. He found Kennedy's muscles so weak that he could not do a single sit-up, yet so taut that his leg muscles felt like 'piano wires. When Kennedy bent over to try and touch the floor, his fingertips could not reach closer than 20 inches. (120) (121)

December 14, 1961

In a rare reference to Kraus that slipped into the press on December 14, 1961, the New York Times reported, "President's Back Reported better. Back apparently is Tremendously Better. About six weeks ago, New York expert Dr. Hans Kraus began coming to the White House to supervise a series of muscle strengthening exercises. Dr. Kraus still makes the visit once or twice a week. Presidential aides said he had done wonders for the President." (122)

March 16, 1962

On March 16, 1962, Dr. Wade, Kennedy's orthopaedic surgeon, and Kraus examined the president. His back treatment was, at long last, in strong and competent hands and the better results were well appreciated by him and others. (123)

May 1962

By May 1962, all that needed to be done to fully control Kennedy's medication was to get rid of Max Jacobson.

The Thirteen Days in October 1962

Health problems continued to dog him during the crisis. He took his usual doses of antispasmodic to control his colitis, antibiotics for a flare-up of his urinary tract problem and a bout of sinusitis, and increased amounts of hydrocortisone and testosterone, as well as salt tablets to control his Addison's disease and increase his energy. Judging from the tape recordings of conversation made during the crisis, his medication was no impediment to long days and lucid thought; on the contrary, Kennedy would have been significantly less effective without them and might not even have been able to function. But the medicine was only one element in helping him focus on the crisis. His strength of will was indispensable.

November 2, 1962

On November 2, 1962, Kennedy took ten additional milligrams of hydrocortisone and 10 grains of salt to boost him before giving a brief report to the American people on the dismantling of the Soviet Missile bases in Cuba.

December 1962

In December, Jackie asked the president's gastroenterologist, Dr. Russell Boles, to eliminate anti-histamines for food allergies. She described them as having a "depressing action" on the president and asked Boles to prescribe something that would ensure "mood elevation without irritation to the gastrointestinal tract."

Boles prescribed 1 milligram twice a day of Stelazine, an anti-psychotic that was also used as an anti-anxiety medication. When Kennedy showed marked improvement in two days, they removed the Stelazine from his daily medications. (124)

March 1963

In March of 1963, Kennedy had developed two trigger points from tension. Kraus easily eliminated both with his trigger point injections but wasn't surprised when Kennedy asked him, "Should I try crutches again?" Kraus was clear, "Don't even think of it – throw those things out."

Kraus vehemently opposed artificial supports, whether canes, crutches, girdles, braces, or back corsets, and he wanted Kennedy to stop using his back corset as soon as possible. He explained, "Because muscles atrophy without physical activity, a person should be strengthening his muscles rather than relying on those things." (125)

Summer of 1963

By the summer of 1963, Kraus considered Kennedy cured. He was playing golf, had not experienced any back pain during his strenuous European tour, and could toss his son in the air. (126)

August 13, 1963

In his notes, Dr. Burkley reported that President Kennedy had discomfort in his right eye. Examination of the eye revealed nothing. But a few hours later, when the President complained of an itching sensation in the right eye, a Bethesda ophthalmologist was summoned. Again the examination showed nothing.

On one occasion, Dr. Burkley began to suspect that the presidents' stomach problem might stem from anxiety. On August 13, 1963, he discussed Kennedy's gastrointestinal ailment with another physician. "We should stress the fact that emotional tension rather than food would be the cause of the president's distress and that no organic change has taken place," Burkley reported. (127)

Burkley makes an excellent observation because when on August 7, 1963, Patrick Bouvier is born and dies on August 9, less than thirty-nine hours later, President Kennedy suffered his most dreadful experience of his life, losing his son. Even a healthy person could have had serious emotional tension or even depression.

August 22-27, 1963

Kennedy had re-injured his back by stepping into a hole on the Hyannis Golf course at the beginning of August and aggravated it by playing more golf two weeks later. X-rays were taken, diagrams drawn, hot packs prescribed, bandages wound around his back and groin, and a misleading story concocted for the press to explain why he appeared to be limping. "I don't want to read anything in the papers about my groin," he told Salinger. "We can attribute it all to the back. I don't want the American public thinking that their president is falling apart. Now he's got a bad back, now his groin is going."

Dr. Kraus was on a climbing holiday in Italy, so his associate, Dr. Willibrand Nagler, examined Kennedy on August 22-27, 1963. He diagnosed a muscle sprain, recommended continuing with hot packs and bandages and told him to avoid walking and climbing stairs.

August 31, 1963

When the pain persisted, Kennedy insisted on seeing Kraus in person. Kraus arrived on August 31, examined Kennedy and confirmed Nagler's diagnoses, a strain of the hip flexor muscle and not a very serious one. He advised him to continue the hot packs and bandages for two or three days and then resume exercising.

October 1963

Kennedy's back had continued bothering him during the weekend, and he asked Dr. Kraus to meet him at the White House when he returned from Camp David. Kraus noted that he was experiencing discomfort on his left side and told him that if he resumed his full exercise program, his pain would disappear. He again urged him to discard his back brace (Dr. Burkley said, "You could hardly call it a brace. It was just a small support rather than any actual brace").

Kennedy promised to get rid of it on January 1, 1964, making it a New Year's resolution. (128) (129)

October 12, 1963

According to Thurston Clarke, Jack Kennedy had recently complained to Red Fay that his face was showing his weight, and he was getting what he called "full jowls." Thurston Clarke wrote that he should have been more concerned about his cholesterol, since on October 13 laboratory report showed it at 353, a dangerously high level.

But in the Red Fay Oral History, there is no mention that Kennedy complained. Fay said, "As he got involved and became president, then his health really got to be awfully good. I mean, he had to watch his weight, and he was a great one for, you know, he thought he was gaining weight under the – you know, he'd call his jowls, you know...I'm getting full jowls." (130) (131)

6.10. Conclusion

Lying and denying are part of human nature – Kennedy wasn't the first president who was hiding his true medical condition from the public. It's even not an all American phenomenon.

France, America's oldest ally, has a few striking examples with Charles de Gaulle, Georges Pompidou and the French cover-up of the century with François Mitterand. When I investigated the scale of John Kennedy's "Health Issues," I was impressed, astonished, and humbled by the way he pulled through all his medical ordeals, from childhood to the end of his very short life. Historians, scholars who doubt Kennedy's character should study my health chronology. Of course, there were the many health cover-ups – getting in the Navy and the Addison denial for becoming president, among others.

Robert Dallek, who, on the health issue, has described as fairly, accurately and honestly as he could, what was in the Kennedy health dossier, said, "There was a cover-up, so to speak, but this was not unusual, other presidents have had health problems, and they hid it from the public." (1)

It took a lot of courage. A force will consist of character, determination – revisionists will call it recklessness on his behalf – to go to war, as a rich man's son, Jack could easily have chosen a quiet desk job. He wanted the image of a healthy man, although he was not. As a dashing young man, congressman, senator and finally president, he displayed an uncommon force of will to reflect a public persona that the public wanted, and nothing wrong with that – the public indeed found him young, beautiful and healthy.

In 1956, he ignored his father's advice to come clean about Addison's disease, which at that time, with medication, was not life-threatening anymore.

I think if he had listened to his father, it would have saved him a lot of trouble in the future on the issue, and failure to come to clean exposed him to claims of secrecy and lying.

Jack Kennedy had a tough medical journey, from Travell, the "naughty" madam, via Burkley, Cohen, Jacobson's amphetamine injections, to the very demanding exercise doctor Hans Kraus, who made Kennedy look better and in the best physical shape at the end of his life.

Of the three back doctors, there's only one who deserves my utmost respect, although I have to be fair to Dr. Travell. She did a good job in the late fifties. On the other hand, "the naughty madam" – Jacqueline Kennedy in her "emotionally distraught" days just after the assassination, called her a "Madame Nhu," had the guts to write in her memoirs on Dr. Kraus, that in the White House gymnasium the two Navy Chief physiotherapists under the direction of Dr. Kraus and it helped him greatly, "I had known Dr. Kraus for years, through a mutual interest in the relief of painful muscle spasm by vapocoolant sprays and I asked him to see President Kennedy late in the summer of 1961 at Hyannis Port," said Travell. (2)

This is a blatant lie because she forgets to mention that she blocked Kraus' entrance in the White House to treat Kennedy for months during summer and autumn 1961.

His first time in the White House to treat Kennedy was on October 17, 1961.

Dr. Kraus put his patient's health first, not looking for publicity or seeking social contacts with the president. He promised Kennedy absolutely secrecy which he proved by writing three books after Kennedy's death, not once mentioning his name. The way John Fitzgerald Kennedy dealt with his medical problems throughout his whole life have my utmost admiration and respect.

Throughout all his medical ordeals, he struggled day in and day out. He proved in the Cuban Missile Crisis that he was a very effective and successful President. He will have a lasting appeal because he was young and charming at the time of his assassination and with a beautiful wife, two beautiful young children, frozen in time by the existence of television.

He wrote a book about courage! Handling and managing his health problems is, for me, his true profile in courage.

How many different medications did Jack Kennedy take a day?

According to James N. Giglio, Dallek revealed that President Kennedy ingested at least seven different prescription drugs daily. Eleven, according to Dr. Forest Tennant, based on medical records kept by Dr. Travell over the course of her 8-years of treatment of JFK. But it was ten to twelve, according to Dr. Kelman. The strange thing is that Robert Dallek was given access to files covering eight years leading up to Kennedy's assassination in 1963, and he examined them with Dr. Jeffrey A. Kelman. But Robert Dallek never mentioned in his Kennedy biography nor in interviews the 7 or 8 prescription drugs. (3) We will never know the exact amount he took every day.

Another Kennedy controversy concerning his health was whether or not the "insomniac story" is true or false, and on the yes's and the no's, they contradict each other.

Janet Travell, in her oral history interview for the Kennedy Library, when she mentioned to Sorensen that he didn't take any sleeping pill and that there is a story around that he was an insomniac, Travell answered that she had seen that and certainly, that's the farthest from the truth. He could lie down almost any place and be asleep in 30 seconds, to which Sorensen agreed. Travell further asserted that he could disconnect completely and pick himself up refreshed. He could carry through without sleep for periods of times, but he was quickly and easily refreshed by sleep. (4)

Dr. Burkley asked "on what kind of a sleeper Kennedy was in his opinion," answered, "The President slept well. I don't know where that insomniac story of that nature would arise." (5)

Asked by Schlesinger if Kennedy never took sleeping pills, Jacqueline said that he had no trouble sleeping, but sometimes, in a campaign, he would take a little sleeping pill. (6)

But Dallek said that when he faced crises, such as the Bay of Pigs and the Cuban Missile Crisis, his dosages of cortisone and salt tablets were increased in order to allow him to cope effectively with the stress that he was under. He was also on sleeping pills, claims Robert Dallek. (7)

Forest Tennant claims that constant pain and excess electrical discharges keep the centralized pain patient awake. JFK had to take barbiturates (Tuinal) to get some sleep, and almost all centralized pain patients require a potent sleep pill. (8)

According to Dr. Jeffrey Kelman, his 10 to 12 medications a day included a Nembutal for sleep. (9)

I found once again a perfect example of how some authors interpret the history and the "historical truth," their own way, apart from being reckless, a cold warrior, a womanizer among others, now Nassir Ghaemi has made Kennedy a psychiatric patient. John Kennedy, he said, had many reasons to be psychiatrically ill. He may

362

have had a family history of mental illness – Addison's disease, when severe, "a lot of authors considered his Addison's as a mild one" – produces clinical depression, and steroids themselves cause mania or depression. But after carefully examining the medical records in the JFK presidential archives, Ghaemi found little medical comment on his mental states.

Most records simply do not discuss psychiatric symptoms. There was no documentation stating that Kennedy ever experienced clinical depression or a manic episode. However, Ghaemi claims that he found documents suggesting he had at least one case of depressive symptoms severe enough to warrant medical attention.

In early December 1962, Kennedy developed another viral cold, with sinus and throat symptoms ("a slight sniffle," according to his press secretary, Pierre Salinger). According to Ghaemi, on December 11, 1962, Jackie, concerned about mental depression, called both Dr. Travell and Dr. Burkley. Here is the note in Dr. Burkley's file, with "X," being his notation for the president, and "X-1," meaning the first lady, "Received a call from X-1, stating that X seemed a little depressed and that she felt that perhaps the antihistamine drugs were responsible for it."

Kennedy received a small dose of Stelazine, which is, in fact, antimanic, antipsychotic, not an antidepressant, for the next three days. (10) (11) (12)

Dallek wrote in the Atlantic article on JFK's medical ordeals that Kennedy used antihistamines for allergies, and on at least one occasion, an antipsychotic (though only for two days) for a severe mood change (13), which Ghaemi blamed on mild depression, but which Jackie Kennedy believed had been brought on by the antihistamines.

My comment on that small viral cold incident when Jackie felt Kennedy was "a little depressed" – aren't we all "a little depressed" from time to time?"

It is well known that during his lifetime, Jack Kennedy injected himself many times. There are two different stories about whether Kennedy injected himself or had somebody else doing the injection; one from his friend Paul B. Fay Jr. and one from his other "friend" George Smathers.

Fay, in his book "The pleasure of his company," tells the following story about ten days he spent with Jack in Palm Beach when he needed to inject himself daily. "Luckily, this was a treatment he had to endure only for a short period." Fay told him, "Jack, the way you take that jab, it looks like it doesn't even hurt." Before Fay had time to dodge, he reached over and jabbed the same needle into Fay's leg, making him scream with the pain. Kennedy remarked flatly, "It feels the same way to me." (14)

George Smathers told in two interviews, the first one with Hersh in 1996, that he learned how necessary Jacobson's shots were while playing golf with the President in Palm Beach. "We played about seven or eight holes," Smathers recalled, "and then Jack said to me, I'm hurting so bad that I can't believe it. I got to get a shot of a painkiller or whatever. But it was something, in addition, some medicine he had. So we go back to his house, and Jack lies down and says to me or Frank, my brother, that somebody got to give him a shot. He told us where the medicine was, and Frank went out and got it. It had a big needle, at least two and a half or three inches long. Jack was lying down, and he said, "Now Frank, here's what you got to do. Get this bottle and take the syringe, and so on. And then I am going to lie down and pull down my britches, and stick the needle in my butt and shoot it in there." Frank did just that," Smathers recounted, adding, "That's what Kennedy had to do. And he had to do that about once every six hours at that time." (15)

In the second interview with Laurence Leamer, Smathers claimed that Jack Kennedy did not mind that an old friend knew about his drug use, "I wasn't sure what it was he was taking – I don't think Jack knew," Smathers reflected. "He just knew it made feel him better. So, he'd say, "Give me the injection. Be damn sure that you take alcohol first and clean it off. I don't want to get infected." I said, "Okay." Then just like a pro, I'd stick him and shoot him in there." Smathers added, "On these physical things, he could stand pain better than anybody I ever saw. I mean, when you stopped to look at what really bothered him, he endured the pain like you wouldn't believe!" (16)

The Story that Red Fay told seems plausible to me because everybody knew that Kennedy injected himself often with Jacobson's prepared hypodermic needles, of which he knew the contents for self-administration and the DOCA pellets he himself put in his body.

The two Smathers stories reveal to me that George is a great storyteller and that Kennedy had two more secret doctors, George Smathers and his brother Frank.

I have great reservations about the authenticity of his stories. They should be catalogued in a chapter called "All the gossip on Jack Kennedy." Had John Kennedy lived, his health problems wouldn't have disappeared, but he's back through the exercises from Dr. Hans Kraus and his team, would have been stabilized with some upsets from time to time, but he wouldn't have been confined to a wheelchair, as Perret and Barnes are claiming.

One final remark on Dr. Jacobson. He left his unpublished memoirs with a 48-page "JFK chapter," but Jacobson's medical records for Kennedy are not available. His widow Ruth Jacobson is certain that he destroyed them. So we have to believe his "Unpublished Memoirs."

During the early 1950s, Kennedy's recurring back problem made it necessary for him to campaign on crutches.
(Copyright: JFK Library)

Kennedy strained his back on May 16, 1961 during a tree-planting ceremony in Ottawa.
(Copyright: JFK Library)

Chapter 7: JFK: The Man, The President, The Character Issue

"A man may die, nations may rise and fall, but an idea lives on. Ideas have endurance without death."

- **JFK at Greenville, North Carolina, 8th February 1963**

"People keep telling me I can be a great man. I'd rather be a good one."

- **John Fitzgerald Kennedy Jr.**

"Forgive your enemies, but never forget their names."
"The Presidency is not a good place to make new friends. I'm going to keep my old friends."
"The point is that you've got to live every day like it's your last day on earth. That's what I am doing."

- **JFK to George Smathers**

In an interview on CBS 60 minutes by Lesly Stahl in 1998, June 7 with Edward Moore Kennedy.
Interviewer Lesly Stahl asked the following question to Edward Moore Kennedy:
"Do you think that it is appropriate for Americans to judge our political figures by their personal behavior?"
Edward M. Kennedy answered: "Yes, to the extent that their personal behavior reflects on their ability to do the job."

- **CBS 60 minutes, June 7, 1998**

7.1. His Best Friend Was Gay

What illustrated JFK's character at its best was his capacity for friendship; he proved it with an almost lifelong relationship with Lem Billings.

It started when Lem was sixteen, and Jack was fifteen at Choate School for boys and lasted until Jack's death in 1963. Lem never recovered from the pain he felt from Jack's assassination and spoke about Jack's capacity for friendship. "I certainly don't think he was cold in any way. He had a warm personality. I think he cared a great deal about people and his feelings of loyalty were far above average. I'd go even further. I never knew anyone with stronger feelings of loyalty."

Lem added, "I think that anytime that he really established in his own mind that a man who was his friend, he never deserted him. His feelings toward that person never lessened. This was true even when his loyalty was sorely tried." (1)

Eunice Kennedy Shriver observed, "Of the nine or ten men who were close to the president, I would say that Lem was number one" – even though Lem had no governmental role. He'd been offered any post he wanted, from the first director of the Peace Corps, first director of the American Tourist Bureau, top positions in the Post Office and Commerce Departments or ambassador to Denmark. Lem turned all of them down. "Can you imagine my best friend becomes president of the United States and I spend his presidency in Denmark?" He exclaimed. (2) (3) (4) (5)

As the administration got underway, Lem came to Washington almost every weekend, flying down from New York, where he was still working for advertising agency Lennen & Newell. He stayed at the White House so often that he was given his own room on the third floor. He even left some of his belongings there, effectively making it Lem's room: no one else used it. "Lem was one of the few people with whom Jack shared his physical suffering," said Chris Lawford, who knew Lem later in life. (6)

But Jack's best long-life friend was gay.

In the 1930s, homosexuality was a gigantic taboo in America and much of the rest of the world at that time, and for decades more. The word was not even mentioned in polite company, and most gays stayed firmly in the closet, fearing rejection, discrimination, or worse. At that time, it is no exaggeration to say, many people thought of gays as almost subhuman – certainly sinful and degenerate.

David Pitts, in his book "Jack and Lem," wrote, "Some advisors no doubt wondered about Lem being gay, but never brought the subject up with Jack. Paradoxically, the climate of homophobia and intolerance in the 1960s might have protected Lem." (7)

I disagree with this point of view. Even in the 1970s, homo's stayed in the closet. A well-known Belgian singer came out of the closet in December 1970. It had disastrous effects on his career. Belgian television let him down.

Now in the 21st century, homosexuality is largely accepted, not by everybody. Only fools and ignorant don't accept that "times are a-changing" like Bob Dylan used to sing.

Lem and Jack met at school at very different times – and Lem fell in love with Jack. His desire for physical intimacy with Jack was so overpowering that he couldn't hide it. He had to find some way of letting Jack know. But Lem didn't want to talk to Jack directly and discuss the matter with him openly. He didn't want to risk admitting to Jack that he was the object of his sexual desires and emotions because he feared it would end their friendship.

So he decided to drop a hint. Boys who wanted sexual activity with other boys exchanged notes written on toilet paper to indicate their interest. So Lem finally took the plunge and sent such a note to Jack. There is no record of what he wrote on the note, but whatever he wrote, it backfired. When Jack received it, he was angry and upset.

On June 27, 1934, while Jack was hospitalized at St. Mary's hospital in Rochester, Jack wrote, "Please don't write to me on toilet paper anymore. I am not that kind of boy."

The letter was a clear indication that Jack did not share his preference, did not want to experiment, and wanted nothing to do with homosexual behavior. Lem wisely backed off. But unlike most straight men confronted with this situation, certainly, at that time, Jack didn't break off the friendship with Lem. (8) (I would have acted differently). The emphasis for Jack was on a close relationship – not the kind of love that Lem felt. Isn't Jack's friendship with Lem an example of true profile in courage on Jack's behalf?

Lem may have considered taking the path of many gay men in the 20th century – a conventional marriage, even children, to hide their homosexuality from the outside world. Lem certainly became close to Jack's younger sister Kathleen, a popular figure known as Kick, with the same witty and self-deprecating humor as Jack. They wrote to each other, especially after she moved to England with Joe and Rose, and there was speculation that they were a courting couple. But Kick wisely put off a proposal from Lem, telling him, "Come on Lem, you know, you're not the marrying kind." (9) (10)

According to Lem's niece, Sally Carpenter, Lem often talked about Kick, even years after she had died. It was Sally's impression that the relationship between them was very close, but it was very unlikely that they were intimate. (11)

Charles L. Bartlett, a journalist and a friend of both Billings and Kennedy, describes their relationship as follows:

"Lem was a stable presence for Jack – his raison d'être was Jack Kennedy. I don't think it's true that he did not have views of his own, as some have said. He had a very independent mind. He had interests of his own that Jack didn't necessarily share. He certainly didn't have the same interest in politics and women that Jack had." (12)

Lem himself said that "Jack made a big difference" in his life. "Because of him, I was never lonely. He may have been the reason I never got married." (13)

Unable to extinguish his own pain stemming from the assassinations of Jack and

Bobby and the death of his mother, he began to drink more and – a sign of the times – began taking drugs, sometimes with the Kennedy children. On May 28, 1981, he died in his sleep in his Manhattan apartment following a heart attack at the age of 65. (14)

7.2. Thomas Jefferson & Sally Hemings Controversy: A Character Issue?

Why put the myth of Thomas Jefferson and Sally Hemings or their illicit affair in a book on John F. Kennedy? Because there is a common thread between Kennedy's womanizing, or his approach to Vietnam, and the Jefferson-Hemings story – enduring controversy.

I will try to find similarities in both controversies.

In September 1802, political journalist James T. Callender, a despicable individual, ruled by venom and racism, and a disaffected former ally of Jefferson, wrote in a Richmond newspaper that Jefferson had, for many years, kept as his concubine one of his own slaves, called Sally, and had several (six) children with her. Jefferson owned 607 slaves over the course of his life. Because of his vicious writings, Callender had already been fined $200 and imprisoned for nine months in 1800 under the federal sedition law but did not relent. While in prison, he authored two more attacking pieces, and in articles written throughout 1802 and 1803, he accused Jefferson, among other things, of "dishonesty," "cowardice," and "gross personal immorality."

After threatening suicide on several occasions, Callender died on July 17, 1803, drowning in three feet of water in the James River, too drunk to save himself. I call this an accidental suicide.

There is a similar story in Kennedy's womanizing, when Phil Graham, alcoholic and manic depressive, who wrote about the Meyer-JFK affair, took the microphone at a convention of American newspapers editors in Phoenix and removed his clothes. He was taken to a private mental institution, finally shooting himself dead later that year, on August 3, 1963.

There's another similarity between Jefferson and Kennedy regarding how journalists and authors deal with stories without sufficient care or sloppy research.

Pulitzer Prize-winning historian James Truslow Adams said, "Almost every scandalous story about Jefferson which is still whispered or believed, can be traced to the lies in Callender's writings."

John C. Miller, a Stanford University historian, described Callender as the most unscrupulous scandal-monger of the day, a journalist who stopped at nothing and stopped at anything. He explains, "Callender made his charges against Jefferson without fear and without research: he had never visited Monticello. He had never spoken to Sally Hemings. He had never made the slightest effort to verify the "facts" he so stridently proclaimed. It was "journalism" at its most reckless, wildly irresponsible, and scurrilous." (1)

Nothing has changed in 200 years. Remember, Heymann's story about Marilyn Monroe calling at the White House, or Hersh using the totally unreliable source Judith Exner carrying $250,000 as a courier to Sam Giancana in Chicago in April 1960, one week after (March 27, 1960) Campbell was introduced by Sinatra to Giancana?

Thomas Jefferson's policy was to offer no public response to personal attacks, and he made no explicit public or private comment on Callender's allegation about Sally Hemings. However, a private letter of 1805 has been interpreted by some individuals as a denial of the story. Sally Hemings herself left no known accounts – it is not known if she was even literate.

Jefferson's daughter, Martha Jefferson Randolph, privately denied the published reports. Two of her children Ellen Randolph Coolidge and Thomas Jefferson Randolph, maintained many years later that such a liaison was not possible, on both moral and practical grounds. They also stated that Jefferson's nephews Peter and Samuel Carr were the fathers of the light-skinned Monticello slaves – some thought to be Jefferson's children because they resembled him.

In 2001, the Thomas Jefferson Heritage society suggested in its April 2001 report, revised in 2011, that Jefferson's younger brother Randolph was likely to be the father of at least some of Sally Hemings' children – and it was suggested that Hemings might have had multiple partners. (2)

In 1787, when she was 14, Jefferson had Hemings accompany his young daughter Maria to Paris, where he was serving as the United States Minister to France. (3) According to accounts from Hemings' son Madison and most historians, their relationship began in France. According to her son Madison, Hemings became pregnant by Jefferson in Paris. She was about 16 at the time.

She agreed to return with him to the US, based on his promise to free their children when they reached the age of 21. (4) Under French law, Sally could have petitioned for her freedom under the 1789 revolutionary constitution in France, which abolished slavery in principle. Hemings had the legal right to remain in France as a free person. If she returned with Jefferson to the United States, it would be as a slave. (5) (6)

One thing is sure. There is a Jefferson-Hemings controversy.

I didn't study their "relationship" as I did on JFK, but I would like to quote Annette Gordon Reed in her book "Thomas Jefferson and Sally Hemings: An American Controversy," "Was Madison Hemings telling the truth when he said that Thomas Jefferson and Sally Hemings were lovers and that Jefferson promised his mother that their children would be free at 21?" Some might say definitely yes, others would say definitely no, and depending upon the time of day, I might agree with either position. What I would bet on is my belief that no fair-minded person could decide that the circumstances I have recounted amount to insufficient evidence that the story could be true or that it would be "irresponsible to believe that Madison Hemings was telling the truth." (7)

Thomas Jefferson freed all of Sally Hemings' children. Beverly and Harriet were allowed to leave Monticello in 1822, and Madison and Easton were released in Jefferson's 1826 will.

Jefferson gave freedom to no other nuclear slave family, and he did not free Sally Hemings, who was only permitted to leave Monticello by his daughter Martha Jefferson Randolph, not long after Jefferson's death in 1826.

In 1998, a DNA study that tested the Y-chromosome of direct male-line descendants of Easton Hemings, coupled with other related tests, showed a near 100% certainty that Thomas Jefferson was the biological father of Easton Hemings. Shortly after the DNA results were released in November 1998, the Thomas Jefferson Foundation formed a research committee consisting of nine Foundation staff members, including four with Ph. D.'s. In January 2000, the committee reported that the weight of all known evidence indicated a high probability that Thomas Jefferson was the father of Easton Hemings and that he was likely the father of all six of Sally Hemings' children. (7) (8)

Did Jefferson support or condemn slavery?

Some say he was an opponent of slavery all his life. Others criticize Jefferson for racism, for holding slaves and for breaking promises, as he never freed most of his slaves while remaining silent on the issue during his presidency.

I am sure Jefferson was the father of Sally Hemings' six children.

But as a founding father, the principal author at the age of 33 of the Declaration of Independence, and third president from 1801 to 1809 – perhaps the brightest of all American presidents – he was spared the harshest criticism over the Sally Hemings controversy.

Kennedy's womanizing, on the other hand, cost him precious points in different presidential rankings. His low standard of personal morality was seen as diminishing the prestige of the office or reducing his effectiveness as president.

If you apply the same standard to Jefferson, who in most polls gets maximum points on morality, then I must conclude that most scholars and historians do not think that Jefferson fathered Sally Hemings' children and that he was not a slave owner.

7.3. JFK More Than a President: A Man

I have some examples of a humane Kennedy; some critics will call it hagiographic, but so be it.

His exercise doctor Hans Kraus had an appointment with the president just before he was to give a key speech at the height of the Cuban Missile Crisis.

Kennedy walked stiffly downstairs to the Dispensary still wearing his thick television make-up, taking Kraus' hand gently, "I know, doctor, you've come a long way to take care of me, but please forgive me, tonight I simply have no time."

Kraus recalled, "I was struck that on such a momentous occasion, Kennedy took the time to personally come down to excuse himself. It only took a minute, but almost anyone else (Kraus rattled off Eisenhower, Nixon, Robert Kennedy, and Lyndon Johnson) would have sent an assistant or secretary down to say, "Get rid of this guy, this doctor, I'm busy."

The incident reinforced Kraus' respect for Kennedy. (1)

On April 28, 1961, Abraham Bolden was standing outside a men's restroom to which he'd been assigned as security when Kennedy stopped in front of him and asked who he was. Bolden told him. Kennedy then asked, "Are you a member of the Secret Service?"

"Yes, Sir," replied Bolden.

Kennedy went on, "Mr. Bolden, has there ever been a Negro member of the White House detail of the Secret Service?"

Bolden said, "No, Sir, there has not."

Kennedy asked, "Would you like to be the first?"

Bolden replied, "Yes, Sir."

Kennedy said, "I'll see you in Washington."

Bolden joined the White House Secret Service detail in June 1961 and had personal experience of John Kennedy's concern for people. Kennedy never passed Bolden without speaking to him, asking about his family in such a way that Bolden knew he meant it. (2)

Another secret service agent, Harry Gibbs, was assigned to the president-elect at Palm Beach. He didn't have time to pack any warm weather clothing, and as soon as he landed, he was directed to stand post at the left corner of the backyard on the seawall. "I was standing there in my wool suit and fedora, the sweat just pouring down my face," Harry said. The president-elect came up to him, asked his name, and asked why he was wearing a wool suit in about eighty-degree heat. Kennedy suggested moving to a different spot, under a tree, where he'd be in the shade. But what Kennedy didn't understand was that moving to a different position because you were hot or cold or wet was not an option.

Gibbs said later, "Of course I told him I couldn't do that, and then, he asked me how many agents were on the post at that time, and turned and walked into the house.

"When he came back out, he had a stack of short-sleeved golf shirts in his arms, in all different colors. He put them down on the ground and said, "Pass these out to the agents with my compliments. I think you'll do a better job of protecting me if you're not uncomfortable."

Unlike Eisenhower, who referred to the secret service as "Agent," Kennedy learned every agent's name. (3)

I have another JFK story – far from the cold, immoral, selfish Jack Kennedy portraited by some historians but never quoted in any Kennedy book.

It reveals a humane emotional JFK and should be mentioned in every Kennedy biography, hagiographic, or iconoclastic.

Ironically it's about one of my favorite actors, the genius Jerry Lewis, his involvement with the MDA (Muscular Dystrophy Association), and his world-famous telethons.

During the presidential campaign, Jerry asked Kennedy to stomp for him in Los Angeles at the Pole Lounge in the Beverly Hills Hotel. Kennedy said to Jerry, "I don't want you to stomp for me, please don't do that. I don't need you to do that, and you will just put yourself in terrible jeopardy."

Jack further said, "Yeah, but come Labor Day, every Republican will turn on you, and you'll hurt your kids."

Throughout the beginning of his presidency, they met six or seven times, the press never knew of their friendship: Jerry was often in disguise or visited at night, in Washington or Hyannis Port. "That was the way he wanted it for me. It was all for me. It had nothing to do with him," said Lewis.

One day, Jerry asked Jack Kennedy if he could organize an audience with Congress in connection with his charity work, explaining, "I've got to do that if I can borrow $500 million, I can get it back in maybe ten telethons." Kennedy said, "I could probably get you to do that. I'll do it for you but understand something. You can get on the phone right now and order a wheelchair, and it'll be delivered to that child's home tomorrow at nine in the morning. You will never have the opportunity to do that again. Congress will be your partner, and they will write a requisition, and you'll never get a wheelchair to a child. Do you want that?"

Jerry recalled later, "I said, "I think I'll continue to do it the way I'm doing it – and here we are now $1.8 billion later, and he (JFK) was right."

Jerry Lewis had never seen Jack Kennedy more emotionally touched by something someone was doing for charity than by Jerry's work with MDA. Jack Kennedy always called Jerry Lewis "The Preacher" and said, "A Jew preacher is the worst." (4)

Throughout my decades of reading about JFK, this is the "true" story that touches me the most, and I hope it will move the reader too.

7.4. Conclusion

When Pierre Salinger was asked in an Oral History interview whether Kennedy would have been a viable presidential candidate in the 1990s, he answered, "I think that in today's climate, there has been such a change in the political mentality in this country – conducting investigations into the private lives of political leaders has become a major point – that Kennedy would probably have a greater problem getting elected." (1)

This is a very Anglo-Saxon way of looking at politics that doesn't exist in European countries. The President of France has had fifty mistresses and named one of them to be prime minister. On May 7, 2017, France elected a new president, Emmanuel Macron, who is married to Brigitte Trogneux, a teacher 24 years older. He met her at the age of fifteen in 1993 as a pupil at her literature and theatre classes. She was married and had three children at that time but divorced to marry Macron. Would Americans elect a president who seduced a married woman at the age of 15 when she was 39? In the United States, that would be the scandal of the century.

Salinger was only asked once about Kennedy's private life as press secretary. A journalist said, "I am beginning to get information that Kennedy has got mistresses." Salinger gave him an answer he could not have given in the 1990s because he said he would have been thrown out as press secretary. Salinger said, "Listen, this man is the President of the United States. He works fourteen or fifteen hours a day. He has to deal with international problems. If he does that all day long and still has time to have a mistress, what the hell difference does it make?"

The journalist laughed and walked out, and that was the end of it. (1)

No honest book about John Kennedy can ignore or avoid discussing his womanizing and thus opening the door to a discussion of his character as a human being, aside from his performance as a political leader.

The problem is, of course, that these topics get us into very difficult areas with considerable speculation. That is true even of those who knew him well, never mind those who never even met the man or did so very casually. So whatever one reads or hears on these subjects has to be viewed through a most skeptical lens.

Furthermore, the biases of the author are stamped very heavily on how he or she deals with these topics. Those who like Kennedy, or any other subject of a biography, tend to brush off discussion of these matters just as those who dislike him and his politics castigate him on these grounds.

One example is constantly referenced to his "recklessness" in his sexual encounters, a value term if I ever read one, whereas the evidence is quite clear. In fact, he was very discreet in such matters, in contrast to people like Bill Clinton and Garry Hart. Be that as it may, there are many mines buried in this field for historians and the general public alike. For one thing, many people with direct knowledge of his sex life specifically and his relations with women generally are dead. The man himself, his wife, Dave Powers, Ken O'Donnell, Evelyn Lincoln and Lem Billings, for example. There are others, of course, who, seeking some limelight or other, give the impression that they know – but do they really? There are always moths who seek to demonstrate how close they were to the flame. We know JFK was a very private person, and he would hardly have trumpeted such matters to a large audience. Secondly, there are all too many women who, for whatever reason, tell stories that may or may not be true and cannot be verified, given the passage of time and people. When Dan Fenn Jr. was director of the Kennedy Library, he received numerous letters from women claiming to have borne Kennedy's child. When Judy Campbell Exner first surfaced and referred to her many contacts with Dave Powers in the White House, Powers ducked press call until he could see a picture of her, thinking that he might have known her under another name. As soon as the first pictures appeared, and he realized he had never seen the woman before, he came out with his famous quote: "The only Campbell I know is chunky vegetable soup."

Sometimes established sources, for whatever reason, get important data wrong. Again on the Exner stories, the Church Committee state that after the famous one-on-one Hoover-Kennedy interview, phone calls in the Oval Office between Kennedy and Campbell ceased. The easily verifiable fact, the telephone logs kept by Evelyn Lincoln, show that all the calls were initiated by Campbell, that Kennedy never took any of them, that they were shelving off before the Hoover visit, and they did continue after that, and JFK never took any of them.

A critical question in the case of John Kennedy is whether or not his philandering affected his professional performance as a political leader throughout his life. Acquiring hard, verifiable data on Kennedy's sex life – or Lyndon Johnson's or Nelson Rockefeller's or Franklin Roosevelt's or anyone else's – is hard enough to come by. Accurately defining someone's character is even more difficult and depends even more on what is in the eye of the beholder. And then, of course, there is the classic dilemma. How are we to reach an overall evaluation of the "character" of the great poet who is cold and even cruel to his family; the great orchestra conductor who is tyrannical with his players; the great artist who never pays bills and leaves creditors penniless; the great comedian who takes advantage of women? Given the booby traps in these areas, and especially in sorting the wheat from the chaff in the reporting of JFK's long sex life, which seems to go back to his youth (stories around Massachusetts were abundant), I am going to avoid the trap of pawing through the stories, and alleged stories, of specific particular encounters and instead concentrate my attention on some general characteristics and the relation, if any, of his sexual activities and presidential performance and then delve into the broader and more important question of JFK's character – who was he as a human being.

In 1991 Thomas C. Reeves wrote that studies show that expectations remain high as far the presidency is concerned. The presidency is venerated by Americans in all walks of life. The inhabitant of the Oval Office is supposed, at best, to reflect the highest virtues and at the very best be trustworthy. In one survey of public opinion on the president's character, 79% favored a president whose private and public life is exemplary. 62% agreed that "a president should give a perfect example for all Americans, at all times."

That some presidents have failed to maintain that standard has not changed the ideal. (2)

In 2013 Larry J. Sabato wrote that the public's tolerance of Kennedy's extramarital affairs while the president is noteworthy. Just a third of the respondents in a poll had major concerns about Kennedy's behavior, and there was essentially no difference based on age. 45% had "only miner" or "no concerns" about JFK's womanizing. As a follow-up, respondents were asked to assess how Kennedy's many extramarital affairs affected their view of him, and many drew a clear distinction between JFK the President and JFK the person.

Only 17% said, "This makes me feel more unfavorable of JFK both as a person and as president," while 44% replied, "This makes me feel unfavorable to JFK as a person, but does not affect my view of him as a president." And another 36% indicated that their view of Kennedy as both a president and a person was completely unaffected by the affairs. But a large partisan political gap emerged about JFK.

Only 19% of Democrats had major concerns about extramarital affairs, compared with 56% of Republicans. And while only 4% of Democrats felt more unfavorable towards Kennedy as a person and a president on account of his affairs, 34% of Republicans rated Kennedy lower as a result.

It's a fact that members of the press knew about JFK's extramarital affairs during his presidency but adhered to an unspoken agreement to ignore his transgressions.

By a 52- 41% margin, respondents believed we were better off in the 1960s when many of the private details of elected officials' personal lives were considered off-limits by the media. Older adults were more inclined to "strongly agree" with the former rules of coverage than younger adults, and party differences emerged on private life, reporting Democrats and independents strongly preferred the old "off-limits" press guidelines, but Republicans were almost evenly divided about which set of journalistic procedures is better. (3)

Every American will agree that they live in a very puritanical country.

Herve Alphand, the French Ambassador in Washington, wrote in his diary that the president's "desires are difficult to satisfy without raising fears of scandal and use by his political enemies. This might happen one day because he does not take sufficient precautions in this puritanical country." (4)

The French President, Salinger was referring to, was François Mitterand. As for the number of mistresses, that was a "Pierre Salinger" exaggeration, but on the Prime Minister Edith Cresson, he was right. French presidents have a reputation for having mistresses, and the French people don't care.

François Hollande, French socialist President from 2012-2017, was caught with his mistress Julie Gayet in the streets of Paris on a scooter with his helmet on.

French greatest stand-up comedian Laurent Gerra made "the helmet story" part of his one-man show, and the French public and I enjoyed it.

"Times are a-changing," sang Bob Dylan in his 1964 legendary song, and if you compare the Reeves survey to the Sabato survey – on the evidence of the 1990's polls of Kennedy's popularity – he wouldn't have had a chance to get elected in that era. But by 2010, his time would have come once again.

Some would say that Kennedy's womanizing was similar to drug and alcohol addictions, but I can assure you that addicts go through a personal hell, as I experienced it in my first marriage.

There was never any indication that Kennedy's sexual escapades made his life a personal hell, but Michael O'Brien says that Kennedy's personal life certainly affected his performance as a president.

His retention of Hoover as FBI director, for example, can partly be explained by his womanizing. But the link between Kennedy's private life and his presidential performance should not be exaggerated. He disconnected his personal life from his work. (5)

Thomas C. Reeves has a totally different opinion. He says, "His reckless liaisons with women and mobsters were irresponsible, dangerous, and demeaning to the office of the chief executive. Kennedy's personal foibles were also dangerous to the welfare of this country and the free world. Had Kennedy lived to see a second term, the realities of his lechery and his dealings with Sam Giancana might have leaked out while he was still in office, gravely damaging the presidency, and that impeachment might well have followed such public disclosure." (6)

Robert Dallek writes that the muckraking about Kennedy's private life has had no significant impact on public administration for his presidential record. (7)

Most Americans consider his health problems, sexual escapades, and dealings with Giancana to be unproven gossip that had no demonstrable effect on his official duties.

The American people elect a president and want him to be a saint, but honestly, do we ask for one moment whether we are saints ourselves?

But I have two last stories about the lies and the truths concerning JFK to demonstrate why readers should never believe all they read, always be careful and critical.

Lawrence Quirk, in his 1996 book "The Kennedys in Hollywood," tells how Joseph P. Kennedy, shortly before his stroke on December 19, 1961, offered Marilyn Monroe a million dollars just to ensure her perpetual silence about the years-long romantic sexual hanky-panky she had been indulging in with Jack.

Quirk expresses surprise that so many Kennedy insiders believe this story, with one source saying, "It's just so characteristic of Marilyn to take it." (8) But in 2011, there was a totally opposite version of the "one million dollar story." Joe desperately wanted Jack to run for a second presidential term in 1964, and he viewed Marilyn as a "walking time bomb," fearing that revelations about her relationship with Jack would destroy his son's political career. Joe called Marilyn and offered a huge financial statement which some sources put at one million dollars, "the price of silence," Joe told Jack.

Marilyn, or so it is said, agreed to make the deal.

But the negotiations lingered into the Christmas Season of 1961, and before the deal was agreed, Joe suffered a stroke! He was left sitting in a wheelchair, helpless, mute, and drooling. Marilyn would soon go to her own death, with very little money left in her checking account and her mortgage not yet paid off. (9)

The second story from Quirk is even more hilarious.

He wrote that Marilyn had become tired of being a "backstreet" woman, however famous. Quirk cited Lem Billings and Peter Lawford as confirming that by then, she had aborted JFK's child in a secret operation in the summer of 1962. (8)

Using such accounts from Lem Billings, who died in 1981, and Peter Lawford, who died in 1984, is pure defamation and libel. I doubt he would have dared to write this when both men were still alive.

There are two stories that prove that Jacqueline Kennedy was well aware of Jack's infidelities.

A French male reporter for Paris Match was taken on a tour around the White House by Mrs. Kennedy, who was a friend. The reporter later told Barbara Gamarekian that they walked into Mrs Lincoln's office and said hello to Mrs Lincoln and to Priscilla (Fiddle) Weir. Mrs. Kennedy turned to the reporter and said, "This is the girl who supposedly is sleeping with my husband" in French -and he was utterly taken aback. At any rate, Gamarekian got the story from the French correspondent who said, "What is going on here?" (10) (11) (12) (13) (14) (15)

But there is another "journalist story," this time involving an Italian named Benno (Gilbert) Graziani. According to David C. Heymann, a friend of Jackie Kennedy and a suitor of her sister, Lee Radziwill, Graziani visited the executive mansion as the guest of the first lady. While Jackie was showing him around the White House, said yellow journalist Francis Lara, she suddenly opened the door to an office in which two young women were seated. Jackie turned to the Italian journalist and said, "Those are my husband's lovers." The pair were known to the President's brother Bobby, who referred to them as Fiddle and Faddle. (16) (17) (18) (19)

Two stories, a French and an Italian one. The first Fiddle, the second Fiddle and Faddle. Two stories, but no author mentioned them both.

In his book "Reckless Youth," Nigel Hamilton wrote, "Though unremarked in the Boston Press and never later published, I was able to find the oration delivered at Faneuil Hall, July 4, 1946, published by The King & Queen Press in 1976 of which only 350 copies were printed.

Very little attention was given to the occasion by Boston newspapers of the day, and even Ted Sorensen in his compilation of the speeches, statements and writings of John F. Kennedy starts only from 1947."

It is strange, indeed, that the speech has been so neglected.

"Some Elements of the American Character" is one of the earliest works by President Kennedy, preceded only by "Why England Slept" (1940) and "As We Remember Joe" (1945), which were his first published address and his earliest political contribution.

I think it's the duty of every scholar or historian to comment on this speech in any study on John F. Kennedy because that speech went to the heart and soul of Jack Kennedy in a mix of idealism and realism. That speech proved Kennedy could have been a writer or a journalist.

In that speech, he approached four elements of the American Character – the Religious, the Idealistic, the Patriotic, and the Individualistic.

The first element he discussed was Religious morality, "Our government was founded on the essential religious idea of the integrity of the individual. Our earliest legislation was inspired by the deep religious sense. George Washington, the first president, was inspired by a deep religious sense. Lincoln, too, was inspired by this religious sense. He said, "That this nation under God, shall have no birth of freedom and that government of the people, by the people, and for the people shall not perish from the earth."

"Today, our basic religious ideas are challenged by atheism and materialism. At home in the cynical philosophy of many of our intellectuals, abroad in the doctrine of collectivism which set up the twin pillars of atheism and materialism as the official philosophical establishment of the state."

Another element was the idealism of our people, "In recent years, the existence of this element in the American character has been challenged by cynics, that American history could be reduced to an economic interpretation alone. And again, the cynics may apply the interpretation for the Civil War. The Industrial North against the Agricultural South, the struggle of the two economics.

Say what they will, it is an undeniable fact that the Northern Army of Virginia and the Army of the Potomac were inspired by devotion to the people, on the one hand, the right of secession on the other, the belief that the "Union must be preserved."

Woodrow Wilson said, "Some people call me an idealist. Well, that is the way I know. I am an American. America is the only idealistic nation in the world."

The third element is the great patriotic instinct of our people, "American patriotism was shown at the Halls of Montezuma. It was shown with Meade at Gettysburg, and it was shown by the flower of the Virginia army when Picket charged at Gettysburg. Wherever freedom has been in danger, Americans with a deep sense of patriotism have ever been willing to stand at Armageddon and strike a blow for liberty and the Lord.

The American character has been not only religious, idealistic, and patriotic, but because of these, it has been essentially individual. The right of the individual against the State has ever been one of our most cherished political principles. Conceived in Grecian thought, strengthened by Christian morality, and stamped indelibly into American political philosophy, the right of the individual against the State is the keystone of our Constitution.

Each man is free. He is free of thought. He is free of expression. He is free in worship. To us, who have been reared in the American tradition, these rights have become part of our very being. They have become so much part of our being that most of us are prone to feel that they are rights universally recognized and universally exercised. But the sad fact is that this is not true. They were dearly won for us only a few short centuries ago, and they were dearly preserved for us in the days just past. And there are large sections of the world today where these rights are denied as a matter of philosophy and as a matter of government. We cannot assume that the struggle is ended. It is never-ending. Eternal vigilance is the price of liberty. It was the price yesterday. It is the price today, and it will ever be the price.

The characteristics of the American people have ever been a deep sense of religion, a deep sense of idealism, a deep sense of patriotism, and a deep sense of individualism.

Let us not blink at the fact that the days which lie ahead of us are bitter ones. May God grant that, at some distant date, on this day, and on this platform, the orator may be able to say that these are still the great qualities of the American character and that they have prevailed."

Nigel Hamilton gave the following comment on Jack Kennedy's speech, "Listening to Jack's speech, his grandfather's heart burst with pride. Others wondered at the difference between the father, Joseph Kennedy and his son, the shy unemotional, scholarly, and sickly looking youth, who could so move his audience by his idealism." (20) (21)

I could add to this comment that Jackie, years later, would call him an idealist without illusions.

I think we have here one of Jack Kennedy's best speeches ever as a young man of 29, not written by Ted Sorensen – a speech full of idealism, passion, vigor at the beginning of his political career.

Did Kennedy's womanizing affect his presidency?

Some authors write that Republicans would have made JFK's womanizing an issue in the 1964 campaign. Why didn't they make Lyndon Johnson's womanizing a campaign issue in 1964?

For Johnson was a womanizer too. Indeed he claimed to have had "more women by accident than Kennedy had on purpose." He had a lengthy affair with Alice Glass, probably one with Madeleine Brown as well, and also had flings with countless White House secretaries. "Next to John Kennedy," writes one student of the sexual lives of chief executives, "Lyndon Johnson likely enjoyed the most active sex life of any American president." (22)

During his presidency, rumors were there, and they would have continued in his second term had he survived, but most reporters were not aware. Walter Cronkite wrote, "Certainly the Kennedy-era reporters were operating in a time almost as different from today as were the years of Lincoln or Washington. In the sixties, the Washington press, like the media elsewhere, operated on a rule of thumb regarding the morals of our public men. The rule had it that, as long as his outside activities, alcohol or sexual, did not interfere with or seriously endanger the discharge of his public duties, a man was entitled to his privacy."

Cronkite further wrote, "Yet it is interesting that none of the White House correspondents I know claimed at the time to have any evidence of John Kennedy's alleged bedroom escapades. Most will tell you today that they knew about the rumors but were never able to come up with enough evidence to go with the story."

This alibi represents a denial of responsibility for gross dereliction of the fourth estate.

Cronkite concluded, "In the light of later revelations that at least one of his lady friends had close Mafia connections, this pardon – a "right to privacy" – was a mistake. If there were news people who knew about this and failed to report it, no wonder they are too embarrassed to confess now." (23)

Steven Walts develops another theory on his philandering. He wrote, "His behavior was so reckless that it threatened not only his own personal integrity but that of his administration. Had he lived longer and won a second term as president, the odds are high that it would have erupted in scandal and threatened his leadership of the most powerful nation in the world." (24)

Mark J. White suggests that the key issue here is whether JFK's personal life was relevant to his political performance as president. It was in several ways. His appointments, specifically his retention of Hoover as director of the FBI, can only be explained by reference to his womanizing. Kennedy's philandering had been a matter of concern for the FBI for two decades. (25) (26)

Some historians seem to forget that J. Edgar Hoover was appointed as the sixth director of the bureau of investigation, the FBI's predecessor, in 1924. He was instrumental in founding the FBI in 1935, where he remained director until his death in 1972, at the age of 77.

And why would Kennedy have to fire Hoover when no president before or after him had the courage to do it?

But Mark J. White concludes on the link between Kennedy's private life and his presidential performance, though, should not be exaggerated. He disconnected his personal life from his work. He was as consistently cautious in his policymaking as he was reckless in private. He refused to send American forces to Cuba when the Bay of Pigs was failing or to deploy combat troops in Vietnam and preferred the blockade option rather than the dangerous air-strike alternative during the Cuban Missile Crisis. (27) (28)

Kennedy's womanizing history, whether a private or public matter or both, will likely remain shrouded in mystery – like the whole Kennedy legend.

Everybody can write his own "truth," which is historically impossible to prove because there is unfortunately not enough evidence in the presidential library. "He was a hard man, casually cruel," concludes Richard Reeves in his study of Kennedy, "I did not like the man who jabbed a needle into his buddy Red Fay's leg to show the pain of his own daily medical regimen." (29) (30) (31)

I disagree. Reeves lacks empathy; there's nothing cruel about that, and Red Fay certainly didn't see it that way.

Paul Fay came to Florida in January 1955. The family was worried about Jack and didn't know whether he was going to live. He flew to Palm Beach and spent ten days with Jack. During his stay, he said to Jack, "the way you take that jab, it looks like it doesn't even hurt." Before Fay had the time to dodge, he reached over and jabbed the needle into his leg. Fay screamed with the pain. "It feels the same way to me," he commented flatly. (32)

I agree with Reeves that Kennedy refused to talk for months to his friend Ben Bradlee to punish him for small criticism.

But on the whole, Reeves exaggerates because Jack Kennedy was a forgiving man who didn't harbor grievances.

John Kennedy cared for working people, not merely in the abstract, but as individuals. He was always putting himself in their shoes. He could project himself into their lives because he was by nature a worker and because he was endowed with a remarkable capacity to feel deeply – he was very empathetic. (33)

Kennedy campaign worker Hyman Raskin said that Kennedy was a genuinely good person, very interested in his associates, his friends, the people he worked with and the people that were around him. When he had the pleasure of being with him, his first question was "How are you" or "How's the law business?" or "How are you doing?" He didn't start out by asking Raskin how he, Kennedy, was doing or how the Party was doing or how the government was doing. (34)

Thomas C. Reeves has a totally different opinion of Jack Kennedy. "Beneath the surface, however, Jack was pragmatic to the point of amorality; his sole standard seemed to be political expediency. Gifted with good looks, youth and wealth (Reeves forgets Kennedy's bad health), he was often, in his personal life, reckless, vain, selfish, petty and lecherous. Jack's character, so much a reflection of his father's single-minded pursuit of political power and personal indulgence, lacked a moral center, a reference point that went beyond self-aggrandizement." (35)

The reader can choose between a genuinely good person and an amoral individual.

Jack and life-long friend LeMoyne "Lem" Billings with "Dunker" in Europe, 1937.
(Copyright: JFK Library)

June 20, 1963, President John F. Kennedy visits with National Poster children for the Muscular Dystrophy Associations of America Inc. (MDAA), with National Chairman for the MDAA comedian Jerry Lewis.
(Copyright: JFK Library)

EPILOGUE

If John Kennedy had been able to read about the myth-making, the debunking of his presidency and the revelations about his personal life, he would probably have been less than pleased. But, as an avid reader of history, he would have agreed that not all historians would approve of his policies and actions.

In writing each of my chapters, I discovered time and again a big clash between the "Camelot" historians, who saw Kennedy as a man who inspired hope for the future, and the revisionists who claim that Kennedy's presidency was more style than substance. The former still hail Kennedy as a man with a mission, an idealistic, passionate human being, a man who wanted peace and put an end to the Cold War, and who had the intention to withdraw from Vietnam. But the revisionists found him a compulsive womanizer, an amphetamine addict, a liar, a reckless, ruthless, corrupt, self-indulgent hypocrite, who only sought his own for self-aggrandizement. His elevation as martyr and pop icon, they argue, only served to obscure his failings as a man and as a president. But this view ignores the many ways in which JFK has influenced American politics in the years following his death. JFK as a president was a work in progress. He matured on the job, and, despite his relatively brief tenure, he left large footprints for those who followed. (1)

Bill Clinton and Barack Obama were inspired by both the man and his presidency. Ronald Reagan echoed and even embraced Kennedy's legacy, not merely in rhetoric but also in policy. In the heat of the 1984 presidential campaign, Republican Reagan even portrayed himself as the heir to Democrat Kennedy, accusing the modern Democratic Party of straying from JFK's policies. (2)

Historian and journalist, Theodore H. White's first impression of John Kennedy was that he was interested in personalities and viewed politics as a game. But personality led on to style, and this was where the image radiating cut through his circle of admiring staff and entranced newsmen became the public persona, the dashing, impeccably tailored, handsome Boston Irishman with the Harvard gloss. Style, to Kennedy, was very relevant to politics. Indeed, the style was the essence of personality, and personality determined the quality of leadership – and leadership was what the country needed and what he offered in the campaign of 1960. White said that Kennedy mixed laughter with pain, truth with nostalgia, the language of the street with the language of the thinking people. He was both realistic and romantic and thus harder to assess in history than almost any other American president of our time. (3)

According to author Bruce Miroff, Kennedy's objectivity limited him to facts, and his detachment divorced him from the emotional dimension of events. Whether it was a question of temperament or of intellectual choice, John F. Kennedy seemed singularly devoid of political passion. In the White House, he kept his emotional distance. (4)

Historian and presidential biographer James McGregor Burns reflected in a

December 19, 1964 "Remembrances of John F. Kennedy" on JFK's "heart" commitment.

Burns said that Kennedy felt during his presidency that he was moving steadily toward a deeper political and intellectual commitment to his program, but that he was not sure of his emotional or "heart" commitment, which upset some of his idolaters. Burns always felt that there was little emotional sentiment in him – almost a reaction against the over-sentimentality of his grandfather Honey Fitz which prevented Kennedy ever throwing himself into any cause blindly. There would always be part of him sitting back and watching with some detachment. His wit reflected this lack of passion, but Burns concluded, these may be good qualities, "It is better that a president does not allow the heart to rule the head. God knows he made enough of a commitment in the end."

Burns found JFK "one of the finest persons he had ever known, engaging, intellectually responsive, simple, direct, remarkably frank and always human." (5)

Jackie Kennedy believed that Jack had a great detachment about things because he had a great capacity to put himself in other people's positions and understand their problems – call it empathy. Maybe that's what made some people – like Burns, who never knew him – describe Kennedy as detached and questions his "heart commitment." Jackie, as well as Jack, resented the closing passage of Burns' 1960 book, "John Kennedy: A Political Profile" when Burns wrote that for Kennedy to bring passion to the presidency would need a commitment not only of mind but also of heart that, up to that time, he had never been required to make. Jackie thought he had the greatest heart when he cared, but he also had detachment. She thought he would have been the greatest courtroom judge. (6)

In an interview with Richard Snyder in 1988, Arthur M. Schlesinger Jr. said that "Kennedy was a man of high intelligence, great charm, and self-control. He had a highly retentive memory, great intellectual curiosity, and a very wide range of human concerns. His weakness was excessive activism. When we all came to Washington in 1961, we were young and ardent, and we believed that if there was a problem, there must be a remedy and that we ought to be applying remedies at once."

Schlesinger said that he thought that "there was a tendency in the first year of the Kennedy administration to react too quickly to situations. (7)

Once, when JFK was walking the White House grounds, thinking aloud, he blurted out, "A politician is a dream merchant." Then he thought a moment and added, "But he must back up that dream." (8) (9)

Kennedy was far too sophisticated to leave the creation of that dream to a chance. Projecting his character was as important to his success as deciding the right policies. His detachment allowed him to recognize how he impressed other people and how he might enhance that impression."

For Bart Lython, finance chairman of the California Democratic State Committee from 1958 to 1960, Kennedy had a sense of a mission. He related to and listened to other people, and didn't pretend to know what he did not know, "He had no hesitation in saying, "I don't understand that" or "what does this mean" or something of the sort. Some people thought he was cold. Actually, he wasn't. He was sometimes diffident, which is a quality not often associated with him." (10)

Maurice Couve de Murville, French Foreign Affairs minister (1958-1968), also thought that John F. Kennedy was a man on a mission. "He took things seriously. He believed in what he said, in what he did. In other words, he really gave the impression, although he still was very young, young in age and young in office, that he was fully aware of the enormous responsibility he had accepted. He was a very keen politician. He was what you call an "intellectual," a man who reads, who thinks, and who believes that life is more complicated than it generally appears." (11)

Paul Kirk, chairman of the Democratic National Committee (1985 to 1989), recalled that the Kennedy era "was a call to greatness – it was the country feeling young and good about itself." (12)

Herbert S. Parmet is more critical of his presidency and is convinced that Kennedy's thousand days led to the nightmare years that followed. The rage that destroyed neighborhoods and the endless search for the "light at the end of the tunnel" only resulted in an "age of disillusionment." And Jack Kennedy, to whom the torch had been passed, became the orphan of failure. At best, he was an "interim" president who had promised but not performed, said Parmet – a president who was rejected along with his era. (13)

In 2008, Ted Sorensen described in his book "Counselor" John Kennedy's administration as a golden era. Nevertheless, Sorensen saw the past more clearly now, just like James Madison writing at age seventy about his "more full and matured view" of his decades in early American politics, including his participation at the Constitutional Convention. But it was not Camelot: President Kennedy made errors, such as the Bay of Pigs. He suffered setbacks, like his failure to obtain passage of such key legislation as Medicare. He dismissed too few medicare officials, placed too much emphasis on civil defense in his first year, and too little on civil rights. He had a blind spot on Cuba and a deaf ear on China. And in his first eighteen months, he gave Vietnam too many military advisors and too little of his attention.

In Sorensen's opinion, Kennedy's determination to build a missile force so powerful that it would never be challenged or used may well have exceeded that track record – spending on those obscenely expensive but idle weapons systems countless billions of dollars that could better have been used in rebuilding American schools, hospitals, and cities. (14)

David E. Kaiser, an American history professor, said that it was Kennedy, not Lyndon Johnson, who in 1963 introduced sweeping civil rights legislation designed to deal with education, voting rights, employment, discrimination, and above all with exclusion from public accommodations. And although Johnson's unparalleled legislative skill eased the bill's passage in 1964, Kaiser is convinced that it would have passed under Kennedy as well.

For Kaiser, Kennedy remains a significant historical figure because he was, for better or for worse, the incarnation of an era, with the Peace Corps and the space program as perhaps the most appropriate symbols of his presidency. (15)

Irving Bernstein is persuaded that the Civil Rights legislation might have passed in 1964 if Kennedy had been alive. If not, then certainly in early 1965 – inside Kennedy's self-imposed 18-months deadline – along with primary and secondary education and medicare. In fact, because of the assassination and Johnson's skillful leadership, the process may have speeded up. (16)

Princess Grace of Monaco, who was befriended by Jack and Jackie, was asked in an interview for the Kennedy library if she thought that "in a sense, President Kennedy died in vain?" She answered, "Well, it might not seem so today, but I, for one, cannot believe that a man of Mr Kennedy's stature and achievements was put upon this earth for no other purpose than to stop an assassin's bullet or that the lesson will be wholly lost. It is only since the 20th century that the majesty of Abraham Lincoln has been appreciated. I believe that God allows these certain tragedies to happen in order to emphasize the man and his achievements, and to inspire those who follow to have the strength and the will to accomplish his unfulfilled dreams." (17)

Princess Grace's words, both touching and moving, are hiding some truth in them as Bill Clinton and Barack Obama represent two wonderful examples of her words and feelings on President Kennedy.

Princess Grace felt that, in addition to his peace efforts, there was still another connection she and her husband, Prince Rainier III of Monaco, felt with President Kennedy, namely his interest in the promotion of all the arts. "From the moment he became president, it seemed as though a wave of excitement ran through all of the young painters, poets, writers and musicians of the United States. Now that someone of their own age was in the White House, there was somehow a better chance for them to be seen or heard. There are some leaders who appear from time to time, who have the great gift of stimulating creative talents." (17)

But according to James N. Giglio, the Kennedy image also contains a lesser-known unflattering side. Despite his promotion of the arts, his tastes were very mundane – ballet and opera bored him, and he knew little about painting. Giglio also highlights the national security threat by his frequent sexual indiscretions, which were little known until the 1970s. And he describes the cover-up of Kennedy's numerous health problems as inexcusable, even though it had no discernible impact on his presidential performance. But Giglio also admits that, to many Americans, John Kennedy's death ended an age of excellence, innocence, hope and optimism. And unlike the deaths of other presidents, Kennedy's assassination left Americans with the image of youth and the promise of greatness, frozen in time. (18)

I have two questions for James N. Giglio. First, must a president love the arts and be a connoisseur to be able to and allowed to promote the arts?

Second, don't you think that if President Kennedy had been candid about his health problems, the public could have been very concerned and perhaps panicked to the point that it could have affected his handling of the presidency? Concerning

Kennedy's frequent "sexual indiscretions," the claim of a threat to national security is a bridge too far for me. The womanizing was indisputable, but it never threatened national security. Of course, there were the rumors, but at the time of his presidency, almost nobody knew about them. The revelations about his womanizing only started in the 1970s.

Thomas C. Reeves is a notorious iconoclast whose writing seems calculated to satisfy the Kennedy haters.

Mr Reeves's Kennedy is a man whose sole standard seemed to be political expediency. "Gifted with good looks, youth and wealth. Kennedy was often, in his personal life, reckless, vain, selfish, petty and lecherous. Jack's character lacked a moral center, a reference point that went beyond self-aggrandizement." According to Reeves, Kennedy had, like his father, a bad character and would probably have been impeached before the end of his second term.

Reeves believes that "a good character is an essential framework for the complex mixture of qualities that make an outstanding president and a model leader for a democratic people. Character is a question of values, inclinations, and judgment, all of which are brought to bear in the day-to-day work of leadership. America needs great presidents, which means that the country must find and elect people of high moral character, as well as intelligence and experience." (19) (20)

But Reeves makes claims about Kennedy's dealings with the Mafia, which are largely fiction, and never substantiated. Reeves is navigating between fact and fiction, presumably applying the criteria in judging the greatness of a man. However, a good character has never guaranteed presidential greatness. If it did, Herbert Hoover and Jimmy Carter would stand in the top five rankings of American presidents.

By definition, Reeves thinks men should be angels!

In a famous passage in the Federalist Paper no 51 of 1788, James Madison made clear he did not believe that men were inherently good. I completely agree with Madison's statement that "If men were angels, no government would be necessary. If angels were to govern men, neither external nor internal controls on government would be necessary." (21)

But in all his debunking of Kennedy's character and record, Reeves also has something positive to say about the president that, in assessing Kennedy's record as a top diplomat and commander-in-chief, it is important to acknowledge his caution as well as courage. Against the recommendations of top advisors, Kennedy dramatically limited America's role in the Bay of Pigs invasion and refused to send American troops into Laos and Vietnam. He chose not to use military force against East Germany when the Berlin Wall was being constructed. During the Cuban Missile Crisis, he did what he reasonably could to avoid an invasion of Cuba, revealing a sensitivity about nuclear war that many others in Washington and elsewhere did not share. Reeves concluded that Kennedy deserved credit for his efforts in 1963 to defuse the Cold War and achieve meaningful disarmament. The

American University speech and the Partial Test-Ban Treaty were significant achievements that signaled a measure of growth in such qualities as compassion and responsibility. (22)

Another author, Richard Reeves, described a John F. Kennedy who did not know what he was doing at the beginning, and in some ways never changed at all, particularly in a certain love for chaos, the kind that kept other men off-balance. He was intelligent, detached, curious, candid, if not always honest (name me, a politician who is always honest), and he could be careless and even dangerously disorganized. (23)

In 1977 Donald C. Lord wrote that historian William E. Leuchtenburg, who once described Kennedy's Partial Test Ban Treaty as a dynamic reversal of a post-war trend, had now concluded that Kennedy would be "swallowed up in history" within 50 years. Leuchtenburg pointed out that presidential scholar and Kennedy consultant devotee Richard Neustadt "sadly echoes this assessment." Indeed, Neustadt, speaking in the 1970s, concluded that JFK "will be just a flicker, forever clouded by the record of his successors" because history is unkind to transitory figures." (24)

But in 1988, Leuchtenburg pondered, "In 2086, when the Kennedy presidency will be a segment of fewer than three years in some three centuries of the Republic, how much space, in Neustadt's phrase, will there be for John Kennedy?"

Leuchtenburg, in a counterfactual history attempt, said that if we were compelled to hazard several guesses about what a historian in 2086 would find significant, they would include the following:

1. that Kennedy accelerated the pace of the civil rights revolution;
2. that Kennedy, under the tutelage of Walter Heller, helped gain the acceptance of the New Economics;
3. that Kennedy, after several false starts, moved American foreign policy to some degree, away from the bipolar assumptions of the Cold War; and
4. that Kennedy was the first American president to commit the United States to the massive effort necessary to put a man on the moon.

But William E. Leuchtenburg also said that John F. Kennedy had to be judged not as a shining knight nor as a failed hero but as a man of his time and place. The America which mourned John F. Kennedy in November 1963 was different – it had not been transformed, but it was better. That was Kennedy's modest and magnificent achievement. (25)

Lewis J. Paper wrote that the finality of any judgment would, in some ways, be as tenuous as a similar analysis of Abraham Lincoln if he had died after delivering the Gettysburg Address. And as with Lincoln, the tragedy of Kennedy's untimely death was that his effect on the continuum of American politics was suspended. (26)

"He was a man who could have become great or could have failed," Norman Mailer said shortly after Kennedy's death, "and now we'll never know. That's what's so awful. Tragedy is amputation, the nerves of one's memory run back to the limb which is no longer there."

In an essay published in Esquire Magazine three weeks before Kennedy's election, titled "Superman Comes to the Supermarket," Mailer depicted the campaign as the outcome of a dramatic morality play rather than as a realignment of voter preferences based on demographics and party promises. JFK was "a prince in the unstated aristocracy of the American dream," while Nixon was described as a man who was "sober, the apotheosis of opportunistic lead." Kennedy would win, Mailer predicted, because the nation was eager for change after eight dull, dispiriting years under President Dwight D. Eisenhower. Looking back many years later, Mailer said, "The country began to speed up, the sexual revolution began with Jack Kennedy, things began to open up." (27) (28)

At one of the so-called Hickory Hill seminars, this time in the yellow Oval Room at the White House, organized by Arthur Schlesinger Jr., Jack Kennedy asked Lincoln historian David Herbert Donald, "Would Lincoln have been as great a president if he'd lived? I mean, would he be judged as great – because he would have had this almost insoluble problem of the Reconstruction, which, you know, either way, you did it, would have dissatisfied so many people." That was Kennedy's question. Donald's answer was that it was better for Lincoln that he died when he did. Kennedy remembered it and recalled it with dry wit after the Cuban missile crisis, telling Jackie, "Well, if anyone's ever going to shoot me, this would be the day to do it." (29)

Alan Brinkley, in his biography on John F. Kennedy, wrote that given Kennedy's almost three years in office, his tangible accomplishments were relatively modest. By most standards by which historians assess presidents, Kennedy seems in many ways to have been a relatively minor president. And a disillusionment set in with the man himself, said Brinkley, "In an age increasingly preoccupied with the personal behavior of public figures, Kennedy's now well- known private life has disillusioned many Americans. They have seen in him a recklessness and even a moral emptiness." (30)

Conversely, Robert Dallek says that the public has other yardsticks for measuring presidential greatness, claiming that the muckraking about Kennedy's private life had no significant impact on public admiration for his presidential record. Most Americans dismissed his health problems, sexual escapades, and dealings with mobster Sam Giancana as unproven gossip that had no demonstrable effect on his official duties.

Dallek further said that the principal reason for Kennedy's popularity was his inspirational rhetoric. Substantial presidential accomplishment seems to have less of a hold on Americans than on memorable presidential language in public addresses. (31) (32)

Nevertheless, Garry Wills claims that the pursuit of style as if it were substance leeches vitality from the style itself, "The Kennedy rhetoric just sounds flashy now." (33)

It is up to the iconoclasts to prove Kennedy's dealings with the mafia. They will have difficulty finding reliable witnesses, not those used by Seymour Hersh and others. And if they do their investigation correctly, they will come to the conclusion that the "Giancana dealings" are not substantiated and are pure gossip.

In 2009 American adults participating in an opinion poll supervised by Peter Hart and Geoff Garin reflected the public's tolerant view of Kennedy's extramarital affairs while president, only a third of the respondents had major concerns about Kennedy's behavior, and there was no difference based on age, while 45% had "only minor" or "no concerns" about JFK's womanizing. As a follow-up, respondents were asked to assess how Kennedy's many extramarital affairs affected their view of him as president and as a person. Only 17% opted for the sentence "This makes me feel unfavorable to JFK, both as a person, and as a president," while 44% ticked the box beside the words, "This makes me feel more unfavorable to JFK as a person, but does not affect my view of him as a president." And another 36% said their view of Kennedy as both a president and a person was completely unaffected by his affairs. By a 59%-41% margin, respondents believed people were better off in the 1960s when many of the private details of elected officials' personal lives were considered off-limits by the media. Older adults were more inclined to "strongly agree" with the old rules than younger adults. (34)

Every Democratic candidate for president since JFK has been analyzed through the lens of Kennedy. Bill Clinton and Barack Obama each ran for the White House as the semi-official new Kennedy. This identification worked well on the campaign trail but less well in office since the press and public eventually discovered that Clinton and Obama were not Kennedy.

On the day before he was inaugurated on January 19, 1993, President-elect Bill Clinton made a pilgrimage to the Kennedy graveside guarded by the eternal flame in Arlington, Virginia, where he knelt, bowed his head, bit his lip, and left a single white rose. Hardly a press briefing passes in which President Clinton, who met President Kennedy as a teenager on the White House lawn, fails to make reference to the man he credits with influencing his decision to pursue a career in politics. (35) (36)

W.J. Rorabaugh ponders that it is unclear just how much about the early sixties John Kennedy understood, although he certainly both expressed and helped sustain the idea that it was a promising time. Like most politicians, he was often vague, and when talking, he preferred to give questions rather than answers, to offer wit rather than conclusions. Or he obfuscated by reciting information. Perhaps the tendency towards witty questioning marks Kennedy as an appropriate symbol for the early sixties, a time caught between the truths of traditional society and those of the postmodern age. (37)

Peter Foster considered the Cuban Missile Crisis, on some subsequent readings of history, was not a triumph of bold statesmanship as it was hailed at the time, but a piece of foolhardy grandstanding that unnecessarily humiliated the Soviets and precipitated the arms race that defined the Cold War. (38)

During the Cuban Missile Crisis, Jack Kennedy did everything possible not to humiliate Chairman Khrushchev, as they respected each other as adversaries. Kennedy's empathy was much too great even to consider humiliating his Soviet counterpart.

Michael O'Brien said that because of Kennedy, Americans re-examined religious bigotry, poverty, racial discrimination, and selfish corporate power. Economic growth averaged 5.6% per year during his presidency, unemployment fell, and inflation amounted to only 1.3%. His administration was also remarkably free from financial scandal and incompetence. (39)

During the Eisenhower presidency, unemployment rose from 2.9% in January 1953 to 6.6% in December 1960. In November 1963 it was at 5.7%.

In 1964, when I was a teenager, I was convinced in my youthful enthusiasm that JFK's assassination was a conspiracy because I thought Jack Kennedy being killed by Oswald alone diminished the meaning of his death. With the conspiracy by the Russians, Fidel Castro, the FBI, the CIA, the Mob, the Mossad and even Lyndon Johnson, he would have died for a cause, wanting equality for the black people or wanting to withdraw from Vietnam.

However, my good friend Dan H. Fenn Jr. always told me Lee Harvey Oswald acted alone, but I did not believe him. Priscilla Johnson McMillan, who was the only person who knew both Kennedy and Oswald – she worked for Kennedy in 1953 – was also convinced that Oswald acted alone. She befriended Marina Oswald in 1964, and the two spent considerable time together, resulting in McMillan writing an article for the Boston Globe describing Lee Harvey Oswald as a classic example of an "embittered psychological loner." She added, "I soon came to feel that this boy was of the stuff of which fanatics are made." (40)

This view is supported by Attorney Vincent Bugliosi, who argued in his 1,518 pages counting book "Reclaiming History: The assassination of John F. Kennedy," in favor of the accuracy of the Warren Commission's conclusion that Lee Harvey Oswald acted alone in shooting Kennedy. (41)

Hundreds of books have been written on the assassination. It was and remains a profitable industry for conspiracy theorists. Conspiracy theories still sell better than books establishing the truth that Oswald acted alone, a fact of which I am now convinced.

JFK will always be remembered for standing up to the Soviets during the Cuban Missile Crisis, for proposing the legislation that became the Civil Rights Act, for the Partial Test Ban Treaty – albeit a first step – and for the launching of the Space program for which he will still be remembered in a thousand years from now – not forgetting his American University speech – my absolute favorite – which will go down in history as a quest for world peace. And the Peace Corps, a pure example of Kennedy's capacity to inspire young people, then and now, will serve his memory eternally.

The Peace Corps was established in a "Special Message" to Congress on March 1,

1961, in which Kennedy said, "Peace Corps members will often serve under primitive conditions among the people of developing nations. For every Peace Corps member service will mean a great financial sacrifice." (42)

Sargent Shriver, Kennedy's brother-in-law, his sister Eunice's husband, became the first director of the Peace Corps.

President Jimmy Carter's mother, in 1966, at the age of 68, applied to join the Peace Corps. After completing a psychiatric evaluation, she did three months of training and was sent to India to work at the Godrej Colony 30 miles from Mumbai. President Carter, who received the Nobel Peace Prize in 2002, and who was the main speaker at the dedication of the JFK library in 1979, felt Jack Kennedy's death as the greatest blow that he had suffered since his father died. It was a great source of pride to President Carter, whenever be compared in any way with JFK. (43)

A young volunteer in Africa wrote shortly after Kennedy's death, "Being in the Peace Corps, we all here felt, we had a special attachment to him. Hell, most of us felt we were working for him and would refer to him as Jack as if he were a Peace Corps volunteer." (44)

Almost all historians forget JFK's commitment to people with intellectual disabilities, frequently referred to in the past as "mental retardation," people on the wrong side of society, neglected and forgotten. His support was at the urging of his sister Eunice Kennedy Shriver, an exceptional human being – Eunice was extremely bright, courageous and socially engaged and could well have been the first female president of the United States if she had lived in the 21 century. Also, the foundation of the President's Committee on Mental Retardation was established in October 1961 by President Kennedy, consisting of distinguished Americans, led by Chairman Leonard Mayo. They launched a plan to respond to the president's charge to review the status of programs for persons with mental retardation. Eunice Kennedy Shriver served as a consultant and liaised between the panel and the White House, and in the spring of 1962, Eunice told JFK she wanted to write a piece for the Saturday Evening Post about Rosemary Kennedy, their mentally retarded sister. JFK replied, "That's fine. Let me see it first." The article appeared in the September 22 issue, and it was one of the biggest moments in perhaps the most important contribution the Kennedys made to the nation. (45)

What is truly stunning about the Kennedys and, most particularly, Eunice Kennedy Shriver's role in changing the way the world treated mentally retarded people is how little noticed it has been. John Kennedy made intellectual disabilities a priority for his new administration.

On October 24, 1963, President Kennedy signed the Maternal and Child Health and Mental Retardation Planning Amendments to the Social Security Act, the first major legislation to contest mental illness and intellectual disabilities in the United States. Furthermore, in 1968, Eunice Kennedy Shriver founded the Special Olympics, an organization dedicated to celebrating and accepting people with intellectual disabilities as athletes. I happen to have a dear friend who is a lawyer, Lawrence

Verhelst, who did quite a lot of legal pro bono work for the Special Olympics, which were being held in Antwerp, Belgium, in 2014.

Senator Mike Mansfield, the Democratic Senate Majority Leader during JFK's presidency, said one of the major achievements of the Kennedy administration was to help tackle mentally retarded and mentally ill. (46)

As President Kennedy said, "mental retardation ranks with mental health as a major problem in this country. It strikes our most precious asset, our children."

Almost 61 years after JFK became president through his inspirational rhetoric, he is still considered a president with idealistic ideas who created hope and appealed to the youth – even 59 years after his death. There are, of course, his tantalizing "might have been," but he left large footprints for presidents to come, and there is no sign that Kennedy's hold on Americans is anywhere in retreat. Yet many people saw him, and still do, as an idealistic and passionate president who would have transformed the nation, and the world had he lived. He reminded many Americans of an age when it was possible to believe that politics could speak to society's moral yearnings, and he harnessed to its highest aspirations. After thoroughly studying John F. Kennedy's presidency for the past few decades, I think he left America better than he found it. Americans said that they felt good, great and happy during his presidency, which is a wonderful compliment and accomplishment attributed to JFK. Almost 61 years after he came to power, I think his legacy is still a work in progress, and his influence continues. His cult of personality is as strong today as in the 1960s, a golden age when people felt good about themselves, the baby-boomer generation.

Apart from the Moon landing project, the handling of the Cuban Missile Crisis, JFK's Peace Corps, and the Alliance for Progress, the changes wrought by Eunice Kennedy Shriver on Mental Retardation have a big place in John F. Kennedy's legacy.

John F. Kennedy in the Polls – Some Statistics

For some historians, Kennedy's reputation may have declined, but 58 years after his death, he is still extremely popular with the public. A few interesting statistics follow below for the reader's consideration.

In 1975, when a Gallup poll asked Americans whom they considered their greatest president, Kennedy was rated highest with 52% ahead of Lincoln and FDR. Ten years later, in 1985, Kennedy remained number one with a backing of 56%.

In 1982, two thousand scholars were asked to categorize American presidents as great, near-great, above average, average, below average, or failure. Kennedy ranked as number 13, in the middle of the "above-average" group.

In 1988, 75 historians and journalists described JFK as "the most overrated public figure in American history."

In 1991, after a period of Kennedy debunking, Abraham Lincoln overtook him in a new popularity poll, but only just – by 40% to 39%.

In 1996, a New York Times/CBS poll asked Americans which of all presidents they would choose to run the country today. The majority answer was John F. Kennedy. More recent polls confirm Kennedy's continued popularity. Like the martyred Lincoln, Kennedy has become the property of the whole nation and both political parties.

In 1997 in the book "Rating the Presidents," US leaders were ranked from the great and honorable to the dishonest and incompetent. The poll consisted of four parts, the most important being quality ratings, based on five categories; Leadership qualities, Accomplishments and Crisis management, Political skill, Appointments, and Character and Integrity.

John Kennedy's overall ranking was 15th. And in the five categories – leadership qualities, 8th, Accomplishments and Crisis management, 16th, Political skill, 10th, Appointments, 7th, Character and integrity, 34th.

In February 1999, a Gallup poll declared Lincoln the greatest of our presidents, with Washington, JFK, Ronald Reagan and Bill Clinton tied for second.

In 2000, in a study, "The American Presidents Ranked by Performance by Charles F. Faben and Richard B. Faber, John F. Kennedy was ranked overall in eighth place. His rankings in policy sectors were, Foreign Relations: 12th (tied); Domestic Programs: 7th (tied); Administration: 4th (tied); Leadership: 11th (tied); Personal Qualities: 12th (tied).

In a 2000 Gallup poll, Kennedy topped the list, followed by Lincoln, FDR and Reagan.

In 2001, stories about Reagan's 90th birthday propelled him to the top spot, with Kennedy second and Lincoln third.

In October 2000, a survey of 78 scholars in history, politics and law, which gave considerable weight to length of presidential service, ranked Kennedy 18th, at the bottom of the "above-average" category.

According to a Rasmussen poll conducted **in 2007**, six presidents were rated favorably by at least 80% of Americans:

1. George Washington   94%
2. Abraham Lincoln   92%
3. Thomas Jefferson   89%
4. Theodore Roosevelt   84%
5. Franklin D. Roosevelt 81%
6. John F. Kennedy   80%

In 2009, American adults participating in an opinion poll, supervised by Peter Hart and Geoff Garin, were asked to rate all the presidents from Dwight Eisenhower to Bill Clinton on a scale from 0 to 10.

John F. Kennedy was the most highly rated by a considerable margin, followed by Ronald Reagan, Dwight Eisenhower and Bill Clinton. John F. Kennedy got a 7.6 rating, Reagan 6.9, Eisenhower 6.8, Clinton 6.7, Ford 5, H.W. Bush 4.9, Johnson 4.9, Carter 4.6, and Nixon 3.7.

In 2010, a Gallup poll demonstrated how remarkably well-regarded Kennedy has been over the past 50 years. As recently as 2010, 85% said they approved of the way Kennedy handled his job as president, the highest retrospective job approval rating of any president measured, and his posthumous approval rating fell no lower than 76% in Gallup polls from 1990 to 2010.

February 2-5, 2011, a Gallop poll about presidential greatness asked 1015 adults in the US, "Who do you regard as the greatest United States president?"

1. Ronald Reagan   (19%)
2. Abraham Lincoln   (14%)
3. Bill Clinton   (13%)
4. John F. Kennedy   (11%)

On **February 18-19, 2011,** a Vision Critical / Angus Reid poll asked respondents whether they considered each of the last 11 US presidents, plus the current president, to be good or bad. John F. Kennedy came in first with 80% approval and 6% disapproval.

In a Public Policy Polling poll taken between September 8-11, 2011, a total of 665 American voters were asked whether, based on what they know or remember about the nine most recent former presidents, from Kennedy to George W. Bush, they held favorable or unfavorable views of how each handled his job in the office. John F. Kennedy came in first with 74% favorability and 15% unfavorability.

A Gallup poll based on telephone interviews on **November 7-10, 2013,** with a random sample of 1039 adults, aged 18 and over, living in all 50 US States and the District of Columbia, asked the following question, "How do you think each of the following presidents will go down in history, as an outstanding president, average, below-average or poor?" **From Eisenhower to Barack Obama.**

	Outstanding	Above Average	Poor
1. John F. Kennedy	74%	19%	3%
2. Ronald Reagan	61%	27%	10%
3. Bill Clinton	55%	29%	15%
4. Dwight Eisenhower	49%	36%	3%
5. Barack Obama	28%	31%	40%
6. George H.W. Bush	27%	48%	22%
7. Jimmy Carter	23%	37%	35%
8. George W. Bush	21%	36%	43%
9. Lyndon Johnson	20%	46%	22%
10. Gerald Ford	16%	56%	20%
11. Richard Nixon	15%	27%	52%

November 7-10, 2013 Job Approval Average for US presidents "Entire Time in Office." From Eisenhower to Obama.

1. Kennedy 70%

A Quinnipiac University poll, taken June 24-30, 2014, asked 1.446 registered voters in the United States who they thought were the best presidents since World War II.
3. John F. Kennedy (15%)

Four years later, January 20-25, 2017, the Quinnipiac poll asked 1.190 voters in the United States who they thought were the best presidents since World War II.
3. John F. Kennedy (12%)

On March 3-5, 2018, the Quinnipiac poll asked 1.122 voters in the United States who they thought were the best presidents since World War II.
3. John F. Kennedy (tie) (10%)
3. Bill Clinton (tie) (10%)

In a 2017 C-Span Presidential Historians Survey, John F. Kennedy's total scores. Overall Rank was in

2000 Total scores 704	Overall Rank	8
2009 Total scores 701	Overall Rank	6
2017 Total scores 722	Overall Rank	8

	18 to 29%	30 to 49%	50 to 64%	65 +%
Outstanding/Above Average	83	71	77	67
Average	12	18	18	26
Below Average/Poor	3	3	3	4

C-Span Presidential Historian Survey 2017

Presidential Job approval ratings following the first 100 days
From Eisenhower to Trump.

	Approval	Disapproval
1953 (April 19-24) Dwight D. Eisenhower	73	10
1961 (April 28-May 3) John F. Kennedy	83	5
1969 (May 1-6) Richard Nixon	62	15
1977 (April 29-May 2) Jimmy Carter	63	12
1981 (May 8-11) Ronald Reagan	68	21
1989 (May 4-7) George Bush	56	22
1993 (April 22-24) William J. Clinton	55	37
2001 (April 20-23) George W. Bush	62	29
2009 (April 21-30) Barack Obama	65	29

A 2017 Morning consult poll, taken February 9-10, asked 1,791 registered voters in the United States who they thought were the best presidents since World War II.
1. Ronald Reagan (26%)
2. Barack Obama (20%)
3. John F. Kennedy (17%)

In a Potus Poll, February 19, 2017, "The best US presidents, as ranked by presidential historians.

	2000	2009	2017
John F. Kennedy	8	6	8

In a poll originally by Ranker Community, updated September 20, 2019, they ranked the Greatest U.S. Presidents of All Time:
1. Abraham Lincoln
2. George Washington
3. Thomas Jeffersons
4. Theodore Roosevelt
5. Franklin D. Roosevelt
6. John F. Kennedy

Abraham Lincoln, Franklin D. Roosevelt and George Washington are most often the three highest-rated presidents among historians. The remaining places in the top ten are often rounded out by Theodore Roosevelt, Thomas Jefferson, Harry S. Truman, Woodrow Wilson, Dwight D. Eisenhower, Andrew Jackson and John F. Kennedy.
These polls I mentioned speak for themselves. Kennedy's popularity with the public, especially with the youth, remains untouched in almost sixty years. Although I respect the historians' evaluation of JFK, there is an old saying in soccer that the supporter of the soccer team is always right. This is also applicable to Kennedy's support from the public too. (47) (48) (49) (50) (51) (52) (53) (54)

16-year-old Bill Clinton meets with President Kennedy in The Rose Garden of the White House, July 24, 1963
(Copyright: Getty images)

JFK signs the Peace Corps Act into law on September 22, 1961. Sargent Shriver, the Corps' first director is at the far left, senator Hubert Humprey standing next to Kennedy, had been the first to propose the idea.
(Copyright: JFK Library)

Commencement Address at American University in Washington, June 10, 1963.
The President spoke at the John M. Reeves Athletic Field on the campus of
American University after being awarded an honory degree of doctor of laws.
(Copyright: JFK Library)

Edwin Schlossberg, Caroline Kennedy, President Barack Obama and Michelle Obama at the 2017 Profile in Courage Award Ceremony, May 7, 2017 (Copyright: John F. Kennedy Library Foundation)

On October 24, 1963, President John F. Kennedy distributes pens at the signing of the Mental Retardation Facilities and Community Mental Health Center Construction Act, 10.00 a.m. President John F. Kennedy (back to camera) hands a pen to Eunice Kennedy-Shriver, consultant to the President's Panel on Mental Retardation.
(Copyright: JFK Library)

*May 24, 1961. Visit of guests Price Rainier III and Princess Grace of Monaco
(actress Grace Kelly) North Portico, White House, Washington D.C.
(Copyright: JFK Library)*

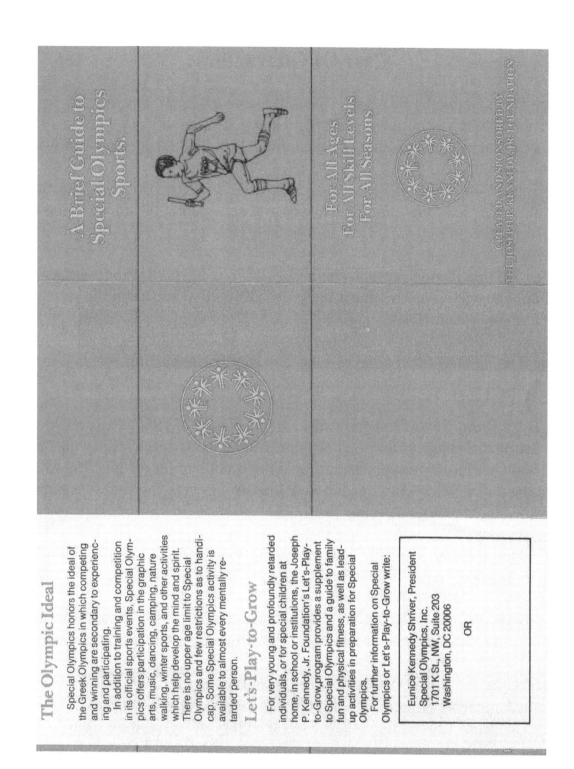

The Olympic Ideal

Special Olympics honors the ideal of the Greek Olympics in which competing and winning are secondary to experiencing and participating.

In addition to training and competition in its official sports events, Special Olympics offers participation in the graphic arts, music, dancing, camping, nature walking, winter sports, and other activities which help develop the mind and spirit. There is no upper age limit to Special Olympics and few restrictions as to handicap. Some Special Olympics activity is available to almost every mentally retarded person.

Let's-Play-to-Grow

For very young and profoundly retarded individuals, or for special children at home, in school or institutions, the Joseph P. Kennedy, Jr. Foundation's Let's-Play-to-Grow program provides a supplement to Special Olympics and a guide to family fun and physical fitness, as well as lead-up activities in preparation for Special Olympics.

For further information on Special Olympics or Let's-Play-to-Grow write:

Eunice Kennedy Shriver, President
Special Olympics, Inc.
1701 K St., NW, Suite 203
Washington, DC 20006

OR

A Brief Guide to Special Olympics Sports.

For All Ages
For All Skill Levels
For All Seasons

CREATED AND SPONSORED BY
THE JOSEPH P. KENNEDY, JR. FOUNDATION

*Eunice Kennedy Shriver, founder of Special Olympics, August 2, 1968.
(Copyright: private collection of Eddy Neyts)*

Cast Of Characters

<u>Acheson Dean Gooderham</u> (April 11, 1893 –October 12, 1971) was a US Secretary of State in the administration of President Henry S. Truman from 1949 to 1953. He played a central role in defining American foreign policy during the Cold War.

<u>Adams John</u> (October 30, 1735 – July 4, 1826) was an American statesman, attorney diplomat, writer and Founding Father, who was the second president of the United States, serving from March 4, 1797 to March 4, 1801.

<u>Adenauer Konrad Herman Joseph</u> (January 5, 1876 – April 19, 1967) was a German statesman who served as the first Chancellor of the Federal Republic of Germany (West Germany) from 1949 to 1963.

<u>Addison Thomas</u> (April 2, 1793 – June 29, 1860) was an English physician and scientist. He discovered Addison disease and Addison's anemia.

<u>Aldrin Buzz</u> (born Edwin Eugene Aldrin Jr.) (January 2, 1930 –) is an American former astronaut, engineer and fighter pilot. Aldrin made three spacewalks as pilot of the 1966 Gemini 12 mission, and as the lunar module pilot on the 1969 Apollo 11 mission, he and mission commander Neil Armstrong were the first two humans to land on the moon.

<u>Alphand Herve</u> (May 31, 1907 – January 13, 1994) was a French diplomat and French ambassador to the United States from 1956 to 1965.

<u>Alsop Joseph Wright</u> (October 10, 1910 – August 28, 1989) was an American journalist and syndicated newspaper columnist from the 1930s through the 1970s.

<u>Anderson Clinton Presba</u> (October 23, 1895 – November 11, 1975) was an American politician. A member of the Democratic Party, he served as US representative from New Mexico from 1941 until 1945, the US secretary of Agriculture from 1945 until 1948, and as a US Senator from New Mexico from 1949 to 1973.

<u>Anderson Rudolf Jr.</u> (September 15, 1927 – October 27, 1962) was a pilot and commissioned officer in the United States Air Force and the first recipient of the Air Force Cross, the US Air Force's second-highest award for heroism. The only person killed by enemy fire during the Cuban Missile Crisis.

<u>Arvad Inga Marie Petersen</u> (October 6, 1913 – December 12, 1973) was a journalist from Denmark, later a US citizen noted for being a guest of Adolf Hitler at the 1936 Summer Olympics and for her romantic relationship with John F. Kennedy during

1941 and 1942.

Attwood William Hollingsworth (July 14, 1919 – April 15, 1989) was an American journalist, author, editor and diplomat. Early in his presidency, President Kennedy appointed Attwood to serve as the 2nd United States Ambassador to Guinea from April 26, 1961, till May 27, 1963.

Auchincloss Hugh Dudley Jr. (August 15, 1897 – November 20, 1976) was an American stockbroker and lawyer who became the second husband of Nina S. Gore, mother of Gore Vidal, and also the second husband of Janet Lee Bouvier, mother of First Lady Jacqueline Kennedy Onassis and Caroline Lee Bouvier.

Auchincloss Hugh D. "Yousha" III (1927 – 2015) was the step-brother of Jacqueline Kennedy Onassis. He was the son of Hugh Dudley Auchincloss Jr., a stockbroker and lawyer who married Nina Gore, the mother of Gore Vidal.

Auchincloss James Lee (March 1947 –) is Jackie's half-brother.

Auchincloss Janet Norton Lee, formerly Bouvier (December 3, 1907 – July 22, 1989), was an American socialite and mother of the former First Lady Jacqueline Kennedy.

Auchincloss Nina Gore Straight (formerly Steers) (January 10, 1937 –) is an American author, journalist and socialite. She is the mother of writer/director Burr Steers and artist Hugh Auchincloss Steers, half-sister of Gore Vidal, step-sister of First Lady Jacqueline Kennedy and socialite Lee Radziwill.

Baker Robert Gene (November 12, 1928 – November 12, 2017) was an American political advisor to Lyndon B. Johnson and an organizer for the Democratic Party. He became the Senate's Secretary to the Majority Leader. In 1963, he resigned during an investigation by the Democratic-controlled Senate into Baker's business and political activities. The investigation included allegations of bribery and arranging sexual favors in exchange for Congressional votes and government contracts.

Baldwin James Arthur (August 2, 1924 – December 1, 1987) was an American novelist, playwright, essayist, poet and activist.

Ball George Wildman (December 21, 1909 – May 26, 1994) was an American diplomat and banker. He served in the management of the US State Department from 1961 to 1966 and is remembered most as the only major dissenter against the escalation of the Vietnam War.

Ball Lucille Désirée (August 6, 1911 – April 26, 1989) was an American actress, comedian, model, studio executive and producer. As one of Hollywood's greatest icons, she was the star and producer of sitcoms: I Love Lucy, The Lucy Show, Here's Lucy, and Life with Lucy, as well as comedy television specials aired under the title: the Lucy-Desi Comedy Hour.

Bartlett Charles Leffingwell (August 14, 1921 – February 17, 2017) was an American journalist who won the 1956 Pulitzer Prize for National Reporting for his original disclosures that led to the resignation of Harold E. Talbott as Secretary of the Air Force.

Beck David Daniel (June 16, 1894 – December 26, 1993) was an American labor leader and president of the International Brotherhood of Teamsters from 1952 to 1975 and was one of the most powerful labor leaders of the time.

Belafonte Harry, born Harold George Bellanfanti, Jr. (March 1, 1927 –), is a Jamaican-American singer, songwriter, activist and actor.

Bell David Elliot (January 19, 1919 – September 6, 2000) was a director of the US Office of Management and budget from January 22, 1961, until December 20, 1962, under President John F. Kennedy.

Berlin Sir Isaiah (June 6, 1909 – November 5, 1997) was a Latvian-born British social and political theorist, philosopher and historian of ideas.

Bernstein Leonard (August 25, 1918 – October 14, 1990) was an American composer, conductor, pianist, music educator, author, and lifelong humanitarian. He was one of the most significant American cultural personalities of the 20th century.

Bessette Carolyn Jeanne Kennedy (January 7, 1966 – July 16, 1999) was a publicist for Calvin Klein and the wife of John F. Kennedy Jr. The couple and Bessette-Kennedy's older sister Lauren died in a plane crash off the coast of Martha's Vineyard July 16, 1999.

Billings Kirk LeMoyne "Lem" (April 15, 1916 – May 28, 1981) was a close and longtime friend of President John F. Kennedy and the Kennedy family. Billings was a prep school roommate of Kennedy, an usher at his wedding and a campaigner for his successful 1960 presidential bid. Joseph Kennedy Sr. called him "my second son," and he sometimes acted as escort for several of the Kennedy women.

Bissell Richard Mervin Jr. (September 18, 1909 – February 7, 1994) was a Central

Intelligence Agency officer responsible for major projects such as the U-2 spy plans and the Bay of Pigs invasion.

Blair James Thomas. Jr. (March 15, 1902 – July 12, 1962) was an American Democratic politician from the state of Missouri. He was the 35th lieutenant Governor of Missouri from 1949 to 1957 and the 44th Governor of Missouri from 1957 to 1961.

Block Joseph Leopold (October 6, 1902 – November 17, 1992) was the chief executive of the Inland Steel Compay in the 1950s and 60s and a prominent Chicago civic leader for more than five decades.

Blough Roger M. (January 19, 1904 – October 8, 1985) was the chairman of the board and chief executive of the US Steel Corporation for 13 ½ years from May 1955 through January 1969.

Boggs Thomas Hale Sr. (February 15, 1914 – disappeared October 16, 1972) was an American Democratic politician and a member of the US House of Representatives from New Orleans, Louisiana. He was the House Majority Leader and a member of the Warren Commission.

Bolden Abraham W. (January 19, 1935 –) is a former the United States Secret Service Agent – the first African-American Secret Service agent assigned to the Presidential Protection Division – appointed by John F. Kennedy in 1961.

Bolshakov Georgi (1922 – 1989) was a Soviet GRU officer under journalist cover who was posted to Washington DC twice, most significantly in the early 1960s. In this capacity, he played a major role in diplomacy between the United States and the Soviet Union during the beginning of the John F. Kennedy administration.

Bouvier John Vernou III (May 19, 1891 – August 3, 1957) was an American Wall Street stockbroker and socialite. He was the father of First Lady Jacqueline Kennedy Onassis and was the father-in-law of John F. Kennedy. His nickname "Black Jack" referred to his perpetually dark-tanned skin and his flamboyant lifestyle.

Bowles Chester Bliss (April 5, 1901 – May 25, 1986) was an American diplomat and ambassador, Governor of Connecticut, Congressman, and co-founder of a major advertising agency, Benton & Bowles, now part of Publicis Groupe. He served as a foreign policy advisor to Adlai Stevenson and John F. Kennedy. His reward was Undersecretary of State from January 25, 1961, to December 3, 1961.

Bradlee Antoinette "Tony" Pinochet (January 15, 1924 – November 9, 2011) was the wife of Washington Post executive editor Ben Bradlee.

Bradlee Benjamin Crowninshield (August 26, 1921 – October 21, 2014) was one of the most prominent journalists of post-World War in America, serving first as managing editor, then as executive editor of the Washington Post from 1965 to 1991. He became a public figure when he joined the New York Times in publishing the Pentagon Papers and gave the go-ahead for the paper's extensive coverage of the Watergate scandal. Bradlee became close friends with then-senator John F. Kennedy, who had graduated from Harvard two years before Bradlee, and lived nearby.

Brinkley David McCLure (July 10, 1920 – June 11, 2003) was an American newscaster for NBC and ABC in a career lasting from 1943 to 1997.

Bulkeley John Duncan (August 19, 1911 – April 6, 1996) was vice-admiral in United States Navy and was one of its most decorated naval officers. He received the Medal of Honor for actions in the Pacific Theater during World War II.

Bundy McGeorge "Mac" (March 30, 1919 – September 16, 1996) was an American academic who served as United States National Security Advisor to Presidents John F. Kennedy and Lyndon B. Johnson from January 20, 1961 through February 28, 1966.

Camus Albert (November 7, 1913 – January 4, 1960) was a French philosopher, author and journalist. He won the Nobel Prize in Literature and, at the age of 44 in 1957, the second-youngest recipient in history. He died in a car accident.

Cannon James M. (February 26, 1918 – September 15, 2011) was a historian, author and former Assistant to the President of the United States for Foreign Affairs during the Gerald Ford administration.

Carter James Earl Jr. (October 1, 1924 –) is an American politician and philanthropist who served as the 39th president of the United States from January 20, 1977, to January 20, 1981. A member of the Democratic Party, he previously served as a Georgian State Senator from 1963 to 1967 and as the 76th governor of Georgia from 1971 to 1975. In 2002, he was awarded the Nobel Peace Prize for his work in co-founding the Carter Center.

Carter Rosalyn (August 18, 1927) is an American who served as first lady of the United States from 1977 to 1981 as the wife of President Jimmy Carter.

Castro Fidel Alejandro Ruz (August 13, 1926 – November 25, 2016) was a Cuban revolutionary and politician who served as Prime Minister from 1959 to 1976 and

President from December 2, 1976, to February 24, 2008.

Castro Raul Modesto (June 3, 1931) is a Cuban retired politician and general who served as the first secretary of the Communist Party of Cuba, the most senior position in the one-party communist state from 2011 to 2021, succeeding his brother Fidel Castro.

Chafin Raymond (January 29, 1917 – March 21, 2008) was a free-wheeling political "boss" from Logan County, West Virginia, who managed political machinery for the elections of several state governors, US senators and in 1960, for John F. Kennedy.

Chaplin Sir Charles Spencer KBE (April 16, 1889 – December 25, 1977) was an English comic actor, filmmaker, and composer who rose to fame in the era of silent films. His career spanned more than 75 years, from childhood in the Victorian era until a year before his death in 1977, and encompassed both adulation and controversy.

"Che" Ernesto Guevara (June 14, 1928 – October 9, 1967) was an Argentine Marxist, revolutionary, physician, author, guerrilla leader, diplomat, and military theorist. A major figure of the Cuban Revolution, his stylized image has become a ubiquitous countercultural symbol of rebellion and global insignia in popular culture.

Chirac Jacques René (November 29, 1932 – September 26, 2019) was a French politician who served as President of France from May 17, 1995, to May 16, 2007. Chirac was previously the Prime Minister of France from 1974 to 1976 and from 1986 to 1988, as well as Mayor of Paris from 1977 to 1995.

Chomsky Noam (December 7, 1928 –) is an American linguist, philosopher, cognitive scientist, historian, social critic and political activist.

Churchill Sir Winston Leonard Spencer (November 30, 1874 – January 24, 1965) was a British statesman, army officer and writer. He joined the British Army in 1895. He was Prime Minister of the United Kingdom twice, once during World War II and again in the early 1950s. He won the Nobel Prize in literature in 1953.

Ciano Gian Galeazzo (March 18, 1903 – January 11, 1944) was an Italian diplomat and politician who served as Foreign Minister in the government of his father-in-law, Benito Mussolini, 1936 to 1943. During this period, he was widely seen as Mussolini's most probable successor as Duce.

Clark Joseph Sill. Jr. (October 21, 1901 – January 12, 1990) was an American author, lawyer and politician. A member of the Democratic Party, he served as the 116th

Mayor of Philadelphia from 1952 to 1956 and as a US Senator from Pennsylvania from 1957 to 1969.

Clark Kenneth Bancroft (July 14, 1914 – May 1, 2005) was an African-American psychologist and was active in the Civil Rights Movement.

Clark William Ramsey (December 18, 1927 – April 9, 2021) is an American lawyer, activist and former federal government official. A progressive New Frontier liberal, he was United States Attorney General from 1967 to 1969. Previously he was Deputy Attorney General from 1965 to 1967 and Assistant Attorney General from 1961 to 1965.

Clemenceau Georges (September 28, 1841 – November 24, 1929) was a French statesman who served as Prime Minister of France from 1906 to 1909 and again from 1917 until 1920.

Clifford Clark McAdams (December 25, 1906 – October 10, 1998) was an American lawyer who served as an important political advisor to democratic presidents Henry S. Truman, John F. Kennedy, Lyndon B. Johnson and Jimmy Carter.

Clinton William Jefferson Blythe III "Bill" (August 19, 1946 –) is an American politician and attorney who served as the 42nd president of the United States from January 20, 1993, to January 20, 2001. Prior to his presidency, he served as governor of Arkansas (1979–1981 and 1983–1992) and as attorney general of Arkansas (1977–1979). A member of the Democratic Party, Clinton was known as a New Democrat, and many of his policies reflected a centrist "Third Way" political philosophy. He was impeached in December 1998 by the House of Representatives. He is the husband of former Secretary of State, former US senator, and two-time candidate for president, Hilary Clinton.

Clinton Hillary Diane Rodham (October 26, 1947 –) is an American politician, diplomat, lawyer, writer and public speaker. She was first lady from Arkansas from 1979 to 1981 and again from 1983 to 1992. She was first lady of the United States from January 20, 1993, to January 20, 2001. She was a Senator from New York from 2001 to 2009 and the 67th United Secretary of State from 2009 to 2013.

Connally John Bowden Jr. (February 27, 1917 – June 15, 1993) served as the 39th Governor of Texas and as the 61st United Secretary of the Treasury. He began his career as a Democrat and later became a Republican in 1973.

Coolidge Calvin (Born John Calvin Coolidge Jr.) (July 4, 1872 – January 5, 1933) was an American politician and lawyer who served as the 30th president of the United

States from August 2, 1923, to March 4, 1929.

Coolidge Grace Anna Goodhue (January 3, 1879 – July 8, 1957) was the first lady in the presidency of her husband Calvin Coolidge from 1923 to 1929.

Cox Archibald Jr. (May 17, 1912 – May 29, 2004) was an American lawyer and law professor who served as US Solicitor General under President John F. Kennedy and as a special prosecutor during the Watergate scandal.

Cresson Edith, born Campion (January 27, 1934 –), is a French politician. She is the first and so far the only woman to have held the office of Prime Minister of France, from May 15, 1991, to April 2, 1992.

Cronkite Walter Leland Jr. (November 4, 1916 – July 17, 2009) was an American news reporter. He was the anchor of CBS News from 1962 to 1981.

Curley James Michael (November 20, 1874 – November 12, 1958) was an American Democratic politician from Boston, Massachusetts. He served four terms as mayor of Boston. He also served a single term as Governor of Massachusetts.

Cushing Richard James (August 24, 1895 – November 2, 1970) was an American prelate of the Roman Catholic Church. He served as Archbishop of Boston from 1944 to 1970 and was made Cardinal in 1958.

Daley Richard Joseph (May 15, 1902 – December 20, 1976) was an American politician who served as the mayor of Chicago from 1955 and the chairman of the Cook County Democratic Party Central Committee from 1953 until his death.

Daniel Jean (July 21, 1920 – February 19, 2020), also known as Jean Daniel Bensaïd, was an Algerian-born French journalist and author. He was the founder and executive editor of "Le Nouvel Observateur," usually now known as L'Obs.

Dassin Julius "Jules" (December 1911 – March 31, 2008) was an American film director, producer, writer and actor. He was a subject of the Hollywood blacklist, and he was a member of the Communist Party USA, and subsequently moved to France, where he continued his career. One of his children was Joseph Ira Dassin, better known as Joe Dassin, a popular French singer in the 1970s.

Davis John Hagy (June 14, 1929 – January 29, 2012) was an American author who wrote several books on the Mafia. Davis was the son of stockbroker John Ethelbert Davis and Maude Reppelin Bouvier, younger sister of John Vernou Bouvier III and, therefore, the first cousin of Jacqueline Kennedy Onassis and Lee Radziwill. His mother and John V. Bouvier III were both children of prominent New York lawyer John Vernou Bouvier Jr.

De Gaulle Charles André Joseph Marie (November 22, 1890 – November 9, 1970) was a French army officer and statesman who led the Free French Forces against Nazi Germany in World War II and chaired the Provisional Government of the French Republic from 1944 to 1946 in order to re-establish democracy in France. He was President of France from January 8, 1959, to April 28, 1969.

DeLoach Cartha Deke (July 20, 1920 – March 13, 2013), known as Deke DeLoach, was deputy associate director of the Federal Bureau of Investigations (FBI) of the United States. During his post, DeLoach was the third most senior official in the FBI after J. Edgar Hoover and Clyde Tolsen.

De Murville Jacques Maurice Couve (January 24, 1907 – December 24, 1999) was a French diplomat and politician who was Minister of Foreign Affairs from 1958 to 1968 and Prime Minister from 1968 to 1969 under the presidency of General de Gaulle.

Dennison Admiral Robert Lee (April 13, 1901 – March 18, 1980) was an American naval officer and aide to President Harry Truman.

De Valera Eamon (October 14, 1892 – August 29, 1975) was a prominent statesman and political leader in 20th-century Ireland, serving several times as head of government and head of state, with a prominent role introducing the Constitution of Ireland. He was the 3rd President of Ireland from June 25, 1959, until June 24, 1973.

Diem Ngo Dinh (January 3, 1901 – November 2, 1963) was a Vietnamese politician. He was the final prime minister of the State of Vietnam (1954-55) and then served as President of South Vietnam (Republic of Vietnam) from 1955 until he was deposed and assassinated during the 1963 military coup.

Dillon Clarence Douglas (August 21, 1909 – January 10, 2003) was an American diplomat and politician who served as US ambassador to France (1953-1957) and as the 57th Secretary of Treasury (1961-1965). He was also a member of the Executive Committee of the Nation of Security Council (ExComm) during the Cuban Missile Crisis.

Dirksen Everett McKinley (January 4, 1896 – September 7, 1969) was an American politician. A member of the Republican Party, he represented Illinois in the United States House of Representatives and the United States Senate. As Senate Minority Leader from January 3, 1959, to September 7, 1969, he played a highly visible and key role in the politics of the 1960s.

Dobrynin Anatoly Fyodorovich (November 16, 1919 – April 6, 2010) was a Russian statesman and a Soviet diplomat and politician. He was Soviet Ambassador to the United States for more than two decades, from 1962 to 1986.

Donovan James Britt (February 29, 1916 – January 19, 1970) was an American lawyer and the United States Navy officer in the Office of Scientific Research and Development and the Office of Strategic Services (OSS. Predecessor of the Central Intelligence agency). Donovan is widely known for negotiating the 1960-1962 exchange of captured American U-2 pilot Gary Powers and American student Frederic Pryor for Soviet Spy Rudolf Abel and for negotiating the 1962 release and return of 9,073 prisoners held by Cuba after the failed Big of Pigs invasion.

Douglas Paul Howard (March 26, 1892 – September 24, 1976) was an American politician and Georgist economist. A member of the Democratic Party, he served as a US Senator from Illinois for eighteen years, from 1949 to 1967.

Douglas William Orville (October 16, 1898 – January 19, 1980) was an American jurist and politician who served as an associate justice of the Supreme Court of the United States. Nominated by President Franklin D. Roosevelt, Douglas was confirmed at the age of 40, one of the youngest justice appointed to the court.

Droney John J. (January 25, 1911 – November 03, 1989) was a Middlesex County District Attorney who met JFK for the first time one day at the Bellevue Hotel at his grandfather's apartment in 1946.
He was involved in John F. Kennedy's House and Senate campaigns and a friend of the Kennedy family.

Dulles Allen Welsh (April 7, 1893 – January 29, 1969) was the first civilian Director of Central Intelligence (DCI) and the longest-serving director to date. Dulles was one of the members of the Warren Commission investigating the assassination of John F. Kennedy.

Dungan Ralph Anthony (April 22, 1923 – October 5, 2013) was an American diplomat and ambassador from the United States to Chili from December 10, 1964, to August 2, 1967. Prior to the appointment, he served as White House Special Assistant to the President in the Kennedy Administration 1961-1963.

Durie Kerr Malcolm Desloge Shevlin Appleton (December 30, 1916 – March 17, 2008), known as Mrs Appleton, is known to have been married four times. But she was perhaps best known for rumors of a secret marriage to John F. Kennedy – an allegation she reportedly denied and often refused to publicly discuss. A brief marriage was alleged to have occurred between the two in early 1947.

Dutton Frederick Gary (June 16, 1923 – June 27, 2005) was a lawyer and Democratic Party power broker, who served as campaign manager and chief of Staff for California Governor Pat Brown, Special Assistant to US President John F. Kennedy, and went on to manage Robert F. Kennedy's campaign for the Presidency.

Dylan Bob, born Robert Allen Zimmerman (May 24, 1941 –), is an American singer-songwriter, author, and visual artist. Widely regarded as one of the greatest songwriters of all time, he has been a major figure in popular culture for more than 60 years.

Eisenhower Dwight David "Ike" (October 14, 1890 – March 28, 1969) was an American politician and soldier. During World War II, he became a five-star general in the Army and served as Supreme Commander of the Allied Expeditionary Force in Europe. He served as the 34th president of the United States from January 20, 1953, until January 20, 1961.

Eisenhower Mamie Geneva (November 14, 1896 – November 1, 1979) was the wife of President Dwight D. Eisenhower and thereby first lady of the United States from 1953 to 1961.

Eisenhower Milton Stover (September 15, 1899 – May 2, 1985) was an American academic administrator. He was the younger brother of US President Dwight D. Eisenhower.

Ellender Allen Joseph (September 24, 1890 – July 27, 1972) was a US Senator from Houma in Terrebonne Parish in South Louisiana, who served from 1937 to 1972 when he died in office in Maryland at the age of 81. He was a Democrat who was originally allied with Huey Long.

Ellsberg Daniel (April 7, 1931 –) is an American economist, political activist and former United States military analyst who, while employed by the Rand Corporation, precipitated a national controversy in 1971 when he released the Pentagon Papers, a top-secret Pentagon study of the US-government decision-making in relation to the Vietnam War, to the New York Times, The Washington Post, and other newspapers.

Evans Courtney Allen (1914 – 2010) was an FBI agent from 1940 to 1964. In 1960, he became assistant director in charge of the Special Investigation Division. He served for a time as the FBI liaison to Attorney General Robert F. Kennedy.

418

Evans Rowland Jr. (April 28, 1921 – March 23, 2001) was an American journalist known best for his decades-long syndicated column and television partnership with Robert Novak.

Evers Medger Wiley (July 2, 1925 – June 12, 1969) was an American civil rights activist in Mississippi, the state's field secretary of the NAACP, and a World War II veteran who had served in the United States Army.

Exner Judith (January 11, 1934 – September 24, 1999) was an American woman who claimed to be the mistress of US President John F. Kennedy and Mafia leaders Sam Giancana and John Roselli. She was also known as Judith Campbell Exner and Judith Campbell. According to Michael O'Brien of the Washington Monthly, on February 7, 1960, Frank Sinatra and Campbell were in Las Vegas, where Sinatra introduced her to John F. Kennedy, then a senator from Massachusetts and presidential candidate.

Fay Paul Burgess Jr. (July 8, 1918 – September 23, 2009) On Kennedy's election as President, Fay was nominated and served as Undersecretary of the Navy over the objections of Defense Secretary Robert McNamara, and then as Acting Secretary of the Navy in November 1963 while Kennedy was US President. He was an usher at JFK's wedding.

Feklisov Alexander (March 9, 1914 – October 26, 2007), known as the alias "Alexander Fomin," was a KGB Colonel who was the top Soviet agent in the United States, gaining information about America's nuclear program and other secrets.

Fenn Dan Huntington Jr. (March 27, 1923 – August 14, 2020) was staff assistant to President John F. Kennedy (1961-1963), Commissioner (1963), Vice-chairman (1964-1967), Tariff Commission, discussed Massachusetts politics in the 1050s, including various state elections and the 1960 presidential election, among other issues. He was the founding director of the Kennedy Library in 1971, left there in 1986.

Fitzgerald John Francis "Honey Fitz" (February 11, 1863 – October 2, 1950) was an American Democratic politician, father of Rose Kennedy and maternal grandfather of President John F. Kennedy. Fitzgerald was a Democratic US Congressman who won two terms as mayor of Boston. He had a theatrical style of campaigning, and charisma earned him the nickname of "Honey Fitz."

Flanders Ralph Edward (September 28, 1880 – February 19, 1970) was an American mechanical engineer, industrialist and politician who served as a Republican US

Senator for the State of Vermont from November 1, 1946, to January 3, 1959. He was president of the Boston Federal Reserve Bank for two years before being elected US Senator from Vermont.

Ford Gerald Rudolph Jr. (born Leslie Lynch King Jr.) (July 14, 1913 – December 26, 2006) was the 38th President of the United States from August 9, 1974, to January 20, 1977. He is the only president to have served both as vice president and president without being elected to either office by the Electoral College.

Forrestal Michael Vincent (November 26, 1927 – January 11, 1989) was one of the leading aides to McGeorge Bundy, the National Security Advisor of President John F. Kennedy.

Freeman Orville Lothrop (May 9, 1918 – February 20, 2003) was an American Democratic politician who served as the 29th Governor of Minnesota from January 5, 1955, to January 2, 1961, and as the US Secretary of Agriculture from 1961 to 1969 under Presidents John F. Kennedy and Lyndon B. Johnson.

Fulbright James William (April 9, 1905 – February 9, 1995) was a United States Senator representing Arkansas from January 1945 until his resignation in December 1974. As a Southern Democrat, he was the longest-serving chairman in the history of the Senate Foreign Relations Committee.

Galbraith John Kenneth (October 15, 1908 – April 29, 2006) was a Canadian-born American economist and public servant known for his support of public spending and for the literary quality of his writing on public affairs. He was active in Democratic Party politics, serving in the administrations of Franklin D. Roosevelt, Harry S. Truman, John F. Kennedy and Lyndon B. Johnson. He served as United States Ambassador to India under the Kennedy administration.

Gargan Ann (1937 –) is a cousin – niece of Joe and Rose Kennedy. Her mother, Agnes Fitzgerald Gargan, was Rose Fitzgerald Kennedy's sister.

Gargarin Yuri Alekseïevich (March 9, 1934 – March 27, 1968) was a Soviet Air Forces pilot and cosmonaut who became the first human to journey outer space, achieving a major milestone in the Space Race. His capsule, Vostok 1, completed one orbit of Earth on April 12, 1961.

Gasa Biuku (July 27, 1923 – November 23, 2005) and Kumana Eroni (1918 – August 2, 2014) were Solomon Islanders of Melanesian descent who found John F. Kennedy and his surviving PT109 crew following the boat's collision with the Japanese destroyer Amagiri near Plum Pudding Island on August 1, 1943. They were from the

Western Province of the Solomon Islands.

Gayet Julie (June 3, 1972 –) is a French actress and film producer. She is also known for being the partner of the former President of the French Republic, François Hollande.

Gerra Laurent (December 29, 1967 –) is a French imitator, humorist, actor and scenarist.

Geyl Pieter (December 15, 1887-December 31, 1966) was a Dutch historian, well known for his studies in early modern Dutch history and historiography.

Giancana Sam (May 24, 1908 – June 19, 1975) was an American mobster who was the boss of the Chicago Outfit from 1957 to 1966.

Gilpatric Roswell Leavitt (November 4, 1906 – March 15, 1996) was a New York City corporate attorney and government official who served as Deputy Secretary of Defense from 1961-1964, where he played a pivotal role in the high-stake strategies of the CMC, advising President John F. Kennedy as well as Robert McNamara and McGeorge Bundy on dealing with the Secret nuclear missile threat.

Glenn John Herschel Jr. (July 18, 1921 – December 6, 2016) was a US Marine Corps aviator, engineer, astronaut, businessman and politician. He was the third person and the first American to orbit the Earth, circling it three times in 1962. Following his retirement from NASA, he served from 1974 to 1999 as the Democratic United States Senator from Ohio. In 1998, he flew into space again at age 77.

Goldberg Arthur Joseph (August 8, 1908 – January 19, 1990) was an American statesman and jurist who served as the 9th US Secretary of Labor, as an Associate Justice to the Supreme Court of the United States and the 6th United States Ambassador to the United Nations.

Goldwater Barry Morris (January 2, 1909 – May 29, 1998) was an American politician, businessman, United States Air Force officer, and author, who was a five-term senator from Arizona (1953-1965, 1969-1987) and the Republican Party nominee for president of the United States in 1964.

Goodwin Richard Naradof (December 7, 1931 – May 20, 2018) was an American writer and presidential advisor. He was an aide and speechwriter to Presidents John F. Kennedy and Lyndon B. Johnson and to Senator Robert F. Kennedy.

Gordon Kermit (July 3, 1916 – June 21, 1976) was director of the United States

Bureau of the Budget (now the Office of Management and Budget) (December 28, 1962 – June 1, 1965) during the administration of John F. Kennedy. He continued to serve in this capacity in the Lyndon Johnson administration.

Gore Albert Arnold Sr. (December 26, 1907 – December 5, 1998) was an American politician who served as a US Representative and as US Senator for the Democratic Party from Tennessee. He was the father of Albert A. Gore Jr., the 45th vice-president of the United States (1993-2001).

Graham Phil (July 18, 1915 – August 3, 1963) was an American newspaperman. He served as publisher and later co-owner of the Washington Post and its parent company, The Washington Post Company.

Griffin Robert Paul (November 6, 1923 – April 6, 2015) was an American politician. A member of the Republican Party, he represented Michigan in the US House of Representatives and US Senate and was a Justice of the Michigan Supreme Court. As a deputy minority leader in the Senate, he called on President Richard Nixon to resign during the Watergate scandal.

Gromyko Andreï Andreyevich (July 18, 1909 – July 2, 1989) was a Soviet and Belarusian communist politician during the Cold War. He served as minister of Foreign Affairs from 1957 until 1985.

Gruening Ernest Henry (February 6, 1887 – June 26, 1974) was an American journalist and politician. A member of the Democratic Party, Gruening was the Governor of Alaska Territory from 1939 until 1953 and US Senator from Alaska from 1959 until 1969.

Guthman Edwin O. (August 11, 1919 – August 31, 2008) was an American journalist and university professor. While at the Seattle Times, he won the paper's first Pulitzer Prize for National Reporting in 1950. Guthman was third on Richard Nixon's "Enemies List."

Harding Warren Gamaliel (November 2, 1865 – August 2, 1923) was the 29th president of the United States from 1921 until his death in 1923. A member of the Republican Party, he was one of the most popular US presidents to that point.

Harriman William Averell (November 15, 1891 – July 26, 1986) was an American Democratic politician, businessman and diplomate. He helped negotiate the Partial Nuclear Tes Ban Treaty during President John F. Kennedy's administration and was deeply involved in the Vietnam War during the Kennedy and Lyndon B. Johnson administrations.

Harris Louis (January 6, 1921 – December 17, 2016) was an American opinion polling entrepreneur, journalist and author. He ran one of the best know polling organization of his time – Louis Harris and Associates – which conducted The Harris Poll.

Harris Seymour Edwin (September 8, 1897 – October 27, 1974) was an American economist, born in New York City and educated at Harvard.

Healey Joseph Peter (1915-1985) was Chief speechwriter for JFK during his early political career. He was appointed by President Kennedy in 1961 to the governing council of the Administrative Council of the US.

Heller Walter Wolfgang (August 27, 1915 – June 15, 1987) was a leading American economist in the 1960s, and an influential advisor of President John F. Kennedy, as chairman of the Council of Economic Advisors, 1961-1964.

Helms Richard McGarrah (March 30, 1913 – October 23, 2002) was an American government official and diplomat who served as Director of Central Intelligence (DCI) from 1966 to 1973. Following the 1947 creation of the Central Intelligence Agency (CIA), he rose in its ranks during the presidencies of Truman, Eisenhower and Kennedy. Helms then was DCI under President Johnson and President Nixon.

Hemings Sarah Sally C. (1773 – 1835) was an enslaved woman of mixed race owned by President Thomas Jefferson.

Herter Christian Archibald (March 28, 1895 – December 30, 1966) was an American Republican who was the 59th Governor of Massachusetts from 1953 to 1957 and United States Secretary of State from 1959 to 1961 and the first United States Trade Representative.

Hilsman Roger (November 23, 1919 – February 23, 2014) was an aide and advisor to President John F. Kennedy on Vietnam.

Hoban James (1755 – December 8, 1831) was a US Irish architect who was the designer and builder of the White House in Washington DC. Hoban was trained in the Irish and English Georgian style and worked in this design tradition throughout his architectural career. He immigrated to the US after the Revolutionary War, first settling in Philadelphia and then in South Carolina.

Hodges Luther H. (March 9, 1898 – October 6, 1974) was a businessman and an American politician. In 1961 he was appointed as United States Secretary of

Commerce under President John F. Kennedy and Lyndon B. Johnson serving until January 15, 1965.

Hoffa James Riddle (February 14, 1913 – disappeared July 30, 1975, declared dead July 30, 1982) was an American labor union leader who served as the president of the International Brotherhood of Teamsters (IBT) from 1957 until 1971. Hoffa became involved with organized crime from the early years of his Teamsters work, a connection that continued until his disappearance in 1975. He is believed to have been murdered by the Mafia and was declared legally dead in 1982.

Hollande François Gérard Georges Nicolas (August 12, 1954 –) is a French politician who served as President of France and ex-office Co-Prince of Andorra from May 15, 2012, to May 14, 2017. He previously was First Secretary of the Socialist Party from 1997 to 2008. Mayor of Tulle from 2001 to 2008 and President of the General Counsel of Corrèze from 2008 to 2012. Hollande also served in the National Assembly twice for the first constituency of Corrèze from 1988 to 1993 and again from 1997 to 2012.

Hoover Edgar John (January 1, 1895 – May 2, 1972) was an American law enforcement administrator who served as the first Director of the Federal Bureau of Investigation (FBI) of the United States. He served from 1924 until his death in 1972 at the age of 77.

Hoover Herbert Clark (August 10, 1874 – October 20, 1964) was the 31st president of the United States from March 4, 1929, to March 4, 1933. He was a world-famous mining engineer and humanitarian administrator.

Howard Lisa (born Dorothy Jean Guggenheim) (April 24, 1926 – July 4, 1965) was an American journalist, writer and television news anchor who previously had a career as an off-Broadway-theater and soap opera actress. In 1965, Howard suffered a miscarriage and depression, dying of an overdose of painkillers.

Hugo Victor Marie (February 26, 1802 – May 22, 1885) was a french poet, novelist, and dramatist of the Romantic Movement. During a literary career that spanned more than sixty years, he wrote abundantly in an exceptional variety of genres: lyrics, satires, epics, philosophical poems, epigrams, novels, history, critical essays, political speeches, funeral orations, diaries, letters public and private, and dramas in verse and prose.

Humphrey Hubert Horatio "Chet" (May 27, 1911 – January 13, 1978) was an American politician who served as the 38th vice-president of the United States from 1965-1969. He twice served in the United States Senate, representing Minnesota from 1949 to 1964 and 1971 to 1978.

<u>Huntley Chester Robert</u> (December 10, 1911 – March 20, 1974) was an American television newscaster, best known for co-anchoring NBC's evening news program, The Huntley-Brinkley Report, for 14 years, beginning in 1956.

<u>Husted John Grinnel Westmore Jr.</u> (May 26, 1926 – May 9, 1999) was an American stockbroker who was briefly engaged to future First Lady of the United States Jacqueline Bouvier.

<u>Irving McNeil Ives</u> (January 24, 1896 – February 24, 1962) was an American politician. A member of the Republican Party, he served as a US Senator from New York from 1947 to 1959. A Liberal Republican, he was known as a specialist in labor and civil rights legislation. Ives voted in favor of the Civil Rights Act of 1957.

<u>Jackson Andrew</u> (March 15, 1767 – June 8, 1845) was an American soldier and statesman who served as the 7th president of the United States from March 4, 1829, to March 4, 1837. Before being elected to the presidency, Jackson gained fame as a general in the United States Army and served in both houses of the US Congress. As president, Jackson sought to advance the rights of the "common man" against a "corrupt aristocracy" land to preserve the Union.

<u>Jackson Henry Martin "Scoop"</u> (May 31, 1912 – September 1, 1983) was an American Democratic politician who served as a US Representative (1941-1953) and US Senator (1953-1983) from the state of Washington.

<u>Jacobson Max Dr.</u> (July 3, 1900 – December 1, 1979) was a German physician and medical researcher who treated numerous high-profile clients in America, including President John F. Kennedy. Jacobson came to be known as "Miracle Max" and "Dr. Feelgood" because he administrated highly addictive "vitamin shots" laced with various substances that included amphetamine and methamphetamine.

<u>Jefferson Thomas</u> (April 13, 1743 – July 4, 1826) was an American statesman, diplomat, lawyer, architect, musician, philosopher, and Founding Father, who served as the third president of the United States from March 4, 1801 – March 4, 1809.

<u>Johnson Lyndon B.</u> (August 27, 1908 – January 22, 1973) served as the 36th president of the United States from 1963 to 1969 and previously as the 37th vice-president from 1961 to 1963.

<u>Jones Clarence Benjamin</u> (January 8, 1931 –) is the former personal counsel, advisor, draft speechwriter and close friend of Martin Luther King.

Katzenbach Nicholas de Belleville "Nick" (January 17, 1922 – May 8, 2012) was an American lawyer who served as the 65th United States Attorney General during the Lyndon B. Johnson administration. He served as Deputy Attorney General appointed by President John F. Kennedy in 1962.

Kaye Danny (born David Daniel Kaminski) (January 18, 1911 – March 8, 1987) was an American actor, singer, dancer, comedian, musician and philanthropist. His performances featured physical comedy, idiosyncratic pantomimes and rapid-fire novelty songs.

Keating Kenneth Barnard (May 18, 1900 – May 5, 1975) was an American attorney, politician, judge, and diplomat from Rochester, New York. A Republican, he was most notable for his service as a US Representative, US Senator, State Appeals, court judge, and as a US Ambassador first to India (1969-1972), then to Israel (1973-1975).

Kelly Grace Patricia (November 12, 1929 – September 14, 1982) was an American film actress who, after starring in several significant films in the early mid-1950s, became Princes of Monaco by marrying Prince Rainier III in April 1956. She died aged 52 at Monaco Hospital on September 14, 1982, succumbing to injuries sustained in a car crash the previous day. She is listed among the American Film institute's 25 Greatest Female Stars of Classical Hollywood Cinema.

Kennedy Bouvier Caroline (November 27, 1957) is an American author, attorney and diplomat who served as the United States' Ambassador to Japan from 2013 to 2017. In 1980, she earned a Bachelor of Arts from Radcliffe Cottage at Harvard University. She married exhibit designer Edwin Schlossberg in 1986 at our Lady of Victory Church in Centerville, Massachusetts. She is president of the Kennedy Library Foundation and daughter of President John F. Kennedy.

Kennedy Edward Moore (February 22, 1932 – August 25, 2009) was an American politician who served as a US Senator from Massachusetts for almost 47 years, from 1962 until his death in 2009. A member of the Democratic Party and the Kennedy political family, he was the second most senior member of the Senate when he died and the fourth-longest-continuously-serving senator in United States history.

Kennedy Eunice Mary Shriver (July 10, 1921 – August 11, 2009) was an American philanthropist and sister of US President John F. Kennedy, US Senators Robert F. Kennedy and Ted Kennedy. She was the founder of the Special Olympics, a sports organization for persons with physical and intellectual disabilities. For her efforts on behalf of the disabled, Shriver was awarded the Presidential Medal of Freedom in

1984.

Kennedy Ethel Skakel (April 11, 1928) is an American human rights advocate. She is the widow of US Senator Robert F. Kennedy as well as the sixth child of George Skakel and Ann Brannack. She married Robert F. Kennedy in 1950, and the couple had 11 children together. Shortly after her husband's 1968 assassination, she founded the Robert F. Kennedy Center for Justice and Human Rights. In 2014 Ethel Kennedy was awarded the Presidential Medal of Freedom by President Barack Obama.

Kennedy Kathleen Agnes Cavendish (February 20, 1920 – May 13, 1948), also known as "Kick" Kennedy, was an American socialite. She was the daughter of Joseph P. Kennedy and Rose Kennedy, sister of future US President John F. Kennedy, and the wife of the Marquess of Hartington, heir apparent to the 10th Duke of Devonshire. Working with the Red Cross in London, she began a romantic relationship with Lord Hartington, who she married in May 1944. He was killed on active service in Belgium only four months later. Kathleen died in a plane crash in 1948, flying to the South of France while on vacation with her new partner, the 8th Earl Fitzwilliam Marchioness of Hartington.

Kennedy Robert Francis (November 20, 1925 – June 6, 1968) was an American politician and lawyer who served as the 64th United States Attorney General from January 1961 to September 1964 and as a US Senator from New York from January 1965 until the assassination in June 1968. He was, like his brothers John and Edward, a prominent member of the Democratic Party and has come to be viewed by some historians as an icon of modern American liberalism.

Kennedy Onassis Jacqueline (July 28, 1929 – May 19, 1994) was the first lady of the United States as the wife of John F. Kennedy and was regarded as an international icon of style and culture. At age 31, she was the third-youngest first lady when her husband was inaugurated, President. On October 20, 1968, Jacqueline Kennedy married Aristotle Onassis, a wealthy Greek shipping migrate on Skorpios, Onassis' private Greek Island in the Ionian Sea. In 1989, she was listed as one of Gallup's Most-Admired Men and Women of the 20th Century.

Kennedy John Jr. (November 25, 1961 – July 16, 1999) was an American lawyer, journalist, and magazine publisher and son of President John F. Kennedy. In 1995, Kennedy and Michael Berman founded "George," a glossy politics-as-lifestyle and fashion monthly, with Kennedy controlling 50% of the shares. He married Carolyn Bessette (who worked in the fashion industry) on September 21, 1996, in a private ceremony on Cumberland Island, Georgia.

Kennedy Joseph Patrick "Joe" (September 6, 1888 – November 18, 1969) was an

American businessman, investor and politician. He was United States Ambassador to the United Kingdom from March 8, 1938, to October 22, 1940. He was the first Chairman of the US Maritime Commission from April 14, 1937, to February 19, 1938.

Kennedy Joseph Patrick Jr. (July 25, 1915 – August 12, 1944) was a United States Navy Lieutenant. He was killed in action during World War II while serving as a land-based patrol bomber pilot. He was the eldest of nine children born to Joseph Kennedy Sr. and Rose Fitzgerald Kennedy.

Kennedy Patrick Bouvier (August 7, 1963 – August 9, 1963) (aged two days) was the infant child of United States President John F. Kennedy and First Lady Jacqueline Kennedy. Born prematurely, Kennedy lived just over 39 hours before dying from complications of hyaline membrane disease (HMD) after desperate attempts to save him failed.

Kennedy Rose Marie "Rosemary" (September 13, 1918 – January 7, 2005) was the eldest daughter born to Joseph P. Kennedy and Rose Fitzgerald Kennedy. She was the sister of President of the United States John F. Kennedy and Senators Robert F. Kennedy and Ted Kennedy.

Kennedy Rose Elizabeth Fitzgerald (July 22, 1890 – January 22, 1995) On October 7, 1914, at age 24, she married Joseph Patrick "Joe" Kennedy after a courtship of more than seven years. They had nine children. Rose Kennedy was a strict Catholic. Even after her 100th birthday, she rarely missed Sunday Mass and maintained an "extremely prudent" exterior.

Kennedy Smith Jean Ann (February 20, 1928 – June 17, 2020) was an American diplomat, activist, humanitarian, and author, who served as United States Ambassador to Ireland from 1993 to 1998.

Kennedy Townsend Kathleen (July 4, 1951) was the eldest of Robert F. Kennedy and Ethel Skakel's eleven children. She is an American attorney who was lieutenant governor of Maryland from 1995 to 2003.

Kennedy Victoria "Vicki" Anne Reggie (February 26, 1954 –) is an American lawyer. She is the second wife and widow of longtime US Senator Ted Kennedy, who was twenty-two years her senior.

Kerr Robert Samuel (September 11, 1896 – January 1, 1963) was an American businessman and politician from Oklahoma. Kerr formed a petroleum company before turning to politics. He served as the 12th Governor of Oklahoma (January 11,

1943-January 13, 1947) and was elected three times to the US States Senate (January 3, 1949-January 1, 1963)

<u>Khrushchev Nikita Sergeyevich</u> (April 15 (O.S. April 3), 1894 – September 11, 1971) was a Soviet politician who led the Soviet Union during part of the Cold War as the first secretary of the Communist Party of the Soviet Union from 1953 to 1964 and as a chairman of the Council of Ministers from 1958 to 1964. He was responsible for the de-Stalinization of the Soviet Union.

<u>Khrushchev Sergei Nikitich</u> (July 2, 1935 – June 18, 2020) was a Russian engineer and the son of the Cold War-era Soviet Premier Nikita Khrushchev. He moved to the United States in 1991 and was a naturalized American citizen. He shot himself on June 18, 2020, at his Cranston, Rhode Island home.

<u>Kilduff Malcolm MacGregor "Mac" Jr.</u> (September 26, 1927 – March 3, 2003) was Kennedy's assistant White House Press Secretary and the ranking press secretary on Kennedy's November 1963 trip to Dallas, Texas, where Kennedy was assassinated.

<u>King Martin Luther Jr.</u> (January 15, 1929 – April 4, 1968) was an American pastor, activist, humanitarian, and leader of the African-American Civil Rights Movement. He was best known for improving civil rights by using nonviolent civil disobedience based on his Christian beliefs.

<u>King Coretta Scott</u> (April 27, 1927 – January 30, 2006) was an American author, activist, civil rights leader and the wife of Martin Luther King Jr.

<u>Kraus Hans</u> (November 28, 1905 – March 6, 1996) was a physician, physical therapist, mountaineer and alpinist. A pioneer of modern rock climbing, he was also one of the fathers of sports medicine and physical medicine and rehabilitation.

<u>Krock Arthur Bernard</u> (November 16, 1886 – April 12, 1974) was a Pulitzer Prize-winning American journalist. In a career spanning several decades covering the tenure of eleven United States presidents, he became known as the "Dean of Washington newsmen."

<u>Krugman Paul Robin</u> (February 28, 1953 –) is an American economist who is the Distinguished Professor of Economics at the Graduate Center of the City University of New York and a columnist for the New York Times. In 2008 he was awarded the Nobel Prize in Economic Sciences for his contributions to New Trade Theory and New Economic Geography.

<u>Krulak Victor Harold</u> (January 7, 1913 – December 29, 2008) was a decorated

United States Marine Corps officer who saw action in World War II, Korea and Vietnam.

La Follette Robert Marion Sr. (June 14, 1855 – June 18, 1925) was an American Republican. He was a Senator from Wisconsin from January 2, 1906, until his death on June 18, 1925. He ran for President in 1924 but lost. He is thought to be one of the greatest Senators of American History.

Landrum Phillip Mitchell (September 10, 1907 – November 19, 1990) was a Democratic US Representative from Georgia. He served from January 3, 1953, until January 3, 1977. A Staunch segregationist in 1956, Landrum signed "The Southern Manifesto."

Lansdale Edward Geary (February 6, 1908 – February 23, 1987) was a United States Air Force officer until retiring in 1963 as a major general before continuing his work with the Central Intelligence Agency (CIA).

Lasky Harold Joseph (June 30, 1883 – March 24, 1950) was an English political theorist and economist.

Lawford Peter Sydney Ernest (September 7, 1923 – December 24, 1984) was an English-American actor, producer, and socialite, who lived in the United States throughout his adult life. He was a member of the "Rat Pack" and the brother-in-law of President John F. Kennedy and Senators Robert F. Kennedy and Edward Kennedy.

Lawrence David Leo (June 18, 1889 – November 21, 1966) was an American politician who served as the 37th Governor of Pennsylvania from 1959 to 1963.

LeMay Curtis Emerson (November 15, 1906 – October 1, 1990) was an American Air Force general who implemented an effective but also controversial strategic bombing campaign in the Pacific theater of World War II. He later served as Chief of Staff of the US Air Force from 1961 to 1965. He then served as Supreme Allied Commander of Nato from 1963 to 1969.

Lemnitzer Lyman Louis (August 29, 1899 – November 12, 1988) was a United States Army General who served as Chairman of the Joints Chiefs of Staff from 1960 to 1962. He then served as Supreme Allied Commander of NATO from 1963 to 1969.

Lenin Vladimir Ilyich Ulyanov (April 22, 1870 – January 21, 1924), better known by his alias Lenin, was a Russian revolutionary politician and political theorist. He served as the head of government of Soviet Russia from 1917 to 1924 and of the

Soviet Union from
1922 to 1924.

Leuchtenburg William Edward (1922 –) is the William Rand Kanan Jr. professor emeritus of history at the University of North Carolina at Chapel Hill. He is a leading scholar of the life and career of Franklin Delano Roosevelt.

Levison Stanley David (May 2, 1912 – September 12, 1979) was an American businessman and lawyer who became a lifelong activist in progressive causes. He was best known as an advisor to and close friend of Martin Luther King Jr., for whom he helped write speeches, raise funds, and organize events.

Lewis Jerry – born Joseph Levitch (March 16, 1926 – August 20, 2017) was an American comedian, actor, singer, and filmmaker and humanitarian, nicknamed "The King of Comedy." In addition to his years as an entertainer and filmmaker, Lewis was also a world "renowned" humanitarian, philanthropist and "number one volunteer" who supported fundraising for research into muscular dystrophy. In 1966 Lewis began hosting the live annual event of The Jerry Lewis MDA Labor Day Telethon, known variously as the Jerry Lewis Telethon.

Lewis John Robert (February 21, 1940 – July 17, 2020) was an American politician, statesman, and civil rights leader who served in the United States House of Representatives for Georgia's 5th congressional district from 1987 until his death in 2020.

Lincoln Abraham (February 12, 1809 – April 15, 1865) was an American statesman and lawyer who served as the 16th president of the United States (1861-1865). He was self-educated and became a lawyer. Lincoln led the nation through the American Civil War, the country's greatest moral, constitutional and political crisis from March 4, 1861, until April 15, 1865. He was assassinated by John Wilkes Booth, a well-known actor and a Confederate spy from Maryland.

Lincoln Evelyn Maurine Norton (June 25, 1909 – May 11, 1995) was the personal secretary to John F. Kennedy from his election to the United States Senate in 1953 until his 1963 assassination.

Lincoln Mary Todd (December 13, 1818 – July 16, 1882) was the wife of the 16th President of the United States. She staunchly supported her husband throughout his presidency and was active in keeping national morale high during the Civil War.

Lippmann Walter (September 23, 1889 – December 14, 1974) was an American writer, reporter and political commentator famous for being among the first to introduce the concept of the Cold War.

Lodge Henry Cabot Jr. (July 5, 1902 – February 27, 1985) was a Republican United States Senator for Massachusetts. In 1963, President Kennedy appointed Lodge to the position of Ambassador to South Vietnam, where Lodge supported the 1963 South Vietnamese coup.

Luce Henry Robinson (April 3, 1898 – February 28, 1967) was an American magazine magnate who was called "the most influential private citizen in the America of his day." He envisaged that the United States would achieve world hegemony, and, in 1941, he declared the century would be the "American Century."

Lumumba Patrice Emery (July 2, 1925 – January 17, 1961) was a Congolese politician and independence leader who served as the first Prime Minister of the independent Democratic Republic of Congo (then Republic of the Congo) from June until September 1960. Lumumba was so subsequently imprisoned by state authorities under Mobutu and executed by a firing squad under the command of Katangan authorities. Belgium formally apologized for its role in the assassination.

MacArthur Douglas (January 26, 1880 – April 5, 1964) was an American five-star general and Field Marshal of the Philippine Army.

MacDonald Torbert Hart (June 6, 1917 – May 21, 1976), nicknamed Torby, was an American politician from Massachusetts. He served as a Democratic member of the United States House of Representatives from 1955 until his death in Bethesda, Maryland, in 1976.

Macmillan Maurice Harold (February 10, 1894 – December 29, 1986) was a British Conservative politician who served as Prime Minister of the United Kingdom from 1957 to 1963. Caricatured as "Supermac," he was known for his pragmatism, wit and unflappability.

Macron Brigitte Marie-Claude Frogneux (April 13, 1953 –) is a French schoolteacher who is the wife and former teacher of Emmanuel Macron, current President of the French Republic.

Macron Emmanuel Jean-Michel, Frédéric (December 21, 1977 –) is a French politician who has been President of France and ex officio co-prince of Andorra since May 14, 2017.

Malcolm X (born : Malcolm Little) (May 19, 1925 – February 21, 1965) was an African-American Muslim minister and human rights activist who was a prominent figure during the civil rights movement.

Mansfield Michael Joseph (March 16, 1903 – October 5, 2001) was an American politician and diplomat. A member of the Democratic Party, he served as a US Representative (1943-1953) and a US Senator (1953-1977) from Montana. He was the longest-serving Senate Majority Leader and served from 1961 to 1977.

Marshall Burke (October 1, 1922 – June 2, 2003) was Assistant Attorney General to Robert F. Kennedy, who was Attorney General in President John F. Kennedy's administration.

Matthews Chris (December 17, 1945 –) is an American retired political commentator, talk show host and author. He hosted his weeknight hour-long talk show "Hardball with Chris Matthews" on America's talking and later in MSNBC, from 1997 until March 2, 2020.

McCarthy Eugene Joseph "Gene" (March 22, 1916 – December 10, 2005) was an American politician and part of Minnesota. He sought the presidency five times but never won. Born in Watkins, Minnesota, McCarthy became an economics professor after earning a graduate degree from the University of Minnesota.

McCarthy Joseph Raymond (November 14, 1908 – May 2, 1957) was an American politician who served as a Republican US Senator from the State of Wisconsin from 1947 until his death in 1957.

McClellan John Little (February 25, 1896 – November 21, 1977) was an American lawyer and politician. A member of the Democratic Party, he served as a US Representative (1935-39) and a US Senator (1943-77) from Arkansas. At the time of his death, he was the second most senior member of the Senate and chairman of the Senate Appropriation Committee.

McCormack John William (December 21, 1891 – November 22, 1980) was an American politician from Boston. An attorney and a Democrat, he became the 45th Speaker of the House of Representatives in 1962. McCormack enjoyed a long House career (1928 to 1971).

McDonald David John (November 22, 1902 – August 8, 1979) was an American labor leader and president of the United Steelworkers of America from 1952 to 1965.

McGovern George Stanley (July 19, 1922 – October 21, 2012) was an American historian, author, US representative, US Senator and the Democratic Party presidential nominee in the 1972 presidential election.

McGrory Mary (August 22, 1918 – April 20, 2004) was an American journalist and columnist. She and JFK were close in age, both of Irish descent and from Boston.

McNamara Robert Strange (June 9, 1916 – July 6, 2009) was an American business executive and the eighth United States Secretary of Defense, serving from 1961 to 1968 under Presidents John F. Kennedy and Lyndon B. Johnson. He played a major role in escalating the United States to involvement in the Vietnam War.

Meany William George (August 16, 1894 – January 10, 1980) was an American labor union leader for 57 years. He was the key figure in the creation of the AFL-CIO and served as the AFL-CIO's first president from 1955 to 1979.

Miller Arthur (October 17, 1915 – February 10, 2005) was an American playright and essayist in the 20th -century American theater. The drama "Death of a Salesman" has been numbered on the shortlist of finest American plays in the 20th Century. In June 1956, Miller left his first wife, Mary Slattery, whom he had married in 1940, and wed filmstar Marilyn Monroe. Miller and Monroe divorced in 1961 after their five years of marriage.

Mitterand François Maurice Adrien Marie (October 26, 1916 – January 8, 1996) was a French statesman who served as President of France from May 21, 1981, to May 17, 1995, the longest time in office in the history of France. As First Secretary of the Socialist Party, he was the first left-wing politician to assume the presidency under the Fifth Republic.

Monroe James (April 28, 1758 – July 4, 1831) was an American statesman, lawyer, diplomat and founding father who served as the 5th president of the United States from March 4, 1817, to March 4, 1825. He is perhaps best known for issuing the Monroe Doctrine, a policy of opposing European colonialism in the Americas.

Monroe Marilyn, born Norma Jeane Mortenson (June 1, 1926 – August 4, 1962), was an American actress, model and singer. She became one of the most popular sex symbols of the 1950s and early 1960s and was emblematic of the era's changing attitudes toward sexuality. Monroe struggled with addiction, depression and anxiety. On August 4, 1962, she died at the age of 36 from an overdose of barbiturates at her home in Los Angeles.

Morrissey Francis Xavier (Frank) (May 21, 1910 – December 27, 2007) was a Massachusetts attorney who served as a judge on the Boston Municipal Court from 1958 to 1980. He was John F. Kennedy's secretary when Kennedy served as a congressman and senator.

Morse Wayne Lyman (October 20, 1900 – July 22, 1974) was an American attorney and the United States Senator from Oregon from January 5, 1945, to January 3, 1969. He was known for his proclivity for opposing his party's leadership and specifically for his opposition to the Vietnam War on constitutional grounds.

Moss John Emerson (April 13, 1915 – December 5, 1997) was an American politician of the Democratic Party, noted for his championing of the Federal Freedom of Information Act (FOIA) through multiple sessions of the United States of Representatives where he served from January 3, 1953, to December 31, 1979.

Moyers Billy Don (June 5, 1934) is an American journalist and political commentator. He served as the ninth White House Press Secretary under the Johnson administration from 1965 to 1967.

Moynihan Daniel Patrick" Pat" (March 16, 1927 – March 26, 2003) was an American politician, sociologist and diplomat. A member of the Democratic Party, he represented New York in the United States Senate and served as an advisor to Republican US President Richard Nixon. He served as an assistant secretary of labor under President Kennedy and President Lyndon B. Johnson.

Muhammad Ali, born Cassius Marcellus Clay Jr. (January 17, 1942 – June 3, 2016), was an American professional boxer, activist and philanthropist. Nicknames "The Greatest," he is widely regarded as one of the most significant and celebrated figures of the 20th century and one of the greatest boxers of all time. In March 1966, Ali refused to be inducted into the armed forces because of his religious beliefs and ethical opposition to the Vietnam War. He was systematically denied a boxing license in every state and stripped of his passport. As a result, he did not fight from March 1967 to October 1970 from age 25 to almost 29, as his case worked its way through the appeals process before his conviction was overturned in 1971.

Muhammad Elijah (born Elijah Robert Poole) (October 7, 1897 – February 25, 1975) was an African-American religious leader who led the Nation of Islam from 1934 until his death in 1975. He was a mentor to Malcolm X, Louis Farrakhan and Muhammad Ali.

Murphy Charles Springs (August 20, 1909 – August 28, 1983) was an American attorney who served as The White House Counsel to US President Harry S. Truman from 1950 to 1953.

Myrdal Karl Gunnar (December 6, 1898 – May 17, 1987) was a Swedish economist and sociologist.

Nasser Gamal Abdel Hussain (January 15, 1918 – September 28, 1970) was an Egyptian politician who served as the second President of Egypt from June 23, 1956 until his death on September 28, 1970.

Nehru Jawaharlal (November 14, 1889 – May 27, 1964) was an Indian independence activist and subsequently the first Prime Minister of India from August 15, 1947, until May 27, 1964.

Neustadt Richard Elliott (June 26, 1919 – October 31, 2003) was an American political scientist specializing in the United States presidency. He also served as an advisor to several presidents.

Nitze Paul Henry (January 16, 1907 – October 19, 2004). During the administrations of President John F. Kennedy and Lyndon B. Johnson, Nitze served in high-level Department of Defense positions and expanded the US military presence in Europe.

Nixon Richard Milhous (January 9, 1913 – April 22, 1994) was the 37th president of the United States, serving from January 20, 1969, until August 9, 1974. In light of his loss of political support and the near-certainty that he would be impeached and removed from office, he resigned from the presidency on August 9, 1974, after addressing the nation on television the previous evening.

Obama Hussein Barack (August 4, 1961 –) was the 44th president of the United States, in office January 20, 2009 – January 20, 2017. October 2009 Nobel Peace Prize was awarded to Obama for his extraordinary efforts to strengthen international diplomacy and cooperation between people.

O'Brien Lawrence Francis Jr. (July 7, 1917 – September 28, 1990). In 1959, he built the foundation for Kennedy's 1960 presidential campaign by touring the United States. He was appointed in 1960 by Kennedy to serve as the director of his presidential campaign nationally.

O'Donnell Kenneth Patrick (March 4, 1924 – September 9, 1977) was an American political consultant and special assistant and appointments secretary to President John F. Kennedy from 1961 until Kennedy's assassination in November 1963. He was a close friend of President Kennedy and Robert Kennedy and was part of the group of Kennedy's close advisors dubbed the "Irish Mafia."

O'Neill Thomas Phillip Jr. "Tip" (December 9, 1912 – January 5, 1994) was an American politician who served as the 47th Speaker of the United States House of Representatives from 1977 to 1987, representing Northern Boston, Massachusetts, as a Democrat from 1953 to 1987.

Patman John Willian Wright (August 6, 1893 – March 7, 1976) was US Congressman from Texas.

Peale Norman Vincent (May 31, 1898 – December 24, 1993) was an American minister and author known for his work in popularizing the concept of positive thinking. He was a personal friend of President Richard Nixon. Donald Trump attended Peale's church while growing up.

Pope Pius XII (Italian Pio XII), born Eugenio Maria Giuseppe, Giovanni Pacelli (March 2, 1876 – October 9, 1958), was head of the Catholic Church and sovereign of the Vatican City State from March 2, 1939, to October 9, 1958, when he died.

Powers David Francis "Dave" (April 25, 1912 – March 28, 1998) was special assistant and assistant appointments secretary to President John F. Kennedy. Powers served as a museum curator of the JFK library and museum from 1964 until his retirement in May 1994.

Pulitzer Joseph Jr III (May 13, 1913 – May 26, 1993) was an American newspaperman and publisher of the St Louis Post-Dispatch for 38 years.

Radziwill Caroline Lee, born Bouvier (March 3, 1933 – February 15, 2019), usually known as Princess Lee Radziwill, was an American socialite, public-relations executive and interior decorator. She was the younger sister of First Lady Jacqueline Bouvier Kennedy and sister-in-law of President John F. Kennedy.

Randolph Asa Philip (April 15, 1889 – May 16, 1979) was an American labor unionist, civil rights activist, and social politician. In 1963, Randolph was the head of the March on Washington, which was organized by Bayard Rustin.

Randolph Jefferson Martha (September 27, 1772 – October 10, 1836) was the eldest daughter of Thomas Jefferson and his wife, Martha Wayles Skelton Jefferson. She was born at Monticello, near Charlottesville, Virginia.

Raskin Hyman B. (February 27, 1909 – August 10, 1995) was a Chicago lawyer who entered the political scene when he helped manage the 1952 and 1956 presidential campaign of Adlai Stevenson. He was recruited into the Kennedy effort by Joe Kennedy in 1957. He was a campaign worker to John F. Kennedy for President (1960).

Rayburn Samuel Taliaferro (January 6, 1882 – November 16, 1961) was an

American politician who served as the 43rd Speaker of the United States of Representatives from January 3, 1955, until November 16, 1961.

Reagan Ronald Wilson (February 6, 1911 – June 5, 2004) was an American politician who served as the 40th president of the United States from January 20, 1981 to January 20, 1989 and became a highly influential voice of modern conservatism. Prior to his presidency, he was a Hollywood actor and union leader before serving as the 33rd governor of California from January 2, 1967 to January 6, 1975.

Reed James Allan (February 2, 1917 – August 23, 2006) was a prominent Springfield attorney who served with Jack Kennedy in the South Pacific during World War II, and later was appointed by the president as an assistant secretary of the US Treasury.

Reuther Walter Philip (September 1, 1907 – May 9, 1970) was an American Leader of organized labor and civil right activist who built the United Automobile Workers (UAW) into one of the most progressive labor unions in American history. He was recognized by Time Magazine as one of the 100 most influential people of the 20th Century.

Ribicoff Abraham Alexander (April 9, 1910 – February 22, 1998) was an American Democratic Party politician from the State of Connecticut. He represented Connecticut in the United States House of Representatives and Senate and was the 80th Governor of Connecticut and Secretary of Health, Education and Welfare in President John F. Kennedy's Cabinet. He was Connecticut's first and, to date, only Jewish governor.

Rockefeller Nelson Aldrich (July 8, 1908 – January 26, 1979) was an American businessman and politician who served as the 41st vice-president from 1974 to 1977 under Gerald R. Ford and previously as the 49th governor of New York from 1959 to 1973. He was a Republican who was often considered to be liberal, progressive or moderate.

Rometsch Ellen Bertha Hildegard Elly (September 19, 1936), born in Kleinitz, Germany, was rumored to be an East German Communist spy who was assigned on diplomatic cover to the West German Embassy in Washington DC. During the early 1960s.

Roosevelt Anna Eleanor (October 11, 1884 – November 7, 1962) was an American political figure, diplomat and activist. She served as the first lady of the United States from March 4, 1933, to April 12, 1945, during her husband Franklin D. Roosevelt's four terms in office, making her the longest-serving first lady of the United States.

Roosevelt Franklin Delano (January 30, 1882 – April 12, 1945) was the 32nd president of the United States from 1933 until his death in 1945. He served 12 years as President dying shortly after beginning his 4th term, the longest ever spent in office.

Roosevelt Franklin Delano Jr. (August 17, 1914 – August 17, 1988) was an American lawyer, politician and businessman. He served as a United States Congressman from New York from 1949 to 1955. He was the son of President Franklin D. Roosevelt and First Lady Eleanor Roosevelt and served as an officer in the United States Navy during World War II. In 1963 he was appointed Under Secretary of Commerce by President John F. Kennedy.

Rostow Walt Whitman (October 7, 1916 – February 13, 2003) was an American economist, professor and political theorist who served as National Security Advisor to the President of the United States Lyndon B. Johnson from 1966 to 1969.

Roush J. Edward (September 12, 1920 – March 26, 2004) was a US Representative from Indiana.

Rusk Dean David (February 9, 1909 – December 20, 1994) was the United States Secretary of State from 1961 to 1969 under presidents John F. Kennedy and Lyndon B. Johnson. He is one of the longest-serving US Secretaries of State, behind only Cordell Hull.

Russell Richard Brevard Jr. (November 2, 1897 – January 21, 1971) was an American politician. A member of the Democratic Party, he served as the 66th Governor of Georgia from 1931 to 1933 before serving in the United States Senate for almost 40 years, from 1933 to 1971, and at his death was the most senior member of the Senate.

Rustin Bayard (March 17, 1912 – August 24, 1987) was an American leader in social movements for civil rights, socialism, non-violence, and gay rights. Rustin worked with A. Philip Randolph on the March in Washington Movement in 1941 to press for an end to racial discrimination in employment

Salinger Pierre (June 14, 1925 – October 16, 2004) was an American journalist, author and politician. He had served as the seventh White House Press Secretary of United States Presidents John F. Kennedy and Lyndon B. Johnson.

Samuelson Paul Anthony (May 15, 1915 - December 13, 2009) was an American economist. The first American to win the Nobel Memorial Prize in Economic Sciences in 1970.

Sarközy Nicolas Paul Stéphane de Nagy-Bocsa (January 28, 1955 –) is a retired French politician who served as President of France and ex-office Co-Prince of Andorra from May 16, 2007, until May 15, 2012. Born in Paris, he is one half Hungarian Protestant, one-quarter Greek Jewish, and one quarter French Catholic origin. Mayor of Neuilly-sur-Seine from 1983 to 2002, he was Minister of the Budget under Prime Minister Eduard Balladur (1993-1995) during François Mitterand's second term. During Jacques Chirac's second presidential term, he served as the Minister of the Interior and as Minister of Finances. He was the leader of the Union for a Popular Movement (UMP) party from 2004 to 2007.

Scali John Alfred (April 27, 1918 – October 9, 1995) was the United States Ambassador to the United Nations from 1973 to 1975. From 1961 he was also a longtime correspondent for ABC News.

Schlesinger Jr. Arthur Meier, born Arthur Bancroft Schlesinger (October 15, 1917 – February 28, 2007), was an American historian, social critic and public intellectual. He served as special assistant to President Kennedy from 1961 to 1963. His book "A Thousand Days: John F. Kennedy in the White House" won a 1966 Pulitzer Prize for biography or autobiography.

Schlossberg Rose Kennedy (June 25, 1988 –) is an American actress, the eldest child of Caroline Kennedy and the first-born grandchild of John F. Kennedy. She is a 2010 graduate of Harvard University. She has been described as a look-alike of her maternal grandmother, First Lady Jacqueline Kennedy Onassis.

Schlossberg Tatiana Celia Kennedy (May 5, 1990 –) is an American journalist and author. She is the daughter of Caroline Kennedy, the former US Ambassador to Japan, and a granddaughter of John F. Kennedy. A reporter for the New York Times covering climate change, she has also written for the Atlantic. She is the author of the book "Inconspicuous Consumption."

Schlossberg John "Jack" Bouvier Kennedy (January 19, 1993 –) is the youngest child and only son of the former Ambassador to Japan, Caroline Kennedy, and the only grandson of John F. Kennedy. He graduated from Yale University in 2015 and entered Harvard Law School in the fall of 2017 and Harvard Business School in the fall of 2018. On May 11, 2018, he made his acting debut as Officer Jack Hammer on the eighth season of the television show Blue Bloods.

Schwarzenegger Arnold Alois (July 30, 1947 –) is an Austrian-American actor, businessman, and former politician and professional bodybuilder. He served as the 38th Governor of California from November 17, 2003, to January 3, 2011.

Seeger Pete (May 3, 1919 – January 27, 2014) was an American folk singer and socialist activist. He was a longstanding opponent of the arms race and of the Vietnam War.

Seaton Frederick Andrew (December 11, 1909 – January 16, 1974) was an American newspaperman and politician. He represented the US state of Nebraska in the US Senate and served as US secretary of the Interior during Dwight D. Eisenhower administration.

Seberg Jean Dorothy (November 13, 1938 – August 30, 1979) was an American actress who lived half her life in France. Her performance in Jean-Luc Godard's 1960 film "Breathless" immortalized her as an icon of French New Wave cinema. Seberg died at the age of 40 in Paris, with police ruling her death a probable suicide.

Seigenthaler John Lawrence (July 27, 1927 – July 11, 2014) was an American journalist, writer, and political figure. He was known as a prominent defender of First Amendment Rights. He was Robert F. Kennedy's administrative assistant.

Shaw Maud (1903 – 1988) served as the governess for the children of Jacqueline and John F. Kennedy during the period 1956 and 1963.

Shepard Alan Bartlett Jr. (November 18, 1927 – July 21, 1998) was an American astronaut, naval aviator, test pilot and businessman. In 1961, he became the first American to travel into space, and in 1971, he walked on the moon.

Shriver Maria Owings (November 6, 1955) is an American journalist, author, former first lady of California, and the founder of the nonprofit organization: The Women's Alzheimer's Movement." She was married to former Governor of California and actor Arnold Schwarzenegger, from whom she filed for divorce in 2011.

Shriver Robert Sargent (November 9, 1915 – January 18, 2011) was an American diplomat, politician and activist. As the husband of Eunice Kennedy Shriver, he was part of the Kennedy family. Shriver was the driving force behind the creation of the Peace Corps. He was the first director of the Peace Corps from 1961 until 1966. He was the 21st ambassador to France from 1968 until 1970.

Sinatra Francis Albert (December 12, 1915 – May 14, 1998) was an American singer, actor and producer who was one of the most popular and influential musical artists of the 20th century. He is one of the best-selling music artists of all time, having sold more than 150 million records worldwide.

Smathers George Armistead (November 14, 1913 – January 20, 2007) was an American lawyer and politician who represented the state of Florida in the United States Senate from 1951 until 1969 and in the United States House from 1947 to 1951 as a member of the Democratic Party.

Smith Stephen Edward (September 24, 1927 – August 19, 1990) was the husband of Jean Ann Kennedy. He was a financial analyst and political strategist in the 1960 United States presidential campaign of his brother-in-law John F. Kennedy.

Sorensen Theodore Chaikin (May 8, 1928 – October 31, 2010) was an American lawyer, writer, and presidential advisor. He was a speechwriter for President John F. Kennedy, as well as one of his closest advisors. President Kennedy once called him his "intellectual blood bank."

Spalding Charles F. (a.k.a Chuck Spalding (April 12, 1918 – December 29, 1999) was an American heir, political advisor, television screenwriter and investment banker. He was a political campaigner during the presidential campaigns of John F. Kennedy and Robert F. Kennedy. He was a screenwriter for Charlie Chaplin.

Spellman Francis Joseph (May 4, 1889 – December 2, 1967) was an American Bishop and Cardinal of the Catholic Church. From 1939 until his death in 1967, he served as the sixth Archbishop of New York. He had previously served as an auxiliary Archdiocese of Boston from 1932 through 1939. He was created a Cardinal in 1946.

Spivack Robert G. (April 28, 1915 – June 25, 1970) was a syndicated columnist and former Washington correspondent for the New York Post.

Stennis John Cornelius (August 3, 1901 – April 23, 1995) was an American politician who served as US Senator from the State of Mississippi. He was a Democrat who served in the Senate for over 41 years, becoming its most senior member for his last eight years.

Stevenson Adlai (February 5, 1900 – July 14, 1965) was an American lawyer, politician and diplomat. He was the 31st Governor of Illinois from January 10, 1949, to January 12, 1953, and he won the Democratic Party's nomination for president in the 1952 and 1956 elections but lost twice against Eisenhower. He became US Ambassador for the United Nations from 1961 until his death in 1965.

Stone Oliver (September 15, 1946 –) is an American movie director, producer and screenwriter. He has become a controversial figure in American filmmaking, with critics accusing him of promoting unsubstantiated conspiracy theories and of misrepresenting real-world events and figures in his works.

Sullivan William Cornelius "Bill" (May 12, 1912 – November 9, 1977) directed Federal Bureau of Investigation (FBI) domestic intelligence operations from 1961 to 1971. Sullivan was forced out at the FBI at the end of September 1971 due to disagreements with FBI director J. Edgar Hoover.

Swanson Gloria Mae Josephine (March 27, 1899 – April 4, 1983) was an American movie, television, stage, voice, radio, silent movie actress, singer and movie producer.

Sylvester Arthur (October 21, 1901 – December 28, 1979) was Assistant Secretary of defense for Public Affairs in JFK's administration.

Symington William Stuart III (June 26, 1901 – December 14, 1988) was an American businessman and Democratic politician. He served as the first Secretary of the Air Force from 1947 to 1950 and was a United States Senator from Missouri from 1953 to 1976.

Taft William Howard (September 15, 1857 – March 8, 1930) was the 27th president of the United States from March 4, 1909, to March 4, 1913. He was the tenth Chief Justice of the United States (1921-1930), the only person to have held both offices.

Taylor Maxwell Davenport (August 26, 1901 – April 19, 1987) was a senior United States Army officer and diplomat of the mid-20th century. After the war, he served as the fifth Chairman of the Joints Chiefs of Staff, having been appointed by President John F. Kennedy.

Thompson Llewellyn E. 'Tommy" Jr. (August 24, 1904 – February 6, 1972) was a United States diplomat. He was a key advisor to President John F. Kennedy during the Cuban Missile Crisis.

Thornberry William Homer (January 9, 1909 – December 12, 1995) was an American politician and judge. He served as the United States Representative from the 10th congressional district of Texas from 1949 to 1963.

Tito Josip Broz (May 7, 1892 – May 4, 1980) was a Yugoslav communist, revolutionary and statesman, serving in various roles from 1943 until his death in 1980. He served as the President of the Socialist Federal Republic of Yugoslavia from January 14, 1953, to May 4, 1980.

Tobin James (March 5, 1918 – March 11, 2002) was an American economist who served on the Council of Economic Advisors and consulted with the Board of Governors of the Federal Reserve System and taught at Harvard and Yale Universities. He developed the ideas of Keynesian economics and advocated government intervention to stabilize output and avoid recessions.

Tobin Maurice J. (May 22, 1901 – July 19, 1953) was a Mayor of Boston, Massachusetts, the Governor of Massachusetts, and United States Secretary of Labor.

Tojo Hideki (December 30, 1884 – December 23, 1948) was a Japanese politician and general of the Imperial Japanese Army (IJA) who served as Prime Minister of Japan and President of the Imperial Rule Assistance Association for most of World War II.

Tolson Clyde Anderson (May 22, 1900 – April 14, 1975) was the second-ranking official of the FBI from 1930 until 1972, from 1947 titled Associate Director, primarily responsible for personnel and discipline. He is best known as the protégé and longtime top deputy of FBI director J. Edgar Hoover.

Travell Janet Graeme (December 17, 1901 – August 1, 1997) was an American physician and medical researcher. She is remembered as President John F. Kennedy's personal physician and a researcher of the concept of trigger points as a cause of musculoskeletal referred pain.

Trujillo Rafael Leonidas Molina, nicknamed El Jefe "The Chief" or "the Boss" (October 24, 1891 – May 30, 1961), was a Dominican dictator who ruled the Dominican Republic from February 1930 until his assassination in May 1961.

Truman Harry S. (May 8, 1884 – December 26, 1972) was the 33rd president of the United States from April 12, 1945, to January 20, 1953, succeeding upon the death of Franklin D. Roosevelt after serving as vice president. He implemented the Marshall Plan to rebuild the economy of Western Europe and established the Truman Doctrine and NATO.

Trump Donald John (June 14, 1946 –) was the 45th president of the United States from January 20, 2017 to January 20, 2021. Before entering politics, he was a businessman and media personality.

Valenti Jack Joseph (September 5, 1921 – April 26, 2007) was a Special Assistant to US President Lyndon B. Johnson and the longtime president of the Motion Picture Association of America.

<u>Vidal Eugene Luther Gore</u> (October 3, 1925 – July 31, 2012) was an American writer and public intellectual known for his epigrammatic wit, erudition, and patrician manner.

<u>Von Braun Wernher Magnus Maximilian Freiherr</u> (March 12, 1912 – June 16, 1977) was a German-born American aerospace engineer and space architect. He was the leading figure in the development of rocket technology in Nazi Germany and a pioneer of rocket and space technology in the United States. Von Braun had an ambivalent and complex relationship with the Nazi third Reich. He applied for membership of the Nazi Party on November 12, 1937, and was issued membership number 5.738.692.

<u>Wallace George Corley Jr.</u> (August 25, 1919 – September 13, 1998) was an American Democratic politician who served as the 45th Governor of Alabama for four terms. He sought the United States presidency as a Democrat three times and once as an American Independent Party candidate, unsuccessfully each time.

<u>Washington George</u> (February 22, 1732 – December 14, 1799) was an American political leader, military general, statesman, and Founding Father who served as the 1st President of the United States from April 30, 1789, until March 4, 1797.

<u>Watkins Arthur Vivian</u> (December 18, 1886 – September 1, 1973) was a Republican US Senator from Utah, serving two terms from 1947 into 1959. He was influential as a proponent of terminating federal recognition of American Indian tribes in the belief that they should be assimilated and all treaty rights abrogated.

<u>Webb James Edwin</u> (October 7, 1906 – March 27, 1992) was an American government official who served as the second appointed administrator of NASA from February 14, 1961, to October 7, 1968.

<u>West James Bernard</u> (July 27, 1912 – July 18, 1983) was the 6th Chief Usher of the White House, serving from 1957 to 1969.

<u>White Byron Raymond "Whizzer"</u> (June 8, 1917 – April 15, 2002) was an American lawyer and professional football player who served as an Associate Justice of the Supreme Court of the United States from 1962 to 1993.

<u>Wicker Thomas Grey "Tom"</u> (June 18, 1926 – November 25, 2011) was an American journalist. He was best known as a political reporter and columnist for the New York Times.

<u>Wiesner Jerome Bert</u> (May 30, 1915 – October 21, 1994) was a professor of

electrical engineering, chosen by President Kennedy as chairman of his Science Advisory Committee (PSAC). He was an outspoken critic of manual exploration of outer space, believing instead in automated space probes.

Wilkins Roy Ottoway (August 30, 1901 – September 8, 1981) was a prominent activist in the Civil Rights Movement in the United States from the 1930s to the 1970s. His most notable role was his leadership of the National Association for the Advancement of Colored People (NAACP), in which he held the title of Executive Secretary from 1955 to 1963 and Executive Director from 1964 to 1977.

Williams Brian Douglas (May 5, 1959 –) is an American journalist at MSNBC, currently serving as the network's chief anchor and host of its nightly wrap-up program, The 11th Hour with Brian Williams.

Williams G. Mennen "Soapy" (February 23, 1911 – February 2, 1988) was the 41st Governor of Michigan, elected in 1948 and serving six two-year terms in office. He later served as Assistant Secretary of State for African Affairs under Presidents John F. Kennedy and Lyndon B. Johnson and chief justice of the Michigan Supreme Court.

Wilson Thomas Woodrow (December 28, 1856 – February 3, 1924) was an American politician and academic who served as the 28th president of the United States from March 4, 1913, to March 3, 1921.

Wofford Harris Llewellyn (April 9, 1926 – January 21, 2019) was an American attorney, civil rights activist and Democratic politician who represented Pennsylvania in the United States Senate from May 8, 1991, to January 3, 1995.

Yates Richard (February 3, 1926 – November 7, 1992) was an American fiction writer identified with the mid-century "Age of Anxiety."

Young Whitney Moore Jr. (July 31, 1921 – March 11, 1971) was an American civil rights leader. In 1961 at age 40, Young became Executive Director of the National Urban League.

Zedong Mao (December 26, 1893 – September 9, 1976), also known as Chairman Mao, was a Chinese communist revolutionary who became the founding father of the People's Republic of China (PRC), which he ruled as the chairman of the Communist Party of China from its establishment on March 29, 1943 until his death in 1976. Ideologically a Marxist-Leninist, his theories, military strategies, and political policies are collectively known as Maoism.

<u>Zorin(e) Valerian Alexandrovich</u> (January 1, 1902 – January 14, 1986) was a permanent Representative of Russia to the United Nations, best remembered for his famous confrontation with Adlai Stevenson on October 25, 1962 during the Cuban Missile Crisis.

Notes

Author's Notes

1. Stern, S. M. 2012. The Cuban Missile Crisis in American Memory. Myths versus Reality – p. 5.
2. White, M. J. 1998. Kennedy. The New Frontier Revisited. p.262 – Transcript, Donahue show, 30 May 1991 – note 15 p. 275.
3. Bradlee, B. C. 1975. Conversations with Kennedy – p. 12
4. Heymann, C.D. 1989. A Woman Name Jackie – p. 364
5. Heymann, C.D. 2014. Joe and Marylin – p. 315
6. Anderson, C. 2013. These Few Precious Days. The Final Year of Jack with Jackie – p. 170
7. Fenn, D. H. Jr. 2014. Young Again. Letter from Dan H. Fenn – April 24, 2014
8. Sabato, L.J. 2013. The Kennedy Half Century – p. 255
9. Martin, R.G. 1995. Seeds of Destruction. Joe Kennedy and his sons – p. 436

Chapter 1: The Influence of The Parents on John F. Kennedy's Preparation for the Presidency

1.1. Who Was Joseph P. Kennedy?
1. Nasaw, D. 2012. The Patriarch. The Remarkable Life and Turbulent Times of Joseph P. Kennedy – Introduction xxiii
2. The Patriarch. December 7, 2012. Interview with David Nasaw by Randy Dotinga
3. Kessler, R. 1996. The Sins of the Father – p. 27-28
4. Kennedy, J. P. 1940. Joseph P. Kennedy's Radio Address on Behalf of Franklin Roosevelt's Third-term Election, October 29, 1940
5. The Patriarch. December 7, 2012. Interview with David Nasaw by Randy Dotinga
6. Koskoff, D. E. 1974. Joseph P. Kennedy: A life and Times — p. 375 – Source Martin, H. 1957. "The Amazing Kennedys Saturday Evening Post, September 7, 1957 p. 19-48 + Standard-Times (New Bedford Mass.) September 12, 1943, also p. 400
7. Nasaw, D. 2012. The Patriarch. The Remarkable Life and Turbulent Times of Joseph P. Kennedy – p. 535-536
8. Bergstrom, S. 2009. Set Your Compass True. The Wisdom of John, Robert, and Edward Kennedy – p. 177
9. Hamilton, N. 1992. JFK Reckless Youth – p. 680 – Source J. Patrick Lannan interview JCBP and JCB, p. 366- 369
10. Kennedy, R. 1974. Times to Remember – p. 201
11. O'Donnell, K. & Powers, D. F. 1970-1972. Johnny, We Hardly Knew Ye… Memoirs of John F. Kennedy – David F. Powers – p. 39
12. Interview with Françoise Pelligrino in Antibes, December 5, 2015
13. Kessler, R. 1996. The Sins of the Father – p. 419
14. Kennedy E.M. 2009. True Compass – A Memoir – p. 292

1.2. When Did Jack Kennedy Decide to Run for Public Office?
1. Kennedy, J. P. 1936. I'm for Roosevelt – inside cover
2. Cutter, J. H. 1962. Honey Fitz – p. 301
3. Ernest Renan: French philosopher (02/28/1823 – 10/02/1892)
4. Goodwin, D. K. 1987. The Fitzgeralds and the Kennedys – p. 705-707
5. Kennedy, R. F. 1974. Times to Remember – p. 305-306
6. Kennedy, E. M. 2009. True Compass a memoir – p. 89-90
7. Hamilton, N. 1992. JFK Reckless youth – p. 673 – source KLB interview CBSI
8. Kennedy Dictabelt Conversation 39. The Miller Center, John F. Kennedy Presidential Recordings: John F. Kennedy on Politics and Public Service
9. Burns, J. M. 1959. John Kennedy A Political Profile – p. 57

10. O'Donnell, K. & Powers, D. F. 1970. Johnny, We Hardly Knew Ye: Memoirs of John F. Kennedy – p. 44-45
11. Blair C. Jr & Blair J. 1976. The Search for JFK – p. 356
12. Fay, P. B. Jr. 1966. The Pleasure of His Company – p. 149-150-151-152
13. Blair C. Jr & Blair J. 1976. The Search for JFK – p. 357
14. Krock, A. 1968. Memoirs – p. 328-329 - Oral History Interview 05/01/1964
15. Gallagher. E. M. 1965. Oral History Interview JFKL – 01/08/1965
16. Lord, D. C. 1977. John F. Kennedy. The Politics of Confrontation and Conciliation – p. 26-27
17. O'Brien, M. 2005. John F. Kennedy A Biography – p. 190-191
18. Parmet, H. S. 1980. Jack: The struggles of John F. Kennedy – p. 125-126
19. Reed, J. A. 1964. Oral History JFKL – 06/16/1964 – p.13
20. O'Donnell, K. & Powers, D. F. 1970. Johnny, We Hardly Knew Ye: Memoirs of John F. Kennedy – p. 46
21. Perry, B. A. 2013. Rose Kennedy, the Life and Times of A Political Matriarch – – p. 184
22. Renehan, E. J. Jr. 2002. The Kennedy's at War — p. 314
23. Cutler, J. H. 1962. Honey Fitz – p. 307
24. Collier, P & Horowitz, D. 1984. The Kennedys - An American Drama – p. 150
25. Widmer, T. 2012. Listening In The Secret White House Recordings of John F. Kennedy – excerpts from Dinner Party conversation January 5, 1960 in Washington DC: JFK and his wife Jacqueline – their guests included Ben Bradlee, then Newsweek's Washington bureau chief, and his then wife Tony and Newsweek correspondent James M. Cannon – p. 27-42

1.3. Joe Jr., 'the Golden Boy' Compared With Jack, 'the Sick One'

1. Hamilton, N. 1992. JFK Reckless Youth – p. 163-299-527-689

1.4. Jack Kennedy's Possible Career Instead of Politics

1. McCarthy, J. 1960. The Remarkable Kennedys – p. 89
2. Droney, J.J. 1964. OH interview JFKL – 11/30/1964
3. Gallagher, E.M. 1965. OH interview JFKL – 01/08/1965
4. Sorensen, T. 1965. Kennedy – p. 15
5. Schlesinger, Jr. A. 1965. A Thousand Days – p. 89
6. Fay, P.B., 1966. The Pleasure of his Company – p. 152
7. Krock. A. 1968. Memoirs – p. 349-350
8. O'Donnell, K. and Powers, D.F. 2013. Johnny, we hardly knew ye: memories of John Fitzgerald Kennedy – p. 46.
9. Goodwin, D.K. 1987. The Fitzgeralds and the Kennedys. – p. 699-700 – source: Russell F. 1976. The President Makers – p. 361

10. Reeves, T.C. 1991. A Question of Character: A life of John F. Kennedy. Charles Spalding Oral History JFKL – p. 73 – source: Charles Spalding Oral History JFKL

11. Kennedy. E.M. 2009. True Compass: A Memoir – p. 89

12. Perry, B.A. 2013. Rose Kennedy: The Life and Times of a Political Matriarch – p. 184

13. Pitts, D. 2009. Jack and Lem: The untold Story of an extraordinary Friendship – p. 105

14. Dallek, R. 2003. An Unfinished Life: John F. Kennedy, 1917-1963 – p. 114-120

15. Blair C. Jr & Blair J. 1976. The search for JFK - p. 586

16. O'Brien, M. 2005. John F. Kennedy: A Biography – p. 181

1.5. How Did Jack Kennedy Meet With Kenneth O'Donnell and David F. Powers

1. O'Donnell, K. and Powers, D. F. 1970-1972. Johnny, We Hardly Knew You: Memories of John F. Kennedy – p. 51-52-53-54-55.

2. Laurence, L. 2001. The Kennedy Men: 1970-1972. The Laws of the father – p. 230.

3. O'Donnell, K. and Powers, D.F. 1970-1972. Johnny, we hardly knew ye: Memories of John F. Kennedy – p. 51-52-53-54-55.

4. O'Donnell, H. 2015. The Irish Brotherhood: John F. Kennedy, His Inner Circle, and the Improbable Rise to the Presidency– p. 23-24.

1.6. The James Michael Curley Pay Off

1. Blair C. Jr & Blair J. 1976. The search for JFK – p. 396.

2. Hamilton, N. 1992. JFK, Reckless Youth. Kane interview RMEEP – p.674.

3. Beatty, J. 1992. The Rascal King: The Life and Times of James Michael Curley (1874-1958) – p. 456.

4. Whalen, T.J. 2000. Kennedy Versus Lodge: The 1952 Massachusetts Senate Race – p. 22.

5. Perret, G. 2001. Jack: A Life Like No Other – p. 134.

6. Laurence, L. 2001. The Kennedy Men: 1901-1963. The Laws of the Father – p. 231.

7. Dallek, R. 2003. An Unfinished Life: John F. Kennedy, 1917-1963 – p. 122.

8. O'Brien, M. 2005. John F. Kennedy: A Biography – p. 191.

9. Nasaw, D. 2012. The Patriarch: The Remarkable Life and Turbulent Times of Joseph P. Kennedy – p. 593.

10. Shaw, J.T. 2013. JFK in the Senate: Pathway to the Presidency – p. 14.

11. Goodwin, D.K., 1991. The Fitzgeralds and the Kennedys – p. 708.

Also on the $ 12,000 pay off: Martin, R.G. 1995. Seeds of Destruction: Joe Kennedy and His Sons – p. 133

1.7. How Many Family Dollars Were Invested in the Campaign?
1. Martin, R.G. and Plaut, E. 1960. Front Runner: Dark Horse – p. 133.
2. Koskoff, D.E. 1974. Joseph P. Kennedy: A Life and Times – p. 407- 598.
3. O'Neill and Novak, W. 1987. Man of the House: The Life and Political Memoirs of Speaker Tip O'Neill – p.77-81.
4. Martin, R.G. 1995. Seeds of Destruction – p. 140.
5. Hersh, S.M. 1997. The dark side of Camelot – p. 41- 42.
6. Thomas, E. 2002. Robert Kennedy: his life – p. 48.
7. Dallek, R. 2003. An Unfinished Life: John F. Kenned, 1917-1963 – p. 130.
8. Dalton, M. 1964. Oral History Interview JFKL – 08/04/1964

1.8. Jack Kennedy's First Campaign for Congress in 1946
1. O'Donnell, K.P., Powers, D.F. and McCarthy, J. 1970. Johnny, We Hardly Knew Ye: Memories of John F. Kennedy – p. 47-48.
2. Goodwin, D.K. 1987. The Fitzgeralds and the Kennedys: An American Sage – p. 706.
3. O'Donnell, K.P., Powers, D.F. and McCarthy, J. 1970. Johnny, We Hardly Knew Ye: Memories of John F. Kennedy – p. 59.
4. John F. Kennedy Presidential Recordings Miller Center John F. Kennedy on Politics and Public Service. Kennedy Dictabelt Conversation 39.
5. Historical Journal of Massachusetts Summer. 2013. p.118.
6. Dallek, R. 2003. An Unfinished Life John F. Kennedy 1917-1963 – p. 128.
7. O'Donnell, K.P., Powers, D.F. and McCarthy, J. 1970. Johnny, We Hardly Knew Ye: Memories of John F. Kennedy – p. 63-64.
8. Cutler, J.H. 1962. Honey Fitz: Three steps to the White House: The Life and Times of John F. (Honey Fitz) Fitzgerald – p. 307.
9. Perret, G. 2001. Jack: A Life Like No Other – p.135.
10. Bzdek, V. 2009. The Kennedy legacy: Jack, Bobby and Ted and a family dream fulfilled – p. 61.
11. Cutler, J.H. 1962. Honey Fitz: Three steps to the White House: The Life and Times of John F. (Honey Fitz) Fitzgerald – p. 308.
12. Goodwin, D. K. 1987. The Fitzgeralds and the Kennedys An American Saga – p. 708.
13. O'Neill and Novak, W. 1987. Man of the House: The life and political memoirs of Speaker Tip O'Neill - p. 77-78
14. Koskoff, D. E. 1974. Joseph P. Kennedy: A Life and Times – p. 408.
15. Nasaw, D. 2012. The Patriarch: The Remarkable Life and Turbulent Times of Joseph P. Kennedy – p. 597.
16. Dalton, M. 1964. OH JFKL 1 – 08/04/1964
17. Droney, J. J. 1964. OH JFKL – 11/30/1964
18. Blair C. Jr & Blair J. 1976. The search for JFK – p. 398.

19. Hamilton, N. 1992. JFK Reckless Youth – p. 750-751.
20. Matthews, C. 2011. Jack Kennedy: Elusive Hero – p. 82.
21. Martin, R.G. 1995. Seeds of Destruction: Joe Kennedy and his sons – p. 137.

1.9. Conclusion

1. Kennedy, J.F. September 12, 1960. Quoted in Newsweek – p. 30
2. Kennedy, R.F. 1974. Times to Remember – p. 308-309.
3. Parmet, H.S. 1980. Jack: The struggles of JFK – p. 138.
4. Dalton, M. 1964. OH interview JFKL – 08/04/1964.
5. Smith, A. 2001. Hostage to Fortune. The Letters of Joseph P. Kennedy – p. 625.
6. Nasaw, D. 2012. The Patriarch: The Remarkable Life and Turbulent Times of Joseph P. Kennedy – p. 598.
7. Goodwin, D.K. 1987. The Fitzgeralds and the Kennedys – p. 707.
8. Dalton, M. 1964. OH Interview JFKL – 08/04/1964
9. Parmet, H.S. 1980. Jack: The struggles of John F. Kennedy – p. 147.
10. Parmet, H.S. 1978. David F. Powers interview – July 24, 1978

Chapter 2: Who Wrote 'Profiles In Courage'?

2.1. Where did the Idea for the Book Come From?

1. Sorensen, T. 1965. Kennedy – p. 66-67-68.
2. O'Brien, M. 2005. John F. Kennedy: A Biography – p. 284-285.
3. Parmet, H.S. 1980. Jack: The Struggles of John F. Kennedy – p. 325.
4. Martin, R. G. and Plaut, Ed. 1960. Front Runner: Dark Horse – p. 200.
5. Shaw, J. T. 2013. JFK in the Senate: Pathway to the Presidency – p. 126.
6. Sorensen, T.C. 2008. Counselor: A Life at the edge of History – p. 145.
7. O'Donnell, K.P., Powers, D.F. and McCarthy, J. 1970. Johnny We Hardly Knew Ye – p. 103-104.
8. Sorensen, T.C. 2008. Counselor: A Life at the edge of History – p. 145-146.
9. Parmet, H.S. 1980. Jack: The Struggles of John F. Kennedy – p. 326-327.
10. Letters Evan Thomas to JFK. May 6, 1955. Profiles in Courage Papers JFKL Box 31.
11. Burns, J.M.G. John Kennedy: A Political Profile – p. 162.
12. O'Brien, M. 2005. John F. Kennedy: A Biography – p. 285.
13. Sorensen, T. 1965. Kennedy – p. 68.
14. Letter JFK to Eunice Shriver. , July 26, 1955. Profiles in courage Papers JFKL Box 31. The . Letters of John F. Kennedy 2013 – p. 48.
15. Letter JFK to Evan Thomas. August 1, 1955 – Evan Thomas to JFK August 4, 1955, Profiles in Courage Papers JFKL Box 31.
16. O'Brien, M. 2005. John F. Kennedy: A Biography – p. 286.
17. Parmet, H.S. 1980. Jack: The Struggles of John F. Kennedy – p. 322.
18. Longford, L. 1976. Kennedy – p. 40.
19. Fenn, D.H. 2016. Email – December 10, 2016
20. Phillips, C. 1956. Men who dared to stand alone. The New York Times, January 1, 1956
21. Poore, C. 1956. Review of Profiles in Courage. New York Times, January 7, 1956
22. Shaw, J.T. 2013. JFK in the Senate: Pathway to the Presidency – p. 130.
23. Parmet, H.S. 1980. Jack: The Struggles of John F. Kennedy – p. 320.
24. O'Brien, M. 2005. John F. Kennedy: A Biography – p. 289.
25. Reeves, T.S. 1991. A Question of Character: A Life of John F. Kennedy – p. 128.
26. Shaw, J.T. 2013. JFK in the Senate: Pathway to the Presidency – p. 131.
27. Silvestri, V.N. 2000. Becoming JFK: A Profile in Communication – p.54.
28. Profiles in Courage. Email. February 16, 2017. Translated in 23 Languages - Right Queries <Right>

2.2. Who Helped Him Write the Book

1. Kennedy, J.F. 1956. Profiles in Courage – preface xxi – xxii – xxiii.
2. Letter Schlesinger, A. to Kennedy, J. July 4, 1955. Department of History Cambridge Mass. Profiles in Courage Papers JFKL Box 31.
3. Parmet, H.S. 1980. Jack: The Struggles of John F. Kennedy – p. 326.
4. Hohenberg, J. 1997. The Pulitzer Diaries inside America's Greatest Prize – p. 49.
5. Kessler, R. 1996. The Sins of the Father: Jospeh P. Kennedy and the Dynasty he founded – p. 348-349.
6. Smith, A. 2001. Hostage to Fortune. The letters of Joseph P. Kennedy – p. 669.
7. O'Donnell, K.P., Powers, D.F. and McCarthy, J. 1970. Johnny We Hardly Knew Ye – p. 101.
8. Krock, A. 1968. Memoirs Sixty years on the Firing Line – p. 355.
Krock, A. 1964. OH JFKL, 05/10/1964 – p. 24-25.
Letter Krock to JFK. April 9, 1954. Presidents Office Files JFKL Box 31.
9. Heymann, C.D. 1989-1994. A Woman Named Jackie: An intimate Biography of . . . . Jacqueline Kennedy Onassis – p. 172-174-175.

2.3. Who Saw Him Write the Book?

1. Krock, A. 1968. Memoirs: Sixty years on the Firing Line – p. 354,376.
2. Travell, J. 1968. Office Hours: Day and Night. The Autobiography of Janet, M.D. – p. 7.
3. Bartlett, C.L. 1965. Oral History Interview JFKL, 01/06/1965 – p. 25.
4. Kennedy, R.F. 1974. Times to Remember – p. 146.
5. Sitrin, G. 1966. Oral History Interview, 06/14/1966 – p. 5-6.
6. Pitts, D. 2007. Jack and Lem: John F. Kennedy and Lem Billings. The Untold story of an extraordinary friendship – p. 145

Further Reading

- O'Brien, M. 2005. John F. Kennedy: A Biography – p. 336.

2.4. The Drew Pearson Episode

1. Parmet, H.S. 1980. Jack: The Struggles of John F. Kennedy – p. 330.
2. Shaw, J.T. 2013. JFK in the Senate: Pathway to the Presidency – p. 134
Seldes, G. May 15, 1957. The Lively Arts. Village Voice.
Sheehy, E. Letter to Kennedy, J. July 17, 1957. John F. Kennedy. File US Senate Library
Kennedy, J. F. July 23, 1957. John F. Kennedy Letter to Emma Sheehy. File US Senate Library.
3. Clifford, C. and Holbroke, R. 1991. Council To The President: A Memoir – p.

306- 307- 308- 309- 310.

4. Abell, T. 1974. Drew Pearson Diaries 1949-1959 – p. 405- 418.

5. O'Brien, M. 2005. John F. Kennedy: A Biography – p. 333 – 334.

6. Martin, R.G. 1995. Seeds of Destruction: Joe Kennedy and his sons – p. 201.

7. Heymann, C.D. 1989-1994. A Woman Named Jackie. An intimate Biography of Jacqueline Kennedy Onassis – p. 176.

8. Clifford, C. 1974. Oral History Interview JFKL – 12/16/1974

9. Collier, P. and Horowitz, D. 1984. The Kennedy's An American Drama – p. 207. Note: Joe Kennedy asked Hoover: See Joseph P. Kennedy FBI File

10. Parmet, H.S. 1980. Jack: The Struggles of John F. Kennedy – p. 330-552, Nichols, L.B. to Tolson, C. May 14, 1957. JFK File FBI.

11. Parmet, H.S. 1980. Jack: The Struggles of John F. Kennedy – p. 330-331.

12. Hohenberg, J. 1997. The Pulitzer Diaries inside America's Greatest Prize – p. 51.

Further Reading

- Kessler, R. 1996. The Sins of the Father: Joseph P. Kennedy and the Dynasty he founded – p. 351-352

- Sorensen, T.C. 2008. Counselor: A Life at the edge of history – p. 148- 149- 150.

- Brogan, H. 1996. Kennedy – p. 36.

- Burns, J.M.G. 1959-1960. John Kennedy: A Political Profile – p. 163.

- Kessler, R. 1996. The Sins of the Father: Joseph P. Kennedy and the Dynasty he founded – p. 351.

- O'Brien, M. 2005. John F. Kennedy: A Biography – p. 334-335.

2.5. Sorensen's Role in Profiles in Courage

1. Kennedy, J.F. 1956. Profiles in Courage – p. 237.

2. Sorensen, T.C. 2008. Counselor: A Life at the edge of history – p. 150.

3. Martin, R.G. and Plaut, E. 1960. Front Runner Dark Horse – p. 199-200-201-202.

4. Sorensen, T.C. 1965. Kennedy – p. 69.

5. Pitts, D. 2007. Jack and Lem: John F. Kennedy and Lem Billings. The Untold story of an extraordinary friendship – p. 145.

6. Parmet, H.S. 1980. Jack: The Struggles of John F. Kennedy – p. 326-327.

7. Letter Davids, J. to Parmet. November 30, 1978. p. 327.

8. Sabato, L.J. 2013. The Kennedy Half-Century: The Presidency, Assassination and lasting legacy of John F. Kennedy – p. 442 note 30.

9. Cohen, P. October 18, 1997. The New York Times Books.

10. Birkner, M.J. November 22, 2010. Ghost's Story.

11. Cohen, P. October 18, 1997. The New York Times Books.
12. Letter Jules Davids to JFK. February 15, 1956. Profiles in Courage papers JFKL Box 32.
13. Letter JFK to Jules Davids. February 27, 1956. Profiles in Courage papers JFKL box 32.
14. Cohen, P. October 18, 1997. The New York Times Books. Selverstone, M.J. 2014. A Companion to John F. Kennedy – p. 115-118.
15. Perret, G. 2001. Jack: A Life Like No Other – p. 213-215.
16. Hellmann, J. 1997. The Kennedy Obsession. The American Myth of JFK – p. 76.
17. Dallek, R. 2003. An Unfinished Life: Kennedy 1917-1963 – p. 199.
18. Parmet, H.S. 1980. Jack: The Struggles of John F. Kennedy. Sorensen interview with Parmet May 17, 1977 – p. 551 notes.
19. Burns, J.M.G. 1965. Oral History interview JFKL, 05/14/1965 – p. 28-29-30-31.
20. Schlesinger, R. 2008. White House Ghosts Presidents and their speechwriters from FDR to George W. Bush – p. 143-144.
21. Sorensen, T.C. 2008. The Counselor: A Life at the edge of History – p. 151.
22. Email from Fenn D. H. Jr. – December 10, 2016.
23. Kennedy, C. 2011. Jacqueline Kennedy Historic Conversations on Life with John F. Kennedy. Interviews with Arthur M. Schlesinger Jr. 1964 – p. 59-62.

2.6. Parmet's Prejudicial Approach

1. O'Brien, M. 2005. John F. Kennedy: A Biography – p. 339.
2. Mannix, J.M.G. 1996. Oral History Interview JFKL – 03/06/1966
3. Parmet, H.S. Jack: The Struggles of John F. Kennedy – p. 325; Jules Davids to Herbert Parmet; November 30, 1978 – p. 551 note 39 – p. 551 note 41 Jean Mannix, JFKL-OH
4. Sitrin, G.L. 06/14/1966. Oral History Interview JFKL. Sorensen interview by Parmet. May 17, 1977.
5. Sorensen, T.S. 1965. Kennedy – p. 68.
6. Parmet, H.S. 1980. Jack: The Struggles of John F. Kennedy – p. 328.
7. Parmet, H.S. 1980. Jack: The Struggles of John F. Kennedy – p. 328.
8. Memorandum. 05/23/1955. Profiles in Courage JFKL Box 31.
9. O'Brien, M. 2005. John F. Kennedy: A Biography – p. 339.
10. Parmet, H.S. 1980. Jack: The Struggles of John F. Kennedy – p. 325.
11. Bartlett, C.L. 1965. Oral History Interview JFKL – 01/06/1965
12. Parmet, H.S. 1983. Oral History Interview JFKL – 08/09/1983
13. Clifford, C. 1974. Oral History Interview JFKL – 10/16/1974
14. Parmet, H.S. 1980. Jack: The Struggles of John F. Kennedy – p. 323.
15. Burns, J.M.G. 1965. Oral History Interview JFKL – 05/04/1965

16. Parmet, H.S. 1980. Jack: The Struggles of John F. Kennedy – p. 332-333.
17. Letter JFK to Evan Thomas. June 23 and August 1, 1955. Profiles in Courage Papers Box 31.
18. Letter JFK to Ernest Hemingway. July 26, 1955

2.7. Did Arthur Krock Lobby for the Pulitzer Prize?

1. Kessler, R. 1996. The Sins of the Father: Joseph P. Kennedy and the Dynasty he founded – p. 349.
"Joe then persuaded Arthur Krock": interview by Joan and Clay Blair Jr. . . . with Krock, Nigel Hamilton papers, MH.
2. Perret, G. 2001. Jack: A Life Like No Other – p. 216.
3. Dallek, R. 2003. An Unfinished Life: John F. Kennedy 1917-1963 – p. 210.
4. Wills, G. 1981. The Kennedy Imprisonment. A Meditation on Power. – p. 137.
5. Brinkley, A. 2012. John F. Kennedy – p. 34.
6. Smith, S.B. 2004. Grace and Power: The Private world of the Kennedy White House. Arthur Krock interview JCBC – p. 84.
7. Leamer, L. 1994. The Kennedy Woman: The Saga of an American Family – p. 467.
8. Matthews, C. 2011. Jack Kennedy: Elusive Hero – p. 227.
9. Parmet, H.S. 1980. Jack: The Struggles of John F. Kennedy – p. 396.
10. Martin, R.G. 1995. Seeds of Destruction: Joe Kennedy and his sons. Oral History interview with Lucus A. Star by Evan Thomas, June 1974 # 1177 PRCQ 52-43, Columbia University – p. 201.
11. Parmet, H.S. 1980. Jack: The Struggles of John F. Kennedy. John Hohenberg Interview, June 18, 1977 – p. 396.

Further Reading

• Wills, G. 1981. The Kennedy Imprisonment: A Meditation on Power – p. 135.

2.8. Conclusion

1. Kennedy, J.F. 1956. Profiles in Courage – p. 18 - p. 240.
2. Longford, L. 1976. Kennedy – p. 41.
3. Burns, J.M.G. 1959-1960. John Kennedy a political Profile – p. 160.
4. Perret, G. 2001. Jack: A Life Like No Other – p. 216
5. Parmet, H.S. 1980. Jack: The Struggles of John F. Kennedy – p. 323.
6. Ted Sorensen to JFK. September 12, August 12, October 20, 1955. Sorensen Papers Box 7 JFKL.
7. O'Brien, M. 2005. John F. Kennedy: A Biography – p. 287.
8. Dallek, R. 2003. An Unfinished Life: John F. Kennedy 1917-1963 – p. 197.
9. Sorensen, T.C. 1965. Kennedy – p. 68.

10. Sorensen, T.C. 2008. Counselor: A Life at the edge of History – p. 147.

11. Burns, J.M.G. 1959-1960. John Kennedy a political Profile – p. 167-168.

12. Schlesinger, A.M. 1965. A Thousand Days: John F. Kennedy in the White House – p. 208.

13. Schlesinger, R. 2008. White House Ghosts Presidents and their speechwriters from FDR to George W. Bush – p. 104.

14. Bartlett, C.L. 1965. Oral History Interview JFKL, 01/06/1965 – p. 28.

15. O'Brien, M. 2005. John F. Kennedy: A Biography – p. 339.

16. Parmet, H.S. 1980. Jack: The Struggles of John F. Kennedy. Ted Sorensen interview May 17, 1977 – p. 324.

17. Dallek, R. 2003. An Unfinished Life: Kennedy 1917-1963 – p. 199.

18. Parmet, H.S. 1980. Jack: The Struggles of John F. Kennedy. Blair Clark interview with the author, March 18, 1977 – p. 330.

19. Heymann, D. 1989-1994. A Woman Named Jackie: An intimate Biography of Jacqueline Kennedy Onassis – p. 173.

20. Willis, G. 1981. The Kennedy Imprisonment: A meditation on Power – p.138.

21. McNamara, R.S. 1964. Oral History Interview JFKL – 04/04/1964

22. Smith, S.B. 2004. Grace and Power: The Private World of the Kennedy White House – p. 84.

23. Schlesinger, A.M. 1965. A Thousand Days: John F. Kennedy in the White House – p. 14.

24. O'Brien, M. 2005. John F. Kennedy: A Biography – p. 290.

Further Reading

- Mills, J. 1988. John F. Kennedy – p. 121-122.

- Reeves, T.C. 1991. A Question of Character: A Life of John F. Kennedy – p. 127-128.

- Lord, D.C. 1977. John F. Kennedy: The politics of Confrontation and Conciliation – p. 60.

- Clinch, N.G. 1973. The Kennedy Neurosis – p. 142-143.

- McElrath, J. 2008. The Everything John F. Kennedy Book – p. 100-101.

- O'Brien, M. 2009. Rethinking Kennedy: An Interpretive Biography – p. 77-78.

- Matthews, C. 1996. Kennedy & Nixon: The Rivalry that shaped Postwar America – p.106.

- Lasky, V. 1963. JFK: The Man and the Myth – p. 224, 225, 226, 229.

Chapter 3: Who Elected JFK: A Rendezvous With History

3.1. His Father Bought Him the Election

1. Finding aid prepared by Karen Garcia Raines. June 12, 2014. OAC Descriptive Finding Guide for Caroline JFK Campaign Aircraft SPASM 50-10023. .

2. Lasky, V. 1963. JFK: The Man and the Myth – p. 321.

3. Pietrusza, D. 2008. 1960 LBJ vs JFK vs Nixon. The Epic Campaign that forged three Presidents – p. 86.

4. Lincoln, E. 1965. My twelve years with John F. Kennedy – p. 125.

5. Kessler, R. 1996. The Sins of the Father: JosephP. Kennedy and the Dynasty he Founded – p. 377.

6. Princeton, NJ. 1962. Financing the 1960 Election by Herbert E. Alexander. Citizins Research Foundation – p. 17-18.

7. Parmet, H.S. 1980. Jack: The Struggles of John F. Kennedy – p. 512.

8. Pietrusza, D. 2008. 1960 LBJ vs JFK vs Nixon. The Epic Campaign that forged three Presidents – p. 86.

9. O'Brien, M. 2005. John F. Kennedy: A Biography – p. 437.

10. Davis, J.H. 1984. The Kennedy Dynasty and Disaster 1948-1983 – p. 234.

11. Rorabaugh, W.J. 2009. The Real Making of the President: Kennedy, Nixon and the 1960 Election – p. 46.

12. Martin, R.G. and Plaut, Ed. 1960. Front Runner Dark Horse – p. 215.

13. Lasky, V. 1963. JFK: The Man and the Myth – p. 321.

14. Whalen, R.J. 1964. The Founding Father. The Story of Joseph P. Kennedy – p. 453.

15. Schwarz, T. 2003. The Mogul, The Mob, The Statesman and the Making of an American Myth Joseph P. Kennedy – p. 392.

16. BZDEK, V. 2009. The Kennedy Legacy: Jack, Bobby and Ted and a family dream fulfilled – p. 74.

17. Pitts, D. 2007. Jack and Lem: John F. Kennedy and Lem Billings. The Untold Story of an extraordinary friendship – p. 158.

18. Bradlee, C.B. 1975. Conversations with Kennedy – p. 26.

19. Dallek, R. 2003. An Unfinished Life: John F. Kennedy 1917-1963 – p. 257.

20. O'Brien, L.F. 1974. No Final Victories: A Life in Politics from John F. Kennedy to Watergate – p. 68-69.

21. O'Brien, M. 2005. John F. Kennedy: A Biography – p. 449.

22. White, T.H. 1961. The Making of the President 1960 – p. 99.

23. Humphrey, H.H. 1991: The Education of a Public Man: My life in Politics – p. 159-160.

24. Chafin, R. and Sherwood, T. 1994. Just good Politics: The Life of Raymond Chafin, Appalachian boss – Jean-Paul Sartre: Kennedy and West Virginia, Morality and History.

25. Lasky, V. 1960. John F. Kennedy: What's behind the image – p. 195.

26. Martin, R.G. and Plaut, E. 1960. Front Runner, Dark Horse – p. 459.

27. Whalen, R.J. 1964. The Founding Father: The Story of Joseph P. Kennedy – p. 453.

28. Hersh, S.M. 1997. The Dark Side of Camelot – p. 90-95-98.

29. Ernst, H.W. 1962. Eagleton Institute: The Primary that Made a President West Virginia – p. 30-31.

30. Humphrey, H.H. 1991. The Education of A Public Man: My life in Politics – p. 159.

31. Fleming, D.B. 1992. Kennedy vs Humphrey West Virginia 1960 – p.127 – p. 185 note 49.

32. Hersh, S.M. 1997. The Dark Side of Camelot – p. 329-330.

33. Kessler, R. 1996. The Sins of the Father: Joseph P. Kennedy and the Dynasty He Founded – p. 379 – notes p. 454.

34. Maas, P. 1990. Father and Son. Harper Collins reprint – p. 65.

35. Schwarz, T. 2003. The Mogul, The Mob, The Statesman and the making of an American Myth Joseph P. Kennedy – p. 399-400.

36. Rorabaugh, W.J. 2009. The Real Making of the President Kennedy, Nixon, and the 1960 Election – p. 55 – 220 note 27.

37. O'Neill, T. 1987. Man of the House: The Life and Political Memoirs of Speaker Tip O'Neill – p. 91-92.

38. Fleming, D.B. 1992. Kennedy vs Humphrey, West Virginia 1960: The Pivotal battle for the Democratic Presidential Nomination. Thomas P. 'Tip' O'Neill Jr.telephone interview with the author, November 2, 1988 – p. 157.

39. Leamer, L. 2001. The Kennedy Men 1901-1963. The Laws of the Father – p. 423.

40. Kessler, R. 1996. The Sins of the Father: Joseph P. Kennedy and the Dynasty he Founded – p. 376.

41. Mahoney, R.D. 1999. Sons & Brothers: The Days of Jack and Bobby Kennedy – p. 53.

42. Fleming, D.B. 1992. Kennedy vs Humphrey, West Virginia 1960: The Pivotal Battle for the Democratic Presidential Nomination – Raymond Chafin, interview with author Omar, July 29, 1985, WVA – p. 100-101.

43. Loughry, A.H. 2006. Don't buy another vote: I won't pay for a landslide. The Sordid and continuing History of Political Corruption in West Virginia – p. 10.

44. Fleming, D.B. 1992. Kennedy vs Humphrey, West Virginia 1960: The Pivotal battle for the Democratic Presidential Nomination – p. 102.

45. Loughry, A.H. 2006. Don't buy another vote: I won't pay for a landslide. The Sordid and continuing History of Political Corruption in West Virginia – p. 10.

46. Chafin, R. & Sherwood, T. 1994. Just Good Politics: The Life of Raymond Chafin. Appalachian Boss – p. 132.

47. Fleming, D.B. 1992. Kennedy vs Humphrey, West Virginia 1960: The Pivotal Battle for the Democratic Presidential Nomination. Barrie interview with the

author – p. 104.

48. Davis, F.K. 2003. West Virginia Tough Boys. Vote Buyers, Fist Fighting And a President Named JFK – p. 139.

49. Fleming, D.B. 1992: Kennedy vs Humphrey, West Virginia 1960: The Pivotal Battle for the Democratic Presidential Nomination. Sargent Shriver, telephone interview with author, October 29, 1985 – p. 104.

50. Chafin, R. & Sherwood, T. 1994. Just Good Politics: The Life of Raymond Chafin. Appalachian Boss – p. 136-137.

51. Chafin, R. & Sherwood, T. 1994. Just Good Politics: The Life of Raymond Chafin. Appalachian Boss – p. 141-142.

52. Davis, F.K. 2003. West Virginia Tough Boys. Vote Buyers, Fist Fighting And a President Named JFK – p. 141.

53. Chafin, R. & Sherwood, T. 1994. Just Good Politics: The Life of Raymond Chafin. Appalachian Boss – p. 143.

54. Davis, F.K. 2003. West Virginia Tough Boys. Vote Buyers, Fist Fighting And a President Named JFK – p. 154.

55. Davis, F.K. 2003. West Virginia Tough Boys. Vote Buyers, Fist Fighting And a President Named JFK – p. 171-172.

Further Reading

- Pietrusza, D. 2008. 1960 LBJ vs JFK vs Nixon: The Epic Campaign that forged Three Presidencies – p. 124-125

3.2. The Franklin Roosevelt Jr. Factor in West Virginia

1. Leamer, L. 2001. The Kennedy Men 1901-1963 – p. 425-426.

2. Martin, R.G. 1995. Seeds of Destruction: Joe Kennedy and his Sons – p. 249.

3. Pietrusza, D. 2008. 1960 LBJ vs JFK vs Nixon – p. 121.

4. O'Donnell, K.P., Powers, D.F. and McCarthy, J. 1970-1972. Johnny We Hardly Knew Ye: Memories of John F. Kennedy – p. 165.

5. Collier, P.and Horowitz, D. 1984. The Kennedys: An American Drama – p. 239.

6. Martin, R.G. 1983. A Hero for our time: An intimate Story of the Kennedy Years – p. 22.

7. Kessler, P. 1996. The Sins of the Father – p. 107.

8. Pietrusza, D. 1960. LBJ vs JFK vs Nixon – p. 121.

9. Martin, R.G. 1983. A Hero For our Times: An Intimate Story of the Kennedy years – p. 122.

10. Pietrusza, D. 2008. 1960 LBJ vs JFK vs Nixon. The Epic Campaign that forged three Presidents – p. 121-122.

11. Martin, R.G. 1995. Seeds of Destruction: Joe Kennedy and his Sons – p. 249.

12. Lawrence, W.K. May 7, 1960. The New York Times.

13. O'Brien, M. 2005. John F. Kennedy: A Biography – p. 453.

14. Fleming, D.B. 1992. Kennedy vs Humphrey West Virginia 1960 – p. 50.

15. Leamer, L. 2001. The Kennedy Men – p. 426.

16. Pietrusza, D. 2008. 1960 LBJ vs JFK vs Nixon. The Epic Campaign that forged three Presidents – p. 123.

17. Schlesinger, A.M. 1978. Robert Kennedy and his Times – p. 201.

18. Heymann, C.D. 1998. RFK – p. 153-154.

19. Wisconsin Rapide Daily Tribune. May 7, 1960. p. 9.

20. O'Brien, L. 1974. No Final Victories – p. 72.

21. Kallina, E.F. 2010. Kennedy vs Nixon. The Presidential Election of 1960– p. 65.

22. Rorabaugh, W.J. 2009. The Real Making of the President. Kennedy, Nixon and the 1960 Election – p. 54.

23. Leamer, L. 2001. The Kennedy Men 1901-1963 – p. 426 – notes p. 792.

24. Fleming, D.B. 1992. Kennedy vs Humphrey, West Virginia 1960. The Pivotal battle for the Democratic Presidential Nomination – p. 51- p. 175 note 88.

25. Lawrence, W.P. 1996. OH JFKL – 4/22/1966

26. Wisconsin Rapide Daily Tribune. May 7, 1960.

27. White, T.H. 1978. In Search of History. A personal Adventure – p. 465.

28. Schlesinger, A.H. 1978. Robert Kennedy and his Times – p. 201.

29. Fleming, D.B. 1992. Kennedy vs Humphrey, West Virginia 1960: The Pivotal battle for the Democratic Presidential Nomination. Powers interview with the author – p. 52.

30. Feldman, M. 1966. OH JFKL – 3/13/1966

31. O'Brien, L.F. 1974. No Final Victories – p. 73.

32. Schlesinger, A.H. 1978. Robert Kennedy and his Times – p. 201.

33. Roosevelt recorded interview by Jean Stein, December 9, 1969

34. Humphrey, H.H. 1991. The Education of a Public Man. My Life in Politics – p. 363.

35. Dalek, R. 2003. An Unfinished Life: John F. Kennedy 1917-1963 – p. 256.

36. Pietrusza, D. 2008. 1960 LBJ vs JFK vs Nixon. The Epic Campaign that forged three Presidents – p. 123.

37. Goldwater, B.M. and Casserly, J. 1988. Goldwater – p. 139.

3.3. Choosing LBJ as Running Mate: A Labyrinth in Search of a Vice President

1. White, T.H. 1961. The Making of the President – p. 172-173.

Graham, K. 1997. Personal History – p. 266.

White, T.H. 1965. The Making of the President 1964. White – p. 407 Appendix B.

Caro, R.A. 2012. The Years of Lyndon Johnson: The Passage of Power – p. 641.

2. Schlesinger, A.H. 1978. Robert Kennedy and his times – p. 206.

3. Rorabaugh, W.J. 2002. Kennedy and the promise of the sixties – p. 152.

4. Graham, K. 1997. Personal History – p. 262.

5. Lincoln, K. 1968. Kennedy and Johnson – p. 96-97.

6. Guthman, E. 1971. We Band of Brothers – p. 78.

7. Shesol, J. 1997. Mutual Contempt – p. 40-41.

8. Gerald S. & Strober, D.H. 1993. Let Us Begin Anew – p. 16.

9. Schlesinger, A.H. 2007. Journals 1952-2000 – p. 78-79.

10. Clifford, C. 1991. Council to the President – p. 318.

11. Lasky, V. 1963. JFK: The Man and the Myth – p. 403.

12. Schlesinger, A.M. 1978. Robert Kennedy and his times – p. 211.

13. Dickerson, N. 1976. Among those present – p. 42-43.

14. Kallina, E.F. 2010. Kennedy vs Nixon – p. 77.

15. Goodwin, D.G. 1987. The Fitzgeralds and the Kennedys – p. 802.

16. Janeway, M. 2004. The Fall of the House of Roosevelt – p. 178-179.

17. Hersh, B. 2007. Bobby and J. Edgar – p. 14.

18. Janeway, M. 2004. The Fall of the House of Roosevelt – p. 178.

19. Guthman, E. 1971. We Band of Brothers – p. 78-79.

20. Schlesinger, A.H. 1965. A Thousand Days – p. 49.

21 Schlesinger, A.H. 1978. Robert Kennedy and his Times – p. 208.

22. Guthman, E.O. and Shulman, J. 1988. Robert Kennedy in his Own Words. The unpublished Recollections of the Kennedy years – p. 21.

23. White, T. 1961. The Making of the President 1960 – p. 175.

24. Lasky, V. 1968. Robert Kennedy. The Myth and the Man – p. 145-146.

25. Caro, R.A. 2012. The years of Lyndon Johnson – p. 124.

26. Schlesinger, A.H. 1965. A Thousand Days – p. 49.
Oral History Interview Charles Bartlett JFKL – 1/6/1965

27. Hilty, J.W. 1997. Robert Kennedy: Brother protector – p.157.

28. Hersh, S.M. 1997. The Dark Side of Camelot – p. 122.

29. Shesol, J. 1997. Mutual Contempt – p. 52.

30. Hilty, J.W. 1997. Robert Kennedy: Brother protector – p.157.

31. Lincoln, E. 1968. Kennedy and Johnson – p. 90-93.

32. Lincoln, E. 1965. My twelve years with John Kennedy – p. 164-165.

33. Johnson, L.B. 1979. Oral History Interview JFKL – 3/9/1979

34. Dickerson, N. 1976. Among those present – p. 43.

35. Dallek, R. 2003. An Unfinished Life – p. 270.

36. Pietrusza, D. 2008. 1960 LBJ vs JFK vs Nixon. The Epic Campaign that Forged Three P. residencies – p. 196.

37. O'Neil, T. 1987. Man of the House: The Life and Political Memoirs of Speaker Tip O'Neill with William Novak – p. 93-94-95.
Shesol, J. 1997. Mutual Contempt – p. 49-50.

38. Hilty, J.W. 1997. Robert Kennedy: Brother protector – p. 160

39. Miller, M. 1980. Lyndon: An Oral Biography – p. 256-257.

40. Caro, R.A. 2012. The Years of Lyndon – p. 127.

41. Caro, R.A. 2012. The Years of Lyndon – p. 128.

42. Sorensen, T.C. 1965. Kennedy – p. 162-163.

43. Dallek, R. 2003. An Unfinished Life – p. 268.
44. Hilty, J.W. 1997. Robert Kennedy Brother Protector – p. 158.
45. Sorensen, T.C. 1965. Kennedy – p.163.
46. Salinger, P. 1966. With Kennedy – p. 46.
47. Smathers, G.A. 1964. Oral History Interview JFKL – 7/10/1964
48. Slatem, E.G. 1988. RFK in his own words – p. 23.

Further Reading
- Fuller, H. 1962. Year of Trial Kennedy's Crucial Decisions – p. 8-9-10.
- O'Donnell, H. and O'Donnell, K. 2015. The Irish Brotherhood: John F. Kennedy His Inner Circle, and the Improbable Rise to the Presidency – p. 358-363.

The Blackmail from the Johnson camp
1. Salinger, P. 1966. With Kennedy – p. 44-45.
2. Hersh, S.M. 1997. The Dark Side of Camelot – p. 128.
3. Salinger, P. 1966. With Kennedy – p. 46.
4. Summers, A. 1993. Official and Confidential: The Secret Life of J. Edgar Hoover – p. 271.
5. Interview with Evelyn Lincoln. Blackmailing the President. Part 2 tube.com.
6. Summers, A. 1993. Official and Confidential: The Secret Life of J. Edgar Hoover – p. 272-. 273.
7. Hersh, S. M. 1997. The Dark Side of Camelot – p. 129.
8. Hersh, S.M. 1997. The Dark Side of Camelot – p. 123-124.
9. Raskin, H.B. 1964. Oral History Interview JFKL –5/8/1964
10. O'Donnell, H. 2018. Launching LBJ. How a Kennedy Insider Helped Define Johnson's Presidency – p. 36-37.

3.4. A Stolen Election with the Help of the Chicago Mob
1. Kallina, E.F. 2010. The Presidential Election of 1960: Kennedy vs Nixon – p. 212-213.
2. White, T.H. 1978. In Search of History: A Personal Adventure – p. 454.
3. Hersh, S.M. 1997. The Dark side of Camelot – p. 131.
4. O'Brien, M. 2005. John F. Kennedy: A Biography – p. 496-497.
5. Thomas, E. 2000. Robert Kennedy: His life – p. 107.
6. Hersh, S.M. 1997. The Dark Side of Camelot – p. 137-138.
7. Greenberg, D. Oct 16, 2000. Was Nixon Robbed? The Legend of the stolen 1960 presidential election.
8. Posner, G. Nov 10, 2009. The fallay of Nixon's graceful exit.
9. Nixon, R. 1978. The Memoirs of Richard Nixon – p. 224.
10. Donaldson, G.A. 2007. The First Modern Campaign. Kennedy, Nixon and the Election of 1960. Donaldson – p. 151.

11. Nixon, R.M. 1962. Six Crises – p. 419
12. Greenberg, D. Oct 16, 2000. Was Nixon Robbed? The Legend of the stolen 1960 presidential election.
13. Bradlee, B.C. 1975. Conversations with Kennedy – p. 33.
14. Bradlee, B.C. 1995. A Good Life – p. 212-213.
15. Kallina, E.F. 2010. The Presidential Election of 1960. Kennedy vs Nixon – p. 208.
16. Nixon, R. 1978. The Memoirs of Richard Nixon – p. 224.
17. Hersh, S.M. 1997. The Dark Side of Camelot – Hersh – p. 133.
18. O'Donnell H. amd O'Donnell, K. 2015. The Irish Brotherhood: John F. Kennedy: His inner Circle and the Improbable Rise to the Presidency – p. 426-427.
19. Nixon, R. 1978. The Memoirs of Richard Nixon – p. 224.
20. Lasky, V. 1977. It didn't start with Watergate – p. 50.
21. Kiel, R.A. 2000. J. Edgar Hoover. The Father of the Cold War – p. 73.
22. Greenberg, D. Oct 16, 2000. Was Nixon Robbed? The Legend of the stolen 1960 presidential election. History Lesson: The History behind current events.
23. Dallek, R. 2003. An Unfinished Life: John F. Kennedy 1917-1963 – p. 295.
24. O'Brien, M. 2005. John F. Kennedy: A Biography – p. 497.
25. Thomas, E. 2000. Robert Kennedy: His Life – p. 107.
26. White, T.H. 1978. In Search of History – p. 489.

3.5. Calling Mrs. Martin Luther King

1. Schlesinger, A. 1978. Robert Kennedy and his Times – p. 214-215.
2. Stein, J. October 3, 1968. Harris Wofford, in an interview by Jean Stein – Stein Papers
3. White, T.H. 1978. In Search of History: A personal adventure – p. 471.
4. Thomas, E. 2000. Robert Kennedy: His Life by Even Thomas – p. 101.
5. Pietrusza, D. 2008. 1960 LBJ vs JFK vs Nixon. The Epic Campaign that Forged Three Presidencies – p. 295.
6. White, T.H. 1961. The Making of the President 1960 – p. 321.
7. Matthews, C. 1996. Kennedy & Nixon: The Rivalry that Shaped postwar America – p. 170.
8. Rorabaugh, W.J. 2009. The Real Making of the President: Kennedy Nixon and the 1960 election – p. 167.
9. White, T.H. 1961. The Making of the President 1960 – p. 322.
10. White, T. 1978. In Search of History: A personal Adventure – p. 472.
11. Hilty, J.W. 1997. Robert Kennedy: Brother protector – p. 172.
12. Rorabaugh, W.J. 2009. The Real Making of the President. Kennedy, Nixon and the 1960 Election – p. 167.
13. Thomas, E. 2000. Robert Kennedy: His Life – p. 101.
14. Dallek, R. 2003. An Unfinished Life. John F. Kennedy 1917-1963 – p. 292.

15. Stossel, S. 2004. Sarge, The Life and times of Sargent Shriver – p. 163.

16. Pietrusza, D. 2008. 1960 LBJ vs JFK vs Nixon. The Epic Campaign that forged Three `Presidencies – p. 295.

17. Schlesinger, A.M. 1978. Robert Kennedy and his Times – p. 216.

18. Wofford, H. 1980. Of Kennedys and Kings: Making Sense of the Sixties – p. 16.

19. Wofford, H. 1980. Of Kennedys and Kings: Making Sense of the Sixties – p. 16.

20. Matthews, C. 1996. Kennedy & Nixon: The Rivalry that shaped postwar America – p. 170 – 171.

21. Schlesinger, A.M. 1978. Robert Kennedy and his Times – p. 216.

22. Pietrusza, D. 2008. 1960 LBJ vs JFK vs Nixon. The Epic Campaign that forged Three Presidencies – p. 295 – 296.

23. Dallek, R. 2003. An Unfinished Life: John F. Kennedy 1917-1963 – p.292.

24. O'Brien, M. 2005. John F. Kennedy: A Biography – p. 485.

25. Thomas, E. 2000. Robert Kennedy: His Life – p. 101.

26. Rorabaugh, W.J. 2009. The Real Making of the President. Kennedy, Nixon and the 1960 Election – p. 168.

27. Thomas, G.S. 2011. A New World to be Won. John Kennedy, Richard Nixon and the tumultuous years of 1960 – p. 229.

28. Hilty, J.W. 1997. Robert Kennedy: Brother Protector – p. 172.

29. Oliphant, T. and Wilkie, C. 2017. The Road to Camelot. Inside JFK's Five-years Campaign – p. 341.

30. White, T.H. 1961. The Making of the President 1960 – p. 322.

31. White, T.H. 1978. In Search of History: A Personal Adventure – p. 472.

32. Wofford, H. 1980. Of Kennedys & Kings: Making Sense of the Sixties – p. 17-18.

33. Sorensen, T.C. 1965. Kennedy – p. 215-216.

34. Wofford, H. 1980. Of Kennedys and Kings: Making Sense of the Sixties – p. 19.

35. Stossel, S. 2004. Sarge: The Life and Times of Sargent Shriver – p. 165.

36. Seigenthaler, J. 1964. Oral History Interview JFKL 1 – 7/22/1964

37. O'Donnell, H. and O'Donnell, K. 2015. The Irish Brotherhood – p. 401-402-403.

38. Gerald S. And Strober, D.M. 1993. Let Us Begin Anew: An Oral History of the Kennedy Presidency – p. 35-36.

39. Gerald S. And Strober, D.M. 1993. Let Us Begin Anew: An Oral History of the Kennedy Presidency – p. 35.

40. Hilty, J.W. 1997. Robert Kennedy: Brother Protector – p. 173.

41. Rorabaugh, W.J. 2009. The Real Making of the President. Kennedy, Nixon and the 1960 election – p. 169.

42. Thomas, E. 2000. Robert Kennedy: His Life – p. 103.

43. O'Brien, M. 2005. John F. Kennedy: A Biography – p. 486.

44. 1995. Seeds of Destruction Joe Kennedy and his Sons – Ralph G. Martin – p. 271

45. Schlesinger, A.M. 1978. Robert Kennedy and his Times – p. 218.

46. Galbraith, J.K. 1969. Ambassador's Journal: A personal Recount of the Kennedy years – p. 6.

47. Kallina, E.F. 2010. Kennedy vs Nixon: The Presidential Election of 1960 – p. 154.

48. Wofford, H. 1980. Of Kennedys and Kings. Making Sense of the sixties – p. 22.

49. O'Brien, M. 2005. John F. Kennedy: A Biography – p. 488.

50. Wofford, H. 1980. Of Kennedys and Kings. Making Sense of the sixties – p. 25.

51. Martin, R.G. 1995. Seeds of Destruction: Joe Kennedy and his Sons – p. 272.

52. Stossel, S. 2004. Sarge: The Life and Times of Sargent Shriver – p. 169.

53. Stossel, S. 2004. Sarge: The Life and Times of Sargent Shriver – p. 169.

54. Stossel, S. 2004. Sarge: The Life and Times of Sargent Shriver – p. 166.

55. Stossel, S. 2004. Sarge: The Life and Times of Sargent Shriver – p. 166-167.

56. Wofford, H. 1980. Of Kennedy and Kings. Making Sense of the Sixties – p. 23.

57. Hilty, J.W. 1997. Robert Kennedy: Brother Protector – p. 174-175.

58. Pietrusza, D. 2008. 1960 LBJ vs JFK vs Nixon – p. 298.

59. Kallina, E.F. 2010. Kennedy vs Nixon: The Presidential Election of 1960 – p. 155.

60. Gerald S. And Strober, D.M. 1993. Let Us Begin Anew: An Oral History of the Kennedy Presidency – p. 37.

61. Thomas, G.S. 2011. A New World to Be Won. John Kennedy, Richard Nixon and the Tumultuous year of 1960 – p. 230.

62. White, T.H. 1961. The Making of the President 1960 – p. 323.

63. Pietrusza, D. 2008. 1960 LBJ vs JFK vs Nixon – p. 298.

64. Rorabaugh, W.J. 2009. The Real Making of the President – p. 170.

65. Kallina, E.F. 2010. Kennedy vs Nixon: The Presidential Election of 1960 – p. 155.

66. Oliphant, T. and Wilkie, C. 2017. The Road to Camelot. Inside JFK's five-year campaign – p. 344-345.

67. Hilty, J.W. 1997. Robert Kennedy Brother Protector – p. 175.

68. Martin, R.G. 1995. Seeds of Destruction: Joe Kennedy and his sons – p. 272.

69. O'Brien, M. 2005. John F. Kennedy: A Biography – p. 487.

70. Nixon, R.M. 1962. Six Crises – p. 419.

71. Rorabaugh, W.J. 2009. The Real Making of the President. Kennedy, Nixon and the 1960 election – p. 168-169.

3.6. The TV Debates

1. Gerald S. And Strober, D.H. 1993. Let us Begin Anew. An Oral History of the Kennedy Presidency – p. 44.
2. O'Donnell, K.P., Powers, D.F. and McCarthy, J. 1970. Johnny, We Hardly Knew Ye: Memories of John F. Kennedy – p. 211.
3. Gerald S. And Strober, D.H. 1993. Let us Begin Anew. An Oral History of the Kennedy Presidency – p. 32.
4. Nixon, R. 1978. The Memoirs of Richard Nixon – p. 218.
5. Dallek, R. 2003. An Unfinished Life. John F. Kennedy 1917-1963 – p. 286.
6. White, T.H. 1961. The Making of the President– p. 282-283.
7. Horebek, A. 2015. The Cambridge Companion to John F. Kennedy – p. 47.
8. Nixon, R.M. 1962. Six Crises – p. 323.
9. Nixon, R. 1978. The Memoirs of Richard Nixon – p. 217.
10. Kraus, S. 1962. The Great Debates. Kennedy vs Nixon 1960 – p. 190.
11. Matthews, C. 1996. Kennedy Nixon. The Rivalry that shaped Postwar America – p. 150.
12. O'Brien, M. 2005. John F. Kennedy: A Biography – p. 480.
13. Sorensen, T. 2008. Counselor: A Life at the Edge of History – p. 190.
14. Selverstone, M.J. 2014. A Companion to John F. Kennedy – p. 66.
15. Rorabaugh, W.J. 2009. The Real Making of the President – p. 154.
16. Nixon, R.M. 1962. Six Crises – p. 346.
17. Donaldson, G.A. 2007. The First Modern Campaign. Kennedy, Nixon, and the Election of 1960 – p. 110.
18. Swisher, C. 2000. People who made History John F. Kennedy – p. 67.
19. Gerald S. And Strober, D.H. 1993. Let Us Begin Anew. An Oral History of the Kennedy Presidency – p. 31.
20. Kallina, E.F. 2010. The Presidential Election of 1960. Kennedy vs Nixon – p. 122.
21. Goodwin, R.N. 1988. Remembering America. A Voice from the Sixties – p. 115.
22. Bradlee, B. 1995. A Good Life. Newspapering and other adventures – p. 211.
23. Matthews, C. 1996. Kennedy & Nixon. The Rivalry that Shaped Postwar America – p. 148.
24. Matthews, C. 1996. Kennedy & Nixon. The Rivalry that shaped Postwar America – p. 149.
25. Horobek, A. 2015. The Cambridge Companion to John F. Kennedy – p. 48.
26. White, T. 1961. The Making of the President 1960 – p. 283-284.
27. Sorensen, T. 2008. Counselor: A Life at the Edge of History – p. 189.
28. Donaldson, 2007. The First Modern Campaign. Kennedy, Nixon and the Election of 1960 – p. 114.
29. Rorabaugh, W.J. 2009. The Real Making of the President. Kennedy, Nixon and the 1960 Election – p. 151.

30. Kraus, S. 1962. The Great Debates. Kennedy vs Nixon 1960 – p. 348-350.

31. Selverstone, M.O. 2014. A Companion to John F. Kennedy – p. 66.

32. Matthews, C. 1996. Kennedy & Nixon. The Rivalry that shaped Postwar America – p. 150.

33. Rorabaugh, W.J. 2009. The Real Making of the President. Kennedy, Nixon and the 1960 Election – p. 151-152.

34. White, T.H. 1961. The Making of the President 1960 – p. 287.

35. Pietrusza, D. 2008. 1960 LBJ vs JFK vs Nixon. The Epic campaign that forged three Presidencies – p. 346.

36. O'Donnell, K.P., Powers, D.F. and McCarthy, J. 1970. Johnny, We Hardly Knew Ye: Memories of John F. Kennedy – p. 214.

37. White, T.H. 1961. The Making of the President 1960 – p. 290.

38. Sorensen, T 2008. Counselor: A Life at the Edge of History – p. 190.

39. Nixon, R.M. 1978. The Memoirs of Richard Nixon – p. 219.

40. White, T.H. 1961. The Making of the President 1960 – p. 293.

41. O'Brien, M. 2005. John F. Kennedy: A Biography – p. 480-481.

42. Nixon, R.M. 1978. The Memoirs of Richard Nixon – p. 220.

43. Nixon, R. 1962. Six Crises – p. 346.

44. White, T.H. 1961. The Making of the President 1960 – p. 290.

45. Kraus, S. 1962. The Great Debates. Kennedy vs Nixon 1960 – p. 190.

46. Donaldson, G.A. 2007. The first Modern Campaign. Kennedy, Nixon and the election of 1960 – p. 112.

3.7. Bobby as a Campaign Manager

1. Kennedy, R.F. 1974. Times to Remember – p. 358.

2. Selverstone, M.J. 2014. A Companion to John F. Kennedy – p. 52-53.

3. Schlesinger, A.M. 1978. Robert Kennedy and his Times – p. 136.

4. Robert Kennedy in interview with John Bartlow Martin. December 7, 1966. Martin Papers, August 14, 1958

5. Davis, J.H. 1984. The Kennedys Dynasty and Disaster 1948-1984 – p. 283 – pocket version

6. Schlesinger, A.M. 1978. Robert Kennedy and his Times – p. 213.

7. Times. October 10, 1960. Sidey: Brother on the spot p. 209.

8. Martin, R.G. 1995. Seeds of Destruction: Joe Kennedy and his Sons – p. 235.

9. Schneider, S.K. 2001. Robert F. Kennedy – p. 32.

10. Thomas, E. 2000. Robert Kennedy His Life – p. 90.

11. Toledano, R.D. 1967. RFK: The Man Who Would Be President – p. 134.

12. Martin, R.G. 1995. Seeds of Destruction: Joe Kennedy and his Sons – p. 236.

13. Kallina, E.F. 2010. Kennedy vs Nixon. The presidential election of 1960 – p. 99

14. The 1960 Democratic Presidential race. People & Events. Internet.

15. Lasky, V. 1968. Robert F. Kennedy. The Myth and the Man – p. 152.
16. Johnson, P. 1997. A History of the American People – p. 851.

3.8. The Jacqueline Kennedy Factor
1. Tracy, K. 2008. The Everything Jacqueline Kennedy Onassis Book. A portrait of an American Icon – p. 112.
2. Schlesinger, A.M. 1965. A Thousand Days. John F. Kennedy in the White House – p. 17.
3. Lowe, J. 1996. Jacqueline Kennedy Onassis: The Making of a first Lady. A Tribute – p. 50.
4. Heymann, C.D. 1989. A Woman Named Jackie – p. 223.
5. Perry, B.A. 2004. Jacqueline Kennedy: First Lady of the New Frontier – p. 52-55 – notes p. 214.
6. Dallek, R. 2003. An Unfinished Life. John F. Kennedy 1917-1963 – p. 253-254.
7. David, L. 1994. Jacqueline Kennedy Onassis. A portrait of her private years – p. 54.
8. Heymann, C.D. 1989. A Woman Named Jackie – p. 221 – 222.
9. O'Donnell, K.P., Powers, D.F. and McCarthy, J. 1970. Johnny, We Hardly Knew Ye: Memories of John F. Kennedy – p. 156-157.
10. Perry, B.A. 2004. Jacqueline Kennedy. First Lady of the New Frontier – p. 53-60
11. Hall, G.L. and Ana Pinchot, A. 1964. Jacqueline Kennedy: A Biography – p. 156.
12. David, L. 1994. Jacqueline Kennedy, Onassis. A portrait of her private years – p. 54.
13. Tracy, K. 2008. The Everything Jacqueline Kennedy Onassis Book: A Portrait of an American Icon – p. 114.
14. Perry, B.A. 2004. Jacqueline Kennedy: First Lady of the New Frontier – p. 62. Notes p. 216 "Campaign Wife", October 27, 1960 (quotation) "Million cheer Kennedy in NY – Washington Post, October 20, 1960 – p. A 22

3.9. The Help of the Media
1. White, T.H. 1961. The Making of the President 1960 – p. 337-338.
2. Bradlee, B.C. 1975. Conversations with Kennedy – p. 18.
3. Kallina, E.J. 2010. The Presidential Election of 1960. Kennedy vs Nixon – p. 212.
4. Nixon, R.M. 1978. The Memoirs of Richard Nixon – p. 225.
3. Kallina, E.J. 2010. The Presidential Election of 1960. Kennedy vs Nixon – p. 213.
6. Donaldson, G.R. 2007. The First Modern Campaign. Kennedy, Nixon and the

Election of 1960 – p. 142.

7. Rorabaugh, W.J. 2009. The Real Making of the President. Kennedy, Nixon and the 1960 election – p. 174.

8. Sorensen, T.C. 1965. Kennedy – p. 169.

9. Krock, A. 1968. Memoirs: Sixty years on the firing Line – p. 366.

10. Nixon, R.M. 1962. Six Crises – p. 419.

3.10. The Economic Factor, Three Recessions

1. Donaldson, G.A. 2007. The First Modern Campaign. Kennedy, Nixon and the Election of 1960 – p. 127.

2. Dallek, R. 2003. An Unfinished Life John F. Kennedy 1917-1963 – p. 287-288 notes p. 756.

3. Sorensen, T.C. 1965. Kennedy – p. 217.

4. Matthews, C. 1996. Kennedy & Nixon. The Rivalry that shaped postwar America – p. 136.

5. Lord, D.C. 1977. John F. Kennedy. The politics of Confrontation and Conciliation – p. 81.

3.11. The Missile Gap

1. Oklahoma Jefferson-Jackson Day Dinner, Oklahoma City, Oklahoma November 7 1957. JFK Library.

2. Parmet, H.S. 1980. Jack: The Struggles of John F. Kennedy – p. 444.

3. Collier, P. & David Horowitz, D. 1984. The Kennedys: An American Drama – p. 232.

4. Papers of John F. Kennedy, Pre-Presidential Papers, Senate files, Serie 12, Speeches and the Press, Box 901. US Military Power, Senate Floor. August 14, 1958.

5. Lasky, V. 1963. JFK: The Man and the Myth – p. 361-362.

6. Collier, P. & David Horowitz, D. 1984. The Kennedys: An American Drama – p. 232.

7. Beschloss, M.R. 1991. The Crisis Years Kennedy and Khrushchev. 1960-1963 – p. 25- 26.

8. Dallek, R. 2003. An Unfinished Life. John F. Kennedy 1917-1963 – p. 289-290.

9. Raymond, J. February 6, 1960, published February 7. The New York Times. Special to the New York Times.

10. Reeves, R. 1993. President Kennedy. Profile of Power– p. 58.

11. Reeves, R. 1993. President Kennedy. Profile of Power– p. 59.

12. News Conference of February 8, 1961 Washington D.C.

13. Chase, H.W. and Lerman, A.H. 1965. Kennedy and the Press. The News Conferences – p. 19.

14. Taylor, M.D. 1972. Swords and Plowshares – p. 205.

15. Reeves, T.C. 1991. A Question of Character – p. 249.

16. Gilpatric, R.L. 1970. Oral History Interview JFKL – 6/30/1970

17. Guthman, E.O. and Jeffrey Shutman, J.1988. Robert Kennedy in his own words. The Unpublished Recollections of the Kennedy years – p. 305.

3.12. The Religious Issue

1. Sorensen, T. 2008. Counselor: A Life at the Edge of History – p. 156.

2. O'Brien, M. 2005. John F. Kennedy: A Biography – p. 414-415.

3. McCarthy, J. 1960. The Remarkable Kennedys – p. 18-19.

4. O'Brien, M. 2005. John F. Kennedy: A Biography – p. 416.

5. Lord, D.C. 1977. John F. Kennedy. The politics of confrontation and conciliation – p. 87.

6. Sorensen, T.C. 1965. Kennedy – p. 188.

7. Lasky, V. 1963. JFK: The Man and the Myth – p. 489.

8. Nixon, R.M. 1962. Six Crises – p. 307.

9. Menendez, A.J. 2011. The Religious Factor in the 1960 Presidential Campaign – p. 39-40.

10. Kallina, E.F. 2010. Kennedy vs Nixon. The Presidential Election of 196 - p. 170.

11. Casey, S.A. 2003. The Making of a Catholic President Kennedy vs Nixon 1960 – p. 192.

12. Meet the Press. Sunday, September 11, 1960.

13. Martin, R.G. 1983. A Hero for our Time – p. 192.

14. O'Donnell, K.P., Powers, D.F. and McCarthy, J. 1970. Johnny, We Hardly Knew Ye: Memories of John F. Kennedy – p. 206- 207.

15. Sabato, L. 2013. The Kennedy Half-Century. The Presidency, Assassination and Lasting Legacy of John F. Kennedy – p. 61.

16. White, T.H. 1961. The Making of the President 1960 – p. 260.

17. Lasky, V. 1963. JFK: The Man and The Myth – p. 490.

18. Sorensen, T.C. 1988. Let the Word go forth – p. 130-131-132- 133-134.

19. Rorabaugh, W.J. 2009. The Real Making of the President. Kennedy, Nixon and the 1960 election – p. 145.

20. Dickerson, N. 1976. Among those Present – p. 54.

21. 1991. A Question of character: A Life of John F. Kennedy – Thomas C. Reeves . . . – p. 192-193

22. The New York Times. September 14, 1960. Poling praises Kennedy's Stand on Religion Issue.

23. Reeves, T.C. 1991. A Question of character. A Life of John F. Kennedy – p. 192.

24. White, T.H. 1978. In Search of History: a Personal Adventure – p. 486.

25. O'Donnell, K.P., Powers, D.F. and McCarthy, J. 1970. Johnny, We Hardly

Knew Ye: Memories of John F. Kennedy – p. 208- 209.

26. Sorensen, T. 1965. Kennedy – p. 190.

27. Gerald S. And Strober, D.H. 1993. Let Us Begin Anew. An Oral History of the Kennedy Presidency – p. 44-45.

28. Martin, R.J. 1983. A Hero for our Time – p. 192-193.

29. Donaldson, G.A. 2007. The First Modern Campaign. Kennedy, Nixon and the Election of 1960 – p.157.

30. Carty, T.J. 2004. A Catholic in the White House – p. 157.

31. Dallek, R. 2003. An Unfinished Life. John F. Kennedy 1917-1963 – p. 283.

32. Ithiel de Sola Pool, Robert P. Abelson, Samuel L. Popkin Candidates. 1964. Issues and Strategies. A Computer Simulation of the 1960 Presidential Elections Cambridge MA, the MIT Press – p. 115-117.

3.13. Nixon's Mistakes

1. White, T.H. 1961. The Making of the President 1960 – p. 308.

2. Kallina, E.F. 2010. Kennedy vs Nixon. The Presidential Election of 1960 – p. 161.

3. White, T.H. 1961. The Making of the President 1960 – p. 309.

4. Nixon, R.M. 1978. The Memoirs of Richard Nixon – p. 221-222.

5. Pietrusza, D. 2008. 1960 LBJ vs JFK vs Nixon. The Epic Campaign that forged three presidents – p. 386.

6. Kallina, E.F. 2010. Kennedy vs Nixon. The Presidential Election of 1960 – p. 162.

7. Nixon, R.M. 1962. Six Crises – p. 418.

8. White, T.H. 1961. The Making of the President 1960 – p. 309- 310.

9. Selverstone, M.J. 2014. A Companion to John F. Kennedy – p. 63.

10. Matthews, C. 1996. Kennedy & Nixon. The Rivalry that shaped postwar America – p. 136.

11. Donaldson, G.A. 2007. The First Modern Campaign. Kennedy, Nixon and the election of 1960 – p. 129.

12. Donaldson, G.A. 2007. The First Modern Campaign. Kennedy, Nixon and the election of 1960 – p. 130-131.

13. Nixon, R.M. 1962. Six Crises – p. 419.

14. Goodwin, R.N. 1988. Remembering America – p. 106.

15. Rorabaugh, W.J. 2009. The Real Making of the president – p. 122.

16. Nixon, R.M. 1978. The Memoirs of Richard Nixon – p. 219.

17. Lasky, V. 1963. JFK: the Man and the Myth – p. 432.

18. Nixon, R.M. 1962. Six Crises – p. 419-420-421.

19. Nixon, R.M. 1962. Six Crises – p. 418-419.

20. Bradlee, B.C. 1975. Conversations with Kennedy – p. 18-19.

21. Dallek, R. 2003. An Unfinished Life. John F. Kennedy 1917-1963 – p. 706.

3.14. What Was the Vote Margin in the 1960 Presidential Election?

1. White T. H. 1978. The Making of the President 1960 – p. 386 Appendix A
2. Lasky V. 1963. JFK, The man and the Myth – p. 494
3. Nixon, R.M. 1978. The Memoirs of Richard Nixon – p. 224
4. Kallina Jr. E. F. 1988. Courthouse over White House: Chicago and the Presidential Election of 1960 – Appendix.
Kallina Jr. E. F. 2010. Kennedy vs Nixon. The presidential election of 1960
5. Reeves, R. 1993. President Kennedy. Profile of Power – p. 18
6. Matthews C. 1996. Kennedy & Nixon, The Rivalry That Shaped Postwar America – p. 181
7. Johnson P. 1997. A History of the American People – p. 854
8. Davis K. F. 2003. West Virginia Tough Boys: Vote Buying, Fist Fighting, and a President Named JFK – p. 174
9. Donaldson G. A. The first Modern Campaign: Kennedy, Nixon, and the Election of 1960, 2007 – p. 153
10. Pietrusza D. 2008. LBJ vs JFK vs Nixon – p. 409
11. Rorabaugh W. J. 2009. The Real Making of the President: Kennedy, Nixon and the 1960 Election – p. 210
12. Thomas G. S. 2011. "A New World to be Won. John Kennedy, Richard Nixon and the Tumultuous Year of 1960" – p. 256
13. Wilkie C., Oliphant T. 2017. The Road to Camelot Inside JFK's Five-Year Campaign – p. 355

Chapter 4: JFK and Cuba - From The Bay Of Pigs To The Cuban Missile Crisis

4.1. The Bay of Pigs: A Brilliant Disaster

1. Gerald S. and Strober, D.H. 1993. Let Us Begin: An Oral History of the Kennedy Presidency – p. 323-324.

2. Martin, R.G. 1983. A Hero for out Time – p. 287.

3. Nixon, R.M. 1962. Six Crises – p. 353-354.

4. Wyden, P. 1979. Bay of Pigs. The Untold Story – p. 67.

5. Giglio, J.N. and Rabe, S.G. 2003. Debating the Kennedy Presidency – p. 32.

6. Dallek. 2003. An Unfinished Life. John F. Kennedy 1917-1963 – p. 362.

7. Lord, D.C. 1977. John F. Kennedy. The politics of Confrontation and Conciliation – p. 182.

8. O'Brien, M. 2005. John F. Kennedy. A Biography – p. 522-523.

9. Wyden, P. 1979. Bay of Pigs. The Untold Story – p. 46.

10. Dean Rusk as told to Richard Rusk. 1990. As I Saw it – p. 208.

11. Kennedy, P. January 10, 1961. The New York Times.

12. Schlesinger, A.M. 1965. A Thousand Days. John F. Kennedy in the White House – p. 238.

13. Schlesinger, A.M. 1965. A Thousand Days. John F. Kennedy in the White House – p. 240-242-243.

14. Wyden, P. 1979. Bay of Pigs. The Untold Story – p. 99-100.

15. Salinger, P. 1966. With Kennedy – p. 146.

16. The Kennedy Presidential Press Conferences. April 12, 1961 – p. 76.

17. O'Brien, M. 2005. John F. Kennedy. A Biography – p. 525-526.

18. Sabato, L.J. 2013. The Kennedy Half Century. The Presidency, Assassination, and Lasting Legacy of John F. Kennedy – p. 82.

19. Dallek, R. 2003. An Unfinished Life. John F. Kennedy 1917-1963 – p. 360-361.

20. Dean Rusk as told to Richard Rusk. 1990. As I Saw it – p. 209-210.

21. Acheson, D.G. 1964. Oral History interview JFKL1 – 4/27/1964

22. Parmet, H.S. 1983. JFK. The Presidency of John F. Kennedy – p. 163.

23. Schlesinger, A.M. 1965. A Thousand Days. John F. Kennedy in the White House – p. 251.

24. O'Brien, M. 2005. John F. Kennedy. A Biography – p. 527.

25. Schlesinger, A.M. 1965. A Thousand Days. John F. Kennedy in the White House – p. 251.

26. Smith, M.E. 1980. John F. Kennedy's 13 Great Mistakes in the White House – p. 82-83-84.

27. Thompson, K. 1985. The Kennedy Presidency Seventeen intimate perspectives of John F. Kennedy. Portraits of American Presidents Volume IV – p. 142-143.

28. O'Brien, M. 2005. John F. Kennedy. A Biography – p. 528.

29. Schlesinger, A. and Schlesinger, S. 2007. Journals 1952-2000 – p.109-110.

30. 1980 John F. Kennedy's 13 Great Mistakes in the White House – Malcolm E. Smith – p.82

31. O'Brien, M. 2005. John F. Kennedy. A Biography – p. 529.

32. Kennedy, J. 2011. Historic Conversation on Life with John F. Kennedy interviews with Arthur M. Schlesinger Jr. 1964 – p. 182.

33. Paterson, T.G. 2000. People who made history John F. Kennedy – p. 119.

34. Giglio, J.N. and Rabe, S.G. 2003. Debating the Kennedy Presidency – p. 32.

35. Reeves, R. 1993. President Kennedy. Profile of Power – p. 91.

36. Dallek, R. 2003. An Unfinished Life. John F. Kennedy 1917-1963 – p. 364-365.

37. O'Brien, M. 2005. John F. Kennedy. A Biography – p. 533.

38. Schlesinger, A. and Schlesinger, S. 2007. Journals 1952-2000 – p.118.

39. Dallek, R. 2003. An Unfinished Life. John F. Kennedy 1917-1963 – p. 371. Taylor, M.D. 1960. The Uncertain Trumpet.

40. Brogan, H. 1996. Kennedy – p. 68.

41. Smith, M.E. 1980. John F. Kennedy. 13 Great Mistakes in the White House – p. 92.

42. Parmet, H.S. 1983. JFK. The Presidency of John F. Kennedy – p. 177.

43. Longford, L. 1976. Kennedy – p. 87.

44. O'Brien, M. 2005. John F. Kennedy. A Biography – p. 536.

45. Wyden, P. 1979. Bay of Pigs. The Untold Story – p. 325-326.

46. McNamara, R.S. 1964. Oral History Interview JFKL – 4/4/1964

47. Rusk, D. 1970. Oral History Interview JFKL3 – 9/19/1970

48. Dallek, R. 2003. An Unfinished Life. John F. Kennedy 1917-1963 – p. 365-366.

49. Selverstone, M.J. 2014. A Companion to John F. Kennedy – p. 232.

50. Hersh, S.M. 1997. The Dark side of Camelot – p. 214.

51. Interviews 1972-1973. The reminiscences of Admiral Robert L. Dennison are available from the U.S. Naval Institute in Annapolis.

52. O'Donnell, K.P., Powers, D.F. and McCarthy, J. 1970. Johnny, We hardly knew ye. Memories of John Fitzgerald Kennedy – p. 275.

53. Guthman, E.O. and Jeffrey Shulman, J. 1988. Robert Kennedy in his own words. The unpublished Recollections of the Kennedy years – p. 246.

54. Schlesinger, A.M. 1965. A Thousand Days. John F. Kennedy in the White House – p. 297.

55. White, M.J. 1998. Kennedy. The New York Frontier Revisited – p. 85.

56. Dallek, R. 2003. An Unfinished Life. John F. Kennedy 1917-1963 – p. 573.

57. Email Dan H. Fenn Jr. – June 22, 2018

58. Rostow, W.W. 1964 Oral History Interview JFKL – 4/11/1964

59. Taylor, M.D. 1972. Swords and Plowshares – p. 193.

60. Galbraith, J.K. 2002. Oral History Interview JFKL2 – 09/12/2002

61. Reeves, R. 1993. President Kennedy. Profile of Power – p. 106.

62. Paterson, T.G. 1989. Kennedy's quest for Victory. American Foreign Policy 1961-1963 – p. 129.

63. The Kennedy Presidential Press Conferences. April 21, 1961. p. 90.

64. Schlesinger, A.M. 1965. A Thousand Days. John F. Kennedy in the White House – p. 289-290.

65. Schlesinger, A.M. 2011. Jacqueline Kennedy. Historic Conversations on Life with John – p. 186-187.

66. Reeves, R. 1993. President Kennedy. Profile of Power – p. 678.

67. Siegel, R. 2007. NPR 24 Hour Program Stream.
https:/www.npr.org/templates/story/story.php?storyId=10785989.

68. Schlesinger, A.M. 1965. A Thousand Days. John F. Kennedy in the White House – p. 283.

69. Wyden, P. 1979. Bay of Pigs. The Untold Story – p. 292.

70. Schlesinger, A.M. 1965. A Thousand Days. John F. Kennedy in the White House – p. 284.

71. The Memoirs of Richard Nixon. 1978. p. 233-234.

72. Kennedy, R.F. 1974. Times to Remember – p. 400.

73. Schlesinger, A.M. 2011. Jacqueline Kennedy. Historic Conversations on Life with John – p. 185-186.

74. O'Donnell, K.P., Powers, D.F. and McCarthy, J. 1970. Johnny, we hardly knew you. Memoirs of John Fitzgerald Kennedy – p. 274-275.

75. Salinger, P. 1995. P.S. A Memoir – p. 110-111.

76. O'Donnell, K.P., Powers, D.F. and McCarthy, J. 1970. Johnny, we hardly knew you. Memoirs of John Fitzgerald Kennedy – p. 272.

77. Reeves, R. 1993. President Kennedy. Profile of Power – p. 95 – 677.

78. Dallek, R. 2003. An Unfinished Life. John F. Kennedy 1917-1963 – p. 366-367.

79. Dr. Janet Travell medical records. Jan-April 1961. JFKL.

80. Clifford, C and Holbrooke, R. 1991.Council to the President. A Memoir – p. 349.

81. Cushing, C.R. 1966. Oral History interview. JFKL – p. 9.

82. Fay, P.B. 1970. Oral History interview. JFKL1 – 11/09/1970

83. Sorensen, T.C. 1965. Kennedy – p. 308.

84. Billings, K.L.M. 1965. Oral History interview. JFKL10 – 06/18/1965.

85. Time Magazine. Friday, May 5, 1961.

4.2. The Cuban Missile Crisis: President Kennedy in Total Control

1. Talbott, S. 1970. Khrushchev Remembers – p. 493-494.

2. Schlesinger, A.M. 1965. A Thousand Days. John F. Kennedy in the White House – p. 795.

3. Stern, S.M. 2012. The Cuban Missile Crisis in American Memory. Myths versus Reality – p. 155.

4. Gerald S. and Strober, D.H. 1993-2003. Let Us Begin anew: An Oral History of the Kennedy Presidency – p. 388.

5. Kennedy, R. 1988. Robert Kennedy in His Own Words – p. 19.

6. Gerald S. and Strober, D.H. 1993-2003. Let Us Begin anew. An Oral History of the Kennedy Presidency – p. 388-389.

7. Sorensen, T.C. 2008. Counselor. A Life at the Edge of History – p. 287.

8. Sorensen, T.C. 1965. Kennedy – p. 676-677-678.

9. Blight, J.G. & Welch, D.A. 1989. On The Brink. Americans and Soviets Reexamine the Cuban Missile Crisis – p. 27-28.

10. The Kennedy Presidential Press Conferences. 1978. p. 379-380.

11. Giglio, J.N. 2006. The Presidency of John F. Kennedy. Second Edition – p. 205.

12. Schlesinger, A.M. 1965. A Thousand Days. John F. Kennedy in the White House – p. 798.

13. The Kennedy Presidential Press Conferences. 1978. p. 384.

14. Giglio, J.N. 2006. The Presidency of John F. Kennedy. Second Edition – p. 205.

15. Dallek, R. 2003. An Unfinished Life. John F. Kennedy 1917-1963 – p. 538.

16. O'Brien, M. 2005. John F. Kennedy. A Biography – p. 657.

17. Sorensen, T.C. 1965. Kennedy – p. 673.

18. Donald, A.D. 1966. John F. Kennedy and the New Frontier – p. 112.

19. O'Brien, M. 2005. John F. Kennedy. A Biography – p. 659.

20. Abel, E. 1966. The Missile Crisis – p. 49.

21. O'Brien, M. 2005. John F. Kennedy. A Biography – p. 659.

22. Dallek, R. 2003. An Unfinished Life. John F. Kennedy 1917-1963 – p. 545-546.

23. Papp, D.S. 1990. As I Saw it: Dean Rusk as told to Richard Rusk – p. 230.

24. Stern, S.M. 2012. The Cuban Missile Crisis in American Memory. Myths versus Reality – p. 21.

25. O'Donnell, K.P., Powers, D.F. and McCarthy, J. 1970. Johnny, We hardly knew ye. Memories of John Fitzgerald Kennedy – p. 317.

26. Weisbrot, R. 2001. Maximum Danger. Kennedy, the Missiles and the Crisis of American Confidence – p. 122.

27. Kennedy, R.F. 1969. Thirteen Days. A Memoir of the Cuban Missile Crisis – p. 31.

28. Weisbrot, R. 2001. Maximum Danger. Kennedy, the Missiles and the Crisis of American Confidence – p. 122-123.

29. Shukman, H. 1988. Memoirs Andrei Gromyko – p. 178.

30. Shukman, H. 1988. Memoirs Andrei Gromyko – p. 179.

31. Kennedy, R.F. 1969. Thirteen Days. A Memoir of the Cuban Missile Crisis – p. 37.

32. Stern, S.M. 2012. The Cuban Missile Crisis in American Memory. Myths versus Reality – p. 57-58-59-67.

33. Shukman, H. 1988. Memoirs Andrei Gromyko – p. 176.

34. Sidey, H. 1964. John F. Kennedy President. New Edition – p. 277.

35. Giglio, J.N. 2005. The Presidency of John F. Kennedy. Second Edition – p. 214.

36. Shukman, H. 1988. Memoirs Andrei Gromyko – p. 176-177.

37. O'Donnell, K.P., Powers, D.F. and McCarthy, J. 1970. Johnny, We hardly knew

ye. Memories of John Fitzgerald Kennedy – p. 319.

38. Shukman, H. 1988. Memoirs Andrei Gromyko – p. 179.

39. Papp, D.S. 1990. As I Saw it: Dean Rusk as told to Richard Rusk – p. 233.

40. Perret, G. 2001. Jack. A Life like no Other – p. 373.

41. Gerald S. and Strober, D.H. 1993-2003. Let Us Begin anew. An Oral History of the Kennedy Presidency – p. 385.

42. Blight, J.G. & Welch, D.A. 1989. On The Brink. Americans and Soviets Reexamine the Cuban Missile Crisis – p. 44.

43. Gerald S. and Strober, D.H. 1993-2003. Let Us Begin anew. An Oral History of the Kennedy Presidency – p. 385.

44. Barnes, J.A. 2005. John F. Kennedy on leadership. The Lessons and Legacy of a president – p. 201-202.

45. Blight, J.G. & Welch, D.A. 1989. On The Brink. Americans and Soviets Reexamine the Cuban Missile Crisis – p. 246.

46. O'Donnell, K.P., Powers, D.F. and McCarthy, J. 1970. Johnny, We hardly knew ye. Memories of John Fitzgerald Kennedy – p. 319-320.

47. Harper, P. and Krieg, J.P. 1988. John F. Kennedy. The Promise Revisited – p. 94.

48. Dallek, R. 2003. An Unfinished Life. John F. Kennedy 1917-1963 – p. 554-555.

49. Goduti, P.A. 2009. Kennedy's Kitchen Cabinet and the pursuit of peace. The Shaping of American foreign policy 1961-1963 – p. 180-181.

50. Dobbs, M. 2008. One Minute to Midnight. Kennedy, Khrushchev and Castro on the brink of Nuclear War – p. 22-23.

51. O'Donnell, K.P., Powers, D.F. and McCarthy, J. 1970. Johnny, We hardly knew ye. Memories of John Fitzgerald Kennedy – p. 318.

52. Suri, J. 2017. The Impossible Presidency. The Rise and Fall of America's Highest Office – p. 197.

53. Sorensen, T.C. 1965. Kennedy – p. 679.

54. Dean Rusk as told to Richard Rusk. 1990. As I Saw it – p. 234.

55. Stern, S.M. 2012. The Cuban Missile Crisis in American Memory. Myths versus Reality – p. 23.

56. Kennedy, R.F. 1969. Thirteen Days. A Memoir of the Cuban Missile Crisis – p. 33.

57. Gerald S. and Strober, D.H. 1993-2003. Let Us Begin anew. An Oral History of the Kennedy Presidency – p. 396.

58. Stern, S.M. 2012. The Cuban Missile Crisis in American Memory. Myths versus Reality – p. 23.

59. Beschloss, M.R. 1991. The Crisis Years. Kennedy and Khrushchev 1960-1963 – p. 482-483.

60. Kennedy, J.F. 1962. Public papers of the Presidents of the United States – p. 806-807-808-809.

61. Sorensen, T.C. 2008. Counselor. A Life at the Edge of History – p. 297.

62. Hersh, S.M. 1997. The Dark side of Camelot – p. 354.

63. Reeves, R. 1991. President Kennedy. Profile of Power – p. 280.
64. Fensch, T. 2001. Top Secret. The Kennedy-Khrushchev Letters – p. 301- 302.
65. Beschloss, M.R. 1991. The Crisis Years. Kennedy and Khrushchev 1960-1963 – p. 485.
66. Sorensen, T.C. 2008. Counselor. A Life at the Edge of History – p. 300.
67. Beschloss, M.R. 1991. The Crisis Years. Kennedy and Khrushchev 1960-1963 – p. 486.
68. Kern, M., Levering, P.W., Levering, R.B. 1983. The Kennedy Crisis. The press, the Presidency and Foreign Policy – p. 126.
69. Barnes, J.A. 2005. John F. Kennedy on leadership. The Lessons and Legacy of a president – p. 151-152.
70. Blight, J.G. & Welch, D.A. 1989. On The Brink. Americans and Soviets Reexamine the Cuban Missile Crisis – p. 245-246.
71. Dobbrynin, A. 1995. In confidence Moscow's Ambassador to America's six cold War Presidents – p. 81-82.
72. Beschloss, M.R. 1991. The Crisis Years. Kennedy and Khrushchev 1960-1963 – p. 486.
O'Brien, M. 2005. Kennedy. A Biography – p. 666-667.
73. Longford, L. 1976. Kennedy – p. 122.
74. Hersh, S.M. 1997. The Dark side of Camelot – p. 351.
75. Stern, S.M. 2012. The Cuban Missile Crisis in American Memory. Myths versus Reality – p. 9.
76. Giglio, J.N. 2006. The Presidency of John F. Kennedy. Second Revised Edition – p. 208.
77. Stern, S.M. 2012. The Cuban Missile Crisis in American Memory. Myths versus Reality – p. 8-11.
78. Safire, W. October 12, 1997. The New York Times Opinion essay: White House Tapes.
79. Stern, S.M. 2012. The Cuban Missile Crisis in American Memory. Myths versus Reality – p. 5 – p. 9.
80. Stern, S.M. 2012. The Cuban Missile Crisis in American Memory. Myths versus Reality – p. 34-135-136.
81. Sorensen, T.C. 2008. Counselor. A Life at the Edge of History – p. XVI – p. 2.
82. Hersh, S.M. 1997. The Dark side of Camelot – p. 346.
83. Talbott, S. 1970. Khrushchev Remembers – p. 492.
84. Kaplan, F. December 19, 2003. Culturebox, Arts, entertainment and more.
85. Stern, S.M. 2012. The Cuban Missile Crisis in American Memory. Myths versus Reality – p. 65.
86. The Fog of War. 2003. An Errol Morris film.
87. Khrushchev, S. 2011. How my father and President Kennedy saved the world – p. 12.
88. Dallek, R. 2003. An Unfinished Life. John F. Kennedy 1917-1963 – p. 563-564.

89. Fensch, T. 2001. The Kennedy-Khrushchev Letters – p. 305-306-307-308.

90. Dean Rusk as told to Richard Rusk. 1990. As I Saw it – p. 237.

91. Newsweek. When One Man Sizes Up Another. December 3, 1962. p. 23.

92. Kennedy, R.F. 1969. Thirteen Days – p. 75-76.

Perret, G. 2001. Jack: A Life Like No Other – p. 376-377.

Dallek, R. 2003. An Unfinished Life. John F. Kennedy 1917-1963 – p. 564-565.

O'Brien, M. 2005. John. F. Kennedy. A Biography – p. 668.

93. O'Donnell, K.P., Powers, D.F. and McCarthy, J. 1970. Johnny, we hardly knew you. Memoirs of John Fitzgerald Kennedy – p. 322-323-334.

94. The Saturday Evening Post. In Time of Crisis. December 18, 1962.

O'Brien, M. 2005. John. F. Kennedy. A Biography – p. 676

95. Reeves, R. 1993. President Kennedy. Profile of Power – p. 389-390.

96. As I Saw it by Dean Rusk as told by Richard Rusk. 1990. p. 234.

97. Fensch, T. 2001. Top Secret. The Kennedy-Khrushchev Letters – p. 320.

98. O'Donnell, K.P., Powers, D.F. and McCarthy, J. 1970. Johnny, we hardly knew you. Memoirs of John Fitzgerald Kennedy – p. 323-324.

99. Donald, A.D. 1966. John F. Kennedy and the New Frontier – p. 113.

100. Kennedy, R.F. 1969. Thirteen Days. A Memoir of the Cuban Missile Crisis – p. 30, 116.

101. Stern, S.M. 2012. The Cuban Missile Crisis in American Memory. Myths versus Reality – p. 99-100.

102. Talbott, S. 1970. Khrushchev Remembers – p. 504.

103. Sorensen, T. 2008. Counselor. A Life at the Edge of History – p. 300.

104. Hilsman, R. 1996. The Cuban Missile Crisis. The Struggle over Policy – p. 131.

105. As I saw it by Dean Rusk as told by Richard Rusk. 1990. p. 241

106. Fensch, T. 2001. Top Secret. The Kennedy-Khrushchev Letters – p. 347-360-361.

107. Khrushchev, S. 2002. How my father and President Kennedy saved the world. American Heritage Magazine October 2002 – Volume 53, Issue 5 – p. 12-14.

108. Dean Rusk as told to Richard Rusk. 1990. As I Saw it – p. 242.

109. Dean Acheson to JFK. 1962. JFKL. October 29, 1962. POF, Box 27

110. Parmet, H.S. 1983. JFK. The Presidency of John F. Kennedy – p. 298.

111. Stern, S.M. 2012. The Cuban Missile Crisis in American Memory. Myths versus Reality – p. 57.

112. Blight, J.G. and Lang, J.M. 2012. The Armageddon letters. Kennedy/Khrushchev/Castro in the Cuban Missile Crisis – p. 234.

113. Giglio, J.N. 2006. The Presidency of John F. Kennedy. Second Edition Revised – p. 224.

114. Stern, S.M. 2012. The Cuban Missile Crisis in American Memory. Myths versus Reality – p. 66.

115. Blight, J.G. and Welch, D.A. 1989. On The Brink. Americans and Soviets Reexamine the Cuban Missile Crisis – p.311-369 N 118.

116. Talbott, S. 1970. Khrushchev Remembers – p. 499.

117. O'Donnell, K.P., Powers, D.F. and McCarthy, J. 1970. Johnny, We hardly knew ye. Memories of John Fitzgerald Kennedy – p. 339.

118. White, M.J. 1998. Kennedy. The New Frontier Revisited – p. 79.

4.3. The Scali-Fomin (Feklisov) Meetings

1. Hilsman, R. 1967. To Move a Nation. The Politics of Foreign Policy in the Administration of John F. Kennedy – p. 216-217.

2. Hilsman, R. 1996. The Cuban Missile Crisis. The Struggle over Policy – p. 121. Fursenko, A. and Naftali, T. 1997. One Hell of a Gamble. Khrushchev, Castro and Kennedy 1958-1964 – p. 264.

3. Dobrynin, A. 1995. In Confidence – p. 94-95.

4. Fensch, T. 2001. The Kennedy. Khrushchev letters – p. 420.

5. Hilsman, R. 1967. To Move a Nation – p. 218-219.

6. Beschloss, M.R. 1991. The Crisis Years. Kennedy and Khrushchev 1960-1963 – p. 514-515-521.

7. Garthoff, R.L. 1989. Reflections on the Cuban Missile Crisis. Revised Edition – p. 80-81.

8. Hilsman, R. 1996. The Cuban Missile Crisis. The Struggle over Policy – p. 140-141.

9. Beschloss, M.R. 1991. The Crisis Years. Kennedy and Khrushchev 1960-1963 – p. 515.

10. Salinger, P. 1966. With Kennedy – p. 274-275-276- 278.

11. Gerald S. and Strober, D.H. 1993-2003. Let Us Begin anew. An Oral History of the Kennedy Presidency – p. 398.

12. O'Donnell, K.P., Powers, D.F. and McCarthy, J. 1970. Johnny, We hardly knew ye. Memories of John Fitzgerald Kennedy – p. 335.

13. Kern, M., Levering, P.W., Levering, R.B. 1983. The Kennedy Crisis. The press, the Presidency and Foreign Policy – p. 129.

14. Khrushchev, S. 2002. How my father and President Kennedy saved the world. American Heritage Magazine October 2002 – Volume 53, Issue 5 – p. 7 of 14.

15. Dobbs, M. 2008. One Minute to Midnight. Kennedy, Khrushchev and Castro on the brink of Nuclear War – p. 167-168.

16. Dobbrynin, A. 1995. In confidence Moscow's Ambassador to America's six cold War Presidents – p. 87-88.

17. Crankshaw, E. 1970. Khrushchev Remembers – p. 497-498.

Further Reading on Scali -Fomin

- O'Donnell, K.P., Powers, D.F. and McCarthy, J. 1970. Johnny, We hardly knew ye. Memories of John Fitzgerald Kennedy – p. 334-335.

- Dean Rusk as told to Richard Rusk. 1990. As I Saw it – p. 238.

- Paterson, T.G. 1989. Kennedy's quest for Victory. American Foreign Policy 1961-1963 – p. 145-146.
- Fursenko, A. and Naftali, T. 1997. One Hell of a Gamble. Khrushchev, Castro and Kennedy 1958-1964 – p. 264-265-269-270-271-279-283-284.

4.4. McNamara's Ambiguous Point of View on the "Castro Assassination"
1. The Church Committee. 1975-1976. p. 157-158-162-164-165-166.
2. Goodwin, R.N. 1988. Remembering America. A Voice from the Sixties – p. 189.
3. Email from Dan Fenn Jr. June 5, 2018

4.5. Three Cuban Cigar Stories
1. Grande, W.M.L & Kornbluh, P. 2014. Back Channel to Cuba – p. 44.
2. Goodwin, R.N. 1988. Remembering America. A Voice from the Sixties – p. 202.
3. Grande, W.M.L & Kornbluh, P. 2014. Back Channel to Cuba. The hidden history of negotiations between Washington and Havana – note 10-16 p. 428
4. The Church Committee. 1975-1976. Information on U.S. Attempts to assassinate foreign leaders – p. 73.
5. Salinger P. issue (Autumn 92) Kennedy, Cuba and Cigars. Cigar Aficionado.com – Proclamation 3447 Embargo on....with Cuba, February 3, 1962
6. Goodwin, R. JFK and Che. Demi Moore Autumn 96.
7. Salinger, P. 1995. P.S. A Memoir – p. 144-150-151-152.

4.6. The William Attwood – Lisa Howard – Jean Daniel – Castro Rapprochement
1. White, M.J. 1998. Kennedy. The New Frontier Revisited – p. 64.
2. Goodwin, R.N. 1988. Remembering America. A Voice from the Sixties – p. 200.
3. Stern, S.M. 2012. The Cuban Missile Crisis in American Memory – p. 5.
4. Goodwin, R. JFK and Che. Demi Moore. Issue/Autumn 96
5. Schlesinger, A.M. 1978. Robert Kennedy and his Times – p. 542.
6. White, M.J. 1999. The Kennedys and Cuba. The declassified Documentary History – p. 339.
7. Bundy, M.G. 1963. Memorandum for the President. January 4,1963
8. Grande, W.M.L & Kornbluh, P. 2014. Back Channel to Cuba. The hidden history of negotiations between Washington and Havana – p. 43.
9. Attwood, W. 1967. The Reds and the Blacks. A personal adventure – p. 142.
10. Talbot, D. 2007. Brothers. The Hidden History of the Kennedy years – p. 228.
11. Parmet, H.S. 1983. JFK. The Presidency of John F. Kennedy – p. 300.
12. The Church Committee. 1975–1976. p. 174.
13. Dallek, R. 2003. An Unfinished Life. John F. Kennedy 1917-1963 – p. 662-663.
14. Public Papers of the Presidents of the United States. 1963. Address in Miami

before the Inter-American Press Association – p. 873-876.

15. Talbot, D. 2007. Brothers. The Hidden History of the Kennedy years – p. 228.
16. Attwood, W. American History: The assassination of JFK. http://spartacuseducational.com/JFK Attwood.htm + source section 3.
17. Sorensen, T. 2008. Councelor. A Life at the Edge of History – p. 353.
18. Kornbluh, P. May/June 2018. The Untold Story of how Lisa Howard's intimate diplomacy with Cuba's revolutionary leader changed the course of the Cold War.
19. Talbot, D. 2007. Brothers. The Hidden History of the Kennedy years – p. 224-225.
20. Kornbluh, P. May/June 2018. The Untold Story of how Lisa Howard's intimate diplomacy with Cuba's revolutionary leader changed the course of the Cold War.
21. Talbot, D. 2007. Brothers. The Hidden History of the Kennedy years – p. 226-227.
22. Kornbluh, P. May/June 2018. The Untold Story of how Lisa Howard's intimate diplomacy with Cuba's revolutionary leader changed the course of the Cold War.
Attwood, W. The Twilight Struggle – p. 262.
Douglass, J.W. 2008. JFK and the Unspeakable. Why he died and why it matters – p. 85.
23. Daniel, J. 1973. Le Temps qui reste – p. 149-150-161-162-164.
24. Daniel, J. December 7, 1963. I was with Fidel Castro when JFK was assassinated.
25. Breuer, W. 1997. Vendetta. Fidel Castro and the Kennedy Brothers – p. 222.
26. Talbot, D. 2007. Brothers. The Hidden History of the Kennedy years – p. 229.
27. Dallek, R. 2003. An Unfinished Life. John F. Kennedy 1917-1963 – p. 664.
28. Giglio, J.N. and Rabe, S.G. 2003. Debating the Kennedy Presidency – p. 45.
29. Dallek, R. 2003. An Unfinished Life. John F. Kennedy 1917-1963 – p. 664.
30. Attwood, W. 1987. The Twilight Struggle: Tales of the cold War. American History. The assassination of JFK – http:/spartacuseducational.com/JFK Attwood.htm + source section 3
31. Richard Nixon's press conference. November 7, 1962.
32. Beschloss, M.R. 1991. The Crisis Years. Kennedy and Khrushchev 1960-1963 – p. 693.
33. Politico. May/June 2018. My dearest Fidel. An ABC Journalist's secret liaison with Fidel Castro. 17/30-25/30

Further Reading

- Giglio, J.N. and Rabe, S.G. 2003. Debating the Kennedy Presidency – p. 36.
- Dallek, R. 2003. An Unfinished Life. John F. Kennedy 1917-1963 – p. 438.
- Grande, W.M.L & Kornbluh, P. 2014. Back Channel to Cuba. The hidden history of negotiations between Washington and Havana – p. 44-47.

4.7. Operation Mongoose

1. Schlesinger, A.M. 1978. Robert Kennedy and his Times – p. 476.
2. RFK handwritten notes. November 7, 1961. RFK papers.
3. Memorandum from President Kennedy, Washington. November 30, 1961. Four X. p. 688-689.
4. Thomas, E. 2000. Robert Kennedy. His Life – p. 148.
5. Schlesinger, A.M. 1978. Robert Kennedy and his Times – p. 477.
6. Talbot, D. 2007. Brothers. The Hidden History of the Kennedy years – p. 96.
7. Thomas, E. 2000. Robert Kennedy. His Life – p. 149.
8. Goodwin, R.N. 1988. Remembering America. A Voice from the Sixties – p. 188.
9. Powers, T. 1979. The Man who kept the secrets. Richard Helms and the CIA – p. 138.
10. Thomas, E. 2000. Robert Kennedy. His Life – p. 150.
11. Freedman, L. 2000. Kennedy's Wars. Berlin, Cuba, Laos and Vietnam – p. 156.
12. Dallek, R. 2003. An Unfinished Life. John F. Kennedy 1917-1963 – p. 467.
13. Mary Hemingway. March 26, 2001. The Nation, p. 17.
14. Beschloss, M.R. 1991. The Crisis Years. Kennedy and Khrushchev 1960-1963 – p. 376.
15. Reeves, T.C. 1991. A Question of Character – p. 277.
16. Stern, S.H. 2012. The Cuban Missile Crisis in American Memory – p. 41.
17. Reeves, R. 1993. President Kennedy. Profile of Power – p. 336.
18. Davis, J.H. 1984. The Kennedys dynasty and Disaster 1948-1983 – p. 328.
19. Hersh, S.M. 1997. The Dark side of Camelot – p. 285.
20. Thomas, E. 2000. Robert Kennedy. His Life – p. 151.
21. The Church Committee. 1975-1976. p. 170.

4.8. Did President Kennedy Order the Assassination of Fidel Castro?

1. O'Brien, M. 2005. John F. Kennedy. A Biography – p. 648.
2. The Church Committee. Information on U.S. Attempts to assassinate foreign leaders. p. 71.
3. The Church Committee. p. 138.
4. Schlesinger, A.M. 1978. Robert Kennedy and his Times – p. 492.
5. Talbot, D. 2007. Brothers. The Hidden History of the Kennedy years – p. 93-94.
6. Hersh, S.M. 1997. The Dark side of Camelot – p. 281.
7. Thomas, E. 2000. Robert Kennedy His Life – p. 157 (158-notes p. 421)
8. Schlesinger, A.M. 1978. Robert Kennedy and his Times – p. 492.
9. The Church Committee. p. 139.
10. Talbot, D. 2007. Brothers. The Hidden History of the Kennedy years – p. 94.
11. Public Papers of the Presidents of the United States John F. Kennedy. 1961. p. 725.
12. Wofford, H. 1980. Of Kennedys and Kings. Making Sense of the Sixties – p.

398.

13. Szulc, T. 1986. Fidel: A Critical Portrait – p. 557-558.

14. Tad Szulc to Arthur M. Schlesinger Jr. June 23, 1961

15. Schlesinger, A.M. June 26, 1961. Memorandum for the President. You will be interested in Tad Szulc's report on his recent conversation with Fidel.

16. Smathers, G.A. 1964. OH Interview. JFKL – 3/3/1964

17. The Church Committee. 1975-1976. p. 123-124.

18. Beschloss, M.R. 1991. The Crisis Years. Kennedy and Khrushchev 1960-1963 – p. 139.

19. Hersh, S.M. 1997. The Dark side of Camelot – p. 200.

20. Talbot, D. 2007. Brothers. The Hidden History of the Kennedy years – p. 123.

21. Powers, T. 1979. The Man who kept the secrets. Richard Helms and the CIA – p. 345 – note 72

22. Schlesinger, A.M. 1978. Robert Kennedy and his Times – p. 498.

23. Powers, T. 1979. The Man who kept the secrets. Richard Helms and the CIA – p. 7.

24. Davis, J.H. 1984. The Kennedys dynasty and Disaster 1948-1983 – p. 329.

25. Paterson, T.G. 1989. Kennedy's quest for Victory. American Foreign Policy 1961-1963 – p. 138.

26. Beschloss, M.R. 1991. The Crisis Years. Kennedy and Khrushchev 1960-1963 – p. 138-139-140.

27. Giglio, J.N. 1991-2006. The Presidency of John F. Kennedy – p. 63 – p. 65.

28. Reeves, R. 1993. President Kennedy. Profile of Power – p. 337.

29. Hersh, S.M. 1997. The Dark side of Camelot – p. 3-220

30. Lumumba, P. Wikipedia.

31. Hilty, J.W. 1997. Robert Kennedy: Brother Protector – p. 420-427.

32. White, M.J. 1998. Kennedy. The New Frontier Revisited – p. 69.

33. Thomas, E. 2000. Robert Kennedy. His Life – p. 154-159-176-177.

34. The Church Committee. 1975-1976. p. 131-132.

35. Freedman, L. 2000. Kennedy's Wars. Berlin, Cuba, Laos and Vietnam – p. 150-151.

36. Hersh, S.M. 1997. The Dark side of Camelot – p. 268-269.

37. O'Brien, M. 2005. John F. Kennedy. A Biography – p. 649-652-653-656-657.

38. Talbot, D. 2007. Brothers. The Hidden History of the Kennedy years – p. 86-87.

39. Dobbs, M. 2008. One Minute to Midnight. Kennedy, Khrushchev and Castro on the brink of Nuclear War – p. 154.

40. The Church Committee. 1975-1976. p. 117-119-120-141-142-146-147-148-149-150-151-168.

41. Davis, J.H. 1984. The Kennedys dynasty and Disaster 1948-1983 – p. 330.

42. Reeves, T.C. 1991. A Question of Character. A Life of John F. Kennedy – p. 277-278.

43. Breuer, W. 1997. Vendetta. Fidel Castro and the Kennedy Brothers – p. 173.

44. The Church Committee. 1975-1976. p. 155-167-168-169.

45. Lucci, S. Sept/Oct 1999. JFK and Castro by Peter Kornbluh.

46. Talbot, D. 2007. Brothers. The Hidden History of the Kennedy years. interview Talbot with Robert Kennedy Jr. – p. 94.

47. Drennen, K. October 19, 2012. NBC Brian Williams interview with Ethel Kennedy.

48. John Kennedy: A Tribute. October 1999. George Magazine.

49. Breuer, W. 1997. Vendetta. Fidel Castro and the Kennedy Brothers – p. 215.

50. Castro Kennedy tactics. September 9, 1963. The New York Times.

51. Johnson, H. 1964. The Bay of Pigs – p. 354.

52. Kennedy, J.F. January 1 to November 22, 1963. Public Papers of the Presidents of the United States – p. 461.

53. Kennedy, J.F. January 1 to November 22, 1963. Public Papers of the Presidents of the United States – p. 524.

54. Nevins, A. 1960. The Strategy of Peace by John Kennedy – p. 132-133.

55. Knebel, L.B. 1977. OH JFKL – 8/1/1977

56. Sorensen, T.C. 1965. Kennedy – p. 306.

57. Parmet, H.S. 1983. Oral History Interview JFKL 1 – 08/09/1983

4.9. Conclusion

1. Talbott, S. 1970. Khrushchev Remembers – p. 493.

2. Khrushchev, S. Wikipedia.

3. Khrushchev, S. 2002. American Heritage Magazine. October Volume 53 Issue 5. How My father and President Kennedy Saved the World – p. 3.

4. Talbott, S. 1970. Khrushchev Remembers – p. 493-494-495-496.

5. Wedge, B. 1968. Khrushchev at a distance: A Study of Public Personality – Society 5, p 24, 28.

6. Lord, D.C. 1977. John F. Kennedy. The politics of Confrontation and Conciliation – p. 203.

7. Khrushchev, S. 2002. American Heritage Magazine. October Volume 53 Issue 5. How My fahter and President Kennedy Saved the World – p. 13.

8. Talbott, S. 1970. Khrushchev Remembers – p. 497-458.

9. Khrushchev, S. 2002. How my father and President Kennedy saved the world. October Volume 53 Issue 5. American Heritage Magazine – p. 4.

10. Talbott, S. 1970. Khrushchev Remembers – p. 500-504-505.

11. Sorensen, T. 2008. Counselor. A Life at the Edge of History – p. 309.

12. Selverstone, M.J. 2014. A Companion to John F. Kennedy – p. 234.

13. White, M.J. May 2011. History Extra 20th Century Bay of Pigs invasion: Kennedy's Cuban Catastrophe. Issue of BBC History Magazine – p. 8.

14. White, M.J. 1998. Kennedy. The New Frontier Revisited – p. 65.

15. Salinger, P. 1995. PS: A Memoir – p. 214-215.

16. Gilpatric, R.L. 1970. Oral History Interview JFKL 2 – 05/27/1970

17. Parmet, H.S. 1983. JFK. The Presidency of John F. Kennedy – p. 285.

18. Rusk, D. 1970. Oral History Interview JFKL 3 – 02/19/1970

19. Gerald S. and Strober, D.H. 1993-2003. Let Us Begin anew. An Oral History of the Kennedy Presidency – p. 393.

20. Hersh, S.M. 1997. The Dark side of Camelot – p. 360.

21. Goduti, P.A. 2009. Kennedy's Kitchen Cabinet and the pursuit of peace. The Shaping of American foreign policy 1961-1963 – p. 184.

22. Giglio, J.N. and Rabe, S.G. 2003. Debating the Kennedy Presidency – p. 42.

23. Martin Luther King's reaction to the Cuban Missile Crisis. 2017. European journal of American studies – 12/2/2017– Leonardo Campus

24. Dallek, R. 2003. An Unfinished Life. John F. Kennedy 1917-1963 – p. 574.

25. Giglio, J.N. 2006. The Presidency of John F. Kennedy. Second Edition – p. 209.

26. Selverstone, M.J. 2014. A Companion to John F. Kennedy. Chapter 12 Alan Mc Pherson – p. 237.

27. Fensch, T. 2001. Top Secret. The Kennedy-Khrushchev Letters – p. 306.

28. Dobrynin, A. 1995. In Confidence – p. 84.

29. White, M.J. 1998. Kennedy. The New Frontier Revisited – p. 73-74-75.

30. Harper, P. and Krieg, J.P. 1988. John F. Kennedy. The Promise Revisited. The Dangerous Legacy: John F. Kennedy and the Cuban Missile Crisis Michael P. Riccards – p. 82.

31. Bohn, M.K. February 13, 2015. Ranking 12 Presidents on Foreign Crisis Management. Real clear Politics.

32. Schlesinger, A.M. 2011. Jacqueline Kennedy. Historic Conversations on Life with John – p. 267.

Chapter 5: Kennedy and The Civil Rights Issue. Did He Act Too Slowly?

5.1. The RFK-Baldwin Meeting May 24, 1963

1. Brauer, C.M. 1977. John F. Kennedy and the Second Reconstruction – p. 242.
2. Reeves, R. 1993. President Kennedy. Profile of Power – p. 497.
3. Schlesinger, A.M. 1978. Robert Kennedy and his Times – p. 330-331.
4. Guthman, E.O. and Jeffrey Shulman, J. 1988. Robert Kennedy in his own words. The unpublished Recollections of the Kennedy years – p. 224-225.
5. Schlesinger, A.M. 1978. Robert Kennedy and his Times – p. 332-333.
6. Hilty, J.W. 1997. Robert Kennedy: Brother Protector – p. 354.
7. Giglio, J.N. and Rabe, S.G. 2003. Debating the Kennedy Presidency – p. 154.
8. Schlesinger, A.M. 1978. Robert Kennedy and his Times – p. 333.
9. Schlesinger, A.M. 1965. A Thousand Days. John Kennedy in the White House – p. 963.
10. Schlesinger, A.M. 1978. Robert Kennedy and his Times – p. 334.
11. Guthman, E.O. and Jeffrey Shulman, J. 1988. Robert Kennedy in his own words. The unpublished Recollections of the Kennedy years – p. 224.
12. Tye, L. 2016. R. The Making of a Liberal icon – p. 197.
13. Gerald S. and Strober, D.H. 1993. Let Us Begin anew. An Oral History of the Kennedy Presidency – p. 291.
Sidey, H. 1964. John F. Kennedy President New Edition – p. 331.
14. Gerald S. and Strober, D.H. 1993. Let Us Begin anew. An Oral History of the Kennedy Presidency – p. 291.
15. Gerald S. and Strober, D.H. 1993. Let Us Begin anew. An Oral History of the Kennedy Presidency – p. 292.
16. Hilty, J.W. 1997. Robert Kennedy: Brother Protector – p. 356.
17. Leamer, L. 2001. The Kennedy Men 1901-1963. The Laws of the father – p. 706.
18. Hoberek, A. 2015. The Cambridge Companion to John F. Kennedy – p. 76.
19. Robinson, L. May 25, 1963. Robert Kennedy Consults Negroes Here about North. New York Times.
20. Hilty, J.W. 1997. Robert Kennedy: Brother Protector – p. 356-357.
21. Reeves, T.C. 1991. A Question of Character. A Life of John F. Kennedy – p. 352.
22. Guthman, E. 1971. We band of brothers – p. 220-221.
23. Livingston, S. 2017. Kennedy and King. The President, the Pastor and the Battle over Civil Rights – p. 386.
24. Belafonte, H. 2005, Oral History Interview. JFKL – 5/20/2005 p. 1-14
25. Booker, S. 1964. Black Man's America – p. 199.

Further Reading on the RFK – Baldwin Meeting New York May 24, 1963

- Brauer, C.M. 1977. John F. Kennedy and the Second Reconstruction – p. 220-221.
- Reeves, R. 1993. President Kennedy. Profile of Power – p. 505-506.
- Hobrerek, A. 2015. The Cambridge Companion to John F. Kennedy – p. 77.
- Livingston, S. 2017. Kennedy and King. The President, the Pastor and the Battle over Civil Rights – p. 387-390.
- Leamer, L. 2001. The Kennedy Men 1901-1963. The Laws of the father – p.704-705-706.
- Goduti, P.A. 2013. Robert F.Kennedy and the Shaping of Civil Rights 1960-1964 – p. 191-192.
- Matthews, C. 2017. Robert Kennedy. A Raging Spirit – p. 242-243.
- Thomas, E. 2000. Robert Kennedy. His Life – p. 244-245.
- Fairlie, H. 1973. The Kennedy Promise. The politics of Expectation – p. 252-253.
- Parmet, H.S. 1983. JFK. The Presidency of John F. Kennedy – p. 268.
- Branch, T. 1988. Parting the Waters. America in the King Years 1954-63 – p. 809-810-811-812.
- Giglio, J.N. 1991. The Presidency of John F. Kennedy – p. 178-179.
- Barner, D. & West, T.R. 1984. The Torch is Passed. The Kennedy Brothers and American Liberation – p. 205-206.
- Stern, M. 1992. Calculating Visions. Kennedy, Johnson and Civil Rights – p. 84-85.
- Cohen, A. 2014. Two Days in June. John F. Kennedy and the 48 hours that made history – p. 231.
- Shesol, J. 1997. Mutual Concept. Lyndon Johnson, Robert Kennedy and the Feud that defined a Decade – p. 159.
- Mahoney, R.D. 1999. Sons & Brothers. The Days of Jack and Bobby Kennedy – p. 249-250.
- Heymann, C.D. 1998. RFK. A Candid Biography of Robert F. Kennedy – p. 286-287-288.
- Swisher , C. 2000. People who made history: John F. Kennedy – p. 106.
- Wofford, H. 1980. Of Kennedy and Kings. Making sense of the sixties – p. 171-172.
- Dallek, R. 2003. An Unfinished Life. John F. Kennedy 1917-1963 – p. 600-601.
- Levison, S. 2014. Dangerous Friendship. Martin Luther King Jr. and the Kennedy Brothers – p. 164.
- Bryant, N. 2016. The Bystander. John F. Kennedy and the Struggle for Black Equality – p. 402-403.
- Giglio, J.N. 2006. The Presidency of John F. Kennedy. Second Edition – p. 192-193.

5.2. The June 11, 1963 Address – August 28, 1963 The March on Washington

1. O'Brien, M. 2009. Rethinking Kennedy. An interpretive Biography – p. 160-161.
2. Lord, D.C. 1977. John F. Kennedy. The politics of Confrontation and Conciliation – p. 157.
3. Stand in the Schoolhouse Door, Part of the Civil Right Movement. Wikipedia – p. 3.
4. Hilty, J.W. 1997. Robert Kennedy: Brother Protector – p. 265-366.
5. Reeves, R. 1993. President Kennedy. Profile of Power – p. 520.
6. Bernstein, I. 1991. Promises Kept. John F. Kennedy's New Frontier – p. 99.
7. Bryant, N. 2006. The Bystander. John F. Kennedy and the Struggle for Black Equality – p. 420.
8. Rowan, C.T. Thursday, September 5, 1991. The Rehabilitation of George: Wallace from the internet. Washingtonpost.com: George Wallace Remembered – p. A21.
9. George Wallace's daughter lives in shadow of past. CBS/AP. – June 11, 2013 1.15 p.m.
10. Wayne, G. June 8, 2012. Son says former Governor George Wallace repended for past. The Tuscaloosa News. Retrieved January 15, 2016

Further Reading on June 11, 1963 Stand in the Schoolhouse Door

- Sidey, H. 1963-1964. John F. Kennedy: President – p. 333.
- Schlesinger, A.M. 1978. Robert Kennedy and his Times – p. 341-342.
- Barner, D. & West, T.R. 1984. The Torch is Passed. The Kennedy Brothers and American Liberation – p. 172-173.
- Mills, J. 1988. John F. Kennedy – p. 252.
- Brogan, H. 1996. Kennedy – p. 168-169.
- Heymann, C.D. 1998. RFK. A Candid Biography of Robert F. Kennedy – p. 289-290.
- Rorabaugh, W.J. 2002. Kennedy and the Promises of the Sixties – p. 111.
- Barnes, J.A. 2005. John F. Kennedy on leadership. The Lessons and Legacy of a president – p. 5.
- Giglio, J.N. 2006. The Presidency of John F. Kennedy. Second Edition – p. 193-194.
- Hersh, B. 2007. Bobby and J. Edgar – p. 352.
- Ling, P.J. 2013. John F. Kennedy – p. 161.
- Whalen, T.J. 2014. JFK and his Enemies. A portrait of Power – p. 145-146.
- Tye, L. 2016. Bobby Kennedy. The Making of a Liberal Icon – p. 244.
- Matthews, C. 2017. Robert Kennedy. A Raging Spirit – p. 244-245.

Two Speeches that changed the course of Civil Rights

1. Schlesinger, A.M. 2007. Journals 1952-2000 – p. 195.
2. Radio and Television Report to the American People on Civil Rights – June 11, 1963 8 p.m.
Public Papers of the Presidents John F. Kennedy 1963 – p. 468-469-470-471
3. May 18, 1963 remarks in Nashville at the 90th Anniversary Convocation of Vanderbilt University
Public Papers of the Presidents John F. Kennedy 1963 – p. 406-407-408-409
4. June 9, 1963 Address in Honolulu before the United States Conference of Mayors
Public Papers of the Presidents John F. Kennedy 1963 – p. 454-455-456-457-458-459
5. Sorensen, T.C. 1965. Kennedy – p. 495-496.
6. Schlesinger, A.M. 1965. A Thousand Days. John F. Kennedy in the White House – p. 965.
7. Schlesinger, A. and Schlesinger, S. 2007. Journals 1952-2000 – p.196.
8. Schlesinger, A.M. 1965. A Thousand Days. John F. Kennedy in the White House – p. 966.
9. Guthman, E.O. and Jeffrey Shulman, J. 1988. Robert Kennedy in his own words. The unpublished Recollections of the Kennedy years – p. 201.
1963 February 28 Special Message to the Congress on Civil Rights – Public Papers of the Presidents John F. Kennedy 1963- p. 221-222-223-224-225-226-227-228-229-230
10. Sorensen, T.C. 1965. Kennedy – p. 494-495.
11. Sorensen, T.C. 2008. The Counselor– p. 278-279.
12. Marshall, B. 1964. Oral History Interview JFKL 6/20/1964 – p. 107-108-109
13. Cohen, A.W. 2014. Two Days in June – p. 283.
14. Guthman, E.O. and Jeffrey Shulman, J. 1988. Robert Kennedy in his own words. The unpublished Recollections of the Kennedy years – p. 200.
15. Marshall, B. 1964. Oral History Interview JFKL – 6/20/1964
16. Cohen, A.W. 2014. Two Days in June – p. 287-391
17. Robert Kennedy's papers in the JFKL PL. A copy of Richard Yate's draft civil rights speech.
18. Hodges, L.H. 1964. Oral History Interview JFKL – 05/18/1964
19. Bryant, N. 2006. The Bystander John F. Kennedy and the Struggle for Black Equality – p. 421.
20. Dallek, R. 2003. An Unfinished Life. John F. Kennedy 1917-1963 – p. 605.
21. O'Brien, M. 2005. John F. Kennedy: A Biography – p. 839.
22. Whalen, T.J. 2014. JFK and his Enemies. A portrait of Power – p. 148-149.
23. Brauer, C.M. 1977. John F. Kennedy and the Second Reconstruction – p. 263.
24. O'Brien, M. 2005. John F. Kennedy: A Biography – p. 839.
25. King, M.L. 1964. Oral History Interview JFKL – 03/09/1964

26. Livingston, S. 2017. Kennedy and King. The President, the Pastor and the Battle over Civil Rights – p. 407.

27. The New York Times. June 12, 1963

28. Branch, T. 1988. Parting the Waters. America in the King Years 1954-63 – p. 824.

29. Sorensen, T.C. 2008. Counselor. A Life at the Edge of History – p. 282.

30. Branch, T. 1988. Parting the Waters. America in the King Years 1954-63 – p. 824.

31. Levison's call to King. June 12, 1963, FLNY – p. 9-126

32. The New York Times. June 12, 1963.

33. O'Brien, M. 2005. John F. Kennedy: A Biography – p. 839-840.

34. O'Brien, M. 2010. Rethinking Kennedy. An interpretive Biography – p. 162.

35. Robinson, J. June 13, 1963. JFKOF Box 97.

36. Bryant, N. 2006. The Bystander: John F. Kennedy and the Struggle for Black Equality – p. 424.

37. Brauer, C.M. 1977. John F. Kennedy and the Second Reconstruction – p. 263.

38. Cohen, A.W. 2014. Two Days in June. John F. Kennedy and the 48 hours that made history – p. 339-340-341.

39. Reeves, T.C. 1991. A Question of Character. A Life of John F. Kennedy – p. 363-355-356.

40. Brauer, C.M. 1977. John F. Kennedy and the Second Reconstruction – p. 259-262.

41. Fairlie, H. 1973. The Kennedy Promise. The politics of Expectation – p. 253-254.

42. Miroff, B. 1976. Pragmatic Illusions. The Presidential Politics of John F. Kennedy – p. 256-257.

43. Kennedy, J.F. 1963. Special Message to the Congress on Civil Rights and Job Opportunities. Public Papers of the Presidents – p. 493.

44. Joseph, P.E. June 10, 2013. Kennedy's finest Moment. The New York Times.

45. Beckwith, B.D. Wikipedia.

46. Sabato, L.J. 2013. The Kennedy Half-Century. The Presidency, Assassination and Lasting Legacy of John F. Kennedy – p. 115.

47. Barnes, J.A. 2005. John F. Kennedy on leadership. The Lessons and Legacy of a president – p. 8.

48. Hobrerek, A. 2015. The Cambridge Companion to John F. Kennedy – p. 85.

49. Cohen, A.W. 2014. Two Days in June – p. 368.

50. JFK to Mrs Medgar Evers. Letter. 2332 Gynce Street Jackson 3, Mississippi

51. Sabato, L.J. 2013. The Kennedy Half-Century. The Presidency, Assassination and Lasting Legacy of John F. Kennedy – p. 115.

52. Bryant, N. 2006. The Bystander: John F. Kennedy and the Struggle for Black Equality – p. 425.

53. Schlesinger, A.M. 1965. A Thousand Days. John F. Kennedy in the White House

– p. 966.

54. Kennedy, J.F. June 19, 1963. Special Message to the Congress on Civil Rights and Job Opportunities. Public Papers of the Presidents – p. 483-493-494.

55. Whalen, T.J. 2014. JFK and his Enemies. A portrait of Power – p. 150.

56. Bryant, N. 2006. The Bystander: John F. Kennedy and the Struggle for Black Equality – p. 427.

57. Dallek, R. 2003. An Unfinished Life. John F. Kennedy 1917-1963 – p. 604.

58. Guthman, E.O. and Shulman, J. 1988. Robert Kennedy in his own words. The unpublished Recollections of the Kennedy years – p. 202-203.

59. Mansfield, M. 1964. Oral History Interview JFKL – 06/23/1964

60. Navasky, V.S. 1971. Kennedy Justice – p. 99.

61. Thompson, K.W. 1985. The Kennedy Presidency. Seventeen Intimate Perspectives of John F. Kennedy – p. 71.

62. Perret, G. 2001. Jack. A Life Like no Other – p. 369.

63. Reeves, R. 1993. President Kennedy. Profile of Power – p. 528.

64. Brauer, C.M. 1977. John F. Kennedy and the Second Reconstruction – p. 269.

65. Schlesinger, A.M. 1978. Robert Kennedy and his Times – p. 349.

66. Reeves, T.C. 1991. A Question of Character. A Life of John F. Kennedy – p. 357.

67. Schlesinger, A.M. 1965. A Thousand Days. John F. Kennedy in the White House – p. 967.

The March on Washington August 28, 1963
The John Lewis Speech Controversy

1. Gerald S. and Strober, D.H. 1993. Let Us Begin anew. An Oral History of the Kennedy Presidency – p. 312.

2. Navasky, V.S. 1971. Kennedy Justice – p. 226.

3. Branch, T. 1988. Parting the Waters. America in the King Years 1954-63 – p. 874.

4. Garrow, D.J. 1986. Bearing the Cross – p. 281-282-283.

5. Guthman, E.O. and Shulman, J. 1988. Robert Kennedy in His Own Words. The unpublished Recollections of the Kennedy years – p. 228-229.

6. Branch, T. 1988. Parting the Waters. America in the King Years 1954-63 – p. 879.

7. Reeves, R. 1993. President Kennedy Profile of Power – p. 582.

8. Goduti, P.A. 2013. Robert F. Kennedy and the Shaping of Civil Rights 1960-1964 – p. 216.

9. Garrow, D.J. 1986. Bearing the Cross – p. 281-282.

10. Feeney, L. July 24, 2003. Moyers & Company John Lewis Marches on Two Versions of John Lewis' Speech.

11. Miroff, B. 1976. Pragmatic Illusions. The Presidential Politics of John F. Kennedy – p. 264-265.

12. Schlesinger, A.M. 1978. Robert Kennedy and his Times – p. 349.

13. Biography Bayard Rustin. Internet 3/6.

14. Garrow, D.J. 1986. Bearing the Cross. Martin Luther King Jr., and the Southern Christian Leadership Conference – p. 276-277.

15. Branch, T. 1988. Parting the Waters. America in the King Years 1954-63 – p. 846-847.

16. Livingston, S. 2017. Kennedy and King. The President, the Pastor and the Battle over Civil Rights – p. 421.

17. Guthman, E.O. and Jeffrey Shulman, J. 1988. Robert Kennedy in his own words. The unpublished Recollections of the Kennedy years – p. 227.

18. Reeves, R. 1993. President Kennedy. Profile of Power – p. 581.

19. Goduti, P.A. 2013. Robert F. Kennedy and the Shaping of Civil Rights 1960-1964 – p. 215.

20. Reeves, R. 1993. President Kennedy. Profile of Power – p. 565.

21. Bernstein, I. 1991. Promises Kept. John F. Kennedy's New Frontier – p. 115.

22. Guthman, E.O. and Jeffrey Shulman, J. 1988. Robert Kennedy in his own words. The unpublished Recollections of the Kennedy years – p. 228.

23. Mills, J. 1988. John F. Kennedy – p. 255.

24. Kennedy, E.M. 2009. True Compass. A Memoir – p. 200.

25. Parmet, H.S. 1983. JFK. The Presidency of John F. Kennedy – p. 273.

26. Schlesinger, A. and Schlesinger, S. 2007. Journals 1952-2000 – p.197.

27. Stern, M.J. 1992. Calculated Visions. Kennedy, Johnson and Civil Rights – p. 97.

28. Dallek, R. 2003. An Unfinished Life. John F. Kennedy 1917-1963 – p. 642.

29. Rauh, J.L. 1965. OH JFK1 – 12/23/1965

30. Schlesinger, A. and Schlesinger, S. 2007. Journals 1952-2000 – p.197-198.

31. Branch, T. 1988. Parting the Waters. America in the King Years 1954-63 – p. 884.

32. Kennedy, J.F. June 6, 1963. Commencement address at San Diego State College. Public Papers of the Presidents – p. 445-446-447-448.

33. Frost, D.B. John F. Kennedy in Quotations. A Topical Dictionary – p. 66.

34. Guthman, E.O. and Jeffrey Shulman, J. 1988. Robert Kennedy in his own words. The unpublished Recollections of the Kennedy years – p. 226.

35. Sabato, L.J. 2013. The Kennedy half-Century. The Presidency, Assassination, and lasting Legacy of John F. Kennedy – p. 115-116.

36. The New York Times. June 26, 1963.

37. Stern, M. 1992. Calculating Visions. Kennedy, Johnson and Civil Rights – p. 100.

38. Reilly, J.R. 1970. OH Interview RFK 2. 10/29/1970

39. Raywid, A. 1974. OH Interview RFK 1. 08/15/1974

40. Thomas, E. 2000. Robert Kennedy. His Life – p. 250.

41. Leamer, L. 2001. The Kennedy Men 1901- 1969. The Law of the father – p.

709.

42. The Kennedy Presidential Press Conferences. 1978. p. 529.

43. Rorabaugh, W.J. 2002. Kennedy and the Promise of the Sixties – p. 119.

44. Parmet, H.S. 1983. JFK. The Presidency of John F. Kennedy – p. 273-274.

45. Brauer, C.M. 1977. John F. Kennedy and the Second Reconstruction – p. 291.

46. Stern, M. 1992. Calculating Visions. Kennedy, Johnson and Civil Rights – p. 104.

47. The Kennedy Presidential Press Conferences. 1978. p. 535.

48. Dallek, R. 2003. An Unfinished Life. John F. Kennedy 1917-1963 – p. 642.

49. Schlesinger, A. and Schlesinger, S. 2007. Journals 1952-2000 – p. 200.

50. Gerald S. and Strober, D.H. 1993. Let Us Begin anew. An Oral History of the Kennedy Presidency – p. 310.

51. Sorensen, T.C. 1965. Kennedy – p. 504.

52. Sorensen, T.C. 1964. OH JFKL – 05/03/1964

53. Brauer, C.M. 1977. John F. Kennedy and the Second Reconstruction – p. 291-292.

54. Oates, S.B. 1982. Let the trumpet Sound. A life of Martin Luther King Jr. – p. 256.

55. Carson, C. 2001. The Autobiography of Martin Luther King Jr. – p. 223.

56. King, M.L. 1963. Why We Can't Wait – p. 145.

57. White House Appointment Books JFKL. August 28, 1963.

58. Parmet, H.S. 1983. JFK. The Presidency of John F. Kennedy – p. 275.

59. Martin, R.G. 1995. Seeds of Destruction. Joe Kennedy and his sons – p. 440.

60. Kennedy, E.M. 2009. True Compass. A Memoir – p. 200-201.

61. Speeches that changed the world. 2005-2010. p. 139-142-143.

62. Giglio, J.N. 2006. The Presidency of John F. Kennedy. Second Edition – p. 201. First Edition – p. 186.

63. Branch, T. 1988. Parting the Waters. America in the King Years 1954-63 – p. 875-876.

64. Rorabaugh, W.J. 2002. Kennedy and the Promise of the Sixties – p. 122.

65. Branch, T. 1988. Parting the Waters. America in the King Years 1954-63 – p. 883.

66. Dallek, R. 2003. An Unfinished Life. John F. Kennedy 1917-1963 – p. 645.

67. Bryant, N. 2006. The Bystander. John F. Kennedy and the Struggle for Black Equality – p. 436.

68. Livingston, S. 2017. Kennedy and King. The President, the Pastor and the Battle over Civil Rights – p. 425.

69. Leamer, L. 2001. The Kennedy Men 1901-1963. The Laws of the father – p.712.

70. Fairlie, H. 1973. The Kennedy Promise. The politics of Expectation – p. 255.

71. Memorandum from William Sullivan to Alan Belmont. 8/30/1963. Church Committee final report p. 83 – p. 1.

72. Levingston, S. 2017. Kennedy and King. The President, the Pastor and the Battle over Civil Rights – p. 426.
73. Humphrey, H. 1991. The Education of a Public Man. My Life and Politics – p. 201.
74. Livingston, S. 2017. Kennedy and King. The President, the Pastor and the Battle over Civil Rights – p. 424.
75. Rorabaugh, W.J. 2002. Kennedy and the Promise of the Sixties – p. 122-123.
76. Bryant, N. 2006. The Bystander. John F. Kennedy and the Struggle for Black Equality – p. 437

Further Reading on the June 11, 1963 Civil Rights Speech
- Bernstein, I. 1991. Promises Kept. John F. Kennedy's New Frontier – p. 100-101-102.
- Giglio, J.N. 2006. The Presidency of John F. Kennedy. Second Edition – p. 193-194-195.
- Lupacova, M. 2008. John F. Kennedy and His Role in the Civil Rights Movement – Master's Diploma Thesis – p. 72-73.

Further Reading on his political Swan Song
- Leamer, L. 2001. The Kennedy Men 1901-1963. The Laws of the father – p.709.
- Dallek, R. 2003. An Unfinished Life. John F. Kennedy 1917-1963 – p. 605.
- Tye, L. 2016. Bobby Kennedy. The Making of a Liberal Icon – p. 229.

Further Reading on the Gallup Poll June 16, 1963
- Lewis J. 1975. The Promise and the Performance – p. 245.
- Parmet, H.S. 1983. JFK. The Presidency of John F. Kennedy – p. 272.

Further Reading on Medgar Evers Assassination
- Reeves, R. 1993. President Kennedy. Profile of Power – p. 522-523.
- Bryant, N. 2006. The Bystander. John F. Kennedy and the Struggle for Black Equality – p. 424.

Further Reading on Special Message to the Congress on Civil Rights and Job Opportunities
- Schlesinger, A.M. 1965. A Thousand Days. John F. Kennedy in the White House – p. 967.
- Sorensen, T.C. 1965. Kennedy – p. 496.
- Miroff, B. 1976. Pragmatic Illusions. The Presidential Politics of John F. Kennedy – p. 257-258-259.
- Brauer, C.M. 1977. John F. Kennedy and the Second Reconstruction – p. 266-

267.

- Reeves, T.C. 1991. A Question of Character. A Life of John F. Kennedy – p. 357.
- Reeves, R. 1993. President Kennedy. Profile of Power – p. 528.
- Dallek, R. 2003. An Unfinished Life. John F. Kennedy 1917-1963 – p. 604.
- Bryant, N. 2006. The Bystander: John F. Kennedy and the Struggle for Black Equality – p. 427.
- Goduti, P.A. 2013. Robert F. Kennedy and the Shaping of Civil Rights 1960-1964 – p. 206-207.

Further Reading on The John Lewis speech Controversy

- Schlesinger, A.M. 1978. Robert Kennedy and his Times – p. 351
- Branch, T. 1988. Parting the Waters. America in the King Years 1954-63 – p. 880.
- Reeves, T.C. 1991. A Question of Character. A Life of John F. Kennedy – p. 359.
- Bernstein, I. 1991. Promises Kept. John F. Kennedy's New Frontier – p. 115-116.
- Rorabaugh, W.J. 2002. Kennedy and the Promise of the Sixties – p. 121.
- Bryant, N. 2006. The Bystander. John F. Kennedy and the Struggle for Black Equality – p. 435-436.
- Ling, P.J. 2013. John F. Kennedy – p. 165-166.
- Sabato, L.J. 2013. The Kennedy Half Century. The Presidency, Assassination, and Lasting Legacy of John F. Kennedy – p. 116.
- Livingston, S. 2017. Kennedy and King. The President, the Pastor and the Battle over Civil Rights – p. 422-423.

5.3. Who Ordered King Wiretaps?
1. Navasky, V.S. 1971. Kennedy Justice – p. 135-139.
2. Nixon supports Hoover on Taps. June 20, 1969. The New York Times.
3. Herbers, J. June 21, 1962. Clark Suggests Hoover Step Out. HerbersSpecial to the NYT.
4. O'Leary, J. 6/10/1969. The Evening Star.
5. Evans, C. 1971. Oral History Interview RFK 5 – 01/08/1971
6. The Church Committee. Book III Final Report of the Select Committee to Study Governmental Operations – p. 102.
7. Gerald S. and Strober, D.H. 1993. Let Us Begin anew. An Oral History of the Kennedy Presidency – p. 314-315.
8. Hersh, B. 2007. Bobby and J. Edgar – p. 357.
9. White House appointment book. June 22, 1963.

10. Reeves, R. 1993. President Kennedy. Profile of Power – p. 530.

11. Branch, T. 1988. Parting The Waters; America in the King Years 1956-63 – p. 564.

Reeves, R. 1993. President Kennedy. Profile of Power – p. 530.

Schlesinger, A.M. 1978. Robert Kennedy and His Times – p. 357-358.

12. The Church Committee. Book III Final Report of the Select Committee to Study Governmental Operations – p. 97.

13. The Kennedy Presidential Press Conferences. 1978. p. 531.

14. Hilty, J.W. 1997. Robert Kennedy: Brother Protector – p. 399.

15. Schlesinger, A.M. 1978. Robert Kennedy and his Times – p. 262 – notes p. 949, 4

16. Garrow, D.J. 1981. The FBI and Martin Luther King Jr. From "Solo" to Memphis – p. 68.

17. Sullivan, W.C. and Brown, B. 1979. The Bureau. My Thirty Years in Hoover's FBI – p. 137.

18. The Church Committee. Final Report of the Select Committee to Study Governmental Operations – p. 106-107.

Guthman, E.O. and Shulman, J. 1988. Robert Kennedy in His Own Words. The Unpublished Recollections of the Kennedy years – p. 141-145-146.

19. Stern, M. 1992. Calculating Visions. Kennedy, Johnson and Civil Rights – p. 98-99.

20. Rorabaugh, W.J. 2002. Kennedy and the Promise of the Sixties – p. 118.

21. Navasky, V.S. 1971. Kennedy Justice – p. 141.

22. Garrow, D.J. 1981. The FBI and Martin Luther King Jr. From "Solo" to Memphis – p. 42-43.

23. Hilty, J.W. 1997. Robert Kennedy: Brother Protector – p. 338.

24. Powers, R.G. 1987. Secrecy and Power. The Life of J. Edgar Hoover – p. 370.

25. Garrow, D.J. 1981. The FBI and Martin Luther King Jr. From "Solo" to Memphis – p. 42-43.

26. Schlesinger, A.M. 1978. Robert Kennedy and his Times – p. 356 note 65 p.960.

27. Hilty, J.W. 1997. Robert Kennedy: Brother Protector – p. 338.

28. Garrow, D.J. 2002. The Atlantic. July/August 2002 Issue. The FBI and Martin Luther King.

29. Garrow, D.J. 1981. The FBI and Martin Luther King Jr. From "Solo" to Memphis – p. 46.

30. The Church Committee. 1976. Book III Final Report of the select Committee to Study Governmental Operations p. 88-89.

31. Schlesinger, A.M. 1978. Robert Kennedy and his Times – p. 355.

32. Reeves, R. 1993. President Kennedy. Profile of Power – source notes p. 732.

33. Wofford, H. 1980. Of Kennedys and Kings. Making Sense of the Sixties – p. 217.

34. Navasky, V.S. 1971. Kennedy Justice – p. 144-145-146-148.

35. O'Brien, M. 2005. John F. Kennedy: A Biography. History and Dr. King – p. 853 – source: Old Myths/New Insights: History and Dr. King – p. 56-57; Michael O'Brien source: The History Teacher, Vol 22, N°1 (Nov 1988) p. 49-65

36. Navasky, V.S. 1971. Kennedy Justice – p. 148.

37. O'Brien, M. 2005. John F. Kennedy: A Biography. History and Dr. King – p. 853-854 – source: Old Myths/New Insights: History and Dr. King – p. 56-57; Michael O'Brien source: The History Teacher, Vol 22, N°1 (Nov 1988) p. 49-65

38. Hersh, B. 2007. Bobby and J. Edgar. The Historic face-off between the Kennedys and J. Edgar Hoover that transformed America – p. 372.

39. Reeves, T.C. 1991. A Question of Character. A Life of John F. Kennedy – notes: Schlesinger Robert K. and His Times p. 382 not found

40. Garrow, D.J. 2002. The FBI and Martin Luther King. The Atlantic. July/August 2002 Issue

41. Sullivan, W.C. and Brown, B. 1979. The Bureau. My Thirty Years in Hoover's FBI – p. 135-136-137-138-139.

42. Garrow, D.J. 1981. The FBI and Martin Luther King Jr. From "Solo" to Memphis – p. 88-89.

43. Sullivan, W.C. Wikipedia 2/4.

44. The Church Committee. Book III Final Report of the Select Committee to Study Governmental Operations – p. 100-101-102.

45. Schlesinger, A.M. 1978. Robert Kennedy and his Times – p. 359-360.

46. Leamer, L. 2001. The Kennedy Men 1901-1963. The Laws of the father – p.710-711.

47. The Church Committee. Book III Final Report of the Select Committee to Study Governmental Operations – p. 115.

48. Branch, T. 1988. Parting the Waters. America in the King Years 1954-63 – p. 906-907.

49. Hersh, B. 2007. Bobby and J. Edgar – p. 371.

50. The Church Committee. Book III Final Report of the Select Committee to Study Governmental Operations – p. 115-116-117.

51. Evans, C. 1971. Oral History Interview RFK 4 – 1/5/1971

52. Schlesinger, A.M. 1978. Robert Kennedy and his Times – p. 360.

53. Wise, D. 1976. The American Police State. The Government Against the People – p. 301.

54. Hersh, B. 2007. Bobby and J. Edgar. DeLoach interview with the author – 5/31/2004

55. Summers, A. 1993. Official and Confidential. The secret Life of J. Edgar Hoover – p. 312-313.

56. Branch, T. 1988. Parting the Waters. America in the King Years 1954-63 – p. 908-909.

57. Sullivan, W.C. and Brown, B. 1979. The Bureau. My Thirty Years in Hoover's FBI – p. 50.

58. Garrow, D.J. 2002. The FBI and Matin Luther King. The Atlantic. July/August 2002 Issue

59. O'Brien, M. 2005. John F. Kennedy: A Biography – p. 851.

60. Clark, R. 1970. Oral History Interview. RFK 3 – 7/20/1970

61. Navasky, V.S. 1971. Kennedy. Justice – p. 140.

62. Turner, W. 1993. Hoover's FBI – p. 101.

63. Kiel, R.A. 2000. J. Edgar Hoover. The Father of the Cold War – p. 103.

64. The Church Committee. April 23 (under authority of the order of April 14) 1976. Book III Final Report of the Select Committee to Study Governmental Operations – p. 117-118.

65. Gerald S. and Strober, D.H. 1993. Let Us Begin anew. An Oral History of the Kennedy Presidency – p. 315.

Further Reading on A Stroll in the Rose Garden on Saturday June 22, 1963

- Reeves, T.C. 1991. A Question of Character. A Life of John F. Kennedy – p. 360.
- Goduti, P.A. 2013. Robert F. Kennedy and the Shaping of Civil Rights 1960-1964 – p. 210-211.
- Gentry, C. 2000. J. Edgar Hoover. The Man and the Secrets – p. 507-508.
- Reeves, R. 1993. President Kennedy. Profile of Power – p. 529-530-531.
- Hersh, B. 2007. Bobby and J. Edgar – p. 355-356.
- Tye, L. 2016. Bobby Kennedy. The Making of a Liberal Icon – p. 233.
- Leamer, L. 2001. The Kennedy Men 1901-1963. The Laws of the father – p.710.
- Hilty, J.W. 1997. Robert Kennedy: Brother Protector – p. 375-376.
- Stern, M. 1992. Calculating Visions. Kennedy, Johnson and Civil Rights – p. 97-98.
- Summers, A. 1993. Official and Confidential. The secret Life of J. Edgar Hoover – p. 306.
- Powers, R.G. 1987. Secrecy and Power. The Life of J. Edgar Hoover – p. 372.
- Navasky, V.S. 1971. Kennedy Justice – p. 143.
- Rorabaugh, W.J. 2003. Kennedy and the Promise of the Sixties – p. 117.
- Schlesinger, A.M. 1978. Robert Kennedy and his Times – p. 357-358.
- Giglio, J.N. and Rabe, S.G. 2003. Debating the Kennedy Presidency – p. 192.
- Kamin, B. 2014. Dangerous Friendship. Stanley Levison, Martin Luther King Jr. and the Kennedy Brothers – p. 24-25-26.

Further Reading on Levison and O'Dell

- Hersh, B. 2007. Bobby and J. Edgar – p. 348-349-350.
- Levingston, S. 2017. Kennedy and King – p. 221-222.

- Leamer, L. 2001. The Kennedy Men 1901-1963 – p. 709-710.
- Gentry, C. 2000. J. Edgar Hoover. The Man and the Secrets – p. 502-503-504-507-508-509.
- Branch, T. 1988. Parting the Waters. America in the King Years 1954-63 – p. 835-836.
- Reeves, R. 1993. President Kennedy. Profile of Power – p. 502.

Further Reading on the King and Jones wiretaps
- Gentry, C. 2000. J. Edgar Hoover. The Man and the Secrets – p. 528.
- Reeves, R. 1993. President Kennedy. Profile of Power – p. 626-627.
- Powers, R.G. 1987. Secrecy and Power. The Life of J. Edgar Hoover – p. 372-373.
- Steel, R. 2000. In Love with Night – p. 160.
- Garrow, D.J. 1981. The FBI and Martin Luther King Jr. From "Solo" to Memphis – p. 64-65-66-67-72-73-74.
- Reeves, T.C. 1991. A Question of Character. A Life of John F. Kennedy – p. 362.
- Martin, R.G. 1995. Seeds of Destruction. Joe Kennedy and his sons – p. 441.
- Hersh, B. 2007. Bobby and J. Edgar – p. 371-372.
- Goduti, P.A. 2013. Robert F. Kennedy and the Shaping of Civil Rights 1960-1964 – p. 213-214.
- Hilty, J.W. 1997. Robert Kennedy: Brother Protector – p. 392-393.

5.4. Was Harris Wofford Sent to Africa, or Was It His Own Decision?
1. Wofford, H.L. 1965. Oral History Interview JFKL1. 11/29/1965
2. Wofford, H.L. 1968. Oral History Interview JFKL2. 5/22/1968
3. Katzenbach, N.B. 2008. Some of it Was Fun. Working with RFK and LBJ – p. 15-16.
4. Brauer, C.M. 1977. John F. Kennedy and the Second Reconstruction – p. 93.
5. Heymann, C.D. 1998. RFK. A Candid Biography of Robert F. Kennedy – p. 192-193.
6. Marshall, B. 1970. Oral History Interview RFK. 1/19-20/1970
7. Wofford, H.L. 1965. Oral History Interview JFKL1. 11/29/1965
8. Wofford, H.L. 1968. Oral History Interview JFKL2. 5/22/1968
9. Wofford, H. 1980. Of Kennedys and Kings. Making Sense of the Sixties – p. 131-132.
10. Wofford, H. 1980. Of Kennedys and Kings. Making Sense of the Sixties – p. 130.
11. Wofford, H.L. 1969. Oral History Interview JFKL3. 02/03/1969
12. Wofford, H. 1980. Of Kennedys and Kings. Making Sense of the Sixties – p.

124.

13. Wofford, H. 1980. Of Kennedys and Kings. Making Sense of the Sixties – p. 153.

14. Wofford, H. 1980. Of Kennedys and Kings. Making Sense of the Sixties – p. 125-157.

15. Hilty, J.W. 1997. Robert Kennedy: Brother Protector – p. 298.

16. Lansford L. PH D., Watson, R.P., Scumski, B., Barbeur, S. 2004. Presidents and their decisions. John F. Kennedy – p. 138 – Kennedy Missed Opportunities to act forcefully on civil Rights by Jackson D.W. & Riddlesperger J.W. Jr.

17. Goodwin, R.N. 1988. Remembering America. A Voice from the Sixties – p. 133.

18. Giglio, J.N. 2006. The Presidency of John F. Kennedy. Second Edition – p. 185.

19. Wofford, H. 1980. Of Kennedys and Kings. Making Sense of the Sixties – p. 133.

20. Branch, T. 1988. Parting the Waters. America in the King Years 1954-63 – p. 587.

21. Billings, K.L. 1965. OH JFK. 03/20-21/1965

22. Fenn, D.H. 2018. Email. January 6, 2018

5.5. Would Kennedy Have Replaced J. Edgar Hoover in 1965?

1. Clifford, C. and Holbrooke, R. 1991. Counsel to the President. A Memoir – p. 331.

2. Neustadt, R. October 30, 1960. Memorandum. TCS 18.

3. Brauer, C.M. 1977. John F. Kennedy and the Second Reconstruction – p. 162.

4. Bradlee, B.C. 1975. Conversations with Kennedy – p. 32-33-34.

5. Schlesinger, A.M. 1965. A Thousand Days. John F. Kennedy in the White House – p. 125.

6. White, T.H. 1978. In Search of History. A personal adventure – p. 492.

7. Sorensen, T.C. 2008. Counselor. A Life at the Edge of History – p. 525.

8. Martin, R.G. 1995. Seeds of Destruction. Joe Kennedy and his sons – p. 99.

9. Perret, G. 2001. Jack. A Life Like no Other – p. 272.

10. Martin, R.G. 1983. A Hero for our Time. An Intimate Story of the Kennedy years – p. 456.

11. O'Brien, M. 2005. John F. Kennedy: A Biography – p. 502-715.

12. Dallek, R. 2013. Camelot's court. Inside the Kennedy White House – p. 76.

13. Reeves, T.C. 1991. A Question of Character. A Life of John F. Kennedy – p. 56.

14. Nasaw, D. 2012. The Patriarch. The Remarkable Life and Turbulent Times of Joseph P. Kennedy – p. 541-559.

15. Summers, A. 1993. Official and Confidential. The secret Life of J. Edgar Hoover – p. 265-266.

16. Blair, J. and Blair C. Jr.. 1976. The Search for JFK – p. 144.

17. Schwarz, T. 2003. Joseph P. Kennedy. The Mogul, The Mob, The Statesman and the Making of an American Myth – p.404.

18. Summers, A. 1993. Official and Confidential. The secret Life of J. Edgar Hoover – p. 274.

19. Blair J. & Blair C. Jr. 1976. The Search for JFK – p. 144.

20. Summers, A. 1993. Official and Confidential. The secret Life of J. Edgar Hoover – p. 266.

21. Fenn, D.H. 2018. Email. February 21, 2018

22. Summers, A. 1993. Official and Confidential. The secret Life of J. Edgar Hoover – p. 266.

23. Blair, J. and Blair C. Jr. 1976. The Search for JFK – p. 144.

24. Dallek, R. 1998. Flawed Geant. Lyndon Johnson and his times 1961-1973 – p. 408.

25. Gerald S. and Strober, D.H. 1993. Let Us Begin anew. An Oral History of the Kennedy Presidency – p. 269.

26. Summers, A. 1993. Official and Confidential. The secret Life of J. Edgar Hoover – p. 148-149-150.

27. Five Myths about J. Edgar Hoover. November 9, 2011

28. Summers, A. 1993. Official and Confidential. The secret Life of J. Edgar Hoover – p. 151-152.

29. Off the record: the Private Papers of Harry S. Truman ed. Robert Ferrell NY, Harper & Row. HT/May 12, 1980... p. 22.

30. Demaris, O. 1975. The Director. An Oral Biography of J. Edgar Hoover – p. 281.

31. Summers, A. 1993. Official and Confidential. The secret Life of J. Edgar Hoover – p. 289.

32. Parmet, H.S. 1983. JFK. The Presidency of John F. Kennedy – p. 127. O'Donnell, K.P. Interview. December 4, 1976

33. Demaris, O. 1975. The Director. An Oral Biography of J. Edgar Hoover – p. 181.

34. Demaris, O. 1975. The Director. An Oral Biography of J. Edgar Hoover – p. 173.

35. Guthman, E.O. and Jeffrey Shulman, J. 1988. Robert Kennedy in his own words. The unpublished Recollections of the Kennedy years – p. 126.

36. Gerald S. and Strober, D.H. 1993. Let Us Begin anew. An Oral History of the Kennedy Presidency – p. 317.

37. Gerald S. and Strober, D.H. 1993. Let Us Begin anew. An Oral History of the Kennedy Presidency – p. 269.

38. Demaris, O. 1975. The Director. An Oral History of J. Edgar Hoover – p. 143.

39. Demaris, O. 1975. The Director. An Oral History of J. Edgar Hoover – p. 166.

40. Gentry, C. 2000. J. Edgar Hoover. The Man and the Secrets – p. 560-561.

41. Bernstein, C. and Woodward, B. 1974. All the President's Men – p. 289.

42. Hunter, M. May 9, 1964. The New York Times. Special to the New York Times.

43. Hersh, B. 2007. Bobby and J. Edgar. Gus Russo private citation quoting Martin Underwood – p. 380.

44. Bradlee, B. 1995. A Good Life. Newspapering and other adventures – p. 271-272.

45. Gentry, C. 1991. J. Edgar Hoover. The Man and the Secrets – p. 560; Dallek, R. 1998. Flawed Giant. Lyndon Johnson and his times 1961-1973 – p. 126; Hersh, B. May 9, 2007. New York Times – p. 380; Bradlee, B. 1995. Good Life – p. 272; J. Edgar Hoover and the FBI. November 1964. Newsweek Article – p. 21.

46. Lyndon B. Johnsons's Daily Diary collection. LBJ Presidential Library. May 8, November 17, December 4, 1964

47. Summers, A. 1993. Official and Confidential. The secret Life of J. Edgar Hoover – p. 11-12-203-373.

48. White House tape transcripts. Oct 8-25, 1971

49. Gerald S. and Strober, D.H. 1993. Let Us Begin anew. An Oral History of the Kennedy Presidency – p. 270.

50. Schlesinger, A.M. 2011. Jacqueline Kennedy. Historic Conversations on Life with John – p. 343.

51. Summers, A. 1993. Official and Confidential. The secret Life of J. Edgar Hoover – p. 304.

52. Evans, C. 1971. Oral History Interview. RFK 5. 1/8/1971

53. Sullivan, W.C. and Brown, B. 1979. The Bureau. My Thirty Years in Hoover's FBI – p. 55.

54. Schwarz, T. 2003. Joseph P. Kennedy. The Mogul, The Mob, The Statesman and the Making of an American Myth – p.406.

55. Mahoney, R.D. 1999. Sons & Brothers. The Days of Jack and Bobby Kennedy – p. 156.

56. Interviews with Anthony Lewis (with Burke Marshall present) NY City, December 4, 1964: Mc Lean Virginia, December 6 & 22, 1964

57. Gentry, C. 1991. J. Edgar Hoover: The Man and the Secrets. Courtney Evans interview
 – p. 536.

58. Thomas, E. 2000. Robert Kennedy. His Life – p. 268.

59. Hoover to Tolson et al. October 29, 1963. Hoover's reward, Rometsch FOIA/FBI. The Attorney General said all such rumors were unfounded and vicious

60. Hosty, J. 1996. Assignment Oswald – p. 154.

61. Kiel, R.A. 2000. J. Edgar Hoover. The Father of the Cold War – p. 105.

62. Reeves, R. 1993. President Kennedy: Profile of Power. Confidential dispatch Time arch – p. 288.

63. Gerald S. and Strober, D.H. 1993. Let Us Begin anew. An Oral History of the

Kennedy Presidency – p. 269.

Further Reading on "Vicious and baseless
- Giglio, J.N. 2006. The Presidency of John F. Kennedy. Second Edition – p. 200.
- Hersh, B. 2007. Bobby and J. Edgar – p. 368-369.

Further Reading on Reappointing Hoover & Dulles – on Hoover & Dulles to remain in their posts
- Damore, L. 1967-1993. The Cape Cod Years of John Fitzgerald Kennedy – p. 230.
- Dallek, R. 2013. Camelot's court. Inside the Kennedy White House – p. 22-76.
- Collier, P. & Horowitz, D. 1984. The Kennedys. An American Drama – p. 253.
- Willis, G. 1981. The Kennedy Imprisonment. A Meditation on Power – p. 36.

Further Reading on the Inga Arvad tapes
- Reeves, T.C. 1991. A Question of Character. A Life of John F. Kennedy – p. 217-218.
- Mills, J. 1988. John F. Kennedy – p. 188.
- Rubin, G. 2005. Forty ways to look at JFK – p. 240.
- Reeves, R. 1993. President Kennedy. Profile of Power – p. 66-67.
- Heymann, C.D. 1989. A Woman named Jackie – p. 154-155.
- Matthews, C. 2011. Jack Kennedy. Elusive Hero – p. 321-322.

Further Reading March 22, 1962 Kennedy, Hoover, O'Donnell meeting
- Mahoney, R.D. 1999. Sons & Brothers. The Days of Jack and Bobby Kennedy – p. 156-157.
- Hersh, B. 2007. Bobby and J. Edgar – p. 297.

Further Reading on "J. Edgar Hoover has Jack Kennedy by the balls"
- Whalen, T.J. 2014. JFK and his Enemies. A portrait of Power – p. 163.

5.6. Conclusion
1. Sorensen, T.C. 2008. Counselor. A Life at the Edge of History – p. 221.
2. Goduti, P.A. 2013. Robert F. Kennedy and the Shaping of Civil Rights 1960-1964 – p. 51-52.
3. Fairlie H. 2000. People who made history: John F. Kennedy, Swisher C. (Book Editor). Kennedy's Failure to work for Civil Rights – p. 95.
4. Thomas, E. 2000. Robert Kennedy. His Life – p. 126.
5. Gerald S. and Strober, D.H. 1993. Let Us Begin anew. An Oral History of the Kennedy Presidency – p. 285-286.

6. Sorensen, T.C. 2008. Counselor. A Life at the Edge of History – p. 272-273.
7. Rauh, J.L. 1965. Oral History Interview JFKL 1. 12/23/1965
8. Logevall, F. 2018. Email. February 19, 2018
9. Wicker, T. 1968. JFK and LBJ. The Influence of personality upon politics – p. 89.
10. Genovese, M.A. 2001. The Power of the American Presidency 1789-2000 – p. 151.
11. Barnes, J.A. 2005. John F. Kennedy on leadership. The Lessons and Legacy of a president – p. 185.
12. Carson, C. 1998. The Autobiography of Martin Luther King Jr. – p. 143-144.
13. Wofford, H. 1980. Of Kennedy and Kings. Making Sense of the Sixties – p. 128-129.
14. Giglio, J.N. 2006. The Presidency of John F. Kennedy. Second Edition – p. 174.
15. Manchester, W. 1967. The Death of a President 1963 – p. 129.
16. Reeves, R. 1993. President Kennedy. Profile of Power – p. 62.
Bruce, P. 1964. Oral History Interview JFKL – 6/16/1964
17. Levingston, S. 2017. Kennedy and King. The President, the Pastor and the Battle over Civil Rights – p. 423-424.
18. Carson, C. 1998. The Autobiography of Martin Luther King Jr. – p. 345.
19. Harris, T.G. Look [Magazine]. November 17, 1964. Eight Views of JFK. The Competent American.
20. Lewis J. 1975. The Promise and the Performance. The Leadership of John F. Kennedy – p. 319-320
21. Booker, S. 1967. Oral History Interview JFKL – 04/02/1967
22. Wilkins, R. 1964. Oral History Interview JFKL – 08/03/1964

Further Reading
- Wofford, H. 1980. Of Kennedys and Kings. Making Sense of the Sixties – p. 99.

Chapter 6: The Health Issue: A Perfect Cover Up And A True Profile In Courage

6.1. Kennedy's Family Members on His Health
1. Kennedy, R.F. 1974. Times to Remember – p. 83-84-85.
2. Kennedy, R.F. 1995. Times to Remember – p. 153-200-201.
3. Kennedy, R.F. 1974. Times to Remember – p. 133-174.
4. Kennedy, R.F. 1995. Times to Remember – p. 145.
5. Kennedy, E.M. 2009. True Compass. A Memoir – p. 24-73-74-400.
6. Smith, A. 2001. Hostage to fortune. The Letters of Joseph P. Kennedy – p. 676.
7. Schlesinger, A.M. 2011. Jacqueline Kennedy. Historic Conversations on Life with John – p. 16-17-18-90-91-161-162-163.
8. Kennedy, R.F. 1964. Profiles in Courage. Memorial Edition with a special foreword by Robert F. Kennedy – p. 9-10.
9. Owen, D. 2008. In Sickness and in Power – p. 158.

6.2. Kennedy's Addison's Disease
1. Blair J. & Blair C. Jr. 1976. The Search for JFK – p. 562-563.
2. Travell, J.M.D. 1968-1969. Office Hours, Day and Night. The Autobiography of Janet Travell M.D. – p. 329-330.
3. Gilbert, R.E. June 10, 2009. JFK and Addison's Disease. From the internet; last updated Friday April 9, 2010
4. Dallek, R. December 2002. The Atlantic Monthly. The Medical Ordeals of JFK – p. 52.
5. O'Brien, M. 2005. John F. Kennedy: A Biography – p. 758.
6. Tennant, F. and MD, D. September 2012. Practical Pain Management John F. Kennedy's Pain Story – p. 63.
7. Dallek, R. 2003. An Unfinished Life. John F. Kennedy 1917-1963 – p. 105.
8. Blair J. & Blair C. Jr. 1976. The Search for JFK – p. 561.
9. Owen, D. 2008. In Sickness and in Power. Illness in Heads of Government during the last 100 years – p. 157.
10. Travell, J. M.D. 1968. Office Hours: Day and Night. The Autobiography of Janet Travell, M.D.. – p. 330.
11. Schlesinger, A.M. 1965. A Thousand Days. John F. Kennedy in the White House – p. 19.
12. Bradlee, B.C. 1975. Conversations with Kennedy – p. 68.
13. Widmer, T. January 5, 1960. A taped interview, Transcript discussion among Bradlee, Cannon and Kennedy JFKL. Smithsonian Magazine October 2012.
14. Clarke, T. 2013. JFK's last Hundred Days – p. 34.
15. Blair J. & Blair C. Jr. 1976. The Search for JFK – p. 576.

16. Braden, J. 1989. Just Enough Rope. An Intimate Memoir – p. 115-116.
17. Dallek, R. December 2002. The Atlantic Monthly. The Medical Ordeals of JFK – p. 50.
18. Parmet, H.S. 1983. JFK. The Presidency of John F. Kennedy. R. Sargent. source: Shriver S.R. Interview January 14, 1980 + Hans Kraus interview, December 8, 1980

6.3. How Did Kennedy Injure His Back?
1. Kennedy, R.F. 1974. Times to Remember – p. 145, 215.
2. Pitts, D. 2007. Jack and Lem. The Untold Story of an Extraordinary friendship – p. 47.
3. Burns, J.M.G. 1960. John Kennedy. A Political Profile – p. 30, 53.
4. Sorensen, T.C. 1965. Kennedy – p. 39.
5. Blair J. & Blair C. Jr. 1976. The Search for JFK – p. 22-24-25.
6. Hamilton, N. 1992. JFK: Reckless Youth – p. 210,296,341.
7. Perret, G. 2001. Jack. A Life Like no Other – p. 58,406,407.
8. Owen, D. 2008. In Sickness and in Power. Illness in Heads of Government during the last 100 years – p. 154.
9. Giglio, J.N. October 2006. Growing up Kennedy: The Role of Medical Ailments in the life of JFK 1920-1957 – Journals of Family History Vol 31 n°4 – p. 369.
10. Tennant, F. and MD, D. September 2012. John F. Kennedy's pain Story. From Autoimmune disease to central Pain. Practical Pain Management – p. 55-56.
11. Dallek, R. 2003. An Unfinished Life. John F. Kennedy 1917-1963 – p. 81.
12. Selverstone, M.J. 2014. A companion to Kennedy – p. 20.
13. Reeves, T.C. 1991. A Question of Character. A Life of John F. Kennedy – p. 69.
14. Barnes, J.A. 2005. John F. Kennedy on leadership. The Lessons and Legacy of a president – p. 216.
15. O'Brien, M. 2005. John F. Kennedy: A Biography – p. 113-114.
16. Travell, Janet Dr. Oral History Interview (by T. Sorensen) JFKL1 – 1/20/1966 – p. 3
17. Collier, P. & Horowitz, D. 1984. The Kennedys. An American Drama – p. 133.
18. Willis, G. 1981-1982. The Kennedy Imprisonment. A Meditation on Power – p. 128.
19. Beschloss, M.R. 1991. The Crisis Years – p. 189.
20. Salinger, P. 1966. With Kennedy – p. 41.

6.5. Three Back Doctors in the White House
6.5.1. Janet Travell "The Procaine injections
1. Travell, J. M.D. 1968. Office Hours: Day and Night. The Autobiography of Janet

Travell, M.D. – p. 5-6-7.

2. Reeves, R. 1993. President Kennedy. Profile of Power – p. 15.

3. Travell, Janet Dr. Oral History Interview (by T. Sorensen). JFKL1 1/20/1966 – p. 1

4. Travell, Janet Dr. Oral History Interview (by T. Sorensen) JFKL1 1/20/1966 – p. 3-4

5. Travell, J. M.D. 1968-1969. Office Hours: Day and Night. The Autobiography of Janet Travell, M.D. – p. 327.

6. Tennant, F. and MD, D. 2012. John F. Kennedy's pain Story. From Autoimmune disease to central Pain – p. 60-61-62.

7. Fay, P.B. 1970. Oral History Interview JFKL2 11/10/1970 – p. 240

8. Fay, P.B. 1966. The Pleasure of his Company – p. 175-176.

9. Tennant, F. and MD, D. John F. Kennedy's pain Story. From Autoimmune disease to central Pain – p. 65.

10. Schlesinger, A.M. 2011. Jacqueline Kennedy. Historic Conversations on Life with John – p. 18.

11. Leamer, L. 2001. The Kennedy Men 1901-1963. The Laws of the father – p.411-525-526.

12. Schier, W.D. July 29, 1964. Lem Billings OH interview, Washington D.C. p. 471-472.

13. Clarke, T. 2013. JFK's Last Hundred Days. The Transformation of a Man and the Emergence of a Great President – p. 37-38.

14. JFKPP. JFKL. Box 58.

15. Leamer, L. 2001. The Kennedy Men 1901-1963. The Laws of the father – p.547.

16. Travell, J. M.D. 1968. Office Hours: Day and Night. The Autobiography of Janet Travell, M.D. – p. 396-397.

6.5.2. Mac Jacobson "The Quack"

1. Lertzman, R.A. and Birnes, W.J. 2013. Dr. Feelgood. Max Jacobson Patient List – p. 61 (from office records supplied by Ruth Jacobson, courtesy of the C. David Heymann Archive)

2. Owen, D. 2008. In Sickness and in Power. Illness in Heads of Government during the last 100 years – p. 165.

3. Saunders, F. and Southwood, J. 1980. Torn Lace Curtain. Life with the Kennedys recalled by their personal chauffeur – p. 206.

4. O'Brien, M. 2005. John F. Kennedy: A Biography – p. 761.

5. Barnes, J.A. 2005. John F. Kennedy on leadership. The Lessons and Legacy of a president – p. 215.

6. Heymann, C.D. 1989. A Woman named Jackie – p. 312.

7. Lertzman, R.A. and Birnes, W.J. 2013. Dr. Feelgood – p. 7.

8. Heymann, C.D. 1989. A Woman named Jackie. An Intimate biography of Jacqueline Bouvier Kennedy Onassis – p. 297,319.

9. Parmet, H.S. 1983. JFK. The Presidency of John F. Kennedy – p. 121.

10. Reeves, R. 1993. President Kennedy Profile of Power – p. 147.

11. Reeves, T.C. 1991. A Question of Character. A Life of John F. Kennedy – p. 295.

12. Heymann, C.D. 1989. A Woman named Jackie. An Intimate biography of Jacqueline Bouvier Kennedy Onassis – p. 308.

13. Reeves, R. 1993. President Kennedy Profile of Power – p. 146-147, 243, 685, 698, 699.

14. Reeves, R. Unpublished Memoirs of Max Jacobson: JFK chapter 10.

15. Hersh, S.M. 1997. The Dark side of Camelot – p. 234.

16. Sorensen, T. 2008. Counselor: A Life at the Edge of History – p. 106.

17. White, M.J. 1998. Kennedy. The New Frontier Revisited – p. 263-264.

18. Leamer, L. 2001. The Kennedy Men 1901-1963 – p. 543, 807.

19. Rubin, G. 2005. Forty ways to look at JFK – p. 265,245-246.

20. Perret, G. 2001. Jack. A Life Like no Other – p. 355.

21. Dallek, R. 2003. An Unfinished Life. John F. Kennedy 1917-1963 – p. 581-582, 792.

22. Barnes, J.A. 2005. John F. Kennedy on leadership. The Lessons and Legacy of a president – p. 216.

23. O'Brien, M. 2005. John F. Kennedy: A Biography – p. 761.

24. Giglio, J.N. 2006. The Presidency of John F. Kennedy. Second Edition, Revised – p. 280-330-331.

25. Selverstone, M.J. 2014. A companion to Kennedy – p. 11-25.

26. Pitts, D. 2007. Jack and Lem. The Untold Story of an Extraordinary Friendship – p. 234-235.

27. Owen, D. 2008. In Sickness and in Power. Illness in Heads of Government during the last 100 years – p. 179-180.

28. Dallek, R. 2003. An Unfinished Life. John F. Kennedy 1917-1963 – p. 581.

29. Ghaemi, N. 2001. A First Rate Madness: Uncovering the links between leadership and Mental Illness – His references are Owen p. 169 & Dallek p. 303-304.

30. Clarke, T. 2013. JFK's last Hundred Days. The Transformation of a Man and the Emergence of a Great President – p. 35-36.

How many Vials were examined?

1. Heymann, C.D. 1989. A Woman named Jackie – p. 312-313.

2. Reeves, T.C. 1991. A Question of Character. A Life of John F. Kennedy – p. 296.

3. Reeves, R. 1993. President Kennedy. Profile of Power – p. 243-699.

4. Hersh, S.M. 1997. The Dark side of Camelot – p. 237.

5. Thomas, E. 2000. Robert Kennedy: His Life – p. 191.

6. Perret, G. 2001. Jack: A Life Like No Other – p. 313.
7. Leamer, L. 2001. The Kennedy Men 1901-1963 – p. 546.
8. White, M.J. 1998. Kennedy. The New Frontier Revisited – p. 265.
9. Dallek, R. 2003. An Unfinished Life. John F. Kennedy 1917-1963 – p. 582.
10. O'Brien, M. 2005. John F. Kennedy: A Biography – p. 763.
11. Owen, D. 2008. In Sickness and in Power – p. 169.
12. Lertzman, R.A. and Birnes, W.J. 2013. Dr. Feelgood – p. 122-123.

6.5.3. Hans Kraus "The Exercise Doctor"

1. Kraus, H. Wikipedia.
2. Schwartz, S.E.B. 2012. JFK's Secret Doctor. The remarkable life of medical Pioneer and legendary rock Climber Hans Kraus – p. 170-171-182-184-185-187.
3. Owen, D. 2008. In Sickness and in Power. Illness in Heads of Government during the last 100 years – p. 177.
4. Dallek, R. 2003. An Unfinished Life. John F. Kennedy 1917-1963 – p. 473.
5. Schwartz, S.E.B. 2012. JFK's Secret Doctor. The remarkable life of medical Pioneer and legendary rock Climber Hans Kraus – p. 188-189-xvi- 190-194-195-199-200.
6. Schwartz, S.E.B. 2012. JFK's Secret Doctor. The remarkable life of medical Pioneer and legendary rock Climber Hans Kraus – p. 207-208-211-212-213.
7. Perret, G. 2001. Jack. A Life Like no Other – p. 355.
8. Reeves, R. 1993. President Kennedy: Profile of Power – p. 242.
9. Barnes, J.A. 2005. John F. Kennedy on leadership. The Lessons and Legacy of a president – p. 215.
10. Lincoln, E. 1965. My Twelve Years with John F. Kennedy – p. 338.
11. Schwartz, S.E.B. 2012. JFK's Secret Doctor. The remarkable life of medical Pioneer and legendary rock Climber Hans Kraus – p. 213-214-219-220-224-225 – notes 86
12. Salinger, P. 1966. With Kennedy – p. 41-90.
13. Giglio, J.N. 2006. The Presidency of John F. Kennedy. Second Edition – p. 283.
14. O'Donnell, K.P., Powers, D.F. and McCarthy, J. 1970-1972. Johnny, we hardly knew you. Memoirs of John Fitzgerald Kennedy – p. 102-103.

6.6. Thursday, June 22, 1961: The day President Kennedy Almost Died in the White House

1. Selverstone, M.J. 2014. A Companion to John F. Kennedy – p. 18.
2. Janet Travell Oral History Interview 1966. JFKL 01/20/1966. p. 21-22.
3. Ghaemi, N. 2011. A First-Rate Madness. Uncovering the links between Leadership and Mental illness – p. 162,164-299-300.
4. Sidey, H. 1964. John F. Kennedy, President. New Edition – p. 174.

5. Reeves, R. 1993. President Kennedy. Profile of Power – p. 181.
6. Leamer, L. 2001. The Kennedy Men 1901-1963. The Laws of the father – p.539.
7. Leaming, B. 2006. Jack Kennedy. The Education of A Statesman – p. 321.

6.7. How Did Health Affect His Presidency?

1. Dallek, R. T. December 2002. The Atlantic Monthly. The Medical Ordeals of JFK – p. 61.
2. Owen, D. 2008. In Sickness and in Power. Illness in Heads of Government during the last 100 years – p. 163-189.
3. Ghaemi, N. 2011. A First Rate Madness: Uncovering the links between leadership and Mental Illness – p. 178.
4. Burkley, A.G.G. October 17, 1967. Washington D.C. Oral History Interview.
5. Gilbert, R.E. 1992. The Mortal Presidency. Illness and Anguish in the White House – p. 162.
6. Barnes, J.A. 2005. John F. Kennedy on leadership. The Lessons and Legacy of a president – p. 216.
7. Tennant, F. and MD, D. September 2012. John F. Kennedy's pain Story. From Autoimmune disease to central Pain. Practical Pain Management – p. 65-66.
8. Rubin, G. 2005. Forty ways to look at JFK – p. 259.
9. Selverstone, M.J. 2014. A companion to Kennedy – p. 26.
10. Travell, J.G. 1966. Oral History Interview JFKL1 – 01/20/1966
11. President Kennedy's Health Secrets – PBS NewsHour. Internet.
12. Illinois pain institute: One President and his debilitating Pain. Internet.
13. Johnson, P. 1997. A History of the American people – p. 849.
14. Martin, R.G. 1995. Seeds of Destruction. Joe Kennedy and his sons – p. 231.
15. Reeves, T.C. 1991. A Question of Character – p. 296.
16. White, M.J. 1998. Kennedy: The New Frontier Revisited. Behind Closed Doors: the Private Life of a Public Man – p. 265-269.

6.8. Was Grace De Monaco the "New Night Nurse" at Jack Kennedy's Bedside Late 1954?

1. Andersen, C. 1996. Jack and Jackie. Portrait of an American Marriage – p. 145.
2. Spoto, D. 2000. Jacqueline Bouvier Kennedy Onassis: A Life – p. 109-110.
3. Bradford, S. 2000. America's Queen. The Life of Jacqueline Kennedy Onassis – p. 98.
4. Klein, E. 1996. All Too Human. The Love Story of Jack and Jackie Kennedy – p. 189.
5. Heymann, C.D. 1989. A Woman named Jackie. An Intimate biography of Jacqueline Bouvier Kennedy Onassis – p. 171.
6. O'Brien, M. 2005. John F. Kennedy: A Biography – p. 282-283.

7. Monaco, G.D. 1965. Oral History Interview. JFKL – 6/19/1965

Further Reading
- Martin, R.G. 1983. A Hero For Our Time. An Intimate Story of the Kennedy Years – p. 83-84.
- Perret, G. 2001. Jack. A Life Like no Other – p. 212.
- Rubin, G. 2005. Forty ways to look at JFK – p. 281.

6.9. An Extensive Chronology

1. Billings, K.L. 1964. Oral History Interview JFKL1 – 03/25/1964
2. Giglio, J.N. October 2006. Growing up Kennedy: The Role of Medical ailments in the Life of JFK 1920-1957. Journal of family history – history Vol 31 N°4
3. Hamilton, N. 1992. JFK: Reckless Youth – p. 42.
4. Blair J. & Blair C. Jr. 1976. The Search for JFK – p. 23.
5. Dallek, R. December 2002. The Atlantic Monthly. The Medical Ordeals of JFK – p. 51.
6. Dallek, R. 2003. An Unfinished Life. John F. Kennedy 1917-1963 – p. 28.
7. Blair J. & Blair C. Jr. 1976. The Search for JFK – p. 23.
8. Smith, A. 2001. Hostage to fortune. The Letters of Joseph P. Kennedy – p. 91.
9. Hamilton, N. 1992. JFK: Reckless Youth – p. 85.
10. Dallek, R. December 2002. The Atlantic Monthly. The Medical Ordeals of JFK – p. 51.
11. Blair J. & Blair C. Jr. 1976. The Search for JFK – p. 23.
12. Giglio, J.N. October 2006. Growing up Kennedy: The Role of Medical ailments in the Life of JFK 1920-1957. Journal of family history Vol 31 N°4
13. Dallek, R. December 2002. The Atlantic Monthly. The Medical Ordeals of JFK – p. 51.
14. Blair J. & Blair C. Jr. 1976. The Search for JFK – p. 23.
15. O'Brien, M. 2005. John F. Kennedy A Biography – p. 60.
16. Blair J. & Blair C. Jr. 1976. The Search for JFK – p. 23.
17. Dallek, R. December 2002. The Atlantic Monthly. The Medical Ordeals of JFK – p. 51.
18. Hamilton, N. 1992. JFK: Reckless Youth – p. 87.
Logevall, F. 2020. JFK Volume One 1917-1956, chapter 4 note 1: Mrs. St John to RK, Choate School Archives – Outline, Box 1, JFKP
19. Dallek, R. December 2002. The Atlantic Monthly. The Medical Ordeals of JFK – p. 51.
20. Tennant, F. and MD, D. September 2012. John F. Kennedy's pain Story. From Autoimmune disease to central Pain. Practical Pain Management – p. 56.
21. Hamilton, N. 1992. JFK: Reckless Youth – p. 98.

22. Dallek, R. December 2002. The Atlantic Monthly. The Medical Ordeals of JFK – p. 51.

23. Blair J. & Blair C. Jr. 1976. The Search for JFK – p. 23.

24. Giglio, J.N. October 2006. Growing up Kennedy: The Role of Medical ailments in the Life of JFK 1920-1957. Journal of family history Vol 31 N°4 – p. 363.

25. Dallek, R. December 2002. The Atlantic Monthly. The Medical Ordeals of JFK – p. 51.

26. Billings, K.L. 1964. Oral History Interview. JFKL1 – 03/25/1964

27. O'Brien, M. 2005. John F. Kennedy A Biography – p. 69.

28. Hamilton, N. 1992. JFK: Reckless Youth – p. 104.

29. Smith, A. 2001. Hostage to fortune. The Letters of Joseph P. Kennedy – p. 134.

30. O'Brien, M. 2005. John F. Kennedy A Biography – p. 70-71.

31. Dallek, R. December 2002. The Atlantic Monthly. The Medical Ordeals of JFK – p. 51-52.

32. Giglio, J.N. October 2006. Growing up Kennedy: The Role of Medical ailments in the Life of JFK 1920-1957. Journal of family history Vol 31 N°4 – p. 363.

33. Dallek, R. December 2002. The Atlantic Monthly. The Medical Ordeals of JFK – p. 52.

34. Kennedy, R.F. 1995. Times to Remember – p. 174.

35. Blair J. & Blair C. Jr. 1976. The Search for JFK – p. 566.

36. Billings, K.L. 1964. Oral History Interview JFKL – 03/25/1964

37. Hamilton, N. 1992. JFK: Reckless Youth – p. 146-147.

38. Pitts, D. 2007. Jack and Lem: John F. Kennedy and Lem Billings. The Untold Story of an Extraordinary Friendship – p. 47.

39. Hamilton, N. 1992. JFK: Reckless Youth – p. 193.

40. O'Brien, M. 2005. John F. Kennedy A Biography – p. 89.

41. Hamilton, N. 1992. JFK: Reckless Youth – p. 196.

42. Tennant, F. and MD, D. September 2012. John F. Kennedy's pain Story. From Autoimmune disease to central Pain. Practical Pain Management – p. 56.

43. Dallek, R. December 2002. The Atlantic Monthly. The Medical Ordeals of JFK – p. 52.

44. Hamilton, N. 1992. JFK: Reckless Youth – p. 219.

45. Giglio, J.N. October 2006. Growing up Kennedy: The Role of Medical ailments in the Life of JFK 1920-1957. Journal of family history Vol 31 N°4 – p. 368.

46. Dallek, R. December 2002. The Atlantic Monthly. The Medical Ordeals of JFK – p. 54;
O'Brien, M 2005. John F. Kennedy: A Biography – p. 347.

47. Giglio, J.N. October 2006. Growing up Kennedy: The Role of Medical ailments in the Life of JFK 1920-1957. Journal of family history Vol 31 N°4 – p.

369.

48. Hamilton, N. 1992. JFK: Reckless Youth. Dr. Vernon Dick to Dr. William Herbst – p. 341-342 – Source: Dr. Vernon Dick to Dr. William Herbst, March 10, 1953 MS 83-38 JFKL

49. Dallek, R. 2003. An Unfinished Life. John F. Kennedy 1917-1963 – p. 81.

50. Hamilton, N. 1992. JFK Reckless Youth – p. 341.

51. Giglio, J.N. October 2006. Growing up Kennedy: The Role of Medical ailments in the Life of JFK 1920-1957. Journal of family history Vol 31 N°4 – p. 369-370.

52. Giglio, J.N. October 2006. Growing up Kennedy: The Role of Medical ailments in the Life of JFK 1920-1957. Journal of family history Vol 31 N°4 – p. 370.

53. Dallek, R. 2003. An Unfinished Life. John F. Kennedy 1917-1963 – p. 82.

54. Giglio, J.N. October 2006. Growing up Kennedy: The Role of Medical ailments in the Life of JFK 1920-1957. Journal of family history Vol 31 N°4 – p. 370.

55. Hamilton, N. 1992. JFK: Reckless Youth – p. 490.

56. Blair J. & Blair C. Jr. 1976. The Search for JFK – p. 150.

57. Hamilton, N. 1992. JFK Reckless Youth – p. 490.
Blair J. & Blair C. Jr. 1976. The Search for JFK – p. 150.

58. Dallek, R. 2003. An Unfinished Life. John F. Kennedy 1917-1963 – p. 86.

59. Hamilton, N. 1992. JFK: Reckless Youth – p. 491.

60. Hamilton, N. 1992. JFK: Reckless Youth – p. 493.

61. Giglio, J.N. October 2006. Growing up Kennedy: The Role of Medical ailments in the Life of JFK 1920-1957. Journal of family history Vol 31 N°4 – p. 372.

62. Hamilton, N. 1992. JFK: Reckless Youth – p. 644.

63. Giglio, J.N. October 2006. Growing up Kennedy: The Role of Medical ailments in the Life of JFK 1920-1957. Journal of family history Vol 31 N°4 – p. 372.

64. Giglio, J.N. October 2006. Growing up Kennedy: The Role of Medical ailments in the Life of JFK 1920-1957. Journal of family history Vol 31 N°4 – p. 372.

65. O'Brien, M. 2005. John F. Kennedy: A Biography – p. 170.

66. Gheami, N. 2011. A First-Rate Madness – p. 295.

67. Giglio, J.N. October 2006. Growing up Kennedy: The Role of Medical ailments in the Life of JFK 1920-1957. Journal of family history Vol 31 N°4 – p. 373.

68. Leamer, L. 2001. The Kennedy Men 1901-1963 – p. 223.

69. Giglio, J.N. October 2006. Growing up Kennedy: The Role of Medical ailments in the Life of JFK 1920-1957. Journal of family history Vol 31 N°4 – p. 374.

70. O'Brien, M. 2005. John F. Kennedy: A Biography – p. 179.

71. O'Brien, M. 2005. John F. Kennedy: A Biography – p. 187-188.

72. Giglio, J.N. October 2006. Growing up Kennedy: The Role of Medical ailments in the Life of JFK 1920-1957. Journal of family history Vol 31 N°4 – p. 374.

73. Blair, J. and Blair, C. 1976. The Search for JFK – p. 476.

74. Giglio, J.N. October 2006. Growing up Kennedy: The Role of Medical ailments in the Life of JFK 1920-1957. Journal of family history Vol 31 N°4 – p. 375.

75. Blair J. & Blair C. Jr. 1976. The Search for JFK – p. 560-561.

76. Giglio, J.N. October 2006. Growing up Kennedy: The Role of Medical ailments in the Life of JFK 1920-1957. Journal of family history Vol 31 N°4 – p. 375.

77. O'Brien, M. 2005. John F. Kennedy: A Biography – p. 225.

78. Dallek, R. December 2002. The Atlantic Monthly. The Medical Ordeals of JFK – p. 56.

79. Blair J. & Blair C. Jr. 1976. The Search for JFK – p. 565.

80. Giglio, J.N. October 2006. Growing up Kennedy: The Role of Medical ailments in the Life of JFK 1920-1957. Journal of family history Vol 31 N°4 – p. 376.

81. Nassaw, D. 2012. The Patriarch Joseph P. Kennedy – p. 654.

82. Perret, G. 2001. Jack. A Life Like no Other – p. 171.

83. Wills, C. 2009. Jack Kennedy – p. 69.

84. Thomas, E. 2000. The Life of Robert Kennedy – p. 59-60.

85. Dallek, R. December 2002. The Atlantic Monthly. The Medical Ordeals of JFK – p. 56.

86. Giglio, J.N. October 2006. Growing up Kennedy: The Role of Medical ailments in the Life of JFK 1920-1957. Journal of family history Vol 31 N°4 – p. 377.

87. Kennedy, R.F. 1964. Profiles in Courage. Memorial Edition – p. 10.

88. Giglio, J.N. October 2006. Growing up Kennedy: The Role of Medical ailments in the Life of JFK 1920-1957. Journal of family history Vol 31 N°4 – p. 377.

89. Giglio, J.N. October 2006. Growing up Kennedy: The Role of Medical ailments in the Life of JFK 1920-1957. Journal of family history Vol 31 N°4 – p. 378.

90. Leamer, L. 2001. The Kennedy Men 1901-1963. The Laws of the father – p.339-340.

91. Dallek, R. 2003. An Unfinished Life. John Fitzgerald Kennedy 1917-1963 – p. 196.

92. Leamer, L. 2001. The Kennedy Men 1901-1963. The Laws of the father – p. 340.

93. Owen, D. 2008. In Sickness and in Power. Illness in Heads of Government during the last 100 years – p. 155.

94. Blair J. & Blair C. Jr. 1976. The Search for JFK – p. 569.

95. Perret, G. 2001. Jack. A Life Like no Other – p. 211.

96. Giglio, J.N. October 2006. Growing up Kennedy: The Role of Medical ailments in the Life of JFK 1920-1957. Journal of family history Vol 31 N°4 – p. 378.

97. Bartlett, C.L. 1965. Oral History Interview. JFKL – 01/06/1965

98. Perret, G. 2001. Jack. A Life Like no Other – p. 214.

99. Dallek, R. 2003. An Unfinished Life. John Fitzgerald Kennedy 1917-1963 – p. 196-197.

100. Goodwin, D.K. 1987. The Fitzgeralds and the Kennedys – p. 776.

101. Dallek, R. 2003. An Unfinished Life. John F. Kennedy 1917-1963 – p. 212.

102. Travell, J.G. 1966. Oral History Interview JFKL – 01/20/1966

103. Travell, J. M.D. 1968. Office Hours: Day and Night. The Autobiography of Janet Travell, M.D. – p. 7.

104. Dallek, R. December 2002. The Atlantic Monthly. The Medical Ordeals of JFK – p. 58.

105. Dallek, R. 2003. An Unfinished Life. John Fitzgerald Kennedy 1917-1963 – p. 212.

106. Dallek, R. December 2002. The Atlantic Monthly. The Medical Ordeals of JFK – p. 58.

107. Giglio, J.N. October 2006. Growing up Kennedy: The Role of Medical ailments in the Life of JFK 1920-1957. Journal of family history Vol 31 N°4 – p. 379.

108. Dallek, R. 2003. An Unfinished Life. John Fitzgerald Kennedy 1917-1963 – p. 745.

109. Travell, J.G. 1966. Oral History Interview JFKL – 01/20/1966

110. Ghaemi, N. 2011.A First–Rate Madness. Uncovering the links between leadership and mental Illness – Nassir– p. 162. note: JFK Presidential Archives Medical Records, PP, Box 45

111. Heymann, C.D. 1989. A Woman named Jackie – p. 297.

112. Widmer, T. January 5, 1960. A taped interview: Transcript of discussion among Bradlee, Cannon and Kennedy, JFKL. Smithsonian Magazine 2012; Clarke, T. 2013. JFK's last Hundred Days – p. 34.

113. Blair J. & Blair C. Jr. 1976. The Search for JFK – p. 576.

114. Dallek, R. 2003. An Unfinished Life. John Fitzgerald Kennedy 1917-1963 – p. 367.

115. Clarke, T. 2013. JFK's last Hundred Days – p. 36-37.

116. Travell, J. 1968. Office Hours: Day and Night. The Autobiography of Janet Travell, M.D. – p. 385.

117. Dallek, R. 2003. An Unfinished Life. John Fitzgerald Kennedy 1917-1963 – p.

398-472.

118. Ghaemi, N. 2011. A First – Rate Madness. Uncovering the links between Leadership and Mental illness – p. 177.
119. Dallek, R. 2003. An Unfinished Life. John Fitzgerald Kennedy 1917-1963 – p. 472.
120. Schwartz, S.E.B. 2012. JFK's Secret Doctor. The remarkable life of medical pioneer and legendary Rock Climber Hans Kraus – p. 184-185-187.
121. Owen, D. 2008. In Sickness and in Power. Illness in Heads of Government during the last 100 years – p. 177-178.
122. Schwartz, S.E.B. 2012. JFK's Secret Doctor. The remarkable life of medical pioneer and legendary Rock Climber Hans Kraus – p. 193.
123. Owen, D. 2008. In Sickness and in Power. Illness in Heads of Government during the last 100 years – p. 179.
124. Dallek, R. 2003. An Unfinished Life. John F. Kennedy 1917-1963 – p. 576.
125. Schwartz, S.E.B. 2012. JFK's Secret Doctor. The remarkable life of medical pioneer and legendary Rock Climber Hans Kraus – p. 220.
126. Clarke, T. 2013. JFK's last Hundred Days. The transformation of a Man and the emergence of a great President – p. 39.
127. O'Brien, M. 2005. John F. Kennedy: A Biography – p. 759-760.
128. Clarke, T. 2013. JFK's last Hundred Days. The transformation of a Man and the emergence of a great President – p. 120 – 235.
129. Burkley, A.G.G. October 17, 1967. Oral History Interview – p. 16.
130. Clarke, T. 2013. JFK's last Hundred Days – p. 224. notes: He had recently complained to Fay, Fay JFKLOH – He should have been more concerned, JFK Personal Papers, Box 48 JFKL
131. Fay, P.B. 1970. Oral History Interview JFKL3 – 11/09/1970

Further Reading on "The Last Rites ?" in Okinawa Japan October-November 1951
Parmet, H.S. 1980. Jack: The Struggles of John F. Kennedy – p. 226.
Owen, D. 2008. In Sickness and in Power – p. 155.
Hilty, J.W. 1997. Robert Kennedy: Brother Protector – p. 65.
Blair J. & Blair C. Jr. 1976. The Search for JFK – p. 581-582.
O'Brien, M. 2005. John F. Kennedy A Biography – p. 236.
Mahoney, R.D. 1999. Sons & Brothers – p. 13.
Leamer, L. 2001. The Kennedy Men -p. 291.
Sorensen, T.C. 1965. Kennedy – p. 41.
Collier, P. & Horowitz, D. 1984. The Kennedys. An American Drama – p. 182.
Gilbert, R.E. 1992. The Mortal Presidency. Illness and Anguish in the White House – p. 147.

6.10. Conclusion

1. Dallek, R. November 14, 2002. The Atlantic Unbound. Interview.

2. Travell, J. 1968-1969. Office Hours: Day and Night. The Autobiography of Janet Travell, M.D.. – p. 388.

3. Selverstone, M.J. 2014. A Companion to John F. Kennedy.

Tennant, F. and MD, D. September 2012. John F. Kennedy's pain Story. From Autoimmune disease to central Pain – p. 61.

One President and His Debilitating Pain. May 7, 2014. In Lifestyle by Illinois Pain Institute "...10 to 12 medications a day, Dr. 6maintains"

Altman, L.K. and Purdum, T.S. November 17, 2002. The New York Times Archives. In JFK File, Hidden Illness, Pain and Pills – 1/8.

4. Travell, J.G. 1966. Oral History Interview JFKL1. 01/20/1966

5. Burkley, A.G. October 17, 1967. Oral History Interview. Washington D.C.

6. Schlesinger, A.M. 2011. Jacqueline Kennedy. Historic Conversations on Life with John – p. 91.

7. Atlantic Unbound – November 14, 2002 – Interview with Robert Dallek "Puling back the curtain".

8. Tennant, F. and MD, D. September 2012. John F. Kennedy's pain Story. From Autoimmune disease to central Pain. Practical Pain Management – p. 62.

9. Kelman, J. Illinois Pain Institute. One President and his Debilitating Pain - From the internet.

10. Ghaemi, N. 2001. A First Rate Madness – p. 174.

11. JFK Presidential Archives. Medical Records. PP, box 46.

12. Burkley, G. December 13, 1962. The Stelazine dose was 1 mg twice daily.

13. Dallek, R. December 2002. The Atlantic Monthly. The Medical Ordeals of JFK – p. 51.

14. Fay, P.B. 1966. The Pleasure of his Company – p. 172-173.

15. Hersh, S.M. 1997. The Dark side of Camelot – p. 234-235.

16. Leamer, L. 2001. The Kennedy Men 1901-1963 – p. 543.

Chapter 7: JFK: The Man, The President, The Character Issue

7.1. His Best Friend Was Gay

1. Pitts, D. 2007. Jack and Lem: John F. Kennedy and Lem Billings. The Untold Story of an Extraordinary friendship – p. 11.
2. Pitts, D. 2007. Jack and Lem: John F. Kennedy and Lem Billings. The Untold Story of an Extraordinary friendship – p. 188.
3. Martin, R.G. 1995. Seeds of Destruction. Joe Kennedy and his sons – p. 336.
4. Hamilton, N. 1992. JFK: Reckless Youth – p. 191.
5. Perret, G. 2001. Jack. A Life Like no Other – p. 339.
6. Pitts, D. 2007. Jack and Lem: John F. Kennedy and Lem Billings. The Untold Story of an Extraordinary friendship – p. 192.
7. Pitts, D. 2007. Jack and Lem: John F. Kennedy and Lem Billings. The Untold Story of an Extraordinary friendship – p. 24.
8. Pitts, D. 2007. Jack and Lem: John F. Kennedy and Lem Billings. The Untold Story of an Extraordinary friendship – p. 22-23.
9. Pitts, D. 2007. Jack and Lem: John F. Kennedy and Lem Billings. The Untold Story of an Extraordinary friendship – p. 69-70..
10. Martin, R.G. 1995. Seeds of Destruction. Joe Kennedy and his sons – p. 57.
11. Pitts, D. 2007. Jack and Lem: John F. Kennedy and Lem Billings. The Untold Story of an Extraordinary friendship – p. 70.
12. Pitts, D. 2007. Jack and Lem: John F. Kennedy and Lem Billings. The Untold Story of an Extraordinary friendship – p. 207.
13. Pitts, D. 2007. Jack and Lem: John F. Kennedy and Lem Billings. The Untold Story of an Extraordinary friendship – p. 24.
14. Pitts, D. 2007. Jack and Lem: John F. Kennedy and Lem Billings. The Untold Story of an Extraordinary friendship – p. 293.

7.2. Thomas Jefferson & Sally Hemings Controversy: A Character Issue?

1. Turner, R.F. July 11, 2012. The Myth of Thomas Jefferson and Sally Hemings – from the internet.
2. Thomas Jefferson and Sally Hemings: A Brief Account. From the Internet.
3. Thompson, K. February 19, 2017. The Washington Post.
4. Hemings, S. Wikipedia
Thomas Jefferson, Slavery and Slaves. Memoirs of Madison Hemings PBS Frontline Schwabach Aaron. Thomas Jefferson law review 33 n°1 (Fall 2010): 160 Academic Search Complete, EBSCO host (accessed October 16, 2014)
5. Hemings, S. Wikipedia, The free encyclopedia.
6. Reed, A.G. 2008. The Hemingses at Monticello – p. 352-374.
7. Reed, A.G. 1997. Thomas Jefferson & Sally Hemings an American Controversy – p. 58.

8. The Jefferson Monticello Plantation and Slavery Menu Thomas Jefferson and Sally Hemings: A Brief account. 2017. From the internet – 03/04/2017

7.3. JFK More Than a President: A Man
1. Schwartz, S.E.B. 2012. JFK's Secret Doctor. The remarkable life of medical pioneer and legendary Rock Climber Hans Kraus – p. 200.
2. Douglas, J.W. 2008. JFK and the unspeakable. Why he died and why it matters – p. 102-103.
3. Hill, C. and McCubbin, L. 2016. Five Presidents. My extraordinary Journey with Eisenhower, Kennedy, Johnson, Nixon and Ford – p. 88-89.
4. Fries, C., Wilson, I. and Green, S. 2003. We'll Never Be Young Again. Remembering the last days of John F. Kennedy – p. 62-64.

7.4. Conclusion
1. Strober, D.H. and Strober, G.S. 2003. The Kennedy Presidency. An Oral History of the Era – p. 479-480.
2. Reeves, T.C. 1991. A Question of Character. A Life of John F. Kennedy – p. 421.
3. Sabato, L.J. 2013. The Kennedy Half Century. The Presidency, Assassination, and Lasting Legacy of John F. Kennedy – p. 413-414.
4. Beschloss, M.R. 1991. The Crisis Years. Kennedy and Khrushchev 1960-1963 – p. 611.
5. O'Brien, M. 2009. Rethinking Kennedy. An interpretive Biography – p. 225.
6. Reeves, T.C. 1991. A Question of Character. A Life of John F. Kennedy – p. 418-19.
7. Dallek, R. 2003. An Unfinished Life. John F. Kennedy 1917-1963 – p. 700-701.
8. Quirk, L.J. 1996. The Kennedy is Hollywood – p. 213-215.
9. The Kennedys: All the Gossip Unfit to Print. 2011. Blood Moon Productions Ltd – p. 181.
10. Gamarekain, B. 1964. Oral History Interview JFKL – 06/10/1964
11. Dallek, R. 2003. An Unfinished Life. John F. Kennedy 1917-1963 – p. 477.
12. Watts, S. 2016. JFK and the Masculine Mystique. Sex and Power on the New Frontier – p. 225.
13. Andersen, C. 1996. Jack and Jackie. Portrait of an American Marriage – p. 304-305.
14. Smith, S.B. 2004. Grace and Power. The Private World of the Kennedy White House – p. 251.
15. Alford, M. 2012. Once Upon a Secret. My affair with President Kennedy and its aftermath – p. 72.
16. Heymann, C.D. 1998. RFK. A Candid Biography of Robert F. Kennedy – p. 235.

17. David, L. 1994. Jacqueline Kennedy Onassis. A portrait of her private years – p. 44.

18. Hagood, W.O. 1997. Presidential Sex from the founding father to Bill Clinton – p. 150.

19. White, M.J. 1998. Kennedy. The New Frontier Revisited – p. 258.

20. Hamilton, N. 1992. JFK: Reckless Youth. JFK Pre Pres, Box 94 – p. 774-775-776.

21. Kennedy, J. July 4, 1946. Some Elements of the American character: An Oration delivered at Faneuil Hall by John Kennedy (350 copies). The King & Queen Press.

22. White, M.J. 1998. Kennedy. The New Frontier Revisited – p. 262.

23. Cronkite, W. 1996. A Reporter's Life – p. 220.

24. Watts, S. 2016. JFK and the Masculine Mystique. Sex and Power on the New Frontier – p. 358.

25. White, M.J. 1998. Kennedy. The New Frontier Revisited – p. 270.

26. O'Brien, M. 2009. Rethinking Kennedy. An interpretive Biography – p. 225.

27. White, M.J. 1998. Kennedy. The New Frontier Revisited – p. 272.

28. O'Brien, M. 2009. Rethinking Kennedy. An interpretive Biography – p. 225.

29. Reeves, R. 1993. American History Lives at American Heritage. My six years with JFK.

30. O'Brien, M. 2009. Rethinking Kennedy. An interpretive Biography – p. 193-194.

31. O'Brien, M. 2005. John F. Kennedy: A Biography – p. 806.

32. Fay, P.B. 1966. The Pleasure of his Company – p. 172-173.

33. Travell, J. 1969. Office Hours: Day and Night. The Autobiography of Janet Travell, M.D. – p. 339.

34. Raskin, H.B. 1964. Oral History Interview. JFKL – 5/8/1964

35. Reeves, T.C. 1991. A Question of Character. A Life of John F. Kennedy – p. 415.

EPILOGUE

1. The Presidency and beyond: A Legacy in Progress. Time Life JFK at 100 – p. 94-95.
2. Stoll, I. 2013. JFK Conservative – p. 206-209.
3. White, T.H. 1978. In Search of History. A personal adventure – p. 460-461-462.
4. Miroff, B. 1976. Pragmatic Illusions. The Presidential Politics of John F. Kennedy – p. 4.
5. Burns, J.M.G. 1964. Remembrances of John F. Kennedy – p. 19-20.
6. Schlesinger, A.M. 2011. Jacqueline Kennedy. Historic Conversations on Life with John – p. 52.
7. Snyder, J.R. 1988. John F. Kennedy Person, Policy, Presidency – p. 1.
8. Bryant, T. and Leighton, F.S. 1975. Dog Days at the White House – p. 102.
9. Rubin, G. 2005. Forty ways to look at JFK – p. 156.
10. Lython, B. 1966. Oral History Interview JFKL. 06/08/1966
11. Murville, M.C. 1964. Oral History Interview JFKL. 05/20/1964
12. Burner, D. 1988. John F. Kennedy and a New Generation – p. 169.
13. Parmet, H.S. 1983. JFK. The Presidency of John F. Kennedy – p. 354.
14. Sorensen, T.C. 2008. Counselor. A Life at the Edge of History – p. 525.
15. Reeves, T.C. 1990. John F. Kennedy: The Man, The Politician, The President. The University of Winconsin Parkside – p. 153-154-155.
16. Bernstein, I. 1991. Promises Kept – p. 296-297.
17. Monaco, G.D. 1965. Oral History Interview JFKL – 06/19/1965
18. Giglio, J.N. 2006. The Presidency of John F. Kennedy. Second Revised Edition – p. 303-305.
19. Dallek, R. June 2, 1991. He was No Jack Kennedy. The New York Times.
20. Reeves, T.C. 1991. A Question of Character. A Life of John F. Kennedy – p. 415-418-419-420.
21. Bernstein, I. 1991. Promises Kept – p. 280.
22. Reeves, T.C. 1991. A Question of Character. A Life of John F. Kennedy – p. 417.
23. Reeves, R. 1993. President Kennedy Profile of Power – p. 18-19.
24. Lord, D.C. 1977. John F. Kennedy. The politics of Confrontation and Conciliation – p. 319.
25. Snyder, J.R. 1988. John F. Kennedy: Person, Policy, Presidency – p. 19-20-22.
26. Lewis, J. 1975. The Promise and the Performance. The Leadership of John F. Kennedy – p. 380.
27. Mailer, N. 1964. The Presidential Papers of Norman Mailer.
28. Mailer, N. 2014. Superman Comes to the Supermarket – p. 9-10.
29. Schlesinger, A.M. 2011. Jacqueline Kennedy. Historic Conversations on Life with John – p. 251.
30. Brinkley, A. 2012. John F. Kennedy – p. 152-153.

31. Dallek, R. 2003. An Unfinished Life. John F. Kennedy 1917-1963 – p. 700-701.

32. Dallek, R. and Golway, T. 2006. John F. Kennedy in His Own Words. Let every Nation Know – p. xii.

33. Willis, G. 1981-1982. The Kennedy Imprisonment. A Meditation on Power – p. 148.

34. Sabato, L.J. 2013. The Kennedy Half Century. The Presidency, Assassination, and Lasting Legacy of John F. Kennedy – p. 406-413-414-420.

35. Goldman, M.S. 1995. John F. Kennedy: Portrait of a President – p. 146.

36. Stoll, I. 2013. JFK Conservative – p. 213.

37. Rorabaugh, W.J. 2002. Kennedy and the Promise of the Sixties – p. 237.

38. Foster, P. November 16, 2013. JFK: The myth that will never die. On the internet.

39. O'Brien, M. 2005. John F. Kennedy: A Biography. Introduction XIV.

40. American History Journalist Priscilia Johnson Mc Millan. From the Internet.

41. Bugliosi, V. 2007. Reclaiming History: The Assassination of President John F. Kennedy. Wikipedia.

42. The Peace Corps. March 1, 1961. A special Message to The Congress, Washington D.C.

43. A Conversation with President Jimmy Carter: JFK Library. November 20, 2014. From the Internet.

44. O'Brien, M. 2005. John F. Kennedy: A Biography. Introduction – p. XV.

45. The Most Lasting Kennedy Legacy. November 7, 1993.

46. Mansfield, M. 1964. Oral History Interview JFKL – 06/23/1964

47. Dallek, R. 2003. An Unfinished Life: John F. Kennedy 1917-1963 – p. 699-700.

48. O'Brien, M. 2005. John F. Kennedy: A Biography. Introduction XVII.

49. Sabato, L.J. 2013. The Kennedy Half Century – p. 406-407.

50. Ridings, W.J. and Iver, S.B. 1997. Rating the Presidents – p. 221.

51. Faber, C.F. and Faber, R.B. 2000. The American Presidents Ranked by Performance – p. 226.

52. Americans Rate JFK as Top Modern President by Andrew Dugan and Frank Newport. November 15, 2013.

53. C Span: Presidential Historians Survey. 2017.

54. Giglio, J.N. 2006. The Presidency of John F. Kennedy. Second Edition – p. 303.

Index

Lightning Source UK Ltd.
Milton Keynes UK
UKHW051020150722
405897UK00002B/54